THE ARDEN SHAKESPEARE

THIRD SERIES
General Editors: Richard Proudfoot, Ann Thompson
and David Scott Kastan

KING LEAR

KT-556-626

THE ARDEN SHAKESPEARE

ALL'S WELL THAT ENDS WELL	edited by G. K. Hunter*
ANTONY AND CLEOPATRA	edited by John Wilders
AS YOU LIKE IT	edited by Agnes Latham*
THE COMEDY OF ERRORS	edited by R. A. Foakes*
CORIOLANUS	edited by Philip Brockbank*
CYMBELINE	edited by J. M. Nosworthy*
HAMLET	edited by Harold Jenkins*
JULIUS CAESAR	edited by David Daniell
KING HENRY IV, Parts 1 & 2	edited by A. R. Humphreys*
KING HENRY V	edited by T. W. Craik
KING HENRY VI, Part 1	edited by Edward Burns
KING HENRY VI, Part 2	edited by Ronald Knowles
KING HENRY VI, Part 3	edited by John D. Cox and Eric Rasmussen
KING HENRY VIII	edited by Gordon McMullan
KING JOHN	edited by E. A. J. Honigmann*
KING LEAR	edited by R. A. Foakes
KING RICHARD II	edited by Charles R. Forker
KING RICHARD III	edited by Antony Hammond*
LOVE'S LABOUR'S LOST	edited by H. R. Woudhuysen
MACBETH	edited by Kenneth Muir*
MEASURE FOR MEASURE	edited by J. W. Lever*
THE MERCHANT OF VENICE	edited by John Russell Brown*
THE MERRY WIVES OF WINDSO	Redited by Giorgio Melchiori
A MIDSUMMER NIGHT'S DREAM	edited by Harold F. Brooks*
MUCH ADO ABOUT NOTHING	edited by A. R. Humphreys*
OTHELLO	edited by E. A. J. Honigmann
PERICLES	edited by F. D. Hoeniger*
THE POEMS	edited by F. T. Prince*
ROMEO AND JULIET	edited by Brian Gibbons*
SHAKESPEARE'S SONNETS	edited by Katherine Duncan-Jones
THE TAMING OF THE SHREW	edited by Brian Morris*
THE TEMPEST	edited by Virginia Mason Vaughan and Alden T. Vaughan
TIMON OF ATHENS	edited by H. J. Oliver*
TITUS ANDRONICUS	edited by Jonathan Bate
TROILUS AND CRESSIDA	edited by David Bevington
TWELFTH NIGHT	edited by J. M. Lothian and T. W. Craik*
THE TWO GENTLEMEN OF VERONA	edited by Clifford Leech*
THE TWO NOBLE KINSMEN	edited by Lois Potter
THE WINTER'S TALE	edited by John Pitcher

*Second Series

THE ARDEN SHAKESPEARE

KING LEAR

Edited by
R.A.FOAKES

The Arden website is at
http://www.ardenshakespeare.com

The general editors of the Arden Shakespeare have been
W. J. Craig and R. H. Case (first series 1899-1944)
Una Ellis-Fermor, Harold F. Brooks, Harold Jenkins and
Brian Morris (second series 1946-82)

Present general editors (third series)
Richard Proudfoot, Ann Thompson and David Scott Kastan

This edition of *King Lear* by R. A. Foakes
first published in 1997 by Thomas Nelson and Sons Ltd

Published by The Arden Shakespeare
Reprinted 2004 and 2006

Editorial matter © 1997 R. A. Foakes

Arden Shakespeare is an imprint of Thomson Learning

Thomson Learning
High Holborn House
50-51 Bedford Row
London WC1R 4LR

Printed in Croatia

British Library Cataloguing in Publication Data
A catalogue record for this book is available from the British Library
Library of Congress Cataloguing in Publication Data
A catalogue record has been requested

ISBN-13 978-1-903436-58-5 (hbk)
ISBN-10 1-903436-58-3 (hbk)
NPN 9 8 76 5

ISBN-13 978-1-903436-59-2 (pbk)
ISBN-10 1-903436-59-1 (pbk)
NPN 11

The Editor

R.A. Foakes is Professor Emeritus at the University of California, Los Angeles.

He has also taught or held fellowships at Yale, Birmingham, Durham, Kent, Toronto, the University of California, Santa Barbara, and the Australian National University, Canberra.

His publications include *Shakespeare, The Dark Comedies to the Last Plays* and *Illustrations of the English Stage 1580–1642*, as well as editions of *Henry VIII* and *The Comedy of Errors*, for the second Arden series, *Troilus and Cressida* and *Much Ado About Nothing* (The New Penguin Shakespeare) and *A Midsummer Night's Dream* (New Cambridge Shakespeare). He has written extensively on *King Lear* in his book, *Hamlet versus Lear, Cultural Politics and Shakespeare's Art* (1993).

For my beloved Mary

Thou'lt come no more,
Never, never, never, never, never …

CONTENTS

LIST OF
ILLUSTRATIONS

GENERAL EDITORS'
PREFACE

The Arden Shakespeare is now nearly one hundred years old. The earliest volume in the first series, Edward Dowden's *Hamlet*, was published in 1899. Since then the Arden Shakespeare has become internationally recognized and respected. It is now widely acknowledged as the pre-eminent Shakespeare series, valued by scholars, students, actors, and 'the great variety of readers' alike for its readable and reliable texts, its full annotation and its richly informative introductions.

We have aimed in the third Arden series to maintain the quality and general character of its predecessors, preserving the commitment to presenting the play as it has been shaped in history. While each individual volume will necessarily have its own emphasis in the light of the unique possibilities and problems posed by the play, the series as a whole, like the earlier Ardens, insists upon the highest standards of scholarship and upon attractive and accessible presentation.

Newly edited from the original quarto and folio editions, the texts are presented in fully modernized form, with a textual apparatus that records all substantial divergences from those early printings. The notes and introductions focus on the conditions and possibilities of meaning that editors, critics and performers (on stage and screen) have discovered in the play. While building upon the rich history of scholarly and theatrical activity that has long shaped our understanding of the texts of Shakespeare's plays, this third series of the Arden Shakespeare is made necessary and possible by a new generation's encounter with Shakespeare, engaging with the plays and their complex relation to the culture in which they were – and continue to be – produced.

THE TEXT

On each page of the play itself, readers will find a passage of text followed by commentary and, finally, textual notes. Act and scene divisions (seldom present in the early editions and often the product of eighteenth–century or later scholarship) have been retained for ease of reference, but have been given less prominence than in the previous series. Editorial indications of location of the action have been removed to the textual notes or commentary.

In the text itself, unfamiliar typographic conventions have been avoided in order to minimize obstacles to the reader. Elided forms in the early texts are spelt out in full in verse lines wherever they indicate a usual late-twentieth-century pronunciation that requires no special indication and wherever they occur in prose (except when they indicate non-standard pronunciation). In verse speeches, marks of elision are retained where they are necessary guides to the scansion and pronunciation of the line. Final -ed in past tense and participial forms of verbs is always printed as -ed without accent, never as -'d, but wherever the required pronunciation diverges from modern usage a note in the commentary draws attention to the fact. Where the final -ed should be given syllabic value contrary to modern usage, e.g.

> Doth Silvia know that I am banished?
> (TGV 3.1.214)

the note will take the form

214 **banished** banishèd

Conventional lineation of divided verse lines shared by two or more speakers has been reconsidered and sometimes rearranged. Except for the familiar *Exit* and *Exeunt*, Latin forms in stage directions and speech prefixes have been translated into English and the original Latin forms recorded in the textual notes.

COMMENTARY AND TEXTUAL NOTES

Notes in the commentary, for which a major source will be the *Oxford English Dictionary*, offer glossarial and other explication of verbal difficulties; they may also include discussion of points of theatrical interpretation and, in relevant cases, substantial extracts from Shakespeare's source material. Editors will not usually offer glossarial notes for words adequately defined in the *Concise Oxford Dictionary* or *Webster's Ninth New Collegiate Dictionary*, but in cases of doubt they will include notes. Attention, however, will be drawn to places where more than one likely interpretation can be proposed and to significant verbal and syntactic complexity. Notes preceded by * involve discussion of textual variants or readings emended from the early edition(s) on which the text is based.

Headnotes to acts or scenes discuss, where appropriate, questions of scene location, Shakespeare's handling of his source materials, and major difficulties of staging. The list of roles (so headed to emphasize the play's status as a text for performance) is also considered in commentary notes. These may include comment on plausible patterns of casting with the resources of an Elizabethan or Jacobean acting company, and also on any variation in the description of roles in their speech prefixes in the early editions.

The textual notes are designed to let readers know when the edited text diverges from the early edition(s) on which it is based. Wherever this happens the note will record the rejected reading of the early edition(s), in original spelling, and the source of the reading adopted in this edition. Other forms from the early edition(s) recorded in these notes will include some spellings of particular interest or significance and original forms of translated stage directions. Where two early editions are involved, for instance with *Othello*, the notes will also record all important differences between them. The textual notes take a form that has been in use since the nineteenth century. This comprises, first: line reference, reading adopted in the text and closing square bracket; then: abbreviated reference, in italic, to the earliest edition to adopt the accepted reading, italic semicolon and noteworthy alternative reading(s), each with abbreviated italic reference to its source.

Conventions used in these textual notes include the following. The solidus / is used, in notes quoting verse or discussing verse lining, to indicate line endings. Distinctive spellings of the basic text (Q or F) follow the square bracket without indication of source and are enclosed in italic brackets. Names enclosed in italic brackets indicate originators of conjectural emendations when these did not originate in an edition of the text, or when this edition records a conjecture not accepted into its text. Stage directions (SDs) are referred to by the number of the line within or immediately after which they are placed. Line numbers with a decimal point relate to centred SDs not falling within a verse line and to SDs more than one line long, with the number after the point indicating the line within the SD: e.g. 78.4 refers to the fourth line of the SD following line 78. Lines of SDs at the start of a scene are numbered 0.1, 0.2, etc. Where only a line number and SD precede the square bracket, e.g. 128 SD], the note relates to the whole of a SD within or immediately following the line. Speech prefixes (SPs) follow similar conventions, 203 SP] referring to the speaker's name for line 203. Where a SP reference takes the form e.g. 38 + SP, it relates to all subsequent speeches assigned to that speaker in the scene in question.

Where, as with *King Henry V*, one of the early editions is a so-called 'bad quarto' (that is, a text either heavily adapted, or reconstructed from memory, or both), the divergences from the present edition are too great to be recorded in full in the notes. In these cases the editions will include a reduced photographic facsimile of the 'bad quarto' in an appendix.

INTRODUCTION

Both the introduction and the commentary are designed to present the plays as texts for performance, and make appropriate reference to stage, film and television versions, as well as introducing the reader to the range of critical approaches to the plays. They discuss the history of the reception of the texts within the theatre and scholarship and beyond, investigating the interdependency of the literary text and the surrounding 'cultural text' both at the time of the original production of Shakespeare's works and during their long and rich afterlife.

ACKNOWLEDGEMENTS

In preparing this edition I have read much more than I can now remember in the massive published commentary about *King Lear*, seen a number of productions, and looked at films of, or based on, the play. Probably I am no longer conscious of many ways in which my thinking has been affected as a result, so let me offer a general acknowledgement, and express the hope that any who find traces of their ideas in what I have written will take it as a compliment. I am immensely grateful to the many individuals who have helped me in however slight ways, and wish I could name them all. Among scholars and critics with a special interest in *King Lear* who have been graciously supportive, whether agreeing or disagreeing with me, I think especially of Tom Craik, Jay Halio, Ernst Honigmann, Grace Ioppolo, Richard Knowles, and the general editors of the series, David Kastan, Ann Thompson and above all Richard Proudfoot, whose comments have been invaluable. It has been a pleasure to have the stimulus of colleagues in the University of California, notably A. R. Braunmuller, Debora Shuger, Michael Warren and Robert Watson. I am grateful for their constant helpfulness to all the staff at the Folger Shakespeare Library, Washington, where I held a National Endowment for the Humanities Fellowship in 1994 that enabled me to draft the commentary to this edition. It was a special pleasure to have the support there of Georgianna Ziegler, and the stimulus of coffee-breaks with readers and other Fellows, most particularly Peter Blayney, who generously shared his expert knowledge of the texts of *King Lear*. I also owe thanks to the staff at the Huntington Library in Pasadena for many courtesies, and to the gracious librarians of the Shakespeare Centre Library in Stratford-upon-Avon, especially Mary White, who became my wife; it was a joy to have her help and her sustaining presence while I was working on this edition. The University of California at Los Angeles has been generous with research funding, making it possible for me to recruit several graduate students, Terri Bays, Billy Phelan, Owen Staley and Curtis Whitaker, to work with me at different times; and students in graduate and senior seminars have prompted me to think through various problems relating to the play. Jeannette Gilkison has saved me from errors with her skill in proofreading. Both Jane Armstrong and her colleagues at Routledge and Jessica Hodge and her associates at Thomas Nelson have been immensely helpful, sharp-eyed and efficient in response. I am also indebted to the participants in a seminar on *King Lear* I co-directed for the World Shakespeare Congress in Los Angeles in 1996 which threw up many challenging ideas.

The research embodied in my book *Hamlet versus Lear: Cultural Politics and Shakespeare's Art* (Cambridge, 1993) made the preparation of this edition much easier than it might have been. Some material in the Introduction is reworked from this book. My ideas about the role of the Fool were developed in 'Textual Revision and the Fool in "King Lear"', *Trivium*, 20 (1985), 33–47. The problem of textual differences between Quarto and Folio in 3.1, discussed briefly in Appendix 1, is analysed more fully in an essay in *Shakespeare Survey*, 49 (1997), 217–23. I have considered the importance of the crown in the play in 'King Lear: monarch or senior citizen?', in *Elizabethan Theater. Essays in Honor of S. Schoenbaum*, ed. Brian Parker and Sheldon P. Zitner (Newark, Delaware, 1996), 271–89.

R.A. Foakes
Los Angeles

INTRODUCTION

King Lear stands like a colossus at the centre of Shakespeare's achievement as the grandest effort of his imagination. In its social range it encompasses a whole society, from king to beggar, and invites us to move in our imagination between a royal palace and a hovel on a bare heath. Its emotional range extends from the extreme of violent anger to the tenderest intimacy of the loving reconciliation between Lear and Cordelia. The play powerfully registers the anguish of the suffering brought about by the inhumanity of man (and woman) to man in the exposure of Lear in the storm and the blinding on stage of Gloucester. It is unsparing in its depiction of human cruelty and misery, but also rich in its portrayals of goodness, devotion, loyalty and self-sacrifice. Through the Fool's commentary, Poor Tom's 'mad' sayings and the insights gained by Lear and Gloucester in their suffering, the play vividly exposes human folly, greed and corruption. It incorporates aspects of pastoral and romance, recalls morality plays, has a protagonist of 'epic' stature, and these features, together with the astonishing imaginative range of its action, its language and its imagery, have encouraged many to see the play in terms of universal values, as a kind of objective correlative for the spiritual journey through life of suffering Man. So it may not seem extravagant for the claim to be made that 'the bent of the play is mythic: it abandons verisimilitude to find out truth, like the story of Oedipus' (Mack, 97).

For long the play was thought to be unactable, either because of its display of cruelty and suffering, or because of its vastness of scope. Between 1681 and 1838 Nahum Tate's reworking with a happy ending formed the basis of all stage representations; and the idea of the play as Shakespeare's 'greatest achievement' but 'too huge for the stage' (Bradley, 247, 261) persisted into the twentieth century. It is in the decades since the Second World

1

War that *King Lear* has come to be fully accepted as a great stage play; in recent times it has been frequently performed, and several film versions have been made for cinema and television. Its exposure of the horror of torture and suffering no longer seems outrageous in the context of concentration camps, napalm bombs, anti-personnel mines, and acts of terrorism such as have become familiar in report to everyone. Its interrogation of authority, of justice and of need finds an echo in current social concerns; and the way Lear, Gloucester and Edgar are cast out of their society and reduced to poverty connects with anxiety about the old and the poor in the modern world. The innovatory dramatic technique of a play that overrides implausibilities by its imaginative power and emotional intensity anticipates the twentieth-century Theatre of the Absurd to the extent that *King Lear* has been seen as a kind of parallel to Samuel Beckett's *Waiting for Godot* and *Endgame*, and 'above all others the Shakespearean play of our time' (Kott, 162). It has seemed to some the play of our time in being open to nihilistic interpretation as showing not the potentially heroic journey or pilgrimage of Man through life, but rather a progression towards despair or mere nothingness. That *King Lear* can elicit such conflicting interpretations is a testimony both to the play's vitality and to the immense range of possibilities it opens up. The first and most substantial part of this introduction is mainly concerned to illustrate some of the different ways in which we can find ourselves reflected in this most capacious of plays, which is so many-faceted that it invites multiple interpretations.

This first part of the introduction is divided into sections that deal with various aspects of the play, starting with language and performance, and going on to consider how it invites us to perceive the action and characters. Some account of ways in which the play has been staged and some reflections on critical responses to it are woven into the narrative; the stage and critical history of the play is so rich that no introduction could do justice to it. The next part of the introduction provides a brief historical survey of changes in critical reaction to *King Lear*, and a documentation of some of the major reworkings of it in drama, fiction and poetry. A section on 'The inception of *King Lear*' is concerned with its date and its context of ideas, sources, analogues and influences. This is followed by a consideration of the problems thrown up by the two texts of the play, the Quarto of 1608 and the first Folio of 1623, which differ in many respects. The next part of the introduction comments on the more important differences between these texts in considering the question of revision or adaptation, and this is followed by a brief note on the way the play may have been cast on the Jacobean stage. The introduction ends with a notation of conventions followed in the presentation of the text, commentary and collation.

READING AND STAGING *KING LEAR*

Wee wondred (Shake-speare) that thou went'st so soone
From the Worlds-stage, to the Graues-Tyring-Roome.
We thought thee dead, but this thy printed worth,
Tels thy Spectators, that thou went'st but forth
To enter with applause. An Actor's Art
Can dye, and liue, to acte a second part.
> (I.M., 'To the Memory of M. *W. Shake-speare*',
> First Folio, 1623)

But it is not our prouince, who onely gather his works, and give them to you, to praise him. It is yours that reade him. And there we hope, to your diuers capacities, you will finde enough, both to draw, and hold you: for his wit can no more lie hid, than it could be lost. Reade him, therefore; and againe, and againe.
> (John Heminge and Henry Condell, foreword to first
> Folio, 1623)

Plays have a double life, in the mind as read, and on the stage as acted; reading a play and seeing it acted are two different but equally valid and valuable experiences. Shakespeare's fellow-actors provided in the First Folio of his works a text for readers, and all later editors have also had readers in mind; even acting versions have first to be read. There has been a fashion in criticism for claiming that the 'real play is the performance, not the text', or that a play is a 'communal construct', and 'exists in relationship to scripts we will never have, to a series of revisions and collaborations that start as soon as there is a Shakespearean text'.[1] It seems to me rather that the 'real play' is as much the text we read, and perhaps act out in the mind, as the performance we watch; and scripts are what directors and actors make for the stage out of the reading texts provided for them by editors. *King Lear* is a special case in that the text of the play in the First Folio (1623) differs in many details from that first printed in the Quarto of 1608, and each text has lines that are not in the other; we thus have variant versions of the same work. The present edition includes, with markers in the form of superscript [Q] (for Quarto) or [F] (for Folio), the passages found in one text but not the other.[2] The aims of this edition are, first, to make available the text(s) in a form that enables readers to understand the relation between them and to appreciate the problems caused by textual differences; secondly, to help the reader to imagine some of the ways in which the action of the play might be staged; and, thirdly, to open up some of the inexhaustible possibilities for shaping and interpreting the play.

The life a play has in the mind may be very different from the life it has on the stage. *King Lear*, which is a long and complex work, may rarely have been acted in full, and has usually been cut, rearranged or reworked for performance. The title-page of the Quarto of 1608 (see Fig. 20, p. 112) claims to present the text

1 Citing Stephen Orgel, 'Shakespeare imagines a theater', in Kenneth Muir, Jay Halio and D. J. Palmer (eds), *Shakespeare, Man of the Theater* (Newark, 1983), 43; Gary Taylor, *Reinventing Shakespeare: A Cultural History from the Restoration to the Present* (1989), 360; and Jonathan Goldberg, 'Textual properties', *SQ*, 37 (1986), 215.
2 See below, p. 110, for a fuller discussion of the text.

'*As it was played before the Kings Maiestie at Whitehall*' on St Stephen's night, 26 December 1606, but the version printed in the Quarto may well derive from a manuscript that was never used for performance. The changes and revisions found in the text of the first Folio (1623) appear to have been made for a revival by Shakespeare's company after 1608, but, apart from evidence of a staging of the play in Yorkshire in 1610,[1] there are no further records of performances until *King Lear* was revived after the restoration of Charles II in 1664.

Long and complex as the play is, it does not call for elaborate staging. It requires a number of commonplace properties such as letters, purses, weapons, torches and chairs, and some less often in use, such as a map, a coronet and the stocks for Kent, but nothing unusual.[2] Some representation of a storm is also required, and on the Jacobean stage thunder could be imitated by beating drums or rolling a cannon-ball on a metal sheet, while lightning was suggested by squibs (Gurr, 186). At 2.1.20 Edmund calls on Edgar to 'descend'; this is the only point in the play where a balcony or some area above the stage is needed. The 'hovel' from which Poor Tom emerges in 3.4 may have been simply a stage door, and the audience may have been expected to imagine the 'bush' (Q) or 'tree' (F) that shelters Gloucester in 5.2. The play makes good use of visual action and effects, processions, fights, disguises, torches, weapons, deaths, torture (the blinding of Gloucester) and even an imagined fall off a cliff, all designed for an open stage like that at the Globe (see Fig. 1), providing varied and often exciting movement and spectacle without scenery or modern lighting effects.

The audience stood or sat on three sides of the stage, in close proximity to it, and in the same light as the actors, so that the

---

1   First noticed by C. J. Sisson, 'Shakespeare's quartos as prompt-copies, with some account of Cholmeley's players and a new Shakespeare allusion', *RES*, 18 (1942), 129–43; see also John J. Murphy, *Darkness and Devils* (1984), and p. 90.
2   For an account of Shakespeare's use of properties, see Frances Teague, *Shakespeare's Speaking Properties* (Lewisburg, 1991); her list of properties needed for *King Lear*, 185–6, omits a crown and chair of state for Lear in the opening scene.

1 Interior of the reconstructed Globe theatre, Bankside, London

relationship between players and spectators was an intimate one. Shakespeare's plays were written for an audience that obtained much of its news, instruction (in sermons, for example) and entertainment through the ear; many people were illiterate, and there were no newspapers. It is hard now in our increasingly visual culture to imagine the excitement of listening to eloquent poetry and prose in stage dialogue, a pleasure that drew thousands to the theatres of London. *King Lear* has a strong action that is easy to follow, but the absence of modern technical devices meant that the atmosphere, the sense of location, time, external scene, as well as ideas and emotions, had to be generated mainly through the dialogue. Shakespeare's use of language shows that he expected his audience to include many capable listeners who could tune in to puns, paradoxes and nuances of meaning. He also expected them to engage with complex metaphors and images, as well as an innovative vocabulary. Some of these nuances are partly lost because of changes in pronunciation, as at 1.4.312–14, where 'slaughter ... halter ... after' were closer to being true rhymes than these words are now.

English as yet lacked formulated rules, and authors were accustomed to bend grammar to their service, to import or invent words, and had little concern, any more than printers did, for consistency or regularity. Over the centuries significant changes in grammatical usage have taken place, such as the virtual disappearance of the 'ethical dative' in phrases like 'wind me into him' (1.2.98), meaning 'obtain his confidence for me, on my behalf'. Meanings of some words, too, have shifted in ways that may not be obvious; for instance, the primary meanings of 'unhappy' (1.1.91) and 'unhappily' (1.2.144) were 'unlucky' and 'unfortunately' (a meaning still carried in 'mishap'), rather than 'discontented' or 'cheerlessly'; and the word 'practice' (as at 2.1.73 and 5.3.149) has lost the negative connotations of trickery or scheming that it had for Shakespeare.

The commentary on the text deals with these matters. Here it may be more helpful to consider other aspects of Shakespeare's use of language that may not be so readily noticed. We are accustomed to the idea of human beings as equal and all addressed as 'you'; Shakespeare reflects his world in making use of differences in his dramas. He does this most obviously by the way he distributes verse and prose to distinguish social levels as well as emotional states among his characters. He also registers different relationships by linguistic usage, notably in this play by some subtle distinctions in the use of 'thou' and 'you': 'thou' usually has 'overtones either of affection towards intimates, or of well-disposed superiority towards social inferiors, or of enmity towards strangers of the speaker's own rank' (Horsman, 225), while 'you' is the common, more neutral form. For example, when Lear encounters Regan in 2.2, he begins using the affectionate and pleading 'thou' to her, expecting kindness from her, but when he realizes that she is as hostile to him as Goneril he changes to a distancing 'you' (see 2.2.383 and n.). Kent and Oswald register their enmity when they quarrel at the beginning of 2.2 by addressing each other as 'thou', as do Edmund and Edgar when challenging one another to fight in 5.3. The moment when Goneril loses control over her passion for Edmund is marked by a kiss; before it she addresses him as 'you', afterwards with the affectionate 'thou', 'To thee a woman's services are due' (see 4.2.22 and 27). Later in this scene, as Albany and Goneril quarrel, they shift from the general 'you' to 'thou' in the bitterness of matrimonial wrangling.

Lear signals that he is well-disposed towards the disguised Kent in 1.4 by addressing him as 'thou', and the changes in Lear's moods in relation to the Fool, alternating between affection and irritation, are also registered in his use of 'you' and 'thou'. It is striking that in the reconciliation scene, 4.7, Cordelia addresses her father as 'thou' only while he is asleep, but when he wakes she relates to him formally as 'your majesty' in a scene that at once brings them together in great intimacy and suggests a certain distance between them, perhaps to remind us that she is now Queen of France, invading his country (though it is possible that, as in the opening scene, she cannot heave her heart into her mouth in addressing her father). In the final scene, by contrast, the pathos of Lear's address to the body of Cordelia is enhanced by his use of the affectionate 'thou' to her, and the common 'you' to everyone else.

What perhaps most distinguishes Shakespeare's language from everyday modern usage is its richness, density and flexibility; the cumulative effect is to open up resonances and implications in such a way that the possibilities for interpretation seem inexhaustible. Among the patterns of verbal imagery in the play, that relating to seeing, blindness and insight has a prominent thematic importance (see Heilman, 41–64), and the reverberations of terms like 'nothing', and of fools and folly, have been much studied. The sense of imminent violence in the action is fostered by the activity of verbs like 'pierce', 'stamp', 'fret', 'pluck', 'strike', 'dart', 'blister', and by the numerous references to animals (see Spurgeon, 338–44; Thompson,

47–88), many of which also relate to the reduction of men to bestiality, symbolized in the stripping away of clothes to a point where 'Man's life is cheap as beast's' (2.2.456). Also of thematic importance are two other features of the play's language. One is seen in the contrast between plain speech and rhetoric; the play generally favours directness and simplicity, but the temptation to align plain speaking with goodness and rhetoric with flattery or hypocrisy should be resisted, for Kent's bluntness in 2.2 earns him the stocks, and arguably does Lear a disservice, while Lear's passion in Act 3 can only be expressed in the magnificent rhetoric of his outcries in the storm.[1] A second feature, which has links with the first, is a concern with the gap that may exist and be exploited between words and intentions, or words and deeds. Kent draws attention to the potential emptiness of the eloquence of Goneril and Regan early on –

> And your large speeches may your deeds approve,
> That good effects may spring from words of love.
>
> (1.1.185–6)

– but Lear learns to understand the difference between word and deed only through harsh experience (see 1.1.55 and n., and 4.6.96–104).

The reader can savour the full text, and notice connections that may be missed in the theatre. It is in the study, for instance, that a reader is able to examine the numerous examples of words beginning with the prefix 'un-', and observe the way that the play begins with Kent remarking of Gloucester's adultery, 'I

---

1 David Aers and Gunther Kress seem to me to oversimplify in finding two languages in the play, one belonging to an upper-class ideology, the other to the ideology of the self-reliant individual; see 'The language of social order: individual, society and historical process in *King Lear*', in David Aers, Bob Hodge and Gunther Kress (eds), *Literature, Language and Society in England 1580–1680* (Dublin, 1981), 75–99. Kenneth J. E. Graham, in *The Performance of Conviction: Plainness and Rhetoric in the Early English Renaissance* (Ithaca, 1994), 190–219, sees plain speech in *King Lear* as 'challenging the corrupt morality of the powerful' (211), but I think he sees plainness too simply as good, and rhetoric as evil. However, both these thoughtful essays offer interesting perspectives on the play.

cannot wish the fault undone', and ends with Lear crying, 'Pray you undo this button.' Kent's wish is positive, but his mode of expression carries negative connotations. Lear has tried to tear off his clothes, crying 'come, unbutton here' at 3.4.107, where the main force of 'unbutton' is negative, since if he were to succeed, he would reduce himself to a beast. 'Pray you undo this button' has obvious positive resonances, as Lear emerges from his fixation on Cordelia to speak gently to someone else; yet it may have the negative force, if he refers to a button on his own clothes, of signalling his death as his heart bursts. Thus many 'un-' words in the play may have a kind of paradoxical quality, embodying contradictions, and enriching meanings, as in Lear's desire to 'Unburdened crawl toward death' (1.1.40, F only), which is vividly qualified by the final entry of the dying old king, burdened with the body of Cordelia.[1]

In the theatre each production necessarily selects one way of performing the play, emphasizing one range of possible meanings at the expense of others. If something is lost, much is gained, as the actions implied by the dialogue may clarify or convey emotion more strongly than the words. In the opening scene, for instance, what Lear does with the map he calls for (there are no stage directions relating to it in the early texts) vividly establishes the political and emotional tensions of the scene in a way that may be missed in reading it. The map of England (or Britain; see p. 18) both symbolizes Lear's power as King, and reduces it to a sheet of paper which he may easily tear up and destroy, or which, as in a recent production (Royal Shakespeare Theatre, Stratford-upon-Avon, 1993), may be made so large that it 'papered the stage floor', and gradually 'ripped and shredded' until it vanished in the final scenes (Holland, 201–2; and see

1 The implications of Lear's final action and words have provoked many differing interpretations; see especially Rosalie Colie, *Paradoxica Epidemica* (Princeton, 1966), who thinks that Lear's 'undoing is his recreation as a man' (481); and Leslie Thomson, '"Pray you undo this button": implications of "un-" in *King Lear*', *SS*, 45 (1993), 79–88. See also p. 78.

Hawkes, 136–7). Readers may also readily fail to notice the force of the image on stage at 2.2.172–92, where editions since the eighteenth century have inserted scene breaks not in the early texts, as if Edgar's speech about disguising himself as Poor Tom, 'I heard myself proclaimed', constituted a separate scene (2.3). Here Kent remains on stage throughout, asleep in the stocks, so that the audience sees two noble characters humiliated, disguised and reduced to wretchedness in a visual emblem of the disorder produced by the actions of Lear and Gloucester.

Hearing the dialogue spoken can also bring home possibilities easily missed in reading. When Regan says

> Sir, I am made of that self mettle as my sister,
> And prize me at her worth.
>
> $$(1.1.69–70)$$

it may be easier to note the quibble on 'metal' and the undertone of 'price' in the theatre than on the page. Only in performance is it possible to make Lear's 'Know that we have divided / In three our kingdom' (1.1.36–7) initiate a nihilistic interpretation of the play by emphasizing the first word as if it were 'No', as Paul Scofield did in Peter Brook's film version of *King Lear*. At 5.3.17, an audience hearing 'Gods spies' (Q and F), rather than 'gods' spies', is likely to interpret the phrase as 'God's spies', a reference to the Christian God, although only pagan gods are mentioned elsewhere in the play. Reading, hearing and seeing *King Lear* are activities that open up a variety of meanings, connections, reverberations and shapings of the action and dialogue. Some of the possibilities that seem especially valid at the present time are considered in the rest of this section, with reference both to critical accounts of the play and to productions in the theatre.

'Every inch a king'

The stage history of the play down to the late nineteenth century is remarkably consistent in one matter of some importance, namely in the presentation of Lear as a king, dressed in robes such as contemporary monarchs might wear.[1] The title-page of the Quarto calls the play the 'True Chronicle Historie of the life and death of King LEAR and his three Daughters', in imitation of the old play of *King Leir* published in 1605, as if it were really about the 'historical' Lear, who reigned, according to Holinshed's *Chronicles*, about 800 BC, before the founding of Rome (see pp. 30–1). The title-page may also have reminded some readers of *Locrine*, published in 1595 as 'Newly set foorth, ouerseene and corrected, By W.S.', a play that shows the civil strife and wars with 'Huns' and 'Scythians' that follow when Brutus, the legendary founder of Britain, divides his kingdom among his three sons, Locrine, Camber and Albanact. The story of Brutus and his sons is told in Holinshed's *Chronicles* a few pages prior to that of Lear (Holinshed, 1.443–4, 446–8). There may have been readers who also recalled Robert Greene's *Selimus*, published in 1594, a play about an early-sixteenth-century Emperor of Turkey and his three sons, the youngest of them, Selimus, rising to power by poisoning his father and murdering his brothers.[2]

Shakespeare's play is unlike these earlier ones not only in being concerned with daughters rather than sons, but also in being curiously disconnected from chronicled time;[3] we know nothing of Lear's antecedents, of how he came to the throne, of

1 Versions of the play by Nahum Tate or George Colman, with a happy ending, held the stage between 1681 and 1838 (see p. 85), but Lear was played as a majestic figure in these.
2 *Selimus* in turn has links with Christopher Marlowe's *Tamburlaine*, Part 2 (1590); the hero of this play also has three sons, though he retains his power to the end. *Gorboduc*, by Thomas Norton and Thomas Sackville (published 1565 and 1570), may have been known to Shakespeare and others; an academic play about the strife that erupts when a pseudo-historical King of Britain divides his kingdom between his two sons, Ferrex and Porrex, it includes among its cast a Duke of Cornwall and a Duke of Albany.
3 Derek Cohen has drawn attention to references to the past in the play in *Shakespearean Motives* (New York, 1988), 119–32; but none of these allusions relates to a specific time or period; they are general, as in the case of the servant in 3.7 who since childhood has served Cornwall, or of the Old Man in 4.1 who has been Gloucester's tenant fourscore years.

how long he has reigned, of his queen, or of how she lived or died; the play has no past, except in general references to vague injustices and neglect of the poor, which might apply to later times. Shakespeare makes use of the antiquity of the legend to the extent that Lear invokes classical deities such as Hecate and Apollo, and unidentified pagan 'gods' are appealed to throughout; in other words, antiquity is evoked in mythic terms, while the historical past is pretty much a blank, and the present is what matters in the action. Many critics and producers have therefore seen the play primarily in relation to the Jacobean age or to their own contemporary world, rather than to the period when Lear is said to have reigned.

A striking feature of productions of *King Lear* from David Garrick in 1756 to F. R. Benson in 1904 is the tradition of dressing Lear in scarlet trimmed with ermine, not only in the opening scene, but throughout most, if not all, of the play (Figs 2 and 5). Now that there are hardly any kings left in western society, and none who wield significant power, this way of playing Lear, with all the panoply of majesty, has gone, and with it, perhaps, an understanding of an important dimension of the action. The opening court ceremonial emphasizes Lear's majesty, and it is proper that one who is addressed by Kent as 'Royal Lear, / Whom I have ever honoured as my king' (1.1.140–1), should make a processional entry (preceded in the Quarto by 'one bearing a coronet'), sit on a throne, and wear royal robes and a crown. He is to conduct state business, in a formal ceremony publishing the division of the kingdom, and determining a husband for his youngest daughter. The date of the play's action is not fixed by any reference in the text, but Cordelia's suitors, representative of 'The vines of France and milk of Burgundy' (1.1.84), seem to belong to Shakespeare's own age, just as Cornwall and Albany have titles current in Jacobean England, and might remind an audience of Prince Henry, created Duke of Cornwall on the accession of James I to the throne in 1603, and Prince Charles, named Duke of Albany at his baptism in 1600. In other ways, not

2   David Garrick in regal costume in the storm scenes in Act 3, from the painting by Benjamin Wilson (1761), engraved by Charles Spencer; Garrick had played the role in 1756, restoring some of Shakespeare's lines changed or omitted by Nahum Tate

least in its frequent allusion to the Bible, and use of Samuel Harsnett's account of recent exorcisms (see pp. 102–4), the play speaks to and of Shakespeare's own age, an age in which King James told his parliament, 'Kings are justly called Gods, for that they exercise a manner or resemblance of Divine power upon earth' (*Works*, 307).

Some have thought that when Lear offers a coronet to Cornwall and Albany at 1.1.140, he takes one from his own head; but Shakespeare and his audience well knew the difference between crowns and coronets: crowns typically had raised sides, were 'archée', that is, had between four and eight arches over the circlet, and were topped with an emblem symbolic of the power belonging to kings. Coronets (the word is a diminutive of 'crown') were circlets worn by princes and dukes. It makes dramatic sense if Lear wears such a crown at the beginning of the play, and gives a coronet intended for Cordelia to Cornwall and Albany; he acts imperiously all through the scene, and if he continues to wear a crown until his exit this would highlight visually the irony of his actions in giving away his power, yet seeking to retain his royal prerogatives, 'The name, and all th'addition to a king' (1.1.137).

If Lear was robed and crowned like a king (Fig. 3), the play would have had further resonances for its original audiences, who might have detected analogies with James I. Some, indeed, have been tempted to find in the play something like a 'fictional portrait of the king himself',[1] but if James were in attendance when the play was performed at court in December 1606, as the title-page of the Quarto claims, he would have noticed the differences from his own situation and behaviour: James had two sons and a daughter, Lear three daughters; and Lear behaves in a way precisely opposite to that James had recommended to his heir:

> And in case it please God to prouide you to all these three Kingdomes, make your eldest son *Isaac*, leauing him all your kingdomes; and prouide the rest with priuate possessions: Otherwayes by deuiding your kingdomes, yee shall leaue the seed of diuision and discord among your posteritie; as befell to this Ile, by the diuision and assignement thereof, to the three sonnes of *Brutus*, *Locrine*, *Albanact*, and *Camber*.[2]

This passage illustrates one way in which *King Lear* had immediate relevance for a Jacobean audience, and it is reasonable to suppose that Lear's crown on stage was not unlike that worn by James himself.

---

1 So Patterson claims, 106–9; and see also Marcus, 148–59; for further discussion of possible topical concerns in the play, see pp. 89–93.
2 *Basilikon Doron* ('The King's Gift', addressed to Prince Henry) (Edinburgh, 1599; London, 1603), in James I, *Works*, 37. James may have read the story of Brutus in Holinshed, where it is twice told, the second time just before his account of the reign of Lear.

BEATI PACIFICI

Crounes haue their compasse, length of dayes their date,
Triumphes their tombes, felicitie their fate :
Of more then earth, can earth make none partaker,
But knowledge makes the KING most like his maker.

Simon *Passeus sculp:Lond.*   *Ioh: Bill excudit.*

3   Portrait of King James I, with crown, orb and sceptre, from the frontispiece to his *Works* (1618)

James had sons in mind as heirs, not daughters. It is not so clear that Lear's action in dividing his kingdom is certain to sow 'the seed of diuision and discord'; but, if he is unwise to give away his power, his distribution of his lands also, in contemporary terms, appears to have been illegal.[1] Queen Elizabeth had sought advice from her counsel on whether she could dispose of property, and her counsel advised her that any property, whether it came by descent from royal ancestors or from other sources, had to be regarded as part of the royal estate, and not as owned by the monarch as an individual. They appealed to the doctrine of the King's two bodies, and argued that the King (they referred always to the monarch as King) could not give away lands to a subject in his own person, but only by an open letter of authorization formally conferring the title, written on parchment and with the great seal attached, as the law prescribed: 'the land shall pass by the King's letters patent only by the course of the common law'.[2]

In marking out divisions on a map ('Give me the map there'), or, as in some productions, tearing it into three parts, Lear symbolically gives away his power and the revenues generated by his ownership of lands:

> Of all these bounds, even from this line to this,
> With shadowy forests and with champaigns riched,
> With plenteous rivers and wide-skirted meads,
> We make thee lady.

> (1.1.63–6)

Here Shakespeare may well have had in mind contemporary maps such as those of Christopher Saxton, which visibly represented

---

1 No character suggests Lear's actions might be illegal, but I think it would have been impolitic, to say the least, for Shakespeare to introduce the idea overtly in a play that was staged before King James, and that was subject to censorship.

2 *Law Reports*, 1.148. Ernst H. Kantorowicz considers this case in *The King's Two Bodies: A Study in Medieval Political Theology* (Princeton, 1957), 9–15 and 405–9, but only in relation to the doctrine of the King's two bodies. It is interesting that James I was chronically short of funds, and Robert Cecil, appointed Lord Treasurer in 1608, determined that Crown lands would have to be sold off to raise revenue.

forests, rivers, villages and towns as if to display the value of the land (Fig. 4). The importance of possessing land is emphasized in the subplot, in which Edmund's aim is to obtain Edgar's inheritance: 'Let me, if not by birth, have lands by wit' (1.2.181); lacking land, Edmund is dependent upon the whims of his father, as Lear, in giving away his kingdom, becomes dependent on the whims of his daughters.

The King's body politic included the body natural, 'but the body natural is the lesser, and with this the body politic is consolidated. So that ... he has not a body natural distinct and divided by itself from the office and dignity royal, but a body natural and a body politic together indivisible, and these two bodies are incorporated in one person' (*Law Reports*, 1.148). Lear divides what is 'indivisible', for in dividing the kingdom he acts in the body natural, doing what is not permitted in the body politic, and so divides not only his lands but himself. He cannot

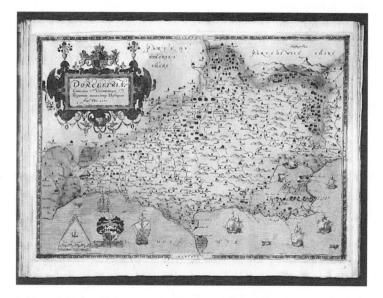

4 Map of part of Devon and Dorset, from Christopher Saxton, *Atlas of the Counties of England* (1579)

stop being King, yet gives his power away. This contradiction Shakespeare exploits to superb effect, as Lear is soon forced by Goneril to sense the split in himself without understanding it:

> Does any here know me? Why, this is not Lear.
> Does Lear walk thus, speak thus? Where are his eyes?
> Either his notion weakens, his discernings
> Are lethargied – Ha! Waking? 'Tis not so.
> Who is it that can tell me who I am?
>
> (1.4.217-21; F)

This last devastating rhetorical question[1] resonates because it highlights at once the rift in Lear himself that will lead to madness, and his failure to perceive the nature of what he has done.

If he has to come to terms with the recognition that he is 'a poor old man' (2.2.461), at the mercy of his daughters, at the same time he remains King, as is shown not only by the way Kent, Cordelia, Albany and Edgar refer to him as King throughout the later acts, but also in the way his enemies continue to think of him so, as when Cornwall and Regan grill Gloucester in 3.7 with questions such as 'Where hast thou sent the King?' It seems that the mental habit of all the characters is to take for granted that their country is a monarchy under Lear, just as it was no doubt taken for granted, both by Jacobean and by much later audiences, that England, or Britain (James was proclaimed King of Great Britain at Westminster in October 1604),[2] was essentially a monarchy. Garrick, Kean, Macready and Edwin Forrest, for example, all played the role dressed in scarlet and

---

1   The response to this question in both texts is also startling. In Q Lear himself cries, 'Lear's shadow', suggesting already a consciousness that he has lost authority; in F the Fool speaks these words, and they come more appropriately from his mouth as an acerbic comment on what he perceives and Lear as yet fails to see. Lear continues to act as if he retains royal authority until well into Act 2, and the change in F makes the action more consistent. See 1.4.222 and n.

2   The play may echo this proclamation in its reference to the armies of Albany and Cornwall as 'the British powers' (4.4.21); possibly Albany and Goneril were given Scotland; Cornwall and Regan the south-west, including Wales, marked out by Lear on the map in 1.1.

ermine. When in the storm scenes Lear tried to tear off his clothes, it was his regal gown, symbol of royalty, that the Fool and Kent prevented him from pulling off.[1] Cordelia returns in 4.3 to describe her father as 'Crowned ... with all the idle weeds that grow / In our sustaining corn', and her words serve as a stage direction for his entry in 4.6, where, as played, for instance, by Edwin Forrest, he still wore in his madness an ornate gown, with a mock crown, archée, tricked out with flowers, and he carried a sceptre made of straw, which enhanced the visual irony of his cry at 4.6.106, 'Ay, every inch a king!' (Fig. 5). The image of the mock-crown parodies Lear's appearance in the opening scene, while reminding us that he is still the King; it also, incidentally, may suggest a transition from the bleak storm scenes into a pleasanter atmosphere of summer and ripeness (see 4.4.3–7 and n.).

In the next scene he is brought on asleep in a chair, and we are told that he has been clothed in 'fresh garments' (4.7.22). His change of clothing is related to other imagery of clothing in the play, and especially to the stripping off by Kent and Edgar of the costume appropriate to their aristocratic status, their adoption of disguises and their shedding of these to appear in their proper roles at the end of the play. It would add to the dramatic irony and poignancy of this scene (4.7) if Lear were dressed again in robes befitting a monarch, as former stage tradition suggests;[2] for visually there is an echo of the opening scene, where Lear sits in his chair of state. Then Goneril and Regan perhaps might kneel before him in homage befitting his majesty, while Cordelia might stand to confront him boldly with the dismissive word 'Nothing'; now she kneels to him, and he tries to kneel to her, in

---

1   See the illustrations by George Scharf of William Macready in the storm scenes (the Fool played by an actress), and the engraving of David Garrick, also in the storm scenes, from a painting by Benjamin Wilson, Figs 8 and 2.

2   Maurice Charney, in *Some Facets*, 77–88, notes how in modern productions Lear has often been clothed in a white robe or 'gown of humility' in 4.7, as if to emphasize a moral contrast to the 'Robes and furred gowns' that hide all in Lear's tirade at 4.6.161.

5 Edwin Forrest costumed royally, with a crown and sceptre of straw in Act 4, Scene 6, when playing Lear in 1871

mutual forgiveness. But whereas Lear's thoughts centre on his new-found humility, his sense of himself as a 'foolish, fond old man', and on dying, 'You do me wrong to take me out o'the grave', Cordelia insists on engaging in a war to restore him to his throne. Her mission in invading England is to return to him his 'right', and the feebler he grows, the more she treats him with reverence, addressing him only as King, not as father:

> How does my royal lord? How fares your majesty?
>
> (4.7.44)

She insists, that is, on restoring him to the role he now, at last, wants to shed.

In Act 5 she draws him into joining her in leading the French forces to do battle against the British powers, so that he is, paradoxically, at the head of enemy forces invading his own country. He is still perceived as King, even when he is taken prisoner, and as 'the old and miserable King' is sent off under guard by Edmund. At the end, when he appears no longer fully aware of those around him, it is entirely appropriate on one level, if ironic on another, that Albany should still regard Lear as King, and propose to

> resign
> During the life of this old majesty
> To him our absolute power.
>
> (5.3.297–9)

Macready was robed as a king at this point, and so brought home to his audience the degree to which the play is about power, and the perception others have of the absolute monarch as symbolic of the body politic. Lear gives away his lands to Goneril and Regan but cannot stop behaving as a king. When he recovers from madness to acknowledge his frailty and wish for reconciliation ('Pray you now, forget and forgive; I am old and foolish.' 4.7.83–4), no one will grant his desire. It is an important aspect of Lear's tragedy that he cannot find release from his role as King, and

'Unburdened crawl toward death', as he proposes in the opening scene (1.1.40, F); the burden of authority remains, and he is always the monarch. It may be that this regal aspect of the play cannot be fully recovered in the present age. Few kings remain, and fewer still have much authority, so that the idea of majesty means less and less; but old, authoritarian rulers and presidents are familar enough, and it is important to try to retain a sense of Lear as an imperious monarch if we are to appreciate fully the interrogation of authority and power that is a central issue in *King Lear*.

'What wouldst thou do, old man?'

If one stage tradition emphasizes the royal authority of Lear, another gives more prominence to the man and father. The play typically offers multiple perspectives on the characters and the action. Different possibilities for playing Lear emerged in the rivalry between the majestic Spranger Barry and David Garrick in the eighteenth century, commemorated in anonymous verses:

> The town has found out different ways
> To praise the different Lears.
> To Barry they give loud huzzas,
> To Garrick – only tears.
> A king, nay, every inch a king,
> Such Barry doth appear,
> But Garrick's quite a different thing,
> He's every inch King Lear.[1]

Edwin Forrest, who played Lear with 'imposing majesty' on the New York stage until 1871, was succeeded by Tommaso Salvini: 'With ... Edwin Forrest one knew from the start and never forgot that Lear was the *king*, but Salvini, with his penchant for realism,

---

1   These lines are cited in Carola Oman, *David Garrick* (1958), 176; see also J. D. Hainsworth, '*King Lear* and John Brown's *Athelstan*', *SQ*, 26 (1975), 471–7, and Leigh Woods, 'Garrick's King Lear and the English malady', *Theatre Survey*, 27 (1986), 17–35.

emphasized the human attributes of *old man*'.[1] Philip Kemble and later Henry Irving also chose to represent Lear as rather decrepit, even palsied, from the beginning. In the twentieth century some powerful Lears renewed the tradition of playing the character with authority, for example, John Gielgud (1940), Donald Wolfit (1943) and Donald Sinden (1976). However, Kenneth Tynan was belated in greeting Peter Brook's production of the play in 1962, with Paul Scofield in the title role, with the cry, 'Lay him to rest, the royal Lear with whom generations of star actors have made us reverently familiar: the majestic ancient'. Tynan thought Brook had discovered a new protagonist, 'an edgy, capricious old man, intensely difficult to live with' (Tynan, 343), but Brook's was by no means the first production to downplay the idea of majesty.

In the opening scene in this production Lear sat on a primitive chair placed on a platform, with a crown standing on a cushion at one side. In his film version (1970), Brook omitted the opening dialogue, and the camera moved from a group of courtiers sitting in a broken circle to a close-up of Scofield, bareheaded, dressed in a garment apparently made of skins, sitting framed within a sort of primitive hooded chair. Many more recent stage productions have further reduced any sense of regality, and some have shown almost from the start an old pensioner with nothing royal about him, white-haired, rather senile, fitter for shuffle-board than to be ruling a kingdom, and losing the last shreds of an uncertain dignity very early on. In the 1990 production at the National Theatre in London, Brian Cox appeared in a wheelchair in the opening scene (Fig. 6). In later scenes Lear has sometimes been costumed in a kind of military greatcoat (Donald Sinden, 1976, and Michael Gambon, 1982), as if he were a superannuated army officer, or simply in shirt and braces, like Robert Stephens (Royal Shakespeare Theatre, 1993). It may be that as the very concept of royalty in the western

1   William Rouseville Alger, *Life of Edwin Forrest, the American Tragedian*, 2 vols (Philadelphia, 1877), 2.781; Charles H. Shattuck, *Shakespeare on the American Stage: From Booth to Sothern and Marlowe*, 2 vols (Washington, 1987), 2.155.

6 Brian Cox as King Lear in a wheelchair in the opening scene of the National
Theatre production by Deborah Warner (1990)

world becomes increasingly hard to grasp, while at the same time a distrust of authority in all its forms becomes more widespread, and anxiety grows about a steadily ageing population, the emphasis in productions of *King Lear* would inevitably reflect these changing conditions. So recent productions have often set out to show 'the overwhelming pathos of an old man humbled and petted, disarmed and then restored to peace and gratitude' (Bratton, 41). Lear as everyman in the modern world tends to be characterized as a victim of violent forces in an uncaring society rather than as an agent, an authoritarian monarch causing the violence that destroys him.

Rather than emphasizing Lear's concern, as the Folio puts it, to divest himself of rule and cares of state (1.1.49–50), such productions give visual prominence to the business with the map. If Lear's action in scrawling boundaries, tearing or otherwise marking the map becomes the focal point, then he may be seen as essentially a patriarch redistributing his property, and Kent's line, 'What wouldst thou do, old man?' (1.1.147), becomes more important than the references to royalty. Peter Brook had the work of Samuel Beckett in mind when he began directing his production, and may have been influenced by Jan Kott's *Shakespeare our Contemporary* (English version 1964), in which *King Lear* is viewed, through the prism of the Theatre of Cruelty, and specifically Samuel Beckett's *Endgame*, as showing the disintegration of both the Renaissance and the modern world (Marowitz, 104, and Leggatt, 46). The characters seemed to be stumbling about blindly in a hostile universe, and words of consolation, repentance or protest, such as the lines given to the servants who take pity on Gloucester at the end of 3.7 (Q), and Edmund's late impulse to do some good (5.3.241, Q and F), were cut, so that the overall effect tended towards nihilism. Brook released and made others aware of the play's potential bleakness, which later productions have softened, and he also made his wilful, arrogant old Lear no better than Goneril and Regan, receiving from them a treatment he perhaps deserved.

Brook's vision of the play had great influence, and helped to reinforce the idea of *King Lear* as Shakespeare's most powerful play, and the one that had most to say to our age (Foakes, 2–5, 54–60; Bratton, 44–6). The numerous stage productions since the 1960s have reconfigured what the play has to say, often restoring much of the text Brook cut, and presenting a Lear who is likely to appear as an increasingly pathetic senior citizen trapped in a violent and hostile environment. Most of these productions have given prominence to the pathos of an old man pushed out of doors by daughters who simply want to get rid of a nuisance, and driven mad by his sufferings until his mind is healed through the love of Cordelia. The image John Wood offered of the mad Lear (4.6) in the 1990 production by Nicholas Hytner at the Royal Shakespeare Theatre (Fig. 7) registers the kind of effect achieved. He is costumed in what look like old jeans, shirt hanging outside them, a worn jacket, and a

7 John Wood as King Lear, with Gloucester and Edgar, in the Royal Shakespeare Theatre production by Nicholas Hytner (1990), Act 4, Scene 6

hat with straws stuck in the brim. The image of Lear 'Crowned' (4.4.3) has gone, and instead we see an old figure garbed, as are Gloucester and Edgar by him, in clothes that might be cast-offs; all three have an immediate contemporary relevance in so far as they represent the old and weak cast out by an uncaring society, and are visually reminiscent of the homeless people who may be encountered in the streets of many cities today.

Such treatments of the play on the stage may be regarded as corresponding to a shift in scholarly criticism towards interpreting it as 'subverting the status quo', and presenting a radical critique of political power and social injustice applicable to the present time as much as to Jacobean England (Ryan, 4–5, 10–12). Readings of this kind may be supported by reference to the strong satirical denunciation of greed and the power of gold, the 'common whore of mankind', in *Timon of Athens* (4.3.43), a play probably close in date of composition to *King Lear*. The first part of the play then becomes a preparation for the crucial episodes in Acts 3 and 4. Lear's great 'Poor naked wretches' speech (3.4.28–36) is likely to carry a special weight, as his cry is spoken by one who is visibly reduced to rags and poverty:

> Take physic, pomp,
> Expose thyself to feel what wretches feel,
> That thou mayst shake the superflux to them
> And show the heavens more just.
>
> (3.4.33–6)

His 'Off, off you lendings!' may be taken as a cue for him to strip off clothes, in contrast to an older tradition in which the Fool and Kent prevent him from doing this (Fig. 8). A key point in the play then comes when the blind Gloucester, who has also called for distribution to undo excess (4.1.73), partners Lear in an attack on injustice and the old king shows a new perception of 'the great image of authority: a dog's obeyed in office' (4.6.154–5). An emphasis on such moments makes plausible a construction of the end of the play as a retreat 'finally into the domestic and familial as

8 Drawing by George Scharf of William Macready in his Covent Garden production (1838), Act 3, Scene 4, attended by Kent and Priscilla Horton as a female Fool, who restrain him from tearing off his robes as he cries 'Off, off, you lendings!'

a shelter from sociopolitical awareness', designed perhaps to avoid giving offence to James I when he saw the play in 1606 (Patterson, 115–16). This kind of approach also may suggest a more immediate relevance in relation to social conditions at the end of the twentieth century in countries such as Britain and the United States, where homelessness and poverty are common problems, and where coping with the elderly and the failings of old age has become a major concern for individuals and governments.

'Let the great gods ... find out their enemies now'

If an emphasis is placed on Lear as a king, then the play may be seen as primarily about what he does; if the emphasis is placed on Lear as an old man, then the play may be seen as primarily about what is done to him. Since William Macready restored most of the original play to the stage in 1838, many productions have sought to incorporate another way of regarding Lear, as an archetypal or quasi-mythic figure. Macready gave the play a setting suggesting an ancient world of prehistoric monoliths, and on his stage 'druid circles' rose 'in spectral loneliness out of the heath' (Odell, 2.210). Such settings, containing or suggesting ancient megaliths or stone circles, often with some reference to Stonehenge (Fig. 9), have been a recurrent feature of the staging of the play, still to be seen in the Granada production for television in 1983, with Laurence Olivier as Lear, which begins 'in a mist-enshrouded replica of a stone circle, incongruously in use as a throne-room' (Bratton, 58).

Although the idea of such visual associations may have been initially prompted in part by a Victorian urge to historicize a play about a king who reigned, according to Holinshed, about 800 BC,

9 The megalith or Stonehenge setting, as used in the opening scene of the Granada television production, directed by Michael Elliott (1983)

they also helped to evoke a sense of the 'elemental and primaeval' (Swinburne, 171), and so worked to dehistoricize it. In part the association of the play with elemental forces and Druid circles may be linked with the elevation of *King Lear* by Romantic writers as the grandest of Shakespeare's plays, in which we find in Lear a 'sublime identification of his age with that of the heavens themselves' (Lamb, 1.107; cited approvingly by Hazlitt, 4.259-60). Keats also gave currency to a lofty idea of the play as a 'fierce dispute, / Betwixt Hell torment & impassioned Clay' (Keats, 1.214–15). Criticism and the stage perhaps fed on one another, as the leading critic of the later nineteenth century, Edward Dowden, found in the play 'some vast impersonal significance', a mystery too grand for critical analysis, so that words were inadequate to respond to such sublimity (Dowden, 257–9, 274). On the stage the visual links with Stonehenge might be used to dissociate the play from the contemporary scene, and suggest instead a remote mythical world detached from ordinary human life.

The effect sought was to reinforce the idea of the play as distanced into prehistory, and so monumental and grand in scope as to transcend political or topical issues, and even to defeat criticism. Lear was treated by a series of critics as representative of Man, capitalized and abstracted from ordinary men, and enduring tribulations beyond the capacity of the reader or audience. This sense of a play of cosmic scope, concerned with universals, showing Man transcending the petty affairs of ordinary life, also alerted critics to its connections with the morality play, and Christian interpreters especially tended to see the play in quasi-allegorical terms as the personal 'pilgrimage' of Lear, a quest often generalized into the journey of suffering mankind on the way to redemption through the agency of the holy figure of Cordelia ('Cor' from the Greek for heart, and 'delia' an anagram of ideal). Perhaps the richest development of such a way of regarding the play is to be found in Maynard Mack's essay *King Lear in our Time* (1965), in which he wrote:

This is what the Morality play was, a vision acted upon a platform whereby the invisible became visible and man's terrestrial pilgrimage was glimpsed whole in its entire arc of pride and innocence, temptation and fall, regeneration and salvation or ruin and damnation. This is also, essentially, what *Lear* is, save that in the case of *Lear* we must add to the arc of pilgrimage Shakespeare's more tragic vision of the creature whose fate it is to learn to love only to lose (soon or late) the loved one, and to reach a ripeness through suffering and struggle, only to die.

(Mack, 117)

Terms like 'pilgrimage', 'salvation' and 'damnation' signal a reading of a play that both recalls and questions Christian teaching, as for example in relation to the idea of suffering and the need for patience in adversity (see 2.2.458–60 and 3.4.28–36 and nn.), or the idea of despair (see 4.6.33–4 and n.). The most explicit echo of Christ's words is also deeply ironic; when Cordelia says 'O dear father, / It is thy business that I go about' (4.4.23–4; Luke, 2.49) she has in mind putting her father back on the throne, not doing God's business.

At the same time, *King Lear* refers directly only to pagan gods, even if Cordelia is given an aura of holiness in the Quarto, and Poor Tom's assortment of devils mockingly recalls exorcisms carried out by recusant priests (see below, p. 102). It has been claimed that *King Lear* was originally played and for the most part has been staged before Christian audiences, who might react to it as a 'Christian play about a pagan world' (Maxwell, 142). On the other hand, stage tradition has sought to bring out the grandeur of the play and a sense of Lear as representative of mankind by visually associating it with pagan mysteries and a world far distanced in time from that of the audience. The gods in the play remain inscrutable, show no sign of being interested in human affairs and may not exist at all. The potential for bleakness in the cruelty of the action, in the sufferings of Lear and

Gloucester and in the death of Cordelia, seemed, in the decades following the Second World War, to give the play a special resonance in relation to the Theatre of the Absurd. Herbert Blau staged a notable production of *King Lear* at the Actors' Workshop in San Francisco in 1961, interpreting the play as 'a provisional summing up of the disturbed questing of our entire theater in a period infected by the demoralizations of the Cold War' (Blau, 279). Like Blau, Brook associated the play with current anxieties about the hydrogen bomb, the Cold War and the concept of mutual assured destruction, but for him there was no sense of a quest, for, he said, according to Charles Marowitz, 'as characters acquire sight it enables them to see only into a void' (Marowitz, 21).

So Brook showed the three outcasts, Lear, Gloucester and Edgar, on a bare stage in 4.6 as if they were the victims of a malignant fate in a hostile universe, clothing them in costumes that appeared to have been put together from old rags (Fig. 10). Giorgio Strehler, in another influential production of the play in 1972, shadowed this time by T. S. Eliot's *The Waste Land*, also put Lear and Gloucester in rags in this scene (Kennedy, 217–19). The effect was very different from the Nicholas Hytner production of 1990 discussed above (pp. 27–8); in this John Wood was dressed in clothes that could have been found as discards on a rubbish dump, but in Brook's production, Paul Scofield and the others were arrayed in robes specially made to look timeless, though they appeared to have been sewn together from old sackcloth, achieving an archetypal effect, as of lost souls groping about in a void. Now such images may seem dated, but these three distinguished directors brought out and made available a potential in the play that the critics had on the whole neglected. Where many had seen *King Lear* as a morality play moving towards regeneration, and leaving unresolved the difficult question, why does Cordelia have to die?, these directors staged an apocalyptic vision in which, as Herbert Blau put it, 'it became possible to ask again about the death of Cordelia, not why should

10 Lear, Gloucester and Edgar (Paul Scofield, Alan Webb and Brian Murray) in Act 4, Scene 6, in the production by Peter Brook for the Royal Shakespeare Theatre (1962)

she die? but why should she want to live?' (Blau, 282).

'Thou art my flesh, my blood, my daughter'

If the figure of Lear dominates the play, whether as king, poor old man, or representative of mankind, it is a work richly peopled with a varied cast of characters. Among them Cordelia has an importance out of relation to the small number of lines she speaks in her few appearances. In the redemptionist interpretations of the play that dominated criticism in the first half of the twentieth century, Cordelia was seen primarily as the agent of Lear's regeneration, and idealized as a saintly figure, or an embodiment of love. If Cordelia could be thought of as representing a 'pure redeeming ardour' (Dowden, 259), or transfigured into the 'perfection of truth, justice, charity' (Danby, 138), then it became possible to find in the image of Lear bending over the dead Cordelia at the end of the play an image of a 'secular Pietà', or even 'the image of Mary bending over another broken child' (Gardner, 28; Mack, 116). The elevation of Cordelia in this manner opened up a way of explaining her death at the hands of a hangman, which otherwise may appear gratuitous and inexplicable, by presenting her as a martyr (Chambers, 32; Foakes, 50).

On the stage idealized Cordelias tended to become sentimental, as in the production by Henry Irving (in 1892), who made the reconciliation scene, 4.7, the climax of his performance, provoking Ellen Terry to weep; he tasted her tears on his fingers, and 'he was restored to faith and peace when Cordelia died to prove her love for him true'.[1] Playing the scene thus for pathos brought out the tenderness of the restoration of love between father and daughter, rather than a religious feeling. By the mid-twentieth century the play began to be staged with a stronger emphasis on the harshness and violence of its world, and the various kinds of resistance built into the dialogue of this scene came more into focus. On the one hand, Lear's opening words to Cordelia in 4.7 are 'You do me wrong to take me out o'the grave', and almost his last are 'Pray you now, / Forget and forgive'; but Cordelia insists on keeping him alive, and does not forgive her sisters (if Lear's words include this meaning). Once Lear is awakened, Cordelia addresses him only as king, not as father, and her aim is to restore him to a throne he keeps reminding her he no longer wants (Rosenberg, 283–91). In place of a feeble Lear going off supported physically by Cordelia, as in Irving's scene, Paul Scofield in Peter Brook's production, like John Gielgud (1940) and Charles Laughton (1959) before him, made his exit alone, and Cordelia, following him, was a powerful Queen of France, not simply an embodiment of tenderness (Fig. 11).

---

1 Bratton, 41, and see also 191–2. David Garrick may have initiated the tradition of playing this scene which culminated in Irving's treatment.

11 Peggy Ashcroft playing Cordelia as Queen of France, with breastplate and sword, Act 4, Scene 4, in the production by John Gielgud and Anthony Quayle, Royal Shakespeare Theatre, 1950

Cordelia is offstage between the opening scene and 4.4. In the Folio text she reappears abruptly and unheralded with drum and colours at the head of a French army, an entrance which makes plausible some toughness in her character. The description of her in Quarto 4.3 as an emblem of pity shedding holy tears is followed by her entry in 4.4 accompanied by a doctor, lending support to a milder conception of her. Her manner in Act 4 is likely to be roughly consistent with her behaviour in Act 1. Nineteenth-century Cordelias usually drew praise for being sweet, innocent and modest in their first appearance (Bratton, 67). It is easier to present Cordelia in this way if she is a Cinderella figure, flanked by two palpably wicked sisters. Twentieth-century directors and critics have come to recognize deeper resonances in the opening scene, which provides no clue as to the ages of Goneril and Regan, no mention of their mother, no hint as to why or how an eighty-year-old monarch comes to have a daughter of marriageable age, young enough to be a grandchild, and no explanation of Lear's apparent desire for Cordelia to marry the Duke of Burgundy.[1] They have also noticed the formal nature of the state ceremony in which Cordelia refuses to play her part by making a public statement of her love for Lear. In Adrian Noble's 1982 production at the Royal Shakespeare Theatre, Goneril and Regan came downstage and addressed their statements of love directly to the audience as if prepared for the occasion. The closeness appropriate to relations between father and daughters is disrupted by the formal distance required in a state ceremony between king and subjects.

Goneril and Regan need not be played as mere flatterers, but rather as married women who, with their aristocratic husbands, have adapted to the court and its conventions. The more the formal nature of the scene is brought out, the more likely it is that

---

1 In *Reading Shakespeare in Performance: King Lear* (Rutherford, 1991), James P. Lusardi and June Schlueter consider problems of interpreting the opening scene with specific reference to Cordelia's situation, and in relation to the BBC and Granada television productions of 1982 and 1983.

Cordelia will be seen as obstinate and self-willed in her response to her king and father. In the Granada film version, Laurence Olivier began as a physically frail but absolute monarch who required everyone, including his daughters, to prostrate themselves before him; but he entered with his arm round Cordelia, displaying her as his favourite. The love-test became a game, and Lear took pleasure in watching how his daughters performed, chortling as Regan went beyond Goneril with 'Only she comes too short' (1.1.72). In this context Cordelia's 'Nothing' was shocking, as an incredulous Lear asked her to speak again. Goneril and Regan were played as older, experienced women, Cordelia as very young. Her defiance of Lear's authority may have recaptured something of the *frisson* it could have elicited on the Jacobean stage.

Everyone seems to know that Cordelia is Lear's favourite, and her stance of confrontation in saying 'Nothing, my lord' to the King might well have seemed astonishing to a Jacobean audience. An appropriate way for a princess to address her father may be illustrated in the letter the newly-married Princess Elizabeth wrote to her father, James I, from Canterbury, some days before she left the country in April 1613; in it she makes no mention of the husband, Prince Frederick of Bohemia, she had married in February; instead, she laments 'the sad effects of separation', and that she may never again see her father:

> My heart, which was pressed and astounded at my departure, now permits my eyes to weep their privation of the sight of the most precious object, which they could have beheld in this world.

She wishes she could 'show to your majesty with what ardent affection she is and will be, even to death, Your majesty's very affectionate, very humble, and very obedient daughter and servant'.[1] If daughters of a king then were expected to show above all

---

1   The letter was printed by Mary Anne Everett Green in *Elizabeth, Queen of Bohemia*, revised by S. C. Lomas (1909), 64, and is cited in Rosenberg, 51. Princess Elizabeth never saw her father again.

obedience, and express themselves to their fathers in a style not unlike that of Goneril and Regan, the behaviour of Cordelia in the opening scene may have appeared outrageous to a Jacobean audience. Now feminist critics especially have drawn attention to several further possible undercurrents in the relation between Lear and his daughters. Lear hoped to set his rest on Cordelia's 'kind nursery' (1.1.125), as if to find in her a mother, and so deliberately puts himself 'in the position of infantile need from which he will experience the rest of the play'.[1] Alternatively, Lear may be seen as harbouring a suppressed incestuous desire for Cordelia, which surfaces late in the play when he envisages a future in her embrace, 'We two alone will sing like birds i'the cage' (5.3.9).[2]

We may sense from the beginning how much like Lear his daughters are, Cordelia in standing up to him against all expectation, Goneril and Regan in their tough dealings with him once they have rule. The Folio text has more lines than the Quarto describing the riotous behaviour of Lear's hundred knights in Goneril's house, which makes more plausible her complaints against her father. If she has some cause for her behaviour, nothing excuses her treatment of him, yet Lear himself comes to recognize that she is behaving as a mirror image of himself in her arbitrary exercise of authority:

> But yet thou art my flesh, my blood, my daughter,
> Or rather a disease that's in my flesh,
> Which I must needs call mine.
>
> (2.2.410–12)

This 'disease' is identified by Lear as the 'mother' (2.2.246) swelling up towards his heart, a hysteria or suffocation that

---

1 Citing Adelman, 116; see also Marianne Novy, *Love's Argument: Gender Relations in Shakespeare* (Chapel Hill, 1984), 150–63, and Kahn, 33–49.
2 See Lynda E. Boose, 'The father and the bride in Shakespeare', *PMLA*, 97 (1982), 325–47, and Kay Stockholder, *Dream Works: Lovers and Families in Shakespeare's Plays* (Toronto, 1987), 118–47. See also the comments on Jane Smiley's *A Thousand Acres* (New York, 1991), pp. 88–9.

afflicted women, especially maids and widows, rose from the womb, and took people with a choking in the throat (Jorden, C1ʳ–C4ᵛ and G2ᵛ). Here may be seen the suppressed presence of the mother of Lear's daughters, who is so notably absent from the play. If they are like him in their masculine qualities, it may be said of Lear that 'in recognizing his daughters as part of himself he will be led to recognize not only his terrifying dependence on female forces outside himself but also an equally terrifying femaleness within himself' (Adelman, 104).

Here may be found an explanation for Lear's gross misogyny in his mad condition:

> Down from the waist they are centaurs, though women all above. But to the girdle do the gods inherit, beneath is all the fiend's.

> (4.6.121–3)

His venom here has been mistaken for the play's or even Shakespeare's misogyny, but it surges out of the experiences of the old king himself. The harsh treatment of him by Goneril and Regan provokes him to reject 'women's weapons, water-drops' (2.2.466) in favour of rage, and it is only after he is restored to sanity that he surrenders to the healing power of tears in being reconciled to Cordelia (4.7.47, 71). Lear's misogyny may also be understood in relation to the generation gap in the play. Lear surrounds himself with his hundred knights, and devotes himself to hunting and the values associated with manliness; he hires the disguised Kent in 1.4 for his 'service' in beating up Oswald. His daughters may be seen as representing a new generation, whose world is more refined, as evidenced in the 'gorgeous' clothes that scarcely keep Regan warm (2.2.456–9; see Fig. 12), and in the appearance of Oswald, who seems foppish to Kent (see 2.2.32, 40, 53–4). In the Olivier/Michael Elliott television version of the play, this sense of change was reinforced by the way Edmund acquired handsome clothes as he rose to become Earl of Gloucester, while Edgar, who was wearing what looked like rich

12 William Larkin, portrait of Frances Howard, Countess of Somerset, 1612,
showing the fashion for very low-cut bodices

satin on his first appearance, became the half-naked beggar Poor Tom.

Goneril and Regan are two of the strongest women characters Shakespeare created. They rarely receive their critical due.[1] They are often treated merely as wicked sisters, embodiments of lust in opposition to the virtue of Cordelia; such accounts hardly do them justice, even if the play finally demonizes their sexuality, while Cordelia seems virginal or sexless, in spite of being married to the King of France (Barker, 18–19). It might seem reasonable to assume that the three sisters are close together in age, given that Goneril and Regan appear to be childless, and that Lear curses Goneril in terms that imply she is not yet a mother ('Into her womb convey sterility', 1.4.270). However, the harder natures of the older sisters, their emotional distance from Cordelia as 'last and least' (F, 1.1.83), as well as their behaviour suggesting they are mature married women, have led directors usually to cast them as some years older than Cordelia. On stage a disparity in age works well, as in Peter Brook's 1962 production, in which Irene Worth as Goneril and Patience Collier as Regan were very much older than Diana Rigg as Cordelia. Talented and forceful actresses have been drawn to the roles of the older sisters, who are inadequately characterized if seen simply as wicked. As the eldest, Goneril might, by the rule of primogeniture, have expected to become queen of a kingdom Lear arbitrarily divides up; also she has been married (like Cordelia, by her father's will?) to a husband she despises, so that she might have good reason to feel hostility towards Lear. Regan is differentiated from her by having a husband who matches her in toughness, so that she is driven to assert her authority, as being of the royal line, by upstaging him. Both daughters, like

1   There have been one or two attempts to make a case for them, as in Stephen Reid's essay, 'In defense of Goneril and Regan', *American Imago*, 27 (1970), 227–44. Elaine Feinstein's play *Lear's Daughters*, staged in London in 1987, presented Goneril and Regan as artistic young women cold-shouldered by their father, who really wanted sons.

their father, enjoy the exercise of power, Goneril in bullying Albany, Regan in maintaining an edge over her husband by interrupting Cornwall when he tries to take charge (as at 2.2.132 and 146–8). If both were given by Lear to much older husbands (Cornwall offers to be a 'dear father' to Edmund, dearer than Gloucester, at 3.5.25), their interest in the young and energetic Edmund becomes explicable. It is ironic that not their ambition but their love for a man, Edmund, a love they denied their father, makes them overreach themselves. If in the end their deaths by poison and suicide are somewhat melodramatic, Shakespeare had to find a way to have them die so that the last scene could display Lear with the bodies of all three daughters, destroyed by a process he started with the division of the kingdom.

'I had a son'

King Lear is the only one of Shakespeare's major tragedies that has a subplot. The story of Gloucester and his two sons has parallels with and significant differences from that of Lear and his three daughters. The opening scene gives prominence to Cordelia's rebellion against her father, and the next scene is dominated by Edmund's rebellion against his father and the gods invoked by Lear. As long as a conception of the play as essentially Lear's pilgrimage to redemption prevailed, critics generally supposed that we should approve the basic order of society assumed in *King Lear*, and saw in the two families a simple moral contrast between a good daughter and bad son. Cordelia was to be treated with devotion and reverence, while Edmund was described by A. C. Bradley (Bradley, 302) as no better than a common thief:

> Practically, his attitude is that of a professional criminal. 'You tell me I do not belong to you', he seems to say to society: 'very well: I will make my way into your treasure-house if I can. And if I have to take life in doing so, that is your affair.'

When, in the wake of the Second World War, J. F. Danby reinterpreted the play in relation to his own society, which he now saw as competitive and corrupt, he reconfigured Lear and Cordelia as representatives of an ideal community, marking perhaps his own yearning for a golden age inevitably located in a far-off, utopian pre-capitalist world. Edmund then took on a new aspect, with Goneril and Regan, as embodying a ruthless, greedy, self-seeking capitalism, and typifying the worst features of modern western societies; they were even linked with the rise of fascism, in opposition to a lost 'communal tradition', based on a 'benevolent thesis Shakespeare's age inherited from the Middle Ages', associated with Lear and Cordelia.[1]

Such a view of Edmund demonizes him as merely evil, and ignores the initial impact he makes. In a play that has few soliloquies of the kind that establish a bond between character and audience, Edmund has three in his first scene, and by his energy, humour and self-command at once engages our interest. As Coleridge remarked, 'Courage, Intellect and strength of Character were the most impressive Forms of Power; and ... to Power in itself, without reference to any moral end, an inevitable Admiration & Complacency appertains' (Coleridge, 2.328; Foakes, 51–4). Coleridge also noted the way Shakespeare provides various circumstances that allow us to admire Edmund, such as his bastardy (not his fault), and his being sent away from home and brought up in a strange house ('He hath been out nine years, and away he shall again', 1.1.31–2). If Gloucester is seen as humiliating Edmund ('the whoreson must be acknowledged') and as representing, like Lear, an old patriarchal and tyrannical power structure, then Edmund may be praised for his 'revolutionary scepticism'. In challenging for Edgar's inheritance, and pursuing wealth and status, Edmund brings out the 'obsession with power, property and inheritance' of a society that screens its authoritarianism behind ideological claims based on meta-

1   See Danby, 50, 194–5; Edwin Muir, 7–8, 15, 23–4; and Foakes, 51–4.

physical notions of values like nobility and justice (Dollimore, 197–8).

The play has often been seen as reflecting a transition from an old order to a new one. Much depends, then, on how this transition is envisaged. It can be seen as showing a beneficent old order, to which Edgar is linked, associated with Nature in its good aspects (as Lear appeals to the 'offices of nature, bond of childhood' at 2.2.367), giving way to a new order based on self-interest, and devoted to Nature in a bad sense, as the goddess to whom Edmund appeals, that is to say Nature as manifested in the law of the jungle ('the lusty stealth of nature', 1.2.11). Alternatively the old order may be seen either as a dictatorial authoritarian order giving way to a bourgeois pattern of values; or, in Marxist terms, as an order collapsing because of its own internal contradictions.[1] As suggested earlier (p. 40), the play also has indications of a transition from a rough physicality that values manliness, represented by Lear and his knights, to a more refined and courtly society. The evaluation of Edmund may turn upon the interpreter's preference for the old order or the new one. Either way, Edmund is a disturbing figure, vital and energetic, and, just as Goneril and Regan offer more rewarding roles for actresses than Cordelia does, so Edmund offers a more satisfying part for a modern actor than the role of Edgar.

Edmund has often been played as a suavely intelligent, rather dashing figure, or as a 'cheery swashbuckler who could engage the audience's complicit laughter'.[2] Edgar, by contrast, is liable to seem bumbling, even stupid, in being so readily tricked by his brother; and attempts to provide a cause for his behaviour, such as presenting him as a naïve student absorbed in books,[3] do not

1 Turner, 101. See also James H. Kavanagh, 'Shakespeare in ideology', in John Drakakis (ed.), *Alternative Shakespeares* (London and New York, 1985), 159.
2 As by Ralph Fiennes in Nicholas Hytner's 1990 production, and see Bratton, 81; the quotation is from Peter Holland's review of Adrian Noble's 1993 production, in which Edmund was played by Owen Teale, *SS*, 47 (1994), 202.
3 In the 1993 production by Adrian Noble; see Holland, 202.

make much difference. Unlike Edmund, Edgar has no particular character at the beginning, and he gains in stature as he takes on a series of disguises, reappearing in his own person only in the final scene of the play. It is too simplistic to idealize him merely as a moral parallel to Cordelia, representing good (though Regan seems to link them in this pagan play by referring to him as Lear's 'godson', 2.1.91). It also diminishes Edgar simply to turn him into a kind of everyman, experiencing what it means to become, in his various disguises, Poor Tom, a peasant, a messenger, a knight, and ending in his final role of ruler, sharing the realm (Danby, 171). Some have argued that a Jacobean audience would have been aware of the historical Edgar, King of England 959–75, whose reign was regarded as something of a golden age for his establishment of codes of law, founding of monasteries and concern for religion, which led to his being made a saint (*Some Facets*, 221–37). The problem with this argument is that Edmund, King of East Anglia 841–69, was perhaps better known as a hero, for his stand against a Viking army, and as a saint, who gave his name to Bury St Edmunds.[1]

Edgar is most vividly present when on the run, and the title-page of the Quarto, which specifically draws attention to his 'sullen and assumed humour of TOM of Bedlam' (see p. 112), suggests that when the play was first staged Edgar was seen as a much more prominent role than Edmund, especially in his assumed disguise as Poor Tom. The figure of such a beggar, half naked and mad, or pretending to be so, must have been familiar to many in Shakespeare's audience, for he is typical of the con-men described in many accounts of vagabonds (see 2.2.185 and n.). Thus Poor Tom had an immediate appeal for the audience at the Globe as linking a play based on ancient history directly with

---

1 David Hugh Farmer, *The Oxford Dictionary of Saints* (Oxford, 1978), 120–2. A later Edmund, also sainted, was Archbishop of Canterbury, 1233–40. All three Saxon names used for characters in *King Lear*, Edgar, Edmund and Oswald, were the names of saints in the Christian calendar.

the notorious underworld of the Jacobean period. The word 'sullen' usually indicates a gloomy bad temper or melancholy, and audiences may have seen in him a figure they feared or hated to meet on highways (Carroll, 431–4); but when he turns into Poor Tom at 2.2.172–92 and shares the stage with Kent in the stocks, the two figures, both of them outcasts and humiliated, are seen together as the victims of Lear's rage and Edmund's scheming. Later he becomes in effect a living representative of the 'Poor naked wretches' neglected by the rich and powerful, since the moment he emerges from the 'hovel' in 3.4 he becomes the focus of Lear's attention. Edgar's role-playing is at once sympathetic and disturbing, as it is later on in Act 4, when he deceives his father, faking a kind of miracle to make the blind old man think he has survived a fall from Dover cliff. Here Edgar denies him the death he seeks:

> Is wretchedness deprived that benefit
> To end itself by death?
>
> (4.6.61–2)

The text opens up varying, even conflicting, perspectives on this episode, in which Gloucester sees himself as a burnt-out candle-end (4.6.39–40), while Edgar speaks of preserving 'the treasury of life' (4.6.43). Is Edgar 'saving' his father, or indulging himself in a kind of game, playing yet another role, that of God? (See 4.6.1–41 and commentary.)

In Nahum Tate's version of the play, which continued to be performed until well into the nineteenth century, Cordelia survives to be married to Edgar. Like her, Edgar tended to be idealized in accounts of *King Lear*, as, for example, by Harley Granville-Barker, who called him a 'Christian gentleman' in a pagan play.[1] A tougher questioning of Edgar's role has put less

---

1 Granville-Barker, 61. Compare Danby's treatment of Edgar, 152, 190–1, as 'the good man' putting on disguises as protective colouring, while his 'Kingly nature' remains 'uncontaminated'.

stress on his suffering, and more on his 'capacity for cruelty' in not revealing himself to his father, and so begrudging him the recovery of his 'eyes':[1]

> O dear son Edgar,
> The food of thy abused father's wrath,
> Might I but live to see thee in my touch,
> I'd say I had eyes again.

(4.1.23–6)

Disguised as Poor Tom, Edgar says his study is 'How to prevent the fiend and to kill vermin' (3.4.155); he becomes a killer in disposing of Oswald and Edmund, and, some would say, in symbolically bringing his father to the point of death. So Edgar may be played in a variety of ways, and it can be difficult to reconcile his 'goodness' with what on stage has often been presented as a vindictive revenge on Oswald or on Edmund. So in one production (Royal Shakespeare Theatre, 1993) he 'was so traumatized by the blinding of his father that he repeatedly sought to revenge it, blinding Oswald with his staff as he killed him and trying to gouge Edmund's eyes with his thumbs at the end of their savage duel' (Holland, 202). It is also possible to play Edgar's duel with Edmund as that of a champion of good emerging out of anonymity to destroy evil, and a fuller understanding of the complexity of Edgar's character might seek to connect the idea of a fiend-haunted game-player capable of mental and physical cruelty with the idea of a 'redemptive or heroic figure'.[2]

---

1 See Cavell, 54–7; he looks for a psychological explanation of Edgar's behaviour. Shakespeare may simply have wanted to avoid a recognition scene that might undercut the effect of the awakening of Lear in 4.7.
2 Harry Berger, Jr, 'Text against performance: the Gloucester family romance', in Peter Erickson and Coppélia Kahn (eds), *Shakespeare's Rough Magic: Essays in Honor of C. L. Barber* (Newark, 1985), 210–29, citing 221. This is a richly nuanced account of Edgar and his relations with Gloucester. See also Janet Adelman's introduction to *Twentieth Century Interpretations of King Lear* (Englewood Cliffs, NJ, 1978), 8–11, and Carroll, 426–41.

The matter is complicated by the differences between the Quarto and Folio texts. In the Quarto Edgar has an expanded role; he participates in the mock-trial in 3.6, moralizes on Lear's sufferings at the end of this scene, and then, in 5.3, he delivers a long report of Kent's coming upon him and the dead Gloucester. These passages, which are not in the Folio, might support an idea of Edgar as a character who repeatedly offers a moral commentary to explain or justify the suffering of others, a commentary which is quickly exposed as inadequate in the face of experience. In the end nothing supports his statement, 'The gods are just' (5.3.168); a 'moral concept of this kind becomes an affront to the human experience the play presents' (Brooke, 52). The optimistic thrust of Edgar's moralizing hints at the possibility of a happy ending, which would not be inappropriate for the subplot, as indeed Gloucester's heart bursts partly in joy. At the same time, his complacencies are shattered by the much more complex main plot, in which the death of Cordelia reveals a worst beyond any worst Edgar could imagine.

The Folio gives the final lines of the play to Edgar, and not to Albany as the Quarto does. In the Quarto it seems that Albany will be the new ruler, with Edgar's support; the Folio text could be interpreted to mean that Albany withdraws, leaving Edgar in charge, and some have taken it for granted that Edgar will be the new King.[1] Edgar has an obvious symbolic function as the 'unaccommodated man' who brings Lear and Gloucester to a new moral consciousness, and as a force of good overcoming evil in battle; once we look deeper into his role in both versions he appears more ambiguous, indeed full of contradictions. He always remains in control of himself, detached, avoiding emotional commitment, and ready with a formula that justifies or

---

1 For example, Danby, 171; Rosenberg, 326. Rosenberg, 245–50, sees cruelty in Edgar in his analysis of 4.1, and he doesn't expect much from the new ruler: 'no summer haloes the new wearer of the crown, Edgar' (326).

makes bearable suffering; perhaps this coolness, as in the way he tricks his father, is especially disturbing.[1]

'Thou wouldst make a good fool'

In the opening scene, when Lear behaves as the very embodiment of regal authority, the Fool is not mentioned in the list of characters who enter with him. When Lear first calls for him in 1.4, the Fool seems to know everything that happened earlier, so it is dramatically effective to have him accompany Lear on his entry at 1.1.32, as he did in Jonathan Miller's BBC film for television with Frank Middlemass in the role (1982). The Fool is most vividly established in 1.4 and 1.5.[2] If he is not present in the first scene, it may be claimed that because the Fool and Cordelia are never on stage together the same actor could have doubled in both roles; but it is very probable that Cordelia was played by a boy, and the Fool by the professional comedian Robert Armin (1568–1616), who had joined Shakespeare's company about 1600, replacing Will Kemp, who had been noted as an improviser, clown and dancer. Armin, who seems to have been small in stature, ugly, and at the same time highly intelligent, combined the physique of a 'natural' fool or clown with the mental agility of a professional wit. He arrived at the Globe in time to play Touchstone in *As You Like It* and Feste in *Twelfth Night*. In his own play *The Two Maids of More-clack* (1608), he doubled in the parts of an idiot clown and a witty steward, and showed off his skill in both.[3] In creating the

---

1 See Foakes, 199. Cavell, 54–7, troubled by Edgar's failure to reveal himself to his father, offers a psychological explanation, suggesting that he feels shame and guilt himself, and cannot bear to see his father maimed and dependent on him. Michael Warren witnesses to the complexities of Edgar's character, but simplifies the differences between Q and F in arguing that in Q Edgar remains 'immature', and ends 'devastated by his experience', while in F he grows into a 'potential ruler', a 'resolute man in a harsh world'; see Warren, 'Albany', 105.

2 The substantial textual changes in the Fool's part as between the Quarto and Folio, and their implications for the conception of his character, are considered below, pp. 133–7.

3 See Wiles, especially 182–91; Bratton, 8–14; and, for a general account of the professional Fool in life and drama, Welsford. Rosenberg, 102–15, also has a full and interesting account of the various ways in which the Fool can be played on stage.

role of the Fool in *King Lear*, Shakespeare may have had in mind
the spectrum of Armin's skills. These skills would have included
singing, and there are indications that the Fool sang some snippets
of ballads and songs, as at 1.4.158–69, where Lear asks 'When
were you wont to be so full of songs, sirrah?' The question suggests that the Fool did not normally sing, and he may have spoken
most of his rhyming passages. Little early music survives that can
be linked with him.[1] It may be worth noting that Armin was
almost forty when he first performed as the Fool, a role in which
Lear frequently addresses him as 'boy'.

In a passage present only in the Quarto, the Fool refers to
himself as 'The one in motley here' (1.4.140), indicating in that
text that he was wearing the long parti-coloured coat, usually a
patchwork of green and yellow, the traditional livery of a fool in
an aristocratic household. He also had the eared hood or coxcomb he offers Kent at 1.4.94, and probably carried a bauble or
marotte, a stick or baton of office surmounted by a carved head
with ass's ears, which he may have used to point his joke
addressed to the audience at 1.5.49–50, and to mock Lear in
various ways. This costume was outmoded by the time *King
Lear* was written, and Shakespeare no doubt wished to avoid
suggesting any direct connection between the character in the
play and Archie Armstrong, a favourite of James I, who came
with him to London in 1603 as his official court jester. Archie
was noted for an impudence verging on arrogance, but retained
considerable influence throughout the reign of James and on
into that of Charles I. A print of uncertain date shows him wearing a long coat, apparently of a rich material, over a matching
doublet, with a falling band at his neck, and carrying a stylish
feathered hat and gloves, so that he looks more like a courtier

---

1   The evidence is gathered in Sternfeld, 158–94. He prints possible settings for 'Then
they for sudden joy did weep', 1.4.166–9; 'He that has and a little tiny wit', 3.2.74–7;
and 'Come o'er the bourn, Bessy, to me', 3.6.25–8.

than a traditional fool (Fig. 13).[1]

The long coat was derived from the coats children wore, as appropriate to the 'natural' with impaired intellect who remained immature, and whose wisdom was instinctive; Shakespeare may have had this image of a natural fool in mind in making Lear address him as 'boy' so frequently, and the Fool call Lear 'nuncle', as if he were an elderly relative. At the same time, the dialogue of this professional 'all-licensed fool', as Goneril calls him at 1.4.191, shows him to be shrewd, witty and very much a conscious entertainer. There is no present-day equivalent for the Fool, and no long stage tradition. The part was omitted by Nahum Tate from his version of the play, and when the Fool was restored by William Macready in 1838, a young actress, Priscilla Horton, played the role (see Fig. 8). The young and pretty actresses who have often since then been cast in the part, providing a visual link with Cordelia, have tended to make the character pathetic, though Emma Thompson (Renaissance Theatre Company, 1990) and Linda Kerr Scott (Royal Shakespeare Company, 1990) in different ways both created a much tougher image of the Fool. In recent times male actors have often associated the part, through costume and style of acting, with modern images of clowning derived from the traditions of music hall or circus (Fig. 14). Although popular music-hall theatre died in the 1950s, giving way to the power of cinema, its forms of comedy have survived by being absorbed into television and into the drama, in the work of Pinter, Beckett and other dramatists (Davison, 13–66). Actors such as Alec Guinness (1946), Frank Middlemass (1970) and most strikingly Antony Sher (1982) have consciously recalled this tradition by their costume or manner of playing.[2]

1 Welsford, 171–81, describes Armstrong's career, and reproduces the print of him here in Fig. 13; see also Wiles, especially 190, and Rosenberg, 104–5.
2 Giorgio Strehler dressed the Fool (Ottavia Piccolo) as a circus clown, and Lear (Tino Carraro) as a ringmaster in his famous production for the Piccolo Teatro in Milan in 1972; see Dennis Kennedy (ed.), *Foreign Shakespeare* (Cambridge, 1993), 152–3.

Archee, *the Ringes Iester.*

13 Archie Armstrong, Fool to King James I, from his *A Banquet of Jests*, 5th edition (1657)

14 Antony Sher as the Fool in the circus or music-hall tradition, in the production by Adrian Noble, Royal Shakespeare Theatre, 1982

Such treatments of the part may vary in emotional range as well as in age and even sex, for, as Stephen Booth has noted, the Fool 'breaks out of every category in which he might be fixed' (Booth, 39). Young or old, humble or aggressive, sad or merry, sensitive or acerbic, most representations of the Fool tend to emphasize his strangeness, his difference from others, and give most weight to his close relationship with Lear (Fig. 15). Just what the balance in this relationship should be is a difficult question. If he is made too dependent on, or interdependent with, Lear, then the Fool may lose his bearings after Act 2 and validate John Bayley's perception of him: 'Made to play his part upon the stage of the court, the Fool shrivels into a wretched little human being on the soaking heath' (Bayley, 61). However, the Fool's unexpected entry on his first appearance at 1.4.92, after having absented himself for two days (as Lear notices at 1.4.70), establishes some measure of his independence, as does his

15 Ian Hughes, with his breeches down, mocking Lear in Act 1, Scene 4, in the production by Adrian Noble, Royal Shakespeare Theatre, 1993

immediate verbal attack on the King's folly, when he is at once threatened with a whipping for telling a bitter truth. Perhaps this is why some directors have preferred to avoid the clown image and omit the trappings of the professional fool, costuming the Fool more or less like other attendants in the court.[1] In Act 3 the Fool drifts apart from Lear, who only notices him, with momentary concern and affection, occasionally (as at 3.2.68 and 3.4.26, Folio only), as he becomes increasingly obsessed with what his daughters have done, and fixated on Edgar as Poor Tom. The Fool, who in Act 1 has a complex intimacy with Lear that combines tenderness with flashes of hostility (Lear calls him 'a pestilent gall to me', 1.4.112), becomes a general voice of common sense in the storm scenes ('This cold night will turn us all to fools and madmen', 3.4.77), and a social critic, more noticeably in the Folio text, which adds his 'prophecy' at the end of 3.2.[2]

In the Quarto the Fool's role ends with his participation in the mad Lear's imaginary trial of his daughters; this is not in the Folio, which gives the Fool an exit line 'And I'll go to bed at noon', responding to Lear's mad topsy-turvy 'we'll go to supper i'the morning' (3.6.81–2) with a proverbial phrase meaning 'I'll play the fool too'. Nothing more is heard of him until the end of the play, when in Lear's last speech the ambiguous line, 'And my poor fool is hanged' (5.3.304), refers most obviously to Cordelia (who we know has been hanged), but recalls the Fool also. No explanation is given for the Fool's disappearance, a matter which some have found troubling. In the notable production by Adrian Noble (Royal Shakespeare Theatre, 1982), the Fool (Antony Sher) was stabbed to death by a mad Lear (Michael Gambon) as

---

1 As Buzz Goodbody did in her production for the Royal Shakespeare Company in 1974.
2 Some, like Stone, 119–21, have disputed the authenticity of the Fool's prophecy, but for a refutation of Stone, and full discussion of the meaning and importance of this passage, see Wittreich, 60–74; see also the note on 3.2.79–96. For further comment on changes in the Fool's role in relation to Q and F, see pp. 133–7.

he retreated downstage in an attempt to escape the old king's indiscriminate fit of rage prompted by his daughters. By contrast, Grigori Kozintsev keeps the Fool alive to the end in his film version (1970). The film ends with a close-up of Edgar, but for Kozintsev the Fool becomes especially important as symbolizing the continuation of life in the sound of the pipe he plays (Kozintsev[1], 198; Foakes, 60–1):

> Rags, and the soft sound of the pipe – the still voice of suffering. Then, during the battle scenes, a requiem breaks out, then falls silent. And once again the pipe can be heard. Life – a none too easy one – goes on.

If directors have anxieties about the disappearance of the Fool, I doubt if anyone watching a performance is troubled by it. Lear has gone mad, and can no longer relate to the wit of the Fool. The action takes a new direction with the blinding of Gloucester in 3.7, and Lear himself is offstage for roughly five hundred lines in the Quarto text, and four hundred or so in the Folio, which makes some substantial cuts between 3.7 and 4.6. When Lear returns in 4.6 he has become, in his madness, a kind of seer, with something of the Fool's wisdom, and himself plays the fool in relation to Gloucester. In Act 1 Lear and the Fool maintain in their dialogue something like the cross-talk act of the music-hall tradition, in which one partner in a double act plays the 'feed' or straight man to the other; as he goes mad, and is engrossed by Poor Tom in Act 3, Lear loses this close relationship with the Fool; and 4.6 establishes a new cross-talk act in which Gloucester has become the 'feed' to Lear, who effectively takes over something of the role of the Fool, though not, of course, his function as professional entertainer.

It is in the role of professional entertainer and 'feed' to Lear in Act 1 especially that the Fool serves, with his generalizing rhymes and songs and direct address to the audience at the end of 1.5 (see 1.5.49–50 and n.), as a connector between the audience and the titanic figure of the old King, who is so absolute in his authority, peremptory in his actions, and given to outbursts of violent rage. The Fool may be thought of as a lightning conductor, earthing the power of majesty, and humanizing Lear. In these early scenes Lear plays straight man to the Fool, whose intellectual superiority in seeing what the consequences of dividing the kingdom will be brings out the aspect of folly in what *King Lear* has done: 'Now thou art an O without a figure; I am better than thou art now. I am a fool, thou art nothing' (1.4.183–5). This function of the Fool in the early scenes can be effective in whatever manner the Fool is played. It is a function that loses its importance when Goneril and Regan bring home the truth of the Fool's perceptions in Act 2 and a function that is no longer necessary when Lear goes mad. Thus in Acts 2 and 3 the Fool's comments are directed more to other characters such as Kent, or to everyone including the audience, and his rhymes and songs usually have a generalizing force as expressing a kind of folk-wisdom. In Act 3 he is more concerned to persuade Lear to take shelter from the storm than to mock him. After 3.6 the Fool has no function, and it is understandable that Shakespeare should let him drop from sight.

The Fool's barbed words often compel assent, but it is assent to a truth, not the whole truth, which is usually more complex. The Fool is a channel for many of the play's ironies and multiple perspectives, which leave no value fixed, and no character unscathed. What seems wisdom from one point of view is folly from another, as the Fool brings out in his advice to Kent that it would be wise to abandon Lear: 'When a wise man gives thee better counsel give me mine again; I would have none but knaves follow it, since a fool gives it' (2.2.264–6). The Fool's mockery of Lear for lacking wisdom ('Thou shouldst not have been old till thou hadst been wise', 1.5.41–2) is spoken by one who has no responsibilities; and his comment springs rather from his perception of the true nature of Goneril and Regan than from folly on Lear's part. It is by no means clear that Lear's retirement and his generosity in dividing the kingdom are in themselves foolish decisions. The Fool's prophecy at the end of 3.2 (Folio only) passes into something like cynicism (see note at 3.2.79–96), and points up a scepticism about human actions and values that enriches the whole play and makes efforts to produce an overall interpretation of it seem reductive. The impact of Montaigne is relevant here, and for further comment see pp. 104–5.

'Tis the time's plague when madmen lead the blind'

It is possible to play Lear as mentally disturbed or senile from the beginning (Rosenberg, 25–7; Bratton, 40–1), in order to provide a psychological explanation for his rages. Some support for regarding him as suffering initially from 'acute hypochondriacal melancholy developing into mania' can be found in Renaissance ideas about madness.[1] The structure of the play, however, brings Lear to a first major climactic moment at the end of Act 2, when Regan takes Goneril by the hand as the two sisters combine to whittle away their father's train of knights: 'What need one?' It is only at this point, when Lear at last recognizes the truth of what the Fool has been telling him, that his emotional outburst in his great speech beginning, 'O, reason not the need!' marks the beginning of a breakdown, as his anger collapses into incoherence:

> I will have such revenges on you both
> That all the world shall – I will do such things –
> What they are yet I know not, but they shall be
> The terrors of the earth! You think I'll weep,
> No, I'll not weep.

> (2.2.468–72)

Here he senses that he will go mad, but until well into the storm scenes in Act 3 he appears in control of his language, and one

---

1 Hoeniger, 330, and see Wittreich, 102. Hoeniger also notes a link between Lear and Nebuchadnezzar, who was punished by God with madness for his fury after he cast Shadrach, Meshach and Abednego into the burning fiery furnace (Daniel, 3–4).

effect of his interaction with the Fool is to confirm that he is in his right mind. As long as Lear can participate in cross-talk with the Fool, he thinks he is sane, and so, I believe, does the audience. At the end of the first act, which Lear has dominated, the Fool's comment, 'Thou shouldst not have been old till thou hadst been wise', provokes his cry, 'O let me not be mad, not mad, sweet heaven!'; and at the end of Act 2, after his wild thoughts of revenge on Goneril and Regan, Lear's perception of what lies ahead is addressed to the Fool: 'O fool, I shall go mad' (2.2.475). It is as if the Fool provides a measure of the King's sanity.

The parallel with Gloucester bears on the peremptory behaviour and anger of Lear in the early part of the play. After casting Cordelia off, Lear's remark, 'I loved her most' (1.1.124), seems at first even more outrageous than his action, but also makes explicable the extremity of his behaviour, in so far as she was for the old man both a fantasy object of sexual desire and a substitute mother.[1] Reacting in a similar way, Gloucester at once denounces Edgar as an 'Unnatural, detested, brutish villain' (1.2.76–7) on hearing Edmund's faked letter. In the Quarto he goes on to express his momentary disbelief:

GLOUCESTER   He cannot be such a monster.
EDMUND   Nor is not, sure.
GLOUCESTER   To his father, that so tenderly and entirely loves him. Heaven and earth!

(1.2.94–7)

This last exchange between Edmund and Gloucester is omitted from the Folio, perhaps because the idea of Gloucester loving Edgar 'tenderly and entirely' seemed absurd or contradictory in relation to his previous fulminations; but his actions here are

---

1   See Kahn, on Lear's 'frustrated incestuous desire for his daughter' (39), and Lynda E. Boose, 'The father and the bride in Shakespeare', *PMLA*, 97 (1982), 325–47; they argue that Lear's desire for Cordelia is deflected into a deeper need for her as 'daughter-mother' (Kahn, 40).

explicable, like those of Lear, in terms of love for a favourite turning to hatred.[1]

If Gloucester's words and actions here recall those of Lear in the previous scene, another reason could be that Shakespeare wished us to see that Lear's behaviour was not abnormal, but rather the ingrained habit of one whose authority had long been taken for granted in a patriarchal society. The old aristocrat Gloucester behaves in a similar way, expecting unquestioning obedience from his children, as if this were a guarantee of their love for him. The rebellion of the children has been seen as marking the transition from an old order to a new, or as exposing contradictions within the absolute monarchy maintained by Lear (see p. 45), but dramatically the immediate conflict is between the old who are set in their ways and have become spiritually blind, and the young who either reject the dishonesty this blindness breeds (Cordelia) or take advantage of the situation for personal gain (Edmund, Goneril, Regan).

Once the parallel between the two old men and their treatment of their children is established, Gloucester diminishes into a background figure, the ineffectual host who would like to help Kent and Lear but accepts the authority now of Cornwall and Regan. His efforts to help Lear, especially in the storm scenes, effect a shift of sympathy towards him, so that the savage blinding of him by Cornwall and Regan in 3.7 is especially shocking. Most Victorian productions cut the scene or had the blinding carried out offstage; in the early twentieth century it was more often done on stage, as Gloucester sat with his back to the audience, but in modern times directors have emphasized the element of sadism, especially since 1962, when, in Peter Brook's production, Cornwall used one of his spurs to gouge out an eye in view of the audience (Bratton, 157; Rosenberg, 242–4).

---

1   In the opening lines Gloucester claims Edgar as his own ('I have a son'), while identifying Edmund as his mother's son: 'Edmund is unequivocally his mother's child' (Adelman, 105). It was proverbial that the greatest hate proceeds from the greatest love (Dent, H210).

It now seems scarcely adequate to say that Gloucester gains insight in losing his physical sight ('I stumbled when I saw', 4.1.21).[1] The violence (considered further in the next section) is too horrible for such neatness. In any case, if Gloucester has moments when he accepts patiently his condition, he keeps returning to thoughts of suicide or dying ('A man may rot even here', 5.2.8), even as Edgar takes it upon himself to 'cure' his 'despair' (4.6.33–4). In this scene the usual roles of father and son are reversed, and Edgar is exercising power over his father, especially in the central episode, when he stages Gloucester's 'death' in mime. As noted above, p. 47, the powerful visual image of Gloucester falling off an imaginary cliff has wider resonances than Edgar's stated aim. Some have seen here another act of gratuitous cruelty, as Edgar plays a rather unpleasant trick on his father (see Rosenberg, 263–5). Critics, directors and actors, who disagree as to whether this episode is tragic, grotesque, absurd or even farcical, also debate 'how much of an illusion his [Shakespeare's] audience might have been under about the presence of a cliff' (Peat, 47–9; Bratton, 175–7). It is arguable that the point of the whole incident would be lost unless the audience is fully aware all the time that there is no cliff. The sequence relates to a conventional stage device of having a character 'die' and return to life, as Bottom, playing Pyramus, does in *A Midsummer Night's Dream*. This device is basically comic, but Shakespeare transforms the convention, as Gloucester is drawn into a charade that raises his hopes for the one thing he wants, death, only to be deprived of what he calls 'that benefit' (4.6.61). The more successful an actor is in conveying an illusion of suicide (Peter Brook made his Gloucester faint as he fell, and regain consciousness convinced that he had died), the more cruel the effect seems to be, as he revives to cry, 'Away and let me die.'

---

1 Heilman's influential study, *This Great Stage* (1948), brought out the importance of blindness and insight in the play, of what he called 'rationalistic obtuseness' as against inward 'illumination'; see especially 277–91.

This episode also brings the gods momentarily into the action, but only as created and stage-managed by Edgar. The spectacle of Gloucester kneeling in prayer, 'O you mighty gods, / This world I do renounce' (4.6.34–5), is at once pathetic and empty, since there is no evidence of another world, except in the words Edgar uses, deceiving his father for the time being into thinking his 'life's a miracle' (4.6.55), and telling him what to believe:

> Therefore, thou happy father,
> Think that the clearest gods, who make them honours
> Of men's impossibilities, have preserved thee.
>
> (4.6.72–4)

Gloucester is anything but a 'happy father', and we get no nearer to the gods than here, as Edgar creates them in his fiction.[1] Many find especially troublesome in this scene the question why Edgar does not reveal himself to a father whom he has heard say,

> O dear son Edgar,
> The food of thy abused father's wrath,
> Might I but live to see thee in my touch,
> I'd say I had eyes again.
>
> (4.1.23–6)

There is no easy answer, as Edgar seems intent on abusing him further, and Stanley Cavell's explanation is worth pondering, that Edgar avoids being recognized partly out of shame and guilt at his own gullibility earlier, and partly because he cannot bear the fact that his father is incapacitated: 'He wants his father still to be a father, powerful, so that *he* can remain a child' (Cavell, 56).

Dramatically Gloucester's passage through a kind of death and restoration to life may be seen as a parallel to Lear's obliviousness in the loss of his wits and subsequent return to sanity;

---

1 The whole play is, of course, a verbal construct; but Edgar appears here within Shakespeare's composition as the author of his own fiction in the layered illusions of reality in the play.

and it prepares for the encounter of the two old men that follows the Dover cliff episode. Lear, who has long been absent from the stage, returns, crowned with flowers, to play both fool and king, delivering through what Edgar calls 'Reason in madness' (4.6.171) a searing indictment of the misuse of authority and perversion of justice. He also 'tries' and 'pardons' Gloucester for his adultery, in a misogynistic outburst against all women. The scene of the three outcasts, the half-mad Lear, blind Gloucester, and Edgar disguised as a peasant, provides a heart-rending stage emblem of the inversion of values and the confusion brought about by the actions of Lear and Gloucester. As Edgar's vexations pale in relation to the miseries of his father, so Gloucester's distresses are overshadowed by those of Lear; yet there is poignancy in Gloucester's wish that he could be mad like Lear, and not endure the conscious knowledge of his 'huge sorrows' (4.6.276). One effect of this scene is to restore Gloucester to a central place in the action, as a victim of physical cruelty, once more paralleling Lear, the victim of psychological cruelty. We have Edgar's narrative account of the moment when, at last, he reveals himself to his father, whose heart could not stand the strain, and

> 'Twixt two extremes of passion, joy and grief,
> Burst smilingly.
>
> (5.3.197–8)

Shakespeare thus avoids another recognition scene that might have undermined that between Lear and Cordelia, and provides a suggestive verbal image that anticipates the death of Lear, though to what extent, and whether it is to be interpreted as analogue or as contrast, remains a matter for debate.

'Then kill, kill, kill, kill, kill, kill!'

King Lear depicts an authoritarian society that takes violence for granted. In the first part of the play this violence is associated chiefly with Lear and his followers. In the opening scene Lear attacks Kent, and the dialogue suggests he draws his sword as if to kill him (1.1.161–3). Goneril says Lear struck her 'gentleman' in 1.3, and we see Lear do this in the next scene, when he hits Oswald, and rewards Kent for tripping and beating him. Goneril and Regan complain about the riotous behaviour of Lear's hundred knights, complaints reinforced in the Folio text by the addition of speeches that stress the outrageousness of his demand to be housed by his daughters with a train of so many:

> 'Tis politic, and safe, to let him keep
> At point a hundred knights! Yes, that on every dream,
> Each buzz, each fancy, each complaint, dislike,
> He may enguard his dotage with their powers
> And hold our lives in mercy.
>
> (1.4.316–20)

The most visibly riotous of Lear's followers is Kent, put in the stocks for beating Oswald. Edmund, who has drawn his sword 'in cunning' on Edgar, and wounded himself to lend conviction to his device for getting rid of his brother, now draws his sword again to stop Kent's onslaught on Oswald.

Oswald reports at 3.7.15 that when Lear walked off into the storm at the end of Act 2 he was accompanied by 'Some five- or six-and-thirty of his knights' as well as other attendants, but in 3.2 he enters with only the Fool by him, and it seems that his knights have deserted him. The violence done to Lear thus far is psychological, symbolically figured in the storm that mirrors his inner turmoil and pushes him into madness. A major shift is effected at the end of Act 3 with the blinding of Gloucester, shocking as an act of gratuitous cruelty done for Cornwall's personal satisfaction ('our power / Shall do a courtesy to our wrath', 3.7.25–6). This act, and the subsequent killing of the servant who has given Cornwall his death-wound, decentre Lear, who has dominated the stage hitherto, and shift attention to Gloucester on the one hand, and to the prospect of war ('the army of France is landed', 3.7.2–3) on the other. The action, so to speak, opens out from this point to deal with the fortunes of Gloucester, but also with the intrigues of Goneril, Regan and Edmund, the return of Cordelia, and the battle between the French and British forces. The focus is less on Lear himself, and more on the confusion he has brought about, a confusion of values marked notably in 3.7, a scene in which 'the traitor, Gloucester' is punished, while his son, Edmund, also confusingly now 'my lord of Gloucester', is praised for his loyalty in betraying his father to Regan and Cornwall. To be loyal to Lear is to be a traitor to the new rulers, and, in aiding her father, Cordelia becomes an enemy who leads French forces in an invasion of England. The bloodshed of 3.7 is a prelude to more violence – to the killing of Oswald, the deaths of Goneril and Regan, the fight between Edgar and Edmund, and the hanging of Cordelia. Though many directors have included some kind of staged warfare, realistic or stylized (Leggatt, 8–9), Shakespeare does not include the battle between the French and English forces in 5.3; the archetypal overthrow of evil by good, brother by brother, symbolized in the fight between Edgar and Edmund, remains the climactic visualization of violence in the action.

In staging the play it is possible to make the violence prominent, or to minimize it, according to whether the emphasis is on the rehabilitation of Lear or on the chaos he brings about. Lear's 'hundred knights' (1.1.134), a larger figure than in any of the sources, to be 'sustained' by Goneril and Regan, become important in this connection: how many of his proposed retinue are seen on stage, and to what purpose? Feudal aristocrats maintained trains of armed retainers, but the custom was in decline in Shakespeare's time, though the royal 'progresses' of Elizabeth and James, as they made state visits with large retinues to great houses in the country, are well documented.[1] Stage directions in

---

1 In 1605 James I went on a 'progress' to Oxford by stages between 16 July and 27 August, lodging for several nights in each of various houses. One day he attended church with nine attendant lords, and was accompanied at Apthorpe by numerous lords of his council, causing Edward Lascelles to report that it made 'the trayne verye

the texts of the play are vague at best about Lear's attendants; four or more are needed in 1.4, but at 2.2.192, when Lear enters to be confronted by Goneril and then Regan, there is no entry for knights in the Quarto, and in the Folio the stage direction specifies only a single knight. Those whose moral sympathies are wholly with Lear from the start may claim that Goneril simply invents her complaints in 1.4 (reinforced by Regan) about the disorderliness of his knights, and may put weight upon the 'sober and judicious comments' of the knight about the lessening of affection and kindness towards the King in Goneril's household (1.4.55–60); it may then be claimed that his function is 'to give the lie to Goneril's account of him and his companions as riotous, insolent and deboshed' (Mahood, 162).

Since Peter Brook, in his 1962 production, brought on enough knights to cause something like a riot in Goneril's house when Lear overturned a table and his knights followed his example in 1.4 (Fig. 16; Rosenberg, 121–2; Marowitz, 28), later productions have often made the knights visually prominent. The action does, after all, provide some support for violent behaviour by the knights. Edmund leads Regan to think that Edgar, accused of plotting to murder his father, was one of 'that consort' (2.1.97), and Kent, hired as one of his train by Lear in 1.4, at once trips and beats Oswald. His fierce verbal and physical onslaught on Oswald again in 2.2 may satisfy the audience's gut feeling that Oswald and Goneril deserve to be castigated, but his violence arguably does his master a disservice, confirms the riotous behaviour of his followers and exacerbates the conflict between Lear and his daughters. The whittling away of Lear's followers marked by Regan's 'What need one?' symbolizes the

greate'. In 1608 another 'progress' by James proved 'as unwelcome as rain in harvest', and the owners of great houses in its path moved their households to other parts of the country (Nichols, 1.517–24). See also Mahood, 160–1; *Some Facets*, 185–220; Paul Delany, '*King Lear* and the decline of feudalism', *PMLA*, 92 (1977), 429–40; and Bruce Thomas Boehrer, '*King Lear* and the royal progress: social display in Shakespearean tragedy', *Renaissance Drama*, n.s. 21 (1990), 243–61.

16 Goneril and Albany (Irene Worth and Peter Jeffrey) seen at the end of Act 1, Scene 4, after Lear and his knights have overturned furniture in their dining hall, in Peter Brook's production for the Royal Shakespeare Theatre, 1962

stripping away of all Lear's power and prerogatives, and the texts leave open the question how many knights actually appear on stage.

The idea of service is important in the play, and Kent has often been seen as 'the quintessence of the good servant' and a model of loyalty.[1] He may well be contrasted with the self-serving Edmund, who is willing to offer his allegiance to any master and 'serve the lust' of any mistress (as Edgar puts it in his satirical portrait of a 'serving-man', 3.4.83–7) to further his own ends. Alternatively, Kent may be compared to Oswald, who is different from Edmund in that he maintains a blind loyalty to Goneril, as, for example, when he refuses to allow Regan to read his mistress's letter (4.5.19–20). Oswald is sometimes compared dismissively to the mannered courtier Osric in *Hamlet*, on account of Kent's abuse of him as foppish in 1.4; or, if the play is regarded in clear-cut moral terms as polarized between good and evil, he may be scorned as a 'serviceable villain', the words Edgar uses after his death at 4.6.247 (Fig. 17). From another perspective, however, Oswald would seem to be the model of a 'trusty servant' (4.2.18) fulfilling the prime requirement of a subject as specified by James I, who demanded obedience above all; the people should regard the King as 'God's Lieutenant in earth, obeying his commands in all thing' (*Works*, 61; he was echoing the 'Homily against Disobedience and wilful Rebellion' included from 1571 in the homilies appointed to be read in churches in the reign of Queen Elizabeth). If Kent shows an equally blind loyalty to Lear when he loses his temper and beats Oswald, he differs from Oswald in offering a disinterested service to Lear that involves disobedience and risks the loss of his life, a service that goes beyond mere loyalty.

---

1 Jonas A. Barish and Marshall Waingrow, '"Service" in *King Lear*', *SQ*, 9 (1958), 349; Mahood's chapter 'Service and servility in *King Lear*', 157–79, is also very relevant here. For a tougher response to Kent's 'rudeness and self-righteousness', see Kent Cartwright, *Shakespearean Tragedy and its Double: The Rythms of Audience Response* (University Park, Pennsylvania, 1991), especially 189–90 and 200.

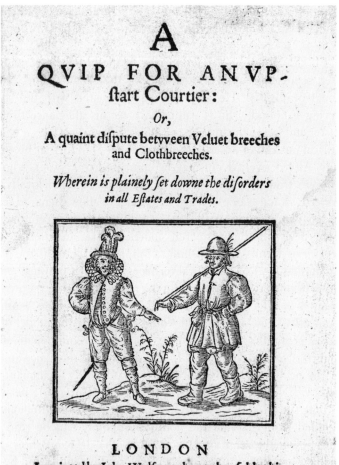

A
QVIP FOR AN VP-
ſtart Courtier:
Or,

A quaint diſpute betvveen Veluet breeches
and Clothbreeches.

Wherein is plainely ſet downe the diſorders
in all Eſtates and Trades.

LONDON
Imprinted by Iohn Wolfe, and are to bee ſold at his
ſhop at Poules chayne. 1592.

17 Title-page of *A Quip for an Upstart Courtier* (1592), showing the contrast beween the style of costume that Oswald, and Edgar in his disguise as a peasant, may have worn in Act 4, Scene 7

It is interesting that in a play staged before James I four characters are prominent for their disobedience, Kent in the opening scene, Gloucester in aiding Lear and ignoring the 'hard commands' of Goneril and Regan (3.4.145), and the servant in resisting Cornwall and trying, by offering a 'better service' (3.7.73), to prevent him from blinding Gloucester. To these must be added Cordelia, who has 'obedience scanted' (1.1.280) in refusing to speak her love for Lear. It has been argued that 'the distinction between virtuous disobedience and improper loyalty' is examined in *King Lear* (Strier, 111), and marks a significant stage in Shakespeare's political thinking. If James I was alert to such considerations when he saw the play in 1606, he may not have been troubled by the presentation of so many disobedient figures, if only because all are punished, by banishment, blinding or death; but the play does unsettle the concept of obedience, just as it raises disturbing questions about the idea of loyalty.

Lear's initial actions are largely responsible for dislodging what appear to have been accepted ideas and values. Gloucester, who has proclaimed his own son Edgar a traitor, himself becomes a 'filthy traitor' (3.7.32) to those in power, Regan and Cornwall, for aiding Lear, and Oswald legitimately seeks his life. Edgar slaughters Oswald and challenges Edmund as a traitor against the 'high illustrious prince' Albany. The fight in 5.3 between the anonymous figure of the disguised Edgar and his brother, who has just won the battle against the French forces on Albany's behalf, marks the climactic point of the violence and confusion of values in the play. It also brings a partial resolution, as good overcomes evil in their symbolic single combat, Abel overthrowing Cain. Yet Edmund fought on the 'right' side – or did he? Albany, who wishes to save Lear and Cordelia, has done battle against them as foreign invaders. Lear and Gloucester have provoked the conflicts that can only end in violence, destroying families, setting brother against brother and sister against sister, as Regan and Goneril die, the one by poison and the other by the knife. The two old men also create the conditions for civil discord as well as a war in which Lear becomes the enemy and Cordelia an invader. If the two old men suffer most, it is they whose actions in the first place help to promote violence and the urge to kill in the world of the play.

'Is this the promised end?'

In his fascinating essay on the play, Stephen Booth begins by arguing that 'Shakespeare presents the culminating events of his *story* after his *play* is over' (Booth, 11). He claims that the formal structure is completed with the deaths of Goneril, Regan and Edmund, marking a 'failure of form' (Booth, 28) that destabilizes evaluation of the play. The restoration of Lear to sanity is accomplished in his reconciliation with Cordelia and his moving readiness to 'forget and forgive' (4.7.83–4). The restoration of Lear to contentment is seen in his acceptance of prison as long as Cordelia is with him: 'We two alone will sing like birds i'the cage' (5.3.9). Lear is then offstage for two hundred lines in the Folio, or rather longer in the Quarto, a period in which an important part of the play's action is completed. Edgar describes the death of his father, Gloucester, and in the Quarto goes on to narrate the story of Kent, whose 'strings of life / Began to crack' (5.3.215–16). The formal challenge to single combat that brings Edmund to face Edgar signals a triumph of good over evil, and for Edmund, Goneril and Regan the wheel comes full circle (5.3.172). Shakespeare has a gentleman enter holding a 'bloody knife', and, while Edmund is on stage, makes Albany order the bodies of Goneril and Regan to be brought on, an unusual demand in a play of the period.[1] This vividly theatrical sequence, which for a time places before the audience the two dead sisters and the dying Edmund, visually registers the completion of one pattern of events.

---

1   Funeral processions, such as those of Henry VI in *R3* and Ophelia in *Ham*, are not uncommon, but it is unusual to have bodies brought on stage for display.

The tableau also distracts attention from Kent, whose entry is ignored by others until he mentions the King, when Albany cries, 'Great thing of us forgot!' (5.3.235). An audience may be so caught up in the action as likewise to forget Lear (Booth, 9, assumes this is what happens). The entry of Lear bearing Cordelia 'in his arms' is startling to the extent that it extends the play beyond one pattern of completion. Albany has ordered Edmund carried offstage, so that three bodies are again visible, those of all Lear's daughters; but, whereas the first group appeared to represent the victory of good over evil, the second group now displays the destruction Lear has brought on his family, as the wheel has come full circle for him too. 'Is this the promised end?' Kent asks, hinting at apocalypse, the end of the world, of everything.[1] What we see is not so great a horror as apocalypse; nor is it the end promised by the pattern I have been describing, which points rather to restoration and a hopeful conclusion, like most other versions of the story Shakespeare knew (see p. 94).

Yet within that pattern are counter-indications that might point to a bleaker ending. As noted earlier (p. 35), the Cordelia we encounter in 4.4 for the first time since Lear's banishment of her in 1.1 is Queen of France, displaying her banners, and accompanied by soldiers (Folio), and her mission is to restore him to his throne, though all he wants is to forget the past and die ('You do me wrong to take me out o'the grave', 4.7.45). His vision of happiness with Cordelia in prison is at once shattered for the audience by Edmund's order for some as yet unspecified cruelty to them ('to be tender-minded / Does not become a sword', 5.3.32–3). It is this unfinished business that requires an alternative ending to the one promised by the restorative pattern. The entry of Lear with Cordelia in his arms may not be 'promised', but neither is it unprepared for.

---

1 Wittreich, especially 103–11, makes the most of what he calls 'the pressure of its apocalyptic myth' in the play.

The texts do not show for certain when Cordelia breathes her last, but, whatever Lear sees or thinks he sees at her lips in his last speech in the Folio, we know before the end that she will come no more. The Quarto has encouraged some critics to give her a halo by emphasizing her saintliness, and associating her, alone among the play's characters, with Christian compassion ('There she shook / The holy water from her heavenly eyes', 4.3.30–1), so that she may appear a sacrificial victim whose death is mitigated by the promise of her ascent to heaven. In the Folio 4.3 is omitted, and she returns to her country as Queen of France commanding a French army. By diminishing the sense of Cordelia as a saintly emblem of pity, reducing her role and showing her as the enemy, leading an invading force into England, the Folio text makes her role more equivocal, and offers some grounds for explaining her death in political terms. At the same time, echoes of the comment of Dr Johnson on the gratuitous violence of the hanging of Cordelia have never been silenced: 'Shakespeare has suffered the virtue of Cordelia to perish in a just cause, contrary to the natural ideas of justice, to the hope of the reader, and, what is yet more strange, to the faith of the chronicles' (Johnson, 222).

The play offers a more disturbing account of justice than Dr Johnson's. Justice in *King Lear* is a shifting concept according to what authority is in power ('change places and handy-dandy, which is the justice, which is the thief?', 4.6.148–50). Perhaps, too, the death of Cordelia seems less outrageous now because we have become accustomed in the modern world to hearing news of random killings on city streets as well as of political murders carried out by terrorists. Shakespeare portrays a play-world in which gratuitous violence seems to be a norm. It begins with Lear's outbursts against Cordelia and Kent in the opening scene, in which he invokes the idea of barbarity and cannibalism in casting off his daughter (1.1.117–21). Kent's unprovoked beating of Oswald is casually vindictive, and Cornwall's blinding of Gloucester viciously cruel. The hanging of Cordelia may be seen as the final and most horrible act of gratuitous barbarity in a series of such acts, initiated by Lear himself; but no way of accounting for it undercuts the emotional impact of the death of the youngest and best of the three daughters, who, in folk- and fairy-tales, generally wins the prince, as, indeed, she did in Nahum Tate's reworking of the play (considered further at p. 85). Bradley confessed that his feelings called for a happy ending (Bradley, 252; Bratton[2], 136), and redemptionist readings of the play, for long so dominant, may have offered critics a way of coping with their own uneasiness at the ending.

The entry of Lear carrying Cordelia does not offer simply the image of horror Kent, Edgar and Albany, speaking momentarily as a chorus, perceive. Lear is reunited with Cordelia, as he wished to be; and as he is oblivious to others he is spared the misery of knowing what the audience knows and what Kent, blunt as usual, tries to tell him, namely, that his other daughters 'desperately are dead' (5.3.290). Lear's own death can be variously interpreted, whichever text is preferred (Figs. 18 and 19). In the Quarto he calls to someone (Edgar? Kent? a bystander?) 'Pray you undo this button' (a button on his own or Cordelia's clothing? another attack of the 'mother'? or a belief that Cordelia is breathing?). Then he groans, faints, and revives to cry, 'Break, heart, I prithee break' (Cordelia's heart or his own?), just before he dies. Though it is not clear here whether he thinks her alive or dead, it seems that he wishes once more for his own death. In the Folio, Lear has the added lines:

> Do you see this? Look on her: look, her lips,
> Look there, look there!

What he sees, or thinks he sees, has been much debated; to some it appears a cruel final delusion if he supposes Cordelia to be alive, while others see a blessed liberation for him in a moment of imagined reunion. On the stage these lines have been hurled at the audience as a cry of pain (Donald Sinden, 1976), used to suggest Lear 'dying grandly in joy at his perception of apotheosis in

The Historie of King Lear.

Kent. That from your life of difference and decay,
Haue followed your sad steps.   *Lear.* You'r welcome hither.
  Kent. Nor no man else, als chearles, darke and deadly,
Your eldest daughters haue foredoome themselues,
And desperatly are dead.   *Lear.* So thinke I to.
  Duke. He knowes not what he sees, and vaine it is,
That we present vs to him.   *Edg.* Very bootlesse.   *Enter*
  Capt. Edmund is dead my Lord.   *Captaine.*
  Duke. Thats but a trifle heere, you Lords and noble friends,
Know our intent, what comfort to this decay may come, shall be
applied : for vs we wil resigne during the life of this old maiesty,
to him our absolute power, you to your rights with boote, and
such addition as your honor haue more then merited, all friends
shall tast the wages of their vertue, and al foes the cup of their de-
seruings, O see, see.
  Lear. And my poore foole is hangd, no, no life, why should a
dog, a horse, a rat of life and thou no breath at all, O thou wilt
come no more, neuer, neuer, neuer, pray you vndo this button,
thanke you sir, O, o, o, o.   *Edg.* He faints my Lord, my Lord.
  Lear. Breake hart, I prethe breake. *Edgar.* Look vp my Lord.
  Kent. Vex not his ghost, O let him passe,
He hates him that would vpon the wracke,
Of this tough world stretch him out longer.
  Edg. O he is gone indeed.
  Kent. The wonder is, he hath endured so long,
He but vsurpt his life.
  Duke. Beare them from hence, our present busines
Is to generall woe, friends of my soule, you twaine
Rule in this kingdome, and the goard state sustaine.
  Kent. I haue a iourney sir, shortly to go,
My maister cals, and I must not say no.
  Duke. The waight of this sad time we must obey,
Speake what we feele, not what we ought to say,
The oldest haue borne most, we that are yong,
Shall neuer see so much, nor liue so long.

FINIS.

18   The end of the play, with the death of Lear, as printed in the Quarto (1608)

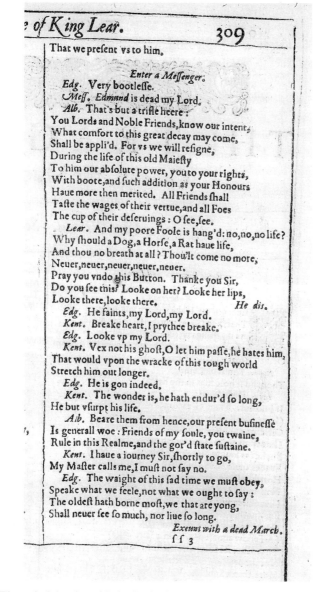

That we prefent vs to him.

Enter a Messenger.

Edg. Very bootleffe.

Mess. Edmund is dead my Lord.

Alb. That's but a trifle heere:
You Lords and Noble Friends, know our intent,
What comfort to this great decay may come,
Shall be appli'd. For vs we will refigne,
During the life of this old Maiefty
To him our abfolute power, you to your rights,
With boote, and fuch addition as your Honours
Haue more then merited. All Friends fhall
Tafte the wages of their vertue, and all Foes
The cup of their deferuings: O fee, fee.

Lear. And my poore Foole is hang'd: no, no, no life?
Why fhould a Dog, a Horfe, a Rat haue life,
And thou no breath at all? Thou'lt come no more,
Neuer, neuer, neuer, neuer, neuer.
Pray you vndo this Button. Thanke you Sir,
Do you fee this? Looke on her? Looke her lips,
Looke there, looke there.   *He dis.*

Edg. He faints, my Lord, my Lord.

Kent. Breake heart, I prythee breake.

Edg. Looke vp my Lord.

Kent. Vex not his ghoft, O let him paffe, he hates him,
That would vpon the wracke of this tough world
Stretch him out longer.

Edg. He is gon indeed.

Kent. The wonder is, he hath endur'd fo long,
He but vfurpt his life.

Alb. Beare them from hence, our prefent bufineffe
Is generall woe: Friends of my foule, you twaine,
Rule in this Realme, and the gor'd ftate fuftaine.

Kent. I haue a iourney Sir, fhortly to go,
My Mafter calls me, I muft not fay no.

Edg. The waight of this fad time we muft obey,
Speake what we feele, not what we ought to fay:
The oldeft hath borne moft, we that are yong,
Shall neuer fee fo much, nor liue fo long.

Exeunt with a dead March.

ff 3

19   The end of the play, with the death of Lear, as it appears in the Folio (1623)

Cordelia' (John Gielgud, 1940; Granville-Barker's notes, Bratton, 213), or allowed to evaporate, as by Paul Scofield (1962), who sat upright, silent, and died without moving (Rosenberg, 320). It is Kent in the Folio who cries, 'Break, heart, I prithee break', referring possibly as much to himself as to Lear, who may already have died (see p. 143).

Both the Quarto and Folio versions of Lear's last moments invite conflicting responses and permit us to see his death as at once cruel and gentle. It is cruel in that his suffering is drawn out through the actions of others so that he cannot, as he once wished, 'Unburdened crawl toward death'; and ironically he is burdened not only by his thoughts ('And my poor fool is hanged ... O thou'lt come no more'), but physically by the body of Cordelia. His repetition of 'never' five times in one astonishing and heart-rending blank verse line brings him and the audience to face death not only as the loss of all that is worth cherishing, but as utter oblivion; there are no flights of angels to hint at some possible compensatory heaven, but only the crushing sense that a process which started with a refusal to speak more than the word 'nothing' finds its culmination in death and the bleakness of 'never'. At the same time, there could be no meaningful future for Lear once Cordelia is dead, so that for him to die looking on her in a final intimacy is a consummation devoutly to be wished for a frail old man, 'fourscore and upward'.

The ending is further complicated by Albany's apparent withdrawals from power, first in favour of Lear (5.3.297–9), and then, after Lear dies, in favour of Edgar and Kent – though he may be inviting them to share the rule:

> Friends of my soul, you twain,
> Rule in this realm and the gored state sustain.

Kent refuses this invitation, and the last lines of the play are spoken by Albany in the Quarto, Edgar in the Folio, which diminishes Albany's role in the later acts. Perhaps Shakespeare decided that to leave Albany in charge might be taken as suggesting that he would like to see Prince Charles, Duke of Albany, succeed James; Edgar, on the other hand, trailed associations with a tenth-century King of Britain (but see p. 46). The variations and uncertainties of the ending may be described in terms of instability or indefinition: 'Even our evaluations of the play are unfixed' (Booth, 56). It is true that the ironic shifts and opposing possibilities of meaning in the final scene confound any attempt to show the Quarto or Folio as validating a fixed interpretation. It seems to me, however, that the ending demands an inclusive response, attuned to the range of conflicting emotions stirred by complexities of action and mean-ing, which render more poignant the simultaneous sense of overwhelming loss and of necessary release that make *King Lear* such a haunting and powerful play.[1]

The last speeches of Albany and Edgar remind us of other issues that reverberate in the play. Edgar, who has become 'preg-nant to good pity' (4.6.219) through suffering himself and witnessing the sufferings of his father and Lear, may offer the prospect of a kinder rule in the 'gored state'; but if for the time being the 'general woe' enables him to claim to speak what he feels, not what he ought to say, will the old patriarchy with its protocols be restored? The last line remains enigmatic, since say-ing what one feels (Lear in his rages? Goneril and Regan expressing their lust for Edmund?) may be just as damaging as saying what one ought to say (Goneril and Regan speaking by the rules in the opening scene?). For a modern audience, the action of the play, the stripping away of Lear's power and pre-rogatives, shows the progressive marginalization of the old king in relation to the economic and power struggles he activates by his division of the kingdom. It is a major irony that as he becomes less a figurehead locked into authority, and more a per-son with a growing awareness of himself as a subject ('Who is it that can tell me who I am?'; 'I am a very foolish fond old man'),

1   The ending of the play has stimulated much debate; see especially Peat, 43–53, McGuire, 106–18, and Matchett, 190–205.

so we learn to appreciate him as a uniquely valuable 'person', even as politically he is reduced to nothing. It is only superficially true to claim that the play retreats 'into the domestic and familial', abandoning the socio-economic message embodied in Lear's 'Take physic, pomp' speech (Patterson, 116). At a deeper level, *King Lear* exposes the contradiction between, on the one hand, the importance we place on individual freedom of expression and fulfilment and, on the other hand, the diminution of the individual to a nobody, another entry in computer lists marking the insignificance of each person in a mass society (Foakes, 213–14). On this deeper level, *King Lear* remains a powerfully political play, and the pathos of the final image of Lear is affected by our awareness of this contradiction, in so far as it is mirrored in what has happened to him.

RESPONSES AND REWORKINGS

The critics and the play

The account I have given so far of the play engages with its critical and stage history to some extent. While this is not the place to review the massive and varied critical commentaries that deal with *King Lear*, it may be helpful to consider some trends in criticism and staging, which have generally related to their own time as much as they do to Shakespeare, so that the play has been perceived in a shifting variety of ways. As long as Nahum Tate's version of 1681 was the only one to be seen on the stage, critics could only relate to the play by reading it. The Romantics found it awesome, but tended to internalize the play, locating the tragedy within the mind of Lear, and reducing the external action to a domestic drama centred on his quarrel with his daughters; Hazlitt, for example, treated the play chiefly in terms of 'the ebb and flow of the feeling' (4.259). Hazlitt made Lear's reconciliation with Cordelia the culminating point of his essay, and prepared the way for the idealization of Cordelia that became a feature of many later accounts of the play.

When Macready in the 1830s distanced the play by setting the first scene among ancient Druidic stone circles (see p. 30), he established an enduring fashion for staging *King Lear*. Many critics went further in seeking analogies for the grandeur of the play by dehistoricizing it, and treating it as transcending period and genre as a work of pure poetic imagination; this way of elevating the play is exemplified in the grouping of *King Lear* with 'works like the *Prometheus Vinctus* and the *Divine Comedy*' (Bradley, 244) by the very influential A. C. Bradley, writing in 1904. Stressing the awesome and mythical aspects of the play in this way paradoxically led to a greater internalization of the play's action, and an emphasis on what became seen as the 'pilgrimage' of Lear.

Bradley went so far as to propose as a title for the play '*The Redemption of King Lear*', arguing that the gods 'lead him to attain through apparently hopeless failure the very end and aim of life' (Bradley, 284–5). Hence his insistence that actors should play Lear as dying in 'unbearable *joy*' (Bradley, 291). Bradley lent his authority to the redemptive readings of the play that flourished until about 1960 and remain influential. Many of these readings promoted a Christian interpretation of the action, or a 'Christian transvaluation of the values of Lear's pagan world' (Heilman, 221). Cordelia, who had been treated as saintly by some earlier critics, took on the aspect of a Christian martyr, Edgar that of a 'Christian gentleman' (Chambers, 25, echoing Harley Granville-Barker; see p. 47), and Lear that of the biblical Job, who suffered in order to shed the old Adam and be born again: so Lear 'loses the world and gains his soul' (Ard², lv). The problem of the death of Cordelia could be bypassed if she was seen as a saint or symbol of divine love (Bickersteth, 25).

Such accounts permitted an understanding of the characters as 'determined by what they are and represent in the total scheme of the play rather than by any form of "life" fluctuating among "motives"' (Mack, 66); the play could thus be regarded as abandoning 'verisimilitude to find out truth' and be seen in mythic terms. In this concern with universals, with the quest of suffering Man on a journey to find redemption, or at least restoration and peace, analogies with legendary epics like those celebrating the fall of Troy may have led to an alternative perception of the action as portraying the fall of a good order of society represented by Lear and his allies, 'an order of society so obviously springing from the nature and needs of man that it can be called natural' (Edwin Muir, 49). The idea that Lear and Cordelia were to be associated with a beneficent natural order, while their enemies might be seen as representing a Machiavellian dissociation of politics from morality, was assimilated notably into the redemptive tradition by J. F. Danby in *Shakespeare's Doctrine of Nature* (1949). He idealized Cordelia and Edgar as embodying the values of an older and better form of society inherited from the Middle Ages, and redeeming the sufferings of the good old man, Lear; by contrast, Edmund, Goneril and Regan represented the competitive self-assertion and ruthless greed of an emergent capitalism. Danby shared Bradley's somewhat sentimental view of *King Lear* as a preparation for *The Tempest*, in which 'Lear and Cordelia find each other again and live happily ever after' (Danby, 195; see also Wickham, 33–9); yet in his vision of the play as showing a transition to a self-seeking society he pulled the play into the twentieth century, but at the same time used it as a way of rejecting what he saw as self-seeking and corrupt in the society of his own time (Danby, 138). The ideas of Bradley and Danby underlie the very influential introduction Kenneth Muir wrote for his 'New Arden' edition that first appeared in 1952 (Ard^2), and affected the thinking of critics like Maynard Mack and Rosalie Colie (Hibbard, 5–6). Danby's perception of the play as based on a conflict between those characters who adhere to a divinely sanctioned benignant order in nature and those who accept a Machiavellian idea of individualism and self-interest looks too simple when the wider context of Shakespeare's ideas of nature, as influenced by Montaigne, is taken into account (Salingar, 126–7, and see pp. 104–5 below).

By the 1960s a remarkable shift was taking place in the interpretation of *King Lear*, as redemptionist readings were largely rejected in favour of an emphasis on bleakness, even despair. If any affirmation was to be found, it was a limited one in the face of 'that universal disruption of Nature, that Descent into Chaos, which for millennia had been a standing dread of mankind' (Holloway, 79). A descent into chaos was portrayed in the famous production by Peter Brook (1962, made into a film in 1970), who consciously conceived Lear in relation to Stalinism in his own time, and the play in nihilistic terms. Brook had a considerable impact on critics, who increasingly stressed the bleakness of an action that seemed to them to deny any affirmation; it was argued that the action of Shakespeare's play was 'calculated to repudiate every source of consolation with which we might greet the final disaster' (Brooke, 57).

This shift towards bleak readings of *King Lear* was prompted by an increasing consciousness of the play's relevance to Europe and America in the wake of the Second World War, the use of the atomic bomb against Hiroshima and Nagasaki (cradle of Christianity in Japan) and the wanton cruelty of concentration camps. So Maynard Mack, who sought in 1965 to repudiate Brooke's interpretation, and to recuperate a way of reading the play both as concerned with personal relationships and in metaphysical terms, acknowledged that 'After two world wars and Auschwitz, our sensibility is significantly more in touch than our grandparents' was with the play's jagged violence, its sadism, madness, and processional of deaths' (Mack, 25). Later criticism has retreated from the heady nihilism of the early 1960s, while recognizing the need to accommodate aspects of the play that may give purchase to bleak interpretations. If Lear progresses neither to redemption nor to despair, the play might be seen to offer the paradox that 'we can only learn through suffering' but 'have nothing to learn from it' (Cavell, 111).

Historicist critics have reinvigorated a sense of the political concerns of the play by seeing the contradictions in it as 'the locus of a distinct, politically dynamic sequence of discursive practices, replete with competing ideologies' (Drakakis, 36), ideologies that are rooted in the age of James I. The play tends to be regarded as a document that interrogates the power of the court (Tennenhouse), or offers a radical analysis of 'the economic structure of his [Shakespeare's] own society' (Patterson), or reinforces patriarchy and a misogynistic attitude to women (McLuskie). If it concerns an emergent form of society displacing an older one, *King Lear* shows 'not an old order succumbing to a new but an old order succumbing to its own internal contradictions' (Turner, 101). This is one of a number of approaches (for instance, new historicist, feminist, deconstructive or cultural materialist) that have contributed to a destabilizing of the play by recognizing contradictions in it, ranges of alternative meanings, indefiniteness and a clash of ideological stances.

It seems that for many critics there can be no return to simple optimistic or pessimistic readings of the play, and the difficulty of reconciling them has helped to promote 'a deep distrust of all attempts at closure' in *King Lear*, a 'negation of the possibility of unity, coherence, and resolution' (Fly, 96; Felperin, 96). Many students of the play who have ready access to film versions rather than staged productions may find such a remark puzzling, since some of the best-known films, such as the Russian film by Grigori Kozintsev and the Michael Elliott film with Laurence Olivier in the title role, achieve in their different ways a coherence and resolution.[1] Deconstructive critics nevertheless have found a radical instability in the play that permits no

---

1 Commentary on films of the play includes Jack Jorgens, *Shakespeare on Film* (Bloomington, 1977), on the films of Brook and Kozintsev; James P. Lusardi and June Schlueter, *Reading Shakespeare in Performance: King Lear* (Rutherford, NJ, 1991), on the television films by Jonathan Miller and Michael Elliott; and Kenneth S. Rothwell, 'Representing *King Lear* on screen: from meta-theatre to "meta-cinema"', *SS*, 39 (1987), 75-90.

confidence in any particular reading, so that evaluations of the play are bound to be 'unfixed' (Booth, 56). A sense of instability has been reinforced by the continuing debate about the significance of the differences between the Quarto and Folio texts (see pp. 116–7). The new awareness of these differences has also made us more sharply conscious that generations of critics and producers, using printed editions of the play with a conflated text, have chosen to emphasize some elements, and ignore or cut others, to suit their particular interpretations.

Reworkings of King Lear

A more direct form of homage to *King Lear* than criticism is represented by reworkings of the play, or other kinds of writings based on it. These have tended to correspond in their emphasis with the prevailing modes of interpretation at the time they were written. Adaptations by Nahum Tate (1681),[1] later revised by George Colman (1768), by David Garrick (1773) and by John Philip Kemble (1808), held the stage until well into the nineteenth century. Tate made many changes, but is best known for his alteration of the ending, which included a tableau of Lear asleep, with his head on Cordelia's lap; soldiers arrive to dispatch them, but Lear wakes and kills two of the attackers before Edgar and Albany arrive to rescue them. Edgar goes off in order to return with his father. Lear gives Cordelia to Edgar as his bride, and the old men (Lear, Gloucester and Kent) plan to retire to a 'cool cell' to meditate. Tate also introduced a companion, Arante, for Cordelia; and a scene in which Edgar rescues them from two ruffians, dependants of Edmund, was still being performed, according to Edwin Forrest's acting text, in 1860.

1   Tate's version, *The History of King Lear*, was reissued in the Regents Renaissance Drama Series, ed. James Black (Lincoln, Nebraska, 1975). The beginning and end of Tate's adaptation are reprinted, with a commentary, in Bratton, 220-37. The reasons why Tate rewrote *King Lear* in 1680, and its political significance, are considered by Nancy Klein Maguire in Jean Marsden (ed.), *The Appropriation of Shakespeare: Post-Renaissance Reconstructions of the Works and the Myth*, (1991), 29–42, and by Michael Dobson, *The Making of the National Poet: Shakespeare, Adaptation and Authorship, 1660–1769* (Oxford, 1992), 80–5.

The emphasis on pathos and sentiment in Tate's version chimed in with the tendency of the Romantics to locate the tragedy in the mind of Lear, and reduce the external action to a domestic drama. William Moncrieff's *The Lear of Private Life* (1828), staged in London, seemed to sum up a common way of treating Shakespeare's play in the nineteenth century. In fact, Moncrieff's play was based on a sentimental novel, Amelia Opie's *Father and Daughter* (1806), a tale of 'filial tenderness and parental suffering' (Bratton[2], 132) which tells the story of a girl who is seduced, elopes from home and returns to find her father mad; she nurses him, but on the day when he recovers his senses he dies. Moncrieff changes the conclusion, borrowing from Shakespeare a reconciliation scene, and from Nahum Tate a happy ending.

Echoes of *King Lear* may be perceived in some of the numerous other nineteenth-century fictional treatments of father–daughter or grandfather–daughter relationships. Of those with the most powerful links to Shakespeare's play the best known is Honoré de Balzac's *Le père Goriot* (1834), in which a growingly senile old man sweats all his life in a flour-mill to enhance the wealth and status of the two daughters he loves, who take all he has to give and waste it. Their quarrel by the bedside of the old man provokes the stroke that kills him, and his elder daughter returns to seek his blessing only after he has lost the power of speech. In this novel a Parisian society driven by greed and snobbery is the source of corruption. Another powerful variant is Ivan Turgenev's *A King Lear of the Steppes* (1870); in this novel an inarticulate giant has an intimation of his death one day in a dream, and cedes his property to his two daughters, seeking only room and board for himself. They gradually take over, withdraw his allowance and turn him out of his house. He takes his revenge by literally tearing the house down, meeting his death when he pulls the roof-tree on himself. Both of these stories turn on the way the daughters learn to tyrannize over their father. In a rather different way Emile Zola's *La Terre* (*The Land*, 1888) also varies the Lear story. In this novel an old peasant, Fouan, who divides his land between his daughter and his two sons, gradually finds himself stripped of everything. In the end he is murdered by his son Buteau and Lise, Buteau's wife, after witnessing Buteau rape and accidentally bring about the death of his own sister-in-law. The peasants depicted in this novel are driven by an obsessive passion to own land and keep it in the family.

In the twentieth century *King Lear* has influenced more plays and films than novels, and the best of these restore the image of a father who tyrannizes over his children.[1] In Hollywood the daughters were changed into sons, not only in the 1949 film *House of Strangers*, directed by Joseph L. Mankiewicz, in which a banker dominates his three sons, but also in the western *Broken Lance* (1954), with a cattle baron as its central figure, and *The Big Show* (1961), which deals with the death of an imperious circus owner and its effect on his sons. Akira Kurosawa also adapted *King Lear* as *Ran* (1985), grafting it on to a superb medieval samurai epic, set in sixteenth-century Japan, with great battle scenes in which a domineering aristocrat's sons fight for succession and power. In changing daughters to sons these films reflect the authority their societies used to give to men and accept the relative marginalization of women, though Kurosawa makes Lady Kaede, wife of Taro, the eldest son of the warlord Hidetora, a powerful 'amalgam of Goneril, Regan, Lady Macbeth and Edmund' (Parker, 416). These films may also perhaps be seen as responses to the daughters in *King Lear* who behave like men (Goneril and Regan) and who have rarely been sympathetically considered by male critics.

The best-known and most powerful dramatic reworking of the Lear story is Edward Bond's *Lear* (performed 1971), in which all personal relationships break down; Cordelia (the

---

1   The chapter on *King Lear* in Ruby Cohn's *Modern Shakespeare Offshoots* (Princeton, 1976) is disappointingly thin, though she does comment briefly on Gordon Bottomley's *King Lear's Wife* (1915) and Robin Maugham's *Mister Lear* (1956); but see Chapter 3, 'Expatriating Lear' in Peter Conrad, *'To be Continued': Four Stories & their Survival* (Oxford, 1995).

Carpenter's wife, no relation to Lear) survives being raped and seeing her first husband butchered by rampaging soldiers only to rebuild in the end a state as horribly cruel and oppressive as Lear's. The final effort of the old, blind Lear, who has at last learned the meaning of pity, seems futile, as he is shot while hacking at the great wall he built originally to protect his possessions. *Lear* offended many because of the outrageous cruelty and violence it depicts, in line with Bond's perception, expressed in his preface (Bond, lvii), of violence as shaping and obsessing modern western society. He saw Shakespeare as a conservative who accepted the ideology of an age that believed in the maintenance of a strong single authority, and he wished in his play to show the state as a source of oppression. The play thus challenges *King Lear* by escalating violence and repression while offering as a positive alternative only an unfocused notion of pity: 'Our lives are awkward and fragile and we have only one thing to keep us sane: pity, and the man without pity is mad' (Bond, 84). Pity in the end, however, does little to modify the play's presentation of a country brutalized by a never-ending cycle of civil war.

Howard Barker's curious play *Seven Lears* (1990) gives Lear a mistress, Prudentia, the mother of Clarissa, Lear's queen, who in turn is the mother of Goneril, Regan and Cordelia. The seven scenes into which the play is divided portray a cruel world in which Prudentia and Clarissa, according to Barker's introduction, are the subject of an unjust hatred 'shared by Lear and all his daughters', a hatred that 'may have been necessary'. Clarissa alone, it seems, has a conscience, speaks the truth, and is capable of love. This play shares with feminist critics an interest in the absent mother of Shakespeare's play. In her finely crafted novel *A Thousand Acres* (1991), by contrast, Jane Smiley focuses on the three daughters of a tyrannical old Midwestern farmer who suddenly decides to transfer his land to his daughters; it is a question whether the land, the demands of farming and fluctuations in costs control people more than people control the land.

As the farmer, Larry Cook (Lear), sinks into alcoholism and madness, Ginnie (recalling Goneril) and Rose (Regan) squabble, losing both their husbands and the land. Caroline (Cordelia), who refuses to have anything to do with the land transfer, moves away to become a lawyer, and seeks unavailingly to have the farm restored to her father. The inability of the narrator, Ginny, and her sister Rose to have satisfying and lasting relationships is linked to the discovery Ginny makes after her father's death that she has been repressing a horrible memory of his forced incest with her and Rose when they were young. In trying to trace the mother she never knew, she finds only her own image. In this novel a potential in *King Lear* that feminist criticism has touched on (e.g. Kahn, 39) is realized in action.[1] The play has also had an impact on poets, as in William Blake's depiction of the aged, blind Tiriel calling on thunder from on high to punish his sons (*Tiriel, c.* 1789). Recent poems alluding to Lear include Adrienne Rich's poem on her father, 'After Dark' (1966), and Paul Muldoon's long, freewheeling autobiographical poem, 'Yarrow', which uses snippets from the play to deepen the sense of his relationship to his parents (*The Annals of Chile*, 1994).

THE INCEPTION OF *KING LEAR*

Date

The play was probably composed in 1605–6, though there is no

---

1   Perhaps I should also mention here two works that turn on the challenge the role of Lear sets for an actor: one is Ronald Harwood's play *The Dresser* (1980, made into a film by Peter Yates in 1983), which gives some idea of the style of playing of the last great actor-manager in England, Donald Wolfit, and of the conditions he endured when performing the role of Lear during the Second World War; the other is Melvyn Bragg's play, *King Lear in New York*, staged at the Chichester Festival Theatre in 1992, in which an ageing actor who has been working in films for years returns to the stage in an attempt to play Lear. Jean-Luc Godard's experimental film about making a film of *King Lear* (1987) is a chaotic medley (Lear becomes Don Learo of the Mafia), even if it has some amusing moments. Randolph Stow also transposed elements of the Lear story into his novel *To the Islands* (1958), in which an elderly white man who has devoted his life to running a mission station for aborigines in Australia finds only disappointment and hatred, and, believing he has killed a native, goes on a walkabout that ends with him facing death.

direct evidence to show when it was written or first performed. A central issue is its relation to the play *The True Chronicle History of King LEIR, and his three daughters*, published, apparently for the first time, in 1605, after being entered in the Stationers' Register on 8 May of that year. This is presumably the same as the old play of 'Kinge leare' staged twice by the Queen's and Earl of Sussex's Men in April 1594 (Henslowe, 21), and entered in the Stationers' Register as the play of 'Leire Kinge of England and his Three Daughters' on 14 May 1594. This play had a powerful impact on Shakespeare, whose close reading of it suggests that he studied the printed book; there is no reason to think that he had prior access to a manuscript of it. The entry for Shakespeare's play in the Stationers' Register for 26 November 1607 records it also as the history of King Lear, and the title-page of the first printed version, the Quarto of 1608, expands this wording into a close parallel of the title-page of the old play, as Shakespeare's *True Chronicle Historie of the life and death of King LEAR and his three Daughters*. It looks very much as if the publisher was anxious to challenge *Leir* by claiming simultaneously that the new play was like the old one, and superior to it. The title-page of *King Lear* draws attention to three differences: one is the new feature of the subplot of Edgar and his disguise as Poor Tom; a second is a performance before James I at Whitehall; the third is the authorship by Shakespeare, whose name is prominently displayed at the top of the page. Many of the quartos of Shakespeare's plays were printed without any attribution of authorship. The title-pages are reproduced in Figs 20 and 21 (pp. 112 and 114).

The performance before James I, which is mentioned in the Stationers' Register entry of 1607, in fact took place during the Christmas period in 1606. Except for this and a production at Gowthwaite Hall, Nidderdale, in Yorkshire by a provincial company patronized by Sir Richard Cholmeley in 1610, for which copies of the printed text, i.e. the 1608 Quarto, were used (Sisson, 135–43), the play's early stage history is a blank. The fact that the two sons of James I included among their titles Duke of Cornwall and Duke of Albany, and the debate in the period 1605–8 about the King's proposal to unite England and Scotland as Great Britain, have occasioned a good deal of speculation about the play's topicality when it was performed at court. Both the idea that the play had a special relevance to St Stephen's Day (Marcus, 155–6) and the suggestion that it came 'perilously close to presenting a fictional portrait of the king himself' (Patterson, 106) seem implausible to me. In dividing the kingdom and bringing about his own downfall, Lear behaves in a way directly contrary to the advice James gave to his son (see p. 15).

Censorship has been claimed as the reason for the omission of some passages present in the Quarto and not in the Folio, especially the Fool's allusion to monopolies (see 1.4.146 and n.) and the dropping of some references to war with France,[1] but in any case, if the title-page can be believed, the Quarto text was played before the King in 1606. The 'late eclipses in the sun and moon' referred to at 1.2.103 could have some connection with the eclipses that occurred in the autumn of 1605; but eclipses were not so infrequent as to require us to think Shakespeare had specific ones in mind (so Ard², xix), and they were commonly described as predicting disasters in the astrological forecasts of the age (see 1.2.103 and n.). Perhaps the only certainty in dating the composition of the play is that Shakespeare could not have written it before the publication of two works that had a pervasive effect on the language of *King Lear*, namely Harsnett's *Declaration of Egregious Popish Impostures* and John Florio's translation of Montaigne's *Essays*, both published in 1603.

Two other possible topical connections should be mentioned,

---

1 For debate of these matters see Taylor, 'Monopolies', 75–117; Patterson², 58–64; Clare², 132–6. A. B. Worden, 'Literature and political censorship in early modern England', in A. C. Duke and C. A. Tamse (eds), *Too Mighty to be Free: Censorship and the Press in Britain and the Netherlands* (Zutphen, 1987), 45–62, is generally sceptical about the impact of censorship, and notes how many works with blatant topical allusions were ignored by the censors. On the war with France, see Appendix 1.

though there is no evidence that Shakespeare knew of either of them. One is the story of Cordell Annesley, whose name and conduct curiously echo the folk-tale and anticipate the play. In 1603–4 the eldest daughter of Brian Annesley, an ageing wealthy gentleman pensioner of Queen Elizabeth, tried to have her father declared a lunatic so that she and her husband could control his affairs. His second daughter seems to have played no part in the matter, but the youngest, Cordell, appealed successfully to Sir Robert Cecil, and when Annesley died in 1604 he left most of his property to her. The case could well have had something to do with the revival and publication of the old play of *King Leir* in 1605, and so, indirectly, with Shakespeare's play.[1] A more prominent case heard in Star Chamber between June 1604 and June 1605 was that of Sir Robert Dudley, bastard son of Robert Dudley, Earl of Leicester, Queen Elizabeth's favourite; he was trying to establish his legitimacy. Leicester had not acknowledged marrying Robert's mother in 1573 so as not to lose the favour of the Queen, and in his will he referred to Robert as bastard or base seventeen times, while leaving him most of his property. Sir Robert lost his case, 'the greatest cause now of England', in part through the intervention of James I, who on 4 May 1605 created the official claimant to the title, Sir Robert's cousin Robert Sidney, Viscount Lisle of Penshurst.[2] In some earlier plays Shakespeare had invented memorable bastards, but Edmund's soliloquy on baseness and bastardy curiously echoes the theme of this lawsuit.

Influences, topicalities and Shakespeare's reading

It often seems to be taken for granted that Shakespeare never

---

1   The case was noticed by C. C. Stopes, *The Life of Henry, Third Earl of Southampton, Shakespeare's Patron* (Cambridge, 1922), 274; the fullest accounts are those by Geoffrey Bullough, '*King Lear* and the Annesley Case', *Festschrift Rudolf Stamm* (Bern, 1969), 43–50, and *Sources*, 7.270–1.
2   See Arthur Gould Lee, *The Son of Leicester: The Story of Robert Dudley* (1964), 100–16, citing a comment by Sir John Hayward on 109.

invented where he could borrow, and searching for the 'sources' of Shakespeare's plays has long been a minor scholarly industry. It is indeed fascinating to trace the dramatist at work, but the word 'source' is too specific and too narrow in relation to most echoes of other works found in *King Lear*. Holinshed's *Chronicles* and Plutarch's *Lives* were at his elbow when he wrote respectively his history plays and Roman plays, but what research has made ever more apparent is that Shakespeare read widely and had a deep and lively engagement with the culture of his own and preceding ages. The philosophical, religious, social and political issues that are interwoven in the dialogue of his plays can rarely be traced to a particular source; for the most part it is more helpful to think in terms of influences or contexts.

In the case of *King Lear* he certainly derived material or ideas from a few works that fed his imagination. The story of Lear and his three daughters has its roots in folk-tales, in which the motif of a father submitting three daughters to a love-test is common. Usually two give answers that please, and the third, the youngest, who fails the test, often by saying she loves her father as meat loves salt, is driven out; she finds a good master, often a prince, whom she marries, and her father, discovering he has been mistaken, is reconciled to her, sometimes when he comes to the wedding feast and is given meat without salt (Young, 309–13). The numerous variations of this motif always end in reconciliation. It has affinities with the even more widespread Cinderella story, some versions of which also have features relating to that of Lear (Perrett, 9–13; Bullough, 271). In his investigation of the recurrent motif of three sisters, Sigmund Freud pushed further back in time to speculate about possible connections with ancient myths. He argued that the third sister, Cordelia in *King Lear*, could be associated both with the goddess of love (Aphrodite in Greek mythology) and with the goddess of death in German mythology; so she 'bids the old man renounce

love, choose death, and make friends with the necessity of dying'
(Freud, 301).[1]

The Lear story itself existed in many versions before
Shakespeare turned to it (see Perrett, 1–142). It is possible, but I
think not necessary, to believe that the dramatist consulted the
earliest of these versions, in the *Historia regium Britanniae* by
Geoffrey of Monmouth (*c*. 1135), which he would have had to
read in manuscript and in Latin, since no English translation
was available. In this account, the love-test occurs when the ageing Leir decides to find husbands for his daughters Gonorilla,
Regan and Cordeilla. Gonorilla and Regan are married to
Henuinus, Duke of Cornwall, and Maglaunus, Duke of Albania,
and are given half the kingdom, while King Aganippus of Gaul
(France) sues for and weds the undowered Cordeilla. Much later,
when Leir becomes infirm, the two Dukes rise in insurrection
and deprive Leir of authority; at first he is allowed sixty attendants, but Gonorilla and Regan whittle these down to one man,
at which point Leir, attended only by his armour-bearer, goes off
to France, where a weeping Cordeilla relieves him. Aganippus
raises an army, and, returning with Leir to England, routs the
sons-in-law and restores Leir to the throne, where he reigns for
three more years before Cordeilla succeeds as Queen. After she
has reigned for five years, the sons of Gonorilla and Regan overthrow her, and, imprisoned by them, she kills herself.

The story is modified in various ways in the many later
reworkings of it, but the general outline remains much the same,
ending with the restoration of Leir to his throne, to be succeeded by Cordeilla, who is subsequently overthrown and
commits suicide. Shakespeare may be presumed to have read the
account (1.446–8) in Holinshed's *Chronicles* (1587), which he
had used for his history plays. This account is derived from

---

1   In *Shakespeare's Ghost Writers: Literature as Uncanny Causality* (1987), Marjorie
    Garber shows how Freud's discussion of the traditional theme of three caskets or
    three daughters relates to his own psychological problems. It nevertheless remains of
    some interest to students of Shakespeare.

Geoffrey via the chronicles of Robert Fabyan (1516) and other sources (Bullough, 273–4). Probably Shakespeare took from Holinshed the titles Duke of Cornwall and Duke of Albany ('Albania', or the country north of the Humber, including Scotland, according to Holinshed, 1.443–4; see 1.1.2 and n.). For the rest, Holinshed's version follows Geoffrey's in its emphasis on civil wars, on the sons-in-law rising against Leir, and their sons rebelling against Cordeilla when she succeeds Leir; in *King Lear* the emphasis is quite different.

In the additions by John Higgins to *The Mirror for Magistrate*s (1574), Cordila tells her story in verse, dwelling at length on the despair that drove her to kill herself; but in her telling, as in Shakespeare's play, Gonerell is married to the King of Albany, and Ragan to the Prince of Cornwall. Cordila reports that Leir stayed first with Gonerell, who stripped him of half the sixty knights he had reserved, and then went to Ragan, who reduced his retinue to ten, then five. He returns to Gonerell, who

> Bereaude him of his seruauntes all saue one,
> Bad him content him selfe with that or none.
> (Bullough, 327)

Higgins also has Cordila marry the King of France, not, as in Holinshed, the Prince of Gallia; and Cordila returns to England with her father at the head of a French army to vanquish her enemies there, leaving her husband in France. Imprisoned in a miserable dungeon by her brothers-in-law, Cordila has to give up beds of down and finds she is glad to have straw to sleep on (Bullough, 330), a detail which may have suggested Cordelia's image of Lear lying in a hovel in 'short and musty straw' (4.7.39–40; see Muir, *Sources*, 198–9).

It is probable, then, that Shakespeare had read this popular work, just as he no doubt knew Edmund Spenser's *Faerie Queene* (1596). In Book 2, Canto 10, a chronicle of British kings includes a brief rehearsal of the story of Leyr and his daughters which includes two variants from the traditional narrative that had an influence on *King Lear*. One is Spenser's revision of the name Cordeilla or Cordila into Cordelia, which not only suggests a link with the heart or feelings in 'Cor' (compare the word 'cordial', connected with Cordella in *Leir*, 709: 'Ah, deare *Cordella*, cordiall to my heart'), but associates the other part of her name with chastity (as in Samuel Daniel's sonnet sequence, *Delia*, 1592), and makes it an anagram of 'ideal' (Anderson, 1–7; see also p. 31). The other variant has to do with the death of Cordelia; in other versions she kills herself in an unspecified way, or by stabbing herself, as in *The Mirror for Magistrates*; in Spenser's poem, however, she hangs herself. In *King Lear* Edmund orders Cordelia to be hanged, intending to 'lay the blame upon her own despair', and report that she committed suicide (5.3.251–3).

No edition of *Leir* is known prior to that of 1605, when the play was reassigned in a new entry in the Stationers' Register on 8 May; this new entry and the title-page both refer to the play as 'lately acted', but there is no other evidence of recent staging. *Leir* preserves many of the main features of the traditional narrative, except that it ends with Leir restored to his throne in England by Cordella and the King of Gallia, her husband, after their army has defeated the forces of the Kings of Cambria and Cornwall, with their wives, Gonorill and Ragan. However, leaving out the events subsequent to the restoration of Leir, the play effectively transforms the story from one that deals with a succession of civil wars to one that focuses on the intrigues and fortunes of Leir and his daughters, and this is what stimulated Shakespeare's imagination. The business of the love-test, the marriages of the daughters and the division of the kingdom take up the first third of the text. The middle part of the action is expanded with much comic or romantic invention involving messengers, murderers, mariners, an ambassador and Mumford (a corruption of Montfort?), a comic companion to the King of Gallia. These two twice appear disguised, first as pilgrims, when they come to Britain to see Leir's daughters, and later, with Cordella, they enter 'disguised like Countrey folke' (2090 SD).

The ending also includes two scenes of English watchmen who get drunk and fail to light a beacon, and turns Mumford into an heroic fighter, who chases the King of Cambria off the stage twice.

Shakespeare compressed the first seven scenes of the old play into the opening scene of *King Lear*, but found in them many ideas he could use. In *Leir* the old king has just buried his queen, and takes advice from counsellors about the succession; he thinks of trying a love-test as a 'sudden stratagem' (78), and a wicked counsellor, Skalliger, reveals his plan to Gonorill and Ragan, who have the opportunity to rehearse their speeches. The King of Gallia comes in disguise to Britain to see Leir's daughters, and happens upon Cordilla, cast out by Leir and wandering on her own. Cordilla accepts the hand of one she thinks is a pilgrim before he reveals himself as the Gallian king. Shakespeare ignored all this material, and seized on what he could use to make a much more dynamic and exciting beginning. Leir is presented as aged and anxious to 'resign these earthly cares' (27), just as Lear wishes to 'shake all cares and business from our age' (1.1.38). The good counsellor, Perillus, who tries to intervene on Cordilla's behalf, and later becomes the sole companion of the old king when he is thrown out by Gonorill and Ragan, has resemblances with Kent. Gonorill and Ragan speak together of their hatred of Cordilla, and contempt for the 'old man' their father, 'Who dotes, as if he were a child agayne' (181), in a dialogue that bears upon the criticism of Lear by Goneril and Regan at 1.1.290–307. Cordilla's response to Lear's love-test, 'I cannot paint my duty forth in words' (277), anticipates Cordelia's 'I cannot heave / My heart into my mouth' (1.1.91–2). Leir's rhetoric lacks the power and ferocity Shakespeare gives to Lear, but his action in disowning Cordilla, 'Call me not father' (314), and casting her out is similar. Leir calls her 'bastard Impe, no issue of King *Leir*' (312), which perhaps prompted Lear's later verbal attack on Goneril, 'Degenerate bastard, I'll not trouble thee' (1.4.245). Leir is absolute in his decision to cast Cordilla off, in spite of the protests of Perillus against his 'ruthlesse doome' (567), and rejects advice:

> sue not to reverse
> Our censure, which is now irrevocable.
> (504–5)

This sequence, with Leir's threat upon the life of Perillus (569), probably suggested the clash between Lear and Kent, where Kent cries to Lear, 'Reverse thy doom' (1.1.150, Q; altered to 'Reserve thy state' in F), and Lear threatens him with loss of life.

The latter part of *Leir* offered Shakespeare less in the way of suggestive ideas or material, but there are some important links. Leir's anger gives way to patience (755) as he puts up with the wrongs inflicted on him by Gonorill; Lear discovers the need for patience just before he goes off into the storm (2.2.460). The wicked counsellor Skalliger, who advises Gonorill to curtail Leir's allowance, drops out of the action when she finds an eager tool in a messenger who is willing to do anything, including murdering Leir, for money; Skalliger and the messenger may together have suggested the idea of Oswald. Goneril's interception of letters from Leir may have given Shakespeare a hint for the use of letters in contriving the clash between Kent and Oswald at the beginning of 2.2 in *King Lear*, as well as the scene in which Regan seeks to persuade Oswald to let her read Goneril's letter to Edmund (4.5). Cornwall in *Leir*, 818–50, does not know of Gonorill's harshness to her father, just as Albany has no knowledge of Goneril's harsh treatment of Lear (1.4. 265–6).

The King of Gallia's companion, Mumford, boasts of his bluntness (386–9), which could have suggested the style of speech the disguised Kent assumes, a 'bluntness' or 'saucy roughness' as Cornwall describes it (*King Lear*, 2.2.94–5). Lear's words to Regan, 'I gave you all' (2.2.439), recall Leir's lament, 'Ah, *Ragan*, did I give thee all . . . ?' (2144). In the scene where Leir is reconciled to Cordilla, 2295–353, Leir, Cordilla and the King of Gallia all kneel to each other for forgiveness and blessing and rise up twice, so that the stage business becomes somewhat absurd, and it ends on a comic note as Mumford then kneels to pray for sexual gratification. Shakespeare saw the potential here for the truly moving reconciliation scene he created in 4.7, in which Cordelia kneels once to Lear, who in turn tries to kneel to her in mutual forgiveness. Towards the end of the play Leir produces letters to prove Ragan's guilt, and she 'snatches them & teares them', according to the stage direction (2586); so in *King Lear* Albany displays a letter to show Goneril's guilt, which she tries to snatch as he says, 'no tearing, lady' (5.3.155). Leir ends by resigning his power to the King of Gallia (2638), just as Albany resigns his power to Lear (5.3.297–9), and then invites Kent and Edgar to 'Rule in this realm'.[1]

The connections are strong enough to suggest that Shakespeare read the old play carefully, and absorbed its emphasis on the good sense of the wise counsellor Perillus who remains with Leir, on the initial rage of Leir that dwindles into patience, on the devotion of Cordilla and her reconciliation with her father, and on the harsh ferocity of Gonorill and Ragan. He turned a tragicomedy into a tragedy, selecting only what would contribute to his bleaker and more powerful vision of the story of Lear. *Leir* is a play in which characters routinely refer to God, and which has from the start, where Leir imagines his dead queen among the 'Cherubins' in heaven, a good deal of Christian religious colouring; this is especially associated with Cordilla, who in one scene has a soliloquy on her way to church to pray (1061–93). In Shakespeare's play, by contrast, characters routinely refer to pagan gods, and only Cordelia is left with residual Christian associations, though the play has many biblical echoes in the dialogue (see p. 105).

---

1 Other verbal parallels, not all convincing, were listed by Greg, 'Date', 388–96, and see Peter Pauls, '*The True Chronicle History of King Leir* and Shakespeare's *King Leir*: a reconsideration', *The Upstart Crow*, 5 (1984), 93–107. Bullough, 278–83, analyses *Leir* in some detail, and has some shrewd comments on links and differences between it and *King Lear*; Muir, *Sources*, gives a more perfunctory account.

One other feature of the old play that Shakespeare may have noticed is its casual indifference to time in the action. Although called a 'history', and using old names for France (Gallia) and Wales (Cambria), various references such as those to costume ('a payre of slops', 'hose ... of the newest fashion', 1834–7, 'sea-gownes and sea-caps', 1990), to artillery and halberds (2424–5), and to the watchmen who go to the inn for 'a pot of Ale and a rasher of Bacon' (2445–6), bring the action into the contemporary world of the Elizabethan audience. Shakespeare also avoided locating his play in any particular time, and it is study of the sources that has led many producers to set it in Druid, Saxon, Roman or other periods in antiquity (see above, p. 30). It has also been given a Jacobean setting and costumes, as by Jonathan Miller (1982, BBC film for television), and a modern ambience, as by Giorgio Strehler in his 1972 Milan production, set in a twentieth-century wasteland, with actors in black leather. *King Lear* is of no particular time, which is to say it accommodates itself to all times, so that it seems just as relevant to the modern world as it did to the age of James I.

The old play has no subplot, and for the action involving Gloucester and his two sons Shakespeare remembered an episode in Sir Philip Sidney's *Arcadia* (1590), Book 2, Chapter 10, where Pyrocles and Musidorus, hiding in a hollow rock from a great storm (suggestive of the hovel in *King Lear*, 3.4?), overhear an old blind man, once the Prince of Paphlagonia, talking with a young man, his son, Leonatus. The old man has begged his son to lead him to the top of the rock so that he can commit suicide by throwing himself off it. He has been cast out of his country by his other son, his bastard, who caused him to hate and seek the death of Leonatus; the bastard son, Plexirtus, has seized power and deprived him of his sight before expelling him. Plexirtus sets upon his father and Leonatus with his followers, aiming to kill Leonatus, but various reinforcements come to the aid of both sides, and Plexirtus escapes. The Prince and Leonatus return to Paphlagonia, where the crown is set on the head of Leonatus, and the old man dies in a condition that anticipates the deaths of Gloucester and Lear, 'weeping teares (both of joy and sorrow)', his heart, broken with affliction, being unable to sustain the 'excess of comfort' (Bullough, 407). Later Plexirtus craftily achieves a reconciliation with his brother.

Shakespeare's changes to Sidney's story in effect transform it. Unlike Leonatus, Edgar does not reveal himself to his father; Edmund is motivated to take pride in his bastardy by hearing Gloucester speak of adultery and the begetting of his bastard son as sport, whereas the Prince has only contempt for 'that base woman' (Bullough, 404), the mother of Plexirtus, who is merely a villain. Edmund does not take part in the blinding of his father, and does not take delight in making him feel his misery (Bullough, 405). Edgar takes on the role of Poor Tom, and Shakespeare develops the incident in which Leonatus disobeys his father and refuses to lead him to the top of the rock into the elaborate charade of Gloucester's mock-suicide as he falls off an imaginary cliff. Shakespeare thus enriches and complicates the characters and their relationships; Sidney's sons are simply heroic or wicked, and the old Prince, presented largely as the victim of the villainy of Plexirtus, feels guilt for the wrongs done to his good son, who becomes an emblem of 'filiall pietie' (Bullough, 406).

Other episodes in *Arcadia* may have stayed in Shakespeare's imagination while he was working on *King Lear*, most notably the story of a credulous king whose wicked second wife causes him to think his good son Plangus seeks his death (Bullough, 409–11). Plangus, tricked into coming armed to overhear the king, his wife, and counsel debate what to do with him, is found by the king with his sword in his hand, and taken prisoner; delivered by the force of his friends, he goes into voluntary exile. Several features of this narrative relate to Edmund's deception of his father in *King Lear*, 2.1. For the rest, the most interesting connections between the play and *Arcadia* are perhaps to be found not in specific verbal or narrative links, but in thematic concerns, as in the treatment of patriarchy, of desire, of nature, of female power in Goneril and Regan, and in the articulation of a sceptical attitude towards the idea that God (the gods in Shakespeare's play) has any providential care of human beings (Bono, especially 122; Elton, 34–62).

Another book that seized Shakespeare's imagination when he worked on *King Lear* was Samuel Harsnett's *A Declaration of Egregious Popish Impostures* (1603). This polemical attack on a group of Catholic priests who conducted exorcism in private houses was written by the chaplain to the Bishop of London as part of an official campaign against exorcism as practised both by some Protestants and by Catholics (Walker, 44–5; Brownlow, 49–66). Harsnett often writes with great verve, and his quirky vocabulary and lively imagery were raided by Shakespeare for his characterization of Edgar as Poor Tom in Act 3, as well as occasionally for words or phrases elsewhere in the play. Harsnett depicted Catholic priests as players, 'cunning Comedians' (Brownlow, 217), and the series of exorcisms they carried out in 1585–6 as the performance of a tragicomedy. Edgar too, pretending in 3.4 to be possessed or pursued by spirits whose names, Flibbertigibbet, Smulkin, etc., are taken from Harsnett, also plays his part 'on the stage with a verie good grace' (Brownlow, 218).

The importance of Harsnett in relation to *King Lear* has been inflated by Stephen Greenblatt, who claims that in the play 'The *Declaration*'s arguments are loyally reiterated, but in a curiously divided form', since Cornwall, Goneril and Edmund are the sceptics, while 'The fraudulent possession and exorcism are given to the legitimate Edgar' (Greenblatt, 121). Shakespeare's use of Harsnett does not, it seems to me, have this kind of structural significance (see also Brownlow, 122 and n.). Edgar's masquerade as the possessed Poor Tom is pretty much confined to one scene, and has little or no effect on the mad Lear, who sees him as a 'learned Theban'; only the Fool is momentarily terrified by him. His 'possession' is not 'fraudulent', since it serves as a protective disguise, not as a means to deceive others. As Poor Tom, Edgar introduces names of devils, and the 'prince of darkness' himself (3.4.139), as fictions to support that disguise, and the action distances itself from the processes of religious exorcism here (which may be fraudulent, as Harsnett argued), just as it is distanced from any specific religious belief elsewhere in the play, in spite of the many allusions to biblical texts scattered through it. It is just possible that some might have seen a connection between Poor Tom and the recusant missionary priests who wandered in disguise in Jacobean England, though they did not travel as beggars (Brownlow, 119–20).

Shakespeare seems to have been attracted by Harsnett's vocabulary and turn of phrase, and recalled a number of unusual words that do not occur in any of his earlier plays (Muir, *Sources*, 202–6; Brownlow, 110–31). His use of them is scattered throughout the play, with a heavy concentration in the storm scenes. Usually they enliven a dramatic moment that has no connection with the event being described by Harsnett, as the image of 'an old corkie woman' (Brownlow, 221) is transferred to Gloucester, when Cornwall cries, 'Bind fast his corky arms' (3.7.29); and Gloucester himself a little later says, 'my hospitable favours / You should not ruffle thus', incorporating a word associated by Harsnett with devils who 'ruffle and rage' (Brownlow, 217). Shakespeare also picked up some ideas for particular moments in the action of his play from Harsnett. The binding of Gloucester to a chair in this scene echoes the way the women subjected to exorcism in Harsnett were bound in a chair (Brownlow, 234, 237, 369, 385, 386).

The idea of Lear as suffering a fit of the 'mother' was suggested by Harsnett's account of Richard Maynie, who had 'a spice of the Hysterica passio ... he himself termes it the Moother' (Brownlow, 223); the 'mother' was usually associated with women (see 2.2.246–7 and n.). Harsnett's description of the adjurations of exorcists in terms of fierce and noisy storms contributed to the rage of the storm scenes in *King Lear* (Brownlow,

113–15). Lear's misogynistic outburst against women, associating their sex with hell, darkness, the devil ('But to the girdle do the gods inherit, beneath is all the fiend's', 4.6.116–27), was no doubt prompted by Harsnett's descriptions of the exorcists' treatment of women, fumigating them to produce 'ugly blacknes, smoake, scorching, broyling and heate' (Brownlow, 287), and their 'assigning the inferiour parts [of women] for a peculiar lodge for the devil' (Brownlow, 252). By attacking exorcisms as merely theatrical, Harsnett was also aligning his tract with Puritan attacks on the stage, so that his book is not likely to have appealed to many of the patrons of the Globe. If the play is 'Shakespeare's reply to Harsnett', as Brownlow claims (128), it is so, I think, not as a response to the latter's offensive 'authoritarianism' (127), but as a recuperation of the power of theatre to embody profound truths in its shows and rituals, and make audiences feel what kings and wretches feel.

Another work that affected Shakespeare's thinking and enriched his vocabulary in *King Lear* was John Florio's translation of Montaigne's *Essays* (1603), where he probably found such unusual terms as 'compeer', 'disnatured', 'goatish', 'handy-dandy', 'marble-hearted', 'sectary' and 'sumpter'.[1] Montaigne's sceptical attitude to human beings, their weaknesses and limitations, enters into the play, notably through the voice of Edmund (in the letter he claims Edgar has written) denouncing the 'oppression of aged tyranny' (1.2.50) in fathers. In his essay 'Of the Affection of Fathers to their Children' Montaigne exclaims against miserly old men who drive their sons 'by some way how unlawfull soever to provide for their necessaries' (2.69). Montaigne also praises the Emperor Charles V for resigning his

---

1   Ard², 236, following on the work of George Coffin Taylor in *Shakspere's Debt to Montaigne* (1925), 58–66, lists ninety-six words common to Florio and Shakespeare, who may, of course, have encountered some of them elsewhere. Taylor also lists a number of parallel passages, only a few of them of much significance. The best discussion of the use Shakespeare made of Montaigne in the play may be found in Salingar, 124–55.

throne to his son when he felt senile, and suggested aged fathers should distribute their wealth to their children. Lear's great speech in the storm, 'Is man no more than this? Consider him well. ...' (3.4.101–6), echoes Montaigne's comparisons of beasts and men in his 'Apologie of Raymond Sebond': 'wretched weake and miserable man: whom if you consider well, what is he, but a crawling and ever-moving Ants-neast?', and so on (2.169, 181). These comparisons relate to two general ideas, major preoccupations in Montaigne's essays, that also affected the writing of *King Lear*: first that 'man is ignorant about his own nature'; and secondly that 'Nature has been obscured or corrupted by civilisation' (Salingar, 136; and see Anderson[2], 179–91).

The undercurrent of scepticism in *King Lear* may be related to the multiplying ironies of the Fool's role and dialogue,[1] and the paradoxes about wisdom and folly in the play (see above, p. 58). Shakespeare was familiar with the Bible, and he knew the Epistles of St Paul, which return to the idea that true wisdom appears foolishness in the eyes of the world, as in the verses, 'hathe not God made the wisdome of this worlde foolish?' (1 Corinthians, 1.20 [Geneva Bible]), and 'If anie man among you seme to be wise in this worlde, let him be a foole, that he may be wise' (1 Corinthians, 3.18). Such paradoxes animate Erasmus's *Praise of Folly*, which Shakespeare may have known either in the Latin or in Sir Thomas Chaloner's translation (1549, reissued in 1577). The narrator, Folly, claiming to be a goddess, turns values inside out in a way that confounds traditional dualities (good/evil; right/wrong, etc.), and exposes the inadequacy of any single perspective. The effect is subtle and complex, questioning without being cynical, and continually makes the reader aware that the best human qualities are inextricably bound up with their opposites (see Kaiser, 88, 96–7).

---

1 See William Empson's chapters on Erasmus and the Fool in *The Structure of Complex Words* (1952), 105–57.

Folly argues, for example, that flattery proceeds from good will, and 'draweth much nearer to a vertue than dooeth her contrarie, that is to say a rough plainnesse, or vnmanerly crabbednesse, to beare with no man' (Chaloner, 67). So in *King Lear* Kent's 'rough plainness' is arguably as harmful as the flattery of Goneril and Regan (see p. 9). Folly's critique of human institutions may be related to Montaigne's devastating onslaught on customary usages and traditions. If Edmund is the character who most obviously rejects custom and traditional values, in his attack on what is traditional or 'legitimate' in favour of nature as the unrestrained pursuit of appetite (see 1.2.3 and n.), the play as a whole moves to Edgar's (Albany's in the Quarto) rather different dismissal of tradition and customary demands as impotent, when he invokes feeling or natural emotion, 'what we feel', as the only proper response to the deaths of Cordelia and Lear. The play's ironic reversals and paradoxes seem to recuperate something of the spirit of Erasmus and Montaigne.[1]

The use of Harsnett and Montaigne in *King Lear* might reinforce the view that the play is essentially a pagan tragedy (Elton, 338). The numerous biblical allusions in the play that have been tracked by Noble, Shaheen and Milward, and that are noted in the commentary to this edition, might lend support to the idea that the story of Lear can be related to the Book of Job (Sewall, Holloway and others), or seen in terms of prophecy and apocalypse (Holloway, Wittreich). In his apocalyptic rage Lear calls on 'all-shaking thunder' to destroy the world at 3.2.6–9, so that the invocation of the last judgement, doomsday, in the final scene, when Edgar glosses Kent's 'Is this the promised end?' with his words 'Or image of that horror?' (5.3.261–2), does not come as a surprise. However, even those who have explored most fully the biblical echoes and resonances of an apocalyptic vision in the play

---

1   Robin Headlam Wells, *Shakespeare, Politics and the State* (1986), 157, noting the importance of Montaigne, comments that in *King Lear* 'Shakespeare appears to endorse the values of virtuous characters only to expose the illusoriness of their intellectual convictions'.

have concluded on the one hand that if it 'rests upon generally assumed Christian principles of morality' it is not a Christian play (Colie[2], 120), and on the other hand that 'The apocalyptic framework of *King Lear* neither discredits a non-Christian, nor credits a Christian reading of the play' (Wittreich, 124).

What we know of Shakespeare's wide reading and powers of assimilation seems to show that he made use of all kinds of material, absorbing contradictory viewpoints, positive and negative, religious and secular, as if to ensure that *King Lear* would offer no single controlling perspective, but be open to, indeed demand, multiple interpretations. Many other works and events contributed something to the play. Shakespeare was familiar with the major literature of his age, and with basic works from earlier periods, not only English, Chaucer for example, but classical, Ovid and Seneca for instance. So the argument that Shakespeare shows us in the wrath or *furor* of Lear a figure who 'thunders in Senecan style' and echoes Seneca's play *Hercules Furens* (Miola, 143–74) should not surprise, any more than the claim that his 'detailed assimilative knowledge' of Books 2 and 3 of Spenser's *Faerie Queene* is recalled at various points (Anderson). It is not implausible that Shakespeare was affected by his knowledge of Ovid in writing *King Lear*, in the idea of metamorphosis or shape-shifting, in the imagery of people behaving like monsters, and in his allusions to centaurs and the myth of Ixion (Bate; Hardison). It is possible that Shakespeare also recalled the play of *Selimus* (1594), which has structural similarities with *King Lear*, since it concerns an emperor with three sons, two of them disloyal, and a character, Aga, who is blinded on stage (Ekeblad; Ronan). Shakespeare is also likely to have noticed the Lord Mayor's pageant of 1605 (Dutton), which celebrated James and the union of Britain, and linked him with Edgar, King of England from 959, who brought Scotland and Wales under his sway, and Edgar Etheling, the hero of the Saxons and 'England's dearling' (Holinshed, 2.15), in the reign of William the Conqueror. It is not necessary to suppose that

Shakespeare came across the connection between Edgar Etheling and James in the curious genealogy compiled by George Owen Harry in 1604,[1] for Holinshed and other writers establish the idea of Edgar as a noble prince (Holinshed, 1.694–5, 756; 2.15–23). Edgar also figures as a somewhat equivocal king in the comedy *A Knack to Know a Knave* (1594), in which he contemplates lustful seduction and murder, but heeds good counsel and in the end does nothing wicked, if also nothing much to justify the praise of him as 'famed for love and vertuous government' (MSR, line 572).

The influence of *Eastward Ho*, a satirical play by Chapman, Marston and Jonson that went through three editions in 1605, has also been detected in *King Lear*, but the evidence is not convincing (Taylor, 'New Source'). No doubt Shakespeare did read or see this play, which could have reminded him of the parable of the prodigal son, a parable that relates to the progress of the prodigal fathers, Lear and Gloucester, in *King Lear* (Snyder); but the prodigal brought to penitence and reconciliation was a common theme of citizen comedy in the period, as in *The London Prodigal*, published in 1605 with a title-page claiming it was acted by the King's Men and written by 'William Shakespeare'. In any case Shakespeare certainly knew the biblical story (Luke, 15).

Identifying influences on Shakespeare's writing is a very uncertain business, if only because it is hard, perhaps impossible, to have much sense of what literate persons absorbed as part of their educational and cultural environment, or what to them was common knowledge. Shakespeare had an extraordinary ability to digest and put to new use elements from romance, folk-tales, morality plays, chronicles, and writings by his contemporaries. He may have been struck by some features of

---

1   Harry's *Genealogy of the High and Mighty Monarch, James* was never reprinted after 1604; it mentions Edgar (42) and Edmund, Earl of Richmond (48), as ancestors of James. Other writers, notably Sir Thomas Elyot in *The Governour*, recorded the greatness of King Edgar; see F. T. Flahiff in *Some Facets*, 229–32.

Thomas Lodge's prose romance, *The Famous, True and Historical Life of Robert Second Duke of Normandy* (1591), which marries the titular story with the legend of Robert of Sicily, or Robert the Devil. Robert progresses from wickedness through suffering to repentance, takes shelter with a hermit in a wood, does penance by taking on the role of a Fool, and fights incognito to save Christendom by defeating the Soldan of Babylon.[1] Shakespeare may also have found suggestive some of the social and political ideas of Justus Lipsius, *Six Books of Politickes, or Civil Doctrine* (translated by William Jones, 1594), especially its neo-stoic emphasis.[2]

If Shakespeare knew the translation by George Pettie of Guazzo's *Civil Conversation* he would have found support in it for Montaigne's attitude to senile parents, and a strong recommendation that old fathers 'ought to acknowledge their insufficiency and want of judgment, and to referre the ordering of their house and liuing to their children, who are of discretion to deale in such waighty matters' (Pettie, 66); Guazzo alludes to the 'many examples' of princes and rulers who have done so, though he is thinking of sons, not daughters.

Contexts for the play include Shakespeare's own earlier and contemporary works. 'Edmund's ancestry' (Danby, 57–101) in particular can be traced back to Aaron the Moor in *Titus Andronicus*, to the bastard Falconbridge in *King John*, to Richard III and to Iago. Other affinities in themes and dramatic incidents with *Titus Andronicus* are brought out in Jonathan Bate's edition of the play (Ard³). Danby sees Edmund as representative of the

---

1 Donna Hamilton, 'Some romance sources for *King Lear*: Robert of Sicily and Robert the Devil', *SP*, 71 (1974), 173–91. Michael Drayton in 1596 published his verse 'Legend of Robert Duke of Normandie', which describes the blinding of this historical Robert, whose story is partly derived from Holinshed, 2.54–7.

2 Arthur F. Kinney, 'Some conjectures on the composition of "King Lear"', *SS*, 33 (1982), 13–25. The general bent of Justus Lipsius seems to me to anticipate the authoritarian writings of James I rather than *King Lear*; but see also Hiram Haydn, *The Counter-Renaissance* (New York, 1950), 642–51, on the stoicism of Kent and Edgar.

'new man' of an emergent capitalist society, where commodity, appetite and authority become key mechanisms (Danby, 100), and as related to the conflict between Prince Hal and Falstaff in the *Henry IV* plays. Edmund is also descended from the Vice of the morality plays, and further analogies may be found with both Lear and Gloucester in the eponymous protagonists of such plays as *Everyman* and *Mankind* (Mack, 57–60). *Timon of Athens* (?1605–8) seems to take off from *King Lear* in its savage depiction of flattery and avarice. *King Lear* has a special connection also with *As You Like It* among Shakespeare's comedies; in both plays a ruler is thrust into the wilderness, out into the winter wind of a harsh natural world away from society, and a good younger son, likewise cast out by an evil elder brother, cares for an old man in his exile. In both plays, too, a daughter of the ruler is also forced into exile, and is reunited with her father at the end. In *As You Like It* the forest of exile becomes a place of healing, love and restoration, and the play ends with the multiple marriages of comedy; *King Lear* is very different, but the sketch for a pastoral romance in it gave credibility to Nahum Tate's reworking in 1681, which ended with the betrothal of Edgar and Cordelia, while Lear and Gloster go off to a 'cool cell', much as the Duke, followed by Jaques, seeks out a 'religious life' (*AYL* 5.4.181). The inversion of pastoral in *King Lear* led Maynard Mack to call the play 'the greatest anti-pastoral ever penned' (Mack, 65).

TEXTS OF *KING LEAR*

On 26 November 1607 there was entered in the Stationers' Register on behalf of John Busby and Nathaniel Butter, booksellers, 'A booke called Mr William Shakespeare his historye of Kinge Lear as yt was played before the kinges maiestie at Whitehall vppon St Stephans night at christmas Last by his mai^{ties} servantes playinge vsually at the globe on Banksyde'. This normal form of entry protected the interests of the booksellers, who arranged to have the book printed by Nicholas Okes, a recently established master printer. In his thorough analysis of the activities of Okes's printing shop, Peter Blayney has shown that the play was printed between early December 1607 and the middle of January 1608 (Blayney, 148–50). The title-page of this first Quarto (Q1) is reproduced in Fig. 20; it adds a reference to Lear's daughters, and advertises the 'sullen and assumed humor' of Edgar, or melancholy disposition affected by him, but otherwise agrees with the wording of the entry in the Register, only changing 'at christmas last' to '*in Christmas Hollidayes*', thus misleading the reader into supposing the play had been performed at Christmas 1607 rather than 1606 (Blayney, 83). Shakespeare's name was no doubt given prominence at the head of the page both for commercial appeal and to establish the play as different from *The True Chronicle History of King LEIR, and his three daughters, Gonorill, Ragan, and Cordella*, known only from the quarto published in 1605 (Fig. 21).

Q1 is 'among Okes's half-dozen worst-printed books of 1607–9', and was set, from a manuscript that was often difficult to read, by two compositors, one of them possibly an inexperienced apprentice, who were working for a printer who had never before printed a play text (Blayney, 26–30, 184–7). It has many errors and muddles, and frequently prints verse as prose or prose as verse. There is no reason to believe that *King Lear* sold well at Nathaniel Butter's shop. A Second Quarto (Q2), issued in 1619, bears on its title-page the false imprint, 'Printed for *Nathaniel Butter*. 1608'; it was in fact printed without authority by William Jaggard for Thomas Pavier, as one of a group of ten plays intended to initiate a collection of plays attributed to Shakespeare. The Pavier quartos may have provoked the King's Men to protest through the Lord Chamberlain, who wrote to the Stationers' Company to demand that no more plays belonging to them should be printed except with their consent (Greg, *First Folio*, 9–16). The Second Quarto of *King Lear* was printed from Q1, but makes some changes, introduces corrections and

M. William Shak-ſpeare:

collated & Perfect ...R-1804.

HIS

True Chronicle Hiſtorie of the life and
death of King L E A R and his three
Daughters.

With the vnfortunate life of Edgar, *ſonne*
and heire to the Earle of Gloſter, and his
ſullen and aſſumed humor of
T O M of Bedlam:

*As it was played before the Kings Maieſtie at Whitehall vpon
S.* Stephans *night in Chriſtmas Hollidayes.*

By his Maieſties ſeruants playing vſually at the Gloabe
on the Bancke-ſide.

George Steevens.

Edw: Palmer

*There is another
copy of this Play,
printed for Nathaniel
Butter. 4°1608. Vol. 119.*

LONDON,
Printed for *Nathaniel Butter,* and are to be ſold at his ſhop in *Pauls*
Church-yard at the ſigne of the Pide Bull neere
S^t. *Auſtins* Gate. 1 6 0 8.

20   Title-page of the First Quarto of *King Lear* (1608)

112

further errors, and is of importance because a copy of it was used in the printing of the Folio text in 1623. In 1655 a Third Quarto (Q3) appeared, which was derived from Q2, and has no independent textual authority.

In *Mr. William Shakespeares Comedies, Histories, & Tragedies. Published according to the True Originall Copies* (1623), otherwise known as the First Folio (F1), William Jaggard, or his son Isaac, who took on the business after his father's death in 1623, included 'The Tragedie of King Lear' between *Hamlet* and *Othello*. This text differs in its title ('tragedy' instead of 'history'), and in hundreds of details, many substantive, from Q1; furthermore it lacks nearly 300 lines found in the Quarto, and has more than a hundred that are not in Q1. Whether the copy for F1 or for Q1 was the 'true original' has been endlessly debated; what is clear is that the texts were based on different copies. The Folio text was reprinted in the Second Folio (F2) in 1632, the Third Folio (F3) in 1663 and the Fourth Folio (F4) in 1685. These reprints correct some obvious errors, but also introduce new ones, and have no independent authority. When Nahum Tate adapted *King Lear* in 1681 for the Restoration theatre, he consulted a Quarto and a Folio text, and used lines from both, while relying mainly on the Folio after the first act. Modern editions begin with those of Nicholas Rowe between 1709 and 1714, who used F4 as the basis for his text. Alexander Pope was the first, in his edition of 1723, to make some comparison and analysis of the Quarto and Folio texts, and he initiated the tradition of conflating them. He was followed by Lewis Theobald, who also assumed that there was one true text of *King Lear*, and that 'theatrical and transmissional corruption of Shakespeare's text' was 'the major source of variants in Quartos and the Folio' (Urkowitz, *Division*, 29). This assumption was generally taken for granted by editors of the play until the 1980s, when the nature of the texts and the relation between them came under intense scrutiny that led to an important revaluation of editorial principles.

THE
True Chronicle Hi.

ſtory of King LEIR, and his three
daughters, *Gonorill, Ragan,*
and *Cordella.*

As it hath bene diuers and ſundry
times lately acted.

LONDON,

Printed by Simon Stafford for Iohn
Wright, and are to bee ſold at his ſhop at
Chriſtes Church dore, next New gate-
Market. 1605.

21 Title-page of the Quarto of *King Leir* (1605)

It is at this point that hypothesis and inference take over, since the copy from which Q and F were printed is lost. Until recently most textual critics assumed that editors should establish a text that would be as close as possible to a supposed lost original, and should aim to provide the reader with a text that 'will be as near to what Shakespeare wrote as ... it is possible to get' (Duthie, 3) In the case of a play like *King Lear*, for which two widely differing printed texts survive, the differences could be explained by corruption of various kinds, by errors in the printing-house, or by cutting and contamination in the playhouse. Some scholars held that Q1 was a reported text, taken down in shorthand during a performance, or reconstructed from memory by one or more of the actors performing it. Others proposed that the verbal errors, mislineation, inadequate punctuation and other confusions in the Quarto could be traced to Shakespeare's 'foul papers', 'which were already confused and illegible through much correction and alteration'.[1] The idea of memorial reconstruction by the entire company of actors formed the basis of G. I. Duthie's critical edition of the play, published in 1949, and was taken over by Kenneth Muir in the Arden edition of 1952. The various arguments for and against seeing Q1 as a reported text or as based on confused rough copy (foul papers) were magisterially summed up by W. W. Greg in *The Shakespeare First Folio* (1955).

Greg also assumed that the Folio text was printed from a copy of the Quarto that had been collated with the prompt-book used for performance, so that passages in Q omitted from F were explained as theatrical cuts, and errors in F were accounted for as introduced by someone, perhaps the collator or book-keeper at the Globe, who 'tampered with the text' (Greg, *First Folio*, 386). The governing idea behind such arguments was that of a

---

1 So Madeleine Doran argued, as reported by Greg, *First Folio*, 379. The phrase 'foul papers' is derived from a letter written by the playwright Robert Daborne in 1613, sending the 'foule sheet' of a scene to the theatre in place of 'the fayr', which he had not finished (Greg, *First Folio*, 92n.).

single lost original text, ideally a fair copy in Shakespeare's hand, the product of his genius, which it was the aim of scholarship to approximate as far as possible; hence all editions of *King Lear* prior to 1986 conflated Q and F, taking what the editors regarded as the best readings from each, and including all the passages found in one but not the other, in an effort to provide readers with all of what Shakespeare wrote. The users of such eclectic texts were presented with what appeared to be a definitive version of the play, and nearly all published criticism has been based upon editions of this kind.

Although a few scholars (notably Doran and Honigmann) had considered the possibility that Shakespeare or someone might have revised the play,[1] it was only in 1978 that Michael Warren argued, in an important essay, that the Q and F texts 'must be treated as separate versions of *King Lear*' (Warren, 'Albany', 105). This imperative was echoed and expanded in a series of re-examinations of the textual problems of the play in the 1980s, most significantly *The Division of the Kingdoms* (1983), a collection of essays aggressively arguing for revision in the Folio text in order to promote the idea that 'The Quarto and Folio texts of *King Lear* are distinct. There is no valid evidence that they derive from a lost archetype' (Wells, 20). Then the one–volume edition of Shakespeare's plays by Stanley Wells and Gary Taylor (Oxf, 1986) for the first time included two modernized texts of the play, based respectively on the Quarto and Folio. *King Lear* was regarded as offering a special, but not a unique, problem, for revision was increasingly seen as the best explanation for differences between the Quarto and Folio texts of other plays, like *Hamlet*, and as accounting for some anomalies and repetitions in plays printed only in the Folio.[2] However, the idea that we

---

1   For an account of the development of the idea that Shakespeare's plays were revised, see Ioppolo.

2   A section headed 'Shakespeare as reviser', by John Kerrigan, was added to the Sphere History of Literature in 1987, reissued as the Penguin History of Literature, vol. 3, *English Drama to 1710* (1993), 255–75. See also Ioppolo.

have two quite distinct versions of *King Lear*, virtually amounting to different plays, has tended to harden into a critical orthodoxy, so that the latest editions either follow one text, the Folio in Jay Halio's Cambridge edition (1992), or present parallel texts of Q and F, as in the facsimile parallel text edition by Michael Warren (University of California Press, 1989), and the modernized versions edited by René Weis (Longman Annotated Texts, 1993).

The idea that some of Shakespeare's plays in the texts that survive may have been revised is based upon a different concept of authorship from that assumed by Greg: instead of regarding the plays as finished products of Shakespeare's mind, they are seen as works in process, affected by the conditions of the stage, the negotiations involved in collaborating with actors, and subject to new influences when revived in performance. It is well known that a great many major writers have revised their works, some tinkering with them endlessly. The example of contemporary dramatists reworking plays in close relation to the companies staging them has also been suggestive in considering Shakespeare's working methods.[1] The reasons it took so long for scholars to recognize the possibility of revision in Shakespeare's plays are complex, but may be traced back to the claims by his fellow actors in their preface to the Folio, first, that they were replacing 'stolne, and surreptitious copies, maimed, and deformed by the frauds and stealths of iniurious impostors' by texts 'cur'd, and perfect of their limbes'; and secondly that they had 'scarse received' from Shakespeare 'a blot in his papers'. The 'papers' from which Q1 of *King Lear* was printed, as Peter Blayney has shown in *The Texts of King Lear and their Origins* (1982), were probably much blotted, and almost illegible in places.

---

1   See Gaskell's commentary, 245–62, on the changes made by actors and the author in
    Tom Stoppard's play *Travesties*.

Those who argued for revision in *King Lear* initially saw themselves as battling a long tradition of criticism and editing that was summed up in Kenneth Muir's words: 'A modern editor will, of course, restore [the] omitted lines, whether his text is based mainly on the Quarto or on the Folio' (Ard², xiv). They proclaimed vigorously what they wished to establish as the new orthodoxy, insisting 'that all further work on the play be based on either Q or F, but not on the conflation of both' (Warren, 'Albany', 105; and see Wells, 18). Certainly the differences between the texts of *King Lear* affect the play in both large and minute ways. For instance, among the larger differences, F omits some passages and reworks others that in Q refer to a French invasion of England in relation to the return of Cordelia; and the minute changes include the significant reassignment in 1.4 of 'This is nothing, Fool' (given to Lear in Q, to Kent in F), and 'Lear's shadow' (given to Lear in Q, to the Fool in F). A conflated edition has to select one alternative, and may at times build in contradictory signals, as in 3.1, where Kent in Q reports that a French force has landed in England, but in F speaks only of a civil war between Albany and Cornwall, and of their servants who are acting as spies for France (see Appendix 1).

Such findings have been taken as requiring editors to adopt the rule that 'we must not conflate any one version with any other' (McKenzie, 29). In defending their position, many of the advocates of revision in Shakespeare have taken a dogmatic and purist stance, which abandons the idea of *King Lear* as a single work of which we have variant versions. Viewed from the perspective of the numerous versions of works by some later writers, the question of the two versions of the play seems a relatively minor matter.[1] In fact none of the differences between Q

1   Jack Stillinger, dealing with multiple versions of Coleridge's poems in *Coleridge and Textual Instability* (New York, 1994), offers 'A practical theory of versions' in chapter 4, 118–40, defining a version as 'a physically embodied text of the work' (132).

and F radically affects the plot of the play, or its general structure, and there is every reason to think that we have two versions
of the same play, not two different plays. In any case, readers
should be free to make up their own minds, just as actors and
directors will see the text(s) as the basis for a script they can use.
The central question, then, for an editor is how best to make
available to readers the play of *King Lear*; and a prime consideration, I think, should be the peculiar nature of dramatic works,
whose form 'may be conceived of as always potential … where
the text is open and generates new meanings according to new
needs in a perpetual deferral of closure' (McKenzie, 29). A play
is realized in performance, either in the mind or on the stage,
and performances are always going to relate to the period when
they are staged. Directors will cut, alter and rearrange to express
their interests and find their audience, and critics will emphasize
different parts of the text to challenge with new interpretations.
It seems to me desirable to offer an edition that seeks to give an
idea of the work, while making the major differences between
the versions easily recognizable; it then becomes the decision of
readers, actors and directors whether to prefer Q to F, F to Q,
or to take readings from both.

A closer look at Q and F

The only evidence we have for the copy that lies behind the text
printed in Q is to be found within it; the nature of the manuscript
has to be inferred, and arguments can never be conclusive in the
absence of external proof. The text is a full one, but its misread-
ings, some apparently based on mishearings (e.g. at 4.6.154–5, 'a
dogge, so bade', corrected to 'a dog's obeyed' in F), mislinings,
and other confusions, lent support to a theory that was for a long
time widely accepted, namely that Q was a corrupt text, pirated in
some way, and was not printed from an authorial manuscript. One
possibility taken seriously for a time was that a stenographer took
down the play in shorthand at a performance, but this idea has
now been generally discredited, since no system of the period was

adequate to the task, and it is difficult to imagine how someone in the audience could have operated without being noticed (the matter is discussed in Stone, 22–5). G. I. Duthie was the principal proponent of another idea, that 'Q was printed from a manuscript written out by a scribe from the actors' dictation, the actors having had to rely upon memory alone' (Duthie, 117). However, the mislineations of verse and treatment of verse as prose in Q led P. W. K. Stone in 1980 to reject the idea of memorial reconstruction by actors, who would be attuned to verse, and to propose that a single reporter repeatedly attended the play, putting together a text by 'a process of piecemeal accumulation', and passing this on to the printer (Stone, 35).

Stone differed from his predecessors in that his explanation of the manuscript behind Q1 enabled him to claim that it could 'be regarded as a true reflection of the original' (Stone, 41), and not a corrupt version. However, no one has been inclined to return to the idea of a reported text since Peter Blayney's exhaustive analysis of the printing of Q appeared in 1982. His concern was 'to allow the Quarto evidence to speak for itself' (Blayney, 8), by studying the production of Q as a printed book in relation to the way the printing-house of Nicholas Okes operated. Although he was not concerned to try to identify the nature of the manuscript from which Q was printed, he was able to demonstrate that *King Lear* was the first play printed by Okes, that it was very badly printed by two compositors,[1] one probably an apprentice, and neither notable for competence, 'from a play-manuscript which required the compositors to impose conventions differing quite substantially from those in most of Okes's other books, and it is perfectly evident that the manuscript itself was a difficult one' (Blayney, 184). Blayney's detailed account of the printing of Q thus indirectly supported the argument put forward by Stephen Urkowitz in 1980 that Q was

---

1 E. A. J. Honigmann had argued for the presence of two compositors in 'Spelling tests and the First Quarto of *King Lear*', *The Library*, 5th series, 20 (1965), 310–15.

based on a manuscript in Shakespeare's own hand (Urkowitz, 129–36, 139–40).

If the best explanation so far produced for the nature of the Quarto text is that it derives from a very messy authorial manuscript that gave the compositors a lot of trouble, the Quarto nevertheless has some puzzling features. If the printing of verse as prose may be accounted for by assuming that Shakespeare did not begin verse lines with capital letters, who then was responsible for the extra-metrical words and phrases that are scattered through the opening scene especially (see 1.1.1 and n.), and are omitted from F? Such additions as 'How' (1.1.90), 'Well' (109), 'Sir' (203) and 'Go to, go to' (235) could possibly be elaborations actors might have made.[1] The curious loose ends and apparent contradictions in Q relating to the matter of the French invasion and war with France, as well as the presence or absence of the King of France, also raise questions about the nature of the manuscript from which it was derived. These questions are considered in more detail in Appendix 1, p. 393, where the possibility is raised that Q offers some intermediate stage in the development of the play rather than an author's final draft.[2]

What appear to be mishearings in Q may have resulted from graphic errors of misreading (Urkowitz, 133–5). So 'in sight' (Q) looks like a mishearing of 'incite' (F), but in context it seems rather that the compositors were more concerned with the look of the final words in a rhyming couplet at 4.4.26–7; in Q 'in sight' rhymes with 'right' (the correct word), while in F 'incite' (the correct word) rhymes with 'Rite', an odd spelling for 'right'.

---

1   Harold Jenkins listed many similar examples of extra-metrical words he thinks were added by actors in the Folio text of *Hamlet*; see 'Playhouse interpolations in the Folio text of *Hamlet*', *SB*, 13 (1960), 31–47. Ard², 4–5, thinks it possible that 'in the heat of rapid composition' Shakespeare 'may not have bothered to count syllables'; see also Stone, 18.

2   As Honigmann argued (Honigmann, 7–21), the idea that Shakespeare composed one draft ('foul papers'), which was then transcribed for the stage ('fair copy'), is too limiting; there is evidence to suggest that Shakespeare may have written 'consecutive authorial drafts' (10) for some plays.

A number of mistakes were noticed while printing was proceeding, and the large number of press variants from sheet C to sheet H and in sheet K shows an awareness of the need for proof correction, and is further evidence of the difficulty of the manuscript; the press variants are listed in Blayney, 592–7. He also provides a considered account of proofreading and of miscorrections in the Quarto; the corrector consulted copy for some of the corrections, but not for all, and some alterations are evidently mistakes (Blayney, 245–52). These can be traced in the textual notes to the present edition.

It was generally in the interest of companies of players to keep the fair copies made for prompt use in the theatre as long as a play was likely to be in repertory, so that the King's Men could have passed on to a printer an author's draft or foul papers. However, it is hard to understand why they would have handed over a manuscript to an unfamiliar and inexperienced printer, especially as the only hitherto unprinted text the King's Men certainly authorized for publication between 1600 and 1619 was the 1604–5 Quarto of *Hamlet*, published in response to what was probably a pirated 'bad' quarto of 1603. It may have cost more money than Okes was willing to lay out to have such a manuscript copied in longhand, and the compositors solved as best they could the many problems they encountered in reading their text, incorporating what were no doubt some authorial spellings at a time when spelling was not fixed, an example being 'ceaze' or 'seaze' for 'seize' (1.1.254, 2.1.117). Much remains obscure about the nature of the manuscript, in particular, why so much verse was interpreted by the compositors as prose, as in the long sequence at 1.4.249–344. Okes presumably wanted to economize on paper, and not use more than ten sheets, which led to crowding on the final page, L4^r (as was his practice, he left L4^v blank), where some verse is set as prose; no better explanation has been offered for the printing of verse as prose elsewhere in *King Lear*. The differences in lineation between Q and F are listed in Appendix 2.

For a long time W. W. Greg's argument, put forward in 1940, that the Folio text was 'set up from a much altered copy of the first quarto',[1] won general acceptance. He demonstrated that the twelve known copies of Q1 had a mixture of corrected and uncorrected formes, and his claim was based largely on one or two instances where F reproduces an error from an uncorrected forme of the Quarto, the most notable occurring at 5.3.48: here the phrase 'and appointed guard' was added in the corrected forme, but is not present in F. However, Madeleine Doran had already noted links between F and Q2 in her pioneer study of *The Text of King Lear* in 1931 (Doran, 110–21), and later investigators have found further evidence of dependence on Q2. Prompted partly by the debate about possible revision of the play by Shakespeare, a flow of essays concerned with the Folio text has appeared since about 1980, and on the whole they confirm that a copy of Q2 was used in printing it.

Meanwhile, in his 1963 analysis of the printing of the Folio, Charlton Hinman established that two compositors shared the setting of *King Lear*, one identified as B, an experienced compositor who was liable to sophisticate his copy, and the other as E, an inexperienced person, perhaps an apprentice, who followed his copy closely, and for the most part worked only from printed copy (Hinman, 1.10–12, 218–26). More recent analyses of the practice of these compositors have produced differing conclusions. Like Hinman, Stone in 1980 found that compositor B set from manuscript, a 'manuscript version of the text derived from Q1', and compositor E from printed copy, a marked-up copy of Q2 (Stone, 129–40, citing 139). In 1983 Stone's views were corroborated by Gary Taylor and MacD. P. Jackson (Taylor, 'Date', 364–7; Jackson, 328–9), but Taylor changed his mind in 1985 to argue that 'The evidence of substantive variants, of spelling, and of punctuation, gives us no reason to doubt that

---

1 Greg, *Variants*, 139. The suggestion seems to have been first made by P. A. Daniel in his Introduction to the Praetorius facsimile of Q1 (1885).

both Folio compositors were setting, throughout *Lear*, from annotated Q2 copy' (Taylor, 'Folio Copy', 69). In 1982, 1985 and 1986 this claim has been challenged by Trevor Howard-Hill, who, in reviewing *The Division of the Kingdoms*, and in a subsequent essay, has argued strongly that both B and E worked from manuscript copy, and the influence of Q2 was mediated through this manuscript. In his analysis of the evidence Peter Blayney concludes that F was probably printed from a transcription of an annotated copy of Q2 (as reported in Halio, 67).

The evidence, from spellings, variants, punctuation, agreements and disagreements between the quartos, and between Q2 and F, is very difficult to interpret, but there is at present a consensus that the text in F has a significant relation with Q2, and no direct link with Q1. What then becomes of Greg's clinching argument to show that F was derived from Q1, that is to say, the absence from F of the phrase 'and appointed guard'? Madeleine Doran had already suggested that the phrase could have been written as an afterthought in the margin of a manuscript, and overlooked or considered to be deleted by the original compositor in setting uncorrected Q1. Stone thought the phrase might have been cut by an adapter. In 1983, in *The Division of the Kingdoms*, Taylor rejected these explanations, in favour of Greg's as the simplest, but since he could show that F had links with Q2, he could only explain the influence of Q1 by assuming that it was exerted through a manuscript, and argued that a transcription of Q1 lay behind F, or, in his own words, 'that Folio agreements with suspicious press variants in Q1 derive from two sources (Q2 copy and a manuscript influenced by Q1)' (Taylor, 'Date', 359–63). In 1985 he revised his view, after a more detailed analysis of compositorial evidence, to conclude that F was set from an annotated copy of Q2, and that errors in it 'stood in the manuscript itself, and were faithfully transcribed from there onto the printed copy' (Taylor, 'Folio Copy', 70). He resisted drawing any conclusions about the nature of this manuscript, but Howard-Hill, tackling again the problem of the phrase 'and appointed guard', argued that it was added in Shakespeare's draft or foul papers 'in such a way as to prompt not only the Q1 compositor but also a scribe (preparing a copy of foul papers) to omit it' (Howard-Hill[3], 431).

It turns out that there are other ways of accounting for what seemed to Greg a simple matter of transference from Q1 to F: indeed, 'For every hypothesis erected as a certainty a new doubt arises' (Howard-Hill[2], 179); and for every explanation of a textual problem an alternative solution is likely to be found. Moreover, explanations tend to be shaped by the categories invented to hypothesize the way Shakespeare worked. So scholars usually assume that Shakespeare prepared two manuscripts for a play, his rough copy or 'foul papers', and a fair transcript, which might then serve as prompt copy; they also suppose that the 'good' quartos, among which Q1 of *Lear* is now usually included, were printed from the author's 'foul papers'. However, in an essay attempting to demystify these categories, Paul Werstine has pointed out that no 'good' quarto can be shown to have been set from 'foul papers', if only because 'no example of Greg's idealized "foul papers" – the author's original and ultimate draft much corrected – has yet been identified';[1] and no manuscript prompt copy of a play by Shakespeare is known. Shakespeare must have written drafts, but Werstine's comment is a useful reminder of how speculative all arguments about Shakespeare's manuscripts are. It is possible that a scribe was employed to make the fair copy of Shakespeare's draft of *King Lear*, and made a deal with Okes for the foul papers.

Enough bibliographical evidence has been established to demonstrate a connection between F *Lear* and Q2, which was printed in William Jaggard's shop from a copy of Q1. Q2 is printed more spaciously than the crowded text of Q1, running to

---

1 Paul Werstine, 'Narratives about printed Shakespeare texts: "foul papers" and "bad" quartos', *SQ*, 41 (1990), 65–86, citing 81, where he notes, 'the marks that have been used to identify "foul papers" as printer's copy are also to be found in extant "promptbooks"'.

85 pages as against 79 in Q1 (Knowles, 192), and so offers more space for annotation. There must have been a manuscript source for the many differences between Q2 and F. Here speculation takes over. If the annotations were made on the wider margins of an untrimmed copy of Q2 some of the manuscript readings could fairly easily have been noted, but it is more difficult to imagine how large changes or expansions, for example, the addition of seven and a half lines, together with seventeen other changes in the text and several more in stage directions in 1.1.26–66, could have been written on to A2^v, which is pretty solidly packed with printed text. It seems likely that the compositors worked from a manuscript, and for ease of setting marked up a copy of Q2 where possible. It has usually been taken for granted that this manuscript derived from prompt copy, and that 'to a considerable degree, the Folio represents actual theatrical practice' (Wells, 9; Cam², 69), since it has what may be theatrical markings, like the repeated direction '*Storm still*' in 3.2 and 3.4.

If Q1 had no direct influence on the printing of F (as suggested by Taylor, 'Folio Copy', 70–1, and Howard-Hill³, 433–4), then variants in Q1 carried over into F would have originated in the manuscript from which Q1 was printed. It would appear that another manuscript was made for use in the theatre, and this, or a transcript made from it, incorporating changes and revisions from the earlier one, and in association with a copy of Q2, formed the basis for the text printed in F. It is possible that the additions in F were written by Shakespeare, who may also have been responsible for, or at least assented to, the cutting of nearly three hundred lines. There is no way of knowing who was responsible for the large number of minor substantive changes between Q1 and F, many of which are indifferent and do not alter the sense to any significant effect, as in the substitution at 1.1.34, 64, 171 and 224 of 'lord' (F) for 'Liege' (Q); 'shadowy' for 'shady'; 'betwixt' for 'betweene'; and 'Should' for 'Could'. Some appear to be the result of deliberate fine tuning, as at

1.1.183, where F has 'dear shelter' in place of 'protection' (Q), 'dear' expressing Kent's affection for Cordelia. There are also instances where F has a simpler reading, like 'stick' for 'rash' (Q) at 3.7.57 and 'stern' for 'dearne' a few lines later (3.7.62). Here, in a difficult speech of Gloucester's, changes could have been made for clarity or ease of speaking (to avoid the repeated 'sh' in 'in his flesh rash boarish fangs'), but it is impossible to know whether Shakespeare was responsible. Yet other changes were made by the compositors in F, who might accidentally omit a word, like 'not' at 1.1.291, or transpose words (for example, 'you to this' for 'this to you' at 1.2.57–8), or introduce errors, like 'will' for 'well' at 1.4.1.

An editor has to juggle with all these uncertainties, and make informed guesses at many points concerning the differences between the texts. Consideration of the possible nature and origin of errors introduced by the author, copyist, or compositors of varying habits and skills can only be speculative. In general this edition prefers Folio to Quarto readings, except where there is good reason for thinking F is in error, since the Folio preserves what is probably the latest state of the play available. The aim is to provide what Philip Gaskell describes as a reading text; he describes the three textual stages of a play as follows: 'There is first the script, the written version of what was originally intended to be said. Secondly, there is the performance text, what is actually said in one or more performances. And thirdly there is the reading text, the version published by author or editor as a record of what might or should have been said' (Gaskell, 245). He was investigating the text of Tom Stoppard's play *Travesties*, and showed that in the opening monologue in the first production the actor made three changes, introducing colloquialisms and an additional phrase; that Stoppard marked for cutting two passages that were included in performance; and that the published text kept one and omitted the other of these passages, and also left out the actor's interpolations (248–9). The reading text of a modern play in which the author collaborated in the production thus may not correspond with what the author initially wrote, or with what was performed. Shakespeare was an actor, a sharer in the Globe theatre, and it is reasonable to assume that he collaborated in the evolution of *King Lear* in performance, conceivably with close attention to details. The Folio version of the play may well show not only the author changing his mind, but the impact of the way the Globe company interpreted and shaped speeches and action. Shakespeare does not seem to have interested himself at all in publication, so that an edited text of *King Lear* can only attempt to provide the fullest materials that will enable the reader to gain a sense of the work and its possible versions. Editors and readers need to keep in mind that 'what we get in the theatre is a living art; plays which evolve with the ideas of the company; performances which are continually affected by the reactions of their audiences' (Gaskell, 261).

REVISION AND ADAPTATION IN *KING LEAR*

Critical debate about the possibility of revision in Shakespearean texts was reanimated in the 1980s with special reference to *King Lear*.[1] The contributors to *The Division of the Kingdoms* in particular presented a forcible and partisan case for authorial revision in the play. Their dogmatism is understandable, since they were concerned to demolish an editorial tradition that regarded both texts as imperfect embodiments of a lost original; they also wished to call in question the common practice in editions of presenting a conflated text. They may well have been right to argue that Shakespeare could have been involved in reworking the play, but less justified in their over-confident assertion that the Quarto and

---

1 Debate was stimulated by Warren, 'Albany', 95–107; by Urkowitz, *Shakespeare's Revision of King Lear*; and by *Division* (1983). For a history of the topic, and an account of recent debates, see Ioppolo and Michael Warren's Introduction in *The Complete King Lear 1608–1623* (Berkeley and Los Angeles, 1989).

Folio texts of the play 'are distinct', 'that the later [i.e. Folio] is the better play', and that new editions should attempt 'to restore each text to an authentic, independent state' (Wells, 20, 18). Their method on the whole sought to justify changes in the Folio as improvements, so that the Quarto was seen as the original play, and the Folio as providing us with a theatrically superior and separate final recension. They did not allow for the possibility of a work which might exist in various versions, no one version essentially superior to another, and for which we cannot with certainty say that we have either a first draft or the final recension. I regard *King Lear* as a single work that is extant in two versions that differ in various ways, and I think readers should be encouraged to decide what constitutes for them the text of the play (see Gaskell, 261; McKenzie, 28–31).

By no means all the changes made in F are likely to be revisions. As noted above, p. 126, there are many indifferent variants, word substitutions that are roughly equivalent in meaning, and might have been introduced by a copyist (conceivably Shakespeare himself) or a compositor. There are many detectable errors in transmission, as at 1.1.74, where eyeskip caused the compositor in F to repeat 'professes' from 72, and Q has the correct reading, 'possesses'; eyeskip again no doubt produced the similar error in Q at 1.1.147, where Q this time is wrong, printing 'When Lear is man' for 'When Lear is mad'. The verse is often mislined in Q, and F restores a number of verses, as at 1.1.119 and 3.4.4, where F adds the words 'to my bosom' and 'here', probably omitted in error from Q, to complete a blank verse line ('To gorge his appetite, shall *to my bosom*', and 'Good my lord, enter *here*. Wilt break my heart?').

The more substantial cuts in the Folio version may have originated in the theatre, although, since he was a member of the King's Men, Shakespeare presumably would have been aware of those made during his lifetime, but there remains an area of uncertainty, as for instance in the omission in F of 'to love my father all' at 1.1.104, or of 'I never got him' at 2.1.78, phrases which could have been dropped by a compositor's error. It is possible that censorship of passages that could have given offence to King James also might have affected the Folio. Edmund's account of 'menaces and maledictions against King and nobles' at 1.2.146–7, the Fool's satirical allusion to monopolies at 1.4.145–6, and a number of references to war with France, in 3.1, 4.3 and 5.1, could have been omitted to avoid displeasing a King who was known for granting monopolies to favourites, and whose motto was *Beati pacifici*, 'Blessed are the makers of peace' (see Patterson[2], 58–73; Clare[2], 133–4).

Setting aside mistakes in reading the manuscript, errors in the printing-house or other possible kinds of corruption, cuts possibly attributable to stage intervention or censorship, corrections and casual variants, there remain a substantial number of changes, small and large, that I think are best explained by deliberate reworking. Not everyone agrees, and it is valuable to be reminded that what looks like an addition in F could be interpreted as an omission in Q; that interpretation of changes varies according to the assumptions with which the interpreter begins; and that in making a case for Shakespeare's involvement as reviser it is tempting to overlook untidinesses and loose ends in F that may be due to intervention by others.[1] Caution is necessary, too, about the scale of the changes: in their anxiety to win converts, advocates of revision have been inclined to overstate their case, to find a 'masterful playwright' creating in effect a new play with 'dramatic boldness, sensitivity and power' (Urkowitz, 147). Many of the changes are fascinating as producing a new effect or shift of emphasis with great economy of means, but neither these, nor the larger alterations, like the omission of 4.3, and the slimming down of the roles of Albany and Edgar in F, affect in more than detailed ways the basic struc-

---

1   See, for example, Sidney Thomas, 'Shakespeare's supposed revision of *King Lear*', *SQ*, 35 (1984), 506–11; Marion Trousdale, 'A trip through the divided kingdoms', *SQ*, 37 (1986), 218–23; and Meyer, 128–46.

ture of the play or the working out of the Lear and Gloucester plots. It is important, then, to try to reassess what effect the changes do have.

In evaluating differences, it is also necessary to bear in mind that a change made in F is not necessarily 'masterful', or an improvement over Q. The problem can be illustrated in considering the entry of Goneril at 2.2.376:

Lear.	This is a slaue, whose easie borrowed pride
	Dwels in the fickle grace of her a followes,
	Out varlet, from my sight.
Duke.	What meanes your Grace? *Enter Gon.*
Gon.	Who struck my seruant, *Regan* I haue good hope
	Thou didst not know ant.
Lear.	Who comes here? O heauens!

(Q, signature F1ᵛ)

Lear.	This is a Slaue, whose easie borrowed pride
	Dwels in the sickly grace of her he followes.
	Out Varlet, from my sight.
Corn.	What meanes your Grace?
	Enter Gonerill.
Lear.	Who stockt my Seruant? *Regan*, I haue good hope
	Thou did'st not know on't.
	Who comes here? O Heauens!

(F, signature rr1ᵛ)

Two small changes, '*Gon.*' to '*Lear.*' in a speech prefix, and 'struck' to 'stockt', alter the sense so that 'seruant', which in Q refers to Oswald, in F refers to Kent. In Q, Goneril enters bursting with anger, as she does in 1.3, but ready to blame Regan; in F a frustrated and angry Lear repeats the question he asked a few lines earlier, at 2.2.371 in Q and in F, and for which he awaits an answer: 'Who put my man i'th'Stockes?' Interpreters have seen here two differing but 'equally striking' dramatic effects; a 'mistaken attribution' in Q corrected to 'absolute rightness' in F; and two acting versions that have both worked well on stage, if in the Q version Lear strikes Oswald on his words, 'Out varlet, from my sight.'[1] However, none of them notes that Q might be seen as following up the rumour of civil discord between Albany and Cornwall at 2.1.7–12, whereas in F Goneril and Regan are united in their nagging opposition to putting up with Lear's rowdy knights. In fact it was Lear who struck Oswald at 1.4.82, and Regan, who has no reason to know about it, takes Goneril by the hand at 2.2.383, so it seems to me that F makes much better dramatic sense of this episode.

In such instances (see also Appendix 1) it is possible to find Q superior to F, F superior to Q, or both as offering equal but different versions; value judgements are always open to challenge. Modern theatrical practice shows that productions have almost always been based on a conflation of Q and F, and have omitted some scenes or passages from each text, so that it is possible to claim that conflation is necessary to preserve all that works best on stage (Richman, 374–82). F has generally been preferred for the opening and closing scenes; 4.3 (Q) has usually been cut or curtailed, but the mock-trial in 3.6 (Q) has invariably been kept (Clare, 46–7). So, for example, the 1990 production by Nicholas Hytner at the Royal Shakespeare Theatre was based on F, but still inserted Edgar's soliloquy and the mock-trial in 3.6.

The mock-trial may serve as a key example, since everyone agrees that it works well on stage, and can be seen as a 'nightmarish reworking of the opening', linking that with the placing of the three bodies of Lear's daughters on the stage in the final scene (Holland, 179–80). The retention of the mock-trial has been strongly defended on the grounds of dramatic coherence (Meyer, 140; Clare, 52–3) against the charge that its omission in F makes for a tauter structure of the play (R. Warren, 45–57).

---

1   Urkowitz, 36–7; Philip Edwards, reviewing Urkowitz's book in *MLR*, 77 (1982), 696; Richman, 380; Michael Warren, 'The theatricalization of text: Beckett, Jonson, Shakespeare', in Dave Oliphant and Robin Bradford (eds), *New Directions in Textual Studies* (Austin, Texas, 1990), 52–4.

Coherence is a difficult notion as applied to a scene in which Lear is mad, and there are plausible reasons why it might have been cut (see pp. 135–6). The debate will continue, and its immediate importance lies in offering a salutary reminder that revisions are not necessarily improvements. This needs to be borne in mind in relation to the major changes, which I assume to be deliberate reworkings in the Folio version, and which involve a series of additions and omissions. These changes affect characterization and the relations between characters in important ways, which can be summarized as follows:

The Fool

The changes in F affect the Fool more than any other character. His dramatic importance in the play seems much greater than his role, which is limited to about 225 lines in six scenes; 54, or almost a quarter, of his lines are changed in F. Critics agree on his importance, but vary enormously in their conception of the character, as do theatre directors (see pp. 52–5). He may be seen as half-witted, a natural whose wisdom is instinctive clairvoyance, or as a sage rationalist, shrewd and thoughtful; he can be thought of as a boy (Lear so addresses him, and he calls Lear 'nuncle'), as a mature, even elderly man (after all, he calls Lear 'boy' too in Q; see 1.4.105 and n.), or as an androgynous youth, perhaps a kind of *alter ego* of Cordelia, as in the productions in 1990 by the Royal Shakespeare Theatre and the English Renaissance Company, in which the Fool was played by an actress. He has also been portrayed as embodying the conscience of the King, as a voice of social protest, and as a court fool who 'shrivels into a wretched little human being on the soaking heath' (Bayley, 61). Two famous representations of the Fool could hardly be more different. In 1982 Antony Sher played him as 'a clown – a Charlie from the late Victorian circus with Dan Leno boots, a Grock violin, and a red button nose on a length of elastic' (Shrimpton, 152). He was a skilled entertainer, an artist enjoying cross-talk acts with Lear and a rapport with the audience (Fig. 14). In his notable film version

sion (1970), on the other hand, Grigori Kozintsev removed 'from the role of the Fool everything that is associated with clownery', and turned him into a youthful village idiot, costumed as a beggar with a shaved head (Kozintsev[2], 71–2).

One of the main reasons for these widely differing interpretations of the Fool is that critics and directors were using editions that conflate Q and F, which to some extent give conflicting signals about the role (see Foakes[2], 35–7). The Fool is established as mocking and needling Lear in long exchanges with him in 1.4, but F omits 1.4.137–48, a sequence in which the Fool answers the question he puts to the King, 'Dost know the difference, my boy, between a bitter fool and a sweet one?', by proving he is the sweet one, and Lear the bitter one. This omission from F not only makes the Fool there more consistently a bitter one (l33), a 'pestilent gall' (112) to Lear, but also removes the only reference in the play to the Fool as wearing motley, i.e. as a professional court fool.[1] Later in the scene F converts Lear's 'Who is it that can tell me who I am? Lear's shadow' (Q) into an exchange with a mocking retort by the Fool: 'Who is it that can tell me who I am? / FOOL Lear's shadow' (1.4.221–2); F also omits the next four lines, so that Lear ignores the Fool's response, and turns at once to address Goneril. Again the effect is to enhance the acerbic quality of the Fool's attack, not only on Lear, but also on Kent, since the line 'This is nothing, fool' (1.4.126) is given to Lear in Q, but to Kent in F, so that the Fool turns his wit against Kent too: 'Then 'tis like the breath of an unfee'd lawyer, you gave me nothing for't.'

The short scene that follows is virtually the same in Q and F, so that in Act 1 the Fool remains close to Lear; but in 2.2, the next scene in which he appears, Lear seems hardly to notice him or his sallies until his exit line, 'O fool, I shall go mad' (2.2.475),

---

1   The cut in F leaves a loose end, for no answer is given to the Fool's question, which should probably also have been omitted. Some think the cut can be explained by censorship, in order to remove an allusion to monopolies; see 1.4.145–6 and n. For a different explanation of the changes in the Fool's role, see Kerrigan, 195–239.

and this could be addressed to himself; any dialogue the Fool has is with Kent. In this scene the Fool in F is given a new rhyming jingle, 'Fathers that wear rags …' (see 2.2.238–43), which, like his other songs and jingles, gives a general satirical force to the particular situation. Towards the end of 3.2 Lear notices the Fool again, but, whereas in Q the Fool leads Lear off to the hovel, in F he remains on stage to deliver to the audience his rhyming 'prophecy', which foregrounds the Fool, and extends his commentary on selfishness and greed, which can be related to the topsy-turvy world Lear has brought about (see 3.2.79–96 and n.).[1] In these scenes the Fool begins to be distanced from Lear, whose incipient madness focuses his attention on his daughters and himself. In 3.4 in both Q and F, the Fool becomes a more marginal figure, for now Edgar appears as Poor Tom, and at once absorbs Lear's attention as a visible projection of his own sense of grievance and loss. In Q Lear seems to ignore the Fool throughout the scene, but two lines are added in F, when Lear notices the Fool before his great 'Poor naked wretches' speech, and urges him to enter the 'hovel':

> In boy, go first. You houseless poverty –
> Nay, get thee in. I'll pray, and then I'll sleep.
> (3.4.26–7)

This momentary display of concern for the Fool probably compensates in F for the omission of 39 lines, the mock-trial of Goneril, which is found only in Q (3.6.17–55). This episode has obvious links with other passages and scenes in a play much concerned with justice, but it arguably flattens out the distinction between the Fool and Poor Tom, who inevitably become much alike when both are equated as 'justicers', and Lear appeals to both of them equally. In Q Lear ignores the Fool in 3.4, and makes much of him in 3.6; in F the quoted addition to 3.4 provides

---

1 Kerrigan, 223, sees these lines as dramatizing 'the Fool's growing sense of his own irrelevance'.

Lear's last expression of affection for the Fool, who has only three short speeches in 3.6, two of them not in Q. The two speeches not in Q both extend the Fool's commentary on the confusion Lear has brought about, and culminate in his mocking exit line, 'And I'll go to bed at noon.'

Although the changes in F are in the main consistent in reinforcing the image of the Fool in his later scenes as something of a choric commentator, whose words and rhymes bring out the general significance of the particular events on stage, so that he provides a bridge between the unlocalized story of Lear and the world of the audience, it would seem that Shakespeare's conception of the character was a complex one in both Q and F. In his early scenes, 1.4 and 1.5, the Fool has a close relationship with Lear, and some would emphasize their mutual devotion as linked by a kind of childishness;[1] but, at the same time, from the beginning the Fool twists the knife in Lear's emotional wounds, and is a 'pestilent gall' and 'bitter fool' to him (1.4.112, 133). In these scenes Lear becomes a partner in a serio–comic duologue in which the Fool scores off him. In 2.2 Kent tends to replace Lear as the Fool's straight man, and in later scenes the Fool's role changes to that of a choric commentator, as Lear increasingly loses touch with him. Even so, two lines were added in 3.4 in F to renew Lear's sympathy with his 'boy'.

Both Q and F offer varying perspectives on the character. On the one hand he can be seen as a faithful attendant on Lear, possibly frail, easily cowed, sensitive, even somewhat feminine, perhaps like Cordelia, with whom the Fool is linked at 1.4.71–2,[2] and hence a reflection of Lear's conscience, a screen on which Shakespeare 'flashes, as it were, readings from the psychic life of

---

1 See, for example, Huntington Brown, 'Lear's Fool: a boy, not a man', *Essays in Criticism*, 13 (1963), 164–71, and Neil McEwan, 'The lost childhood of Lear's Fool', *Essays in Criticism*, 26 (1976), 209–17.

2 It is possible for the same actor to play both roles, and Booth, 32–3, 129 and 153–5, considering Lear's words, 'And my poor fool is hanged', revived the idea that the parts might have been doubled. I think it is far more likely that an adult actor, Robert Armin, played the Fool, and a boy-actor Cordelia. See 5.3.304 and n., Wiles, 144–55, and above p. 50.

the protagonist'.[1] On the other hand, the Fool may be seen as a sharp, mature professional, deliberately needling Lear, and as a voice of social protest in the play. The Fool's later scenes, in Acts 2 and 3, develop this second range of possibilities, but small additions in F still keep alive the King's feelings for his 'knave' even as the Fool is displaced by Edgar at the centre of Lear's attention.

The Folio makes more consistent the growing separation between them, but does not diminish the complexity of the character. He is not seen again after his exit in 3.6, perhaps because Lear himself in his madness takes on the role of Fool, at once mad and rational, riddlingly speaking 'matter and impertinency mixed', as Edgar puts it (4.6.170). As first Lear and then Kent act as 'feeds' to the Fool, so in Act 4 the blind Gloucester has that function in relation to Lear. So there is no need for the Fool in the last part of the play, and he disappears, unthought of until Lear's last speech; his first words there, 'And my poor fool is hanged', are usually taken as referring to Cordelia, but they also remind us of the Fool, and gather him into our, and Lear's, overwhelming sense of loss, 'No, no, no life!'

Lear and Cordelia

The most significant changes to the role of Lear are additions made at the beginning and the end of the play in F (see Clayton, 121–41). Although slight in quantity, their effect is great because of their placing, and because the later acts are substantially shorter in F, so that Lear's role becomes larger proportionally. In staging the Q text Lear's announcement of the division of the kingdom appears arbitrary and unexplained (Richman, 376–7); but in F seven lines are added, in which Lear explains his motives, and initiates what becomes a significant thread of imagery in the play.

---

1   Maynard Mack, 'The Jacobean Shakespeare: some observations on the construction of the tragedies', in John Russell Brown and Bernard Harris (eds), *Jacobean Theatre* (1960), 10–42, citing 24.

In F Lear announces that he will 'Unburdened crawl toward death'; he addresses Cornwall and Albany directly in expressing his wish to prevent 'future strife'; and he says that he will 'divest' himself of rule, lands and power. Each of these remarks is ironic in relation to his later inability to give up his authority, and they soften a little the impression of capricious absolutism suggested by Q. The first phrase announces the underlying potency of confrontation with death, which is what Lear and Gloucester have in mind and later actively desire. The second hints at the strife that will indeed erupt; and the third introduces the idea of disrobing, anticipating Lear tearing at his clothes later, 'Off, off, you lendings: come, unbutton here' (3.4.106–7; 'come on bee true' in Q, corrected to 'come on', may be an error, but if not, F has here another significant change from Q).

The sequence in Q at 3.6.17–55 where the mad Lear conducts a mock-trial of Goneril is not in F. The cut leaves an apparent loose end, when Lear cries, in lines retained in F, 'Then let them anatomize Regan …' (3.6.73), for this would naturally follow his 'arraignment' of Goneril in the omitted lines; but this passes unnoticed on stage, since Lear's mad dialogue is inconsequential anyway. The mock-trial has been criticized as too difficult to play well, and defended as stunningly effective (R. Warren, *Division*, 45–57; Richman, 382; Meyer, 136–40); it is rarely left out of productions of the play, yet the five powerful lines about justice added to Lear's part at 4.6.161–6, beginning, 'Plate sins with gold, / And the strong lance of justice hurtless breaks', suggest an explanation. For 4.6 contains another pseudo-trial ('I pardon that man's life. What was thy cause?'), and F avoids duplication by removing the external play-acting of the mock-trial, and concentrating the issue of justice in the poignant encounter between Lear and Gloucester.

At the end of the play in Q Lear thanks whoever undoes a button for him, groans ('O, o, o, o.'), and faints, recovering only to wish for death, 'Break, heart, I prithee break.' The page is crowded, and there are no stage directions. F is significantly different:

> Do you see this? Looke on her? Looke her lips,
> Look there, look there.   *He dies.*
> *Edg.* He faints, my Lord, my Lord.
> *Kent.* Breake heart, I prythee breake.

> (5.3.309–11)

The addition in F allows us to suppose Lear may die in the joyful delusion of thinking Cordelia is still alive, and it is Kent who wishes either for his own or for Lear's death, or perhaps both. Lear's death in F is more richly nuanced, though in both Q and F death comes to him as a release from suffering, a kind of bitter benefit.

There are other small expansions in the part of Lear in the opening scene, most notably in his confrontation with Cordelia: Q's '*Cord.* Nothing my Lord. / *Lear.* How, nothing can come of nothing, speake againe.' becomes in F:

> *Lear.* ... speake.
> *Cor.* Nothing.
> *Lear.* Nothing?
> *Cor.* Nothing.
> *Lear.* Nothing will come of nothing, speake againe.

> (1.1.86–90)

The effect is to intensify the clash between King and subject, father and daughter, and the change here bears on Cordelia as much as Lear, for it makes her appear more inflexible, and this seems to me consistent with other alterations in F that affect her. These alterations, which include the omission of 4.3, a scene in which a Gentleman describes her at some length as weeping tears of pity for her father, diminish her presence, it is true,[1] but also change her from a saintly figure, emblematic of pity, to a warrior

---

1   Grace Ioppolo, 167–83, argues that a 'powerful and active' Cordelia in Q is revised to become 'incidental and subordinate' in F (citing 173). Cordelia's impact in Q is certainly more extended, but I think she is altogether softer and less powerful there (see Foakes, 109–10).

determined to put her father back on the throne. So the entry in
4.4 in Q, her first appearance since 1.1, calls for her to come on
simply with '*Doctor and others*', whereas in F she enters '*with
Drum and Colours*', and accompanied by '*Souldiours*'. Her warlike
presence as a general leading invading troops is reinforced in F in
5.2, where again in F the entry specifies '*Drumme and Colours*' (see
5.2.0.1 and n.). The Cordelia of the Folio is a less prominent
figure than in the Quarto, where the emphasis is on her 'heavenly'
quality (4.3.31), but more active and warlike.

The war with France

In an attempt to explain why some references in Q to an invasion
of Britain by French forces were omitted or changed in F, Gary
Taylor ('War', 27–34) argues that the two texts provide different
versions of what he called the war in *King Lear*. In F, he claimed,
the action presents 'not an invasion, but a rebellion', a civil war.[1]
He draws attention to a very significant group of differences
between the texts, though his explanation does not survive close
scrutiny. It is true that some references to a French invasion were
omitted from F, as follows: in 3.1 in Q Kent reports that the French
have secretly sent 'a power / Into this scattered kingdom';
Gloucester refers to an invading force as having 'landed' at 3.3.13;
at 4.2.57 Goneril calls Albany to arms because 'France spreads his
banners in our noiseless land'; in 4.3 Kent reports that the King of
France has returned home leaving 'the Marshal of France' in command of his forces; and at 5.1.25 Albany protests that he fights not
against Lear, but only because 'France invades our land'.

Although F leaves these references out, enough remain to
make it clear in F as well as in Q that Cordelia arrives in or near

1 Taylor says, in 'War', 31, that Q and F 'treat the nationality of Cordelia's army in
   consistently different ways', and in 'Monopolies', 80, that F 'consistently eliminates
   references to France in Acts Four and Five'. Neither of these statements is true, and
   he does not consider what the display of 'colours' required in 4.4 and 5.2 might signify. See E. A. J. Honigmann's review of Michael Warren's *The Complete King Lear,
   1608–23* in *The New York Review of Books*, 25 October 1990, 58–60; also Foakes,
   106–7, and Knowles[2], 42–3.

Dover at the head of a French army. In both Q and F Cornwall tells us at 3.7.2 that 'the army of France is landed'; the news that British powers are on the march makes Cordelia grateful at 4.4.25 for the army 'great France' has provided; Edmund is with the 'British party' (Q) or 'English party' (F) according to Oswald at 4.6.246; and Lear wakes from sleep at 4.7.76 to imagine he is in France, suggesting that there may have been French insignia on stage. In F, but not in Q, stage directions call for the British and French forces to display their 'colours' in 4.4, 5.1 and 5.2, the French display perhaps echoing banners or coats of arms shown when the King of France appeared in the opening scene.

The introduction of the King of France here may be a clue to the reason for the differences between Q and F as far as war with France is concerned. France is an ambiguous term that could mean the King, as at 1.1.127, or the country. The changes in F seem designed to remove any possible allusions to the possible presence of the King of France, as in the specific references to him in Q at 4.2.57, 4.3.1–8 and 5.1.25. It seems to me that Q retains traces of a version of *King Lear* in which the King of France played an active role, as he does in other versions of the story known to Shakespeare, such as those in Holinshed and the old play of *Leir*. In these and other retellings the King of France returns to England at the head of an army intending to place Lear back on the English throne. This whole matter is connected with the conflicting passages in Q and F 3.1, and is considered further in relation to this scene in Appendix 1, p. 393. The omission of passages referring to France has also been seen as linked with other larger omissions in F between 3.6 and the end of Act 4 that together, it has been argued, increase the 'narrative momentum' (Taylor, 'War', 29), and clarify the course of the action; but the presence of Cordelia at the head of a French invading army in both Q and F marks the final horrific stage in the process by which Lear's division of the kingdom goes on turning the world upside-down.

Edgar, Albany, Kent and pathos

In Q Edgar, Kent and Albany all have substantially larger parts in the later acts of the play. Edgar and Kent are both present in the mock-trial in 3.6, which is omitted from F. The rhyming moralizing speech Edgar has in Q at 3.6.99–112 is not in F, and his report of meeting Kent, and of Kent's 'piteous tale' of Lear, at 5.3.203–20 (Q) is also omitted. In F Albany has two half-line speeches at 1.4.254 and 266 that are not in Q, and it is he who introduces the idea of patience here. But the main changes in Albany's role occur in 4.2, where his denunciation of Goneril is curtailed in F, and his vision of potential anarchy ('Humanity must perforce prey on itself, / Like monsters of the deep') unless the heavens intervene (4.2.32–51) is left out. Albany's role is also enhanced in 5.1 in Q, where he defines his moral position as fighting against the French invaders, not against Lear (5.1.23–8), and where Edmund appears to defer to him, though he might speak sarcastically, with the phrase 'Sir, you speak nobly', and adds, 'I shall attend you presently at your tent' (5.1.28, 34), in lines found only in Q. If Albany has a stronger moral presence in the later acts in Q, he is given a different kind of authority in F in controlling the duel between Edgar and Edmund at 5.3.102–15, which is dominated by Edmund in Q (see Appendix 1). Edgar nevertheless has more weight in F, where he sheds two long speeches that have no more than a choric function, but gains by the diminution of Albany, two of whose speeches he takes over. In F it is Edgar, not Albany, who gives the order, 'Haste thee for thy life' (5.3.249), as someone is sent to try to save the lives of Lear and Cordelia, and it is Edgar, not Albany, who has the final lines of the play. In Q Albany offers to withdraw, or perhaps share the rule ('Friends of my soul, you twain, / Rule in this realm'), but ends in authority with Edgar silent and Kent declining; in F, on the other hand, Edgar may be seen as taking over, and accepting Albany's retirement.[1]

---

1 See Warren, 'Albany', 95–105. I think he goes too far in claiming that Edgar and Albany are radically reconstructed, and that 'Q and F embody two different artistic visions' (105).

Kent's part likewise is diminished in F, notably by the omission of 4.3, a 56-line scene commenting on Cordelia and Lear, presenting her as 'a paragon of sensitivity', and Lear as overcome with shame (Warren, 'Kent', 66). Another dialogue in Q between Kent and the Gentleman at the end of 4.7 is not in F (see 4.7.85–97 and n.), and the omission of Edgar's tale of Kent's service to Lear at 5.3.203–20 also reduces Kent's presence. In Q Edgar, Albany and Kent all have speeches in the later acts that moralize or exert emotional pressure on the audience, like Kent's comments on 'the poor distressed Lear':

> A sovereign shame so elbows him. His own unkindness
> That stripped her from his benediction, turned her
> To foreign casualties, gave her dear rights
> To his dog-hearted daughters, these things sting
> His mind so venomously that burning shame
> Detains him from Cordelia.
>
> (4.3.43–8)

In such passages we are invited to have compassion for the suffering Lear or Cordelia or Gloucester, and they may have been cut in revision in order to remove lines that are emotionally coercive in a way the play generally is not; the exchange in Q between the servants who plan to relieve the bleeding Gloucester at the end of 3.7 may have been omitted for the same reason. More prominence is given in F to what Edgar, Albany and Kent do, and less to what they say. In the case of Kent, he has little left to say in F between 3.6, where he has a few lines not in Q as he bears Lear off to Dover with the aid of the Fool, and the end of 5.3, where he is given the line 'Break, heart, I prithee break' (Lear's in Q), which could be addressed to himself, or to Lear, or to both of them, and links him in death with the master he has served devotedly.

Goneril, Regan and Edmund

The reduction in the parts of Edgar, Albany and Kent in the later acts in F makes them more ambiguous, and less simply the spokesmen for a moral judgement. The modification in the roles of Goneril and Regan in Acts 1 and 2 has a parallel effect. Goneril's intransigent stance towards her father in 1.3 (Q) is qualified in F by the omission of six lines in which she shows immediate contempt for her father as an 'Idle old man', implies that he is in his second childhood, 'Old fools are babes again', and announces her intention to stir up discord, 'I would breed from hence occasions' (1.3.17–21 and 25). The removal of these lines softens her hostility, and puts the weight of emphasis here on the violence of Lear ('Did my father strike my gentleman ... ?'), and on the riotous behaviour of his retinue. When she returns at 1.4.179, her anger in Q and F is directed against Lear's quarrelsome knights, his disordered and debauched train (233), but F adds two more speeches at 1.4.315–27 in which she extends her complaint by suggesting that the safety of her house is at risk from his hundred knights. A further speech on the same theme is added for Regan at 2.2.330–4, again alluding to the 'riots' of Lear's followers. The effect is thus, on the one hand, to provide Goneril and Regan with a more reasonable basis for their attitude towards their father in these scenes, since they perceive his retinue as a threat to their power, and to peace and order; and, on the other, to point up the unruly actions of Lear and Kent in striking Oswald and tripping him up in 1.4. The alteration at 2.2.376 discussed above, p. 131, is also relevant here in relation to the obsession of Goneril and Regan in F with the riotousness of the knights.

The main changes in Edmund's part in 1.2 may have been made for practical reasons. In Q Edmund spells out the prediction he has been reading at 1.2.144–9 in lines not in F, where a parallel prediction is added to a speech of Gloucester earlier in the scene at 109–14.[1] F focuses more directly on the way Edmund makes Edgar afraid of his father's anger, and adds lines

---

1   The changes here have been related to possible censorship by Patterson[2] and Clare[2]; Taylor, 'Monopolies', 81–8, makes a reasoned case for rejecting censorship as responsible for the alterations in 1.2.

at 164–9 in which he offers Edgar the key of his lodging, and twice advises him to 'go armed', as against once in Q. The most notable difference in the treatment of Edmund occurs in relation to his fight with Edgar in 5.3 (see Appendix 1, p. 402): Edmund's role is bolder in Q, where he takes more initiative, first in telling Albany that 'The question of Cordelia and her father / Requires a fitter place' (5.3.55–60, not in F), and then in the matter of the challenge. In Q Edmund defiantly calls for Albany to sound his trumpet, shouts for a herald and then again cries 'Sound'; in F it is Albany who cries 'Let the trumpet sound' (5.3.91), and a herald then takes over and orders the trumpet to sound three times. In Q Edmund behaves with confidence as though he expects to win, whereas in F Albany is in control, and Edmund seems trapped and at bay.[1]

There are other interesting differences between Q and F, for instance, in some of the bit parts discussed in Mahood, 163–76, like the Gentleman of 3.1 and 4.3, whose role is diminished in F in parallel with that of his chief companion, Kent; or the Captain who in Q vividly illustrates man's potential inhumanity to man with his willingness to kill Cordelia and Lear:

> I cannot draw a cart, nor eat dried oats.
> If it be man's work, I'll do't.
>
> (5.3.39–40)

These lines may have been dropped from F to avoid distracting attention from the immediate entry of Albany to demand Edmund's prisoners. Some tiny changes can carry considerable weight, like the addition in F of Goneril's words 'An interlude!' at 5.3.90, an interjection that points up for actors and audience the grotesque and comic aspects of the competition between Goneril,

---

1 I take issue here with Gary Taylor, who, in 'War', 32–4, argues that Edmund 'becomes more dangerous, and the outcome less predictable' in F; his claim is based partly on the incorrect statement that Edmund in F dismisses his army so that he can plot the murder of Lear and Cordelia; in fact, both in Q and in F it is Albany who discharges Edmund's soldiers.

married to Albany, and Regan, already poisoned by her sister, for the love of Edmund. The differences in the parts of the principal characters, however, generally enhance in F the social commentary in the play, as in the part of the Fool, diminish the moral commentary in the roles of Edgar, Albany and Kent, and make it less clear who is right and who wrong in the relations between Lear and his daughters.

CASTING *KING LEAR*

The play has ten major roles, seven men and three women. Shakespeare's company had ten sharers who were the principal actors, and an unknown number of apprentices, boys to play women's parts, and hired men. There has been much speculation about the casting of the play, most of it based on the assumption that the King's Men worked with the smallest number of players needed to stage it, that is to say twelve men and four boys (Ringler), or fourteen or fifteen actors (Howard). It would be possible to double various roles; Howard, for instance, proposed doubling Cordelia and the Fool, France and Edgar, Burgundy and Oswald, Kent and the Old Man, Gloucester and the Herald. The argument for 'conceptual doubling', matching roles for an actor so that the parts relate to one another,[1] would lend support to the most obvious possibility for doubling, that of Cordelia and the Fool, who are linked in the text emotionally not only as the Fool pines away (1.4.71–2) when Cordelia is banished, but because they are closest to Lear. As Shakespeare conceived it the part of the Fool was probably written for an actor who specialized in such roles, Robert Armin (see above, p. 50), so it is unlikely that doubling the part with that of Cordelia

---

1 The phrase is derived from Ralph Berry's article, 'Hamlet's doubles', *SQ*, 37 (1986), 204–12, where he described it as a 'modern phenomenon', but Giorgio Melchiori argues, *MLR*, 78 (1983), 777–92, in relation to *Romeo and Juliet*, that Shakespeare built in an 'art of doubling' as part of his dramaturgy; see also 'Speculations on doubling' in Booth, 129–55.

was in his mind. No entries are marked for the Fool in Q or F in scenes when Cordelia is on stage, but I know of few modern productions in which these parts are doubled, the most notable being those by Giorgio Strehler in Milan, 1972, and by Deborah Warner in her Kick Theatre production, in London and Edinburgh, 1985.

Some directors have pointedly introduced the Fool as an observer in the opening scene (as in Jonathan Miller's television production for the BBC in 1982). The wise Fool seems, indeed, to me a part tailor-made for the great comic actor Robert Armin, as argued by Wiles. Ringler, however (192–3), claimed that Armin might have played Edgar, and assumed the Fool was staged as a young and childish boy; but the Fool's dialogue belongs to the world of experience, not innocence, and he has been played with success as a kind of counterpart to Lear in age, for example by Frank Middlemass in Jonathan Miller's Nottingham Playhouse production in 1969–70, and again in Miller's BBC film for television; one reviewer described the Fool in this production as a 'broken down Cockney music hall Napoleon, very much Lear's alter ego'.[1]

Minor roles such as Burgundy and the King of France, who only appear in the opening scene, Curan, who is seen only in 2.1, and the Old Man in 4.1 could readily have been doubled with other parts. In his speculative casting of the play as performed by the King's Men, T. J. King (91 and tables 69–70) identified ten principal roles, which he thought were not doubled: Lear, whose part is twice as long as any other, Kent, Gloucester, Edgar and Edmund, whose parts are next in length, followed by the Fool, Regan, Goneril and last, with about a hundred lines, Cordelia. He assumed that the part of Cordelia was not doubled. These main roles, together with France, possibly doubling with

---

1 Anthony Curtis, *Financial Times*, 11 February 1970. Irving Wardle, writing in *The Times*, 11 February 1970, found this 'superannuated' Fool very funny. In the BBC film, by contrast, he is savage, a 'pestilent gall' to Lear, bitterly upset by what Lear has done.

Oswald, and Cornwall, possibly doubling with the Gentleman, he noted constitute 96 per cent of the dialogue. Skiles Howard proposes a different pattern of doubling, pairing Cordelia with the Fool, France with Edgar, Burgundy with Oswald, and Kent with the Old Man; she notes that, though Q has more speaking parts, F has more mutes.

Like most of those who speculate about doubling, Howard (187) starts by assessing the smallest number of players needed to stage the play; however, it is possible that the King's Men staged their plays as lavishly as their resources allowed, and if they had a hectic daily repertory like that at the Rose and Fortune (as listed in Henslowe) actors may have welcomed an alternation between large and small roles, and there may have been less doubling than is often suggested. Q has speaking parts not in F, such as the two servants who seek to help the blind Gloucester at the end of 3.7, the Doctor in 4.7 and the Captain who is ordered by Edmund to execute Lear and Cordelia in 5.3. The cutting of these parts in F seems more related to the general economy of a revision that refurbished the play than to a specific need to lessen the number of roles. If Richard Burbage, the leading actor in the King's Men, played Lear, he would have been about forty-two years old when *King Lear* was staged before James I in 1606, and, in the context of Othello and Macbeth, is likely to have presented a powerful figure. In major productions in modern times, Paul Scofield, who was forty when he acted the part of Lear in 1962 with an enormous if somewhat austere sense of arrogance and innate power, and Donald Sinden, who was forty-three when he played Lear in 1976 as a wilful, obstinate and self-destructive character, perhaps offer the closest comparison.

USAGES IN THIS EDITION

The main conventions used in the series are described in the General editors' preface, p. xii. The present edition seeks to offer the reader such guidance towards following both Quarto and Folio texts as can be presented in printing the play as a single work.

I have used the title *King Lear* rather than '*The Historie of King Lear*', the running title in the Quarto, or '*The Tragedie of King Lear*', the running title in the Folio. Categories were used loosely in Shakespeare's time, the play in both versions has the same basic pattern, and it is generally known now as one of his major tragedies. The title I have preferred is what the play is now commonly called, and puts an emphasis on the word 'King', which is significant, since Lear's behaviour as a monarch is so important in the play (see p. 13).

As I noted earlier, words and passages found only in the Quarto are framed in this edition by superscript ^{Q}, and words and passages found only in the Folio by superscript^F; no reference is made to these in the textual notes. Where the texts differ, I have generally preferred Folio readings; variants in the texts and substitutions in the Folio for words or passages in the Quarto are recorded in the textual notes at the foot of the page. In the Quarto of 1608 eight formes (sets of four pages printed on one side of a sheet of paper) out of twenty-one exist in corrected and uncorrected states, as proof correction took place while the book was being printed. In the Folio twelve formes exist in corrected and uncorrected states.[1] Variants are recorded in the textual notes as observed in Qu (uncorrected Quarto), Qc (corrected Quarto), Fu (uncorrected Folio) and Fc (corrected Folio). The relation between the Folio and the Second Quarto (Q2), issued in 1619, remains something of a puzzle, but it appears that the Folio shows evidence of some dependence on Q2 (see p. 123). Q2 was printed from a copy of Q1 that had a mixture of corrected and uncorrected pages, and the textual notes show whether Q2 agrees with corrected or uncorrected

---

1   The Quarto was analysed by Greg, *Variants*, and, more fully in the context of the printing house of Nicholas Okes, by Blayney. The variants in the Folio text were analysed by Hinman. The issues are summarized in *The Parallel King Lear 1608–1623*, prepared by Michael Warren (Berkeley and Los Angeles, 1989).

states in Q and F, in addition to listing variants and corrections in Q2. In two places, 3.1.17–39 and 5.3.102–15, the radical differences between Q and F warrant more explanation than is practicable on a page of text, and these passages are separately analysed in Appendix 1.

The text is modernized, and variants of spelling or punctuation are recorded in the textual notes or commentary only where they make a substantive difference. Some unusual spellings are noted, especially where they may suggest the way a word was pronounced, but common variants such as 'I' for 'Ay' (as at 1.2.154), 'vild' for 'vile' (as at 3.2.71), 'least' for 'lest' (as at 4.6.229), 'loose' for 'lose' (as at 5.1.18), 'travail' for 'travel' (as at 2.2.153), or 'then' for 'than' (as at 3.2.60 in F) are not recorded unless some ambiguity seems to be involved. The common form 'and', meaning 'if', is silently changed to 'an'. In the early texts 'of the', 'in the' and other such prepositional forms are often abbreviated to 'o'th', 'i'th' before consonants as well as vowels; the printers casually used these abbreviations not only in verse, where they might possibly indicate the metrical pattern, but also in prose, as for example, in 'i'th'middle', twice in the Fool's prose speech at 1.4.151–3. Since usage in the early texts is inconsistent, in the present edition all such abbreviations are silently expanded to 'i'the middle', etc., in accordance with the way they are now generally spoken. Simple misprints in Q or F, such as 'ahy' (F) for 'thy' (Q), 2.2.197, are not collated.

The names of characters in stage directions and speech prefixes vary in spelling and style in Q and F, and are made consistent in the present edition. Edmund is generally listed as '*Bastard*' in entries and '*Bast.*' in speech prefixes in Q, but appears more often as '*Edmund*' ('*Edm.*') in F, while Oswald is usually '*Steward*' ('*Stew.*') in Q and F. Both Albany, in scenes where no confusion is likely, 1.4 and 5.3 for instance, and Cornwall, in 2.2, appear as '*Duke*' in entries and speech prefixes in Q. In 2.2 (F) Cornwall's name is abbreviated in speech prefixes sometimes to '*Cor.*' and sometimes to '*Corn.*', while in 1.1 (F) Cordelia appears as '*Cor.*', so that it is not clear which of them '*Cor.*' signifies at 1.1.163 and 189 (see commentary notes). Q also has '*Dutchesse*' for Regan in 2.2, and '*the two Ladies*' in an entry for Goneril and Regan in 5.3. Unnamed characters are variously referred to in 1.5 as '*Seruant*' (Q), '*Gentleman*' (F); in 2.4 as '*Knight*' (Q), '*Gentleman*' (F); in 4.2 '*Gentleman*' (Q), '*Messenger*' (F); in 4.7 '*Doctor*' (Q), '*Gentleman*' (F); and in 5.3 '*Captain*' (Q), '*Messenger*' (F). Where these variants have some possible susbstantive importance, they are discussed in the commentary.

In this edition 2.2 is treated as a single scene, which is how it must have been staged, as explained in the commentary. Since the eighteenth century it has conventionally been divided into three scenes, and for ease of reference the conventional scene and line numbers are added in square brackets in the right margin. 4.3 is found only in the Quarto, so that scene numbers from 4.3 to 4.6 do not correspond to those in F, which are noted in italic brackets. The Folio jumps from scene 5 to scene 7 and has no scene 6 in this act, so 4.7 returns to the standard scene division.

Editorial additions in stage directions within the text are enclosed in square brackets. The commentary draws attention to points of difficulty and problems of interpretation; commentary notes that include consideration of textual issues are marked with an asterisk. It is often difficult to decide what is verse and what prose in the play, and there are numerous differences in lineation between Q and F, which are listed separately in Appendix 2. For further details concerning the presentation of textual notes, see the section 'Abbreviations and references', pp. 416–29.

KING LEAR

LIST OF ROLES

LEAR	King of Britain
GONERIL	*his eldest daughter*
REGAN	*his second daughter*
CORDELIA	*his youngest daughter*
DUKE of ALBANY	*married to Goneril*
DUKE of CORNWALL	*married to Regan*
KING of FRANCE	
DUKE of BURGUNDY	
EARL of GLOUCESTER	
EDGAR	*his elder son*
EDMUND	*his younger bastard son*
EARL of KENT	
FOOL	*attendant on Lear*
OSWALD	*Goneril's steward*
CURAN	*a follower of Gloucester*
OLD MAN	*Gloucester's tenant*

[A Herald, a Captain, an Officer,
a Doctor (Q only), Knights, Gentlemen,
Attendants, Servants and Messengers]

LIST OF ROLES Rowe first included a list, expanded by later editors, in his edition of 1709.

1 LEAR A spelling perhaps chosen to distinguish Shakespeare's play from the old play of *King Leir*. 'Leir' is the commonest spelling in other versions of the Lear story.

2 GONERIL 'Gonorilla' in Holinshed; 'Gonorill' in Q and *King Leir*; 'Gonerill' in F

3 REGAN Holinshed's spelling; 'Ragan' in *King Leir*

4 CORDELIA 'Cordeilla' in Holinshed, 'Cordella' in *King Leir*; Shakespeare adopted the spelling he found in Spenser's *Faerie Queene*, possibly having in mind an association with the heart ('cor' from the Greek; compare *coeur* in French) and the anagram of 'ideal' in 'delia'; see Introduction, pp. 31 and 34

5 ALBANY According to Holinshed, 1.443–4, Brutus, first King of Britain, divided the kingdom among his sons, giving his third son, Albanact, 'all the north part of the Ile, afterward called Albania, after the name of the said Albanact: which portion of the said Ile lieth beyond the Humber northward'. Harrison identifies Albania as Scotland, or the country north of the Solway, in Holinshed, 1.195, 197. Prince Charles, second son of James I, had the title Duke of Albany; see 1.1.2 and n.

6 CORNWALL Brutus gave his second son Wales or Camber, according to Harrison, and the King of Cambria is Ragan's husband in *King Leir*; but Holinshed says Lear married one of his daughters to Henuinus, Duke of Cornwall. The third of his kingdom Lear gives to Cornwall and Regan may be thought of as the West Country and Wales. Prince Henry, James I's elder son, included among his titles Duke of Cornwall; see 1.1.2 and n.

7 **King of** FRANCE usually called 'France' in the play. Shakespeare modernized the Roman name 'Gallia' used by Holinshed and in *King Leir*. He appears only in the opening scene, but remains a shadowy presence in Q; see Appendix 1.

8 BURGUNDY Shakespeare's invention as a suitor for Cordelia, and present only in the opening scene. Like 'France', the name is anachronistic in relation to the date of Lear's reign according to the chronicles, about 800 BC.

9 GLOUCESTER often spelled 'Gloster' in F, and always in Q, indicating the pronunciation of the name. The names in the subplot were invented by Shakespeare, and are again anachronistic in relation to the chronicled date of Lear's reign.

10 EDGAR a Saxon name, recalling both the historical Edgar, King of England 959–75, a famous hero but also noted for cruelty (Holinshed, 1.694–6), and after his death made a saint, and Edgar Etheling, heroic leader of the Saxons in the reign of William the Conqueror (Holinshed, 2.15). See Introduction, p. 46. He is named as Lear's godson at 2.1.91.

11 EDMUND like Edgar, the name of several Saxon kings (Holinshed, 1.689, 721), and especially Edmund, King of East Anglia from AD 841, who was reputed as a hero and as a saint, and after whom Bury St Edmunds is named. Edmund is occasionally so named in stage directions in Q and F, but is also called simply 'Bastard', and generally 'Bast.' in speech prefixes.

12 KENT Shakespeare's invention, though partly modelled on the good counsellor Perillus in *Leir*. Once, in the final scene, Kent identifies the name he used when in disguise as Caius; see 5.3.281 and n.

13 FOOL Shakespeare's most original addition to the story, and a role probably designed for Robert Armin, though it could have been doubled by the boy-actor playing Cordelia. See Introduction, p. 50.

14 OSWALD another Saxon name, recalling two British saints, the better known being the tenth-century St Oswald of Worcester, Archbishop of York.

15 CURAN A member of Gloucester's household, he appears only briefly in 2.1. It is unusual for a character with so small a role to be named by Shakespeare, who may have initially envisaged a larger part for him. The name could be a version of Ciaran; a noted sixth-century Irish abbot of this name was made a saint.

16 OLD MAN He leads the blind Gloucester on stage in 4.1, and, like Adam in *As You Like It*, embodies values of loyalty and kindness.

17 **Knights** In 1.4 Lear is attended by at least four knights, and stage directors have often crowded the stage with as many as could be managed, in order to give some sense of his train of 100 knights. In 2.2 the entry in F calls for a Gentleman (Knight in Q speech headings) to accompany Lear, and there are no more entries for knights after this point. Q confuses them with servants in 1.4, while F generally calls an attendant who speaks 'Gentleman', several being required in the course of the action. It is thus not certain how many of Lear's knights were represented on stage at the Globe, but the directions require no more than four.

KING LEAR

1.1   *Enter* KENT, GLOUCESTER *and* EDMUND.

KENT   I thought the King had more affected the Duke of
Albany than Cornwall.

GLOUCESTER   It did always seem so to us: but now, in the
division of the kingdom, it appears not which of the
dukes he values most, for qualities are so weighed that   5

1.1 Here, as throughout, words, phrases, or longer passages found only in the Quarto are marked by a raised ^Q at the beginning and end, and those found only in the Folio are marked by a raised ^F. In the opening scene the lineation of blank verse in Q is erratic, and verse is sometimes printed as prose. In this scene especially, but also in later scenes to a lesser extent, Q has many short words or phrases not in F that are extra-metrical, e.g. *do*, 55; *Sir*, 69; *But*, 82; *How*, 90; and *Well*, 109. These are puzzling in relation to the commonly accepted theory that Q was derived from Shakespeare's 'foul papers'. For further comment, see Introduction, p. 121.

0.1 Presumably a throne or chair of state was placed on stage to signal a ceremonial scene, and prepare for the entry of the King; there may have been banners also, with badges or emblems to mark the court as English; see 4.4.0.1 and n. Although the play takes place nominally in the mythical reign of a king who ruled in antiquity, the characters may well have worn contemporary cos-

tume; see 2 and n. Probably Kent carried a rolled-up map; see 36 and n.

1–32 The scene begins and ends with informal prose dialogue between people speaking familiarly with one another, so framing the formal state ceremony in which Lear aims to announce his retirement and arrange Cordelia's betrothal.

1   **affected** favoured

2   **Albany . . . Cornwall** The names are appropriate both to ancient times, and to Shakespeare's own age, since Prince Henry became Duke of Cornwall on the accession of James I to the English throne in 1603, and Prince Charles was created Duke of Albany (the territory north of the Humber, named after Albanact, son of the legendary Brute, first King of Britain) at his baptism in 1603; after the death of Prince Henry (in November 1612) Charles assumed both titles. See Introduction, p. 13.

4   **division** Kent and Gloucester know of Lear's intention to divide the kingdom, and here raise no objection.

5   ***qualities** their qualities. This makes better sense than 'equalities' (Q).

TITLE] Q1 title: M. William Shak-speare: / *HIS* / True Chronicle Historie of the life and / death of King LEAR and his three / Daughters. / *With the vnfortunate life of* Edgar, *sonne* / and heire to the Earle of Gloster, and his / sullen and assumed humor of / TOM of Bedlam. Q1 head title: M. William Shak-speare / *HIS* / Historie, of King Lear. Q1 running title: *The Historie of King Lear*. F catalogue: *King Lear*. F head title: THE TRAGEDIE OF KING LEAR. F running title: *The Tragedie of King Lear*.

1.1] *F (Actus Primus, Scœna Prima)*   0.1 EDMUND] *F (Edmond); Bastard Q*   4 kingdom] *F; kingdomes Q*   5 qualities] *F; equalities Q*

157

curiosity in neither can make choice of either's moiety.

KENT   Is not this your son, my lord?

GLOUCESTER   His breeding, sir, hath been at my charge.
I have so often blushed to acknowledge him that now I
am brazed to't.   10

KENT   I cannot conceive you.

GLOUCESTER   Sir, this young fellow's mother could;
whereupon she grew round-wombed, and had, indeed,
sir, a son for her cradle ere she had a husband for her
bed. Do you smell a fault?   15

KENT   I cannot wish the fault undone, the issue of it being
so proper.

GLOUCESTER   But I have a son, sir, by order of law, some
year elder than this, who yet is no dearer in my account.
Though this knave came something saucily to the world   20
before he was sent for, yet was his mother fair, there was
good sport at his making, and the whoreson must be

6   **curiosity** scrupulousness; but also
both the curiosity of Albany and
Cornwall about their shares, and
inquisitiveness on the part of others
moiety usually a half, which could
explain Lear's 'darker' purpose, 35 and
n., to divide his kingdom into three
parts; but sometimes 'moiety' was used
simply to mean 'share', as by Hotspur
at *1H4* 3.1.95
8   **breeding . . . charge** birth and up-
bringing have been at my expense
(*OED* charge *sb.* 10e)
10   **brazed** brazened or unashamed
11   **conceive** understand. Gloucester
picks up the quibble on 'become pregnant'.
12–24 If Edmund hears his father's
coarse joking and boasting, it could
help to account for his later behaviour.
Adelman, 105, notes that Gloucester
speaks of Edmund as his mother's son

(14), while he claims Edgar as his own
son (18).
15   **smell a fault** smell a sin or wrongdo-
ing, with a punning allusion to the
female genitals (Rubinstein, 98; and
see John H. Astington, ' "Fault" in
Shakespeare', *SQ*, 36 (1985), 330–4).
This line initiates a strain of imagery
(see, for example, 1.4.110–11 and
1.5.22–3) that culminates in Lear's
denunciation of women at 4.6.120–7.
16   **issue** quibbling on two meanings,
'outcome' and 'offspring'
17   **proper** handsome
18   **by . . . law** i.e. legitimate
18–19 **some year** about a year; see
1.2.5–6
20–2 **knave . . . whoreson** playfully
= boy . . . fellow; but both terms
contemptuously evoke Edmund's
condition as inferior and a bastard
20   **something** somewhat

18 a son, sir] *F;* sir a sonne *Q*   19 account.] *Theobald;* account, *Q, F*   20 to] *F;* into *Q*

acknowledged. Do you know this noble gentleman,
Edmund?

EDMUND   No, my lord.   25

GLOUCESTER *[to Edmund]*   My lord of Kent: remember
him hereafter, as my honourable friend.

EDMUND   My services to your lordship.

KENT   I must love you, and sue to know you better.

EDMUND *[to Kent]*   Sir, I shall study deserving.   30

GLOUCESTER   He hath been out nine years, and away he
shall again. The King is coming.

Sennet. Enter ᵠ*one bearing a coronet, then*ᵠ LEAR,
CORNWALL, ALBANY, GONERIL, REGAN, CORDELIA
and attendants.

LEAR

Attend the lords of France and Burgundy, Gloucester.

---

28 **services** respects

30 **study deserving** i.e. make it my aim
to earn your favour. (Is Edmund
consciously obsequious here?)

31 **out** away from home. Sons of
noblemen often gained their training
in the houses of other aristocrats in
Britain or abroad, as Prince Henry,
elder son of James I, was placed in the
household of the Earl of Mar; but
Gloucester may also have sought to
distance himself from Edmund.

32.1–3 The first entry for the Fool in Q
and F is in 1.4, and it is possible that
Shakespeare kept him out of the opening scene so that the part could be
doubled with that of Cordelia.
However, the Fool has been brought
on stage at this point, as by Jonathan
Miller in the BBC television version
(see Introduction, p. 50), making a

splash of colour in the otherwise
black-costumed court. In 1.4 the Fool
seems to know exactly what takes place
in 1.1.

32.1 *Sennet* a set of notes played on wind
instruments to herald a ceremonial
entrance
*one . . . then not in F, and on stage
sometimes Lear has taken a coronet
from his own head to give to Albany
and Cornwall at 140–1; but I
think Lear should be crowned (see
Introduction, pp. 14–15), and the
direction in Q points up both the ceremonial nature of the occasion and
Lear's intention to give the coronet to
Cordelia when he passes control of her
third of the kingdom to her.

33 **Attend** wait upon. Traditionally
Lear has been discovered seated on, or
has ascended, a throne on his entry

25+ SP EDMUND] *F (Edm.); Bast. Q*   26 SD *to Edmund] Oxf*   30 SD *to Kent] Oxf*   32.1–3] *as
in F; Sound a Sennet, Enter one bearing a Coronet, then Lear, then the Dukes of Albany, and Cornwell,
next Gonorill, Regan, Cordelia, with followers. Q*   33 the] *F;* my *Q*

GLOUCESTER

I shall, my lord.   [F]*Exit.*[F]

LEAR

Meantime we shall express our darker purpose.   35
[F]Give me[F] the map there. Know [F]that[F] we have divided
In three our kingdom; and 'tis our fast intent
To shake all cares and business from our age,
Conferring them on younger strengths, [F]while we
Unburdened crawl toward death. Our son of Cornwall,   40
And you, our no less loving son of Albany,

(see Bratton, 61–3), and it is visually
important for him to do so in relation
to 4.7, where he is carried on stage in a
chair for the reconciliation with
Cordelia, who seeks to make him king
again; see 4.7.20.1, 44 and n.
34 SD Editors since Capell have often
given Edmund an exit here; none is
provided for him in the scene in Q or
F, but if he witnesses what happens at
court, and leaves with the rest at 268,
the rebellion of a daughter against the
King could be seen as related to his
plot against Edgar and his father, and,
as Horsman suggests, Goneril and
Regan may already begin to notice him
with 'speaking looks' (4.5.27) in this
scene.
35 we Lear uses the royal plural, as is appropriate for a state occasion.
  darker more secret (Kent and
Gloucester already know of his plan to
divide the kingdom at 1–5 above, but
they mention only Cornwall and
Albany; has Lear kept secret his intention to give Cordelia a third of his
kingdom?). As commonly used, 'darker' also hints at something more
wicked than the overt purpose of the
formal court meeting, which is to
arrange a marriage for Cordelia.
36 map Who hands the map to Lear? It

would make sense if Kent does so,
assuming he carried it on at 0.1, where
it could prompt the opening lines
about the division of the kingdom. In
many productions an attendant carries
it.
37 *fast fixed; also speedy. Q has 'first',
or first in importance.
39 *Conferring so F. Q has 'Confirming', which also makes sense; the
words could be confused in secretary
hand.
39–44 *while . . . now These lines, found
only in F, provide motives for what
Lear is doing, introduce the idea of
dying, and add an ironic note, as Lear's
actions would have been seen as likely
to guarantee *future strife* rather than
prevent it.
40 crawl . . . death Some actors have
made Lear frail and doddery here, as if
he meant literally that he was about to
crawl toward death (Macready, for
instance, entered leaning on a physician; see Bratton, 61–3); but Taylor
notes that F's alterations of Q remove
hints of senility in the early scenes, so
that a vigorous Lear speaks figurat-
ively here ('Monopolies', 96–7, cited
in Cam[2]).
  son son-in-law

34 lord] *F; Liege Q* SD] *F; not in Q; Exeunt Gloucester and Edmund / Capell* 35 shall] *F; will
Q* purpose] *F; purposes Q* 37 fast] *F; first Q* 38 from our age] *F; of our state Q*
39 Conferring] *F; Confirming Q* strengths] *F; yeares Q*

160

We have this hour a constant will to publish
Our daughters' several dowers, that future strife
May be prevented now.^F
The ^Qtwo great^Q princes, France and Burgundy,   45
Great rivals in our youngest daughter's love,
Long in our court have made their amorous sojourn,
And here are to be answered. Tell me, my daughters –
^FSince now we will divest us both of rule,
Interest of territory, cares of state –^F   50
Which of you shall we say doth love us most,
That we our largest bounty may extend
Where nature doth with merit challenge. – Goneril,
Our eldest born, speak first.

GONERIL
    Sir, I ^Qdo^Q love you more than word can wield the
        matter,   55

---

42 **constant will** settled purpose
43 **several** separate
44 **prevented** forestalled
49 **divest us** This begins a sequence of
clothing images that culminate in Lear
trying to strip off his garments at
3.4.106–7. See Heilman, 71–7.
    both often used in relation to more
than two objects (*OED adv.*, 1b). Cam²
compares *WT* 4.4.56.
50 **Interest** right to possession
    state government
53 ***Where . . . challenge** where natural
affection and merit both lay claim to it
(our generosity). Q has 'Where merit
doth most challenge it'.
54 F tidies the metre here, and the short
line may indicate a pause before
Goneril speaks. It is also possible that
she kneels, and Regan after her; this
would add visual point to the image of
Lear kneeling to Regan at 2.2.343, and
Lear and Cordelia both kneeling at
4.7.57–9, especially if Cordelia in the

present scene remains standing at 87.
The scene has been performed in
this way; see Bratton, 65, and
Introduction, pp. 20–2.
55–76 The words of Goneril and Regan
here can be seen as simply hypocriti-
cal, but should be understood in relation to their situation; Lear has invited
flattery, whether he intended it or no,
and their lines might suggest the sisters are delivering rehearsed speeches
designed for the occasion, a public ceremony to confirm what has already
been decided. See Introduction, p. 37.
55 **more . . . matter** more than words
can express. The relation between
words, matter or meaning, and deeds
comes under recurrent scrutiny in the
play as at 71, 185–6, 237–9, 1.2.63,
3.2.81. The gap between what people
say and what they mean or do becomes
especially poignant in 4.6, where Lear
rejects the flattery he once accepted;
see 4.6.96–104.

---

53 nature . . . merit] *F*; merit doth most *Q*   challenge] *F*; challenge it *Q*   55 word] *F*; words *Q*

Dearer than eyesight, space and liberty,
Beyond what can be valued, rich or rare,
No less than life, with grace, health, beauty, honour.
As much as child e'er loved, or father found,
A love that makes breath poor and speech unable,   60
Beyond all manner of so much I love you.

CORDELIA [*aside*]

What shall Cordelia speak? Love, and be silent.

LEAR

Of all these bounds, even from this line to this,
With shadowy forests ^Fand with champaigns riched,
With plenteous rivers ^F and wide-skirted meads,   65
We make thee lady. To thine and Albany's issues
Be this perpetual. – What says our second daughter,
Our dearest Regan, wife of Cornwall? ^QSpeak.^Q

REGAN

^QSir^Q I am made of that self mettle as my sister,
And prize me at her worth. In my true heart   70
I find she names my very deed of love:

56 **Dearer . . . eyesight** It is Goneril who cries 'Pluck out his eyes' to punish Gloucester in 3.7.
space and liberty possession of land, as at 81 below (though often explained as 'freedom from confinement'), and freedom of action (Kittredge)

59 **found** met with (love)

60 **breath poor** utterance ineffectual
unable inadequate

61 **all . . . much** all kinds of answer to the question 'how much?' (Horsman)

63 **from . . . to this** The map becomes an important property here, as Lear points to it, or draws on it, or tears part of it off and hands it to Goneril as a token of his gift; see Introduction, pp. 17–18.

64 **shadowy** shady
champaigns open country

65 **wide-skirted meads** wide-bordered meadows, presumably lying alongside rivers

68 *****Speak** Q, not in F, but see 86, where the same word is in F and not in Q. Here it seems required to complete a blank verse line, and continues the demand first made of Goneril at 53–4.

69 *****self mettle** same substance (metal) and spirit (mettle). Either spelling could be used for both words, and Q has 'selfe same mettall'.

70 **prize . . . worth** value myself (and my love to you) at the same rate that she does

71 **deed** performance; also contract, or

56 and] *F;* or *Q*   59 ²as] *F;* a *Q*   found] *F;* friend *Q*   62 SD] *Pope*   speak] *F;* doe *Q*
64 shadowy] *F;* shady *Q*   66 Albany's issues] *F; Albaines* issue *Q; Albanies* issue *Q2*   68 of] *F;* to
Q   69 that self mettle] *F (*selfe-mettle*);* the selfe same mettall *Q*   as my sister] *F;* that my sister
is *Q*   70 worth.] *F;* worth *Q*

Only she comes ᶠtooᶠ short, that I profess
Myself an enemy to all other joys
Which the most precious square of sense possesses,
And find I am alone felicitate   75
In your dear highness' love.
CORDELIA [*aside*]   Then poor Cordelia,
And yet not so, since I am sure my love's
More ponderous than my tongue.
LEAR
To thee and thine hereditary ever
Remain this ample third of our fair kingdom,   80
No less in space, validity and pleasure
Than that conferred on Goneril. – �QBut ᵠ now our joy,
Although our last and least, to whose young love
ᶠThe vines of France and milk of Burgundy
Strive to be interested,ᶠ what can you say to draw   85
A third more opulent than your sisters? ᶠSpeak.ᶠ

---

legal document. Regan speaks as though words were deeds; see 55 and n.

72 **that** in that
74 **square of sense** unexplained: probably the most sensitive part of the body or mind. Some find a link with a carpenter's square, and interpret as rule or criterion of sensibility.
  *possesses Q must be correct; 'professes' (F) is probably due to eyeskip from *profess*, 72.
75 **felicitate** made happy
78 **ponderous** weighty, substantial
  tongue words
81 **validity** value
83–5 *and . . . interested** F alters Q's 'not least in our deere loue', which might be taken as an internal direction for Lear to embrace Cordelia, and diminishes her importance, adding a

reminder that the main purpose of the occasion is to determine whom she will marry.

84 **milk** Burgundy became identified with wine only at the end of the seventeenth century. Did Shakespeare intend to suggest something insipid about the character? See 260 and n.
85 **be interested** lay claim. 'Interest' is a variant spelling of this past participle, from the verb 'interess', which gradually gave way to the modern form 'interested' in the seventeenth century.
  draw as in a lottery?
86 **more opulent** The thirds of the country cannot be equal in resources, and Lear has presumably reserved the richest for Cordelia (probably the rest of England, if Goneril is to have Scotland and Regan Wales and Cornwall. He may be anxious to hand

72 comes] *F;* came *Q*   74 possesses] *Q;* professes *F*   76 SD] *Pope*   78 ponderous] *F;* richer *Q*
82 conferred] *F;* confirm'd *Q*   83 our . . . least] *F;* the last, not least *Q*   to . . . young] *F;* in our
deere *Q*   85 interested] *Theobald (*int'ress'd*); interest *F*   draw] *F;* win *Q*   86 opulent] *Q;* opi-
lent *F*

CORDELIA   Nothing, my lord.

^FLEAR   Nothing?

CORDELIA   Nothing.^F

LEAR

^QHow,^Q nothing will come of nothing. Speak again.   90

CORDELIA

Unhappy that I am, I cannot heave

My heart into my mouth. I love your majesty

According to my bond, no more nor less.

LEAR

How, how, ^FCordelia?^F Mend your speech a little,

Lest you may mar your fortunes.

CORDELIA   Good my lord,   95

You have begot me, bred me, loved me. I

Return those duties back as are right fit,

Obey you, love you and most honour you.

Why have my sisters husbands, if they say

They love you all? Haply when I shall wed,   100

That lord whose hand must take my plight shall carry

---

over her share during his lifetime.

*Speak found only in F, which expands and reworks Q in 82–9; see textual notes, and also 68 and n.

88–9 added in F, so hammering on the word *nothing*, echoed at 1.2.31–5, 1.4.126–30, 178, etc., and emphasizing Lear's inability to believe that anyone would speak (or fail to speak) in this way to him

90 **nothing . . . nothing** proverbial; Dent, N285

93 **bond** a complex word that suggests filial obligation, or bond of natural affection between child and parent; shackle, as in the term *bondage* at 1.2.49; and legally binding agreement (see also 1.2.108, 2.1.47 and 2.2.367).

As Cam² notes, Salingar, 96–7, relates the term here to other uses by Shakespeare.

94 ***How, how** Here and at 235 Lear says in Q 'Goe to, goe to'; Taylor, 'Monopolies', 96, may be right to suggest that the changes in F make Lear a stronger figure in F. See above, 40 and n.

98 **Obey** Cordelia's behaviour here is tantamount to disobedience, as Goneril remarks at 280; but her words (echoing the marriage service, as Reibetanz, 31, observes) anticipate the way she becomes a surrogate wife or mother to her father from 4.7 onwards; see 124–5, and Adelman, 120–2.

100 **Haply** perhaps

101 **plight** pledge; promise to marry

---

90 will] *F;* can *Q*   93 no] *F;* nor *Q*   94 How, how] *F;* Goe to, goe to *Q*   speech a] *Q, Fc;* speec ah *Fu*   95 you] *F;* it *Q*

Half my love with him, half my care and duty.
Sure I shall never marry like my sisters
ᵠTo love my father all.ᵠ

LEAR   But goes thy heart with this?   105

CORDELIA   Ay, my good lord.

LEAR   So young and so untender?

CORDELIA   So young, my lord, and true.

LEAR

ᵠWellᵠ, let it be so. Thy truth then be thy dower,
For by the sacred radiance of the sun,   110
The mysteries of Hecate and the night,
By all the operation of the orbs
From whom we do exist and cease to be,
Here I disclaim all my paternal care,
Propinquity and property of blood,   115
And as a stranger to my heart and me
Hold thee from this for ever. The barbarous Scythian,

102–4 Half . . . all Like her stress on *bond* and *duties*, Cordelia's measurement of love seems, at the least, tactless. As Antony says, 'There's beggary in the love that can be reckoned' (*AC* 1.1.15). Her words might invite comparison with the bargaining over Lear's knights by Goneril and Regan at 2.2.390–452, and especially Lear's remark at 2.2.447–9. The half-line 104 may have been omitted from F by oversight.

104 all altogether, exclusively

107 untender unkind; the first use recorded in *OED*

108 true loyal, virtuous and speaking the truth. Cordelia evades the question Lear raises, with a firmness that matches his: the likeness between them is 'Shakespeare's first important dramatic effect' in the play, in Granville-

Barker's view, 189, as Horsman notes.

111 *mysteries . . . night secret rites of the goddess of the infernal regions, associated also with night and the moon, and with witchcraft. This is F2's correction of 'miseries' (F); Q has 'mistresse', which must be an error. Q also has 'might' for 'night', perhaps a desperate attempt to make sense of the line.

112 operation . . . orbs influence on human fate of heavenly spheres, the planets and stars. Compare Gloucester's acceptance of astrological influence at 1.2.103–9.

115 Propinquity kinship
property of blood rights of possession or disposal due by their blood-relationship

117 this this moment; but, as Cam² notes, possibly indicating a gesture. Does

---

105 thy . . . this] *F;* this with thy heart *Q*   106 my good] *F;* good my *Q*   107 untender?] *F;* vntender. *Q*   111 mysteries] *F2;* mistresse *Q;* miseries *F*   night] *F;* might *Q*   112 operation] *Q, F;* operations *F2*

Or he that makes his generation messes
To gorge his appetite, shall ^Fto my bosom^F
Be as well neighboured, pitied and relieved,   120
As thou my sometime daughter.

KENT   Good my liege –

LEAR

Peace, Kent,
Come not between the dragon and his wrath!
I loved her most, and thought to set my rest
On her kind nursery. [*to Cordelia*] Hence and avoid
    my sight.   125
So be my grave my peace, as here I give
Her father's heart from her. Call France. Who stirs?
Call Burgundy.   [*Attendants rush off.*]
                        Cornwall and Albany,
With my two daughters' dowers, digest this third.
Let pride, which she calls plainness, marry her.   130

Lear point to his heart, the map or the coronet?

Scythian The savagery of people from the area around the Black Sea and Asia Minor was legendary; compare *Tit* 1.1.131, and Marlowe's dramatization of a Scythian shepherd in *Tamburlaine*.

118 **he . . . messes** cannibals who eat their offspring

120 **neighboured** helped in time of need (Weis)

121 **sometime** former

123 **wrath** i.e. object of anger

124 **set my rest** stake all (from 'rest' as remainder, all that is left); rely for my repose (from 'rest' as tranquillity, with a hint of dying, or being laid to rest)

125 **nursery** care, nursing; ironically, Cordelia does in the end nurse him, in 4.7; see also 98 and n.

avoid get out of; addressed to Cordelia, who presumably moves away from him, giving place to Kent

126 **So . . . as** may my rest in the grave be peaceful in as much as
    give a paradoxical use of 'give' to mean remove or detach

127 **Who stirs?** Jump to it! (Cam²). Lear is peremptory, as usual in the first scene, but it is possible, as Muir (Ard²) suggested, that the courtiers are 'shocked into immobility'.

129 ***this** This (Q) corresponds to *these bounds* (63) and *this ample third* (80), suggesting that Lear may again point to or hand over part of the map; 'the' (F) may be a casual slip.

130 **plainness** Plain-speaking, or putting matter before words (see 55 and n.), relates to Kent's bluntness in this scene and later (see 2.2.94–8), and to Lear's

---

121 liege –] *Rowe* (liege, –); Liege. *Q*, *F*   125 SD] *Rowe*   128 Burgundy.] *Rowe* (Burgundy –); Burgundy, *Q*, *F*   SD] *this edn; Exit an Attendant. / Capell*   129 dowers] *F; (*Dowres); dower *Q*   this] *Q;* the *F*

I do invest you jointly with my power,
Pre-eminence and all the large effects
That troop with majesty. Ourself by monthly course,
With reservation of an hundred knights
By you to be sustained, shall our abode   135
Make with you by due turn; only we shall retain
The name, and all th'addition to a king: the sway,
Revenue, execution of the rest,
Beloved sons, be yours; which to confirm,
This coronet part between you.

KENT   Royal Lear,   140
Whom I have ever honoured as my king,
Loved as my father, as my master followed,
As my great patron thought on in my prayers –

LEAR

The bow is bent and drawn; make from the shaft.

KENT

Let it fall rather, though the fork invade   145
The region of my heart: be Kent unmannerly

recovery at 4.7.60–2. See Introduction, p. 9.
marry her find her a dowry and a
husband
132 **large effects** lavish marks or
insignia; compare 2.2.368
133 **troop** are associated; perhaps hinting that Lear sees his retinue symbolically as a company or troop of
soldiers
133–9 **Ourself . . . yours** Lear uses the
royal plural here; he wishes to keep the
distinctions and ceremonies accorded a
king (*th'addition*), and is probably wearing the crown, even as he ostensibly
gives away his *power* (131). Shakespeare
makes his proposed retinue of 100
knights larger than in any of the
sources. See Introduction, pp. 65–9.

134 **reservation** the right to retain.
The term has legal implications; see
2.2.441.
137 **addition to** honours belonging to
sway control of government
138 **Revenue** accented on the second
syllable
140 **This . . . part** Lear presumably
takes the coronet, intended for
Cordelia, from an attendant (see 32.1
above). Perhaps Cornwall and Albany
each grasp it at first, but they cannot
divide (*part*) it literally; it is a token of
the extra third of the kingdom they
can now share. Lear gives it to his *sons*,
not to Goneril and Regan; how do they
react? See Introduction, p. 14.
144 **make from** avoid
145 **fork** forked head of the arrow

131 with] *F;* in *Q*   136 turn] *F;* turnes *Q*   shall] *F;* still *Q*   137 addition] *F;* additions *Q*
140 between] *F;* betwixt *Q*   143 prayers –] *Rowe;* prayers. *Q, F*

When Lear is mad. What wouldst thou do, old man?
Think'st thou that duty shall have dread to speak,
When power to flattery bows? To plainness honour's
    bound
When majesty falls to folly. Reserve thy state,   150
And in thy best consideration check
This hideous rashness. Answer my life my judgement,
Thy youngest daughter does not love thee least,
Nor are those empty-hearted, whose low sounds
Reverb no hollowness.

LEAR   Kent, on thy life, no more.   155
KENT

My life I never held but as ^Qa^Q pawn
To wage against thine enemies, ne'er fear to lose it,
Thy safety being ^Qthe^Q motive.

LEAR   Out of my sight!
KENT

See better, Lear, and let me still remain

---

147 **mad** Kent may merely mean 'extremely foolish', but sets up reverberations that close in later on Lear, beginning at 1.5.43.

thou . . . man It is a notable breach of decorum so to address a king at a formal meeting of the court with Lear in state, but Kent calls his and our attention to what the King is brought eventually to acknowledge at 2.2.343, 'I confess that I am old'.

149 **plainness** plain-speaking; see 55 and 2.2.90–102, also Introduction, p. 9

150 **Reserve thy state** retain your power. F alters Q's 'Reuerse thy doome'; in Q Kent is thinking of Cordelia, in F of Lear, and F is more consistent with the general drift of the

speech. Q echoes *Leir*, 505–6, 'sue not to reverse / Our censure', and 567, 'Whose deeds haue not deserved this ruthless doom' (as Duthie noted, 125). Q may represent Shakespeare's first thoughts; see also Jackson, 337–8 (so Cam²).

152 **Answer . . . judgement** I stake my life on (the validity of) my judgement

155 **Reverb** re-echo; Shakespeare's coinage, from 'reverberate'
hollowness insincerity, as at 1.2.113, and emptiness, recalling the proverb 'Empty vessels make most sound' (Dent, V36)

156 **pawn** pledge to fight; see 5.3.94 and *R2* 1.1.74

157 **wage** risk; another image related to chance or gambling; see 85–6 and 124

---

147 mad] *Q2, F;* man *Q*   wouldst] *F (*wouldest*);* wilt *Q*   150 falls] *F;* stoops *Q*   folly.] *Johnson (Rowe);* folly, *Q, F*   Reserve . . . state] *F;* Reuerse . . . doome] *Q*   154–5 sounds / Reverb] *F;* sound / Reuerbs *Q*   156 as a] *Q, F2;* as *F*   157 thine] *F;* thy *Q*   ne'er fear] *F;* nor feare *Q;* ne'er fear'd *Riv (Var)*

The true blank of thine eye.   160

LEAR

Now by Apollo –

KENT   Now by Apollo, King,

Thou swear'st thy gods in vain.

LEAR   ᶠOᶠ vassal! Miscreant!

ᶠALBANY, CORNWALL   Dear sir, forbear!ᶠ

KENT

ᵠDo,ᵠ kill thy physician, and thy fee bestow

Upon the foul disease. Revoke thy gift,   165

Or whilst I can vent clamour from my throat

I'll tell thee thou dost evil.

LEAR

Hear me, ᶠrecreant,ᶠ on thine allegiance, hear me:

That thou hast sought to make us break our vows,

Which we durst never yet, and with strained pride   170

To come betwixt our sentences and our power,

---

160 **blank** the white spot at the centre of a target (*OED sb.* 2). Kent invites Lear to look to him for good advice. Both Lear and Gloucester will learn to 'See better' in the course of the play.

161 **Apollo** pagan (ancient Greek and Roman) god of the sun, noted as an archer (compare 144, 160), and for being clear-sighted

162 **vassal** insultingly = slave
*Miscreant heretic (the original sense); insultingly = vile wretch! So F, substituted from 'recreant' (Q), which means much the same, in order to avoid repetition in 168.

163 *This line is not in Q. In F the speech heading is '*Alb. Cor.*', which has been taken to mean Albany and Cordelia (Goldring, 145–7, and Oxf). But Cordelia was dismissed from Lear's sight at 125, and Albany and Cornwall

are paired throughout the scene; if, as stage tradition suggests (Bratton, 73; Rosenberg, 72), they prevent Lear here from drawing his sword or doing violence to Kent, the action is more appropriate to men. See also 189 and n.

165 ***Revoke . . . gift** Q has 'doome' instead of 'gift', and F here reinforces Kent's concern to stop Lear from abdicating; see 150 and n.

166 **vent clamour** utter protest

168 **recreant** villain; one who breaks faith

169 **That** seeing that, because

170 ***strained** unnatural, forced; Q has 'straied', interpreted by Weis as 'forced beyond its proper limits'. A misreading of minims could account for the difference.

171 ***sentences** pronouncements or

---

162 Miscreant] *F;* recreant *Q*   163 SP ALBANY, CORNWALL] *F (Alb. Cor.); * ALBANY *and* CORDELIA *Oxf*   164 thy fee] *F;* the fee *Q*   165 gift] *F;* doome *Q*   168 thine] *F;* thy *Q*
169 That] *F;* Since *Q*   vows] *F;* vow *Q*   170 strained] *F;* straied *Q*   171 betwixt] *F;* betweene *Q*
sentences] *Fc;* sentence *Q, Fu*

Which nor our nature, nor our place can bear,
Our potency made good, take thy reward.
Five days we do allot thee for provision,
To shield thee from disasters of the world,   175
And on the sixth to turn thy hated back
Upon our kingdom. If on the next day following
Thy banished trunk be found in our dominions,
The moment is thy death. Away! By Jupiter,
This shall not be revoked.   180

KENT

ᵠWhyᵠ, fare thee well, King, since thus thou wilt
    appear,
Freedom lives hence and banishment is here.
[*to Cordelia*] The gods to their dear shelter take thee,
    maid,
That justly think'st and hast most rightly said;

---

decisions, to divide the kingdom and to
give Cordelia's portion to her sisters
and their husbands. This is the correction in Fc; Q and Fu have 'sentence'.
172 **nor . . . nor** neither . . . nor; common
usage in Shakespeare's time
173 **potency . . . good** power carried into
effect. Lear seems to be reclaiming the
power he gave to Albany and Cornwall
at 131, or perhaps looking to them for
support. Coleridge saw here evidence
of Lear's '*moral* incapability of resigning the Sovereign power in the very
moment of disposing of it' (*Lectures*,
2.329).
175 **disasters** misfortunes, as at 1.2.120
177 ***next** This is Blayney's ingenious
suggestion, assuming the word was
misread as 'tenth' (Q and F), which
makes no sense.

178 **trunk** body
179 **Jupiter** See 161 and n. According to
Harrison, in Holinshed, 1.39, 444–8,
after the time of Brutus, idolatry
increased, and the ancient Britons worshipped Apollo and Jupiter amongst
other pagan gods. Lear was the ninth
ruler to follow Brutus (so Perrett).
180 **This** emphatic in relation to the
many ways in which Kent has given
offence
181–8 Kent's rhyming couplets mark a
return to calmness after his stormy
exchange with Lear (so Ard[1]).
182 **Freedom . . . here** a first indication
of the inversion of order and values
brought about by Lear's actions, and
later a constant theme of the Fool, as
in his prophecy at 3.2.79–96 (so Cam[1]
notes, xxviii)

---

174 Five] *F;* Foure *Q*   175 disasters] *F;* diseases *Q*   176 sixth] *F (sixt); fift Q*   177 next] *Oxf
(Blayney);* tenth *Q, F;* seventh *Collier*   181 since] *Q;* sith *F*   182 Freedom] *F;* Friendship *Q*
183 SD] *Hanmer*   dear shelter] *F;* protection *Q*   thee, maid] *F (thee Maid);* the maide *Q*
184 justly think'st . . . rightly] *F;* rightly thinks . . . iustly *Q*

[*to Goneril and Regan*] And your large speeches may
    your deeds approve,   185
That good effects may spring from words of love.
Thus Kent, O princes, bids you all adieu;
He'll shape his old course in a country new.   ᶠ*Exit.*ᶠ

ᶠ*Flourish.*ᶠ *Enter* GLOUCESTER *with* FRANCE, *and* BURGUNDY
                [*and*] ᶠ*attendants.*ᶠ

CORNWALL
Here's France and Burgundy, my noble lord.
LEAR
My lord of Burgundy,   190
We first address toward you, who with this king
Hath rivalled for our daughter. What in the least
Will you require in present dower with her,
Or cease your quest of love?
BURGUNDY   ᶠMostᶠ royal majesty,
I crave no more than hath your highness offered –   195

185–6 See 55 and n. for the importance of the relation between words and deeds; *approve* = demonstrate, confirm; compare 2.2.158
    large high-flown
188.1 *Flourish* fanfare. It is not known how this differs from a *Sennet* at 32.1 above.
    FRANCE, *and* BURGUNDY Banners, coats of arms, or other insignia probably established these characters as foreigners in the English court; the 'colours' of England and France are displayed in 5.1 and 5.2; see also 4.4.0.1 and n.
189 SP *CORNWALL Q has '*Glost.*', who is the obvious character to announce the arrival of France and Burgundy; the change in F may have been made to allow Lear to see Kent off the stage

before he notices Gloucester's entry by another door. *Cor.*, in F, has been interpreted as Cordelia (see above, 163 and n.), introducing her suitors, which is possible, and fits modern ideas; but it seems to me more likely to represent Cornwall, since Lear told Cordelia to avoid his sight at 125, and it would be inappropriate for her to put herself forward here. He may look around for her, or even pull her forward to exhibit her to her suitors.
189 **Here's** See 241 and n.
191 **address toward** address our words to
192 **rivalled** competed; the first use of 'rival' as a verb recorded in *OED*
193 **in present dower** by way of an immediate dowry

185 SD] *Hanmer*   188.1–2] *As F subst.; Enter France and Burgundie with Gloster. Q*   189 SP
CORNWALL] *F (Cor.); Glost. Q;* CORDELIA *Oxf*   191 toward] *F;* towards *Q*   this] *F;* a *Q*
195 hath] *F;* what *Q*

Nor will you tender less?

LEAR   Right noble Burgundy,
When she was dear to us, we did hold her so,
But now her price is fallen. Sir, there she stands:
If aught within that little–seeming substance,
Or all of it, with our displeasure pieced,   200
And nothing more, may fitly like your grace,
She's there, and she is yours.

BURGUNDY   I know no answer.

LEAR

ᵠSirᵠ, will you, with those infirmities she owes,
Unfriended, new adopted to our hate,
Dowered with our curse and strangered with our oath,   205
Take her or leave her?

BURGUNDY   Pardon me, royal sir;
Election makes not up in such conditions.

LEAR

Then leave her, sir, for, by the power that made me,
I tell you all her wealth. [*to France*] For you, great
   king,
I would not from your love make such a stray   210
To match you where I hate, therefore beseech you

---

196 **less?** so in Q and F. Burgundy is
asking a question, not making a
demand.
197 **so** dear, meaning both precious,
and beloved
199 **little-seeming** *Seeming* goes with
little, as referring to Cordelia's little-
seeming, or refusal to 'seem' or to
flatter Lear; it may also connect with
substance, pointing to her as little (a
boy-actor) and worthless (*substance* as
matter or reality, and as wealth).
200 **pieced** joined, added on
201 **fitly like** aptly please

203 **infirmities she owes** defects she
possesses
205 *****Dowered** F, in effect rephrasing
the question he asked at 192–4; Q has
'Couered' or overshadowed, which is
less apt in the context
strangered disowned; see 116
207 **Election . . . up** it is impossible to
choose; 'makes up' seems to be used in
the sense of making up one's mind (so
Schmidt)
209 **tell** describe and count out
210 **make . . . stray** deviate so far

199 aught] *Q*, *F* (ought*)*   little-seeming] *Collier (W. S. Walker);* little seeming *Q*, *F*   201 more]
F; else *Q*   205 Dowered] *F* (Dow'rd*);* Couered *Q*   207 in] *F;* On *Q*   209 SD] *Pope*

T'avert your liking a more worthier way
Than on a wretch whom nature is ashamed
Almost t'acknowledge hers.

FRANCE   This is most strange,
That she who even but now was your ᵠbestᵠ object,   215
The argument of your praise, balm of your age,
The best, the dearest, should in this trice of time
Commit a thing so monstrous, to dismantle
So many folds of favour. Sure her offence
Must be of such unnatural degree   220
That monsters it, or your fore-vouched affection
Fall into taint, which to believe of her
Must be a faith that reason without miracle
Should never plant in me.

CORDELIA

I yet beseech your majesty,   225
If for I want that glib and oily art
To speak and purpose not – since what I well intend,
I'll do't before I speak – that you make known

---

212 to turn your fancy in a worthier direction, or on someone more deserving. The intensifying double comparative, *more worthier*, was in common use in Shakespeare's age; see 2.2.100 (Abbott, 242).

215 *who* 'Whom' in F may be an error caught from 213.
   best object most favoured object of your love: *best* (Q) is necessary to complete the line metrically

216 **argument** theme

217 *The . . . the* F; 'Most . . . most' in Q, altered perhaps so as not to anticipate 252–3 (so Duthie, 52–3)

218 **dismantle** strip off; compare *divest*,

49 and n., and *unfold*, 282

221 **monsters it** makes it monstrous
   your . . . affection the love you previously declared

222 **Fall into taint** must (from 220) be discredited

222–4 **believe . . . me** France emphatically rejects the first alternative.

226 **If for** if because. Cordelia does not complete this sentence; the broken syntax could reflect her emotional state, as Cam² and others suggest.
   want lack

227 **purpose not** intend not to do what I say

228 **I'll . . . speak** putting deeds before

---

215 who] *F2; whom F; that Q*   217 The best, the] *F; most best, most Q*   221 your fore-vouched affection] *F; you for voutch'd affections Q*   222 Fall] *F; Falne Q*   224 Should] *F; Could Q*
225 majesty,] *Q; Maiestie. F*   226–8 If . . . not – . . . I speak –] *Oxf; If . . . not, . . . I speake, Q, F; (If . . . not, . . . I speak) Theobald*   227 well] *Q; will F*   228 make known] *F; may know Q*

It is no vicious blot, murder, or foulness,
No unchaste action or dishonoured step, 230
That hath deprived me of your grace and favour,
But even for want of that for which I am richer,
A still soliciting eye and such a tongue
That I am glad I have not – though not to have it
Hath lost me in your liking.

LEAR   ᵠGo to, go to,ᵠ better thou 235
Hadst not been born than not to have pleased me better.

FRANCE
Is it ᵠno moreᵠ but this? – a tardiness in nature,
Which often leaves the history unspoke
That it intends to do? My lord of Burgundy,
What say you to the lady? Love's not love 240
When it is mingled with regards that stands
Aloof from th'entire point. Will you have her?
She is herself a dowry.

BURGUNDY   Royal King,
Give but that portion which yourself proposed,
And here I take Cordelia by the hand, 245

words; see 55 and n.
229 **vicious blot** stain of dishonour due
    to vice in me
    foulness immorality
230 **dishonoured** dishonourable
232 **even for want** merely for lack
233 **still soliciting** ever begging
235 **lost . . . liking** blotted me out of your
    love. Cordelia picks up Lear's own
    term for affection, used at 212.
237 **tardiness in nature** natural slow-
    ness or hesitation
238 **history** tale, narrative
238–9 **unspoke . . . do** Cordelia may have
    failed to say what she meant to do
    (227–8), but France neatly shifts from
    words to deeds, recognizing that what

she does matters more than what she
has left unspoken. See 55 and n.
240–2 ***Love's . . . point** Sonnet 116
    develops a similar argument; *regards* =
    considerations that have nothing to do
    with the central issue, love. Q has
    'respects', which yields much the same
    sense.
241 **stands** A singular verb with a plur-
    al subject was common usage in
    Shakespeare's age (Abbott, 333).
242 **entire point** essential matter, i.e.
    love
245 **take . . . hand** symbolizing the
    marriage union. Burgundy takes her
    hand, and drops it again when he hears
    Lear's reaction, only for France to

230 unchaste] *F;* vncleane *Q* 232 for want] *Q, F;* the want *Oxf (Hanmer)* richer] *F;* rich *Q*
234 That] *F;* As *Q* 236 to have] *Q;* t haue *F* 238 Which] *F;* That *Q* 239 do?] *Pope;* do, *Q;* do:
F 240 Love's *F;* Love is *Q* 241 regards] *F;* respects *Q* 243 a dowry] *F (*a Dowrie*);* and dowre
Q King] *F; Leir Q; Lear Q2*

Duchess of Burgundy.

LEAR   Nothing. I have sworn, ᶠI am firm.ᶠ

BURGUNDY [*to Cordelia*]

I am sorry then you have so lost a father

That you must lose a husband.

CORDELIA   Peace be with Burgundy.

Since that respect and fortunes are his love,   250

I shall not be his wife.

FRANCE

Fairest Cordelia, that art most rich being poor,

Most choice forsaken and most loved despised,

Thee and thy virtues here I seize upon,

Be it lawful I take up what's cast away.   255

Gods, gods! 'Tis strange that from their cold'st neglect

My love should kindle to inflamed respect.

Thy dowerless daughter, King, thrown to my chance,

Is queen of us, of ours and our fair France.

Not all the dukes of waterish Burgundy   260

Can buy this unprized, precious maid of me.

Bid them farewell, Cordelia, though unkind;

seize Cordelia's hand at 254. The visual importance of this stage action is brought home at 2.2.383, where Regan takes Goneril by the hand.

248 **so** in such a manner (Weis)

250 *respect and fortunes* esteem (the honour due to his rank) and wealth. Q has 'respects / Of fortune' = considerations of wealth.

252 **most . . . poor** recalling biblical paradoxes relating to Christ, such as 2 Corinthians, 6.10, 'as having nothing, and yet possessing all things', and 8.9, 'though hee was riche, yet for your sakes hee became poore, that yee through his povertie might be made rich' (Noble, Shaheen)

254 **seize upon** take possession of

(Weis)

255 **Be it** if it be

256–9 These rhyming couplets formally conclude the state business of the scene.

257 **inflamed respect** fervent regard. France echoes Cordelia's word *respect*, 250, but with a different meaning.

258 **thrown . . . chance** cast (as in throwing dice) to my (good) fortune; see 156–7 and nn.

260 **waterish** (as a place) abounding in water; (as a person) vapid, wishy-washy; see 84 and n.

261 **unprized** unvalued (by her father), but heard also as 'unpriced', without price, or priceless (to France)

262 **though unkind** though they have

250 respect . . . fortunes] *F;* respects / Of fortune *Q*   254 seize] *Q2, F;* ceaze *Q*   256 cold'st] *Q2, F;* couldst *Q*   258 my] *F;* thy *Q*   260 of] *F;* in *Q*   261 Can] *F;* Shall *Q*

Thou losest here a better where to find.

LEAR

Thou hast her, France; let her be thine, for we
Have no such daughter, nor shall ever see   265
That face of hers again. Therefore, be gone,
Without our grace, our love, our benison.
Come, noble Burgundy.

ᶠ*Flourish.*ᶠ *Exeunt* ᵠ*Lear and Burgundy*ᵠ [, *Cornwall, Albany,*
Gloucester, Edmund and attendants].

FRANCE

Bid farewell to your sisters.

CORDELIA

The jewels of our father, with washed eyes   270
Cordelia leaves you. I know you what you are,
And like a sister am most loath to call
Your faults as they are named. Love well our father.
To your professed bosoms I commit him,
But yet, alas, stood I within his grace   275
I would prefer him to a better place.
So farewell to you both.

been wanting in natural affection;
compare 3.4.70 (Horsman)
263 **here . . . where** functioning as
nouns, a common usage in Shakespeare's age (see *OED* Where 14)
267 **benison** blessing
268.1–2 a processional and ceremonial
exit for the court, as Lear sweeps off,
banishing Cordelia; it is marked by
another 'flourish'; see above, 188.1 and
n. If Edmund has remained on stage
throughout the scene, as is possible,
not least to swell the numbers in the
court, he would leave with the others
here; see 34 SD and n.

270 **jewels** treasures, darlings
    washed washed with tears, as she is
    rejected; seeing clearly what her sisters
    are
272–3 **call . . . named** designate (or pro-
    claim) your faults by their plain names
274 **professed bosoms** professèd; *pro-*
    fessed bosoms = the love you have
    professed. For *bosom*, compare 5.3.50.
276 **prefer . . . place** literally, promote
    him to a better position or office. She
    seems already to be thinking of restor-
    ing Lear to the throne he has just
    relinquished; see 4.7.83–4 and n.

268.1–2 *Flourish . . . attendants*] *Cam²; Flourish. Exeunt. F; Exit Lear and Burgundie. Q*   270 The]
Q , F; Ye Rowe, Oxf   273 Love] *F;* vse *Q*

REGAN

Prescribe not us our duty.

GONERIL   Let your study

Be to content your lord, who hath received you

At fortune's alms. You have obedience scanted,   280

And well are worth the want that you have wanted.

CORDELIA

Time shall unfold what plighted cunning hides,

Who covert faults at last with shame derides.

Well may you prosper.

FRANCE   Come, ᶠmyᶠ fair Cordelia.

Exeunt France and Cordelia.

GONERIL   Sister, it is not ᵠaᵠ little I have to say of what   285

most nearly appertains to us both. I think our father

will hence tonight.

REGAN   That's most certain, and with you. Next month

with us.

---

278 **study**   aim, solicitous concern; see
30 above
280 **At fortune's alms**   as a charitable
gift of fortune (relieving her poverty)
scanted   withheld, neglected
281 **are . . . wanted**   deserve the loss of
what you have both lacked and desired
(i.e. a dowry, and parental love). The
two meanings of *wanted* create a sense
of paradox.
282–3 ***Time . . . derides**   varying the
commonplace 'Truth is the daughter of
Time' (*Veritas filia temporis*); Time,
who finally mocks with shame covert
faults, will reveal what cunning hides in
the folds (as of a cloak; see *dismantle*,
218). *Plighted* is the same as 'pleated',
the spelling in Q. F changes 'shame
them' (Q) to 'with shame', but the line
then makes little sense for an audience,

and, like Cam¹ and Oxf, I have accepted Rann's emendation of 'covers' to
'covert'. For further comment, see
Andresen, 155–7 (cited Cam²).
284 **Well . . . prosper**   Cordelia crowns
her sarcasm with an allusion to
Proverbs, 28.13, 'He that hideth his
sins, shall not prosper' (cited by Noble
and Shaheen).
285–309 a return to prose, which frames
the scene; see 1–32 and n. above
286 **nearly appertains**   closely concerns (Weis)
288 **with you**   See 133–6; it would be
natural for Lear to go to his eldest
daughter first (so Cam²).
289 **us**   Is she already using the royal
plural, or referring to herself and
Cornwall?

---

278 SP REGAN . . . GONERIL] *F; Gonorill . . . Regan Q*   duty.] *F;* duties? *Q*   280 At . . . alms] *Q,*
F; As . . . alms *Capell;* At . . . arms *(Stone)*   281 want] *F;* worth *Q;* worst *Oxf*   282 plighted] *F;*
pleated *Q*   283 covert] *Rann (Mason);* couers *Q, F;* cover *Jennens;* cover'd *Hanmer*   with shame]
F; shame them *Q*   284 SD *Exeunt] F3; Exit. Q, F*

GONERIL You see how full of changes his age is. The observation we have made of it hath [Q]not[Q] been little. He always loved our sister most, and with what poor judgement he hath now cast her off appears too grossly.

REGAN 'Tis the infirmity of his age, yet he hath ever but slenderly known himself.

GONERIL The best and soundest of his time hath been but rash; then must we look from his age to receive not alone the imperfections of long-engrafted condition, but therewithal [F]the[F] unruly waywardness that infirm and choleric years bring with them.

REGAN Such unconstant starts are we like to have from him as this of Kent's banishment.

GONERIL There is further compliment of leave-taking between France and him. Pray [F]you[F] let us hit together. If our father carry authority with such

291 ***not** no doubt omitted from F by oversight

293 **grossly** plainly, palpably

294–5 **he . . . himself** 'Know thyself' (*Nosce teipsum*, the title of a long poem of 1597 on the human condition by Sir John Davies) was a humanist rallying cry; only by understanding the relation, in Sir Philip Sidney's words, between 'erected wit', or intelligence, and 'infected will', or the desires prompted by the senses, could human beings, sharing the nature of angels on the one hand and beasts on the other, conduct their lives well. These words give us a rare glimpse into Lear's past, if Regan can be believed.

297 **look . . . age** expect in his old age

298 **long-engrafted condition** long-implanted (engrafted) and so habitual mental disposition

299 **therewithal** in addition to that

300 **choleric** prone to anger. The term derives from 'choler', in early physiology one of the four humours or body-fluids that were supposed to govern temperament.

301 **unconstant starts** sudden outbursts (as in the phrase 'fits and starts')

303 **compliment** ceremony. Goneril seems to be misinformed; see 1.2.23.

304 **France** So Q, F. After the way France and Cordelia are sent packing at 264–8, Burgundy's name might rather be expected here. A matter of authorial inadvertence?

***hit** agree (so *OED* Hit *v.* 17, citing this as the first example), or perhaps strike. This is the reading of Q; F's 'sit', perhaps with the idea of consulting, is weaker.

305–7 **If . . . us** If Lear continues to exercise authority with his habitual disposition (see 298–9), this most recent abdication of his will merely do us harm. Goneril perceptively observes

293 grossly] *F;* grosse *Q* 297 from . . . receive] *F;* to receiue from his age *Q* 298 imperfections] *F;* imperfection *Q* 304 let us] *F;* lets *Q* hit] *Q;* sit *F*

disposition as he bears, this last surrender of his will
but offend us.

REGAN We shall further think of it.

GONERIL We must do something, and i'the heat. *Exeunt.*

1.2 *Enter* [EDMUND, *the*] *Bastard* [, *holding a letter*].

EDMUND

Thou, Nature, art my goddess; to thy law
My services are bound. Wherefore should I
Stand in the plague of custom, and permit

that Lear has so identified himself
with power that he may not be able to
relinquish it.

309 **do . . . i'the heat** act while we are
worked up about it (or strike while the
iron is hot). They apparently go off
together as if they will at once devise a
plan, which is good theatre, though
nothing comes of it.

1.2 The first scene is mainly in verse, but
framed by two prose sequences; this
scene inverts the arrangement, and is
in prose, framed by two verse soliloquies of Edmund. He has, in fact,
three soliloquies in the scene, including a prose one at 118–33, and so is
given a sympathetic prominence
through direct address to the audience.

0.1 holding a letter Edmund may draw it
from a pouch or pocket at 19 rather
than hold it as he comes on stage, but a
property letter is needed. The setting
is Gloucester's *house*, so called at 2.2.2
and 2.2.477, where Regan says it is
little, or not large enough to accommodate Lear and his train.

1–2 Thou . . . bound 'Nature' has various meanings in the play, most notably
in its frequent reminders of the bonds
of nature, the ties of natural affection
between parent and child, what Lear
calls 'The offices of nature, bond of

childhood' (2.2.367; for extended
discussion see Danby, *Shakespeare's
Doctrine of Nature*, and Elton, *King
Lear and the Gods*). In rejecting these
ties, Edmund appeals to the law of the
jungle in effect, and aligns himself
with beasts (*lusty stealth*) as against
custom, morality and order, as a way of
justifying himself. He has something
of the morality Vice and something of
the stage Machiavel in him, but his
energy, his humour and the contemptuous treatment of him by his father
make him initially very engaging. For a
meditation on the 'music of ideas' suggested by the curious juxtaposition
here of 'nature' and 'art', see Stephen
Booth, in Russ McDonald (ed.),
Shakespeare Reread (Ithaca, 1994),
42–55.

3 **Stand . . . custom** remain subject to
the evil of customary usage or laws,
which denied a bastard any share by
inheritance in his father's property; see
2.1.84–5. As Salingar notes, 122–3,
Shakespeare makes Edmund subscribe
to Montaigne's attack on the tyranny
of the violent prejudice of custom,
which we see 'upon every occasion to
force the rules of Nature' ('Of
Custom', Montaigne, 1.105). See
Introduction, pp. 104–5.

306 disposition] *F;* dispositions *Q*   308 of it] *F;* on't *Q*   **1.2]** *F (Scena Secunda); not in Q*
0.1 *Enter . . . letter*] *Theobald (Rowe); Enter Bastard Solus. Q; Enter Bastard. F*   1+ SP EDMUND]
Bast. Q throughout; F to 158

The curiosity of nations to deprive me?
For that I am some twelve or fourteen moonshines   5
Lag of a brother? Why bastard? Wherefore base?
When my dimensions are as well compact,
My mind as generous and my shape as true
As honest madam's issue? Why brand they us
With base? With baseness, bastardy? ᶠBase, base?ᶠ   10
Who in the lusty stealth of nature take
More composition and fierce quality
Than doth within a dull stale tired bed
Go to the creating ᵠofᵠ a whole tribe of fops
Got 'tween a sleep and wake. Well, then,   15
Legitimate Edgar, I must have your land.
Our father's love is to the bastard Edmund

4 **curiosity** fastidiousness, over-refine-
ment.
deprive me i.e. of his rights, though,
as a younger son, he has no rights of
inheritance
5 **For that** because
5–6 **moonshines / Lag of** months
behind, or younger than; compare
1.1.18–19
6 **base** illegitimate, and so unworthy;
also inferior
7 **dimensions . . . compact** bodily
parts are as well formed
8 **generous** magnanimous; befitting
one of noble birth
true true to my father's likeness; or
perhaps well proportioned, as in
Sonnet 62, 5–6, 'Methinks no face so
gracious is as mine, / No shape so
true'
9 **honest** chaste
10 **base? . . . base?** Edmund harps on
base, baseness, bastard and *bastardy* as if
to bring out, and reject in relation to
himself, the various senses that express

an aristocratic society's contempt for
the low-born: vile, despicable, illegitimate, spurious, inferior; meanness and
cowardice. See also Introduction, p.
44.
11–12 **take . . . quality** have a better
form or make-up and a more active or
ardent disposition
13 ***dull . . . bed** as F; this correction of
'stale dull lyed bed' (Q) may be a
sophistication, if the compositor misread 'dull eyed'; see textual note.
Edmund depicts lovemaking in a marriage bed as jaded and routine.
14 **fops** fools (not 'dandies', a meaning
first recorded by *OED* in the 1670s)
15 **Got** begot. See also 2.1.78.
wake a noun = the state of watchful-
ness (*OED sb.*¹ 1)
16 **land** As Lear gives away his land, so
Edmund plots to gain Edgar's inheritance, Gloucester's lands; see Introduction, pp. 17–18.
17–18 **Our . . . legitimate** recalling
what Gloucester said at 1.1.19

4 curiosity] *Q*, *F*; courtesy *Theobald* me?] *F*; me, *Q* 6 brother?] *F*; brother, *Q* base?] *F*; base
Q 7 dimensions] *F*; dementions *Q* 9 issue?] *F*; issue, *Q* 10 base? With basenes] *F*; base,
base *Q* 13 dull stale tired] *F*; stale dull lyed *Q*; dull eyed *Oxf (Blayney)* 15 a sleep] *Q*, *F*;
asleep *Capell* then] *F*; the *Q*

As to the legitimate. ⌜Fine word, 'legitimate'!⌝
Well, my legitimate, if this letter speed
And my invention thrive, Edmund the base   20
Shall top the legitimate. I grow, I prosper:
Now gods, stand up for bastards!

Enter GLOUCESTER.

GLOUCESTER

Kent banished thus? and France in choler parted?
And the King gone tonight? Prescribed his power,
Confined to exhibition? All this done   25
Upon the gad? – Edmund, how now, what news?

EDMUND [*Pockets the letter.*]   So please your lordship, none.

GLOUCESTER   Why so earnestly seek you to put up that
letter?

EDMUND   I know no news, my lord.   30

GLOUCESTER   What paper were you reading?

---

19 **speed** meet with success
20 **invention** plan
21 ***top** 'To' ('tooth' Q, 'to'th'' F) has
been defended, by Cam² amongst
others, as meaning 'advance to', or
'take the place of', but it would be hard
to put this across on the stage.
Honigmann¹, 164–5, suggests 'Shall
too!', meaning 'Edmund shall also
thrive, or have your land'; this makes
reasonable sense, but leaves 'The legitimate' as a phrase that seems out of
place. Capell's emendation to 'top'
requires only that a single letter was
overlooked or dropped, and fits the
sequence of ideas, the 'base' or low
exceeding the legitimate in height, and
outdoing or surpassing Edgar, as
Edmund grows. The Q/F reading is
defended in notes by Thomas Clayton
and Malcolm Pittock in *N&Q*, n.s. 31

(1984), 206–10.
23–6 ***Kent . . . gad?** Gloucester appears
not to notice Edmund's presence; it is
as if he has just heard amazing news,
and in a few lines he informs the audience about the sudden (*upon the gad*, as
if pricked with a goad or spike) departure of France in unexplained anger,
and also about Lear's departure for
Goneril's palace, but with his power
limited (*prescribed*; Q has 'subscribed',
perhaps meaning signed away or sur-
rendered), and restricted to an
allowance (*exhibition*) for his maintenance. Gloucester's house may be anywhere, and the reference to *tonight*
seems to telescope time, as though the
action here takes place later in the
same day as 1.1.
28 **put up** stow away, or pocket

---

21 top the] *Capell (Edwards);* tooth' *Q;* to'th' *F;* too! *(Honigmann¹, 164–5)*   23 thus? . . . parted?]
F; thus, . . . parted, *Q*   24 tonight?] *F (*to night?*);* tonight, *Q*   Prescribed] *F;* subscribd *Q*
25–6 exhibition? . . . gad?] *F;* exhibition, . . . gadde; *Q*   27 SD] *this edn (Rowe)*

EDMUND   Nothing, my lord.

GLOUCESTER   No? What needed then that terrible
    dispatch of it into your pocket? The quality of nothing
    hath not such need to hide itself. Let's see. – Come, if   35
    it be nothing, I shall not need spectacles.

EDMUND   I beseech you, sir, pardon me. It is a letter from
    my brother that I have not all o'er-read; ^Fand^F for so much
    as I have perused, I find it not fit for your o'er-looking.

GLOUCESTER   Give me the letter, sir.   40

EDMUND   I shall offend, either to detain or give it. The
    contents, as in part I understand them, are too blame.

GLOUCESTER   Let's see, let's see.

EDMUND   I hope, for my brother's justification, he wrote
    this but as an essay, or taste of my virtue.   45

GLOUCESTER (^F*Reads*^F.)   'This policy, ^Fand reverence^F of age,
    makes the world bitter to the best of our times, keeps
    our fortunes from us till our oldness cannot relish
    them. I begin to find an idle and fond bondage in the
    oppression of aged tyranny, who sways not as it hath   50
    power, but as it is suffered. Come to me, that of this I

---

32 **Nothing** echoing Cordelia's response
to her father at 1.1.87

34 **dispatch**   hasty removal

39 **o'erlooking**   inspection

42 **too blame** too blameworthy. According to *OED* Blame *v.* 6, a confusion
about the expression 'be to blame' led
to 'blame' being used as an adjective;
see 2.2.157. *OED* cites 'you are too wilful blame', *1H4* 3.1.175.

45 **essay, or taste**   trial (assay) or test;
the words were virtual synonyms

46 **This . . . reverence**   I assume
Gloucester reads silently at first, then
aloud; there is no antecedent for *This
policy*, which has therefore been taken

as meaning the policy of reverencing
age (so Schmidt), or alternatively as
the craftiness of the old (Kittredge,
Horsman), and both senses are possible.

47 **best . . . times** prime years, as at
1.1.296

48 **relish** suggested by *taste*, 45, and
bitter, 47 (so Whiter)

49 **idle . . . fond** useless and foolish

50–1 **aged . . . suffered** By absorbing his
father *who sways* (i.e. rules) not
through power, but on sufferance, into
an abstraction, *aged tyranny*, Edmund's
phrase reaches out to remind us of
Lear in the opening scene.

---

33 needed] *F;* needes *Q*   37 SP EDMUND] *Qc, Q2, F (Ba., Bast.); not in Qu*   39 o'er-looking] *F;*
liking *Q*   46 SD Reads] *F; A Letter Q (opp. 45)*

may speak more. If our father would sleep till I waked
him, you should enjoy half his revenue for ever and live
the beloved of your brother. Edgar.' Hum! Conspiracy!
'Sleep till I wake him, you should enjoy half his   55
revenue' – My son Edgar, had he a hand to write this?
A heart and brain to breed it in? When came this to
you? Who brought it?

EDMUND   It was not brought me, my lord, there's the
cunning of it. I found it thrown in at the casement of   60
my closet.

GLOUCESTER   You know the character to be your brother's?

EDMUND   If the matter were good, my lord, I durst swear
it were his; but, in respect of that, I would fain think it
were not.   65

GLOUCESTER   It is his?

EDMUND   It is his hand, my lord; but I hope his heart is
not in the contents.

GLOUCESTER   Has he never before sounded you in this
business?   70

EDMUND   Never, my lord. But I have heard him oft
maintain it to be fit that, sons at perfect age and fathers

52–3 **would . . . him** were dead and
would never wake
60 **casement** window opening on hinges
61 **closet** private room
62 **character** writing
63 **matter** substance, meaning; see 1.1.55
and n.
durst would dare
64 **that** the matter
fain gladly
66 ***his?** so Q; F has 'his.', but
Edmund's response indicates that
Gloucester is asking for confirmation.
67 **hand** handwriting
69 **sounded you** sounded you out, tried

to discover your views
71–4 **But . . . revenue** The idea that
sons in their prime should manage the
affairs of fathers who cling on to
power and possessions when well past
their best, or have 'declined / Into the
vale of years' (*Oth* 3.3.265–6), was
debated, as Ard[2] noted, in the *Civil
Conversation* of Guazzo, 2.65–73, and
by Montaigne in his essay 'Of the
Affection of Fathers to their Children', 2.68–9. Lear, indeed, handed
over the management of his 'revenue'
to his sons-in-law, at 1.1.131–3. See
Introduction, pp. 104, 109.

---

55 Sleep . . . wake] *F;* slept . . . wakt *Q*   57–8 this to you] *Q;* you to this *F*   66 his?] *Q;* his. *F*
69 Has] *F;* Hath *Q*   before] *F;* heretofore *Q*   71 heard him oft] *F;* often heard him *Q*
72 perfect] *Q (*perfit*), F*

declined, the father should be as ward to the son and the son manage his revenue.

GLOUCESTER   O villain, villain! His very opinion in the   75
letter. Abhorred villain! Unnatural, detested, brutish
villain – worse than brutish! Go, sirrah, seek him. I'll
apprehend him. Abominable villain, where is he?

EDMUND   I do not well know, my lord. If it shall please
you to suspend your indignation against my brother till   80
you can derive from him better testimony of his intent,
you should run a certain course; where, if you violently
proceed against him, mistaking his purpose, it would
make a great gap in your own honour and shake in
pieces the heart of his obedience. I dare pawn down   85
my life for him, ᶠthatᶠ he hath writ this to feel my
affection to your honour and to no other pretence of
danger.

GLOUCESTER   Think you so?

EDMUND   If your honour judge it meet, I will place you   90
where you shall hear us confer of this and by an
auricular assurance have your satisfaction, and that
without any further delay than this very evening.

GLOUCESTER   He cannot be such a monster.

---

76 **Abhorred . . . detested** odious . . .
detestable
77 **sirrah** a form of address expressing
Gloucester's authority; compare 1.4.44
***I'll** 'I' (Q) could represent 'Ay',
instructing Edmund to arrest his
brother.
78 **abominable** 'abhominable' in Q and
F, meaning 'inhuman', in accordance
with the mistaken Elizabethan belief
that the word derived from the Latin
ab, away from, and *homine*, man (so
Cam²)

82 **run . . . course** pursue a reliable
course of action
where whereas
85 **pawn down** stake, put at risk
86 **feel** test, sound out
87–8 **pretence of danger** dangerous
purpose; compare 1.4.68
90 **meet** fitting
92 **auricular assurance** certainty derived
from hearing what is said; *auricular*
means 'pertaining to the ear'
have . . . satisfaction have your
doubts resolved (Weis)

---

73 declined, the] *F;* declining, his *Q*   74 his] *F;* the *Q*   77 sirrah] *F;* sir *Q*   I'll] *F;* I *Q;* I, *Q2;*
ay *Cam (anon.)*   79 lord.] *Q (*Lord,*), F (*L.*)*   81 his] *F;* this *Q*   86 writ] *F;* wrote *Q*
87 other] *F;* further *Q*   92 auricular] *F;* aurigular *Q*

ᵠEDMUND   Nor is not, sure.   95

GLOUCESTER   To his father, that so tenderly and entirely
loves him. Heaven and earth!ᵠ Edmund, seek him out.
Wind me into him, I pray you: frame the business after
your own wisdom. I would unstate myself to be in a
due resolution.   100

EDMUND   I will seek him, sir, presently, convey the
business as I shall find means and acquaint you withal.

GLOUCESTER   These late eclipses in the sun and moon
portend no good to us. Though the wisdom of Nature
can reason ᶠit ᶠ thus and thus, yet nature finds itself   105
scourged by the sequent effects. Love cools, friendship
falls off, brothers divide: in cities, mutinies; in
countries, discord; ᶠin ᶠ palaces, treason; ᶠand ᶠ the bond
cracked 'twixt son and father. ᶠThis villain of mine
comes under the prediction – there's son against father.   110

95–7 *EDMUND . . . **earth!** Not in F,
these lines may have been omitted
because they contradict Gloucester's
words at 75–8 and 114–15; but they
could be taken as showing that he is
'full of changes' (1.1.290), like Lear.
98 **Wind . . . him** insinuate yourself on
my behalf (*me* is an ethical dative) into
his confidence (*OED* Wind v.¹ 11b)
frame fashion
99–100 **unstate . . . resolution** give up
my rank and wealth to be properly
convinced, either of his guilt (F), or
perhaps of his innocence (Q, where
the phrase follows on from 95–7)
101 **presently** immediately
convey manage discreetly
102 **withal** therewith
103 **late eclipses** Recent (*late*) eclipses of
the moon and sun took place in
September and October 1605, and it is
possible that Shakespeare had these in
mind. Catalogues of disasters similar
to Gloucester's were, however, com-

mon in astrological forecasts of the
period; so Himbert de Billy in *Certaine
wonderful predictions* (1604), A5ᵛ,
writes of 'many great Eclipses' occurring in a few years, 'wherby greeuous
and most wretched accidents are pre-
saged . . . all piety and charity shal
waxe colde, truth and iustice shal be
oppressed . . . and finally nothing else
shall be expected, but spoyle and ruine
of the common society'.
104–6 **Though . . . effects** Although
natural philosophy or science can provide explanations, the world of nature
(including man) is afflicted by the
effects that follow as a consequence.
106–7 **friendship falls off** friends
become estranged
107 **mutinies** quarrels or riots
108 **bond** See 1.1.93 and n. Cordelia
there used the word, and Lear appeals
to the same 'bond' at 2.2.367.
109–14 *This . . . graves This passage,
from F, seems intended as a replace-

The King falls from bias of nature – there's father
against child. We have seen the best of our time.
Machinations, hollowness, treachery and all ruinous
disorders follow us disquietly to our graves.ᶠ Find out
this villain, Edmund; it shall lose thee nothing. Do it   115
carefully. – And the noble and true-hearted Kent
banished, his offence honesty! ᶠ'Tisᶠ strange, ᵠstrange!ᵠ

ᶠ*Exit.*ᶠ

EDMUND   This is the excellent foppery of the world, that
when we are sick in fortune, often the surfeits of our
own behaviour, we make guilty of our disasters the sun,   120
the moon and ᵠtheᵠ stars, as if we were villains on
necessity, fools by heavenly compulsion, knaves, thieves
and treachers by spherical predominance; drunkards,
liars and adulterers by an enforced obedience of
planetary influence; and all that we are evil in by a   125
divine thrusting on. An admirable evasion of

ment for 144–51, lines found only in
Q. The effect is to tighten the dialogue
between Edmund and Edgar (138ff.),
to cut from Edmund's part lines in
which he repeats Gloucester's super-
stitious anxieties, and to add to
Gloucester's speech here a specific
comment on his own and on Lear's situation. The addition here in F also
enlarges the theme of order inverted,
the world turned upside-down, begun
in the opening scene; see 1.1.182 and
n.

111 **bias** tendency, bent; a metaphor from
the weighting of bowls on one side
112 **best . . . time** recalling 47
113 **hollowness** deception, insincerity, as
at 1.1.155
118 **excellent foppery** utter stupidity;
'excellent' is used caustically, as we

might now say 'that's a fine way to
behave'. For *foppery* see 14 above and
n.
119–20 **sick . . . behaviour** have bad
luck, or lose our wealth, often (a result
of) the excesses of our own behaviour;
surfeits suggests a morbid condition
brought about by too much eating and
drinking, and so continues the idea of
sickness
121 **on** by
122 **heavenly** planetary or extra-terres-
trial
123 **treachers** traitors
****spherical predominance** the ascen-
dancy or predominant influence of
some planet or sphere; Q has 'spirituall'
126 **divine thrusting on** celestial impo-
sition

117 honesty!] F *(*honesty.*)*; honest *Q*   119 surfeits] F *(*surfets*)*; surfeit *Q*   121 on] F; by *Q*
123 treachers] F; Trecherers *Q*   spherical] F; spirituall *Q*   predominance;] F *(*predominance.*)*;
predominance, *Q*

whoremaster man, to lay his goatish disposition on the
charge of a star. My father compounded with my
mother under the dragon's tail and my nativity was
under Ursa Major, so that it follows I am rough and   130
lecherous. ^QFut!^Q I should have been that I am had the
maidenliest star in the firmament twinkled on my
bastardizing.

Enter EDGAR.

Pat he comes, like the catastrophe of the old comedy.
My cue is villainous melancholy, with a sigh like Tom   135
o'Bedlam. – O, these eclipses do portend these
divisions. ^FFa, sol, la, mi.^F

EDGAR   How now, brother Edmund, what serious

127 **whoremaster** given to lechery
   goatish lustful. Goats were proverbial
   for their sexual prowess (Dent, G167),
   hence Othello's cry, 'Goats and monkeys!' (*Oth* 4.1.263), when he thinks
   Desdemona an adulteress.
128 **charge** responsibility
129 **dragon's tail** 'the descending node
   of the moon's orbit' (*OED*), with overtones of evil, as Satan was familiarly
   called the 'dragon' or 'serpent'
130 **Ursa Major** the Great Bear, hence
   'rough and lecherous'; the constellation also known as the Big Dipper, and
   the Plough. Its seven bright stars were
   also sometimes called the 'seven stars',
   as in the Fool's question at 1.5.33–4.
131 ***Fut!** Q only; abbreviating 'Christ's
   foot'. This, the most profane oath in
   Q, could have been omitted from F as
   a result of censorship following the
   'Act to Restrain Abuses of Players' in
   1606; see Duthie, 170, and Taylor,
   'Monopolies', 77–8, 109–10.
134 **catastrophe . . . comedy** arbitrary

or contrived denouement as in old-
fashioned comedy; compare *LLL*
4.1.77, 'The catastrophe is a nuptial'
(so Horsman). Edmund is construct-
ing his own 'comedy', and, as in his
soliloquies, taking the audience into
his confidence. On his role as comic
intriguer and stage manager, see
Reibetanz, 58–9.
135 ***My cue** replacing and explaining
   'mine' (Q)
135–6 **Tom o'Bedlam** a name commonly taken by a beggar who claimed to
   have come from Bedlam, or Bethlehem
   Hospital for the insane in London. See
   also 2.2.185 and n.
137 **divisions** discords (see 106–14); and
   in music, variations on, or accompani-
   ments to, a theme
   Fa . . . mi Edmund sings, as if
   unaware of Edgar's approach, in order
   the fourth, fifth, sixth and third notes
   of the scale of C major, a discordant
   motto, Hunter suggests, appropriate to
   the character of Edmund: 'He thus

127 whoremaster man] *Q*, *F* (Whore-master-man)   127–8 on . . . a star] *F*; to . . . Starres *Q*
132 maidenliest] *F3*; maidenlest *Q*, *F*   in] *F*; of *Q*   133 bastardizing.] *F*; bastardy *Edgar*; *Q*;
bastardy; *Edgar Q2*   133.1 *Enter* EDGAR] *as Q2, F; in left margin, opp. 134 Q*   134 Pat] *F* (Pat:); and
out *Q*   135 My cue] *F*; mine *Q*   135–6 sigh . . . Tom o'] *F*; sith like them of *Q*; sigh like them of *Q2*

contemplation are you in?

EDMUND   I am thinking, brother, of a prediction I read   140
this other day, what should follow these eclipses.

EDGAR   Do you busy yourself with that?

EDMUND   I promise you, the effects he writes of succeed
unhappily, ᵠas of unnaturalness between the child and
the parent, death, dearth, dissolutions of ancient   145
amities, divisions in state, menaces and maledictions
against King and nobles, needless diffidences,
banishment of friends, dissipation of cohorts, nuptial
breaches and I know not what.

EDGAR   How long have you been a sectary astronomical?   150

EDMUND   Come, come,ᵠ when saw you my father last?

EDGAR   ᵠWhy,ᵠ the night gone by.

EDMUND   Spake you with him?

EDGAR   ᶠAy,ᶠ two hours together.

EDMUND   Parted you in good terms? Found you no   155
displeasure in him, by word nor countenance?

EDGAR   None at all.

EDMUND   Bethink yourself wherein you may have offended
him, and at my entreaty forbear his presence until some

---

moves across the interval of the augmented fourth, called *diabolus in musica* (the devil in music).'

143 *writes Taylor, 'Monopolies', 86, argues that the change in F from 'writ' (Q; see textual note) indicates that Edmund has a book in his hand, and was probably reading from it at 136–7.

143–4 succeed unhappily follow on wretchedly

144–51 *as . . . come Q only; see note on 109–14 above. Ironically, all that Edmund forecasts here is fulfilled in the play.

145 dearth famine

146 divisions disagreements; recalling the 'division of the kingdom', 1.1.4

147 diffidences doubts or instances of mistrust, as at *KJ* 1.1.65, 'wound her honour with this diffidence'

148 dissipation of cohorts dispersal of companies of soldiers. Was Shakespeare thinking of Lear's hundred knights?

150 sectary astronomical disciple of astrologers. Astrology and astronomy overlapped in meaning until the eighteenth century.

156 countenance bearing, appearance

159 forbear avoid

---

142 with] *F;* about *Q*   143 writes] *F;* writ *Q*   146 amities] *Q;* armies *Q2*   156 nor] *F;* or *Q*
159 until] *F;* till *Q*

little time hath qualified the heat of his displeasure; 160
which at this instant so rageth in him that with the
mischief of your person it would scarcely allay.

EDGAR   Some villain hath done me wrong.

EDMUND   That's my fear. ^FI pray you have a continent
forbearance till the speed of his rage goes slower; and, 165
as I say, retire with me to my lodging, from whence I
will fitly bring you to hear my lord speak. Pray ye, go:
there's my key. If you do stir abroad, go armed.

EDGAR   Armed, brother?^F

EDMUND   Brother, I advise you to the best, ^Qgo armed.^Q I 170
am no honest man if there be any good meaning toward
you. I have told you what I have seen and heard – but
faintly; nothing like the image and horror of it. Pray
you, away!

EDGAR   Shall I hear from you anon? 175

EDMUND   I do serve you in this business.   *Exit Edgar.*
A credulous father and a brother noble,
Whose nature is so far from doing harms
That he suspects none – on whose foolish honesty
My practices ride easy. I see the business. 180
Let me, if not by birth, have lands by wit;

160 **qualified** moderated
161–2 **with . . . allay** with you disabled,
or perhaps dead (the image is of Edgar
being attacked physically), it would
hardly subside
164–9 ***I . . . brother?** This passage,
found only in F, gives Edgar a hiding-
place, Edmund's *lodging* within Gloucester's house, and anticipates the
opening of 2.1.
164–5 **have . . . forbearance** restrain
yourself and avoid him
167 **fitly** at a suitable time
170 ***go armed** Q only. It is likely that

164–9 were added in F, and this phrase
omitted as repetitive; but some think
the lines were cut from Q, and this
phrase, by oversight, retained.
171 **meaning** intention
173 **image and horror** horrifying picture (hendiadys)
175 **anon** shortly
179 **honesty** uprightness, decency
180 **practices** intrigues
181 **lands** As Lear gives away his lands in
1.1, so Edmund, who cannot inherit
land (see 3 and n. above), schemes to
gain lands in this scene; on the impor-

162 person] *Q*, *(*parson*) F*   scarcely] *F;* scarce *Q*   171 toward] *F;* towards *Q*   172–3 heard –
but faintly;] *F (*heard: But faintly.*);* heard, but faintly, *Q*   176 I do] *Q, F;* Ay, I do *(Oxf)*   SD] *as
Q; opp. 175 Q2, F*

All with me's meet that I can fashion fit.   *Exit.*

1.3   *Enter* GONERIL *and* [OSWALD, *her*] *steward.*

GONERIL   Did my father strike my gentleman for chiding
of his fool?
OSWALD   Ay, madam.
GONERIL

By day and night he wrongs me. Every hour
He flashes into one gross crime or other   5
That sets us all at odds. I'll not endure it.
His knights grow riotous and himself upbraids us
On every trifle. When he returns from hunting,
I will not speak with him; say I am sick.
If you come slack of former services   10
You shall do well; the fault of it I'll answer.   [*Horns within.*]
OSWALD   He's coming, madam, I hear him.
GONERIL

Put on what weary negligence you please,

---

tance of land, see Introduction, p. 17.
182 **All . . . fit** everything is all right by
me that I can frame to my purposes. As
Ard² notes, Edmund is saying the end
justifies the means.
1.3 Some (fictional) time has elapsed
since 1.1, for Lear and his train of
knights are established in the house of
Goneril and Albany, the setting of this
scene.
0.1 *steward* an important official, as controller of Goneril's household; Oswald
is not named in the text until 1.4.320.
In Q he enters as '*Gentleman*' in this
scene, and should be costumed as one,
perhaps with some extravagance in
view of Kent's comments at 2.2.15–16,
and 53–4, 'a tailor made thee'.

1-2 **Did . . . fool?** Lear initiates the physical violence in the play, attacking Kent
at 1.1.162, and now striking an attendant of Goneril's. This is the first
mention of the Fool.
4 **By . . . night** an oath, as at *H8* 1.2.213;
meaning 'all the time', merging into
'every hour'
5 **flashes** breaks out; the first use in
this sense according to *OED*
crime offence
10 **come . . . services** are more lax in
serving him than you used to be
11 **answer** be responsible for
SD *Horns within* not in Q or F, but
suggested by *hear him*, 12, and 1.4.7
SD

1.3] *F (Scena Tertia); not in Q*   0.1 SD OSWALD *her*] *Collier*   SD *Steward*] *F; Gentleman Q*
3+ SP OSWALD] *Collier; Gent. Q; Ste. F*   3 Ay] *F (I); Yes Q*   7 upbraids] *Q (obrayds), Q2, F*
8 trifle. When] *F; trifell when Q*   11 SD] *Capell*

You and your fellows; I'd have it come to question.
If he distaste it, let him to my sister, 15
Whose mind and mine I know in that are one,
ᵠNot to be overruled. Idle old man,
That still would manage those authorities
That he hath given away. Now by my life
Old fools are babes again and must be used 20
With checks as flatteries, when they are seen abused.ᵠ
Remember what I have said.

OSWALD   ᵠVery ᵠ well, madam.

GONERIL

And let his knights have colder looks among you,
What grows of it no matter; advise your fellows so.
ᵠI would breed from hence occasions, and I shall, 25
That I may speak.ᵠ I'll write straight to my sister
To hold my ᵠvery ᵠ course. ᵠGo,ᵠ prepare for dinner.

Exeunt.

---

14 **I'd . . . question** I'd like to provoke
him to quarrel
15 ***distaste** dislike (the word in Q)
17–21 ***Not . . . abused** These lines,
and 25–6, 'I . . . speak', are from Q, in
speeches printed as prose. Their omission from F softens the character of
Goneril here, by removing both her
insulting words about her father, and
her conscious plotting against him; see
Introduction, p. 144.

17 **Idle** frivolous, worthless
21 **With . . . abused** with reprimands as
well as flatteries when they are seen to
be misguided
25 **occasions** opportunities for taking
offence
26 **straight** immediately
26–7 **I'll . . . course** See 1.1.308–9, where
the sisters talked of planning together;
it turns out they have no prepared
course of action.

14 fellows] *F;* fellow seruants *Q*   to] *F;* in *Q*   15 distaste] *F;* dislike *Q*   my] *F;* our *Q*   22 have
said] *F;* tell you *Q*   27 SD] *F; Exit Q*

1.4　　　　　　　　　　*Enter* KENT [*disguised*].

KENT
If but as well I other accents borrow
That can my speech diffuse, my good intent
May carry through itself to that full issue
For which I razed my likeness. Now, banished Kent,
If thou canst serve where thou dost stand condemned　　5
ᶠSo may it comeᶠ thy master whom thou lov'st
Shall find thee full of labours.

ᶠ*Horns within.*ᶠ *Enter* LEAR ᶠ*and*ᶠ [*four or more* Knights *as*]
ᶠ*attendants.*ᶠ

LEAR　　Let me not stay a jot for dinner; go, get it ready.
　　　　　　　　　　　　　　　　　　　　[*Exit 1 Knight.*]

1.4.0.1 Identifying himself as *banished Kent* at 4, Kent turns up in a disguise that remains impenetrable, by stage convention, to everyone in the action, a disguise that allows him to give full expression to his true nature as a faithful follower of Lear. In productions he may be costumed in various ways, usually as a serving-man or a rough soldier. At 5.3.281 he gives his new name as Caius, but it is never otherwise mentioned in the play. The setting is still the house of Goneril and Albany.

1 **as well** as well as he has disguised himself

2 **diffuse** make indistinct, confuse

2–4 **my . . . likeness** my good purpose may be carried through to the perfect outcome for which I erased my appearance (and ?shaved myself, a possible meaning)

6 **come** happen

7 **labours** services on his behalf (Weis)

7.1–2 *This is Lear's first entry with

some of his train of knights, if not the hundred he required at 1.1.134. Q has '*Enter Lear*', and calls the knights 'servants' in speech prefixes; F calls for '*Attendants*' in the entry, but has '*Knigh.*' or '*Knight.*' in speech prefixes. It would seem from the number of times Lear sends knights off on errands that he has to be accompanied on stage by four or more of them. As suggested by 1.3.7–8, on stage they have often been presented as armed, undisciplined, noisy and aggressive, and sometimes they have been accompanied by hunting dogs. The more rowdy the knights, the more Goneril's complaints at 191–4 and later may be justified, so their behaviour here is of considerable importance; see also 49–72 and n.

8 **Let . . . dinner** Lear's prose here contrasts with his formal verse in the ceremonial opening scene, but he is just as peremptory. Dinner, the main meal, was commonly eaten in the middle of

1.4] *F (Scena Quarta); not in Q*　0.1 *disguised*] *Rowe*　1 well] *Q; will F*　2 diffuse] *Theobald; defuse Q, F; deface Capell*　7 thee] *F; the Q*　labours] *F; labour Q*　7.1–2 *four . . . as*] *this edn*　8 SD] *Hunter (Capell)*

[*to Kent*] How now, what art thou?

KENT   A man, sir.   10

LEAR   What dost thou profess? What wouldst thou with
us?

KENT   I do profess to be no less than I seem; to serve him
truly that will put me in trust, to love him that is
honest, to converse with him that is wise and says little,   15
to fear judgement, to fight when I cannot choose – and
to eat no fish.

LEAR   What art thou?

KENT   A very honest-hearted fellow, and as poor as the
King.   20

LEAR   If thou be'st as poor for a subject as he's for a king,
thou art poor enough. What wouldst thou?

KENT   Service.

LEAR   Who wouldst thou serve?

KENT   You.   25

LEAR   Dost thou know me, fellow?

KENT   No, sir; but you have that in your countenance
which I would fain call master.

LEAR   What's that?

KENT   Authority.   30

LEAR   What services canst ᶠthouᶠ do?

KENT   I can keep honest counsel, ride, run, mar a curious

---

the day.

11 **What . . . profess?** 'What is your occupation?', or 'What skill do you have?' Kent replies as if the sense were 'claim', as at 1.1.72 (Horsman).

15 **converse** associate

16 **fear judgement** do no evil. The audience might pick up an allusion to God's judgement of 'the ungodly' (Psalm 1.6, cited Noble), the 'day of judgement' (Matthew, 10.15), or last judgement; see 5.3.261 and n.

17 **eat no fish** The incongruity of the phrase is enough to provoke laughter, but Kent may be signalling that he is a proper man, and eats only meat (so Capell); or that he is a Protestant, and does not fast on Fridays (so Warburton); or that he has nothing to do with women (so Cam¹), or all of these things.

27 **countenance** bearing, appearance
28 **fain** gladly
30 **Authority** a term Lear disowns at 4.6.154
32 **keep honest counsel** keep secret

9 SD] *Oxf*   21 be'st] *F;* be *Q*   24 Who] *Q, F;* Whom *F2*   31 thou] *Q2, F; not in Q*

tale in telling it and deliver a plain message bluntly.
That which ordinary men are fit for I am qualified in,
and the best of me is diligence.   35

LEAR   How old art thou?

KENT   Not so young, ᶠsirᶠ, to love a woman for singing,
nor so old to dote on her for anything. I have years on
my back forty-eight.

LEAR   Follow me, thou shalt serve me; if I like thee no   40
worse after dinner, I will not part from thee yet.
Dinner, ho, dinner! Where's my knave, my fool?
Go you and call my fool hither.   [*Exit 2 Knight.*]

Enter OSWALD.

You, ᶠyouᶠ, sirrah, where's my daughter?   44

OSWALD   So please you –   ᶠ*Exit.*ᶠ

LEAR   What says the fellow there? Call the clotpoll back.

                                                 [*Exit 3 Knight.*]

Where's my fool? Ho, I think the world's asleep.

Enter 3 Knight.

How now, where's that mongrel?

3 KNIGHT   He says, my lord, your daughter is not well.

---

confidential matters that are honourable
curious complicated. Kent plays on
the proverb, 'A good tale ill told is
marred in the telling' (Dent, T38).
42 **knave** servant, as at 95 below
44 **sirrah** a form of address expressing
authority and/or contempt
45 **So please you** 'excuse me, I'm busy'
(Camᴵ); an example of the *weary negligence* Goneril recommended at 1.3.13.

Like others, Oswald is following
Goneril's instructions, for Lear never
does get the dinner he calls for.
46 **clotpoll** blockhead
49–72 Mahood argues, 162, that here 'the
Knight's function is to give the lie to
Goneril's account of him and his
companions as riotous, insolent and
deboshed'; but the behaviour of Lear
and Kent verges on the riotous in this
scene. Hunter thinks the Knight's

40–1 serve me; . . . dinner,] *Q*, *F* (serue, . . . dinner,); serve me, . . . dinner. *Jennens*   43 SD]
Hunter (Dyce)   43.1 OSWALD] *Capell; Steward Q*, *F (after 44)*   45+ SP OSWALD] *Collier;
Steward. Q; Ste. F*   46 clotpoll] *F* (Clot-pole); clat-pole *Q*   46 SD] *Hunter (Dyce)*   47.1] *this
edn (Hunter and Dyce)*   49 SP 3 KNIGHT] *Hunter; Knigh. F; Kent. Q*   daughter] *Q*; Daughters *F*

LEAR   Why came not the slave back to me when I called   50
him?

3 KNIGHT   Sir, he answered me in the roundest manner,
he would not.

LEAR   He would not?

3 KNIGHT   My lord, I know not what the matter is, but to   55
my judgement your highness is not entertained with
that ceremonious affection as you were wont. There's a
great abatement ᶠof kindnessᶠ appears as well in the
general dependants as in the Duke himself also, and
your daughter.   60

LEAR   Ha? Sayst thou so?

3 KNIGHT   I beseech you pardon me, my lord, if I be
mistaken, for my duty cannot be silent when I think
your highness wronged.

LEAR   Thou but rememberest me of mine own   65
conception. I have perceived a most faint neglect of
late, which I have rather blamed as mine own jealous
curiosity than as a very pretence and purpose of
unkindness. I will look further into't. But where's my
fool? I have not seen him this two days.   70

3 KNIGHT   Since my young lady's going into France, sir,

---

function is rather 'to emphasize the
isolation of Lear'. See 7.1–2 and n.
52 **roundest** most plain-spoken
56 **entertained** treated
57 **ceremonious affection** 'the affection
due to a father and the ceremony
appropriate to a King' (Hunter)
were wont used to be
58 **kindness** good will, affection
59 **general dependants** servants as a
group
as . . . Duke As Hunter notes, this is
inconsistent with Albany's assertion
that he is *guiltless* at 265–6. It is likely
that Shakespeare wished to emphasize

the first moves in the exclusion of
Lear, even as the scene shows him in
his most imperious and demanding
vein.
65 **rememberest** remindest
66 **faint** lazy, intensifying the sense of
negligence; also slight
67–8 **jealous curiosity** suspicious or
watchful fastidiousness; compare 1.2.4
68 **very pretence** actual intention; compare 1.2.87
71–2 **Since . . . away** the first mention of
Cordelia since the opening scene, linking the Fool with her

52+ SP 3 KNIGHT] *Hunter; Knigh.* F; *seruant.* Q   54 He] *Q2, F;* A *Q*   58 appears] *Q (*apeer's*), F*
68 purpose] *F;* purport *Q*   69 my] *F;* this *Q*   70 this] *Q, F;* these *Pope*

195

the fool hath much pined away.

LEAR   No more of that, I have noted it [F]well[F]. Go you and
tell my daughter I would speak with her.   74

[*Exit 3 Knight.*]

Go you; call hither my fool.   [*Exit 4 Knight.*]

[F]*Enter* OSWALD.[F]

O you, sir, you, come you hither, sir: who am I, sir?

OSWALD   My lady's father.

LEAR   My lady's father? My lord's knave, you whoreson
dog, you slave, you cur!

OSWALD   I am none of these, my lord, I beseech your   80
pardon.

LEAR   Do you bandy looks with me, you rascal?   [*Strikes him.*]

OSWALD   I'll not be strucken, my lord.

KENT [*Trips him.*]   Nor tripped neither, you base football
player.   85

LEAR   I thank thee, fellow. Thou serv'st me and I'll love
thee.

KENT   Come, sir, [F]arise, away,[F] I'll teach you differences.
Away, away; if you will measure your lubber's length
again, tarry; but away, [F]go to,[F] have you wisdom? [F]So![F]   90
[*Pushes him out.*]

82 **bandy looks** exchange glances (*bandy* meant striking the ball to and fro in games such as tennis). It would be insolent of Oswald to stare directly at the King.

83 **strucken** another act of violence on Lear's part; see 1.3.1 and n., and Introduction, pp. 64–6.

84 **tripped** Oswald is sent sprawling, and then yanked to his feet, as is made clear by 88–90.

84–5 **base football player** football was a lower-class game of 'beastly fury and extreme violence', to be 'utterly abjected of all noblemen' (Sir Thomas Elyot, *The Governor* (1531), Everyman edn, 92, cited Cam[1]), in contrast to tennis, 'a good exercise for young men', which lies behind the word *bandy*, 82.

88 **differences** distinctions of rank

89 **lubber's** clumsy lout's

90 **go to** 'come, come' (in modern idiom)

74 SD] *Hunter (Dyce)*   75 SD] *this edn (Hunter and Dyce)*   75.1] *F (Enter Steward, after sir?, 76);
not in Q*   80 these] F; this *Q*   80–1 your pardon] *F;* you pardon me *Q*   82 SD] *Rowe*
83 strucken] *F;* struck *Q*   84 SD] *Rowe (Tripping up his heels)*   90 have you] *F;* you have *Q;* if you
have *Oxf (Blayney)*   wisdom? So!] *Theobald;* wisedome, so. *F;* wisedome *Q*   90.1] *Theobald subst.*

LEAR   Now, ᶠmyᶠ friendly knave, I thank thee. There's
 earnest of thy service.   [*Gives him money.*]

Enter FOOL.

FOOL   Let me hire him too; [*to Kent, holding out his cap*]
 here's my coxcomb.

LEAR   How now, my pretty knave, how dost thou?   95

FOOL [*to Kent*]   Sirrah, you were best take my coxcomb.

KENT   Why, fool?

FOOL   Why? For taking one's part that's out of favour.
 Nay, an thou canst not smile as the wind sits, thou'lt
 catch cold shortly. There, take my coxcomb. Why, this 100
 fellow has banished two on's daughters and did the
 third a blessing against his will – if thou follow him,
 thou must needs wear my coxcomb. [*to Lear*] How now,
 nuncle? Would I had two coxcombs and two daughters.

LEAR   Why, my boy?   105

---

92 **earnest of** earnest-money, a first
payment for
 SD *Enter* FOOL So in Q and F, but it
makes sense if the Fool enters in time
to see Kent's *service* in tripping Oswald
95 **pretty knave** fine lad. *Knave* could be
used of a boy or an adult male
servant; for *pretty* compare 182
96 **coxcomb** professional fool's cap, with
a crest like a cock's comb
97 *so Q; '*Lear*. Why my Boy', F, an error
anticipating 105?
99–100 **an . . . shortly** a cryptic way of
saying 'if you cannot please those in
power, you'll soon suffer for it'
100–2 **Why . . . will** The Fool harps in
this scene on the inversion of order
Lear has brought about; *banished*
echoes Kent's 'banishment is here',
1.1.182, and Lear's curses on her

helped to make Cordelia Queen of
France.
101 **on's** of his; a common usage (Abbott,
182)
104 **nuncle** a variant of 'uncle', contracted from 'mine uncle' (as 'Ned'
from 'Edward', etc.). The initial 'n'
could be associated with 'n' in 'nothing' and 'never', words that reverberate in the play, so perhaps here rather
suggesting a negative, 'not uncle'.
105 **boy** a term of familiar address, especially to a servant, which had no necessary reference to age. The Fool has
been played both as very young and as
an old man; his wisdom has seemed to
many to spring from maturity; see
Rosenberg, 106–7. He calls Lear 'boy'
at 134.

---

92 SD] *Capell subst.* 93 SD *to Kent*] *Collier* SD *holding . . . cap*] *this edn (Rowe)* 96 SD] *this
edn (Oxf)* 97 KENT Why, fool?] *Q; Lear.* Why my Boy? *F* 98 Why? For] *F;* Why for *Q* one's]
*Q2, F (*ones*);* on's *Q* 101 has] *F;* hath *Q* did] *F;* done *Q* 103 SD] *this edn*

FOOL   If I gave them all my living, I'd keep my coxcombs
         myself. There's mine; beg another of thy daughters.

LEAR   Take heed, sirrah, the whip.

FOOL   Truth's a dog ^Q^that^Q^ must to kennel; he must be
         whipped out, when the Lady Brach may stand by the   110
         fire and stink.

LEAR   A pestilent gall to me.

FOOL   Sirrah, I'll teach thee a speech.

LEAR   Do.

FOOL   Mark it, nuncle: 115
                  Have more than thou showest,
                  Speak less than thou knowest,
                  Lend less than thou owest,
                  Ride more than thou goest,
                  Learn more than thou trowest,   120
                  Set less than thou throwest,
                  Leave thy drink and thy whore

106–7 **If . . . myself** echoing the proverb,
'He that gives all before he dies is a
fool' (Dent, A187, cited by Cam¹)

106 **living** estates, lands; compare
1.2.181

108 **whip** It seems that Fools were liable
to be whipped if they overstepped the
mark; in a letter of March 1604–5,
Dudley Carleton notes: 'There was
great Execution done lately upon *Stone
the Fool*, who was well whipt in
Bridewell for a blasphemous Speech,
That there went sixty Fools into Spaine
besides my Lord Admiral', who had
travelled there to confirm peace with
that country (Ralph Winwood,
Memorials of State Affairs, 3 vols
(1725), 2.52).

110 **Brach** bitch. Truth cast out may suggest Cordelia, Kent or the Fool, while
'the Lady Brach' welcomed in might
refer to Goneril or Regan.

112 **gall** source of irritation. Is Lear
referring to the Fool, Cordelia, or
both?

113 **Sirrah** normally used by those in
authority to address inferiors or boys,
as Lear does at 172. The Fool addresses Kent as 'Sirrah' at 96, and Rowe,
who thought the Fool would not risk
such insolence to Lear, added here the
SD '*To Kent*'.

116–20 **Have . . . trowest** The lines
sound proverbial, and Dent, A202,
cites 'Speak not all you know, do not all
you can, believe not all you hear' as
similar.

118 **owest** ownest (the original meaning
of 'owe')

119 **goest** walkest (the original meaning
of 'go')

120 **trowest** believest; see note to 116–20

121 don't stake all on a single throw (of
the dice)

---

106 all my] *F*; any *Q*   110 the Lady] *F*; Ladie oth'e *Q*; Lady the *Steevens*   112 gall] *F*; gull *Q*
115 nuncle] *F*; vncle *Q*

And keep in-a-door,
And thou shalt have more
Than two tens to a score. 125

KENT   This is nothing, fool.

FOOL   Then ᶠ'tisᶠ like the breath of an unfee'd lawyer, you
gave me nothing for't. [*to Lear*] Can you make no use of
nothing, nuncle?

LEAR   Why no, boy; nothing can be made out of nothing. 130

FOOL [*to Kent*]   Prithee tell him, so much the rent of his
land comes to; he will not believe a fool.

LEAR   A bitter fool.

FOOL   Dost ᶠthouᶠ know the difference, my boy, between a
bitter fool and a sweet one? 135

LEAR   No, lad, teach me.

�۹FOOL

That lord that counselled thee to give away thy land,
Come place him here by me; do thou for him stand.

---

123 **in-a-door** indoors
124–5 **have . . . score** save money and
make a profit
126–30 **nothing . . . nothing** recalling
1.1.87–90 and 1.2.31–5; see also 178
and 186 below
127–8 **like . . . for't** Lawyers were
proverbially mercenary: 'A lawyer will
not plead but for a fee' (Dent, L125).
128 **use** profit, interest
130 **nothing . . . nothing** proverbial;
Dent, N285
131–2 **so . . . to** Lear has given away his
land, the source of his *living* (106) and
power. There may also be a pun on *rent*
= torn, alluding to the division of the
kingdom.
136 **lad** serving-man, man of low birth
(with no reference to his age)
137–48 ***FOOL . . . snatching** a passage
found only in Q. It may have been

omitted from F because of censorship
(see 146 below and n.), or because it
merely continues the Fool's attack on
Lear (a) for giving away his land and
(b) by showing him to be a fool. It also
contains the only explicit reference to
the Fool wearing the motley of the
professional court Fool, and perhaps
using his bauble to represent the *bitter*
fool (133, 135); see 1.5.49–50 and n. It
would seem that F should also have
omitted 134–6, as Cam² does. See
Introduction, p. 51. Allan R. Shickman,
'The Fool's Mirror in *King Lear*',
ELR, 21 (1991), 75–86, argues for an
association of Fools with mirrors, and
thinks the Fool here hands his looking-
glass to Lear, who sees himself in it,
'The other found out there'.
137–40 The jingle 'proves' that Lear is
really the bitter fool.

---

123 in-a-door] *Capell;* in a doore *Q, F*   126 SP KENT] *F; Lear. Q*   128 SD] *this edn*
129 nuncle] *F;* vncle *Q*   131 SD] *Rowe*   134 thou] *Q2, F; not in Q*   135 one] *F;* foole *Q*

The sweet and bitter fool will presently appear,
The one in motley here, the other found out there.   140
LEAR   Dost thou call me fool, boy?
FOOL   All thy other titles thou hast given away; that thou
wast born with.
KENT   This is not altogether fool, my lord.
FOOL   No, faith, lords and great men will not let me; if I   145
had a monopoly out, they would have part on't; and
ladies too, they will not let me have all the fool to
myself, they'll be snatching.[Q] Nuncle, give me an egg
and I'll give thee two crowns.
LEAR   What two crowns shall they be?   150
FOOL   Why, after I have cut the egg i'the middle and eat
up the meat, the two crowns of the egg. When thou
clovest thy crown i'the middle and gav'st away both
parts, thou bor'st thine ass on thy back o'er the dirt.
Thou hadst little wit in thy bald crown when thou   155
gav'st thy golden one away. If I speak like myself in

---

139 **presently** at once
140 **there** pointing to Lear, or offering his bauble to him?
146 **monopoly** exclusive privilege of trading in a commodity, or with a particular country. James I, like Elizabeth before him, granted monopolies as a way of rewarding courtiers, but it was only late in his reign that the number of awards grew so large as to lead to a parliamentary campaign against them in 1620–1 (Lockyer, 190–6). This is when censorship, or self-censorship, might have led to the cutting of these lines. See Introduction, p. 130.
146 **on't** of it (Abbott, 182)
147 **fool** quibbling on the idea of folly and *fool* as a dessert made with cream and eggs, a kind of custard
149–54 **crowns . . . parts** See Introduction, p. 13, for the importance of

Lear's crown in the play.
152 **meat** edible part
153 **clovest . . . middle** divided the kingdom
154 **thou . . . dirt** In the fable attributed to Poggio Bracciolini (1380–1459) by Roger L'Estrange, *Fables of Æsop and other eminent Mythologists* (1692), 329, and also printed in *Tales and quicke answeres* (1532), an old man riding his ass tries to please everyone, and when someone says he is overloading the poor animal, he carries his ass to market; everyone laughs at him, and in anger he throws the ass in the river. The moral is that in trying to please all he pleases no one. The fable also, as Cam[2] notes, provides another image of the inversion of order.
156–7 **If . . . so** If I speak (truth) like a fool in saying this, let him (Lear) be

---

146 out] *Q;* on't *Pope*   146–7 on't; and ladies] *Capell;* an't, and lodes *Qu;* an't, and Ladies *Qc;* on't and loads *Collier*   148 Nuncle . . . egg] *F;* giue me an egge Nuncle *Q*   153 crown] *Q;* Crownes *F* 154 bor'st] *F (*boar'st*);* borest *Q*   thine . . . thy] *F;* thy asse at'h *Q;* thy asse on thy *Q2*

this, let him be whipped that first finds it so.

[*Sings.*] Fools had ne'er less grace in a year,
    For wise men are grown foppish,
      And know not how their wits to wear,   160
    Their manners are so apish.

LEAR   When were you wont to be so full of songs, sirrah?

FOOL   I have used it, nuncle, e'er since thou mad'st thy daughters thy mothers; for when thou gav'st them the rod and putt'st down thine own breeches,   165

[*Sings.*] Then they for sudden joy did weep
    And I for sorrow sung,
      That such a king should play bo-peep,
    And go the fools among.

Prithee, nuncle, keep a schoolmaster that can teach thy   170
fool to lie; I would fain learn to lie.

whipped who first finds it to be foolish. See 108–10 and 175–6, where the Fool is threatened with the whip for speaking truth. Wiles, 190, suggests the Fool may have plucked off his cap to reveal his own *bald crown* (155), shaven as a precaution against lice.

158–9 **had . . . foppish** were never so out of favour, because wise men have become foolish (and taken their place)

160 ***to wear** to show off, display. Q has 'doe weare', presumably wear out or deteriorate.

161 **Their . . . apish** wise men are behaving like fools; *apish* = absurdly imitative

162 **When . . . songs** implying that the Fool did not usually sing? He may have spoken most of the rhyming passages, like his 'speech' at 116–25; see 2.2.238–43 and n.

163 **used it** made a habit of singing

163–5 **mad'st . . . breeches** See

Introduction, p. 39 on the significance of the image of Lear as a child, and his daughters as mothers. The Fool varies the proverb, 'He has made a rod for his own (tail or) back'; Dent, R153.

166–7 **Then . . . sung** adapting the first two lines of a ballad of John Careless, a Protestant martyr, printed in 1564 and 1586, 'Some men for sudden joy do weep / And some in sorrow sing'; see H. E. Rollins, *MLR*, 15 (1920), 87–90. Manuscript notation of music for it in a book of 1609 was noted by Peter Seng, *SQ*, 9 (1958), 583–5, and is reprinted by Sternfeld, 175–7.

168 **bo-peep** a game in which a child alternately hides and peeps out unexpectedly in order to frighten or excite (the modern 'peek-a-boo'), but also associated with playing the fool (Dent, B540)

170 **Prithee** I pray thee

158, 166 SD] *Rowe*   158 grace] *F;* wit *Q*   160 And] *F;* They *Q*   to] *F;* doe *Q*   163 e'er] *F* *(*ere*);* euer *Q*   164 mothers] *F;* mother *Q*   169 fools] *Q;* Foole *F*   170 Prithee] *Q (*prethe*), F (*Pry'thy*)*   171 learn to] *Qc, Q2, F;* learne *Qu*

LEAR   An you lie, ᶠsirrah,ᶠ we'll have you whipped.

FOOL   I marvel what kin thou and thy daughters are. They'll have me whipped for speaking true, thou'lt have me whipped for lying, and sometimes I am whipped   175 for holding my peace. I had rather be any kind o'thing than a fool, and yet I would not be thee, nuncle. Thou hast pared thy wit o'both sides and left nothing i'the middle. Here comes one o'the parings.

Enter GONERIL.

LEAR

How now, daughter? What makes that frontlet on?   180 �QMethinksQ you are too much of late i'the frown.

FOOL   Thou wast a pretty fellow when thou hadst no need to care for her frowning. Now thou art an O without a figure; I am better than thou art now. I am a fool, thou art nothing. [*to Goneril*] Yes, forsooth, I will hold my   185 tongue; so your face bids me, though you say nothing. Mum, mum!

He that keeps nor crust nor crumb,
Weary of all, shall want some.

172 **An** if

176 **peace** Does the Fool draw attention to his conspicuous codpiece, or covering of his genitals, to point up a quibble here? See 3.2.27–30 and n.

178 **wit** intelligence

180 **frontlet** frown; strictly an ornamental band worn on the forehead. Cam² suggests Goneril may have sported a bandage, for she has informed Lear that she is sick, at 1.3.9, and 49 above.

181 **Methinks**   it seems to me

183–4 **O . . . figure** cipher, or zero, with

no number before it to give it value

184–5 **thou art nothing** So, after playing in various ways on the word, the Fool finally reduces Lear to nothing; see 126–30 and 178 above.

185 **forsooth** truly

187 **Mum, mum!** Hush, hush! (as in 'mum's the word')

188–9 figuring Lear as one who, weary of responsibility (see 1.1.37–40), has given away everything (his whole loaf, crust and crumb), and will find himself in need

172 An] *Knight;* And *Q*, *F;* If *Q2*   174 thou'lt] *F;* thou wilt *Q*   175 sometimes] *F;* sometime *Q* 176 o'thing] *F;* of thing *Q*   178 o'both] *F;* a both *Q*   181 of late] *F;* alate *Q*   183 frowning. Now thou] *F;* (frowning, now thou); frowne, thou, thou *Qu, Q2;* frowne, now thou *Qc*   185 SD] *Pope*   188 nor crust] *F;* neither crust *Q*   nor crumb] *Q* (nor crum); not crum *F*

[*Points to Lear.*] That's a shelled peascod.   190

GONERIL

　　Not only, sir, this your all-licensed fool,
　　But other of your insolent retinue
　　Do hourly carp and quarrel, breaking forth
　　In rank and not to be endured riots. Sir,
　　I had thought by making this well known unto you   195
　　To have found a safe redress, but now grow fearful
　　By what yourself too late have spoke and done,
　　That you protect this course and put ᶠitᶠ on
　　By your allowance; which if you should, the fault
　　Would not scape censure, nor the redresses sleep,   200
　　Which in the tender of a wholesome weal
　　Might in their working do you that offence
　　Which else were shame, that then necessity
　　Will call discreet proceeding.

FOOL　　For you know, nuncle,   205
　　　　The hedge-sparrow fed the cuckoo so long
　　　　That it's had it head bit off by it young.

---

190 **shelled peascod** an emptied pod, and so nothing; but with overtones of sexual impotence, reinforced by the echo of 'codpiece'; see 3.2.27–30 and n.
191 **all-licensed** allowed to do and say what he pleases
194 **rank** violent, gross
　　endured endurèd
196 **safe redress** sure remedy or reformation
197 **too late** all too recently
198 **put it on** encourage it
199 **allowance** approval
201 **tender . . . weal** tender concern for a well-ordered society
202–4 **Might . . . proceeding** The restraints necessary to effect *redresses*

(200) might be harmful to you, which would in other circumstances be disgraceful, but now, because such actions are necessary, they will be seen as judicious. Some have seen Goneril in this scene as showing a 'calculated venom' (Hunter), but she may also be played as having a legitimate grievance, and as veiling her threat in abstractions and obscure syntax in an attempt to be easy on Lear; she is now queen of half of Britain, concerned with order and rule. How we see her on stage may depend on what sense, if any, a director gives that Lear's knights are riotous and *disordered* (233); see 7.1–2 and n.
207 ***it's . . . young** F, perhaps anxious about the repeated 'it', changes 'it had'

190 SD] *Johnson*　192 other] *Q*, *F;* others *Johnson*　194 not . . . endured riots. Sir,] *as Capell;* (not . . . indured riots,) Sir *Q;* (not . . . endur'd) riots Sir. *F*　200 redresses] *F;* redresse *Q* 203 Which] *F;* that *Q*　204 Will] *F;* must *Q*　proceeding] *F;* proceedings *Q*　205 know] *F;* trow *Q*　207 it's had it] *F;* it had it *Q;* it had its *F3*　by it] *F;* beit *Q;* by its *F3*

So out went the candle and we were left darkling.

LEAR   Are you our daughter?

GONERIL

^QCome, sir,^Q   210

I would you would make use of your good wisdom,

Whereof I know you are fraught, and put away

These dispositions, which of late transport you

From what you rightly are.

FOOL   May not an ass know when the cart draws the   215
horse? Whoop, Jug, I love thee.

LEAR

Does any here know me? ^QWhy^Q, this is not Lear.

Does Lear walk thus, speak thus? Where are his eyes?

Either his notion weakens, ^Qor^Q his discernings are

lethargied – Ha! ^Qsleeping or^Q waking? ^QSure^Q 'tis not   220

so. Who is it that can tell me who I am?

(Q) to 'it's had'; 'it' was commonly used as the possessive, = 'its', as in the other two occurrences in this line, and all three may be meant, as Cam[2] suggests, to represent baby-talk that 'heightens the grotesqueness'. The young cuckoo, notorious for its greed, is usually imaged, as at *1H4* 5.1.60–6, as taking over the nest of the sparrow, which leaves or is driven out; the Fool makes the image more savage, implying a kind of cannibalism on Goneril's part.

208 **darkling** in the dark. Does the Fool here perceptively anticipate the afflictions soon to come (see 243–6), or does he provoke them by his hatred of Goneril?

212 **fraught** supplied

213 **dispositions** inclinations, tendencies
transport you carry you away emotionally

215–16 **May . . . horse?** Even a fool can see the inversion of order in Goneril's behaviour to her father. The Fool keeps returning to this theme; see 100–2 and n., 163–5 and 226.

216 **Jug** Joan. It may be that Goneril makes a face at the Fool, or moves as if to threaten him, and this is his evasive response.

217 **this . . . Lear** Lear's dawning recognition of a gap between his role (as king) and his identity (as human being) begins here.

219–20 **Either . . . lethargied** either his intellect weakens or his powers of discrimination are dulled

220–1 ***Ha! . . . so** It may be that 'Lear pinches or shakes himself to be sure he is not sleeping or dreaming' (Cam[2]), and to convince himself his perceptions are normal; compare 4.7.55–7. The sense in Q (see textual notes) is

---

211 your] *F;* that *Q*   213 which] *F;* that *Q*   transport] *F;* transforme *Q*   217 Does] *F;* Doth *Q*
218 Does] *F;* doth *Q*   219 notion weakens] *F;* notion, weaknes, or *Q*   220 lethargied – Ha!]
Rowe; Lethargied. Ha! *F;* lethergie, sleeping, or *Q*

ᶠFOOLᶠ Lear's shadow.

ᵠLEAR I would learn that, for by the marks of sovereignty,
knowledge and reason, I should be false persuaded I
had daughters.   225

FOOL Which they will make an obedient father.ᵠ

LEAR Your name, fair gentlewoman?

GONERIL
This admiration, sir, is much o'the savour
Of other your new pranks. I do beseech you
ᶠToᶠ understand my purposes aright: 230
As you are old and reverend, should be wise.
Here do you keep a hundred knights and squires,
Men so disordered, so debauched and bold,
That this our court, infected with their manners,
Shows like a riotous inn. Epicurism and lust   235
Makes ᶠitᶠ more like a tavern or a brothel
Than a graced palace. The shame itself doth speak

different; there Lear thinks his *discern-ings* are dulled, 'sleeping or waking', but then cries, 'ha! sure tis not so'. Q's extra words turn into prose what F prints as blank verse: 'Are Lethargied – Ha! Waking? 'Tis not so? / Who is it that can tell me who I am?'

222 *FOOL . . . shadow a significant change in F from Q, in which Lear speaks these words. Q is simpler, as Lear calls himself a *shadow* or semblance in contrast to the substance or real person. In giving the words to the Fool, F is more complex: does the Fool mean both that he is Lear's shadow (or the mirror-image in which Lear may see himself as a fool), and that Lear has become a shadow of his former self, a mere appearance of a king lacking authority? In Q Lear at once (as shown in 223–6, omitted from F) becomes conscious of a split in himself which in

F is as yet marked only by the Fool's acerbic comments.

223 **sovereignty** The phrase in Q suggests that Lear displays some insignia of royalty, as if he were still King.

228 **admiration** (pretended) astonishment
savour nature or character

229 **Of . . . pranks** of your other new mischievous tricks

233 **disordered** disorderly
debauched 'debosh'd' (F) was a variant spelling that indicates how the word was pronounced.
bold impudent

234 **our court** Goneril thinks of herself as Queen, and speaks in the royal plural; see 202–4 and n.

235 **Epicurism** gluttony

237 **graced** dignified
shame disgrace (to me)

226 they will] *Q3;* they, will *Q*   228 This] *F;* Come sir, this *Q*   sir, is] *F;* is *Q*   232 a hundred] *F;* a 100. *Q;* one hundred *Q2*   233 debauched] *Pope, after F (*debosh'd*);* deboyst *Q*
236 Makes it] *F;* make *Q*   or a] *F;* or *Q*   237 graced] *F;* great *Q*

For instant remedy. Be then desired,
By her that else will take the thing she begs,
A little to disquantity your train,   240
And the remainders that shall still depend
To be such men as may besort your age,
Which know themselves, and you.

LEAR   Darkness and devils!
Saddle my horses; call my train together.
Degenerate bastard, I'll not trouble thee: 245
Yet have I left a daughter.

GONERIL

You strike my people, and your disordered rabble
Make servants of their betters.

Enter ALBANY.

LEAR

Woe that too late repents! – ^QO sir, are you come?^Q
Is it your will? Speak, sir. – Prepare my horses.   250
                                                              [*Exit a Knight.*]

238 **desired** requested
240 **disquantity . . . train** reduce the
  number of your followers
241 **remainders** rest, those who remain
  depend be dependent on you
242 **besort** befit (Shakespeare's coinage,
  used also as a noun at *Oth* 1.3.238)
243 **Which . . . you** who know how they
  and you should behave; see 1.1.295
243–5 **Darkness . . . thee** Lear erupts in
  an outburst of anger that takes control
  of him, just as he had done with
  Cordelia in the opening scene. 'Saddle
  my horses' can be taken as prompting
  the knights to wreck the palace, as in
  Peter Brook's film version; or as a signal for one or more attendants to rush
  out; or, since Lear repeats the order at

250, as an order ignored by followers
  shocked by the turn of events.
245 **bastard** equating her with Edmund.
  In his anger Lear imagines Goneril,
  and later Regan (see 2.2.319–20), as
  illegitimate; by contrast, Cordelia
  seems entirely her father's child, not
  associated with a mother; see
  Adelman, 108–9.
247 **people** attendants
249 **Woe** woe to him
249–50 *O sir . . . sir. 'O sir, are you
  come?' (Q, in lines printed as prose)
  may have been omitted from F by
  oversight; this phrase – together with
  either Q's 'that wee' or F's substitution
  'Speak, sir.' – makes two lines of verse.

238 then] *F;* thou *Q*   241 remainders] *F;* remainder *Q*   243 Which] *F;* that *Q;* and *Q2*
248.1 ALBANY] *F; Duke. Q*   249 Woe . . . repents] *F;* We . . . repent's *Q;* We . . . repent's vs *Q2*
250 Speak, sir] *F;* that wee *Q*   my] *F;* any *Q*   SD] *this edn; Exit one or more Oxf*

Ingratitude, thou marble-hearted fiend,
More hideous when thou show'st thee in a child
Than the sea-monster.

^FALBANY
    Pray, sir, be patient.

LEAR^F [*to Goneril*]   Detested kite, thou liest.
    My train are men of choice and rarest parts   255
    That all particulars of duty know,
    And in the most exact regard support
    The worships of their name. O most small fault,
    How ugly didst thou in Cordelia show,
    Which like an engine wrenched my frame of nature   260
    From the fixed place, drew from my heart all love
    And added to the gall. O Lear, Lear^F, Lear^F!
    [*striking his head*] Beat at this gate that let thy folly in
    And thy dear judgement out. Go, go, my people.
                    [*Exeunt Kent, Knights and attendants.*]

---

253 **sea-monster** Sea-monsters abound in legend, as in the biblical accounts of Leviathan (see e.g. Psalms 74.14–15), and in classical myth, as in the story of Hercules rescuing Hesione, daughter of the Trojan Laomedon, from a sea-monster to which, by command of Neptune, she was about to be sacrificed (see *MV* 3.2.54–7).

254 *****ALBANY . . . patient** apparently an addition in F, like 321, strengthening Albany's role; see Introduction, p. 142. The phrase is an extra-metrical interruption in the flow of Lear's speech. This first call for patience, God's medicine to heal grief and sorrow, and 'the virtue that alone can offer effective medicine to cure intemperate passion' (Hoeniger, 325), is echoed later in the play, most notably when Lear acknowledges his need for it at 2.2.459–60, and see also 3.2.37.

kite a bird of prey associated by Shakespeare with 'meanness, cruelty and death' (Armstrong, 12), and listed in Leviticus, 11.14, as 'an abomination'

255 **parts** personal qualities

257–8 **in . . . name** are punctilious in every particular to uphold the dignity of their reputations

260–1 **like . . . place** like a lever or implement wrenched my natural affection away from where it should be centred. The image is of levering or tearing a structure from its foundations.

262 **gall** bitterness

263 **folly** acknowledging at last what the Fool has been pointing out to him, as at 98–107 (Q and F) and 137–40 (Q)

264 **Go . . . people** Perhaps Lear's remaining attendants, including Kent, leave the stage here; Lear and the Fool must remain on stage.

---

254 SD] *Rowe*   liest] *F;* list *Q*   255 are] *F;* and *Q*   260 Which] *F;* that *Q*   263 SD] *Pope*
264 SD] *this edn; Knights and Kent go Cam¹*

ALBANY

 My lord, I am guiltless as I am ignorant   265
 ^FOf what hath moved you.^F

LEAR   It may be so, my lord.

 Hear, Nature, hear, dear goddess, ^Fhear^F:
 Suspend thy purpose if thou didst intend
 To make this creature fruitful.
 Into her womb convey sterility,   270
 Dry up in her the organs of increase,
 And from her derogate body never spring
 A babe to honour her. If she must teem,
 Create her child of spleen, that it may live
 And be a thwart disnatured torment to her. 275
 Let it stamp wrinkles in her brow of youth,
 With cadent tears fret channels in her cheeks,
 Turn all her mother's pains and benefits
 To laughter and contempt, that she may feel
 How sharper than a serpent's tooth it is   280
 To have a thankless child. Away, away!

        ^F*Exeunt*^F [*Lear and Fool*].

ALBANY

 Now gods that we adore, whereof comes this?

GONERIL

 Never afflict yourself to know more of it,

---

267 **Nature** recalling Edmund's appeal to Nature at 1.2.1, but with a difference; Lear invokes Nature as a creative force, but his horrible curse would make nature unnatural (*disnatured*, 275), and almost aligns him with Edmund
272 **derogate** degenerate
273 **teem** give birth
274 **spleen** violent ill-temper
275 **thwart disnatured** churlish unnatural
277 **cadent** falling

fret gnaw, wear away
278 **benefits** pleasures or advantages gained from having a child
281 SD *Exeunt* not in Q; F has '*Exit*', and possibly Lear goes off alone here, but I think the Fool stays close to him. Cam² has all Lear's train leave the stage at this point, but Alexander and Duthie seem to me right in sending off Kent and the knights at 264.
283 **afflict . . . know** try to find out what will pain you

---

265+ SP ALBANY] *F (Alb.); Duke. Q* 267 Hear] *F;* harke *Q* 275 thwart disnatured] *F;* thourt disuetur'd *Q* 277 cadent] *F;* accent *Q* 279 feel] *Q2, F;* feele, that she may feele *Q* 281 Away, away] *F;* goe, goe, my people *Q* SD] *this edn (Oxf); Exit. F; not in Q* 283 more of it] *F;* the cause *Q*

But let his disposition have that scope
As dotage gives it.   285

^F*Enter* LEAR^F [*followed by the* FOOL].

LEAR
What, fifty of my followers at a clap?
Within a fortnight?
ALBANY   What's the matter, sir?
LEAR
I'll tell thee. [*to Goneril*] Life and death, I am ashamed
That thou hast power to shake my manhood thus,
That these hot tears, which break from me perforce,   290
Should make thee worth them. Blasts and fogs upon
      ^Fthee^F!
Th'untented woundings of a father's curse
Pierce every sense about thee. Old fond eyes,
Beweep this cause again, I'll pluck ye out,

---

284 **disposition** inclination, mood, as at 213
284–5 **that ... it** that freedom of action senility allows, i.e. 'violent talk and little action' (Hunter). In F her words here are contradicted by 315–20, which seem to mark a change in Shakespeare's conception of Goneril. *As* = that.
286 **at a clap** at a stroke, at once
286–7 **fifty ... fortnight** The 'bold foreshortening' (Hunter) of the action (Lear has been gone for only four lines) makes it seem that Goneril, who has been on stage all the time, gave this order before confronting her father in this scene, though she spoke only of reducing the number by 'a little' at

240. A fortnight may be the time allowed for their dismissal, for she refers to a hundred knights at 315 and 326 (F), or the time Lear has spent with her so far.
290–1 **That ... them** that you should appear to deserve these hot tears that pour from me uncontrollably (*perforce*); see 2.2.465–7 for the further unmanning of Lear by tears or *women's weapons*.
291 **Blasts and fogs** foul air bearing infection and disease
292 **untented woundings** wounds too deep to be cleansed with a roll of lint, or *tent* (*OED sb.* 3).
293 **fond** foolish
294 **Beweep** if you weep for

---

285 As] *F; that Q*   SD] *this edn (Oxf); Enter Lear. F; not in Q*   288 SD] *Theobald*   290 which] *F; that Q*   291 thee worth them.] *F; the worst Q*   292 Th'untented] *Qc, F; the vntender Qu;* thee! / Untented *Oxf*   293 Pierce] *Qc, F; peruse Qu*   thee] *F; the Q*   294 ye] *F; you Q*

And cast you with the waters that you loose   295
To temper clay. ^QYea, is't come to this?^Q
^FHa? Let it be so.^F I have another daughter,
Who I am sure is kind and comfortable:
When she shall hear this of thee with her nails
She'll flay thy wolvish visage. Thou shalt find   300
That I'll resume the shape which thou dost think
I have cast off for ever. ^QThou shalt, I warrant thee.^Q ^F*Exit*^F.

GONERIL   Do you mark that, ^Qmy lord^Q?

ALBANY

I cannot be so partial, Goneril,
To the great love I bear you –

GONERIL   ^FPray you, content.^F   305
^QCome, sir, no more.^Q ^FWhat, Oswald, ho?^F

[*to the Fool*] You, ^Fsir,^F more knave than fool, after
    your master.

FOOL   Nuncle Lear, nuncle Lear, tarry, ^Qand^Q take the
    fool with ^Fthee:^F

---

295 **loose**   release, pour forth (or possibly 'lose', commonly spelled 'loose'; see Introduction, p. 150)
296 **temper clay**   mix with earth
297 ***Ha? ... so**   often said to be substituted in F (so Cam²) for 'Yea, is't come to this?' (Q), but, if so, I think (as do Duthie and Stone) by mistake, for the phrase in F is a natural sequel to that in Q, and completes the blank verse lines. Q is here printed as prose, and so gives no guide to lineation.
298 **kind and comfortable**   affectionate and comforting; compare 2.2.162
301 **shape**   Lear is still thinking of himself as King, hence Goneril's reaction.
302–3 ***I have ... lord?**   Lear's speech is printed as prose in Q, and ends 'thou shalt I warrant thee.' (*warrant* = assure or promise), a phrase not in F;

Q also adds *my lord* in 303. F prints Lear's speech as verse, and there Goneril's 'Do you mark that?' completes the half-line on which Lear exits, 'I have cast off for ever.'
303 **mark**   take note of
304–5 **partial ... / To**   biased because of (Hunter)
305–6, 320, 328–9   *The changes here between Q and F may be due to reworking and represent alternatives, if 'Pray you, content' is a substitution for 'Come, sir, no more'. Goneril's cry, 'What, Oswald, ho!' (F, 329) may have been intended as a replacement for his response, 'Here madam.' (Q, 328).
305 **Pray ... content**   Goneril snubs Albany by cutting him off in mid-sentence, though less fiercely than in Q.

---

295 cast you] *F;* you cast *Q*   loose] *F;* make *Q;* lose *F3*   297 I . . . another] *F;* yet have I left a *Q*
298 Who] *F;* whom *Q*   300 flay] *Q, F* (flea); fley *Q2*   302 SD] *Q2, F; not in Q*   305 you –]
Theobald; you, *Q;* you. *F*   307 SD] *Johnson*

A fox when one has caught her,   310
And such a daughter,
Should sure to the slaughter,
If my cap would buy a halter;
So the fool follows after.   ᶠ*Exit*ᶠ.

GONERIL
ᶠThis man hath had good counsel – a hundred knights!   315
'Tis politic, and safe, to let him keep
At point a hundred knights! Yes, that on every dream,
Each buzz, each fancy, each complaint, dislike,
He may enguard his dotage with their powers
And hold our lives in mercy. Oswald, I say!   320

ALBANY   Well, you may fear too far.

GONERIL   Safer than trust too far.
Let me still take away the harms I fear,
Not fear still to be taken. I know his heart;
What he hath uttered I have writ my sister.   325
If she sustain him and his hundred knights

313–14 **halter . . . after** closer to true rhymes with *slaughter* than they seem now (see Dobson, §423); *halter* = both a rope to lead her like a beast, and a hangman's noose

315–27 **This . . . unfitness** – an addition in F that seems to fit in with other changes to Goneril's role, and makes somewhat more plausible her treatment of her father; see Introduction, p. 144. Another line is added for the cautious Albany.

315 **This . . . counsel** putting Lear in his place as a mere man (see 301 and n.), and pouring scorn on his *good* (ironically = bad) judgement. *Counsel* is used in the Bible to mean 'judgement', as at Job, 12.13, 'he [i.e. God] hathe counsel and vnderstanding' (Geneva version).

316 **politic** prudent. Goneril is, of course, being ironic, as at 315.

317 **At point** in readiness, armed

317, 326 **hundred knights** At 286 Lear has been told to send away fifty of his followers, but here, in lines found only in F, Goneril speaks as though he is to retain a hundred. Shakespeare seems to have changed his conception of Goneril; see 284–5 and n.

318 **buzz** rumour

319 **enguard** protect; 'en-' is intensive, as in 'encircle'

320 **in mercy** in his power (= at his mercy)

323–4 **still . . . still** always, continually

324 **to be taken** to be seized or afflicted (by such harms)

325 foreshortening the action again, as at 286–7. Oswald has not been present to hear what Lear uttered, and no instructions have been given to him, though Goneril said she would write at 1.3.26. The effect dramatically is to

320 Oswald, I say!] *F;* What Oswald, ho. *Oswald* Here Madam. *Q, after 314*

When I have showed th'unfitness –^F

^F*Enter* OSWALD.^F

^QOSWALD   Here, madam.^Q

GONERIL   ^FHow now, Oswald?^F What, have you writ
    that letter to my sister?   330

OSWALD   Ay, madam.

GONERIL

Take you some company and away to horse.
Inform her full of my particular fear,
And thereto add such reasons of your own
As may compact it more. Get you gone,   335
And hasten your return.   [*Exit Oswald.*]
                    No, no, my lord,
This milky gentleness and course of yours,
Though I condemn not, yet, under pardon,
You are much more attasked for want of wisdom
Than praised for harmful mildness.   340

ALBANY

How far your eyes may pierce I cannot tell;
Striving to better, oft we mar what's well.

---

hint that Goneril has planned more in
advance than the scene shows. Oswald
is her steward, controller of the household, and it would be appropriate for
him to transact business on her behalf,
as her confidential agent.

333 **full** fully
    particular private, special
335 **compact** consolidate, confirm
337 **milky . . . course** mild (or effemi-
    nate) gentleness and course of action
339 ***attasked** censured, taken to task.

Most recent editions accept Greg's
emendation of Qu's 'alapt' as a misreading of 'ataxt'; 'attask'd' (Qc) and
'at task' (F) yield much the same
meaning, since 'tax' and 'task' overlap
in early usage, and were once almost
synonymous (*OED sb.* 1).

340 **harmful mildness** leniency that
    does harm
342 This sounds proverbial, varying
    Dent, W260, 'Let well alone'.

---

330 that] *F*; this *Q*   331 SP OSWALD] *Q (Osw.)*, *F (Stew.)*   Ay] *F (I)*; Yes *Q*   333 fear] *F*; fear-
es *Q*   336 hasten] *Qc, F*; after *Qu, Q2*   SD] *Rowe*   No, no] *F*; now *Q*   337 milky] *Qc, F*; mildie
Qu, Q2   338 condemn] *F*; dislike *Q*   339 You are] *F2*; y'are *Q*; Your are *F*   attasked for] *Qc*;
alapt *Qu, Q2*; at task for *F*; ataxt for *Duthie (Greg)*   340 praised] *F*; praise *Q*   342 better, oft] *F*;
better ought *Q*; better aught *Halio*

GONERIL   Nay then –

ALBANY   Well, well, th'event.   *Exeunt.*

1.5   *Enter* LEAR, ^FKENT *[disguised] and* FOOL.^F

LEAR *[to Kent]*   Go you before to Gloucester with these
    letters. Acquaint my daughter no further with anything
    you know than comes from her demand out of the
    letter. If your diligence be not speedy, I shall be there
    afore you.   5

KENT   I will not sleep, my lord, till I have delivered your
    letter.   *Exit.*

FOOL   If a man's brains were in's heels, were't not in
    danger of kibes?

LEAR   Ay, boy.   10

FOOL   Then I prithee be merry; thy wit shall not go
    slipshod.

---

344 **th'event** the outcome; equivalent to
'we'll see'
1.5.0.1–1 *Enter . . .* **Gloucester** F
includes 'Gentleman' in the entry SD,
but he has no speaking part, and most
editions and productions omit him,
assuming the direction anticipates the
'*Gent.*' ('*Seru.*' Q) required at 47–8. In
a concern to resolve the ambiguity of
Gloucester (person or place?), Oxf
retains the gentleman as a messenger
to Gloucester, sending Kent with a
letter for Regan; Regan indeed receives
Lear's letter (see 2.1.124), but no
letters arrive for Gloucester. It is
possible that *Gloucester* refers to the
place, as a staging-post between
Goneril's palace and Cornwall's house,

but it seems more likely that
Shakespeare anticipated here the
arrival of Cornwall and Regan at
Gloucester's house in the next scene,
as if Lear could already know they
would be there; for other foreshorten-
ings of the action, see 1.4.286–7, 325
and nn. It is unnecessary to follow Oxf,
or Cam¹, which changes 'Gloucester'
to 'Cornwall'.
3   **demand out of** questions arising
from
8   **were't** were his brains (as singular)
9   **kibes** chilblains
10 **boy** See 1.4.105 and n.
11–12 **thy . . . slip-shod** your brains will
not need slippers. The Fool implies
that Lear is brainless in setting off to

---

344 th'event] *Q (the* euent*); the'uent F*

1.5] *F (Scena Quinta); not in Q*   0.1 *Enter . . .* FOOL] *Q2; Enter Lear. Q; Enter Lear, Kent,
Gentleman, and Foole. F   disguised] Riv (disguised as Caius)*   1 SD] *Hunter; to the Gentleman,
giving him a letter   Oxf*   5 afore] *F;* before *Q*   8 were] *Q2, F;* where *Q*   were't] *Q, F (*wert*)*
11 not] *F;* nere *Q*

LEAR   Ha, ha, ha.

FOOL   Shalt see thy other daughter will use thee kindly,
        for though she's as like this as a crab's like an apple, yet   15
        I can tell what I can tell.

LEAR   ^QWhy,^Q what canst ^Qthou^Q tell, ^Qmy ^Q boy?

FOOL   She will taste as like this as a crab does to a crab.
        Thou canst ^Qnot^Q tell why one's nose stands i'the
        middle on's face?   20

LEAR   No.

FOOL   Why, to keep one's eyes of either side's nose, that
        what a man cannot smell out he may spy into.

LEAR   I did her wrong.

FOOL   Canst tell how an oyster makes his shell?   25

LEAR   No.

FOOL   Nor I neither; but I can tell why a snail has a house.

LEAR   Why?

FOOL   Why, to put's head in, not to give it away to his
        daughters and leave his horns without a case.   30

LEAR   I will forget my nature: so kind a father! Be my
        horses ready?

FOOL   Thy asses are gone about 'em. The reason why the

---

see Regan.

14 **kindly** playing on the meanings 'with
affection' and 'according to her kind or
nature', i.e. cruelly. Compare 31 below.

15 **this** this one, i.e. Goneril

16 **I . . . can tell** varying the proverb, 'I
know what I know', Dent, K173 = I
am in on a secret

18 **crab** crab-apple, noted for its sourness

20 **on's** of his (Abbott, 182)

24 **I . . . wrong** usually taken as referring
to Cordelia, as a follow-up of 1.4.258–
64, but possibly, as D. G. James, 94–6,
thought, to Goneril. From this point
Lear only half attends to what the Fool

says and wanders in mind.

27–30 **why . . . case** The snail proverbially stayed at home (Dent, S580), where
at least he would have a covering for
his (cuckold's) horns. The Fool refers
to the common joke that being cuc-
kolded was the fate of all married men;
compare *AYL* 4.2.13–18.

31 **nature** natural affection or kindness;
compare 14 above

32 **horses** The King would travel in a
coach or on horseback; Lear calls for
horses at 1.4.250 and again at 2.2.487,
but always appears on foot.

33 **asses** servants (implying they are fools

---

16 can tell what] *F;* con, what *Q*   18 She will] *F;* Sheel *Q*   does] *F;* doth *Q*   19 stands i'the] *F*
(stands i'th'); stande in the *Q;* stands in the *Q2*   20 on's] *F;* of his *Q*   22 one's] *F;* his *Q*   of] *F;*
on *Q*   23 he] *Q2, F;* a *Q*   30 daughters] *F;* daughter *Q*   33 'em] *F;* them *Q*

seven stars are no more than seven is a pretty reason.

LEAR   Because they are not eight.   35

FOOL   Yes ^Findeed,^F thou wouldst make a good fool.

LEAR   To take't again perforce – monster ingratitude!

FOOL   If thou wert my fool, nuncle, I'd have thee beaten
for being old before thy time.

LEAR   How's that?   40

FOOL   Thou shouldst not have been old till thou hadst
been wise.

LEAR   O let me not be mad, ^Fnot mad^F, sweet heaven! ^QI
would not be mad.^Q

Keep me in temper, I would not be mad.   45

[*Enter a* Gentleman.]

^FHow now,^F are the horses ready?

GENTLEMAN   Ready, my lord.

LEAR   Come, boy.   ^Q*Exeunt* ^Q[*Lear and Gentleman*].

FOOL

She that's a maid now, and laughs at my departure,   49

---

34 **seven stars** a common name for the constellation of the Pleiades, and also applied to the seven bright stars that form the Plough or Great Bear, referred to by Edmund at 1.2.130

37 **To . . . perforce** to take it (i.e. the kingdom?) back by force, recalling 1.4.300–2. In his performance, Brian Cox used this moment to display the crown (a coronet in fact): 'Throughout the earlier scene with the Fool, 1/4, I am fondling the crown – though you can't see what it is – and may be giving it a little clean and polish, and then in 1/5 I hold it out and say, "Take it again perforce." It seems to work quite well' (Cox, 66).

43 **let . . . mad** Lear's first thought of madness. Hoeniger, 330, supposes that Lear is ill more or less from the start of the play with hypochondriac melancholy, brought about by the clash of two passions, anger and grief, but, though Kent calls him mad at 1.1.147, the dialogue seems to me to show a process of change in Lear. In performance the line can be an ironic moment of lucidity for a Lear already mad, or, as often staged, a terrible premonition for a still sane Lear of what is shortly to come; see Rosenberg, 140.

45 **temper** mental balance

49–50 **FOOL . . . shorter** direct address to the audience, marking a significant break in the action; see also 3.2.79–96

---

34 more] *Q;* mo *F*   41 till] *F;* before *Q*   45.1] *Theobald*   47 SP GENTLEMAN] *F; Seruant Q*
48 SD] *Capell; Exit. Q; not in F*   49 that's a] *F;* that is *Q*

Shall not be a maid long, unless things be cut shorter.   *Exit.*

2.1   *Enter* EDMUND *and* CURAN *severally.*

EDMUND   Save thee, Curan.

CURAN   And you, sir. I have been with your father and
given him notice that the Duke of Cornwall and
ᶠReganᶠ his Duchess will be here with him this
night.   5

EDMUND   How comes that?

CURAN   Nay, I know not. You have heard of the news
abroad? – I mean the whispered ones, for they are yet
but ear-bussing arguments.

EDMUND   Not I; pray you, what are they?   10

CURAN   Have you heard of no likely wars toward 'twixt

and n., and Introduction, p. 57.
Laughter was proverbially associated
with sexual surrender, as in the phrase
'Laugh and lie down' (Dent, L69).
Wiles, 190–1, suggests that the Fool
put his *marotte*, or fool's head on a
stick, the traditional bauble, between
his legs as a phallus to illustrate *things*,
and notes a possible pun on *departure*
and 'deporter', French for bauble.
Wiles also notes that the bauble was no
longer used in late-sixteenth-century
fooling, and claims that 'Lear's fool
belongs to a vanished world, not to the
social reality of 1605'; if so, Shakespeare may have been anxious to avoid
comparison with Archie Armstrong,
King James's fool. See 1.4.137–48 and
n.

2.1.0.1 *severally* separately. Curan and
Edmund meet as if coming from different parts of Gloucester's house,

where Edgar has been in hiding in
Edmund's *lodging* (1.2.166); see 20
and n.

1   **Save thee** short for 'God save thee', a
common greeting
    Curan He appears only in this scene,
and seems to be a member of
Gloucester's household. Perhaps
Shakespeare at first thought of developing the character, and so, unusually
for so minor a role, gave him a name.

8   **abroad**   current in the world

9   ***ear-bussing** F's 'ear-kissing' means
the same, but is likely to be a sophistication, for Shakespeare had already
used *buzz* at 1.4.318 to mean 'rumour',
and the pun here would have been hard
to resist.
    arguments topics, as at 1.1.216

11   **wars toward** impending civil war; the
first hint, following on Albany's
distress at seeing Goneril and Lear

50 unless] *F;* except *Q*   SD] *Q; Exeunt. F*

2.1] *F (Actus Secundus. Scena Prima); not in Q*   0.1 EDMUND] *Rowe; Bast. Q; Bastard F*
severally] *F; meeting Q; meetes him Q2*   1+ SP EDMUND] *Theobald; Bast. Q , F*   2 you] *Q;* your *F*
4 this] *F;* to *Q*   8 abroad? –] *this edn;* abroad, *Q , F;* abroad? *Ard²;* abroad – *Hunter*   they] *F;*
there *Q*   9 ear-bussing] *Q;* ear-kissing *F*   10 Not I;] *F (*Not I:*);* Not, I *Q*   11–13] *Q , F; not in
Q2*   11 toward] *F;* towards *Q*

216

the ^Qtwo^Q dukes of Cornwall and Albany?

EDMUND Not a word.

CURAN You may ^Fdo^F then in time. Fare you well, sir. ^F*Exit.*^F

EDMUND

The Duke be here tonight? The better – best!   15
This weaves itself perforce into my business.
My father hath set guard to take my brother,
And I have one thing of a queasy question
Which I must act. Briefness and fortune work!
Brother, a word; descend, brother, I say.   20

Enter EDGAR.

My father watches; O ^Fsir^F, fly this place!
Intelligence is given where you are hid:
You have now the good advantage of the night.
Have you not spoken 'gainst the Duke of Cornwall
   ^Qaught^Q? –

quarrel in 1.4, of a theme picked up again in 3.1. Lear's division of the kingdom into gifts and rewards for his daughters ironically is at once rumoured to bring about a 'division' or rift between his sons-in-law. See also 24–7 and n.

15 **The better – best!** So much the better – best thing of all!

16 **perforce** of necessity

18 **one . . . question** one deed (in the nature) of a dangerous uncertainty

19 *so F; Q has 'which I must aske breefnes and fortune helpe'. Weis makes sense of this by inserting 'to' before 'help', but F seems to me an improvement.

20 **descend** At 1.2.166–8 Edmund gave Edgar the key to his *lodging* within Gloucester's house, from which he now descends. Edgar probably appeared on the balcony as Edmund

called, and descended by internal stairs, since he is wearing a sword (see 30), rather than jumping down, as the continuity of the dialogue might suggest. No other use of a balcony or upper stage is required in the play. At 1.2.168 Edmund advised Edgar to 'go armed'.

21 **watches** remains awake, is on the look-out

22 **Intelligence** information

24–7 **spoken . . . Albany?** If Edmund's opportunist intention (he has only just heard of *likely wars*, 11) is to make Edgar anxious, his questions also reinforce the hints of 'division' as civil dissension, and of voices speaking for one side or cause ('Upon his party') against the other.

24 **aught** at all. The speech is printed as prose in Q, where this word does not

14 SD] *Q2, F; not in Q*   15 better –] *this edn; better Q, F; better, Rowe; better! Pope*   19 I must act] *F; must aske Q, Q2*   work] *F; helpe Q, Q2; to help Weis*   20.1] *as Q2, F (opp. 19); in left margin opp. 16 Q*   24 Cornwall] *F; Cornwall ought Q*

He's coming hither, now, i'the night, i'the haste,   25
And Regan with him. Have you nothing said
Upon his party 'gainst the Duke of Albany?
Advise yourself.

EDGAR   I am sure on't, not a word.

EDMUND

I hear my father coming – pardon me;
In cunning I must draw my sword upon you.   30
ᶠDraw,ᶠ seem to defend yourself; now quit you well.
[*loudly*] Yield, come before my father! Light, ho, here!
[*to Edgar*] Fly, brother, ᵠfly ᵠ! [*loudly*] Torches,
    torches! – [*to Edgar*] So farewell.   ᶠ*Exit Edgar.*ᶠ
Some blood drawn on me would beget opinion
Of my more fierce endeavour.   [*Cuts his arm.*]
                                       I have seen drunkards   35
Do more than this in sport. Father, father!
Stop, stop, no help?

Enter GLOUCESTER, ᶠ*and servants, with torches.*ᶠ

GLOUCESTER   Now, Edmund, where's the villain?

spoil the metre.

28 **Advise yourself** take thought
on't of it

30 ***In cunning** as a device; Q has 'crauing', a possible misreading of secretary
hand

31 **quit you well** do your part (modern
'acquit yourself well'), with a quibble
on *quit* = depart.

32 **Yield . . . father!** intended for
Gloucester's ears, to give the impression that Edmund is defending him

32–3 **Light . . . torches!** Heilman, 46,
notes the irony of Edmund calling for
torches as if to throw light on a dark

plot by Edgar, while Gloucester still
fails to see what is really happening (so
Cam²).

34–5 **beget . . . endeavour** make people
think I have put up a tremendous fight

35–6 **I . . . sport** It seems to have been a
common practice for gallants to cut
their arms and mix their blood with
wine to drink healths to their mistresses;
so Witgood renounces his follies, such
as 'Stabbing of arms for a common
Mistris', in Middleton's *A Trick to
Catch the Old One* (1605–6), 5.2.188
(cited by Kittredge).

27 'gainst] *F;* against *Q*   28 yourself] *F;* your – *Q*   29–30 me; / In cunning] *F;* me in crauing *Q*
32 SD] *this edn (Hunter)*   ho] *F (*hoa*);* here *Q*   33 SD *to Edgar . . . loudly . . . to Edgar*] *this edn*
(Hunter)   35 SD] *this edn (Rowe)*   37 no] *Q, F;* Ho *Oxf (Stone)*

EDMUND

Here stood he in the dark, his sharp sword out,

Mumbling of wicked charms, conjuring the moon

To stand^Qs^Q auspicious mistress.

GLOUCESTER   But where is he?   40

EDMUND

Look, sir, I bleed.

GLOUCESTER   Where is the villain, Edmund?

EDMUND

Fled this way, sir, when by no means he could –

GLOUCESTER [*to servants*]

Pursue him, ^Fho!^F Go after!   [*Servants rush off.*]

                              – 'By no means' what?

EDMUND

Persuade me to the murder of your lordship,

But that I told him the revenging gods   45

'Gainst parricides did all their thunders bend,

Spoke with how manifold and strong a bond

The child was bound to the father. Sir, in fine,

Seeing how loathly opposite I stood

---

39 ***Mumbling** suggesting he was being quietly cautious; 'warbling' (Q) might link him rather with the Weird Sisters in *Macbeth* as chanting his spells

the moon Hecate, goddess of witchcraft; see 1.1.111 and n. Edmund does not answer the question, and tries to play on his father's superstitions (see 1.2.103–14), perhaps to divert attention and give Edgar time to escape. As Hunter notes, there may be some comedy in the cross-purposes of Gloucester and Edmund here.

40 **stand's . . . mistress** act as his favourable patroness

42 **this way** presumably pointing in the wrong direction (so Capell), since Edgar might reveal the truth if he were caught; but see 58 and n.

46 *****their thunders bend** aim their thunderbolts (as if shooting from a bow; see 1.1.144 and 2.2.416). This is from Q; 'the thunder' (F) is more vague and may be due to careless transcription.

47 **bond** Cordelia's word (see 1.1.93 and n.) echoes in the play; see also 1.2.108 and 2.2.367.

48 **in fine** in short, to sum up

49–50 **how . . . / To** with what loathing I opposed (Hunter)

---

39 Mumbling] *F*; warbling *Q*   40 stand's] *Q*; stand *F*; stand his *Q2*   43 SD *to servants*] *this edn (Capell and Dyce)*   SD *Servants . . . off*] *this edn (Dyce)*   45 revenging] *F*; reuengiue *Q*   46 their thunders] *Q*; the thunder *F*   47 manifold] *Q (*many fould*), F*   48 in] *F*; in a *Q*

To his unnatural purpose, in fell motion,   50
With his prepared sword, he charges home
My unprovided body, latched mine arm;
But when he saw my best alarumed spirits,
Bold in the quarrel's right, roused to th'encounter,
Or whether ghasted by the noise I made,   55
Full suddenly he fled.
GLOUCESTER   Let him fly far:
Not in this land shall he remain uncaught,
And found – dispatch! The noble Duke, my master,
My worthy arch and patron, comes tonight;
By his authority I will proclaim it,   60
That he which finds him shall deserve our thanks,
Bringing the murderous coward to the stake:
He that conceals him, death!
EDMUND
When I dissuaded him from his intent,
And found him pight to do it, with curst speech   65
I threatened to discover him. He replied,
'Thou unpossessing bastard, dost thou think,

---

50 **fell motion** fierce thrust. In sword-
fighting a *motion* was a practised movement; compare *Ham* 4.7.101.
51 **prepared** preparèd; unsheathed
charges home aims directly at
52 **unprovided** unprotected
***latched** caught; Q has 'lancht', often
emended to 'lanced', but F's *latched*
more appropriately suggests the slight
wound Edmund has given himself
53 **when** Richard Proudfoot suggests this
might be a misreading of 'whe'r'
(= whether) in manuscript.
alarumed spirits energies stirred to
action
55 **ghasted** frightened (compare the

modern 'ghastly')
56 **Full** very
58 **found – dispatch!** Gloucester presumably gestures to suggest cutting his
head off or some other mode of execution. He is heedlessly sentencing
Edgar without even giving him a trial.
59 **arch and patron** chief patron (hendiadys)
62 **to the stake** to the place of execution
65 **pight** determined, set (past participle
of 'pitch', as in 'to pitch a tent')
65 **curst speech** angry words
66 **discover him** reveal his purpose
67 **unpossessing** bastards could not
inherit property; see 85 and n.

50 in] *F;* with *Q*   52 latched] *F;* lancht *Q;* lanc'd *Theobald*   53 But] *Q;* And *F*   54 quarrel's
right] *Q2, F;* quarrels, rights *Q*   56 Full] *F;* but *Q*   58 found – dispatch!] *this edn (Steevens);*
found, dispatch, *Q;* found; dispatch, *F*   62 coward] *F;* caytife *Q*

If I would stand against thee, would the reposal
Of any trust, virtue or worth in thee
Make thy words faithed? No, what I should deny,   70
As this I would, ᵠay,ᵠ though thou didst produce
My very character, I'd turn it all
To thy suggestion, plot and damned practice;
And thou must make a dullard of the world
If they not thought the profits of my death   75
Were very pregnant and potential spurs
To make thee seek it.'   ᶠ*Tucket within.*ᶠ
GLOUCESTER   ᶠOᶠ strange and fastened villain,
Would he deny his letter, ᶠsaid he?ᶠ ᵠI never got him.ᵠ
Hark, the Duke's trumpets; I know not why he comes.
All ports I'll bar, the villain shall not scape;   80
The Duke must grant me that. Besides, his picture
I will send far and near, that all the kingdom

---

68 **I would** I were to
68–9 **would the . . . worth** would the
placing of any trust (as by your father),
or would any virtue or merit
70 **faithed** believed
70–7 **No . . . it** With an irony of which
Gloucester remains unaware, Edmund
attributes to Edgar what is true of
himself.
72 **character** handwriting, as at 1.2.62
73 **damned** damnèd
*practice treacherous scheming. Q
has 'pretence', meaning purpose or
aim, as at *Mac* 2.3.131.
74 **make . . . world** suppose people to be
stupid
75 **not thought** did not think
76 ***pregnant . . . spurs** compelling and
powerful incentives. F has 'spirits',
which would oddly introduce the
notion of evil spirits here, and which I
think is a corruption, perhaps by
attraction from *spirits*, 53, and *profits*,
75. Sisson, Ard² and Cam² retain F, but

their reasons are more ingenious than
convincing.
77 SD *Tucket* a flourish played on a
trumpet, here recognized as Cornwall's signature notes
strange and fastened unnatural (as
opposed to *natural*, 84) and determined
78 ***I . . . him** Q only (*got* = begot). F has
'said he?' (referring to 70–1), leaving a
short line, possibly marking a pause as
Gloucester notices the trumpet sound;
but, as Duthie argued, this phrase
could be an addition, clarifying the
connection with 70–1, not a substitution, even though, with 'I never got
him', it makes an irregular long line.
Gloucester's denial that he is Edgar's
father here matches Lear disclaiming
his kinship with Cordelia at 1.1.114–
17.
80 **ports** gates of towns, or seaports, or
perhaps both
81 **picture** description

---

68 would the reposal] *F;* could the reposure *Q*   70 I should] *Q;* should I *F*   73 practice] *F;*
pretence *Q*   76 spurs] *Q;* spirits *F*   77 O strange] *F;* Strong *Q*   79 why] *Q;* wher F

May have ᶠdueᶠ note of him; and of my land,
Loyal and natural boy, I'll work the means
To make thee capable.   85

Enter CORNWALL, ᶠREGAN *and attendants.*ᶠ

CORNWALL

How now, my noble friend? Since I came hither,
Which I can call but now, I have heard strange news.

REGAN

If it be true, all vengeance comes too short
Which can pursue th'offender. How dost, my lord?

GLOUCESTER

ᶠOᶠ madam, my old heart is cracked, it's cracked.   90

REGAN

What, did my father's godson seek your life?
He whom my father named, your Edgar?

GLOUCESTER

O lady, lady, shame would have it hid.

REGAN

Was he not companion with the riotous knights
That tended upon my father?   95

GLOUCESTER

I know not, madam; 'tis too bad, too bad.

---

84 **natural** properly loving to his father
(compare *strange*, 77); the word could
also mean both 'legitimate, born in
wedlock', and 'illegitimate'. The ambi-
guities here are very rich.

85 **capable** qualified to inherit. *OED a.* 7
cites this as the earliest use, but also
quotes John Gwillim, *A Display of
Heraldry* (1611), 53: 'Bastards are not
capable of their fathers patrimonie.'

91–2 **my . . . Edgar?** Lear invokes only

pagan gods in Act 1, but this reference
to his acting as godfather to Edgar
links them in Christian terms, and also
hints that Edgar is the son Lear might
have wished for.

94 **riotous** Regan repeats Goneril's word
at 1.4.235.

95 **tended upon** waited on, served.
Regan uses the past tense, as if to distance herself from her father and his
train.

85.1 SD CORNWALL] *F; the Duke of Cornwall Q* 87 strange news] *Q;* strangenesse *F* 89 dost]
Q, F; does *F2* 90 it's] *F;* is *Q* 93 O] *F;* I *Q* 95 tended] *F;* tends *Q;* tend *Theobald*

EDMUND

    Yes, madam, he was ^Fof that consort^F.

REGAN

    No marvel, then, though he were ill affected.

    'Tis they have put him on the old man's death,

    To have th'expense and waste of his revenues.   100

    I have this present evening from my sister

    Been well informed of them, and with such cautions

    That if they come to sojourn at my house

    I'll not be there.

CORNWALL   Nor I, assure thee, Regan.

    Edmund, I hear that you have shown your father   105

    A child-like office.

EDMUND   It was my duty, sir.

GLOUCESTER [*to Cornwall*]

    He did bewray his practice, and received

    This hurt you see, striving to apprehend him.

CORNWALL   Is he pursued?

GLOUCESTER   Ay, my good lord.   110

---

97 **of that consort** of that company (F). Edmund seizes another opportunity, stressed in F, to blacken Edgar's name, and, as Hunter suggests, may begin to establish a rapport with Regan; see 1.1.34 and n.

98 **though** if

   ill affected ill disposed, given to evil ways

99 **put him on** incited him to, put him up to; compare 1.4.198

100 ***th'expense and waste** the using up and squandering (hendiadys). So F; it seems the Q compositor could not make out what was in his manuscript, and printed 'these – and wast', which Qc changed to 'the wast and spoyle'. F

may restore what was in the manuscript, or be 'a deliberate rewriting' (*TxC*, 514).

   revenues accented on the second syllable

102 **informed of them** told about Lear's knights (by Oswald; see 1.4.333–6)

103 **my house** Regan asserts her personal authority in the scene, as here and when she takes over from Cornwall at 121, even if both join in using the royal plural from 115 onwards.

106 **child-like office** service proper to a son

107 **bewray his practice** expose Edgar's treachery (compare 73)

---

100 th'expense . . . his] *F;* these – and wast of this his *Qu, Q2;* the wast and spoyle of his *Qc;* th'expense and spoil of his *Oxf*   105 hear] *F;* heard *Q*   106 It was] *F;* Twas *Q*   107 SD] *Oxf* bewray] *F;* betray *Q*

CORNWALL

    If he be taken, he shall never more
    Be feared of doing harm, make your own purpose
    How in my strength you please. For you, Edmund,
    Whose virtue and obedience doth this instant
    So much commend itself, you shall be ours.   115
    Natures of such deep trust we shall much need;
    You we first seize on.

EDMUND

    I shall serve you, ^Fsir^F, truly, however else.

GLOUCESTER   For him I thank your grace.

CORNWALL

    You know not why we came to visit you?   120

REGAN

    Thus out of season, threading dark-eyed night?
    Occasions, noble Gloucester, of some poise
    Wherein we must have use of your advice.
    Our father he hath writ, so hath our sister,
    Of differences, which I best thought it fit   125
    To answer from our home. The several messengers

---

112 **Be feared of** cause fear with regard to

112–13 **make . . . please** achieve your aim (to seize Edgar) using my authority and resources as you please

116–18 These lines are full of irony, not only in the echo of 1.1.254, where the King of France seizes on Cordelia and her virtues, but also in relation both to Edmund's lies about Edgar at 68–70 and to his later adulterous affair with Regan established in 4.5. Cornwall's 'need' for support may hint again at the civil strife mentioned at 11–12 above.

121 **out of season** inconveniently
    threading making a difficult passage through (like threading the eye of a needle; compare *KJ* 5.4.11), as at *Cor* 3.1.124, where soldiers 'would thread the gates' of an enemy city

122 ***poise** weight, importance. This is the reading of Qc; Qu has 'prise' (F 'prize'), which has roughly the same meaning, and the word may have been emended to avoid the rhyme with *advice*, 123.

124 **father . . . writ** Regan knows Kent has arrived, but it seems Gloucester, to whom Lear's letter was addressed, does not know; see 1.5.1–2. The exchanges of letters in the play are not easy to follow; see 4.5.0.1 and n.

125 **which** in letters which

126 **from our home** If Regan is away from home, Lear cannot descend on

---

121 threading] *F;* threatning *Q*   122 poise] *Qc;* prise *Qu, Q2;* prize *F*   125 differences] *Qc, F;* defences *Qu, Q2* best] *Qu, F;* lest *Qc;* least *Oxf* thought] *Q;* though *F*   126 home] *Qc, F;* hand *Qu, Q2*

From hence attend dispatch. Our good old friend,
Lay comforts to your bosom, and bestow
Your needful counsel to our business,
Which craves the instant use.

GLOUCESTER   I serve you, madam.   130
    Your graces are right welcome.   *Exeunt.* ᶠ*Flourish.*ᶠ

2.2   *Enter* KENT [*disguised*] *and* OSWALD, ᶠ*severally.*ᶠ

OSWALD   Good dawning to thee, friend. Art of this
    house?

KENT   Ay.

OSWALD   Where may we set our horses?

KENT   I'the mire.   5

OSWALD   Prithee, if thou lov'st me, tell me.

KENT   I love thee not.

OSWALD   Why then, I care not for thee.

KENT   If I had thee in Lipsbury pinfold, I would make
    thee care for me.   10

OSWALD   Why dost thou use me thus? I know thee not.

KENT   Fellow, I know thee.

---

her. As Bradley, 449, and others have
noted, Shakespeare contrives to bring
all the main characters except Cordelia
together at Gloucester's house for the
climactic rejection of Lear by Goneril
and Regan in Act 2.
127 **attend dispatch** await permission to
go
130 **craves . . . use** demands immediate
action
2.2.0.1 *severally* separately, as if meeting
outside Gloucester's house
1 ***dawning** The imagined time is
before dawn, for it is still *night* (30),

and later Kent is stocked all day
(131–2). Qu has 'deuen' (= 'dawn'?),
miscorrected to 'euen' in Q.
3 **Ay** a surly refusal to talk? Kent is not
of, i.e. a servant in, Gloucester's house.
6 **if . . . me** be so kind as to
9 **in Lipsbury pinfold** usually taken to
mean 'trapped between my teeth'.
Lipsbury = lips-town (there is no place
of this name), and a *pinfold* is a pound
for stray animals.
10 **care for me** be concerned about me
(because of what I might do)
11 **use** treat

129 business] *Q;* businesses *F*

2.2] *F (Scena Secunda); not in Q* 0.1 *disguised*] *Riv (disguised as Caius)* OSWALD] *Collier;*
Steward Q, F 1+ SP OSWALD] *Collier; Ste. / Stew. / Steward. Q, F* 1 dawning] *F;* deuen *Qu;*
euen *Qc, Q2* this] *F;* the *Q, Q2* 6 lov'st] *F;* loue *Q*

OSWALD   What dost thou know me for?

KENT   A knave, a rascal, an eater of broken meats; a base,
proud, shallow, beggarly, three-suited-hundred-pound,   15
filthy, worsted-stocking knave; a lily-livered, action-
taking ^Qknave, a^Q whoreson, glass-gazing, super-
serviceable, finical rogue; one trunk-inheriting slave,
one that wouldst be a bawd in way of good service and
art nothing but the composition of a knave, beggar,   20
coward, pander and the son and heir of a mongrel
bitch; ^Fone^F whom I will beat into clamorous whining if

14–38 Kent's violent verbal onslaught, insulting Oswald as a base menial (he has a superior office as steward, see 1.3.0.1 and n.), and then his physical attack, are hardly warranted by anything Oswald has done; at 217–33 Kent explains his actions as relieving his feelings at the cold reception given him by Regan and Cornwall. Kent is himself disguised as a servant, and appears at best the equal of Oswald, probably his inferior, for Oswald calls him a *ruffian*, 60, and is himself well, perhaps foppishly, dressed (see 53–4). Dramatically Kent's outburst channels the audience's feelings; but see Introduction, pp. 67–8.

14 **broken meats** scraps left after a meal

15 **three-suited-hundred-pound** Oswald is elegantly dressed as a steward, or head of Goneril's household. Three suits seem to have been the allowance of such a servant; see 3.4.83–4 and 131–2. F's hyphens, not in Q, suggest that clothes and pay go together; a hundred pounds would have been a handsome income. Some have seen here a possible allusion to the selling of knighthoods by James I for this sum.

16 **worsted-stocking** wool stockings, inferior to silk, and a servant's wear

lily-livered cowardly, as having no blood in the liver, thought to be the source of courage; cf. *2H4* 4.3.104–5

16–17 **action-taking** litigious; taking legal action (rather than fighting)

17 **whoreson** a term of abuse, much as 'bastard' is used in modern times
glass-gazing vain; given to admiring one's reflection in a glass or mirror

17–18 **super-serviceable** anxious to do any kind of service (compare 19)

18 **finical** affected, fussy
one trunk-inheriting one who possesses (see 4.6.125) or will inherit no more than would go into a trunk. Often hyphenated to 'trunk' by editors to give the sense 'inheriting only one trunk', but not so in Q or F, and I take 'one' to mark a shift from 'a' (see 14, 16, 17); *one* is repeated in 19 and in 22 (F).

19 **bawd** Oswald later carries letters from Goneril to Edmund, but remains loyal to Goneril; see Introduction, p. 69.

20 **composition** combination

22 *****clamorous** Q; 'clamours' (F) is a possible spelling. Compare 'maruel's' (Q and F) in 'she has a marvellous white hand', *TC* 1.2.136.

15 suited] *F;* snyted *Qu;* shewted *Qc, Q2*   16 worsted-stocking] *F (*woosted-stockin*g); wosted stocken *Qu;* worsted-stocken *Qc, Q2*   17–18 superserviceable, finical] *F;* superfinicall *Q*
22 clamorous] *Qc, Q2;* clamarous *Qu;* clamours *F*

thou deniest the least syllable of thy addition.

OSWALD ᶠWhy,ᶠ what a monstrous fellow art thou, thus
to rail on one that is neither known of thee, nor knows 25
thee!

KENT What a brazen-faced varlet art thou to deny thou
knowest me? Is it two days ᵠagoᵠ since I tripped up thy
heels and beat thee before the King? Draw, you rogue,
for though it be night, ᶠyetᶠ the moon shines. [*Draws* 30
his sword.] I'll make a sop o'the moonshine of you.
ᵠDrawᵠ you whoreson cullionly barber-monger! Draw!

OSWALD Away, I have nothing to do with thee.

KENT Draw, you rascal! You come with letters against the
King, and take Vanity the puppet's part against the 35
royalty of her father. Draw, you rogue, or I'll so
carbonado your shanks! – draw, you rascal, come your
ways!

OSWALD Help, ho! Murder, help!

KENT Strike, you slave. Stand, rogue, stand you neat slave, 40

---

23 **addition** attributes or distinctions.
Kent is being ironic; compare
1.1.131–7 and 137n.

27 **brazen-faced varlet** shameless rogue

31 **sop . . . you** make mincemeat of you
(Cam¹); literally, beat you into soggi-
ness, like a piece of bread soaked in
liquid

32 **cullionly barber-monger** rascally
fop, always at the barber's shop. The
phrase seems to be Shakespeare's
coinage.

35 **Vanity . . . part** the part of Goneril,
conceived as like 'a Morality-play
figure of Self-Regard, performed in a
puppet play' (Hunter); to call a woman
a *puppet* was also to express contempt
for women who 'make themselves
such pictures, puppets and peacockes

as they doe' (Arthur Dent, *Plain
Man's Pathway to Heaven* (1601), 48,
cited in *OED*). Meagher, 252–4, thinks
this passage points to Shakespeare's
conception of Goneril as beautiful (see
2.2.355), and as an icon of Lady
Vanity, gorgeously clothed (see
2.2.456–8, lines that may be addressed
to Regan or to Goneril), her costume
including a hand-mirror, 'hung from
the girdle on a ribbon', and perhaps
referred to by the Fool at 3.2.35–6.

37 **carbonado** score or slash, as if for
grilling meat

37–8 **come your ways** come on then!
Oswald wears a sword, but refuses to
draw it, and backs away rather than
stand (40) and fight.

40 **neat** trim, alluding again, as at 32, to
Oswald's elegance or foppishness

---

23 deniest] *F;* denie *Q* thy] *F;* the *Q* 28–9 tripped . . . thee] *F;* beat thee, and tript vp thy heeles *Q* 30 SD] *this edn (Rowe)* 31 of you] *F;* a'you *Q* 34 come with] *F;* bring *Q*

strike! [*Beats him.*]

OSWALD   Help, ho! Murder, murder!

Enter EDMUND, ^Q*with his rapier drawn,*^Q CORNWALL, REGAN,
GLOUCESTER [*and*] ^F*servants.*^F

EDMUND   How now, what's the matter? ^FPart!^F

KENT [*to Edmund*]   With you, goodman boy, if you please.
Come, I'll flesh ye; come on, young master.   45

GLOUCESTER   Weapons? Arms? What's the matter here?

CORNWALL   Keep peace upon your lives: he dies that
strikes again. What is the matter?

REGAN   The messengers from our sister and the King.

CORNWALL [*to Kent*]   What is your difference? Speak.   50

OSWALD   I am scarce in breath, my lord.

KENT   No marvel, you have so bestirred your valour, you
cowardly rascal; nature disclaims in thee – a tailor made
thee.

CORNWALL   Thou art a strange fellow – a tailor make a man?   55

KENT   ^QAy,^Q a tailor, sir; a stone-cutter or a painter could
not have made him so ill, though they had been but two

42.1 EDMUND . . . *drawn* Edmund,
hearing a disturbance, rushes in ahead
of others who outrank him, with sword
drawn (SD in Q), breaching decorum,
and taking the opportunity to show
how well he serves Cornwall; see
2.1.118.

44 With . . . boy I'll fight with you, whip-
per-snapper; *goodman* is mildly insulting, as a term for a yeoman or an
innkeeper. Capulet uses the same
phrase to put down Tybalt at *RJ*
1.5.77.

45 flesh ye initiate or show you; also
insulting, as if Edmund has never
fought before

50 difference quarrel

53 disclaims in thee denies having anything to do with you

53–4 a . . . thee proverbial (Dent, A283
and T17). Kent again suggests
Oswald's clothes are fine, and the man
inside them worthless; compare 32, 40.

57–8 *two years i.e. out of a seven-
year apprenticeship. F corrects
'houres' (Q), which could just have

---

41 SD] *Rowe*   42 Murder, murder] *F (*murther, murther*);* murther, helpe *Q*   42.1 EDMUND] *Q;*
Bastard F   42.1–2 CORNWALL, REGAN, GLOUCESTER] *F; Gloster the Duke and Dutchesse. Q*   43
SP EDMUND] Bast. *Q , F*   Part] *F; not in Q; as SD Dyce*   44 SD] *this edn*   if] *F;* and *Q*   45 ye]
F; you *Q*   47 SP CORNWALL] *F (Cor. or Corn.);* Duke *Q*   50 What is] *F;* Whats *Q*   difference?
Speak.] *Rowe;* difference, speake? *Q , F*   57 they] *F;* hee *Q*

years o'the trade.

CORNWALL [*to Oswald*] Speak yet: how grew your quarrel?

OSWALD This ancient ruffian, sir, whose life I have   60
spared at suit of his grey beard –

KENT Thou whoreson zed, thou unnecessary letter! My
lord, if you will give me leave, I will tread this unbolted
villain into mortar and daub the wall of a jakes with
him. [*to Oswald*] Spare my grey beard, you wagtail?   65

CORNWALL Peace, sirrah. You beastly knave, know you
no reverence?

KENT Yes, sir, but anger hath a privilege.

CORNWALL Why art thou angry?

KENT

That such a slave as this should wear a sword,   70
Who wears no honesty. Such smiling rogues as these
Like rats oft bite the ᶠholyᶠ cords atwain
Which are too intrince t'unloose; smooth every passion

been a careless misreading of 'yeares' in secretary hand.

61 **at suit of** literally, at the petition of (as if Kent has begged for his life)

62 **zed** showing how the letter Z, 'a consonant much heard amongst us, and seldom sene', *Mulcaster's Elementarie* (1582), ed. E. T. Campagnac (1925), 136, was pronounced. The letter was *unnecessary* because most of its functions could be served by 's', and it does not occur in Latin.

63 **unbolted** unsifted or lumpy, perhaps with a quibbling suggestion of effeminacy, for a 'bolt', or arrow with a thick head, could have sexual implications, as in 'Boult', the name of a bawd in *Per*

64 **jakes** latrine

65 **wagtail** a contemptuous allusion to

Oswald's obsequiousness, or readiness to bow and scrape and wag his tail; see 76–7 and 101–2

68 **anger . . . privilege** i.e. the right to speak out in defiance of propriety; proverbial (Dent, P595.1)

72 **holy cords** recalling the *bond* spoken of by Cordelia at 1.1.93, and Edmund at 1.2.108, but with the wider sense of all the bonds that unite families and societies (compare Dent, C4); also anticipating Oswald's readiness to act as go-between for Goneril and Edmund (see 4.2.18–19)

73 ***intrince** abbreviated from 'intrinsicate' (see *AC* 5.2.304), the word means intricate, involved. F has 't'intrince', correcting 'to intrench' (Q), though the compositor may have thought he

58 years o'the] *F;* houres at the *Q*   59 SP CORNWALL] *F; Glost. Q*   SD] *this edn*   61 grey beard –] *Rowe;* gray-beard. *Q, F*   64 wall] *F;* walles *Q*   jakes] *Q (*iaques*), F (*Iakes*)*   66 sirrah] *F;* sir *Q*   know you] *F;* you have *Q;* have you *Ridley*   68 hath] *F;* has *Q*   71 Who] *F;* That *Q*   72 the holy] *Fc;* those *Qu, Q2;* the holly *Fu*   atwain] *F;* in twaine *Q*   73 too intrince t'unloose] *Malone, after F (*t'intrince, t'vnloose*);* to intrench, to inloose *Q*

That in the natures of their lords rebel,
Bring oil to fire, snow to their colder moods,   75
Renege, affirm and turn their halcyon beaks
With every gale and vary of their masters,
Knowing naught, like dogs, but following.
[*to Oswald*] A plague upon your epileptic visage.
Smile you my speeches as I were a fool?   80
Goose, if I had you upon Sarum plain,
I'd drive ye cackling home to Camelot.
CORNWALL   What, art thou mad, old fellow?
GLOUCESTER   How fell you out, say that.
KENT
  No contraries hold more antipathy   85

---

was printing an infinitive verb; Oxf emends Q to 'too entrenched', which is possible, but makes poor sense.
smooth indulge

74 **rebel** i.e. against reason, which should control the passions (Cam²)

75 ***Bring** Q; 'Being' (F) has been defended by Duthie, 141–2, and adopted by Cam², as meaning 'flatterers *are* oil to the flame of their masters' wrath'; but the sequence 'Smooth . . . Renege, affirm . . . ' seems to demand an active verb, and a careless compositor might confuse the words, just as he printed 'Reuenge' for 'Reneag' (Q) in the next line

76 ***Renege** deny
halcyon beaks The kingfisher (halcyon) was supposed, when dried and hung up, to turn its beak with the wind; so fawning servants support every shift of their masters' moods.

77 ***gale and vary** shifting wind (hendiadys); *gale* is from Q, and continues the image of the previous line. Oxf and Cam² retain 'gall' = irritation, but I suspect this is another compositor error; see 75 and n.

79 **epileptic** Is Oswald 'twitching with terror' (Hunter) while trying to smile, or is this another of Kent's exaggerated insults?

80 **Smile you** smile you at. The spelling in Q and F (Smoile) may indicate how the word was pronounced.
as as if (Abbott, 107)

81–2 **if . . . Camelot** unexplained. The general sense is apparent: 'if I had you at my mercy, I'd make you run for your life'. Oswald's laughter, the cackling of a goose, emblem of stupidity, provokes Kent, but it is not clear why this should be associated with Sarum, near Salisbury, or Camelot, the legendary home of King Arthur. Camelot is linked with Winchester as well as other places further west, and 'Winchester goose' was a name for venereal disease and for a prostitute (*OED* Goose *sb.* 3), so some hidden chain of association may have been at work here.

83 **old fellow** See also 124–5. Kent says he is forty-eight at 1.4.39; that he is *old* has a bearing on the audience's perception of Lear's great age.

---

75 Bring] *Q*; Being *F*   fire] *F*; stir *Q*   their] *Q*; the *F*   76 Renege] *Q (Reneag); Reuenge *F*
77 gale] *Q*; gall *F*   78 dogs] *F*; dayes *Q*   79 SD] *Oxf*   80 Smile] *Q (smoyle)*, *F (Smoile)*
81 if] *F*; and *Q*   82 drive ye] *F*; send you *Q*   Camelot] *F*; Camulet *Q*

Than I and such a knave.

CORNWALL

Why dost thou call him knave? What is his fault?

KENT His countenance likes me not.

CORNWALL

No more perchance does mine, nor his, nor hers.

KENT

Sir, 'tis my occupation to be plain: 90
I have seen better faces in my time
Than stands on any shoulder that I see
Before me at this instant.

CORNWALL This is some fellow
Who, having been praised for bluntness, doth affect
A saucy roughness and constrains the garb 95
Quite from his nature. He cannot flatter, he;
An honest mind and plain, he must speak truth;
An they will take it, so; if not, he's plain.
These kind of knaves I know, which in this plainness
Harbour more craft and more corrupter ends 100
Than twenty silly-ducking observants
That stretch their duties nicely.

KENT

Sir, in good faith, ^Qor^Q in sincere verity,
Under th'allowance of your great aspect,
Whose influence, like the wreath of radiant fire 105

---

88 **likes** pleases, as at 1.1.201
90 **occupation** business or habit
95–6 **constrains . . . nature** coerces the manner (of speaking the truth bluntly) quite against its nature, and so turns it into a mode of deception. See Introduction, p. 9.
98 **An** if
100 **more corrupter** The double com-

parative gives emphasis (Abbott, 11).
101 **silly-ducking observants** absurdly obsequious attendants, constantly *ducking* or bowing
102 **stretch . . . nicely** strain to carry out their duties punctiliously
104 **Under th'allowance** given the approval
104–5 **aspect . . . influence** astrological

---

87 What is] *F;* What's *Q* fault] *F;* offence *Q* 89 nor his, nor] *F;* or his, or *Q* 92 Than] *Q2, F* (Then); That *Q* 93 some] *F;* a *Q* 95 roughness] *F;* ruffines *Q* 97 An . . . and] *F;* he must be *Q* 98 take it, so;] *Rowe;* tak't so, *Q;* take it so, *F* 103 faith] *F;* sooth *Q* 104 great] *F;* graund *Q*

On flickering Phoebus' front –

CORNWALL   What mean'st ᵠthouᵠ by this?

KENT

To go out of my dialect, which you discommend so
much. I know, sir, I am no flatterer. He that beguiled
you in a plain accent was a plain knave, which for my
part I will not be, though I should win your displeasure   110
to entreat me to't.

CORNWALL [*to Oswald*] What was th'offence you gave him?

OSWALD

I never gave him any.
It pleased the King his master very late
To strike at me upon his misconstruction,   115
When he, compact and flattering his displeasure,
Tripped me behind; being down, insulted, railed
And put upon him such a deal of man
That worthied him, got praises of the King
For him attempting who was self-subdued;   120
And in the fleshment of this dread exploit
Drew on me here again.

---

terms. Cornwall's countenance becomes
a star affecting human destiny in
Kent's parody of a sycophantic style of
address.
106 **Phoebus' front** the sun-god's forehead (the original meaning of *front*)
107 ***dialect** idiom or manner of
speaking. Q's 'dialogue' is probably an
error arising from confusion of two
terms that both relate to speech and
stem from a similar Greek root; see
OED under 'Dialect'.
110–11 **though . . . to't** unexplained.
Kent seems to be mocking Cornwall
by saying 'I will not be a plain knave,
even if I could prevail upon your anger

to beg me to be one'.
114 **late** recently; see 1.4.197
115 **upon his misconstruction** as a
result of his misinterpretation. For
what actually happened, see 1.4.76–90.
116 ***he, compact** Kent, in collusion
(with the King). Q's 'coniunct' has
more or less the same meaning
117 **being down, insulted** once I was
down, he boasted
118–19 **put . . . him** adopted such tough
behaviour as made him seem a hero
120 **him . . . self-subdued** attacking one
who offered no resistance
121 **fleshment** first success; see 45 above

---

106 On flickering] *Pope;* In flitkering *Q;* On flicking *F*   front –] *Rowe;* front, *Q*, *F*   107 dialect]
F; dialogue *Q*   112 SD] *Oxf*   What was] *F;* What's *Q*   116 compact] *F;* coniunct *Q*   118–19
man / That] *F;* man, that, / That *Q*   121 fleshment] *F;* flechuent *Q*   dread] *Q;* dead *F*

KENT   None of these rogues and cowards
But Ajax is their fool.

CORNWALL   Fetch forth the stocks, ^Qho^Q!

[Exeunt one or two servants.]

You stubborn, ancient knave, you reverend braggart,
We'll teach you.

KENT   ^FSir,^F I am too old to learn.   125
Call not your stocks for me; I serve the King,
On whose employment I was sent to you.
You shall do small respect, show too bold malice
Against the grace and person of my master,
Stocking his messenger.

CORNWALL   Fetch forth the stocks!   130
As I have life and honour, there shall he sit till noon.

REGAN

Till noon? Till night, my lord, and all night too.

KENT

Why, madam, if I were your father's dog
You should not use me so.

---

123 **Ajax . . . fool** They beguile and make a fool of a great warrior like Ajax (or Cornwall). Ajax was notoriously stupid or 'blockish' (*TC* 1.3.374), and his name recalls a jakes or privy, so Cornwall's anger at this compound insult is understandable.

stocks commonly used to confine the ankles of disorderly offenders, and of household servants who misbehaved. G. M. Young's report of manuscript rules for the household of the Earl of Huntingdon, dating from 1604 or later (*TLS*, 30 September 1949, 633), has been cited by several editors: 'if any doe unseamly behave themselves towards their betters, the offence to be punnyshed first by the stockes'; but see also 138–42 (Q).

124–5 **ancient . . . old** See 83 and n.

126 **I . . . King** Lear has given away his power, so the title of King is merely ceremonial now, and Kent's appeal means little; but it is significant that Lear is still thought of as King, as by Oswald at 114 and 119 and Gloucester at 143; see Introduction, pp. 19–20.

129 **grace and person** the dignity (as King) and the person (as a man)

132 Regan typically intervenes, asserting her authority; see 2.1.103 and n. For the time, see 1 and n. above.

---

123 Ajax] *F (Aiax); A'Iax Q* Fetch] *F; Bring Q* SD] *this edn (Oxf (Blayney))* 124 ancient] *F; ausrent Qu; miscreant Qc, Q2* 127 employment] *F; imploments Q* 128 shall] *F; should Q* respect] *Q; respects F* 130 Stocking] *F; Stobing Qu; Stopping Qc, Q2* 131 sit] *F, Qc, Q2; set Qu* 134 should] *F; could Q*

REGAN   Sir, being his knave, I will.

^F*Stocks brought out.*^F

CORNWALL

This is a fellow of the selfsame colour   135

Our sister speaks of. Come, bring away the stocks.

GLOUCESTER

Let me beseech your grace not to do so.

^QHis fault is much, and the good King, his master,

Will check him for't. Your purposed low correction

Is such as basest and contemnedst wretches   140

For pilferings and most common trespasses

Are punished with.^Q

The King, ^Fhis master, needs^F must take it ill

That he, so slightly valued in his messenger,

Should have him thus restrained.

CORNWALL   I'll answer that.   145

REGAN

My sister may receive it much more worse

To have her gentleman abused, assaulted,

^QFor following her affairs. Put in his legs.^Q

[*Kent is put in the stocks.*]

---

134 **being his knave** (you) being his servant

135 **colour** character or kind

136 **bring away** bring here at once. The
stocks must be placed in some part of
the stage that makes it practicable for
Edgar to deliver his soliloquy at
172–92 and exit without noticing
Kent.

138–42 ***His . . . with** not in F, and perhaps omitted as mere elaboration; but
see 123 and n. above

139 **check** rebuke
low correction disreputable punishment

140 ***contemnedst** most despised. Oxf
may be right in reading 'contemned',
but the rarer superlative perhaps led to
the confusion in Q, which corrects
'contaned' (Qu) to 'temnest' (Qc).

146–9 **My . . . away** Regan has the last
word here in Q; her 'Come, my good
lord, away' may be addressed to
Cornwall, so that Gloucester is simply
left behind. F changes to 'Come my
lord, away' and gives the line to
Cornwall, who speaks to Gloucester,
lingering as Kent is put in the stocks,
and summons him to leave the stage.
Line 148 may have been omitted by

---

135 colour] *F;* nature *Q*   136 speaks] *Q2, F;* speake *Q*   140 basest] *Qc, Q2;* belest *Qu*   con-
temnedst] *Capell;* contaned *Qu;* temnest *Qc, Q2;* contemned *Oxf (Blayney)*   144 he] *F;* hee's *Q*
147 gentleman] *Q2, F;* Gentlemen *Q*   148 SD] *Pope (Rowe)*

ᶠCORNWALLᶠ   Come, my ᵠgood ᵠ lord, away.
                                    ᶠ*Exeunt*ᶠ [*all but Gloucester and Kent.*]

GLOUCESTER

    I am sorry for thee, friend; 'tis the Duke's pleasure,   150
    Whose disposition all the world well knows
    Will not be rubbed nor stopped. I'll entreat for thee.

KENT

    Pray ᵠyouᵠ do not, sir. I have watched and travelled
       hard.
    Some time I shall sleep out, the rest I'll whistle.
    A good man's fortune may grow out at heels.   155
    Give you good morrow.

GLOUCESTER

    The Duke's too blame in this; 'twill be ill taken.   ᶠ*Exit.*ᶠ

KENT

    Good King, that must approve the common saw,
    Thou out of heaven's benediction com'st
    To the warm sun.   160
    Approach, thou beacon to this under-globe,

---

oversight from F, or possibly because Kent was already thus *restrained* (145).

152 **rubbed** sidetracked. In the game of bowls a 'rub' is anything that diverts or impedes the course of the bowl.

153–71 **Pray . . . wheel** Kent in the stocks becomes emblematic of 'Virtue Locked Out', of 'a situation timeless and recurrent, catching in a mirror the world's way with virtue when separated from power' (Mack, 56–7). There are analogies with figures like Pity or Charity being stocked in morality plays; the difference is that Kent has deserved his punishment (see 123 and n). In the stocks he also becomes an emblem of the confusion of social and moral values Lear has brought about (so Cam², citing Salingar, 99).

153 **watched** stayed awake
travelled journeyed and laboured; 'trauail'd' (Q, F) is a spelling variant of what was originally the same word

155 **grow . . . heels** Kent jokingly applies the proverbial 'out at heels' (Dent, H389), or worn out, to his condition, as his heels are displayed in the stocks.

157 **too blame** See 1.2.42 and n.

158 ***approve . . . saw** confirm the saying. Qu has 'say' as a noun, which is possible, and has the same meaning.

159–60 **out . . . sun** meaning from good to bad, or bad to worse; a common proverbial saying (Dent, G272)

161 **beacon** sun. It is still early morning; see 1 and 131–2.

149 good] *Q; not in Q2, F*   SD] *Dyce; Exit. Q2, F; not in Q*   150 Duke's] *Q; Duke F*   154 out] *Q2, F; ont Q*   157 too] *Q2, F; to Q*   taken] *F; tooke Q*   SD] *Q2, F; not in Q*   158 saw] *Qc, Q2, F; say Qu*

That by thy comfortable beams I may
Peruse this letter. Nothing almost sees miracles
But misery. I know 'tis from Cordelia,
Who hath most fortunately been informed   165
Of my obscurèd course, [*reading the letter*] 'and shall
     find time
From this enormous state, seeking to give
Losses their remedies'. All weary and o'erwatched,
Take vantage, heavy eyes, not to behold
This shameful lodging.   170
Fortune, good night: smile once more; turn thy wheel.
ᵠ*Sleeps*.ᵠ

Enter EDGAR.   [2.3]

this under-globe the earth, as below heaven; see *R2* 3.2.37–8. Perhaps another sardonic joke for Kent, if he pointed to the structure of the Globe theatre above him.

162 **comfortable** comforting

163–4 **Nothing . . . misery** Almost none except the wretched see miracles (because to the desperate any relief seems miraculous).

166 **obscured** obscurèd
obscured course covert mode of life (in his disguise)

166–8 **and . . . remedies** perhaps best interpreted as 'and who (i.e. Cordelia) will find time, away from the monstrous (*enormous*) conditions here, as she seeks to make good what has been lost'. Kent could be reading from Cordelia's letter here. Q and F agree in this obscure passage, regarded by most scholars as corrupt. Oxf and Cam²

accept Rowe's emendation of 'From' to 'For', so the phrase could mean '[Cordelia] will find time to do something about the terrible state of affairs in this country'. It would then be possible to interpret the letter as anticipating 3.1 (Q) in hinting to Kent that France is planning an invasion; there is no reference to a French invading force in 3.1 in F; see Appendix 1.

168 **o'erwatched** exhausted through lack of sleep (see 153)

169 **vantage** the opportunity (to sleep)

170–1 The short line suggests that Kent makes himself comfortable in order to sleep and then makes his appeal to Fortune.

171 **wheel** See 5.3.172 and n.

171.1 *Enter* EDGAR Q and F have no scene-break here, but most editors and many stage directors have made one, and treat Edgar's soliloquy as 2.3.

163 miracles] *F;* my rackles *Qu;* my wracke *Qc, Q2* 165 most] *Qc, Q2, F;* not *Qu* 166 course, and] *Q;* course. And *F* SD] *Jennens* 167 From] *Q, F;* For *Oxf (Rowe)* enormous] *F;* enormious *Q* 168 their] *Qc, Q2, F;* and *Qu* o'erwatched] *F;* ouerwatch *Qu, Qc;* ouer-watcht *Q2* 169 Take] *Qc, Q2, F;* Late *Qu* 171 smile once more;] *Johnson;* Smile once more, *F;* Smile, once more *Q* SD] *Q; not in F;* He sleepes. *Q2*

2.3] *Steevens (Pope)*

EDGAR

I heard myself proclaimed,
And by the happy hollow of a tree
Escaped the hunt. No port is free, no place
That guard and most unusual vigilance   175
Does not attend my taking. While I may scape
I will preserve myself, and am bethought
To take the basest and most poorest shape
That ever penury in contempt of man
Brought near to beast. My face I'll grime with filth,   180
Blanket my loins, elf all my hair in knots   [10]
And with presented nakedness outface
The winds and persecutions of the sky.
The country gives me proof and precedent
Of Bedlam beggars, who, with roaring voices,   185

Edgar does not see Kent and appears to be out in the country, not by Gloucester's house; but for the audience this inset brings together, as humiliated, banished and in disguise, two characters who (even though Kent has brought his disgrace on himself) provide a powerful visual emblem of the *enormous state* produced by Lear's folly and Edmund's machinations. See Introduction, p. 151.

172 **proclaimed** i.e. as an outlaw; compare *MM* 2.4.151
173 **happy** timely, opportune
174 **port** gate or seaport, as at 2.1.80
176 **attend my taking** look out for me to be arrested
177 **bethought** resolved
178 **most poorest** an intensifying double superlative; see 100 above, and Abbott, 11
179 **in . . . man** scorning man's claim to be superior to beasts
180–92 **My face . . . am** On stage it has

become customary for Edgar to tear off his clothes as he speaks these lines, and transform himself in front of the audience into a poor, almost naked, Bedlam beggar. This makes visual sense, and links Edgar with Lear, who, at 3.4.106–7, also tries to strip off his clothes. However, Edgar speaks of what he will do, and his abrupt emergence as Poor Tom at 3.4.44 might be more startling if he remains in costume as Edgar here. See Bratton, 117.
181 **elf** tangle or mat together
182 **presented** displayed
184 **proof and precedent** evidence and example
185 **Bedlam beggars** Bedlam refers to Bethlehem Hospital, which was established in London by the fifteenth century as a place to hold the insane; Bedlam beggars or abram-men 'be those that feign themselves to have been mad, and have been kept in Bethlem or in some other prison a

---

172 heard] *F*; heare *Q*   175 unusual] *Q*; vnusall *Q2, F*   176 Does] *F (Do's)*; Dost *Q*   taking.] *F*; taking *Q*   While] *Q*; Whiles *F*   181 elf] *F (elfe)*; else *Q*   hair] *Q*; haires *F*   in] *F*; with *Q*   183 winds] *F*; wind *Q*   persecutions] *F*; persecution *Q*   184 precedent] *Q, F (president)*

Strike in their numbed ᶠandᶠ mortified ᵠbareᵠ arms
Pins, wooden pricks, nails, sprigs of rosemary;
And with this horrible object, from low farms,
Poor pelting villages, sheepcotes and mills,
Sometime with lunatic bans, sometime with prayers,   190
Enforce their charity. Poor Turlygod, poor Tom,   [20]
That's something yet: Edgar I nothing am.   *Exit.*

Enter LEAR, ᶠFOOL *and a* Knight.ᶠ   **[2.4]**

LEAR
'Tis strange that they should so depart from home

good time' (Thomas Harman, *A Caveat for Common Cursitors* (1567), in Judges, 83–4); they commonly walked 'bare-legged and bare-armed', and called themselves Poor Tom, according to John Awdeley, *The Fraternity of Vagabonds*, 1561, in Judges, 53. See 1.2.135–6 above.

186 **mortified** deadened (to the pain)
187 **pricks** spikes
188 **object** sight, spectacle
189 **pelting** paltry
   mills windmills for grinding corn
190 **bans** curses
191 *Turlygod** unexplained, and no explanation is necessary if he is putting on the cries of madness here, though various ingenious possibilities are canvassed by *TxC*, 515. 'Tuelygod' (Qu) is just as impenetrable, if closer to 'Truelygood', which makes a kind of sense.
192 **something . . . nothing** As Poor Tom he has an identity, as Edgar he is non-existent. *Nothing* here is adver-

bial, meaning 'in no way' (Abbott, 55); see 1.1.88–9 and n.
192.1 Q and F have no scene-break here, but editors have traditionally marked a new scene, 2.4, as commencing at this point. There is, however, good reason why Kent should remain on stage throughout the sequence, and the action is continuous; see 171.1 and n.
*Knight** so Q, in speech prefixes (Q has no entry for him); F has 'Gentleman'. He appears to be one of Lear's train of knights, as Kent asks at 252–3 why Lear has such a small retinue. If Lear is attended here only by this one knight, visually it is as if his train has already been reduced (see 348 and 420 and n.; at 3.7.15 Lear has regained some thirty-five or thirty-six knights). The Knight does not speak after 251, but may remain until Lear's exit at 475. Kent, unobserved at first by Lear, wakes up at some point, perhaps on Lear's entry.
193 **they** Regan and Cornwall

186 numbed and] *Qc, Q2, F;* numb'd *Qu*   187 Pins] *Qc, Q2, F;* Pies *Qu*   wooden pricks] *Q2;* wodden prickes *Q;* Wodden-prickes *F*   188 from . . . farms] *F;* frame . . . seruice *Qu;* from . . . seruice *Qc, Q2*   189 sheepcotes] *Q;* Sheeps-Coates *F*   190 Sometime] *Q;* Sometimes *F*   191 Turlygod] *Qc, Q2, F;* Tuelygod *Qu, Oxf*

2.4] *Steevens (Pope)*   192.1 LEAR, FOOL . . . *Knight*] *this edn; Lear, Foole, and Gentleman F; King Q; King, and a Knight Q2; Lear, Fool . . . First Gentleman Oxf*   193 home] *F;* hence *Q*

And not send back my messenger.

KNIGHT   As I learned,
The night before there was no purpose ^Fin them^F   195
Of this remove.

KENT [*Wakes.*]   Hail to thee, noble master.

LEAR
Ha? Mak'st thou this shame thy pastime?

^FKENT   No, my lord.^F

FOOL   Ha, ha, ^Qlook^Q, he wears cruel garters. Horses are
tied by the heads, dogs and bears by the neck, monkeys
by the loins and men by the legs. When a man's   200
overlusty at legs, then he wears wooden nether-stocks.

LEAR [*to Kent*]
What's he that hath so much thy place mistook   [10]
To set thee here?

KENT   It is both he and she,
Your son and daughter.

LEAR   No.   205

KENT   Yes.

LEAR   No, I say.

KENT   I say, yea.

^QLEAR   No, no, they would not.

KENT   Yes, they have.^Q   210

---

194 *messenger Kent; see 1.5.1–7. So
Q; F has 'Messengers', but Kent was
sent alone.
196 remove change of residence (Muir)
198 cruel garters the stocks, with a
pun on 'crewel', a thin worsted yarn
used to make hose
201 overlusty at legs given either to
running away, or to sexual activity
nether-stocks stockings for the lower
legs (upper-stocks were the wider
parts for the thighs)

202 place office
209–12 *LEAR. . . do't The changes in F,
omitting 209–10 where Lear merely
denies Kent's 'Yes' for a third time,
and adding Kent's more powerful
rejoinder, 'By Juno, I swear ay', at 212,
strengthen this exchange, an important
one, since it echoes Lear's amazed
incredulity in his confrontation with
Cordelia at 1.1.86–90, and his inability
to comprehend any kind of opposition
to the power he had taken for granted

194 messenger] *Q;* Messengers *F*   SP KNIGHT] *Q; Gent. F*   196 this] *F;* his *Q*   SD] *Staunton*
197 Ha?] *F;* How, *Q*   198 cruel] *F, Q (*crewell*)*   199 heads] *F;* heeles *Q*   200 man's] *Q2;* mans
Q; man *F*   201 wooden] *Q;* wodden *F*   202 SD] *Oxf*

LEAR   By Jupiter, I swear no.

^FKENT   By Juno, I swear ay.

LEAR^F   They durst not do't: [20]
    They could not, would not do't – 'tis worse than
        murder
    To do upon respect such violent outrage.
    Resolve me with all modest haste which way   215
    Thou mightst deserve or they impose this usage,
    Coming from us.

KENT   My lord, when at their home
    I did commend your highness' letters to them,
    Ere I was risen from the place that showed
    My duty kneeling, came there a reeking post,   220
    Stewed in his haste, half breathless, panting forth
    From Goneril, his mistress, salutations;   [30]
    Delivered letters, spite of intermission,
    Which presently they read; on those contents
    They summoned up their meiny, straight took horse,   225
    Commanded me to follow and attend
    The leisure of their answer, gave me cold looks;
    And meeting here the other messenger,
    Whose welcome I perceived had poisoned mine,
    Being the very fellow which of late   230

---

for so long. Lear appeals to pagan gods, as always; see 1.1.179.

214 **upon respect** upon consideration; or upon the respect due to the King's messenger

215 **Resolve . . . haste** make clear to me quickly but soberly

217 **from us** Lear drops into the royal plural, his habit in 1.1, for the last time; Cornwall and Regan have already taken over this speech habit of power, see 2.1.103 and n.

220–1 **reeking . . . / Stewed** a courier

drenched in sweat. Weis notes the hints of sexual corruption in these terms, recalling Kent's verbal attack on Oswald at 14–23.

223–7 **Delivered . . . answer** The letters are those Regan 'thought it fit / To answer from our home' at 2.1.125–6.

223 **spite of intermission** even though he interrupted me

224 **presently** immediately
on . . . contents on reading the contents of the letters

225 **meiny** retinue

---

213 could . . . would] *F;* would . . . could *Q*   216 mightst] *F;* may'st *Q*   impose] *F;* purpose *Q*
221 panting] *Q;* painting *F*   224 read; on those] *F;* read, on whose *Q*   225 meiny] *F;* men *Q*
230 which] *F;* that *Q*

Displayed so saucily against your highness,

Having more man than wit about me, drew.   [40]

He raised the house with loud and coward cries.

Your son and daughter found this trespass worth

The shame which here it suffers.   235

ᶠFOOL   Winter's not gone yet, if the wild geese fly that

    way.

               Fathers that wear rags

                  Do make their children blind,

               But fathers that bear bags   240

                  Shall see their children kind:

               Fortune, that arrant whore,   [50]

                  Ne'er turns the key to the poor.

But for all this thou shalt have as many dolours for thy

daughters as thou canst tell in a year.ᶠ   245

LEAR

O, how this mother swells up toward my heart!

Hysterica passio, down, thou climbing sorrow,

---

231 **Displayed so saucily** behaved so
insolently; see 1.4.76–90. Kent's words
here may recall his own display of
'saucy roughness' before Cornwall at
90–3 above; he did more to deserve
being put in the stocks than he admits
in this speech.

232 **more . . . wit** more courage than
good sense

236–7 a cryptic way of saying that Kent's
story means more trouble, or stormy
weather is on the way: 'If Geese doe
flye aloft crying and cackling, it is a
token of foule weather to follow'
(*Perpetual and natural prognostications
of the change of weather*, translated
from the Italian by I.F. (1598), B4ᵛ)

238–43 At 1.4.162 Lear remarks on the
Fool being 'full of songs'; neither Q
nor F has directions for him to sing in
this scene, and it is not clear how many

of his rhyming passages were sung (for
lists and commentary, see Sternfeld,
174–5, and Hunter, 337–43). As Cam²
notes, actors now often deliver passages such as this in a sing-song, or a
kind of discordant *Sprechgesang*.

239 **blind** to their father's welfare

240 **bags** money-bags

243 **turns the key** opens the door

244 **for all this . . . dolours** The Fool
plays ironically on two meanings: in
spite of (the hostility of Fortune) Lear
will have dollars; and on account of
(his poverty) he will have sorrows. The
pun on 'dollars' derives from a
German silver coin called a 'thaler'.

245 **tell** count; relate

246–7 **mother . . . *passio*** a disease mainly of women (see Hoeniger, 320–3)
that arose from the womb and took
them 'with choking in the throat'. It

235 The] *F; This Q*   236 wild] *F (wil'd)*   247 *Hysterica*] *F4; Historica Q, F*

Thy element's below. Where is this daughter?

KENT   With the Earl, sir, ^Fhere^F within.   249

LEAR   Follow me not; stay here.   ^F*Exit.*^F

KNIGHT   Made you no more offence but what you speak of?

KENT   None. How chance the King comes with so small a   [60]
number?

FOOL   An thou hadst been set i'the stocks for that
question, thou hadst well deserved it.   255

KENT   Why, fool?

FOOL   We'll set thee to school to an ant, to teach thee
there's no labouring i'the winter. All that follow their
noses are led by their eyes but blind men, and there's
not a nose among twenty but can smell him that's   260
stinking. Let go thy hold when a great wheel runs down
a hill lest it break thy neck with following ^Qit^Q; but the   [70]
great one that goes upward, let him draw thee after.
When a wise man gives thee better counsel give me

was called 'Passio Hysterica', or, in English, the mother, or the suffocation of the mother (Jorden, *A Brief Discourse of a Disease Called the Mother* (1603), C1r–C2r). Shakespeare found the term in Harsnett, who cites Richard Maynie as saying in his confession that his eldest brother died of the disease, and he himself had 'a spice of the Mother . . . It riseth . . . of a wind in the bottome of the belly, and proceeding with a great swelling, causeth a very painfull collicke in the stomack, and an extraordinary giddines in the head' (Brownlow, 401). Lear's disease thus offers another image of order turned upside-down in the play. Feminist readings of the play have focused on this passage as showing us 'the place of the repressed mother' as Lear 'discovers his origin in the suffocating maternal womb' (Adelman,

114). This is the only scene in which Lear mentions the mother of his children (320), and sees them as part of his own flesh (410–14), so the word *mother* has resonances beyond the reference to a disease. See Introduction, pp. 39–40.

248 **element** sphere or proper place

252 **the King** F's 'the the King' may have resulted from a misreading of scribal abbreviations, 'y^t y^e' = that the.

254 **An** if

257–8 **We'll . . . winter** there's no profit to be gained in the winter, echoing biblical counsel to study the ant: 'consider her wayes, and learne to be wise, . . . in the Sommer shee prouideth her meate' (Proverbs, 6.6)

260 ***twenty** so F, reflecting 'so small a number', 252–3. Q has 'a 100', the original number of Lear's retainers.

261 **stinking** of downfall and loss, like Lear

250 here.] *F;* there? *Q*   251 but] *F;* then *Q*   252 None] *F;* No *Q*   the King] *Q;* the the King *F*
253 number] *F;* train *Q*   254 An] *Pope;* And *Q, F;* If *Q2*   255 thou hadst] *Q;* thoud'st *F*
260 twenty] *F;* a 100. *Q*   263 upward] *F;* vp the hill *Q*   264 gives] *Q, Q2, Fc;* giue *Fu*

mine again; I would have none but knaves follow it,   265
since a fool gives it.

>   That sir which serves ꟻand seeksꟻ for gain,
>   And follows but for form,
>   Will pack when it begins to rain,
>   And leave thee in the storm;   270
>   But I will tarry, the fool will stay,
>   And let the wise man fly: [80]
>   The knave turns fool that runs away,
>   The fool no knave perdy.

KENT   Where learned you this, fool?   275
FOOL   Not i'the stocks, ꟻfool.ꟻ

Enter LEAR *and* GLOUCESTER.

LEAR

> Deny to speak with me? They are sick, they are
>   weary,
> They ꟻhaveꟻ travelled all the night? – mere fetches
>   ᵠayᵠ,
> The images of revolt and flying off.
> Fetch me a better answer.

GLOUCESTER   My dear lord,   280
> You know the fiery quality of the Duke,
> How unremovable and fixed he is   [90]

267 **sir** referring to Lear's knights
268 **form** outward appearance, with no deeper loyalty
269 **pack** be off, depart
273–4 The Fool here rejects the worldly wisdom of what he has just said, in favour of a deeper truth: 'The knave (servant) who deserts his master must eventually be seen as a fool; but this fool will stay, and so, in God's name

(perdy) is no knave' (Hunter). The Fool seems to imply that many of Lear's knights have abandoned him, but see 192.1 and n.
277 **Deny** refuse
278 **fetches** dodges, evasions
279 **flying off** desertion. Lear still speaks as if he were in authority as King.
281 **quality** disposition
282 **unremovable** immovable

267 sir which] *F;* Sir that *Q*   269 begins] *Q2, F;* begin *Q*   276.1] *Q; after 273 F*   277 They are . . . they are] *F;* th'are . . . th'are *Q*   278 travelled] *Q, F (*trauail'd*)*   all the] *F;* hard to *Q*   fetches] *F;* Iustice *Q*   ay] *Q (*I*); not in Q2, F*

In his own course.

LEAR

    Vengeance, plague, death, confusion!

    Fiery? What quality? Why, Gloucester, Gloucester,   285

    I'd speak with the Duke of Cornwall and his wife.

ᶠGLOUCESTER

    Well, my good lord, I have informed them so.

LEAR

    'Informed them'? Dost thou understand me, man?ᶠ

GLOUCESTER   Ay, my good lord.

LEAR

    The King would speak with Cornwall, the dear father   290

    Would with his daughter speak, commands – tends –

        service.

    ᶠAre they informed of this? My breath and blood!   [100]

    'Fiery'?ᶠ The fiery Duke, tell the hot Duke that

      �QLearᏃ –

    No, but not yet, maybe he is not well;

    Infirmity doth still neglect all office   295

    Whereto our health is bound. We are not ourselves

    When nature, being oppressed, commands the mind

    To suffer with the body. I'll forbear,

    And am fallen out with my more headier will

287–8, 292 In F only, these lines take the heat off Gloucester by playing on the word 'inform'; all Gloucester could do is convey a message, not give orders in the way Lear wants.

291 *commands – tends – service As Lear slips from *King* to *father*, so he slides from giving orders to *tends* = attends, or waits for. F makes dramatic sense, and is supported by Qu, 'come and tends', flattened in Qc to 'commands her'.

293 *Fiery? The repetition of this word in F sharpens the dramatic effect of the line, by making Lear break off abruptly at 'that –'; in Q the line ends 'that Lear'.

295–6 Infirmity . . . bound when ill we always neglect the performance of duties we are bound to carry out when in health

299 am . . . will quarrel with or reject my more headstrong impulse

---

284 plague, death] *F;* death, plague *Q*   285 Fiery? What] *F;* what fierie *Q*   290 father] *Qc, Q2, F;* fate *Qu*   291 his] *Qc, Q2, F;* the *Qu*   commands – tends] *F (*commands, tends*);* come and tends *Qu;*   commands her *Qc, Q2*   293 The fiery] *Qu, F;* Fierie *Qc, Q2*   294 No] *Qc, Q2, F;* Mo *Qu*   297 commands] *Q2, F;* Cōmand *Q*

To take the indisposed and sickly fit   300
For the sound man.   [*Notices Kent.*]
                Death on my state! Wherefore
Should he sit here? This act persuades me   [110]
That this remotion of the Duke and her
Is practice only. Give me my servant forth.
^FGo^F tell the Duke and's wife I'd speak with them,   305
Now, presently: bid them come forth and hear me,
Or at their chamber door I'll beat the drum
Till it cry sleep to death.
GLOUCESTER   I would have all well betwixt you.   ^F*Exit.*^F
LEAR

O ^Fme,^F my heart! My ^Frising^F heart! ^FBut down!^F   310
FOOL   Cry to it, nuncle, as the cockney did to the eels
when she put 'em i'the paste alive: she knapped 'em   [120]
o'the coxcombs with a stick, and cried 'Down, wantons,
down!' 'Twas her brother that in pure kindness to his

---

301 **Death . . . state!** The common oath
(compare 'Life and death', 1.4.288)
takes on a special meaning here as *state*
relates both to Lear's condition as an
old man, and to his power as King,
which is, as Hunter notes, already
'dead'. The sight of Kent, however,
makes Lear again give commands and
act for the moment as if he were still
all-powerful.
303 **remotion** departure from their own
house to Gloucester's, and perhaps
remoteness or failure to present themselves
304 **practice only** merely a device
Give . . . forth i.e. release Kent from
the stocks
306 **presently** at once
308 **cry . . . death** puts sleep to death by
the noise, and keeps everyone awake
309 SD, 315.1 F marks an exit and re-
entry for Gloucester, who goes to fetch
Cornwall and Regan, both directions

absent from Q. Gloucester has no lines
before 475, where he goes off with
Lear, Kent and the Fool, to return
shortly (483.1) to report on what Lear
is doing. The knight attending on Lear
also may remain silent on stage
through the later part of the scene; see
192.1 and n.
310 **My . . . down!* Q's prose, 'O my
heart, my heart', is stretched into a
blank verse line in F that recalls 246–8,
as Lear is again afflicted with the
'mother'.
311–14 **Cry . . . down!** The point of the
joke is that the *cockney* (a nice or
affected woman) acts too late in striking live eels on their heads (*coxcombs*)
when they are already in the pastry for
the pie, and crying 'Down!' to the
frisky creatures (*wantons*), as Lear is
doing to his unruly heart.
314–15 **in . . . hay** another example of
folly; horses refuse to eat greasy hay, so

---

301 SD] *this edn (Johnson)*   304 practice only.] *F;* practise, only *Q*   305 I'd] *F (*I'd'*);* Ile *Q*
312 'em . . . knapped 'em] *F;* vm . . . rapt vm *Q*   313 o'the] *F (*o'th'*);* ath *Q*

horse buttered his hay.   315

Enter CORNWALL, REGAN, ^FGLOUCESTER [*and*] *servants.*^F

LEAR
  Good morrow to you both.
CORNWALL   Hail to your grace.
  ^F*Kent here set at liberty.*^F
REGAN   I am glad to see your highness.
LEAR
  Regan, I think you are. I know what reason
  I have to think so. If thou shouldst not be glad,
  I would divorce me from thy mother's tomb,   320
  Sepulchring an adultress. [*to Kent*] O, are you free?
  Some other time for that. – Beloved Regan,   [130]
  Thy sister's naught. O, Regan, she hath tied
  Sharp-toothed unkindness, like a vulture, here.

it would be unkindness to give it them
315.1 CORNWALL, REGAN Regan wears *gorgeous* clothes that scarcely keep her warm (457–8; and see Introduction, p. 40), and, if she and Cornwall are dressed for the day, their 'social excuse' of being sick and weary (277) is exposed as a fiction; it is less likely that they have put on night attire, but see Rosenberg, 161–2. It is notable that the Fool remains silent for the rest of the scene.
318 Regan . . . are Many Lears have greeted Regan with tenderness (Henry Irving noted, 'Regan now the only daughter left. All his tenderness goes to her'); others, like Paul Scofield, have remained harsh, but if Lear's anger melts away briefly his greeting of Regan can be very affecting; see Bratton, 123, and Rosenberg, 161–2.

Lear's expectation of kindness from Regan is shown in his use of the intimate *thou* from 319 on, which only changes to a more formal *you* at 383.
320 mother's tomb the only direct mention of Lear's wife in F; see 246–7 and n. In Q Kent wonders at 4.3.35 how one 'mate and make', or husband and wife, could produce children so unlike one another as Cordelia and her sisters.
321 adultress As Adelman, 108–9, observes, Lear invents a fantasy of illegitimacy, so linking his daughters (he called Goneril *degenerate bastard* at 1.4.245) with Edmund's bastardy, and siting the origin of viciousness in the female, anticipating his misogynistic outburst at 4.6.116–25.
322 Beloved belovèd
323 naught wicked
324 vulture alluding to Prometheus, who

315.1 CORNWALL] *F; Duke and Q*   318 you] *Q;* your *F*   320 divorce] *Qc, Q2, F;* deuose *Qu*
mother's] *Q;* Mother *F*   tomb] *Qc, Q2, F;* fruit *Qu;* shrine *Oxf*   321 SD] *Rowe* O] *F;* yea *Q*
322 for that.] *Riv (Ringler²) adds SD, Exit Kent*   323 sister's] *F (Sisters); sister is Q*

[*Lays his hand on his heart.*]

I can scarce speak to thee; thou'lt not believe   325
With how depraved a quality – O, Regan!

REGAN

I pray ᶠyouᶠ, sir, take patience. I have hope
You less know how to value her desert
Than she to scant her duty.

ᶠLEAR   Say? how is that?

REGAN

I cannot think my sister in the least   330
Would fail her obligation. If, sir, perchance
She have restrained the riots of your followers,   [140]
'Tis on such ground and to such wholesome end
As clears her from all blame.ᶠ

LEAR

My curses on her.

REGAN   O, sir, you are old: 335
Nature in you stands on the very verge
Of her confine. You should be ruled and led
By some discretion that discerns your state

---

stole fire from the gods and was punished by being chained to a rock,
where a vulture gnawed endlessly at
his liver. The legend was common
knowledge, and is mentioned, as Ard²
notes, by Harsnett (Brownlow, 260).
326 **quality** nature, disposition, as at 281
327 **patience** See 1.4.254, and lines 419,
459–60 below, where Lear acknowledges his need for patience.
328–9 **You . . . duty** You are less capable
of valuing her merit than she is of
neglecting her duty. Regan's meaning
is plain, even if her syntax is clumsy.
329–34 *a passage adding in F another
reference to the riotous behaviour of
Lear's train; see Goneril's complaint at

1.4.315–20
332 **riots** Originally debauchery or unrestrained revelry, the word later came to
mean violent disturbance of the peace;
perhaps both senses are felt in the play.
337 *her confine** the allotted space of
life, with a possible suggestion of
death as an escape from the dungeon
of the flesh (if *confine* = prison, as at
Ham 1.1.155). Nature is commonly
personified as female, but F's 'his'
makes a kind of sense as drawing the
emphasis towards Lear.
338 **some discretion** someone able to
judge
    state condition; see 301 and n.

324.1] *Hunter (Pope)*   326 With] *F;* Of *Q*   depraved] *F;* deptoued *Qu;* depriued *Qc, Q2*   quality
–] *Rowe;* qualitie, *Q;* quality. *F*   329 scant] *F;* slacke *Q*   336 in] *F;* on *Q*   337 her] *Q;* his *F*

Better than you yourself. Therefore I pray ^Fyou^F
That to our sister you do make return;   340
Say you have wronged her, ^Qsir.^Q

LEAR   Ask her forgiveness?
Do you ^Fbut^F mark how this becomes the house?   [150]
[*Kneels.*] Dear daughter, I confess that I am old;
Age is unnecessary. On my knees I beg
That you'll vouchsafe me raiment, bed and food.   345

REGAN

Good sir, no more. These are unsightly tricks.
Return you to my sister.
LEAR [*Rises.*]   Never, Regan:
She hath abated me of half my train,
Looked black upon me, struck me with her tongue
Most serpent-like, upon the very heart.   350
All the stored vengeances of heaven fall
On her ingrateful top! Strike her young bones,   [160]

---

342 **becomes the house** befits the family, or royal line. Lear is being ironic.

343 SD   Lear kneeling here to his daughter offers a visual emblem of the inversion of order in the play; the restoration of order is marked by Cordelia kneeling to Lear at 4.7.57–9, where she restrains him from kneeling to her. See David Bevington, *Action is Eloquence* (1984), 169–71, on the 'erosion of proper custom' in the play.

344–5 **Age . . . food** Lear's sarcastic words carry a home truth: by his division of the kingdom he has become dependent on her charity.

346 **unsightly** ugly

348 **abated** deprived; the word was used by Spenser, *Faerie Queene*, 2.10.30, where, in order to get rid of her father, Regan maltreats him: 'Her bountie she abated, and her cheare empayrd'
half my train Shakespeare turns

the screw: Goneril called at 1.4.286 for Lear to dismiss fifty followers within a fortnight, and at the end of 1.4.326 was still speaking of Lear's hundred knights, as Lear himself does at 420 below; see 192.1 and n. Regan seeks to cut Lear's train by half at 393. Dramatically, an impression is conveyed that Lear's train has already been slashed.

349 **struck** 'Strooke' (Q and F), a common form of the past participle, as at *R3* 3.1.92, points to the way it was pronounced.

349–50 **tongue . . . serpent-like** It was generally supposed that a serpent's venom was in its tongue (*OED sb*. 1d).

352 **ingrateful top** ungrateful head
young bones In the old play Leir says Goneril is tetchy because she 'breeds young bones', or is with child (*Leir*, 844–6), and it is not clear

---

343 SD] *Johnson (Hanmer)*   347 SD] *Dyce (Collier)*   Never] *F; No Q*   349 struck] *Q, F (strooke)*

248

You taking airs, with lameness!

CORNWALL   Fie, sir, fie!

^FLEAR^F

You nimble lightnings, dart your blinding flames
Into her scornful eyes! Infect her beauty,   355
You fen-sucked fogs, drawn by the powerful sun
To fall and blister!

REGAN   O, the blest gods!

So will you wish on me when the rash mood ^Fis on.^F

LEAR

No, Regan, thou shalt never have my curse.
Thy tender-hafted nature shall not give   360
Thee o'er to harshness. Her eyes are fierce, but
    thine
Do comfort and not burn. 'Tis not in thee   [170]
To grudge my pleasures, to cut off my train,
To bandy hasty words, to scant my sizes
And, in conclusion, to oppose the bolt   365
Against my coming in. Thou better knowst
The offices of nature, bond of childhood,
Effects of courtesy, dues of gratitude.

---

whether Lear's curse here applies to
Goneril, or to any child she may have.

353 **taking** blasting, noxious
Fie, sir, fie! expressing disgust or dis-
approval

357 ***blister** raise blisters on her. Q has
'blast her pride', and F may be a corruption, though blistering seems more
appropriate to the action of fogs.

360 **tender-hafted** set in a delicate bodily frame, and hence gentle; from 'haft'
or handle. Rosenberg, 162–3, sees in
Regan a 'more feminine mode of offering tenderness to Lear' than her sister
shows, and her manner is certainly dif-

ferent from the abrasive way of
Goneril in 1.4; but, for all that, Lear's
lines here represent wishful thinking;
Regan will act like Goneril, whom she
takes by the hand at 383.

364 **scant my sizes** curtail my
allowances (of food and drink)

365 **oppose the bolt** lock the doors.
Ironically it is Regan who orders Lear
to be locked out at 494.

367 **offices of nature** natural obligations
bond recalling the uses of this important term at 1.1.93, 1.2.108 and 2.1.47

368 **Effects of courtesy** outward marks

353 sir, fie] *F; fie sir Q*   354 SP LEAR] *Q2, F (Le.); not in Q*   357 blister] *F; blast her pride Q;*
blister her *Ard²*   360 Thy tender-hafted] *F (Thy tender-hefted); The teder hested Q; Thy tender-
hearted Rowe*   361 Thee] *Q2, F; the Q*

Thy half o'the kingdom hast thou not forgot,
Wherein I thee endowed.

REGAN   Good sir, to the purpose   370

        ᶠ*Tucket within.*ᶠ

LEAR

Who put my man i'the stocks?

Enter OSWALD.

CORNWALL   What trumpet's that?

REGAN

I know't, my sister's. This approves her letter   [180]
That she would soon be here. [*to Oswald*] Is your
        lady come?

LEAR

This is a slave whose easy borrowed pride
Dwells in the fickle grace of her he follows.   375
Out, varlet, from my sight!

CORNWALL   What means your grace?

Enter GONERIL.

LEAR

Who stocked my servant? Regan, I have good hope
Thou didst not know on't. Who comes here? O
        heavens!

---

of proper behaviour

370 **purpose** ironically recalling Lear's
attention to the stocking of Kent

370 SD *Tucket* a flourish played on a
trumpet, as at 2.1.77 SD

371 **Who . . . stocks?** Something of an
anticlimax after Lear's build-up, his
question has to be asked three times, as
Cam² notes, before it is answered at

388.

372 **approves** confirms, as at 158

374 **easy** casual or effortless

375 ***fickle grace** uncertain favour. F
has 'fickly', probably an error, but
some editions, following F3, print
'sickly', which makes a kind of sense in
relation both to Oswald and Goneril.

377–8 ***LEAR . . . on't** so F; in Q these

371 SD OSWALD] *Collier; Steward Q (after 373), F*   372 letter] *F;* letters *Q*   373 SD] *Riv*
375 fickle] *Qu, Qc;* fickly *F;* sickly *F3*   her he] *Q2, F;* her a *Qu;* her, a *Qc*   377 SP LEAR] *F;*
Gon. Q   stocked] *F;* struck *Q*   378 on't] *F;* ant *Q*   Who comes] *F; Lear.* Who comes *Q*

If you do love old men, if your sweet sway
Allow obedience, if ᶠyouᶠ yourselves are old,   380
Make it your cause. Send down, and take my part!
[*to Goneril*] Art not ashamed to look upon this beard?   [190]
O, Regan, will you take her by the hand?

GONERIL

Why not by the hand, sir? How have I offended?
All's not offence that indiscretion finds   385
And dotage terms so.

LEAR   O sides, you are too tough!
Will you yet hold? How came my man i'the stocks?

CORNWALL

I set him there, sir; but his own disorders
Deserved much less advancement.

LEAR   You? Did you?

REGAN

I pray you, father, being weak, seem so.   390
If till the expiration of your month
You will return and sojourn with my sister,   [200]

---

words are given to Goneril, with the
difference that she asks Regan who
'struck' her servant. In Q she thus
seems to be already quarrelling with
her sister, whereas in F Lear repeats
the question he asked at 371. I think Q
for some reason has it wrong, for it is
Lear who strikes Oswald at 1.4.82, and
here Regan takes Goneril by the hand
at 383, visually displaying their soli-
darity. See Introduction, p. 131.

379–80 **sway / Allow** controlling influence sanction; compare 1.4.199

380 **obedience** a concept of some importance in the play; see Introduction, pp.
69–71.

383 **you . . . hand** symbolizing their
union, and recalling the visual image
of Burgundy taking and relinquishing
Cordelia's hand as in promise of marriage, only for France to 'seize upon'

her (1.1.245, 254). See also 360 and n.
This is a critical moment for Lear,
as Granville-Barker, 171, says, 'is
brought to a stand and to face the real-
ities arrayed against him', and his shift
from the intimate *thou* to the more distanced *you* signals his recognition of it.

385 **indiscretion finds** your lack of
judgement finds (to be so)

386–7 **O . . . hold?** His rhetorical question is addressed to his bodily frame,
still holding down his *rising heart*
(310).

389 **much less advancement** Cornwall's sarcasm, meaning 'much worse
punishment'

390 **I pray you** As earlier, Regan charac-
teristically interrupts to prevent
Cornwall responding and to divert
attention to herself; see 2.1.103 and n.

392 **sojourn** reside for a time

---

379 your] *F;* you *Q*   382 SD] *Johnson*   383 will you] *F;* wilt thou *Q*   389 You? Did] *F;* You, did *Q*

Dismissing half your train, come then to me.
I am now from home and out of that provision
Which shall be needful for your entertainment.   395

LEAR

Return to her? And fifty men dismissed?
No! Rather I abjure all roofs and choose
To wage against the enmity o'th' air –
To be a comrade with the wolf and owl –
Necessity's sharp pinch! Return with her?   400
Why, the hot-blooded France, that dowerless took
Our youngest born, I could as well be brought   [210]
To knee his throne and squire-like pension beg,
To keep base life afoot. Return with her?
Persuade me rather to be slave and sumpter   405
To this detested groom.   [*Points at Oswald.*]

GONERIL   At your choice, sir.

LEAR

ᵠNowᵠ I prithee, daughter, do not make me mad:
I will not trouble thee, my child. Farewell:
We'll no more meet, no more see one another.

---

393 **Dismissing . . . train** See 192.1, 348
and notes.
394 **from** away from
   provision supply of necessities
395 **entertainment** maintenance
397 **abjure** swear to abandon
398 **wage** struggle, do battle
   enmity o'th' air anticipating the
   affliction of the storm in Act 3
399 **wolf and owl** nocturnal creatures
   that prey ferociously on others. Lear's
   image is typically an extreme one.
400 ***Necessity's sharp pinch** a
   phrase in apposition with, and summing up, Lear's angry and incoherent
   choice in the previous three lines; as
   Hunter notes, necessity means both
   poverty and fate. Transposing 398 and

399 (Theobald, followed by Oxf) is
   unnecessary, and does not improve the
   sense.
401 ***hot-blooded France** so F, meaning
   the King of France, as at 1.1.189, 265.
   Q has 'hot blud in *France*', 'blood'
   meaning a young buck, a hot-blooded
   man, as at *KJ* 2.1.278.
403 **knee** kneel before
   squire-like like a retainer or vassal
404 **base life afoot** a menial existence on
   the go
405–6 **sumpter . . . groom** packhorse to
   this detested servant (or stableman);
   groom carries both senses
407 **do . . . mad** glimpsing what is to
   come; see 475, and also 1.5.43 and n.

398–9 To . . . owl –] *lines transposed by Theobald*   401 hot-blooded] *Fu;* hot blud in *Q;* hot-
bloodied *Fc*   403 beg] *F;* bag *Q*   406 SD] *Dyce (Johnson)*

But yet thou art my flesh, my blood, my daughter, 410
Or rather a disease that's in my flesh,
Which I must needs call mine. Thou art a boil, [220]
A plague sore, or embossed carbuncle
In my corrupted blood. But I'll not chide thee:
Let shame come when it will; I do not call it, 415
I do not bid the thunder-bearer shoot,
Nor tell tales of thee to high-judging Jove.
Mend when thou canst, be better at thy leisure:
I can be patient, I can stay with Regan,
I and my hundred knights.

REGAN   Not altogether so, ᵠsir ᵠ. 420
I looked not for you yet, nor am provided
For your fit welcome. Give ear, sir, to my sister; [230]
For those that mingle reason with your passion
Must be content to think you ᵠareᵠ old, and so –
But she knows what she does.

LEAR   Is this well spoken ᵠnow ᵠ? 425

410–14 **But . . . blood** Lear finds the
source of his own corruption in that of
his daughters, and cannot disown them
after all: 'if they are his, then he is
intolerably implicated in their femaleness' (Adelman, 109). See 246–7, 321
and n. In cursing them, he thus curses
himself.
413 **embossed** embossèd
    embossed carbuncle bulging tumour
414 **blood** lineage, from *blood* = that
    part of the body parents and children
    share, as at 410 (*OED sb*. 8)
416 **thunder-bearer shoot** Jupiter send
    his thunder-bolts. Lear invokes Jupiter
    at 211.
417 **high-judging** judging from on high
    (Weis)
418 **Mend** improve
419 **patient** See 327 and n.
420 **hundred knights** See 348 and n.

423 **mingle . . . passion** apply cool
    judgement to your passionate out-
    bursts. The play questions the conven-
    tional wisdom of Shakespeare's age,
    which assumed that reason was given
    to human beings to control their pas-
    sions. The idea is summed up in Sir
    John Davies's lines on the fall of Adam
    and Eve: 'Ill they desir'd to know, and
    Ill they did, / And to give Passion eyes,
    made Reason blind' (*Nosce Teipsum*
    (1599), 27–8). The play shows a more
    complex relation between reason and
    passion; Regan and Goneril here can
    appeal to reason in the light of Lear's
    outbursts, but Lear makes a more pow-
    erful appeal to reason at 453. See 73–4
    above and 74n.
424 **and so –** Regan breaks off as if she
    were about to repeat what she said at
    335–9.

411 that's in] *F;* that lies within *Q*   412 boil] *Q* (bile*); Q2, F* (Byle*)   413 or] *F;* an *Q*
421 looked] *F;* looke *Q*   424 so –] *Rowe;* so, *Q, F*

253

REGAN

> I dare avouch it, sir. What, fifty followers?
> Is it not well? What should you need of more?
> Yea, or so many, sith that both charge and danger
> Speak 'gainst so great a number? How in one house
> Should many people, under two commands,   430
> Hold amity? 'Tis hard, almost impossible.

GONERIL

> Why might not you, my lord, receive attendance   [240]
> From those that she calls servants or from mine?

REGAN

> Why not, my lord? If then they chanced to slack ye
> We could control them. If you will come to me –   435
> For now I spy a danger – I entreat you
> To bring but five and twenty: to no more
> Will I give place or notice.

LEAR

> I gave you all –

REGAN   And in good time you gave it.

LEAR

> – Made you my guardians, my depositaries,   440
> But kept a reservation to be followed
> With such a number. What, must I come to you   [250]

---

426 **avouch** confirm
427 **What . . . need** what need should you have
428 **sith . . . danger** since both the expense and the danger of riotous behaviour (*danger* recalls Regan's words added in F at 331–4)
429–31 **How . . . amity?** In asking how friendly relations can be preserved, Regan has a point; see *Cor* 3.1.108–12, where Coriolanus raises a similar question, as to 'how soon confusion' can

result when 'two authorities are up', neither supreme.
434 **slack ye** be wanting in their duty to you. Goneril in fact encouraged *negligence* towards Lear at 1.3.13–14.
438 **place or notice** houseroom or recognition
440 **my . . . depositaries** the managers of my affairs, my trustees
441 **kept a reservation** reserved the right; see 1.1.134 (so Weis)

426 sir. What,] *Rowe;* sir, what *Q, F*   429 Speak] *F;* Speakes *Q*   one] *F;* a *Q*   434 ye] *F;* you *Q*
435 control] *Q (*controwle*), F (*comptroll*)*

With five and twenty? Regan, said you so?

REGAN

And speak't again, my lord: no more with me.

LEAR

Those wicked creatures yet do look well favoured   445

When others are more wicked; not being the worst

Stands in some rank of praise. [*to Goneril*] I'll go

   with thee;

Thy fifty yet doth double five and twenty,

And thou art twice her love.

GONERIL   Hear me, my lord:

What need you five and twenty? Ten? Or five?   450

To follow in a house where twice so many

Have a command to tend you?

REGAN   What need one?   [260]

LEAR

O, reason not the need! Our basest beggars

Are in the poorest thing superfluous;

Allow not nature more than nature needs,   455

Man's life is cheap as beast's. Thou art a lady;

If only to go warm were gorgeous,

Why, nature needs not what thou gorgeous wear'st,

---

445 **well favoured** good-looking
447 **Stands . . . praise** deserves some
  commendation
449 **twice her love** See 1.1.51. Lear has
  to learn that love cannot be quantified,
  any more than *true need* can at 459.
451 **follow** be your followers
453 **reason . . . need** don't argue ration-
  ally about the need; *need* cannot finally
  be calculated, any more than love; see
  423, 449 and nn.
453–4 **Our . . . superfluous** the poorest
  beggars have some miserable possession that is superfluous to their needs.

455–6 ***Allow . . . beast's** If you do not
  allow (human) nature more than
  (animal) nature needs, then man's life
  is as worthless as that of a beast.
  Hunter, who notes the two senses of
  nature, thinks Lear is exploding with
  anger here, not arguing, and he places
  a dash after 'needs', making 'Man's life
  is cheap as beast's' into a statement on
  its own, expressing the attitude of his
  daughters. Q has a comma, F a colon at
  this point.
458–60 **needs . . . need!** Lear shifts from
  bodily need, which is scarcely met by

---

443 twenty? Regan] *F;* twentie, *Regan Q;* twenty, Regan? *Capell*   445 look] *F;* seem *Q*
447 SD] *Hanmer*   452 need] *F;* needes *Q*   453 need] *F;* deed *Q*   455 nature needs,] *Q, Q2, Fc;*
Nattue needs: *Fu*   456 life is] *F;* life as *Q;* life's as *Q2*

Which scarcely keeps thee warm. But for true need –
You heavens, give me that patience, patience I need!   460
You see me here, you gods, a poor old man,
As full of grief as age, wretched in both: [270]
If it be you that stirs these daughters' hearts
Against their father, fool me not so much
To bear it tamely; touch me with noble anger,   465
And let not women's weapons, water-drops,
Stain my man's cheeks. No, you unnatural hags,
I will have such revenges on you both
That all the world shall – I will do such things –
What they are yet I know not, but they shall be   470
The terrors of the earth! You think I'll weep,
No, I'll not weep.   ᶠ*Storm and tempest.*ᶠ
I have full cause of weeping, but this heart   [281]

the sumptuous clothes Regan or Goneril is wearing (his *thou* could be addressed to either), to spiritual need, the capacity to endure suffering, which is beyond calculation. Although Lear goes on to appeal to the *gods*, his cry for *patience* has Christian overtones: 'tribulation worketh patience; And patience, experience; and experience, hope' (Romans, 5.3–4). See also 327 and 419 above, and 3.4.28–36 and n. The word *gorgeous*, suggesting brilliant colours, provides an unusual textual indication of costume.

461–2 **poor . . . both** a recognition of his own basic *nature*, shedding for the moment his regal manner

464 **fool . . . much** do not make me so foolish as

465–75 **touch . . . mad** Lear calls for anger appropriate to a male greatness of mind, but it evaporates in the empty and absurd flourish of unimaginable

revenges; in spite of Lear's verbal rejection of tears as feminine, as unmanning him, actors such as Garrick and Irving have wept or sobbed as they left the stage here, recalling Lear's *hot tears* shed at 1.4.290 when Goneril first shakes his *manhood* (1.4.289). Lear finally yields to the healing power of women's tears, symbolic of love and pity, when he is reconciled to Cordelia; see 4.7.47 and 71. On Lear's 'progress towards acceptance of the woman in himself', see Kahn, 45–6, Adelman, 113–14, and Introduction, pp. 39–40.

472 SD *after *weeping* (473) in F, where the verse is mislined; not in Q. The *heavens*, 460 (or Jupiter the *thunderbearer*, 416), may be responding with ambiguous clamour to Lear's outburst; if so, against whom is the thunder directed?

459 warm. But . . . need –] *Steevens (Warburton)*; warme, but . . . need, *Q*; warme, but . . . need: *F*
461 man] *F*; fellow *Q*   463 daughters' hearts] *Q*, *Q2*, *Fc*;   464 so] *F*; to *Q*; too *Q2*   465 tamely] *F*; lamely *Q*   466 And] *F*; O *Q*   469 shall –] *Q2*, *F*; shall, *Q*   things –] *Hanmer*; things, *Q*, *F*
470 are yet] *Q*; are, yet *Q2*; are yet, *F*   472 SD] *F (after* weeping, *473); not in Q*

Shall break into a hundred thousand flaws
Or e'er I'll weep. O fool, I shall go mad.   475
      Exeunt ^Q*Lear, Gloucester, Kent, Fool*^Q [*and Knight*].

CORNWALL
Let us withdraw; 'twill be a storm.

REGAN
This house is little; the old man and's people
Cannot be well bestowed.

GONERIL
'Tis his own blame; hath put himself from rest
And must needs taste his folly.   480

REGAN
For his particular, I'll receive him gladly,
But not one follower.

GONERIL   So am I purposed.   [290]
Where is my lord of Gloucester?

            Enter GLOUCESTER.

CORNWALL
Followed the old man forth – he is returned.

GLOUCESTER   The King is in high rage.   485

---

474 **flaws** fragments
475 **Or e'er** before; see Abbott 131
SD *Q names Kent as leaving the
stage here, although he says nothing in
the scene after he is set at liberty (F) at
316, and if he goes off into the storm
with Lear it seems odd that he returns
shortly in 3.1 asking 'Where's the
King?' (3.1.3). The general '*Exeunt*' in
F might be taken as allowing him an
earlier unmarked exit, perhaps after he
is released from the stocks. See
Appendix 1.

O . . . mad touchingly addressed to
the Fool, who has remained a silent
supporter of Lear from the entry of
Cornwall and Regan at 315.1
478 **bestowed** lodged
479 **put . . . rest** removed or turned himself away from (*OED* Put *v.*[1] 27b) both
a place to sleep and peace of mind
481 **For . . . particular** as far as he per-
sonally is concerned
482–8 ***So . . . himself** Q and F differ in
the attribution of lines here; 482–3 are
spoken by Goneril in F, Cornwall

---

474 into . . . flaws] *F*; in a 100. thousand flowes *Q*   475 mad] *Q*, *Q2*, *Fc*; mads *Fu*   SD *Lear . . .
Fool*] *Q2*, *Q* (*reading 'Leister' for 'Gloster'); not in F*   SD *and Knight*] *this edn (Ard²)*   476+ SP
CORNWALL] *F (Corn.); Duke Q*   477 and's] *F (an'ds); and his Q*   479 blame; hath] *Capell
(blame; he hath); blame hath Q, F*   482 SP GONERIL] *F; Duke Q*   purposed] *Q2, F; puspos'd Q*
484, 488 SP CORNWALL] *F (Corn.); Reg., Re. Q*

257

^FCORNWALL   Whither is he going?

GLOUCESTER

He calls to horse,^F but will I know not whither.

CORNWALL

'Tis best to give him way; he leads himself.

GONERIL [*to Gloucester*]

My lord, entreat him by no means to stay.

GLOUCESTER

Alack, the night comes on, and the high winds   490
Do sorely ruffle; for many miles about
There's scarce a bush.

REGAN   O sir, to wilful men   [300]
The injuries that they themselves procure
Must be their schoolmasters. Shut up your doors.
He is attended with a desperate train,   490
And what they may incense him to, being apt
To have his ear abused, wisdom bids fear.

CORNWALL

Shut up your doors, my lord; 'tis a wild night.
My Regan counsels well; come out o'the storm.   *Exeunt.*

('*Duke*') in Q; 488 by Cornwall in F, Regan in Q. In addition, a line split between Cornwall and Gloucester is added at 486–7 in F, reporting that Lear calls for horses, as at 1.4.250 and 1.5.31–2. F gives Cornwall and Goneril more prominence, at the expense of Regan, who has had the lion's share of the dialogue with Lear for some time. See Appendix 1 for some further comment.

488 It's best to yield to him; he insists on going his own way.

491 **ruffle** rage, bluster

493 **themselves procure** bring on themselves

494, 498 **Shut . . . doors** The repetition presses home the symbolic force of

shutting Lear out; see 365 and n. How the end of the scene was played at the Globe is not known; later productions have sometimes 'made great closed doors a central visual image of Lear's alienation' (Rosenberg, 182, and see also 136), as Kozintsev did in his film.

495 **with** by; a common usage (Abbott 193); cf. 442 above
    desperate train reckless band. Regan again harps on her fear of Lear's riotous knights; see 332, 428.

496 **incense him to** incite him to do

497 **have . . . abused** be misled by their tales; compare 1.3.21. The verb 'abuse' has now almost lost its old meaning, 'to deceive'.

487 but] *F;* & *Q*   488 best] *F;* good *Q*   490 high] *F;* bleak *Q*   491 ruffle] *F;* russel *Q;* rustle *Capell*   492 scarce] *F;* not *Q*   498 wild] *Q;* wil'd *F*   499 Regan] *Q2, F; Reg. Q*   o'the] *F* (oth')*;* at'h *Q*

258

3.1   ᶠ*Storm still.*ᶠ *Enter* KENT [*disguised*] *and a* Knight
                                              severally.

KENT   Who's there, besides foul weather?
KNIGHT   One minded like the weather, most unquietly.
KENT   I know you. Where's the King?
KNIGHT

    Contending with the fretful elements;
    Bids the wind blow the earth into the sea,   5
    Or swell the curled waters 'bove the main,
    That things might change, or cease; ᵠtears his white
      hair,

3.1.0.1 *Storm still* Directions for the
storm to continue, repeated four times
in F, at 3.2.0.1, 3.4.3, 61 and 158,
together with indications in the text
like Kent's 'Fie on this storm!', 3.1.45,
have fostered a stage tradition of giving great importance to it. From the
late eighteenth century onwards
increasingly naturalistic effects have
been devised, even to simulating real
rain on the stage, as in the Trevor
Nunn production of 1976, and the
Kenneth Branagh production of 1991;
see Bratton, 26–30. It has often proved
more effective to symbolize the storm,
as Peter Brook did by lowering
copper thundersheets from the flies
(Rosenberg, 184–5). The actor playing
Lear has to compete in voice with the
noise of the storm, which at the Globe
was probably suggested by rolling iron
balls on a metal sheet (Ben Jonson, in
the Prologue to *Every Man in his
Humour,* refers to a 'rolled bullet heard
/ To say, it thunders'), beating drums
or letting off squibs.
0.1 **Knight** Q and F have 'Gentleman' in
the speech prefixes, as Q does for the
Knight in 2.2, but, since Kent
recognizes him (17), and he has been

with Lear, he appears to be the knight
who came on with Lear in 2.2, and is
best played by the same actor; see
2.2.192.1 and n.
0.2 *severally* separately, as at 2.1.0.1, or
by different doors (as Q)
2 **minded . . . unquietly** disturbed like
the storm. Here is established, as
Hunter notes, the link between the
outer world of the storm and inner
turmoil in the mind that runs through
the storm scenes.
4 **fretful elements** turbulent water
(rain), air (wind) and fire (lightning);
see 3.2.14–16
5–7 **Bids . . . cease** Lear cries out for the
return of chaos, or the end of the
world, an image recalled at 5.3.261–2.
6 **curled** curlèd
    main mainland
7–15 ***tears . . . all** These lines seem to
have been neatly excised from F so as
to maintain the metre; in Q in effect
they repeat 4–7, do not advance the
action, and describe what we can see
Lear do in 3.2; but the image of Lear
hatless and tearing his white hair has
been suggestive for actors, and the idea
of his 'little world of man' as a micro-
cosm or epitome of the external world

3.1] *F (Actus Tertius. Scena Prima); not in Q* **0.1** *disguised] Riv (disguised as Caius)   severally] F;*
at seuerall doores Q **1** Who's there, besides] *F;* Whats here beside *Q* **2+** SP KNIGHT] *this edn;*
Gen. or Gent. Q , F **4** elements] *F;* element *Q*

Which the impetuous blasts with eyeless rage
Catch in their fury and make nothing of,
Strives in his little world of man to outscorn   10
The to and fro conflicting wind and rain;
This night wherein the cub-drawn bear would couch,
The lion and the belly-pinched wolf
Keep their fur dry, unbonneted he runs,
And bids what will take all.^Q

KENT   But who is with him?   15

KNIGHT

None but the fool, who labours to outjest
His heart-struck injuries.

KENT   Sir, I do know you
And dare upon the warrant of my note
Commend a dear thing to you. There is division,
Although as yet the face of it is covered   20
With mutual cunning, 'twixt Albany and Cornwall,
^FWho have, as who have not that their great stars

establishes the link between the storm
in nature and the storm in Lear's mind
that is dramatized in the next scenes.
8 **eyeless** blind
9 **make nothing of** blow about
   contemptuously (*OED* Make *v.*[1] 21)
12 **cub-drawn** sucked dry by her cubs,
   and so ravenous
   couch go to ground or find its lair
13 **belly-pinched** belly-pinchèd; starv-
   ing
14 **unbonneted** hatless, and therefore
   reckless; see 3.2.60 and n.
15 **bids . . . all** says anyone who wants the
   world can have it, i.e. let all go to ruin,
   echoing 5–7. The cry of the
   gambler staking all on a final throw is
   'Winner takes all'. For *what =*

whoever, compare 5.3.98 (Abbott,
254).
17–39 *See Appendix 1.
17 **heart-struck** recalling 2.2.349–50
18 **warrant . . . note** assurance of my
   observation (of you)
19 **Commend . . . thing** entrust an
   important matter
   division conflict; first hinted at by
   Curan at 2.1.11
22 **stars** fortunes, or influence of the
   stars
22–9 *Who . . . furnishings Here Q (see
   textual notes) has a different version of
   Kent's news from that in F. Q explicitly refers to a secret landing in England
   by French forces, now ready to show
   their banners, and implying that they

10 outscorn] *Q*; outstorm *Ard*[2] *(Steevens)*   14 fur] *Qc*; surre *Qu*   17 struck] *Q, F (strooke)*
18 note] *F*; Arte *Q*   20 is] *F*; be *Q*   22] *Here Q includes these lines not in F (see Appendix 1):* But
true it is, from *France* there comes a power / Into this scattered kingdome, who alreadie wise in our
negligéce, / Have secret feet in some of our best Ports, / And are at point to shew their open banner,

Throned and set high, servants, who seem no less,
Which are to France the spies and speculations
Intelligent of our state – what hath been seen,   25
Either in snuffs and packings of the dukes,
Or the hard rein which both of them hath borne
Against the old kind King, or something deeper,
Whereof, perchance, these are but furnishings. –ᶠ
�QNow to you: 30
If on my credit you dare build so far
To make your speed to Dover, you shall find
Some that will thank you, making just report
Of how unnatural and bemadding sorrow

are already at Dover. The report in F is much more oblique, hinting only that English spies are conveying intelligence to France. I have omitted four lines from Q (see textual notes), but have included 30–7, lines found only in Q, which seem necessary to give directions to the Gentleman, and which provide the first mention of Dover. The change in F at 22–9 may have been made so as to postpone to 3.6 and 3.7 references to a French invasion. In both Q and F Edmund says in 3.5 that Gloucester is spying for France, and F repeats there the word *intelligent* from the present scene. At 3.7.2–3 we are told that a French army has landed, and Cordelia herself receives news of 'British powers' marching to meet hers in 4.4; it thus seems premature for the French to have landed in 3.1. The differences between Q and F here can, however, be interpreted in various ways; see Appendix 1.

23 **who . . . less** who appear servants (but are in fact spies)
24 **France** the country? or the King of France, as at 1.1.189?
24–5 **speculations / . . . of** observers passing information about; compare 3.5.11–12

26 **snuffs and packings** resentments and intrigues. To 'take in snuff' meant to take offence at something.
27–8 **hard . . . King** the harsh way they have oppressed the old, kind King; the metaphor is from riding a horse on a tight rein. Albany was said to treat Lear harshly at 1.4.57–60, but later claims he knows nothing of Goneril's actions and has had no part in afflicting Lear (1.4.265–6). It is notable that he is absent from 2.2, the scene in which Goneril, Regan and Cornwall join together in driving Lear into the storm.
29 **furnishings** decorations, window dressing. Kent breaks off, perhaps with a shrug, as if to say 'Trouble of some kind is brewing, and the French know about it, and that's all I can tell you.'
30–8 *These lines, from Q, are not in F, where they may have been accidentally omitted; but the textual differences between Q and F here are very problematic; see Appendix 1.
32 **Dover** the first hint that Lear is on his way there, and that help of some kind awaits him. Kent received a letter from Cordelia earlier; see 2.2.163–6.
33 **just** accurate
34 **bemadding sorrow** affliction that is driving him mad

27 hath] *F;* have *F2*

The King hath cause to plain. 35
I am a gentleman of blood and breeding,
And from some knowledge and assurance
Offer this office to you.^Q

KNIGHT

I will talk further with you.

KENT   No, do not.
For confirmation that I ^Fam^F much more 40
Than my out-wall, open this purse and take
What it contains. If you shall see Cordelia,
As fear not but you shall, show her this ring,
And she will tell you who your fellow is
That yet you do not know. Fie on this storm; 45
I will go seek the King.

KNIGHT   Give me your hand.
Have you no more to say?

KENT   Few words, but to effect
More than all yet: that when we have found the King,
^FIn which your pain^F that way, I'll this, 49
He that first lights on him holla the other. *Exeunt.*

---

35 **plain** complain
36 **blood and breeding** noble birth and education
37 **assurance** confidence, certainty
38 **office** duty or service
41 **out-wall** appearance or clothing
43 **fear not but** be assured that
44 **your fellow** your companion; perhaps

also, as 'that fellow' (Q) suggests, servant (in appearance) as at 1.4.46 and 86
47 **to effect** i.e. in their importance
49 **pain** labour, effort
that . . . this They go off, as they came on stage, by different doors.
50 **lights on** comes across

39 further] *F*; farther *Q*   41 out-wall,] *Q* (outwall,); out-wall; *F*   44 your] *Q*; that *F*
49 that . . . this] *F*; Ile this way, you that *Q*

3.2 *┌Storm still.┐* *Enter* LEAR *and* FOOL.

LEAR

Blow winds and crack your cheeks! Rage, blow!
You cataracts and hurricanoes, spout
Till you have drenched our steeples, drowned the cocks!
You sulphurous and thought-executing fires,
Vaunt-couriers of oak-cleaving thunderbolts,   5
Singe my white head! And thou, all-shaking thunder,
Strike flat the thick rotundity o'the world,
Crack nature's moulds, all germens spill at once

3.2.0.1 *Storm still* Although directors are often tempted to invent strong visual and sound effects for the storm, Lear's words effectively create it, and need to be heard. His first two speeches especially, in which he calls for a second flood and the destruction of the world, seem to demand powerful utterance; in his later speeches in this scene and in 3.4 he moves from self-pity to pity for others, and his fragility may be more evident than his grandeur. For any actor the scene is a challenge after the climax of 2.2, and many different ways of playing it have been tried; see Bratton, 135–7. There is a bitter sexual undercurrent, feeding his misogyny, in Lear's wish to destroy all the seeds that make man; for comment on this see Rosenberg, 191–2, and Adelman, 110–12.

1 **crack your cheeks** winds are often shown on old maps as faces puffing from the corners
2 **cataracts and hurricanoes** deluges falling from the skies and spouting from the seas. In his only other use of the word 'hurricano', Shakespeare defines it as 'the dreadful spout / Which shipmen do the hurricano call'

(*TC* 5.2.171–2).
3 *drowned F's 'drown' could possibly be an imperative, parallel to *Blow* and *crack*.
  cocks weathercocks (on the steeples)
4 **thought-executing** Is Lear calling on lightning to destroy thought, or to carry out his wishes, or both?
5 **Vaunt-couriers** forerunners
5–6 **oak-cleaving . . . thunder** Prospero claims to have split 'Jove's stout oak' (*Tem* 5.1.45), and Lear is addressing Jupiter (*thou*) here. An audience might also connect these lines with God, who 'thundereth marveilously with his voice' in addressing Job; see Job, 37.4–5.
7 **Strike** F's *Strike* is more euphonious in the context than Q's 'smite', which means the same, but carries a biblical echo as the word often used by or about God as punishing the sinful in the Old Testament.
  thick rotundity as if the world were pregnant; see 0.1 above and n.
8 **Crack nature's moulds** break the moulds that give shape to all natural forms; another in a series of metaphors for the destruction of the world
  germens seeds

3.2] *F (Scena Secunda); not in Q*   1 winds] *F;* wind *Q*   2 cataracts] *F;* caterickes *Q*   hurricanoes] *F (*Hyrricano's*);* Hircanios *Q*   3 our] *F;* The *Q*   drowned] *Q;* drown *F*   5 Vaunt-couriers of] *F (*Vaunt-curriors of*);* vaunt-currers to *Q*   7 Strike] *F;* smite *Q*   8 moulds] *F;* Mold *Q*   germens] *Q (*Germains*), F (*germaines*)

That make ingrateful man!

FOOL   O, nuncle, court holy-water in a dry house is better   10
        than this rain-water out o'door. Good nuncle, in, ^Qand^Q
        ask thy daughters blessing. Here's a night pities neither
        wise men nor fools.

LEAR

        Rumble thy bellyful! Spit fire, spout rain!
        Nor rain, wind, thunder, fire are my daughters;   15
        I tax not you, you elements, with unkindness.
        I never gave you kingdom, called you children;
        You owe me no subscription. ^QWhy^Q then, let fall
        Your horrible pleasure. Here I stand your slave,
        A poor, infirm, weak and despised old man.   20
        But yet I call you servile ministers
        That will with two pernicious daughters join
        Your high-engendered battles 'gainst a head
        So old and white as this. O ^Fho!^F 'tis foul.

FOOL   He that has a house to put's head in has a good   25
        headpiece:

                    The codpiece that will house
                    Before the head has any,

---

10 **court holy-water** flattery or fair
words; a proverbial expression (Dent,
H532)
12 **ask . . . blessing** ask your daughters
for their blessing
15 **fire** perhaps disyllabic as spoken
16 **tax . . . with** accuse of
    elements See 3.1.4 and n.
18 **subscription** approval, support; or
perhaps allegiance (so *OED* 6b, citing
only this passage)
21 **ministers** agents (of the gods; see
5–6)
23 **high-engendered battles** armies

brought into being in the heavens; for
'battle' = army, compare *1H4* 4.1.129,
'What may the King's whole battle
reach unto? / To thirty thousand.'
26 **headpiece** covering; brain
27–34 *Oxf, following Capell, adds the
SD 'Sings', which is not in Q or F; see
2.2.238–43 and n.
27–30 **The . . . many** He who houses
his penis (by fornication) before he has
a home for his head will end up lousy
all over, in beggary, and with a train of
sluts. The Fool's acerbic comments on
sexual appetite relate to undercurrents

---

9 make] *Q;* makes *F*   10 court holy-water] *F, Q2 (*Court holy water*);* Court holly water *Qu;*
Court holy water *Qc*   11 o'door] *F;* a doore *Q*   12 neither] *Q2, F;* nether *Q*   13 wise men] *F
(*Wisemen*);* wise man *Q*   fools] *F;* foole *Q*   16 tax] *F;* taske *Q*   22 will] *F;* haue *Q*   join] *F;*
ioin'd *Q*   23 battles] *F (*Battailes*);* battel *Q*   28 head] *F;* head, *Q*

The head and he shall louse:

    So beggars marry many.   30

The man that makes his toe

    What he his heart should make,

Shall of a corn cry woe

    And turn his sleep to wake.

For there was never yet fair woman but she made   35
mouths in a glass.

Enter KENT [*disguised*].

LEAR

No, I will be the pattern of all patience,

I will say nothing.

KENT   Who's there?

FOOL   Marry, here's grace and a codpiece – that's a wise   40
man and a fool.

KENT [*to Lear*]

Alas, sir, are you here? Things that love night

---

in Lear's storm speeches; see 0.1 and n. A codpiece was the appendage at the front of breeches used both to hide male sex organs and to emphasize their presence; the Fool may have worn a prominent one (see 40), or have thrust his bauble, a stick with fantastic head carved on the end, between his legs (so Wiles, 190–1, and see 1.5.49–50 n. above). Behind the Fool's cryptic words lie proverbs such as Dent, H749, 'Before thou marry be sure of a house wherein to tarry'. Lear seems not to notice the application of the Fool's remarks to himself, nor, indeed, to be listening.

31–4 The man who spurns or kicks away what he should love (Cordelia?), or misplaces his affection on baseness, will find pain and sleeplessness; the

Fool varies a common proverb (Dent, H317) in glancing at Lear's treatment of his daughters and Gloucester's treatment of his sons. In the hierarchy of the members of the body, the toe was the 'lowest, basest, poorest', as Menenius points out at *Cor* 1.1.157.

35–6 made . . . glass practised faces in a mirror; an oblique allusion to the vanity of Goneril (see 2.2.35 and n.), or to her hypocrisy and Regan's?

37 patience See 2.2.459–60 and n.

40 grace . . . codpiece the King (see, e.g., 3.4.121) and the Fool (see 27–30 and n.). Kent and the audience are left to decide which of them is the *wise man*. For *codpiece*, see 27–30 and n.

42 *are F; Q has 'sit', which may be a pointer to the way Shakespeare envisaged Lear standing to challenge the

---

33 of] *F;* haue *Q*   35 but] *Qc, Q2, F;* hut *Qu*   36.1 *Enter* KENT] *as F; opp. 37 Q*   disguised] *Oxf*
42 SD *to Lear] Oxf* are] *F;* sit *Q*

Love not such nights as these. The wrathful skies
Gallow the very wanderers of the dark,
And make them keep their caves. Since I was man   45
Such sheets of fire, such bursts of horrid thunder,
Such groans of roaring wind and rain I never
Remember to have heard. Man's nature cannot carry
Th'affliction, nor the fear.

LEAR   Let the great gods
That keep this dreadful pudder o'er our heads   50
Find out their enemies now. Tremble, thou wretch,
That hast within thee undivulged crimes,
Unwhipped of justice. Hide thee, thou bloody hand,
Thou perjured, and thou simular of virtue
That art incestuous. Caitiff, to pieces shake,   55
That under covert and convenient seeming
Has practised on man's life. Close pent-up guilts
Rive your concealing continents and cry

skies ('I stand', 19), then sitting to show patience (37); see Urkowitz, *Division*, 36–7

44 **Gallow** frighten
  the . . . dark even the creatures that roam at night

45 **keep** remain inside
  Since . . . man Kent is forty-eight (1.4.39), so he is looking back over more than thirty years, if the reference is to puberty.

48–9 ***carry . . . fear** endure the physical suffering or the fear of the gods brought on by the storm (which will cause their *enemies*, the guilty, to reveal themselves, 51). Q has 'force', referring only to physical power, for *fear* (F).

50 **pudder** pother, uproar
52 **undivulged** undivulgèd
53 **bloody hand** murderer

54 **simular of virtue** pretender to chastity. Compare Lear's image of a *simp'ring dame* at 4.6.116–19.
55 **Caitiff** villain
56 **convenient seeming** deception fitted to the purpose
57 **practised on** plotted against
57–8 ***Close . . . continents** Let the secret buried consciousness of guilt burst from the hiding-places where you have concealed it. A *continent* is what contains or bounds something in, as at *MND* 2.1.92, where rivers 'have overborne their continents', or flooded. F makes better sense than 'concealed centers' (Q).
58–9 **cry . . . grace** beg for mercy from these terrifying summoners (to the justice of the gods). A summoner was an officer who cited people to appear in an ecclesiastical court.

44 wanderers] *F;* wanderer *Q*   45 make] *F;* makes *Q*   47 never] *F;* ne're *Q*   49 fear] *F;* force *Q*
50 pudder] *F;* Powther *Q;* Thundring *Q2;* pother *Johnson*   54 of] *F;* man of *Q*   55 to] *F;* in *Q*
57 Has] *F;* hast *Q*   58 concealing continents] *F;* concealed centers *Q*

These dreadful summoners grace. I am a man
More sinned against than sinning.

KENT   Alack, bareheaded?   60
Gracious my lord, hard by here is a hovel:
Some friendship will it lend you 'gainst the tempest.
Repose you there, while I to this hard house –
More harder than the stones whereof 'tis raised,
Which even but now, demanding after you,   65
Denied me to come in – return and force
Their scanted courtesy.

LEAR   My wits begin to turn.
[*to the Fool*] Come on, my boy. How dost my boy? Art
    cold?
I am cold myself. [*to Kent*] Where is this straw, my
    fellow?
The art of our necessities is strange,   70
And can make vile things precious. Come; your hovel.
[*to the Fool*] Poor fool and knave, I have one part in my
    heart

59–60 **I . . . sinning** Lear is no hypocrit-
ical sinner, but if he is seen as still
refusing to admit his own shortcom-
ings, and failing to realize that the gods
may be trying and punishing him as
well as others, this remark will seem
self-pitying.

60 **bareheaded** In the opening scene
Lear should probably have a crown
(see 1.1.33.1 and n.); when he comes in
(from hunting?) with his knights in
1.4, and when he sets off to travel to
Regan at the end of 1.5, he should no
doubt wear a hat, as any gentlemen
would have done. Kent's concern here
shows how unusual it would have been
for a king to be out of doors with no
hat, let alone in a storm.

63 **hard** cruel
65 **demanding after you** when I asked
urgently for you
66 **Denied . . . in** refused to let me in;
compare 2.2.277
67 **scanted** withheld (*OED* Scant *v.* 5)
68–9 **my boy . . . my fellow** Addressing
the Fool, then Kent, Lear becomes for
the first time in the storm 'aware of the
sufferings of others' (Cam¹).
70–1 **The . . . precious** The power of the
hardships we suffer is strange, and can
make us value wretched stuff (like
straw) as precious. Lear may be seen as
redefining *true need*; see 2.2.459, and
glancing at the proverb 'make a virtue
of necessity' (Dent, V73).

60 than] *F;* their *Q*   63 while] *F;* whilst *Q*   64 harder] *F;* hard *Q*   the stones] *F;* is the stone *Q*
65 you] *F;* me *Q*   67 wits begin] *F;* wit begins *Q*   68 SD *to Fool*] *Oxf*   69 SD *to Kent*] *this edn*
71 And] *F;* that *Q*   your] *F;* you *Q*   71–2 hovel. / Poor] *F;* houell poore, *Q*   72 SD *this edn*   in] *F;*
of *Q*

That's sorry yet for thee.

FOOL

He that has ᶠandᶠ a little tiny wit,
With heigh-ho, the wind and the rain,   75
Must make content with his fortunes fit,
Though the rain it raineth every day.

LEAR

True, �520my goodᵠ boy. [*to Kent*] Come, bring us to this
hovel.   [*Exeunt Lear and Kent.*]

ᶠFOOL   This is a brave night to cool a courtesan. I'll speak
a prophecy ere I go: 80

74–7 Adapted from the song Feste sings
at the end of *TN*, 'When that I was
and a little tiny boy'. The same actor,
Robert Armin, probably played both
Feste and the Fool; see Introduction, p.
50, and Wiles, 144–5. A musical setting by Joseph Vernon dating from
1772 that may be adapted from earlier
sources is printed in Sternfeld, 188–92.
76 must make his happiness conform to
his fortunes
79 **brave . . . courtesan** great night to
cool the lust of a courtier's mistress.
These words seem unrelated to previous lines, but link with the *whores* of 90
and the later emphasis on lust, as at
3.4.83–8, and also in 4.2, 4.5 and 4.6.
79–96 *Not in Q, this prophecy foregrounds the Fool, and gives him
another direct address to the audience,
as at the end of 1.5; in F the Fool
becomes much more a general satirical
commentator than he is in Q; see
Introduction, pp. 135–6. Some think
the speech is 'irrelevant' and not by
Shakespeare (see Stone, 119), but it
has been strongly defended as authentic by Kerrigan and by Taylor, 'Date',
in *Division*, 221–6 and 382–5. The first
part of the prophecy relates riddlingly
to abuses of the age, priests concerned

with words not substance (see 1.1.55
and n.), brewers diluting their beer
with water, nobles devoting themselves
to the latest fashions, lovers *burned* by
syphilis; the second part describes an
ideal that will never come, the opposite
of what in fact was happening daily in
England. The promise of confusion is
ironically appropriate to the first part
of the prophecy, while the promise of
good sense prevailing (people using
their feet to walk on) is more appropriate to the utopian images of the
second; many editors, including Cam²,
therefore accept Warburton's proposal
and move 91–2 to follow 84; but I think
Terence Hawkes is right to see here a
deliberately confusing parody of a
tradition of Merlinesque prophecies
predicting 'downfall for a state'
(*N&Q*, n.s. 7 (1960), 331–2). The first
six lines echo pseudo-Chaucerian
verses printed in William Thynne's
edition of Chaucer (1532; Skeat,
7.450), and also in George
Puttenham's *The Arte of English Poesie*
(1589), ed. Gladys Willcock and Alice
Walker (1936), 224. Shakespeare could
have drawn on either of these, and an
argument for his use of Puttenham is
developed by Gary Taylor in 'Date',

---

73 That's sorry] *F;* That sorrowes *Q*   74] *Capell adds SD: Sings*   74 little tiny] *Q (little tine), F*
(little-tyne)   77 Though] *F;* for *Q*   78 SD *to Kent*] *Capell*   SD *Exeunt . . . Kent.*] *Exit. F; not in Q*

When priests are more in word than matter,
When brewers mar their malt with water,
When nobles are their tailors' tutors,
No heretics burned but wenches' suitors;
When every case in law is right   85
No squire in debt, nor no poor knight;
When slanders do not live in tongues,
Nor cut-purses come not to throngs,
When usurers tell their gold i'the field,
And bawds and whores do churches build,   90
Then shall the realm of Albion
Come to great confusion:
Then comes the time, who lives to see't,
That going shall be used with feet.
This prophecy Merlin shall make, for I live before 95
his time.   *Exit.*[F]

3.3   *Enter* GLOUCESTER *and* EDMUND, [Q]*with lights*[Q].

GLOUCESTER   Alack, alack, Edmund, I like not this

382–5. The lines there run:

> When faith failes in Priestes sawes,
> And Lords hestes are holden for
>   lawes,
> And robberie is tane for purchase,
> And lechery for solace
> Then shall the Realme of Albion
> Be brought to great confusion.

Skeat, lxxxi, prints another manuscript version attributing the prophecy to Merlin.

89 **tell** count
91 **Albion** ancient name for Britain, thought by the Romans to be derived from *albus* meaning white, and to refer to the white cliffs of Dover. According to Harrison (Holinshed, 1.6), Albion was a son of Neptune who conquered Britain and changed its name to his own.

92 **confusion** perhaps pronounced as four syllables

95 **Merlin** legendary prophet of the time of King Arthur. Lear's reign is located in the eighth century BC by Holinshed, and Arthur's in the sixth century AD, so in some sense the Fool does 'live before the time' of Merlin.

3.3.0.1 **with lights* Q; not in F, but the usual theatrical technique at the Globe, where plays were performed by daylight, for suggesting an interior night scene, here in Gloucester's house

83 nobles . . . tailors'] *F*; tailors . . . nobles' *(Oxf)*   91–2 Then . . . confusion] *transposed after 84 / Warburton, Oxf*

3.3] *F (Scaena Tertia); not in Q*   0.1 EDMUND] *F; the Bastard Q*

unnatural dealing. When I desired their leave that I
might pity him, they took from me the use of mine own
house; charged me on pain of perpetual displeasure
neither to speak of him, entreat for him, or any way   5
sustain him.

EDMUND   Most savage and unnatural.

GLOUCESTER   Go to, say you nothing. There is division
between the dukes, and a worse matter than that: I have
received a letter this night – 'tis dangerous to be spoken   10
– I have locked the letter in my closet. These injuries
the King now bears will be revenged home. There is
part of a power already footed; we must incline to the
King. I will look him and privily relieve him. Go you
and maintain talk with the Duke, that my charity be not   15
of him perceived. If he ask for me, I am ill and gone to
bed. If I die for it – as no less is threatened me – the
King my old master must be relieved. There is strange
things toward, Edmund; pray you, be careful.   *Exit.*

EDMUND

This courtesy, forbid thee, shall the Duke   20

---

2   **unnatural dealing** unnatural con-
     duct; a phrase, as Ard² notes, echoing
     the account of a wicked son in
     Sidney's *Arcadia;* see Bullough, 403
3   **pity** relieve, assist
6   **sustain him** provide him with neces-
     saries
8–9 **division . . . dukes** repeating Kent's
     information at 3.1.19–21
11   **closet** private room (as at 1.2.61), or
     cabinet
12   **home** to the full, thoroughly
13   ***footed** F's *footed* is a more ambigu-
     ous word than Q's 'landed', which
     implies a landing by the French army;
     I think the change is deliberate, and

made to remove explicit references to a
French invasion before 3.7. There
'footed in the kingdom' (3.7.45, Q and
F) does seem to mean 'landed', but,
since the line follows after a straight-
forward announcement that the army
of France has arrived in England
(3.7.2–3), there was no need to change
it in F. For discussion of the implications, see Appendix 1, p. 393.
14   **look** seek
16   **of** by
19   **toward** about to happen
20   **courtesy . . . thee** kindness in helping
     Lear, which you were forbidden to do

---

3 from me] *Q2, F;* me from me *Q*   4 perpetual] *F;* their *Q*   5 or] *F;* nor *Q*   7+ SP EDMUND]
Bast. Q , F   8 There is] *F;* there's a *Q*   9 between] *F;* betwixt *Q*   13 footed] *F;* landed *Q*
14 look] *F;* seeke *Q*   17 bed. If] *Johnson (Rowe²);* bed, though *Q;* bed, if *F*   18 is] *Q, F;* are
Pope   18–19 strange things] *F;* Some strānge thing *Q*

Instantly know and of that letter too.
This seems a fair deserving and must draw me
That which my father loses, no less than all.
The younger rises when the old doth fall.   *Exit.*

3.4   *Enter* LEAR, KENT [*in disguise*] *and* FOOL.

KENT

Here is the place, my lord: good my lord, enter;
The tyranny of the open night's too rough
For nature to endure.   ᶠ*Storm still* .ᶠ

LEAR   Let me alone.

KENT

Good my lord, enter ᶠhereᶠ.

LEAR   Wilt break my heart?

KENT

I had rather break mine own. Good my lord, enter.   5

LEAR

Thou think'st 'tis much that this contentious storm
Invades us to the skin: so 'tis to thee,
But where the greater malady is fixed,
The lesser is scarce felt. Thou'dst shun a bear,

---

22 **fair deserving** fair reward (for what
his father has done; Edmund is being
typically ironic)
  draw me attract or bring to me
3.4.1   **the place** the hovel mentioned at
3.2.61. Possibly a curtained area at the
rear of the stage was used, or another
door than the one the characters enter
by, or, as in some modern productions,
a trap-door; see 36.1 and n.
2   **open night** night in the open air
3   **nature** human nature, as at 3.2.48–9
4–5 **Wilt . . . own** The storm diverts

Lear's attention from the ingratitude
of his daughters (14), which would
otherwise break his heart (so Ard²).
Kent's desire to save his master here
ironically contrasts with his longing
for Lear's death at 5.3.311.
6   ***contentious storm** Compare *Oth*
2.1.92, 'The great contention of the
sea and skies'; *contentious* is F's correction of 'crulentious' (Qu), altered to
'tempestious' in Qc.
8   **fixed** rooted (in the mind, as explained
in 12–14)

---

21 instantly] *Q2, F;* instāly *Q*   24 The] *F;* then *Q*   doth] *F;* doe *Q*

3.4] *F (Scena Quarta); not in Q*   0.1 *in disguise*] *Oxf (Riv)*   2 The tyranny] *Qc, Q2, F;* the the
tyrannie *Qu*   6 contentious] *F;* crulentious *Qu;* tempestious *Qc*   7 skin: so 'tis] *Fu (*skin. so 'tis*);*
skin, so tis *Q;* skinso: 'tis *Fc*

271

But if thy flight lay toward the roaring sea,   10
Thou'dst meet the bear i'the mouth. When the mind's
   free,
The body's delicate: this tempest in my mind
Doth from my senses take all feeling else,
Save what beats there, filial ingratitude.
Is it not as this mouth should tear this hand   15
For lifting food to't? But I will punish home;
No, I will weep no more. ᶠIn such a night
To shut me out? Pour on, I will endure.ᶠ
In such a night as this? O, Regan, Goneril,
Your old, kind father, whose frank heart gave ᵠyouᵠ
   all –   20
O, that way madness lies, let me shun that;
No more of that.

KENT   Good my lord, enter ᶠhereᶠ.

LEAR

Prithee go in thyself, seek thine own ease.
This tempest will not give me leave to ponder
On things would hurt me more. But I'll go in;   25
[*to the Fool*] ᶠIn boy, go first. You houseless
   poverty –

11 **meet . . . i'the mouth** confront the bear face to face
11–12 **When . . . delicate** when the mind is untroubled, the body is sensitive (and then the mind notices discomfort and pain)
14 **beats there** a stage direction within the text for the actor to point to his head or his heart?
15 **as** equivalent to the modern 'as if' (Abbott, 107)
16 **home** thoroughly, as at 3.3.12
17–18 **In . . . endure* F, not in Q; Stone, 243, thinks Lear does not know he has been shut out of Gloucester's house, but, if he has not been told directly, Kent has made it obvious at 3.2.65–6. Whether this passage is a revision, or was omitted accidentally from Q through a compositor's eyeskip due to the repetition of 'In such a night', its effect is to enhance the pathos of Lear's situation.
20 **frank** generous
21 **that way** i.e. dwelling on his own griefs

10 thy] *Q;* they *F*   roaring] *Qc, F;* raging *Qu, Q2*   12 body's] *Q, F (*bodies*)*   this] *Qc;* the *Qu, Q2, F*   14 beats there, filial ingratitude.] *Fc;* beares their filiall ingratitude, *Qu, Q2;* beates their filiall ingratitude, *Qc;* beates there Filliall Ingratitude, *Fu*   16 home;] *F;* sure, *Q*   20 all –] *Rowe;* all, *Q, F*   21 lies, let] *Q, Fc;* lie, slet *Fu*   23 thine own] *F;* thy one *Q;* thy owne *Q2*   26 SD] *Johnson*

Nay, get thee in. I'll pray, and then I'll sleep.   *Exit*ᶠ [*Fool*].
[*Kneels.*] Poor naked wretches, wheresoe'er you are,
That bide the pelting of this pitiless storm,
How shall your houseless heads and unfed sides,   30
Your looped and windowed raggedness, defend you
From seasons such as these? O, I have ta'en
Too little care of this. Take physic, pomp,
Expose thyself to feel what wretches feel,
That thou mayst shake the superflux to them   35
And show the heavens more just.

[*Enter* FOOL, *as from the hovel.*]

28 SD **Kneels** Not in Q or F, but Granville-Barker, 175, took it for granted that Lear would do so, and actors have found kneeling appropriate (Bratton, 143), no doubt because it marks a stage in Lear's progress towards humility, from the moment when he kneels in mockery to Regan (2.2.343) to the moment when he kneels in contrition to Cordelia (4.7.58); see Introduction pp. 20–2.

28–36 These lines exemplify Protestant teaching about the value of adversity: 'To haue pitye and compassion of people, that are in misery and distresse, is a Chrysten and a necessary vertue. But he that neuer felt no temptation, aduersitie nor affliction him selfe, can haue but litle pity and compassion of other'; hence 'Suffering and patience is a token of wisdom' (Otto Werdmuller, *A Spiritual and most Precious Pearl*, tr. Miles Coverdale (1593 edn), 151, 322). Compare 2.2.458–60 and n., and see also 3.4.69–74 and 5.3.322–5 and nn.

29 **bide** endure
31 **looped** full of holes (like loopholes)
33 **physic** usually meaning a purge
33–4 **pomp . . . thyself** personifying magnificent display of any kind, but

with special reference to himself, and perhaps to the regal costume stage tradition suggests he wore. See Introduction, p. 13.

35 **superflux** Shakespeare's coinage, according to *OED*, meaning 'surplus, superfluous possessions', but disconcertingly hinting at 'flux' or discharge from the bowels (see 33). In an essay in Richard Strier and Donna Hamilton (eds), *Albion's Conscience: Religion, Literature and Politics in Post-Reformation England 1540–1688* (Cambridge, 1996), Debora Shuger shows that a tradition derived from medieval canon law defined 'the basic obligations of the rich towards the poor' as being to distribute superfluities to those in need, and she argues that Lear's prayer 'does not voice subversive heterodoxies . . . but the social teachings of the medieval Church. In his painful epiphany, the pagan king for a moment grasps the nature of Christian *caritas*.'

36.1 *Q has no entry SD, and F prints 'Enter Edgar, and Foole', but Edgar must emerge in response to Kent's call at 43, and it makes theatrical sense if the Fool is driven out by Edgar's first words, and helped up by Kent.

27 SD] *Rowe (opp. 26); Exit.* F; *not in Q*   28 SD] *Oxf*   29 storm] F; *night Q*   31 looped] *Q (*loopt*); lop'd F*   36.1] *Hunter (Theobald); Enter Edgar, and Foole.* F; *not in Q*

^FEDGAR [*within*]   Fathom and half, fathom and half: Poor Tom!^F

FOOL   Come not in here, nuncle, here's a spirit. Help me, help me!   40

KENT   Give me thy hand. Who's there?

FOOL   A spirit, ^Fa spirit.^F He says his name's Poor Tom.

KENT

What art thou that dost grumble there i'the straw? Come forth.

Enter EDGAR[, *disguised as Poor Tom.*]

EDGAR   Away, the foul fiend follows me. Through the   45
sharp hawthorn blows the ^Qcold ^Q wind. ^FHumh,^F go to
thy ^Qcold^Q bed and warm thee.

LEAR   Didst thou give all to thy ^Qtwo^Q daughters? And art thou come to this?

37–8 ***Edgar . . . Tom!** In F (not in Q) Edgar calls as if he were taking soundings from a boat, or measuring the depth of water in the 'hovel' (the use of a trap-door would be appropriate here; see 1 and n.). On *Poor Tom*, see 2.2.185 and n.

43 **grumble** mutter or mumble

45 **Away . . . me** Shakespeare had Samuel Harsnett's *Declaration of Egregious Popish Impostures* (1603) in mind in his creation of Poor Tom in this scene especially. Its elaborate satirical account of the methods practised by exorcizing priests to draw devils out of people said to be possessed gave him the idea for a figure pursued by the *foul fiend*. Harsnett describes in chapter 21, Brownlow, 304–11, the strange shapes devils are supposed to take in haunting people. See Introduction, pp. 102–4.

46 ***Humh** 'Edgar shivers with cold' (Hunter, after Kittredge), as at 56–7;

but *Humh* is in F only, and F removes the word *cold* which occurs twice in Q, so *Humh* could indicate Edgar's startled recognition of Lear, not unlike his father's *Hum* when he discovers conspiracy at 1.2.54. If Edgar is visibly half naked and shivering, the references here to *cold* may have been dropped in F as superfluous, and conflicting with his talk of fire and flame at 51.

48 **Didst . . . daughters?** A poor naked wretch suddenly appears, and Lear projects on to him his own grievances; Poor Tom more or less displaces the Fool, and becomes the centre of Lear's attention. Here for many commentators and actors is the point when Lear goes mad (see Bratton, 143–4, and Rosenberg, 207–10), but Hoeniger, 307–38, argues that Lear would have been seen in Shakespeare's time as afflicted almost from the beginning of

---

37 SD] *Theobald*   44.1] *Hunter (Theobald); Enter Edgar, and Foole. F (after 36); not in Q*
45 Through] *Q2, F;* thorough *Q*   46 blows . . . wind] *Q;* blow the windes *F*   48 Didst . . . give]
F; Hast . . . giuen *Q*

EDGAR   Who gives anything to Poor Tom? Whom the foul   50
    fiend hath led through fire and ᶠthrough flame,ᶠ
    through ford and whirlpool, o'er bog and quagmire;
    that hath laid knives under his pillow and halters in his
    pew; set ratsbane by his porridge, made him proud of
    heart, to ride on a bay trotting horse over four-inched   55
    bridges, to course his own shadow for a traitor. Bless
    thy five wits, Tom's a-cold. ᶠO do, de, do, de, do, de:ᶠ
    bless thee from whirlwinds, star-blasting and taking.
    Do Poor Tom some charity, whom the foul fiend vexes.
    There could I have him now, and there, and there   60
    again, ᶠand there.ᶠ   ᶠ*Storm still.*ᶠ

the play with 'acute hypochondriac melancholy developing into mania' (330).

50–8 **foul . . . taking** In this speech, as noted first by Theobald, and shown in full by Ard² and Brownlow, Shakespeare begins to use material, words, phrases, ideas, he found in Samuel Harsnett's *Declaration*; see Introduction, p. 103.

53–4 **knives . . . ratsbane** Knives and halters figure in Harsnett, but the devil was traditionally conceived of as offering to those in despair such aids to suicide, encouraging them to kill themselves and bring their souls to damnation; hence suicide was regarded as a 'diabolical deed' (see Michael Macdonald and Terence R. Murphy, *Sleepless Souls: Suicide in Early Modern England* (1990), 38 and 59). Marlowe's Faustus and Spenser's Red Cross Knight are both offered swords or knives, halters or ropes, and poison to 'draw them to perdition' (*Doctor Faustus*, 2.3.21–2; *Faerie Queene*, 1.9.50).

53–4 **in his pew** even in church
54 **porridge** soup
55–6 **ride . . . bridges** Supernatural aid would be needed to ride over bridges four inches wide; 'four-archt' (F2, Rowe) flattens the image into the mundane.
56 **course** chase or hunt
57 **five wits** five faculties of the mind, paralleling the five senses. Malone noted that in *The Pastime of Pleasure* (1517), by Stephen Hawes, they are identified as common wit, imagination, fantasy, estimation and memory (EETS No. 173, 108).
O . . . de the sound of chattering teeth?
58 **star-blasting and taking** baleful influence of the stars and seizure by disease (*OED* Taking Sb.3); compare 1.4.291, and 66 below
60–1 **There . . . there** Does Edgar attack an imaginary devil outside himself, or, as Hunter and others think, search on his body 'for lice and devils at the same time'?

51 led through] *Q;* led though *F*   52 ford] *Q;* Sword *F*   whirlpool] *F (*Whirle Poole*);* whirli-poole *Q*   53 hath] *F;* has *Q*   54 pew] *Pope²;* pue *Q, F*   porridge] *F;* pottage *Q*   55 four-inched] *Q, F (*foure incht*);* foure archt *F2*   56 Bless] *Q;* Blisse *F*   58 bless] *Q;* blisse *F*   star-blasting] *F;* starre-blusting *Q*   60–1 and there again, and there] *F;* and and there againe *Q;* and there againe *Q2*

LEAR

Have his daughters brought him to this pass?

Couldst thou save nothing? Wouldst thou give 'em all?

FOOL   Nay, he reserved a blanket, else we had been all
shamed.   65

LEAR [*to Edgar*]

Now all the plagues that in the pendulous air

Hang fated o'er men's faults light on thy daughters.

KENT   He hath no daughters, sir.

LEAR

Death, traitor! Nothing could have subdued nature

To such a lowness but his unkind daughters.   70

Is it the fashion that discarded fathers

Should have thus little mercy on their flesh?

Judicious punishment, 'twas this flesh begot

Those pelican daughters.

EDGAR

Pillicock sat on Pillicock hill,   75

Alow, alow, loo, loo!

---

62 **pass** predicament
64 **reserved** kept for himself
66–7 **in . . . faults** Diseases are imagined
as overhanging (*pendulous*), and striking from the air by planetary influence
to punish *faults*. Harsnett has the
phrase 'pendulous in the ayre'
(Brownlow, 326).
67 **light** alight
69 **subdued nature** reduced man's vital
powers. On the meanings of *nature*, see
1.2.1–2 and n.
70 **lowness** degradation
72 Edwin Booth took this as a direction,
plucked a thorn or twig out of Edgar's
arm and stuck it in his own; see
Rosenberg, 220.
74 **pelican daughters** alluding to the
ancient fable that the pelican feeds its

young with its own blood (see *R2*
2.1.126–7: 'That blood already, like the
pelican, / Hast thou tapped out')
75 **Pillicock** slang for penis (compare the
modern 'pillock' as a term of abuse),
suggested, as Horsman notes, in sound
by *pelican* (74) and in sense by *flesh
begot* (73); *Pillicock hill* then refers to
the mount of Venus or female genitals
(so Partridge, 165). *The Oxford
Dictionary of Nursery Rhymes*, 432,
cites a version of 1810, 'Pillycock,
pillycock, sate on a hill, / If he's not
gone – he sits there still.'
76 **Alow . . . loo!** 'Halloo' and 'loo' were
cries to incite dogs to the chase (*OED*),
but Edgar may be simply exclaiming;
the modern 'hello' is a variant.
75–6 Up to this point the Fool has been

---

62 Have] *Theobald;* Ha's *F;* What *Q*   63 Wouldst] *F;* didst *Q*   'em] *F;* them *Q*   67 light] *F;* fall
Q   75 ²Pillicock] *F;* pelicocks *Q*   76 Alow . . . loo!] *F* (alow: alow, loo, loo.)*;* a lo lo lo. *Q;* halloo,
halloo, loo, loo! *Theobald*

FOOL   This cold night will turn us all to fools and madmen.

EDGAR   Take heed o'the foul fiend; obey thy parents, keep
thy word justly, swear not, commit not with man's
sworn spouse, set not thy sweet-heart on proud array.   80
Tom's a-cold.

LEAR   What hast thou been?

EDGAR   A serving-man, proud in heart and mind, that
curled my hair, wore gloves in my cap, served the lust
of my mistress' heart and did the act of darkness with   85
her; swore as many oaths as I spake words and broke
them in the sweet face of heaven. One that slept in the

given the rhyming jingles and songs that function as part of his satirical commentary on Lear and the world in general, culminating in F in the prophecy at the end of 3.2. Edgar as Poor Tom now absorbs Lear's attention, and takes over something of the Fool's function, as is marked in the way he, not the Fool, now has rhyming jingles; compare 117–20, 133–5 and 178–80. See also 3.6.63–70 and n.

78–80 *obey . . . array   parodying several of the Ten Commandments in the Bible (Exodus, 20.3–17), to honour one's parents, not to bear false witness (in other words, maintain the righteousness or justice of your words in accordance with divine law), not to take the Lord's name in vain (or swear; see also Matthew, 5.34), not to commit adultery, and to avoid covetousness. For other possible biblical echoes, see Milward, 178–9. I have accepted Pope's emendation at 79 (see textual notes) because I suspect that here, as at 4.6.161 and 5.3.148 SD, the 's' in 'words' (Q, F) may be due to a misreading of a tail on MS 'd', and that the correct reading should be 'word justly'.

80 **proud array**   luxurious clothes;

compare 2.2.35, 455–8 and nn.

83–96   This speech resembles other contemporary satirical attacks on revelling, lust and corruption in courts, such as that in *The Revenger's Tragedy* (?1606, also acted by Shakespeare's company), where 'Impudence, / Thou goddess of the palace' (1.3.5–6) is worshipped by courtiers pursuing adultery or rape. Such attacks appear to reflect popular feeling about extravagance and corruption at the court of James I. A *serving-man* might be an attendant (like Oswald, who as steward has a superior rank and is dressed like a courtier; see 2.2.14–38 and 53–4), and perhaps a 'servant' or lover (like Edmund, welcoming an adulterous relationship with Goneril at 4.2.18–28).

83–92   **proud . . . prey**   As Malone noted, Harsnett associates curling the hair with pride, and goes on in the same passage to write of the Seven Deadly Sins taking the form of animals, among them the dog and the wolf (Brownlow, 411). Weis compares the allegorizing of the deadly sins in Spenser's *Faerie Queene*, 1.4.17–36.

84   **gloves . . . cap**   i.e. as a favour or pledge from a mistress

79 word justly] *Pope, Oxf;* words iustly *Q;* words Iustice *F*   80 sweet-heart] *F (*Sweet-heart);
sweet heart *Q*   83 serving-man,] *Q (*Seruingman,); Seruingman? *F*

contriving of lust and waked to do it. Wine loved I
deeply, dice dearly; and, in woman, out-paramoured
the Turk: false of heart, light of ear, bloody of hand;   90
hog in sloth, fox in stealth, wolf in greediness, dog in
madness, lion in prey. Let not the creaking of shoes,
nor the rustling of silks, betray thy poor heart to
woman. Keep thy foot out of brothels, thy hand out of
plackets, thy pen from lenders' books, and defy the foul   95
fiend. Still through the hawthorn blows the cold wind,
says suum, mun, nonny, Dauphin my boy, ^Qmy ^Q boy,
cessez! Let him trot by.   ^F*Storm still.*^F

LEAR   ^QWhy^Q, thou wert better in a grave than to answer
with thy uncovered body this extremity of the skies.   100
Is man no more than this? Consider him well. Thou
ow'st the worm no silk, the beast no hide, the sheep

89–90 out-paramoured the Turk had
more lovers than the Grand Turk or
Sultan, noted for his harem of wives
and concubines

90 light of ear busy listening (compare
'light-fingered'); or perhaps 'credulous
of evil' (Johnson)

91–2 dog in madness because dogs
carried rabies

92 prey seizing prey

95 plackets openings in the front of
petticoats and skirts for convenience in
putting them on and taking them off

96 Still . . . wind recalling 45–6 above

97–8 *suum . . . by unexplained, and
presumably deliberate 'mad' nonsense:
suum, mun may imitate the sound of
the wind (Knight); *nonny* sounds like a
refrain from a song ('hay no on ny' in
Q). Edgar then seems to tell an imaginary horse named Dauphin to stop
doing something (cease or *cessez*; Q has
'caese', Q2 'cease' and F '*Sesey*'; see
also 3.6.71), before calling on all to let

the horse go by. *Dauphin* was commonly spelled and pronounced 'Dolphin'
(Q, F, and throughout *H5*; see comment at Ard³, 1.2.222); the French
suggestion goes with *cessez*, and is a
possible name for a horse, after the title
of the eldest son of the King of
France, whose crest was a dolphin.

99 answer encounter

100 extremity violent outburst

101–3 Is . . . perfume echoing (a)
Montaigne, 2.169: 'Miserable man;
whom if you consider well what is he?'
and 2.181: 'when I consider man all
naked . . . We may be excused for borrowing those [i.e. from those creatures]
which nature had therein favored more
than us . . . and under their spoiles of
wooll, of haire, of feathers, and of silks
to shroud us'; (b) and perhaps Psalms,
8.4 or Hebrews, 2.6 (Bible): 'What is
man, that thou art mindefull of him:
and the son of man that thou visitest
him?' (cited by Noble and Shaheen)

---

89 deeply] *Q;* deerely *F*   93 rustling] *F;* ruslings *Q*   94 woman] *F;* women *Q*   brothels] *F;*
brothell *Q*   95 plackets] *F;* placket *Q*   books] *F;* booke *Q*   97 says . . . nonny] *F;* hay no on ny
Q   Dauphin] *Oxf;* Dolphin *Q, F*   my boy] *Q;* boy *Q2, F*   98 *cessez*] *Oxf (Johnson);* caese *Q;*
Sesey F   99a] *F;* thy *Q*   101 than] *F;* but *Q*

no wool, the cat no perfume. ᶠHa?ᶠ Here's three on's
us are sophisticated; thou art the thing itself.
Unaccommodated man is no more but such a poor,   105
bare, forked animal as thou art. Off, off, you lendings:
come, unbutton ᶠhereᶠ.

[*Tearing at his clothes, he is restrained by Kent and the Fool.*]

ᶠ*Enter* GLOUCESTER, *with a torch*.ᶠ

FOOL   Prithee, nuncle, be contented; 'tis a naughty night
to swim in. Now a little fire in a wild field were like an
old lecher's heart, a small spark, all the rest on's body   110

103 **cat** civet cat. A perfume is derived
from a gland in its anal pouch.

104 **sophisticated** no longer simple or
natural; Shakespeare's only use of the
word, which he may have found in
Montaigne, 3.305 (cited by Cam¹)

105 **Unaccommodated** unprovided
with comforts, such as clothes; see
4.6.81 and n., also *2H4* 3.2.69–80

106–7 **Off . . . here** Many editors have
repeated Rowe's SD here, '*Tearing off
his clothes*', but a strong stage tradition
has Kent and the Fool prevent Lear
from doing this (see Rosenberg, 223,
Bratton, 142, and Introduction, pp. 14
and 20). Lear spoke of divesting himself of rule (1.1.49), and now, symbolically, he may be seen as stripped and
reduced to the *thing itself* (104). If he is
literally unclothed, it could be argued
that he would be reduced to a beast, and
his clothes are what give him the marks
of royalty that make sense of
Gloucester's addressing him as *your
grace* (138), and Kent as *my lord* (157);
such forms of address may be seen,
however, as poignant or ironic if, as in
many modern productions, Lear is
reduced to a shirt or undershirt. See
also 4.7.21–2 and n.

106 **lendings** See 'borrowing' in passage
(a) cited in the note to 101–3.

107 ***unbutton here** Q has 'come on bee
true'. Clayton, 126–8, argues that F is
a revision, not a correction, and if so, it
looks forward to 5.3.308 and Lear's
final unbuttoning, when he sheds 'this
muddy vesture of decay' (*MV* 5.1.64),
or the body, in death.

108 **naughty** nasty (*OED a.* 5)

109–11 **little . . . fire** appropriate to
Gloucester, the *old lecher*, who
becomes visible as he enters here in F
carrying a torch. The staging is puzzling: perhaps Lear, Kent and the Fool
are huddled together, while Kent
makes sure Lear is covered up after his
attempt to take off his clothes, hence
Kent's question at 121; meanwhile
Edgar may keep Gloucester occupied
until the latter becomes aware of the
others, and calls out 'What are you
there?' In Q Gloucester's entry comes
after 111, but in the imagined darkness
of the stage he may at first wander like
a *walking fire* (111) without noticing
anyone.

109 **wild field** rough stretch of country-
side

106 lendings] *Qc, F*; leadings *Qu, Q2*   107 come, unbutton here] *F*; come on bee true *Qu*; come
on *Qc*   SD] *this edn (Capell); Tearing off his clothes / Rowe*   107.1 *Enter . . . torch*] *F*; *Enter Gloster
Q (opp. 111)*   108 contented] *F*; content *Q*   'tis] *F*; this is *Q*   110 on's] *F*; in *Q*

cold: look, here comes a walking fire.

EDGAR   This is the foul ^Qfiend^Q Flibbertigibbet: he begins
at curfew and walks till the first cock; he gives the web
and the pin, squinies the eye and makes the harelip;
mildews the white wheat and hurts the poor creature of   115
earth.
        Swithold footed thrice the wold; `
        He met the nightmare and her nine foal,
        Bid her alight and her troth plight,
        And aroint thee, witch, aroint thee.   120

KENT   How fares your grace?

LEAR   What's he?

KENT   [*to Gloucester*]   Who's there? What is't you seek?

GLOUCESTER   What are you there? Your names?

---

112 **Flibbertigibbet** the name of a devil
in Harsnett; see 4.1.64 and 61–6n.

113 **at curfew . . . cock** from nightfall till
dawn, or first cockcrow (the period
when spirits could walk abroad; see
MND 3.2.382–7)

113–14 **web . . . pin** filming and opacity
of the eyes, or cataracts

114 ***squinies** squints. Greg's suggestion, *Variants*, 165–7, makes sense of
'squemes' (Qc), and is based on two
arguments: one is that Shakespeare
nowhere else uses the verb 'squint', so
that 'squints' (F) may well be a sophistication, and the second is that the
verb 'squiny' is Shakespeare's preferred form, used again at 4.6.133.

115 **white** ready for harvesting; see John,
4.35, 'white alreadie unto harvest'
(Ard², Cam¹)

115–16 **creature of earth** animals
and/or men

117–20 *nonsense verses, and a kind of

charm against demons. Here, as at
133–5 and 178–80, Edgar/Poor Tom
now has rhyming jingles, and seems to
take over something of the Fool's
function; see also 3.6.63–70 and n.
Swithold probably = St Withold,
known from a reference in *The
Troublesome Reign of King John* (1591),
1184; 'old' (Q and F) is an obsolete
form of *wold* or upland; the *nightmare*
was a female spirit (from 'mare', *OED*
sb. 2, meaning 'goblin'), but slides into
mare = horse, if 'ninefold', as seems
likely, is an error for *nine foal* (Oxf),
though 'ninefold' could possibly refer,
as Oxf suggests, to coils in a serpent's
body. The saint makes the demon
swear to do no harm (*her troth plight*),
and drives her away.

120 **aroint thee** be off with you. Here
and at *Mac* 1.3.6 Shakespeare uses
what may be a term from Midlands
dialect; see Hulme, 17–19, 216–17.

---

112 Flibbertigibbet] F; *Sriberdegibit Qu; fliberdegibek Qc; Sirberdegibit Q2*   113 till the] *Q;* at *F*
gives] *Qc,* F;'gins *Qu, Q2*   114 and the pin, squinies] *Duthie (Greg);* the pin. queues *Qu;* & the pin,
squemes *Qc;* the pinqueuer *Q2;* and the Pin, squints *F*   harelip] *Qc,* F; harte lip *Qu, Q2*
117 Swithold] *Q (*swithald*),* F; St. Withold *Theobald;* Swithin *Oxf*   wold] *Theobald;* old *Q,* F
118 He . . . nightmare] *Qc,* F; a nellthu night more *Qu, Q2 (*anel-thu night *Moore)*   nine foal]
Oxf; nine fold *Q;* nine-fold *F*   119 alight] *F;* O light *Q*   120 aroint . . . aroint] *F;* arint thee, with
arint *Qu, Q2;* arint thee, witch arint *Qc*   123 SD] *Hunter*

EDGAR   Poor Tom, that eats the swimming frog, the toad,   125
the tadpole, the wall-newt and the water – ; that in the
fury of his heart, when the foul fiend rages, eats cow-
dung for salads; swallows the old rat and the ditch-dog;
drinks the green mantle of the standing pool; who is
whipped from tithing to tithing and stocked, punished   130
and imprisoned – who hath ^Qhad^Q three suits to his
back, six shirts to his body,
Horse to ride and weapon to wear.
But mice and rats and such small deer
Have been Tom's food for seven long year.   135
Beware my follower. Peace Smulkin, peace, thou
fiend.

GLOUCESTER
What, hath your grace no better company?

125–80 Edgar may show anxiety about being recognized by his father; he sharpens his act as Poor Tom, and hangs about Lear, perhaps using him as a shield to hide from Gloucester, so adding to the poignancy of the latter's words at 162–5.

126 **wall-newt . . . water –** the lizard on the wall and newt in the water

128 **ditch-dog** dead dog thrown in a ditch (Delius)

129 **mantle . . . pool** scum or vegetable matter that covers a stagnant pond like a cloak; compare *AC* 1.4.61–3. The image links with the recurrent concern with clothing, as at 101–7, and recalls 1.1.218–19, 'to dismantle / So many folds of favour'.

130 **from tithing . . . tithing** from one parish to the next. Householders were supposed to pay one-tenth or a tithe of their wealth to the Church. A statute of 1598 orders that any vagabond apprehended in a 'Parish or Tything'

shall 'be openly whipped untill his or her body be bloudye, and shalbe forth-with sent from Parish to Parish . . . the next streighte way to the Parish where he was borne' (Chambers, *ES*, 4.324; 'common Players of Enterludes' were included among rogues and vaga-bonds).

131 **three suits** an echo of Kent's comment on Oswald at 2.2.15. Edgar represents himself as formerly a *serving-man* at 83–6.

134–5 **But . . . year** adapted from a couplet found in the version of the medieval romance of *Sir Bevis of Hampton* published in 1503: 'Rates and myce and suche smal dere / Was his mete that seuen yere' (EETS No. 46, 75)

134 **deer** animals

136 **Smulkin** Smolkin, a minor devil who takes the form of a mouse in Harsnett (Brownlow, 240), and see 155 and n. below

126 tadpole] *F* (Tod-pole*); tode pold *Qu, Q2;* tod pole *Qc*   wall-newt] *Qc, F;* wall-wort *Qu*
127 fury] *Q , F;* fruite *Q2*   130 stocked, punished] *F;* stock-punisht *Q*   135 Have] *F;* Hath *Q*
136 Smulkin] *F;* snulbug *Q*

EDGAR   The prince of darkness is a gentleman. Modo
    he's called, and Mahu.   140

GLOUCESTER

    Our flesh and blood, my lord, is grown so vile

    That it doth hate what gets it.

EDGAR   Poor Tom's a-cold.

GLOUCESTER [*to Lear*]

    Go in with me. My duty cannot suffer

    T'obey in all your daughters' hard commands.   145

    Though their injunction be to bar my doors

    And let this tyrannous night take hold upon you,

    Yet have I ventured to come seek you out,

    And bring you where both fire and food is ready.

LEAR

    First let me talk with this philosopher: 150

    [*to Edgar*] What is the cause of thunder?

KENT   Good my lord,

    Take his offer, go into the house.

139–40 **prince of darkness . . . Mahu**
The immediate source is Harsnett
(Brownlow, 317): 'the graund Prince of
darknes doth combine and unite his
forces', including '*Maho* and *Modu*
(the two Generals of the infernal
furies)'; compare Ephesians, 6.12
(Geneva version), '*the princes* of the
darkenes of this worlde'. Edgar's *company* (138) is at least of high rank!

141 **flesh and blood** kindred, here
specifically children. Gloucester
groups Edgar with Goneril and Regan.

142 **gets** begets

150 **philosopher** natural scientist; or
perhaps magician, if Lear sees Poor
Tom as an occult scientist in view of
his acquaintance with devils; see 153
and n.

151 **What . . . thunder?** a mystery that
some marvelled at, according to the

narrator of Chaucer's 'Squire's Tale',
258, and a question that crops up in
early religious instructional dialogues
(see G. S. Gordon, *Shakespearian
Comedy* (1944), 126–8). In asking 'the
cause of thunder' in his encylopedic
Batman upon Bartholome (1582), f163ᵛ,
Stephen Batman provides a quasi-
scientific definition, 'that thunder is a
spirit of windes received in the bosome
of clowds, & breaketh by the vertue of
his mooving, and renteth all the partes
of the Clowde, and maketh great quak-
ing, noise, and sound, and thunder'.
But Lear may be seen as questioning
divine providence here, in contrast to
his earlier sense of thunder as the voice
of God; see 3.2.5–6 and n.; compare
the atheist, D'Amville, who declares
that thunder 'is a mere effect of
Nature' in Cyril Tourneur's *The*

---

141 my . . . vile] *F* (vilde*)*; is growne so vild my lord *Q*   144 SD] *this edn*   149 fire . . . food] *F*;
food and fire *Q*   151 SD] *Hunter*   Good my] *F*; My good *Q*

LEAR

    I'll talk a word with this same learned Theban:

    What is your study?

EDGAR   How to prevent the fiend and to kill vermin.   155

LEAR   Let me ask you one word in private.

KENT [*to Gloucester*]

    Importune him ^Fonce more^F to go, my lord;

    His wits begin t'unsettle.

GLOUCESTER   Canst thou blame him?

    ^F*Storm still.*^F

    His daughters seek his death. Ah, that good Kent,

    He said it would be thus, poor banished man.   160

    Thou sayest the King grows mad; I'll tell thee, friend,

    I am almost mad myself. I had a son,

    Now outlawed from my blood; he sought my life,

    But lately, very late. I loved him, friend,

Atheist's Tragedy, 2.1.142. See also Elton, 201–8, for a fuller discussion of the matter.

153 **learned Theban** learnèd; probably, as F. G. Butler suggests, *English Studies*, 67 (1986), 511–14, the 'Thebane Crates', cynic philosopher and follower of Diogenes, described in William Baldwin's very popular *Treatise of Moral Philosophy* (1600 edn), Cv^r; the *good Athenian*, 176, would then be Diogenes himself. The cynics chose to live in rags and poverty, despised wealth and power, and were sharp in reproving vices. The shift to Athens may have been triggered by Harsnett's devil, 'Modu', which becomes *Modo* (139), and may have recalled for Shakespeare a famous passage where Horace, *Epistles*, 2.1.213, celebrates the poet who can transport him like a magician now to Thebes, now to Athens ('et modo me Thebis, modo ponit Athenis'). See Edmund Blunden, 'Shakespeare's significances' (1929), in Anne Bradby (ed.),

Shakespeare Criticism 1919–35 (1936), 331–2. Diogenes was brought on stage as a character in John Lyly's *Campaspe* (1584).

155 **prevent** baffle or frustrate (*OED v.* 5, 10)

    kill vermin an idea perhaps suggested by the devils in Harsnett, who frequently take the form of animals, like Smolkin the 'Mouse-devil' (Brownlow, 315)

156 **Let . . . private** in effect a stage direction within the text for Lear and Edgar to move away from the others

157 **Importune** urge

159 **His . . . death** This charge adds to the pathos of Lear's situation, though so far there is no evidence to support it; see 17–18 and n. At 3.6.86 Gloucester reports overhearing a plot to kill Lear.

163 **outlawed . . . blood** banished as a criminal (see 2.1.80–5), and from Gloucester's lineage or blood, as at 3.5.23.

164 **late** recently

153 same] *F;* most *Q*   157 SD] *Oxf*   159 Ah] *F;* O *Q*   163 he] *Q2, F;* a *Q*

No father his son dearer. True to tell thee,   165
The grief hath crazed my wits. What a night's this?
[*to Lear*] I do beseech your grace.

LEAR   O, cry you mercy, ᶠsir.ᶠ

[*to Edgar*] Noble philosopher, your company.

EDGAR   Tom's a-cold.

GLOUCESTER

In, fellow, there, into the hovel; keep thee warm.   170

LEAR   Come, let's in all.

KENT   This way, my lord.

LEAR   With him;

I will keep still with my philosopher.

KENT

Good my lord, soothe him; let him take the fellow.

GLOUCESTER   Take you him on.

KENT   Sirrah, come on; go along with us.   175

LEAR   Come, good Athenian.

GLOUCESTER   No words, no words; hush.

EDGAR

Childe Rowland to the dark tower came,

---

167 **cry you mercy** beg your pardon
170–80 It is not easy to work out what is
   happening on stage here. Gloucester
   tells Poor Tom to go into the hovel,
   and Lear tries to follow ('let's in all'),
   while Kent may urge Lear to go in a
   different direction (returning to some
   part of Gloucester's house?). Edgar
   hangs back (avoiding recognition by
   his father?) with Lear, who wants his
   philosopher by him. 'Take you him on'
   (174) may refer to Poor Tom or to the
   Fool, silent since Gloucester came on
   at 107.1. Kent then goes off with the
   Fool ('Sirrah, come on'), followed by
   Gloucester, while Edgar brings up the
   rear with Lear. See 3.6.1 and n. for further comment on the location of the

action.
172 **keep still** stay constantly
173 **soothe** humour
174 **you him** Both Q and F have 'him
   you', which is awkward syntactically,
   and it seems likely that the words were
   accidentally transposed.
176 **good Athenian** See 153 and n.
178 **Childe** a title of dignity for a young
   noble aspiring to knighthood
178–80 **Childe . . . man** nonsense
   verses. A line possibly from a lost
   ballad concerning Roland, famous as
   related to Charlemagne, and as hero of
   Le Chanson de Roland, is tied into a
   familiar cry from some version of Jack
   the Giant-killer. The lines may also
   point to Edgar, who will turn into a

---

166 hath] *Q*, *F*; has *Q2*   167 SD] *Oxf*   168 SD] *Hunter*   170 into the] *Q2*, *F* (into th'); in't *Q*
171–2 him; / I . . . still] *F*; him I . . . stil, *Q*   178 tower came] *F*; towne come *Q*; tower come *Capell*

His word was still 'Fie, foh and fum,   179
I smell the blood of a British man.'   [F]*Exeunt.*[F]

3.5   *Enter* CORNWALL *and* EDMUND.

CORNWALL   I will have my revenge, ere I depart his house.

EDMUND   How, my lord, I may be censured that nature thus gives way to loyalty something fears me to think of.

CORNWALL   I now perceive it was not altogether your   5
brother's evil disposition made him seek his death, but
a provoking merit set a-work by a reprovable badness in
himself.

EDMUND   How malicious is my fortune, that I must
repent to be just? This is the letter [F]which[F] he spoke of,   10
which approves him an intelligent party to the
advantages of France. O heavens! That this treason
were [F]not[F], or not I the detector.

hero and kill the 'giant' Edmund.
Rowland, a young gentleman in
Fletcher's play *The Woman's Prize*
(?1611), is teasingly called 'Childe
Rowland' (2.1.16), but this could be
echoing *King Lear.*
180 **British** not 'English' as the traditional tale has it, but Lear was King of
Britain in the chronicles, and James I
liked to be known as 'King of Great
Brittaine' (title-page of his *Works*,
1616). See 4.6.246 and n., and
Introduction, p. 19.
3.5.1   **his house** making it clear that the
scene imagined is Gloucester's house
2–23 Edmund's oily hypocrisy here in his
subservience to Cornwall shows him at
his worst, without the jauntiness that
made him engaging in 1.2 and 2.1;
compare Kent's description of 'smiling rogues' at 2.2.70–8.
2   **nature** natural affection for a father

(cf. 2.2.367), as opposed to loyalty to
the ruler, Cornwall
3   **something fears** somewhat frightens
6–8   **his . . . himself** Probably 'it was not
simply Edgar's evil disposition that
made him seek Gloucester's death, but
a sense of his own worth inciting him
(*provoking merit*), stimulated by a rep-
rehensible wickedness in Gloucester'.
The pronouns are confusing, but the
logic of the sentence parallels *evil disposition* and *provoking merit*, and in 3.3
Gloucester has just shown his *badness*
(7) by his *treason* (12) to Cornwall.
11   **approves** confirms
     intelligent party spy, passing infor-
mation (or intelligence; echoing Kent's
words at 3.1.25 in F; see p. 261);
Edmund has stolen the letter, which
Gloucester locked in his closet at
3.3.11.

3.5] *F (Scena Quinta); not in Q*   0.1 EDMUND] *F; Bastard Q*   1 his] *F; the Q*   2+ SP
EDMUND] *Theobald; Bast. Q , F*   12 this] *F; his Q*

CORNWALL   Go with me to the Duchess.

EDMUND   If the matter of this paper be certain, you have   15
mighty business in hand.

CORNWALL   True or false, it hath made thee Earl of
Gloucester. Seek out where thy father is, that he may be
ready for our apprehension.

EDMUND [*aside*]   If I find him comforting the King, it   20
will stuff his suspicion more fully. [*to Cornwall*] I will
persever in my course of loyalty, though the conflict be
sore between that and my blood.

CORNWALL   I will lay trust upon thee and thou shalt find a   24
dear father in my love.   *Exeunt.*

3.6   *Enter* KENT [*disguised*] *and* GLOUCESTER.

GLOUCESTER   Here is better than the open air; take it
thankfully. I will piece out the comfort with what
addition I can. I will not be long from you.

KENT   All the power of his wits have given way to ᶠhisᶠ
impatience. The gods reward your kindness.   5
                                              Exit [*Gloucester*].

15 **matter** substance or meaning; see
1.1.55 and n.
19 **for our apprehension** for us to
arrest him
20 **comforting** giving help to
22 **persever** accented on the second syllable; Shakespeare's habitual usage
23 **my blood** my lineage, what I owe to
my family
3.6.1   **Here** The location is not specified,
but it seems that Lear and his companions have been led away from the
'hovel' and back to some outhouse or
room connected with Gloucester's

house; see 3.4.170–80 and n. This
explains why Gloucester can augment
(*piece out*) comforts for Lear by making
use of the resources of his own house,
and convey him through the gates on
his way to Dover at 3.7.14–19; it also
explains why Edmund has no difficulty in finding his father *comforting
the King* (3.5.20). The presence of
seats (21, 22, 51, Q), cushions (34, Q)
and possibly a curtained bed (79–80, Q
and F) also suggests an interior space
that is part of a house.
5   **impatience** inability to endure, or

20 SD] *Theobald*   21 SD] *this edn; Aloud / Duthie*   22 persever] *F;* persevere *Q*   25 dear] *F;*
dearer *Q*   SD] *F; Exit. Q*

3.6] *F (Scena Sexta); not in Q*   0.1 *F; Enter Gloster and Lear, Kent, Foole and Tom Q*   disguised]
Riv (disguised as Caius)   5 reward] *F;* deserue *Q*   SD] *Capell; Exit F (opp. 3); not in Q*

Enter LEAR, EDGAR *[disguised as Poor Tom] and* FOOL.

EDGAR   Frateretto calls me, and tells me Nero is an angler
in the lake of darkness. Pray, innocent, ᶠandᶠ beware the
foul fiend.

FOOL   Prithee, nuncle, tell me whether a madman be a
gentleman or a yeoman?   10

LEAR   A king, a king.

ᶠFOOL   No, he's a yeoman that has a gentleman to his son;
for he's a mad yeoman that sees his son a gentleman
before him.

LEARᶠ

To have a thousand with red burning spits   15
Come hizzing in upon 'em!

ᵠEDGAR   The foul fiend bites my back.

FOOL   He's mad that trusts in the tameness of a wolf, a

loss of self-control. Lear had promised
to be 'the pattern of all patience' at
3.2.37.
   reward   Gloucester's *reward* is to be
tortured and blinded in 3.7.
6–7 **Frateretto . . . darkness** Poor
   Tom's nonsense is prompted by
   Harsnett; Frateretto is named as one of
   the devils (Brownlow, 242) after whom
   'the Fidler comes in with his Taber
   and Pipe'. The fiddler in hell perhaps
   suggested Nero, and Chaucer's
   'Monk's Tale', where Nero is depicted
   as an angler who delighted 'To fisshe
   in Tybre, when hym liste pleye'. In
   classical mythology the dead had to
   cross the 'stygian lake', mentioned by
   Harsnett (Brownlow, 238), or river
   Styx, to enter the infernal regions.
7   **Pray, innocent** addressed possibly to
   the Fool (as *innocent* may mean
   'simpleton'), or perhaps ironically to
   Lear
9–10   **whether . . . yeoman** In the BBC
   television production of 1982 the Fool

showed with this question that he had
penetrated Edgar's disguise (Bratton,
151). The *gentleman* may be Lear, and
the *yeoman*, or freeholder of lower
rank, Edgar, both qualifying as a *madman*.
12–14 ***No . . . him** This addition in F to
   the role of the Fool, like 82,
   compensates in some measure for the
   absence of his four speeches in 17–55,
   found only in Q. The Fool here glances
   at Lear, who has given his 'sons' (see
   1.1.40–1) and daughters a higher status than his own.
15–16   **red . . . upon 'em** Lear imagines
   Goneril and Regan in hell. Harsnett
   has many images of burning, broiling
   and hell-fire; see, for example,
   Brownlow, 255–6.
17–55 ***EDGAR . . . scape?** Debate continues as to whether the F version of the
   play is better or worse for the omission
   of this mock-trial sequence. Struc-
   turally it seems to me better, since (a)
   the same motif occurs at 4.6.108–14,

5.1] *as F; at 0.1 in Q   disguised . . . Tom*] *this edn; as a Bedlam beggar Oxf*   6 Frateretto] *F;
Fretereto Q*

horse's health, a boy's love or a whore's oath.

LEAR

It shall be done, I will arraign them straight.   20
[*to Edgar*] Come, sit thou here, most learned justicer;
[*to the Fool*] Thou sapient sir, sit here. No, you she-
    foxes –

EDGAR   Look where she stands and glares! Want'st thou
    eyes at trial, madam?
                    Come o'er the bourn, Bessy, to me.   25
FOOL   Her boat hath a leak,
                    And she must not speak
                    Why she dares not come over to thee.
EDGAR   The foul fiend haunts Poor Tom in the voice of a

where Lear 'tries' Gloucester; (b) the
Fool has been increasingly distanced
from Lear, and the omission of the
mock-trial makes his role in his later
scenes as a general sardonic commentator more consistent; and (c) the mock-
trial is too theatrically powerful in relation to the climax of this sequence of
scenes in the blinding of Gloucester in
3.7. Directors like to include it, even
when generally following the F text,
because it is good theatre, and enhances
our sense of Lear's madness. See
Introduction, pp. 132–3.

19 **horse's health** See Biondello's catalogue of the numerous diseases that
might afflict horses in *TS* 3.2.48–56.
20 **arraign** indict or put on trial
21 **learned** learnèd
    ***justicer** judge. Q has 'justice', but the
line runs better with *justicer*, as at 55.
23 ***she** Q's 'he' is probably an error, for
the emphasis here is on the imagined
presences of Goneril and Regan, but
Edgar could be referring to the devil,
or even to Lear.
23–4 **Want'st thou eyes** perhaps 'Do

you lack eyes?', or: 'Are you afraid to
look up and face Lear?'; usually interpreted as 'Do you want spectators?'
25–8 **Come . . . thee** The first line is
from an old song; a fool, Moros,
singing 'the foot of many songs as fools
were wont', includes it in William
Wager's play *The longer thou livest, the
more fool thou art* (?1559–69), 94, and it
begins a ballad by William Birch in
praise of Queen Elizabeth or 'Bessy'
(1564), included in *The Penguin Book
of Renaissance Verse*, ed. H. R.
Woudhuysen (1992), 92. Music for it
from a sixteenth-century manuscript
in the British Library is printed in
Sternfeld, 180–8; and Hunter, 342–4,
prints a different setting from a
Cambridge manuscript for the lute.
The Fool completes the quatrain with
lines that have obscene possibilities, if
the *leak* refers to menstruation or gon-
orrhoea (Partridge, 76, and see *Tem*
1.1.47–8).
29–30 **voice . . . nightingale** Is Edgar, as
Weis thinks, referring to the Fool
singing?

19 health] *Q;* heels *Warburton*   21 SD] *Capell*   justicer] *Theobald;* Iustice *Q*   22 SD] *Capell*
No] *Q;* Now *Q2*   23 she] *Theobald;* he *Q*   Want'st] *Q2;* wanst *Q*   24 trial, madam] *Q2 (*triall
madam*);* tral madam *Q;* troll-madam *Oxf*   25 bourn] *Capell;* broome *Q;* burn *Oxf*

nightingale. Hoppedance cries in Tom's belly for two   30
white herring. Croak not, black angel, I have no food for
thee.

KENT

How do you, sir? Stand you not so amazed.
Will you lie down and rest upon the cushions?

LEAR

I'll see their trial first. Bring in their evidence.   35
[*to Edgar*] Thou robed man of justice, take thy place.
[*to the Fool*] And thou, his yoke-fellow of equity,
Bench by his side. [*to Kent*] You are o'the commission;
Sit you too.

EDGAR   Let us deal justly.   40
          Sleepest or wakest thou, jolly shepherd?
          Thy sheep be in the corn;
          And for one blast of thy minikin mouth
          Thy sheep shall take no harm.
Purr, the cat is grey.   45

30 **Hoppedance** from Harsnett (Brownlow, 242), where this devil's name is 'Hoberdidance', and is associated with music

31 **white** fresh, or salted but unsmoked
Croak rumble; compare Harsnett (Brownlow, 352): 'having the said croaking in her belly . . . they [the priests] said it was the devill that . . . spake with the voyce of a Toade'

34 **cushions** Q's 'cushings', a variant spelling, may indicate Shakespeare's pronunciation; compare 'javeling's' for 'javelin's', *VA* 616.

35 **their evidence** the evidence against them

36 **robed** robèd. Poor Tom has only a blanket for covering; see 2.2.181 and 3.4.64.

37 **yoke-fellow of equity** partner in impartiality, but possibly alluding to

courts of equity, such as the Court of Chancery, which attempted to settle cases according to natural justice

38 **Bench** join him on the judges' bench
o'the commission as if appointed a Justice of the Peace under the Great Seal

41–4 **Sleepest . . . harm** nonsense verses, which have no obvious application. The sleeping shepherd has allowed his sheep to trespass into the cornfield, where they can get bloated and die, but he can summon them back with one shrill cry. Poor Tom in this scene seems to take over the Fool's role as commentator in rhymes and songs, and he may be glancing at Lear as a ruler (shepherd) whose subjects have gone astray.

45 **Purr . . . grey** suggested probably by Harsnett's '*Puffe* and *Purre*', the names

34 cushions] *Q2; Q (*cushings*)* 35 in their] *Q; the* Pope 36 SD] *Capell* robed] *Pope;* robbed *Q* 37 SD] *Capell* 38 SD] *Capell* 40–1 justly. / Sleepest] *Theobald;* iustly sleepest *Q;* iustly, sleepest *Q2*

LEAR   Arraign her first, 'tis Goneril – I here take my oath
        before this honourable assembly – kicked the poor King
        her father.

FOOL   Come hither, mistress: is your name Goneril?

LEAR   She cannot deny it.   50

FOOL   Cry you mercy, I took you for a joint-stool.

LEAR

        And here's another whose warped looks proclaim
        What store her heart is made on. Stop her there!
        Arms, arms, sword, fire, corruption in the place!
        False justicer, why hast thou let her 'scape?^Q   55

EDGAR   Bless thy five wits.

KENT

        O pity! Sir, where is the patience now
        That you so oft have boasted to retain?

EDGAR [*aside*]

        My tears begin to take his part so much
        They mar my counterfeiting.

LEAR   The little dogs and all,   60
        Trey, Blanch and Sweetheart, see, they bark at me.

EDGAR   Tom will throw his head at them: avaunt, you curs!

---

of two 'fat devils' (Brownlow, 242–3)

51 **Cry . . . joint-stool** proverbial (Dent,
    M897), as a mocking excuse for over-
    looking someone; a *joint-stool* was one
    properly fitted together by a joiner
    rather than by rough carpentry. These
    are the Fool's last words in Q (in F he
    has line 82), but he remains on stage,
    and helps to carry Lear off; see 97.

52 **another** i.e. Regan

53 **store** abundance, plenty. Lear's word
    is ironic.

    made on made of (Abbott, 182)

54 **fire . . . place** The place of justice
    suddenly becomes hell in Lear's imag-

ination; compare 4.6.123–5.

56 **five wits** See 3.4.57 and n.

61 **Trey . . . Sweetheart** suggestive of
    Goneril, Regan and Cordelia. *Trey*
    could mean 'pain', or 'betray'; *Blanch*
    make pale with fear, as at *Mac* 3.4.115;
    and Cordelia is to be Lear's darling.

62 **throw . . . them** unexplained; some
    action is indicated, repeated at 69, per-
    haps bending the head and glaring. In
    the nineteenth century the usual stage
    business was for Poor Tom to throw a
    straw hat at imaginary dogs; see
    Bratton, 229, Rosenberg, 236.

    avaunt be off!

---

47 kicked] *Q;* she kicked *Q2*   51 joint-stool] *Q2 (*ioynt stoole*);* ioyne stoole *Q*   53 store] *Q;* stuff
(Jennens); stone *Collier²*   on] *Capell;* an *Q;* of *Theobald*   54 place] *Q;* palace *Grant White*
57 O pity! Sir] *F (*O pitty: Sir*);* O pity sir, *Q*   59 SD] *Rowe*   60 They] *F;* Theile *Q*

Be thy mouth or black or white,
Tooth that poisons if it bite;
Mastiff, greyhound, mongrel grim,   65
Hound or spaniel, brach or him,
ᶠOrᶠ bobtail tyke or trundle-tail,
Tom will make him weep and wail;
For with throwing thus my head,
Dogs leap the hatch and all are fled.   70
Do, de, de, de. ᶠ*Cessez!*ᶠ Come, march to wakes and fairs
and market towns. Poor Tom, thy horn is dry.

63–70 In these lines in Q and F Edgar as
Poor Tom has the last rhyming jingle
in the play; in Q he shares 25–8 with
the Fool, and then takes over from him
at 41–4; see also 3.4.75–6 and n.

63 **or . . . or** either . . . or; also at 67

64 **poisons** with rabies? (so Weis)

66 ***brach or him** unexplained. A *brach*
is a bitch-hound, as at 1.4.110, and *him*
(Q), or 'Hym' (F), ought, it seems, to
offer an alternative to *spaniel*. Edgar
could simply point to an imaginary
him, or even to the Fool or Kent. Many
editors accept Hanmer's emendation
to 'lym', i.e. 'lyam', or leash, as short
for 'lyam-hound', or 'liemer', that
excelleth in smelling and swift running' (Harrison in Holinshed, 1.387),
but Blayney, in the unpublished second part of *The Texts of King Lear and
their Origins*, cited in Cam², shows how
implausible this is; and in any case *him*
should parallel *spaniel*, not *hound*. To
take *him* to mean male dog as opposed
to *brach* is not very plausible either,
and no similar use has been noticed.
Shakespeare may have had a hard time
finding a rhyme.

67 **bobtail tyke** a mongrel with a docked
or bobbed tail
trundle-tail curly-tailed dog

70 ***leap** The Q reading ('leape') is consistent with the tenses in the speech as
a whole; 'leapt' (F) may result from a
misreading of final 'e', a letter easily
confused with 'd' in secretary hand.
hatch closed lower half of a divided
door

71 ***Do . . . de** See 3.4.57; Tom presumably chatters with cold again. Q has
'loudla, doodla', which Weis thinks
may represent a rallying cry of beggars, or the sound of Poor Tom's horn,
72.
***Cessez!** Stop! F has 'sese' which is
close to 'Sesey' (F) at 3.4.98. Katherine
Duncan-Jones notes in *MLR*, 91
(1996), 265, that 'sess' is recorded in a
single entry in *OED* as meaning a call
to a dog when giving it food, but the
dogs have fled, so that it seems more
likely that Poor Tom ceases to address
imaginary dogs, and turns again to
speak to Lear.
wakes annual parish festivals.
Autolycus 'haunts wakes', and no
doubt other vagabonds did; see *WT*
4.3.102.

72 **horn** drinking-horn. Beggars carried
horns for drink, and also to collect
alms, and, according to ?Thomas
Dekker in *O per se O* (1612), it was the

65–6 mongrel grim, / Hound] F (Mongrill, Grim, / Hound); mungril, grim-hoūjd Q   66 him]
Q; Hym F; lym *Hanmer*   67 tyke] Q (tike); tight F   trundle-tail] Q; Troudle taile F   68 him]
F; them Q   69 head,] Q; head; F   70 leap] Q; leapt F   71 Do, de, de, de] F; loudla, doodla Q
Cessez] *Oxf*; sese F; sessa *Pope*; see, see *Collier*

LEAR   Then let them anatomize Regan; see what breeds
about her heart. Is there any cause in nature that make
these hard hearts? [*to Edgar*] You, sir, I entertain ᵠyouᵠ   75
for one of my hundred; only I do not like the fashion of
your garments. You will say they are Persian ᵠattireᵠ,
but let them be changed.

KENT   Now, good my lord, lie here ᶠand restᶠ awhile.

LEAR   Make no noise, make no noise, draw the curtains.   80
So, so, ᵠsoᵠ; we'll go to supper i'the morning ᵠso, so, so.ᵠ
[*He sleeps.*]

ᶠFOOL   And I'll go to bed at noon.ᶠ

style of Bedlam beggars to cry 'give poor Tom one cup of the best drink' (Judges, 373). These are Poor Tom's last words in the scene (and in the play in F, which omits his lines at 99–112) and could mean that he has gone dry and has no more to say (Steevens).

73–5 **anatomize . . . heart** Lear seems to think of Regan's heart as physically hard, hence his desire to dissect or anatomize it. Some Lears may 'act out dissection: plunging the hand in the imaginary body, holding up the heart, striking it with the imagined knife' (Rosenberg, 236). Michael Gambon in Adrian Noble's production of 1982, enraged, 'stabbed at Regan, represented by a pillow the Fool held – accidentally killing him' (Bratton, 153), thus explaining the disappearance of the Fool after this scene. In the Bible metaphorical or moral hardness of heart is frequently attributed to, or inflicted as a punishment on, the wicked; see, for example, Matthew, 19.8, John, 12.40, and Romans, 2.5.

75 **entertain** take into service
76 **hundred** hundred knights
77 **Persian** Persia was noted for its luxury, and for producing fine silk, and Lear's words are ironic in relation to the rags on Edgar's *uncovered body*; see

3.4.100–3.

78 **changed** recalling biblical allusions to the 'law of the Medes and Persians, which altereth not' (citing Daniel, 6.8)
79–80 **lie . . . curtains** If they are in a furnished room (see 1 and n.), there may be a property bed in it, with curtains to enclose it, as was usual (compare *The Revenger's Tragedy*, 2.3.1–10). Alternatively, Lear could lie on the *cushions* (34, Q) or on the stage, and order Kent to draw imaginary curtains, as if round a canopied bed.

81 SD   In Q Kent tells us at 94 that Lear sleeps; in F too he has to be carried off ('Take up, take up', 92), and has presumably passed out or gone to sleep.

82 **And . . . noon** proverbial for 'I'll play the fool too' (Dent, B197). 'Go to bed at noon' was also a name for salsify or goat's beard, the flower of which 'shutteth it selfe at twelve of the clocke, and sheweth not his face open untill the next daies sunne do make it flower anew' (John Gerard, *The Herbal* (1597), 594–5). Kerrigan, 229, argues that the Fool here identifies himself with this flower, as his 'kingly sun' declines. These are the Fool's last words, found only in F, and neatly cap Lear's last mad utterance. On the absence of the Fool from the last two

74 make] *F;* makes *Q*   75 these hard hearts] *F;* this hardnes *Q*   SD] *Capell*   77 garments. You will say] *F;* garments youle say, *Q*   81 SD] *Oxf*

292

Enter GLOUCESTER.

GLOUCESTER

Come hither, friend; where is the King my master?

KENT

Here, sir, but trouble him not; his wits are gone.

GLOUCESTER

Good friend, I prithee take him in thy arms.   85
I have o'erheard a plot of death upon him.
There is a litter ready; lay him in't
And drive toward Dover, friend, where thou shalt meet
Both welcome and protection. Take up thy master:
If thou shouldst dally half an hour his life,   90
With thine and all that offer to defend him,
Stand in assured loss. Take up, take up,
And follow me, that will to some provision
Give thee quick conduct.

^QKENT   Oppressed nature sleeps.

acts, see Introduction, pp. 56–7.

82.1 so Q; Gloucester's entry after 78 in F is presumably anticipatory, since his question at 83 shows he does not see or hear Lear

86 **upon** against

87–8 **litter . . . drive** The litter, or couch within a curtained frame, is imagined to be placed on a horse-drawn cart.

88 **Dover** the only place certainly named in the play (*Gloucester* at 1.5.1 may be the person rather than the place), here mentioned for the first time in F (but see 3.1.32), and implying that Cordelia is there; in Q the reference might be to a French invading force, which has already landed according to Kent in 3.1. See Appendix 1, p. 393.

90 **dally** delay

92 **assured** assurèd

*Take . . . up Qu has 'Take vp to keepe', which looks like a misreading

corrected in F; the press-reader emended Qc to 'Take vp the King', which makes sense but is less forceful.

93–4 **to . . . conduct** lead you quickly to some necessary supplies (for the journey)

*94–112 KENT . . . **lurk!** With the exception of Gloucester's 'Come, come, away!' (98), which ends the scene in F, this passage is found only in Q. Edgar drops his mask as Poor Tom to speak moralizing rhyming couplets in his own voice, directly addressing the audience, and emphasizing the links between the Lear and Gloucester plots. Edgar could be seen as taking over the Fool's role as commentator, substituting for the Fool's social criticism (as at 3.2.79–96, also direct address to the audience) an emotional appeal on behalf of the sufferings of Lear and Gloucester. Edgar's lines add nothing to

82.1] *as Q (opp. 81); after 78 in F*   88 toward] *F;* towards *Q*   92 Take up, take up] *F;* Take vp to keepe *Qu;* Take vp the King *Qc*

This rest might yet have balmed thy broken sinews,   95
Which if convenience will not allow
Stand in hard cure. [*to the Fool*] Come, help to bear thy
    master;
Thou must not stay behind.ᵠ

GLOUCESTER   Come, come away!
    Exeunt [*all but Edgar; Kent and the Fool supporting Lear*].
ᵠEDGAR

When we our betters see bearing our woes,
We scarcely think our miseries our foes.   100
Who alone suffers, suffers most i'the mind,
Leaving free things and happy shows behind.
But then the mind much sufferance doth o'erskip,
When grief hath mates and bearing fellowship.
How light and portable my pain seems now,   105
When that which makes me bend makes the King bow,
He childed as I fathered. Tom, away;
Mark the high noises, and thyself bewray
When false opinion, whose wrong thoughts defile thee,
In thy just proof repeals and reconciles thee.   110

the action, and, for reasons why they might have been deliberately omitted from F, see Introduction, p. 142.

95 **balmed . . . sinews** soothed your shattered nerves

97 **Stand . . . cure** will be difficult to heal
Come . . . master Kent must be addressing the Fool, who has been silent in Q since 51.

99–100 **When . . . foes** When we see our superiors afflicted by our troubles, we find it easier to bear our own miseries. Edgar's first eight lines play variations on the proverb 'It is good to have company in misery' (Dent, C571).

102 **free things** carefree actions

103 **sufferance** suffering

104 **bearing** endurance of suffering

105 **portable** bearable, supportable

106 **bend . . . bow** yield . . . submit; *bow* is the stronger term, as suggesting the obeisance normally due to a king like Lear

107 **childed . . . fathered** Shakespeare seems to have coined both terms ('fathered' occurs in *JC* 2.1.197); as Lear has been cast out by his daughters, so Edgar has been banished by his father.

108 **Mark . . . noises** take note either of serious reports or of rumours about the court (or both)
bewray reveal

110 by showing you to be virtuous recalls you (from banishment) and reconciles you (to your father)

97 SD] *Theobald*   98 SD] *this edn (Theobald); Exit. Q; Exeunt F*   101 suffers, suffers most] *Theobald;* suffers suffers, most *Q;* suffers most *Q2*   103 o'erskip] *Q2 (*ore-skip*), Q (*or'e scip*)*

What will hap more tonight, safe 'scape the King.
Lurk, lurk!^Q   [*Exit.*]

3.7   *Enter* CORNWALL, REGAN, GONERIL, EDMUND
              ^F*and* Servants.^F

CORNWALL [*to Goneril*] Post speedily to my lord your
  husband. Show him this letter: the army of France is
  landed. [*to Servants*] Seek out the traitor, Gloucester.
REGAN   Hang him instantly!   [*Some Servants rush off.*]
GONERIL   Pluck out his eyes!   5
CORNWALL Leave him to my displeasure. Edmund, keep
  you our sister company; the revenges we are bound to
  take upon your traitorous father are not fit for your

---

111 **What** whatever (Abbott, 254)
112 **Lurk, lurk!** Keep out of sight! Edgar
  becomes Poor Tom again momentarily.
3.7.0.1 Servants It would seem that five
  are called for in Q, which specifies
  'two or three' at 2.7.1, but requires one
  to be killed (81), one to drag off the
  body (95–6), one to lead off
  Gloucester (96 SD), and two more
  who remain on stage to speak of helping Gloucester. F omits the dialogue of
  these two (98–106), so reducing the
  number of actors needed in the scene.
  The brutality of Cornwall and Regan
  towards Gloucester is the more horrible because they are guests in his
  house, the setting for this scene; see 30
  and n.
1 **Post** hurry
2 **letter** seized by Edmund from
  Gloucester's *closet*; see 3.3.11 and
  3.5.10
2–3 **army . . . landed** See 3.1.22–9 and
  n., 3.3.13 and 3.6.88. In Q French
  forces are already in English ports in

3.1, but F postpones the landing until
now, except for an ambiguous hint at
3.3.13. The problem of the French
invasion is considered in detail in
Appendix 1.
3 *****traitor** 'vilaine' in Q. F strengthens
the idea of Gloucester as a traitor
(which he is, to the new rulers
Cornwall and Regan), thus stressing
the confusion of values in the play; to
be loyal to Lear is to be a traitor to his
daughters; see also 86.
5 **Pluck . . . eyes** an appropriate punishment since it was sight that attracted
men to commit adultery. Blinding had
been a medieval penalty for rape; 'Let
him thus lose his eyes which gave him
sight of the maiden's beauty' (see
Bridget Gellert Lyons, in *Some Facets*,
28). It is Goneril who first thinks of
blinding Gloucester, and so she too is
incriminated in what Regan and
Cornwall do to him later in the scene.
7 **sister** sister-in-law (Goneril)
   bound obliged

---

112 SD] *Theobald*

3.7] *F (Scena Septima); not in Q*   0.1 REGAN] *Q2, F; and Regan Q*   EDMUND *and servants*] *F*
(Bastard, and Seruants); and Bastard Q   1 SD] *Rowe*   3 SD] *this edn*   traitor] *F; vilaine Q*
4 SD] *this edn; Exeunt some of the servants. / Capell (opp. 3)*   7 revenges] *F; reuenge Q*

beholding. Advise the Duke where you are going to a
most festinate preparation; we are bound to the like.   10
Our posts shall be swift and intelligent betwixt us.
Farewell, dear sister; farewell, my lord of Gloucester.

Enter OSWALD.

How now, where's the King?

OSWALD

My lord of Gloucester hath conveyed him hence.
Some five- or six-and-thirty of his knights,   15
Hot questrists after him, met him at gate,
Who with some other of the lord's dependants
Are gone with him toward Dover, where they boast
To have well-armed friends.   19

CORNWALL   Get horses for your mistress.   [*Exit Oswald.*]

GONERIL   Farewell, sweet lord and sister.

CORNWALL

Edmund, farewell.   *Exeunt* ᵠ*Goneril and Edmund*ᵠ.
[*to Servants*]   Go, seek the traitor Gloucester;
Pinion him like a thief, bring him before us.

[*Servants leave.*]

10 **festinate preparation** speedy preparation (for war)
are . . . like aim likewise to go and prepare for war. With *bound* compare 'outward bound'.
11 **posts** couriers
intelligent keeping us informed, as at
3.1.24–5
12 **Gloucester** Edmund, named so by
Cornwall at 3.5.17–18; but confusing
(see 3 and n.), as at 3 and 14 Edmund's
father is still called Gloucester

15–16 **Some . . . gate** We never see this
remnant of Lear's hundred followers,
who exist in imagination, not on stage,
where only one or two are explicitly
called for, and none are with him in the
storm scenes; see 2.2.192.1 and n., and
Introduction, pp. 65–9.
16 **questrists** seekers; Shakespeare's
coinage, from 'quest'
17 **lord's** Gloucester's
23 **Pinion him** bind his arms; a shocking way to treat an aristocrat

9 Advise] *Q;* Aduice *F*   10 festinate] *F2;* festiuate *Q;* festiuate *F*   11 posts] *F;* post *Q*
intelligent] *F;* intelligence *Q*   12.1 OSWALD] *Collier; Steward Q (opp. 13), F*   14 SP OSWALD] *Stem.
Q, F*   16 questrists] *F;* questrits *Q;* questants *Oxf*   18 toward] *F;* towards *Q*   20 SD] *Staunton*
22 SD *Exeunt . . . Edmund*] *Q (Exit Gon. and Bast.); Exit F (after 22)*   SD *to Servants*] *this edn
(Capell)*   23 SD] *this edn (Capell)*

Though ᶠwellᶠ we may not pass upon his life
Without the form of justice, yet our power   25
Shall do a courtesy to our wrath, which men
May blame but not control. Who's there? The traitor?

Enter GLOUCESTER, �\^Q*brought in by two or three*ᵠ ᶠServants.ᶠ

REGAN   Ingrateful fox, 'tis he.
CORNWALL
    Bind fast his corky arms.
GLOUCESTER   What means your graces?
    Good my friends, consider; you are my guests.   30
    Do me no foul play, friends.
CORNWALL   Bind him, I say –
    [*Servants bind his arms.*]
REGAN   Hard, hard. O, filthy traitor!
GLOUCESTER
    Unmerciful lady as you are, I'm none.
CORNWALL
    To this chair bind him. [*to Gloucester*] Villain, thou
        shalt find –   [*Regan plucks his beard.*]

24 **pass . . . life** pass a death sentence
on him
25 **form of justice** formal procedure
(*OED* Form *sb.* 11) of a trial
26 **do a courtesy** defer (curtsy) or give
way to
28 **Ingrateful fox** Gloucester has been
ungrateful to his 'worthy arch and
patron' (2.1.59), Cornwall, and
behaved like a fox, proverbial for its
craftiness (Dent, F629, F645), in
secretly corresponding with Cordelia.
29–32 **Bind . . . hard** The servants first
pinion Gloucester by the arms (perhaps, as Cam² notes, reluctantly, since
Cornwall gives the order twice), then

tie him to a chair (34).
29 **corky** dry, withered. Harsnett may
have first used it in this sense (*OED* 2),
describing 'an old, corkie woman'
(Brownlow, 221).
30 **guests** For *friends* to attack their host
Gloucester in his own house is an especially brutal violation of hospitality;
compare 39–41 and *Mac* 1.7.14–16.
32 **Hard . . . traitor!** Regan typically
intervenes by an action that cuts off
Cornwall's sentence; see 2.1.103 and
2.2.132.
33 ***none** Q's 'true' yields much the same
meaning.

27 control] *Q* (controule), *F* (comptroll)   27.1] *Hunter, after Q and F; Enter Gloster brought in by
two or three Q; Enter Gloucester, and Seruants F (opp.* control)   29 means] *Q, F;* mean *F4*
31 SD] *Rowe (They bind him)*   33 I'm none] *F;* I am true *Q*   34 SD *to Gloucester*] *this edn*
find –] *Q;* finde. *F*   SD *Regan . . . beard*] *Johnson*

GLOUCESTER

   By the kind gods, 'tis most ignobly done   35
   To pluck me by the beard.

REGAN

   So white, and such a traitor?

GLOUCESTER   Naughty lady,
   These hairs which thou dost ravish from my chin
   Will quicken and accuse thee. I am your host;
   With robber's hands my hospitable favours   40
   You should not ruffle thus. What will you do?

CORNWALL

   Come, sir, what letters had you late from France?

REGAN

   Be simple answered, for we know the truth.

CORNWALL

   And what confederacy have you with the traitors,
   Late footed in the kingdom?

REGAN   To whose hands   45
   You have sent the lunatic King. Speak.

GLOUCESTER

   I have a letter guessingly set down

---

37 **Naughty** wicked; see 2.2.323
38 **ravish** pluck out, but suggesting violation as by rape
39 **quicken** come to life
40 **robber's** or perhaps *robbers'*, if Gloucester's change from 'thou' to 'you' means he is addressing both Regan and Cornwall
   hospitable favours welcoming features or face (*OED sb.* 9b, c, compare *1H4* 3.2.136); see next note
41 **ruffle** handle roughly; compare 2.2.491
42, 45 **late** of late, lately
43 **Be simple answered** give a straight answer
45 **Late footed** recently landed; here

Cornwall is thinking of an invasion from France, as at 2–3 above; but see 3.3.13 and n.
45–6 **kingdom? . . . King.** Many editors place a dash after *kingdom* and a question-mark after *King*, in accordance with Regan's liking for interrupting her husband (see 32 and n.), but Q and F suggest that she converts Cornwall's question into a statement; after all, Regan knows what Gloucester has done (see 18–19).
47 **letter** Cornwall in fact has it, passed on by Edmund; see 3.3.10 and 3.5.10–16.
   guessingly set down written as conjecture

43 answered] *F;* answerer *Q*   45 Late] *Q, F;* lately *Q2*   46 You have] *Q, F;* haue you *Q2*

Which came from one that's of a neutral heart,
And not from one opposed.

CORNWALL   Cunning.

REGAN   And false.

CORNWALL

Where hast thou sent the King?

GLOUCESTER   To Dover.   50

REGAN

Wherefore to Dover? Wast thou not charged at peril –

CORNWALL

Wherefore to Dover? Let him ᵠfirstᵠ answer that.

GLOUCESTER

I am tied to the stake and I must stand the course.

REGAN   Wherefore to Dover, ᵠsirᵠ?

GLOUCESTER

Because I would not see thy cruel nails   55
Pluck out his poor old eyes; nor thy fierce sister
In his anointed flesh stick boarish fangs.
The sea, with such a storm as his bare head
In hell-black night endured, would have buoyed up
And quenched the stelled fires.   60

51 **at peril** at the risk of punishment (referring to Regan's *injunction* to Gloucester at 3.4.146–7); see 3.3.2–6

53 **I . . . course** Gloucester sees himself as a bear tied to the stake and forced to endure the *course* or bout of being assailed or baited by hounds (as in coursing hares, etc.). It was a popular Jacobean spectator-sport; compare *Mac* 5.7.1–2.

57 **anointed flesh** alluding to the practice of anointing English kings and queens since the Middle Ages with holy oil at their coronation service (another anachronism in the play). The consecration of the monarch with

this unction remains to this day the sacramental centre of the ceremony, conferring on him or her the spiritual gifts of kingship; see *R2* 3.2.54–5.

*stick F; 'rash' (Q) is preferred by many editors, as a rarer term meaning to cut or slash, but the thrice repeated 'sh' sound in 'flesh rash boarish' is difficult for a speaker, and the substitution of 'stick' could have been made for the sake of euphony by the author or by an actor.

59–60 **buoyed . . . fires** surged or billowed up and put out the fires of the stars; *stelled* ('stellèd') = starry, from Latin *stella*, a star, but could mean

57 anointed] *Qc, F;* aurynted *Qu*   stick] *F;* rash *Q*   58 as . . . bare] *F;* of his lou'd *Qu, Q2;* on his lowd *Qc;* as his bowed *(Blayney, after Greg)*   59 buoyed] *F;* layd *Qu, Q2;* bod *Qc*
60 stelled] *Qc, F;* steeled *Qu, Q2*

299

Yet, poor old heart, he holp the heavens to rain.
If wolves had at thy gate howled that stern time,
Thou shouldst have said, 'Good porter, turn the key,
All cruels else subscribed'; but I shall see
The winged vengeance overtake such children.   65

CORNWALL

See't shalt thou never. Fellows, hold the chair;
Upon these eyes of thine I'll set my foot.

GLOUCESTER

He that will think to live till he be old,
Give me some help! – O cruel! O you gods!

REGAN

One side will mock another – th'other too.   70

'fixed', from Old English 'stellan', as at
Luc 1444
61 **holp** old form of 'helped'
*to rain i.e. by his tears, emblematic
of pity. Lear was anxious not to weep
at 2.2.465–75, but tears mark his
reconciliation with Cordelia in 4.7. Q
has 'to rage', which makes good sense,
but is less resonant.
62 ***stern** Q has 'dearn' = dreary, dire, a
rarer word, only used once elsewhere
by Shakespeare, and in a deliberately
archaic context, the Chorus of Gower
to Act 3 of *Per.* The change in F could,
like 'stick', 57, be an actor's intervention, but F corrects a lot of Q errors in
this speech (see textual notes), and all
the changes are likely to be revisions
by the same hand, possibly the
author's.
63–4 ***turn . . . subscribed** unexplained;
perhaps 'open the door and let him in,
whatever other forms of cruelty you
have complied with'. This is a noted
crux, because (a) it is not certain
whether what is *said* ends at *key* or
subscribed; (b) it is not clear what *cruels*
means, and whether it refers to creatures like wolves; (c) several meanings

are possible for 'subscribe' (F) or 'sub-
scrib'd' (Q) since the subject of this
verb may be *porter* or *cruels*. Stone proposed emending 'else' to 'I'll', which
Oxf adopts, but this is not much of an
improvement. Compare *subscription* at
3.2.18.
65 **winged vengeance** wingèd; vengeance
of the gods: see 2.2.351–2
67–9 **set . . . cruel!** The text suggests that
Cornwall puts out one of Gloucester's
eyes, throws it down and squashes it
underfoot. In the nineteenth century
the blinding was done offstage or was
concealed from the audience, with
Gloucester seated and facing upstage
so that his eyes were not visible. This
has remained a common way of staging a deed so violent as to seem for
generations of critics and actors too
appalling to enact in view of the audience. Only since Peter Brook's production in 1962, in which Cornwall
gouged out an eye with one of his
spurs, have some producers attempted
to register the horror of the deed in
full view of the audience; see Bratton,
157, and Introduction, pp. 61–2.

61 holp] *F;* holpt *Q* rain] *F;* rage *Q* 62 howled] *F;* heard *Q* stern] *F;* dearne *Q* 64 else sub-
scribed] *Q;* else subscribe *F;* I'll subscribe *Oxf (Stone)* 67 these] *F;* those *Q* 69 you] *F;* ye *Q*

CORNWALL
    If you see vengeance –
1 SERVANT   Hold your hand, my lord.
    I have served ᶠyouᶠ ever since I was a child,
    But better service have I never done you
    Than now to bid you hold.
REGAN   How now, you dog?
1 SERVANT
    If you did wear a beard upon your chin,   75
    I'd shake it on this quarrel. What do you mean?
CORNWALL   My villein?   [*They*] ᵠ*draw and fight.*ᵠ
1 SERVANT
    Nay then, come on, and take the chance of anger.
    [*He wounds Cornwall.*]
REGAN [*to another Servant*]
    Give me thy sword. A peasant stand up thus?
    ᵠ*She takes a sword and runs at him behind.*ᵠ ᶠ*Kills him.*ᶠ
1 SERVANT
    O, I am slain. My lord, you have one eye left   80
    To see some mischief on him. O!   [*He dies.*]
CORNWALL
    Lest it see more, prevent it. Out, vile jelly,
    Where is thy lustre now?
GLOUCESTER
    All dark and comfortless? Where's my son Edmund?
    Edmund, enkindle all the sparks of nature   85
    To quit this horrid act.

---

76 **shake it** fight with you
77 **villein** serf; compare *peasant*, 79. Q
    and F both spell the word 'villaine'.
78 **chance of anger** i.e. as to who is hurt
    or killed

81 **mischief on him** harm done to him
    O! perhaps signalling that Regan stabs
    him again (so Oxf)
85 **nature** filial affection, as at 3.5.2
86 **quit** requite, avenge

71 vengeance –] *Q;* vengeance. *F*   71, 75, 78, 80 SP 1 SERVANT] *Capell; Seruant, Seru., Ser. Q , F*
72 you] *Q2, F; not in Q*   78 Nay] *F;* Why *Q*   SD] *Rowe subst.*   79 SD *to . . . servant*] *Johnson*
80 you have] *F;* yet haue you *Q*   81 SD] *Q2*   85 enkindle] *F;* vnbridle *Q*

REGAN   Out, ᶠtreacherousᶠ villain,
Thou call'st on him that hates thee. It was he
That made the overture of thy treasons to us,
Who is too good to pity thee.

GLOUCESTER

O my follies! Then Edgar was abused?   90
Kind gods, forgive me that and prosper him.

REGAN [*to a Servant*]

Go, thrust him out at gates and let him smell
His way to Dover. How is't, my lord? How look you?

CORNWALL

I have received a hurt. Follow me, lady.
[*to Servants*] Turn out that eyeless villain. Throw this
slave   95
Upon the dunghill.
                    Exeunt [*Servants*] ᶠ*with Gloucester*ᶠ [*and the body*].
                              Regan, I bleed apace;
Untimely comes this hurt. Give me your arm.
                              Exeunt [*Cornwall and Regan*].

Q2 SERVANT
I'll never care what wickedness I do

---

treacherous villain recalling ironi-
cally Gloucester's condemnation of
Edgar as a 'brutish villain', at 1.2.76–9.
F adds *treacherous*, which is not in Q.
See 3 and n.

88 **overture** disclosure

90 **abused** imposed upon, wronged;
compare 4.7.77

93 **How look you?** How are you feeling? (Or what does the way you look
mean?)

96 **apace** at a great rate

98–106 *2 SERVANT . . . Exeunt* These
lines are not in F, and may have been
omitted (a) to economize on the number of actors needed in the scene; see

0.1 and n; (b) as Cam¹ notes, because of
inconsistency: Edgar as a banished
man would have avoided of all places
his father's house (see 2.2.172–6), and
in 4.1 it is an old man who reluctantly
hands Gloucester over to Poor Tom;
(c) so as to emphasize Gloucester's
'treachery' to Cornwall and Regan (see
3 and 86). The two speaking servants
in these lines are additional to the two
or three needed to bring in Gloucester,
bind him, and, minus one who is killed
by Regan, take off Gloucester and the
dead body. Q by contrast channels
audience response through the servants' comments on the wickedness of

95 SD] *Oxf*   96 SD *Exeunt . . . Gloucester*] *this edn. (Hunter); Exit. Q; Exit with Gloster. F (after
Dover, 93)*   SD *and the body*] *this edn, after Oxf (at 97)*   97 SD] *F; Exit. Q*   SD *Cornwall and
Regan*] *this edn, after Theobald*   98 SP 2 SERVANT] *Capell; Seruant Q*

If this man come to good.

3 SERVANT   If she live long

And in the end meet the old course of death,   100

Women will all turn monsters.

2 SERVANT

Let's follow the old Earl and get the bedlam

To lead him where he would. His roguish madness

Allows itself to anything.

3 SERVANT

Go thou: I'll fetch some flax and whites of eggs   105

To apply to his bleeding face. Now heaven help him!

Exeunt.^Q

4.1   *Enter* EDGAR[, *disguised as Poor Tom*].

EDGAR

Yet better thus, and known to be contemned

Than still contemned and flattered. To be worst,

Cornwall and Regan, and elicits pity
for Gloucester by directing attention
to his *bleeding face* (106).
100 **meet . . . death** die in the normal
way (of old age)
101 **Women . . . monsters** because they
see her wickedness prosper
102 **bedlam** Edgar as Poor Tom; the
word was used in the sixteenth century as a common noun to mean a dis-
charged lunatic who was licensed to
beg (*OED* 5); see 2.2.185 and n.
103 **roguish** characteristic of vagabonds; in Qu, but cut in Qc, for no
apparent reason, since the excision
leaves an incomplete verse line
104 **Allows . . . anything** will take on
anything we ask him to do (because he
is mad and cannot be held responsible)

105 **flax . . . eggs** a way of soothing and
protecting a hurt eye. In his *Treatise of
Chyrurgie* (1575), 49, John Banister
recommends using the white of an egg
laid on 'bombase', or cotton wool, for
this purpose.
4.1.0.1 *Enter* EDGAR Lear went on his
way to Dover at the end of 3.6; it is
now the day after the storm (see 34),
and a location some way from
Gloucester's house; Edgar is a wanted
man, and has to keep his distance from
others. See 3.7.98–106 and n.
1–2 **Yet . . . flattered.** It is better to be as
I am, and openly despised, than (as
at court) to be still despised while
being openly flattered. Pope's interpretation of the punctuation in F,
'flatter'd,' (see textual note), might be

99, 105 SP 3 SERVANT] *Capell; 2 Seruant, 2 Ser. Q*   102 SP 2 SERVANT] *Capell; 1 Ser. Q*
103 roguish] *Qu, Q2; not in Qc*   106 SD Exeunt] *Theobald; Exit. Q*

4.1] *F (Actus Quartus. Scena Prima); not in Q*   0.1 disguised . . . Tom] *this edn; as a Bedlam beggar
Oxf*   2 flattered. To be worst,] *Pope; flattered to be worst, Q; flatter'd, to be worst: F*

The lowest and most dejected thing of fortune,
Stands still in esperance, lives not in fear.
The lamentable change is from the best,   5
The worst returns to laughter. ᶠWelcome then,
Thou unsubstantial air that I embrace;
The wretch that thou hast blown unto the worst
Owes nothing to thy blasts.ᶠ

Enter GLOUCESTER, *led by an* Old Man.

ᶠButᶠ who comes here? My father, poorly led?   10
World, world, O world!
But that thy strange mutations make us hate thee,
Life would not yield to age.

---

supported by the further comment on
what it is to be *worst* in 6–9 (F only).
3 **dejected** cast down
4 ***esperance** hope, correcting 'experience' (Q), which may be due to a misreading of the manuscript
6 **The . . . laughter** 'When things are at
the worst they will mend' was a common proverb (Dent, T216), cited in
Mac 4.2.24–5.
6–9 ***Welcome . . . blasts** F, not in Q;
these lines recall the storm scenes, and
the *wretch* refers to Lear as much as to
Edgar being at the worst. Edgar's
confidence is premature; see 27–8.
9 **Owes . . . blasts** Being at the worst,
Edgar can welcome (*embrace*) the air
freely, because he has nothing to thank
the winds for; see 3.2.18.
9.1 **Old Man** Like the Old Man in *Mac*
2.4, he is the only character who
belongs to ordinary life outside the
court, and who has a sense of time
past; he is older even than Lear, and,
like old Adam in *AYL*, he emblema-
tizes ideals of service and of charity
that are no longer valued in a country
ruled by Goneril and Regan. Through

the dialogue between him and
Gloucester, Edgar learns that his
father knows the truth about himself
and Edmund. For a discussion of the
dramatic importance of this episode,
see Mahood, 171–5.
10 ***poorly led** in a way unworthy of his
rank, and by a poor man. Qu has 'poorlie,leed', corrected in Qc to 'parti,eyd',
which is accepted by many editors as
closest to Shakespeare's manuscript,
and meaning 'parti-eyed', or with eyes
of various colours, as suggested by the
blood on Gloucester's face (see 57). F
makes better dramatic sense, however,
as Edgar first sees his father in surpris-
ingly mean company, and only later, at
27–8, realizes also that Gloucester is
blind. In a note forthcoming in *RES*,
R. J. C. Watt suggests the manuscript
behind Q had 'gory-eyed', which
makes sense, and 'gory' is often used
by Shakespeare, but it is not easy to
confuse 'g' and 'p' in secretary hand.
12–13 If it were not that the unaccount-
able changes in the world make us hate
it (and hence willing to let it go), we
would not submit to growing old.

4 esperance] *F;* experience *Q*   9.1] *as F; opp. 13 Q*   SD *led by*] *Q; and F*   10   who comes] *F;*
Who's here *Q*   poorly led] *Qu (*poorlie, leed*), Q2, F;* parti,eyd, *Qc*

OLD MAN O my good lord, I have been your tenant and
your father's tenant these fourscore ᶠyearsᶠ –   15

GLOUCESTER

Away, get thee away; good friend, be gone.
Thy comforts can do me no good at all,
Thee they may hurt.

OLD MAN ᵠAlack, sir,ᵠ you cannot see your way.

GLOUCESTER

I have no way, and therefore want no eyes: 20
I stumbled when I saw. Full oft 'tis seen
Our means secure us and our mere defects
Prove our commodities. O dear son Edgar,
The food of thy abused father's wrath,
Might I but live to see thee in my touch,   25
I'd say I had eyes again.

OLD MAN   How now? Who's there?

EDGAR [*aside*]

O gods! Who is't can say 'I am at the worst'?
I am worse than e'er I was.

OLD MAN [*to Gloucester*]   'Tis poor mad Tom.

EDGAR [*aside*]

And worse I may be yet; the worst is not

14–15 *Q sets as prose, and registers
Gloucester's impatience in interrupting the Old Man. F prints as two
rough lines of verse, adding 'yeares.' to
complete the line and sentence; this
was set by compositor B, who may be
responsible for the sophistication.
18 **may hurt** if he is caught helping a
proclaimed traitor
21 **I . . . saw** Gloucester acknowledges his
own sin and spiritual blindness in
words that echo a biblical theme, e.g.
Isaiah, 59.9–10, 'We walke in the
darke. We grope like the blind upon

the wall, we grope euen as one that
hath no eyes, we stumble at the noone
day, as though it were toward night'
(see Colie, in *Some Facets*, 131–2;
Milward, 185).
22–3 **Our . . . commodities** our wealth
makes us over-confident, while our
outright (*mere* = sheer, pure) defects
are found to be beneficial
24 **abused** abusèd; misled, imposed
upon, as at 3.7.90
27–30 **O . . . worst** rejecting the false
optimism of 1–9 above; Edgar finds in
4.5 that there is indeed worse to come.

15 theṣe] F; this Q (see Comm.)   23 O] F (Oh); ah Q   27, 29, 39, 55, 57 SD aside] Johnson

So long as we can say 'This is the worst.'   30
OLD MAN [*to Edgar*]
    Fellow, where goest?
GLOUCESTER   Is it a beggar-man?
OLD MAN   Madman, and beggar too.
GLOUCESTER
    He has some reason, else he could not beg.
    I'the last night's storm I such a fellow saw,
    Which made me think a man a worm. My son   35
    Came then into my mind, and yet my mind
    Was then scarce friends with him. I have heard more
        since:
    As flies to wanton boys are we to the gods,
    They kill us for their sport.
EDGAR [*aside*]   How should this be?
    Bad is the trade that must play fool to sorrow,   40
    Angering itself and others. [*to Gloucester*] Bless thee,
        master.
GLOUCESTER
    Is that the naked fellow?
OLD MAN   Ay, my lord.
GLOUCESTER
    ^QThen prithee^Q get thee away. If for my sake

---

33 **reason** sanity
35 **think . . . worm** think of men as insignificant and defenceless, echoing another biblical theme, e.g. Psalms, 22.6, 'I am a worme, and no man', and Job, 25.6 (Milward, 185)
38–9 **As . . . sport** Gloucester sees the gods as like destructive children who kill flies in sport. The irony is that he remains unaware that he has been given his desire, expressed in 25–6, to 'see' Edgar again. He teeters on the brink of despair in his recurrent thoughts of suicide, as at 76–81. See

4.6.55 and n.
40 **trade** course of action (or practice, as at *MM* 3.1.148, 'Thy sin's not accidental, but a trade'). Edgar's words here might be taken as a comment on the Fool and Poor Tom, as well as on his immediate role *vis-à-vis* his father.
40–1 **must . . . others** For the moment Edgar *must* play the fool as Poor Tom in spite of his father's misery, vexing himself and others (because he feels forced to conceal his real identity?); but see 57 and n.
43 ***Then . . . away** F repeats the abrupt

---

30 So] *F*; As *Q*   33 He] *Q2, F*; A *Q*   38 to wanton] *F*; are toth'wanton *Q*   39 kill] *F*; bitt *Q*
40 fool] *F*; the foole *Q*   41 SD] *this edn; Aloud Ard²; He comes forward Oxf*   43 away] *F*; gon *Q*

306

Thou wilt o'ertake us hence a mile or twain
I'the way toward Dover, do it for ancient love, 45
And bring some covering for this naked soul,
Which I'll entreat to lead me.

OLD MAN   Alack, sir, he is mad.

GLOUCESTER

'Tis the time's plague when madmen lead the blind.
Do as I bid thee, or rather do thy pleasure; 50
Above the rest, be gone.

OLD MAN

I'll bring him the best 'pparel that I have,
Come on't what will. ᶠ*Exit.*ᶠ

GLOUCESTER   Sirrah, naked fellow.

EDGAR

Poor Tom's a-cold. [*aside*] I cannot daub it further – 55

GLOUCESTER   Come hither, fellow.

EDGAR [*aside*]

ᶠAnd yet I must.ᶠ [*to Gloucester*] Bless thy sweet eyes,
they bleed.

'Get thee away' from 16, leaving a short line, and compositor B, who omits words elsewhere, may have omitted 'Then prithee' (Q); see Werstine², 282–4. Oxf and Cam² follow F.

45 Dover following Lear (see 3.7.50, 92–3), though Gloucester has suicide in view at 76–81
ancient love the attachment or concern for me you felt in former times

49 the time's plague the affliction or evil of our time
madmen . . . blind recalling the proverb 'If the blind lead the blind they both fall into the ditch' (Dent, B452, from Matthew, 15.14, Luke, 6.39)

50 do thy pleasure do what you will; Gloucester realizes he has no power to command any more

51 Above the rest above all

52 'pparel apparel, clothing

53 Come . . . will whatever happens (to me) as a result (Hunter)

55 *daub it further put on a false show any more (as if covering a wall with plaster). Q has 'dance it farther', which could refer to his jerky movements as Poor Tom, and allows a pun on 'father'.

57 *And . . . must Edgar's *must* at 40 makes sense, since as Poor Tom he does not want to let the Old Man know who he really is; but it is hard to see why he still *must* conceal himself from his father, except in terms of the needs of the plot. See Introduction, pp. 47–8, 63 on Edgar's failure to reveal himself. This phrase, in F, not Q, completes the sense of Edgar's aside,

---

44 hence] *F;* here *Q*   45 toward] *Q, F;* to *Q2*   47 Which] *F;* Who *Q*   52 'pparel] *Rowe;* parrell *Q, F*   55 daub] *F;* dance *Q*   further] *F;* farther *Q*   57 SD *to Gloucester*] *this edn; Aloud / Hunter*

GLOUCESTER   Knowst thou the way to Dover?

EDGAR   Both stile and gate, horseway and footpath. Poor
Tom hath been scared out of his good wits. Bless thee,   60
goodman's son, from the foul fiend. ^QFive fiends have
been in Poor Tom at once, of lust, as Obidicut;
Hobbididence, prince of darkness; Mahu, of stealing;
Modo, of murder; Flibbertigibbet, of mopping and
mowing, who since possesses chambermaids and   65
waiting-women. So, bless thee, master.^Q

GLOUCESTER

Here, take this purse, thou whom the heaven's plagues

and completes a blank verse line he
speaks in his own person, not as Poor
Tom; it may be an addition, to go with
the correction of 'dance' (Q) to 'daub'
(F).

58, 74 **Dover** Gloucester has sent Lear to
Dover (3.7.14–19), which becomes
convenient not only as Cordelia's
landing-place but for the blind old
man's attempted suicide, a motif
Shakespeare borrowed from Sidney's
Arcadia (Bullough, 403–4), where the
blind Prince of Paphlagonia tries to
persuade his good son to lead him to
the top of a rock so that he can throw
himself off it; see Introduction, p. 100.

59 **stile . . . footpath** A gate is needed to
give access to the *horseway* or
bridlepath, and a stile to enter the footpath.

61 **goodman's son** addressing his father
as if he were the son of a yeoman or
innkeeper, but also a 'good man'; see
2.2.44 and n.

61–6 **Five . . . master** The names of the
devils are from Harsnett: Hoberdicut
(Brownlow, 295); Hoberdidance and
Flibberdigibbet (Brownlow, 242, and
see 2.2.44 and n.); Maho and Modu
(Brownlow, 241, 243; see also 3.4.139–

40 and n.). In Harsnett, Maho is a
devil attached to Sara Williams, a
chambermaid, and Modu affects
'mimpes, mops and idle holy women',
who are ready to cry out 'at the mowing of an apish wench' (Brownlow,
331). The passage was omitted from F,
perhaps as too much like repetition of
3.4.

63 ***darkness** Q's 'dumbnes' seems an
obvious error, since this passage recalls
3.4.139–40, with its reference, borrowed from Harsnett, to the 'prince of
darkness'; in Harsnett Hobbididance
appears 'like a *whirlwind*, turning
round like a flame of fire' (Brownlow,
312).

64–5 **mopping and mowing** making
faces and grimacing (as chambermaids
do behind the back of their mistress?)

67 ***thou** so Q; F has 'y^u' in a crowded line
where abbreviation was necessary. The
context suggests that 'thou' is prefer-
able to 'you'.

67–74 **Here . . . enough** Gloucester
echoes Lear's 'Poor naked wretches'
speech (see 3.4.28–36 and n.), but
shifts the emphasis from 'what wretches
feel' to the failure of the rich and powerful to feel for others. For the impor-

60 scared] *Q* (scard)*;* scarr'd *F*   thee] *F*; the *Q*   61 goodman's son] *F* (good mans)*;* good man *Q*
62 of lust, as Obidicut] *Q*; as Obidicut, of lust *Cam¹ (W. S. Walker)*   63 darkness] *Capell*; dumbnes *Q*   64 Flibbertigibbet] *Pope*; *Stiberdigebit Q*   64–5 mopping . . . mowing] *Theobald*; Mobing,
& *Mohing Q*; mocking and mowing *Cam¹*; mocking and mouthing *(Blayney)*   67 thou] *Q*; ÿ *F*

Have humbled to all strokes. That I am wretched
Makes thee the happier. Heavens deal so still!
Let the superfluous and lust-dieted man   70
That slaves your ordinance, that will not see
Because he does not feel, feel your power quickly:
So distribution should undo excess
And each man have enough. Dost thou know Dover?

EDGAR   Ay, master.   75

GLOUCESTER
There is a cliff whose high and bending head
Looks fearfully in the confined deep:
Bring me but to the very brim of it,
And I'll repair the misery thou dost bear
With something rich about me. From that place   80
I shall no leading need.

EDGAR   Give me thy arm,
Poor Tom shall lead thee.   ᶠ*Exeunt.*ᶠ

tance of seeing and feeling, see
Introduction, p. 79, and also 5.3.323–5
and n.

68 **humbled . . . strokes** subdued to bear
all kinds of affliction

70 **superfluous . . . man** man who has
more than he can use and indulges his
appetite for pleasure (the earliest
meaning of *lust*); *superfluous* recalls
superflux at 3.4.35 (and see 2.2.454),
while *lust-dieted* is also a reminder of
Gloucester's adultery

71 ***slaves your ordinance** subjects your
injunction (that we should love and
help one another) to his own will.
Behind these lines lie such biblical passages as Mark, 10.21, 'Go and sell all
that thou hast, and giue to the poor,
and thou shalt haue treasure in heav-
en'. Cam² notes that in the Geneva

Bible (1560 edn) there is a marginal
gloss on the parable of Dives and
Lazarus at Luke, 16.19–31, 'By this
storie is declared what punishment
thei shal haue, which liue deliciously &
neglect the poore'. Q has 'stands', perhaps a nonce usage for 'withstands'
(*OED v.* 55, citing this line).

71–2 **will . . . feel** Gloucester begins to
'see' in the sense of an acquired insight
into how others might feel.

73 **undo** eliminate, abolish

77 ***fearfully in** timorously into. The
cliff becomes a person terrified by the
sight of the sea far below. Q has
'firmely', which makes good sense, but
fits the idea of a *bending head* less well.
confined confinèd; in the straits of
Dover, between England and France

80 **about me** on my person

71 slaves] *F;* stands *Q*   73 undo] *F;* vnder *Q*   77 fearfully] *F;* firmely *Q;* sternly *Halio*

4.2   *Enter* GONERIL, EDMUND [*followed by*] OSWALD.

GONERIL

Welcome, my lord. I marvel our mild husband
Not met us on the way. [*to Oswald*] Now, where's your
    master?

OSWALD

Madam, within; but never man so changed.
I told him of the army that was landed;
He smiled at it. I told him you were coming;   5
His answer was 'The worse.' Of Gloucester's treachery
And of the loyal service of his son,
When I informed him, then he called me sot,
And told me I had turned the wrong side out.
What most he should dislike seems pleasant to him,   10
What like, offensive.

GONERIL [*to Edmund*]   Then shall you go no further.
It is the cowish terror of his spirit,
That dares not undertake. He'll not feel wrongs
Which tie him to an answer. Our wishes on the way

4.2.0.1 *Goneril, Edmund and Oswald
set off in 3.7 to join Albany, and are to
be imagined as at his house or palace.
In Q Oswald's entry is placed after
master, 2; Oxf follows F, but assumes
Oswald enters by a different door, as if
meeting Goneril.

3–11 Madam . . . offensive Albany has
not been on stage since 1.4, where he
was merely hesitant about Goneril's
behaviour to Lear; there has been news
of friction between him and Cornwall,
as at 2.1.11–12 and 3.1.19–21, so the
change in him now reported is not
surprising (and is not unlike the
change in Cordelia between Act 1 and
4.4, when she returns; see 4.4.0.1n.).

His moral rejection of Goneril makes
her pursuit of Edmund more plausible.
4 army the French army; see 3.7.2–3
8 sot idiot
9 turned . . . out got the matter the
wrong way round (Horsman). The
idea is from clothing, as if the lining of
a garment were placed on the outside
(*OED a.* 10b, citing *Oth* 2.3.52).
11 What like what he should like
12 cowish cowardly
13 undertake take responsibility
13–14 He'll . . . answer He'll not respond
to injuries that demand retaliation.
14 wishes either about furthering their
love (the first hint of this), or about
getting rid of Albany

4.2] *F (Scena Secunda); not in Q*   0.1 EDMUND] *Q, F (Bastard)   followed by*] *this edn; and F; not
in Q*   OSWALD] *F (Steward); Enter Steward. Q (after 2)*   3+ SP OSWALD] *Stew. Q, F*   10 most .
. . dislike] *F;* hee should most desire *Q;* he should most defy *Oxf*   11 SD] *Hanmer*   12 terror] *Qc
(*terror), *F;* curre *Q;* tenor *(Stone)*

May prove effects. Back, Edmund, to my brother;   15
Hasten his musters and conduct his powers.
I must change names at home and give the distaff
Into my husband's hands. This trusty servant
Shall pass between us. Ere long you are like to hear –
If you dare venture in your own behalf –   20
A mistress's command. Wear this.
[*She places a chain about his neck.*]

                              Spare speech,
Decline your head. This kiss, if it durst speak,
Would stretch thy spirits up into the air.
Conceive, and fare thee well –

EDMUND

Yours in the ranks of death.   ^F*Exit.*^F

GONERIL   – my most dear Gloucester.   25
^FO, the difference of man and man!^F
To thee a woman's services are due;

---

15 **prove effects** turn out to be fulfilled
brother brother-in-law, Cornwall
16 **Hasten his musters** speed up his
assembling of troops
17–18 ***change . . . hands** For Goneril,
Albany has become womanish, and
should have the *distaff*, or staff on
which flax was wound for spinning,
while she takes the sword, a man's
weapon; compare *Cym* 5.3.33–4. Q has
'armes' for 'names', and the change in
F may have been made to avoid a confusion between literal and figurative
arms; the meaning in Q is roughly the
same.
19 **like** likely
21 **mistress's command** in terms both
of her power as ruler, and of her desire
as lover. Goneril's words here and
down to 28 are full of sexual implications.

21–2 **Wear . . . head** implicit stage directions. It seems probable that she places
a chain, symbolic of grace and of high
office, round his neck, or she may put
a favour in his hat; either action would
explain why she stops him speaking,
and orders him to bend.
23, 27 **thy . . . thee** After the kiss,
Goneril shifts from the formal 'you',
acknowledging her intimacy with
Edmund.
23 **spirits** vital powers, suggestive of sexual potency. Hints of sexual arousal
continue in words like *conceive*, *services*
and *bed* in the lines that follow.
24 **Conceive** imagine (what we may do).
He is free to imagine conception in the
sense of pregnancy.
26 *F, not in Q; probably an addition
designed to enhance Goneril's moment of rapture

15 Edmund] *Q2*, *F*; *Edgar Q*   17 names] *F*; armes *Q*   21 command] *Qc*, *F*; coward *Qu*, *Q2*
this.] *F* (this;*)*; this *Qu*, *Q2*; this, *Qc*   24 fare thee] *F*; far you *Q*; farye *Q2*   25 SP EDMUND]
Bast. Q, *F*   27 a woman's] *Qc*, *F* (a Womans*)*; womans *Qu*, *Q2*

A fool usurps my bed.

OSWALD Madam, here comes my lord. ^Q*Exit.*^Q

^F*Enter* ALBANY.^F

GONERIL

I have been worth the whistling.

ALBANY   O Goneril,   30

You are not worth the dust which the rude wind

Blows in your face. ^QI fear your disposition;

That nature which contemns its origin

Cannot be bordered certain in itself.

She that herself will sliver and disbranch   35

From her material sap perforce must wither,

And come to deadly use.

GONERIL   No more, the text is foolish.

---

28 ***A . . . bed** So Qc; F has 'body' for *bed*
(see textual notes), and is followed by
Oxf. The sense is much the same, for
both words extend the meaning of *services* to include the bedchamber as well
as the court and battlefield, but one
must be an error.

30 **worth the whistling** worth watching
out for. She marks Albany's reluctance
to encounter her by recalling the
proverb 'It's a poor dog that is not
worth the whistling' (Dent, D488).

31 **rude** rough and unmannerly

32–51 ***I . . . deep** This is the first of
three passages in this scene found only
in Q (see 54–60 and 63–70 for the
others); in F the scene is shortened by
the abbreviation of the quarrel
between Albany and Goneril, and the
removal of Albany's moral generaliza-
tions. The effect is to speed the action,
at the cost of some excellent lines; see
Introduction, p. 142.

33 **contemns its origin** spurns its cre-
ator (i.e. Lear)

34 cannot assuredly be kept within
bounds (or the limits of moral behaviour)

35–6 **sliver . . . sap** split and break off
(like a sliver or branch of a tree) from
the stock (material or substance) that
nourished her

36 **perforce** of necessity

37 **come . . . use** come to a bad end, or
end up causing death, as Goneril does,
stabbing herself, and poisoning Regan;
see 5.3.289–90

38 'Spare me the sermon' (Cam¹); alluding to biblical injunctions to children
to honour their parents, as in the First
Commandment in Exodus, 20.12,
repeated in the Gospels, e.g. at
Matthew, 15.4, and by St Paul,
Ephesians, 6.2–3: 'Honour thy father
and mother . . . That thou mayest
prosper, and liue long on earth'

---

28 A fool . . . bed] *Qc;* My foote . . . body *Qu;* My foote . . . head *Q2;* My Foole . . . body *F*   29.1]
Q2 (Enter the Duke of Albany), F   30 whistling] *Qc;* whistle *Qu, Q2, F*   33 its] *Q3;* it *Qu, Q2;* ith
Qc

ALBANY

Wisdom and goodness to the vile seem vile;
Filths savour but themselves. What have you done?   40
Tigers, not daughters, what have you performed?
A father, and a gracious aged man
Whose reverence even the head-lugged bear would lick,
Most barbarous, most degenerate, have you madded.
Could my good brother suffer you to do it?   45
A man, a prince, by him so benefitted?
If that the heavens do not their visible spirits
Send quickly down to tame these vile offences,
It will come:
Humanity must perforce prey on itself,   50
Like monsters of the deep.^Q

GONERIL   Milk-livered man,

That bear'st a cheek for blows, a head for wrongs,
Who hast not in thy brows an eye discerning

39–40 **Wisdom . . . themselves** Milward refers to Titus, 1.15, 'Vnto the pure are all things pure: but vnto them that are defiled and vnbeleeuing is nothing pure, but even the mind and conscience of them is defiled.'

40 **Filths . . . themselves** Vile creatures sense, or relish, only their own vileness or stink.

42 **aged** agèd

43 **head-lugged** pulled by the head or baited, and so enraged

45 **brother suffer** brother-in-law allow

46 **benefitted** i.e. by his (Cornwall's) share of the kingdom

47–51 No *visible spirits* or avenging angels (Weis) appear in the play, and this emphatic appeal to the heavens appears only in Q; in both Q and F Albany welcomes the news of Cornwall's death as showing heavenly powers intervening (see 79–81), but

there is little otherwise in the play to suggest that the gods, if they exist at all, have any interest in human affairs.

50–1 **Humanity . . . deep** The idea that 'great fish eat the small' was commonplace (see Dent, F311; Tilley, R102), but Shakespeare turns it into a horrifying vision of cannibalism, as at *TC* 1.3.123–4, and compare *STM*, 86–7, 'men like ravenous fishes / Would feed on one another' (*Riv*, p. 1691).

51 **Milk-livered** chicken-hearted. Cowardice was associated with a lack of blood in the liver, and milk with effeminacy.

52 **cheek for blows** See Luke, 6.29, 'vnto him that smiteth thee on the one cheek, offer also the other', and Matthew, 5.39 (Shaheen).

53–4 **discerning . . . suffering** distinguishing what should be resented (as offensive to your rank or dignity) from what may be honourably tolerated

---

46 benefitted] *Qc;* beniflicted *Qu, Q2;* benefacted *Oxf*   48 these] *Jennens;* the *Qu;* this *Qc*
50 Humanity] *Qc;* humanly *Qu, Q2*   53 discerning] *F;* deseruing *Q*

Thine honour from thy suffering; ^Qthat not knowst
Fools do those villains pity who are punished   55
Ere they have done their mischief. Where's thy drum?
France spreads his banners in our noiseless land;
With plumed helm thy state begins to threat,
Whilst thou, a moral fool, sits still and cries,
'Alack, why does he so?'^Q

ALBANY   See thyself, devil: 60
Proper deformity shows not in the fiend
So horrid as in woman.

GONERIL   O vain fool!

^QALBANY
Thou changed and self-covered thing, for shame

54–60 *that . . . so Q, not in F; see
32–51, and 57n.

55–6 Fools . . . mischief It is foolish to
pity villains (like Gloucester, Lear and
Cordelia?) who are to be prevented
from committing wrongs by being
punished beforehand.

56 drum the sound of military preparation; see 4.4.0.1

57 France the King of France; see
1.1.189. He is said to have returned to
France at the beginning of 4.3; the references to him in 4.3 and in the present
scene are omitted from F; see
Appendix 1 for further discussion.
noiseless quiet and unprepared

58 plumed plumèd
*state . . . threat a difficult crux: this
emendation (see textual notes) has the
merit both of making good sense (if it
means that France begins to threaten
England) and of keeping *state begins*,
altered in Qc from 'slayer begin' (Qu).
The ingenious emendation in Oxf
invents a 'flaxen biggin' or cap, an
implausible association with an aristocrat like Albany; see *Division*, 488. For

confusion between 'threat' and 'thereat', see also textual note to 76. Weis
retains Qc, 'thy state begins thereat',
glossing as 'the true exercise of your
political power starts with this situation', but this seems to me to be
wrenching the meaning of *state*.

59 moral full of moral sentiments, as at
MA 5.1.30

61–2 Proper . . . woman The deformity
of the devil is less horrible (because it
is *proper*, or characteristic of him) than
that of a woman. Albany refers to
physical and moral deformity, to
Goneril's malice and temper, shown in
her expression here. Goneril's deformity is seen as abnormal, and Albany's
words here may be taken to show how
wrong Lear is to condemn all women
at 4.6.122–5.

63 changed changèd
self-covered thing in changing into a
fiend Goneril has concealed or covered
over her womanly features, and
become a *thing*.

63–70 *These lines are not in F, except
for the SD at 69, where F has

---

55 those] *Q;* these *Q2* 57 noiseless] *Qc, Q2;* noystles *Qu* 58 state . . . threat] *Jennens;* slayer
begin threats *Qu, Q2;* state begins thereat *Qc;* flaxen biggin threats *Oxf* 59 Whilst] *Qc;* Whil's
Qu; While *Capell;* Whiles *Oxf* 61 shows] *Qc (shewes);* seems *Q, Q2, F* 63 self-covered] *Q;*
self-converted *Theobald;* false-cover'd *Singer*

Be-monster not thy feature. Were't my fitness
To let these hands obey my blood,   65
They are apt enough to dislocate and tear
Thy flesh and bones. Howe'er thou art a fiend,
A woman's shape doth shield thee.
GONERIL   Marry, your manhood, mew! –^Q

Enter a Messenger.

^QALBANY   What news?^Q   70
MESSENGER
O my good lord, the Duke of Cornwall's dead,
Slain by his servant, going to put out
The other eye of Gloucester.
ALBANY   Gloucester's eyes?
MESSENGER
A servant that he bred, thrilled with remorse,
Opposed against the act, bending his sword   75
To his great master, who, thereat enraged,
Flew on him and amongst them felled him dead;
But not without that harmful stroke which since
Hath plucked him after.
ALBANY   This shows you are above,

'*Messenger*', Q 'Gentleman'; see 32–51
and n.
64 **Be-monster . . . feature** Do not make
your beauty hideous. For *feature*, see
R3 1.1.19, 'Cheated of feature by dis-
sembling nature'.
Were't my fitness if it were proper
for me
65 **blood** temper
67 **Howe'er** despite the fact that
69 **Marry . . . mew!** – 'Why, now see
what passes for manliness with you –

mew!' *Mew* or 'miaou' is derisory
(compare 'catcall').
73, 82 **other** second, or remaining
74 **bred** trained up
thrilled pierced
75 **Opposed against** resisted
75–6 **bending . . . / To** aiming . . . at (as
at 2.1.46)
77 **them** the group of servants? Several
are present in 3.7.
79 **plucked . . . after** i.e. into death
79–81 **This . . . venge** See 47–51 and n.

69 mew] *Qc;* now *Qu, Q2* 69.1 Messenger] *F (after 62);* Gentleman Q *(opp. 70)* 71+ SP
MESSENGER] *F (Mes.);* Gent. Q 73 eyes?] *Q;* eyes. *F* 74 thrilled] *F;* thrald Q 76 thereat
enraged] *Q;* threat-enrag'd *F*

You justicers, that these our nether crimes   80
So speedily can venge. But, O, poor Gloucester,
Lost he his other eye?

MESSENGER   Both, both, my lord.
[*to Goneril*] This letter, madam, craves a speedy answer;
'Tis from your sister.

GONERIL [*aside*]   One way I like this well;
But being widow, and my Gloucester with her,   85
May all the building in my fancy pluck
Upon my hateful life. Another way
The news is not so tart.
[*to the Messenger*]   I'll read and answer.   ᵠ*Exit.*ᵠ

ALBANY
Where was his son when they did take his eyes?

MESSENGER
Come with my lady hither.

ALBANY   He is not here.   90

MESSENGER
No, my good lord; I met him back again.

ALBANY
Knows he the wickedness?

---

80 **justicers** judges
nether belonging to the earth, as opposed to the heavens or upper regions
81 **venge** avenge
Gloucester To Albany here and at 73 and 95, *Gloucester* is the old Earl, whereas for Goneril (85) Edmund is 'Earl of Gloucester' so named by Cornwall at 3.5.17–18.
84 **One . . . well** She wants to possess Edmund (*my Gloucester*), and to rule the kingdom herself, so the news is both bad, since she fears Regan's ambition, and good, since Cornwall is removed, reducing Regan's power.

85 **being** i.e. she being. The construction was common (Abbott, 378), and Keightley's emendation (see textual notes) is unnecessary.
86–7 **May . . . life** may bring to ruin my dream of possessing Edmund. The image is of a building crashing down to crush an existence that has become hateful.
87 **Another** reverting to her first thought at 84
88 **news . . . tart** i.e. as bringing nearer the possibility of undivided rule over Britain (Hunter)
91 **back** on his way back

80 You justicers] *Qc;* your Iustices *Qu, Q2;* You Iustices *F*   83 SD] *this edn*   84 SD] *Johnson*
85 being] *Q, F;* she being *Keightley*   86 in] *F;* on *Q*   88 tart] *F;* tooke *Q*   SD *to . . . Messenger*] *this edn (Delius)*

MESSENGER

Ay, my good lord, 'twas he informed against him
And quit the house on purpose that their punishment
Might have the freer course.

ALBANY   Gloucester, I live   95
To thank thee for the love thou showd'st the King
And to revenge thine eyes. Come hither, friend,
Tell me what more thou knowst.   *Exeunt.*

[**4.3**]   ᵠ*Enter* KENT [*disguised*] *and a* Gentleman.

KENT   Why the King of France is so suddenly gone back,
    know you no reason?

GENTLEMAN   Something he left imperfect in the state
    which since his coming forth is thought of, which
    imports to the kingdom so much fear and danger that   5
    his personal return was most required and necessary.

KENT   Who hath he left behind him General?

GENTLEMAN   The Marshal of France, Monsieur la Far.

KENT   Did your letters pierce the queen to any demonst-
    ration of grief?   10

4.3 *This scene, from Q, is not in F; for possible reasons why it was omitted, see Appendix 1, pp. 400–1. It has three obvious functions, one to explain why the King of France, said to have landed in England at 4.2.57 (Q), has returned home; a second, to establish a saintly image of Cordelia; and the third, to let us know that Lear has reached Dover. None of these advances the action of the play; the 'Marshal of France', 8, is never heard of again; and Cordelia alone appears with the French army in 4.4 (F) and 5.2 (Q and F). Kent was last seen in 3.6, where he went off from the hovel supporting Lear; Kent has accompanied Lear to Dover, and Lear is now in the town; see 39, 51–2, and Appendix 1.

0.1 Gentleman the same one, presumably, Kent spoke with in 3.1

1 gone back i.e. to France. Shakespeare's first thought, at 4.2.57, may have been to have the King of France lead his army in England, his second to replace the King by the Marshal, 8, and his third to get rid of both King and Marshal, who disappear from F; see Appendix 1.

3 imperfect unfinished

5 imports carries as a consequence

6 required requested

9 letters At 3.1.40–5, Kent sent the Gentleman to Cordelia with a verbal

---

94 their] *Q2, F;* there *Q*   97 thine] *F;* thy *Q*   98 SD] *F; Exit. Q*

4.3] *Pope*   0.1 *disguised*] *Oxf; not in Q*   2 no] *Q;* the *Q2*

GENTLEMAN

Ay, sir. She took them, read them in my presence,
And now and then an ample tear trilled down
Her delicate cheek. It seemed she was a queen
Over her passion, who, most rebel-like,
Sought to be king o'er her.

KENT   O, then, it moved her?   15

GENTLEMAN

Not to a rage; patience and sorrow strove
Who should express her goodliest. You have seen
Sunshine and rain at once, her smiles and tears
Were like a better way. Those happy smilets
That played on her ripe lip seemed not to know   20
What guests were in her eyes, which parted thence
As pearls from diamonds dropped. In brief,
Sorrow would be a rarity most beloved
If all could so become it.

message and a ring as token, but the inconsistency is not likely to be noticed by an audience.

12 **trilled** rolled

16 **rage** violent outburst
patience endurance; see 2.2.460 and 458–60n.

17 **Who . . . goodliest** which might portray her best; *patience* and *sorrow* are personified as female figures

18–22 **Sunshine . . . dropped** To cry with one eye and laugh with the other was proverbially associated with dissimulation (Dent, E248, L92a); Cordelia's little smiles (*smilets*) and tears were like sunshine and rain, but in a better sense, neither being aware of the other, and both being good, as the *smilets* seem like fruit on her *ripe* lip, and her tears and eyes like precious stones. The Gentleman's rather florid

description idealizes Cordelia, turning her into an emblem of compassion, with a hint perhaps, as Milward suggests, 188, of a *pietà*, of the Virgin Mary mourning the death of Christ. The immediate suggestion for these lines, noted by Ard[2] after Danby, may have come from Sidney, *Arcadia*, 329, where Philoclea weeps: 'Her tears came dropping down like rain in sunshine, and she not taking heed to wipe the tears, they ran down her cheeks and lips as upon cherries, which the dropping tree bedeweth.'

20 **ripe** red, like ripe fruit, as at *MND* 3.2.139–40, 'O how ripe in show / Thy lips, those kissing cherries, tempting grow'

23 **Sorrow . . . rarity** sorrow would be precious, like pearls and diamonds

24 **become** grace, adorn

11 Ay, sir] *Capell;* I say *Q*   16 strove] *Pope;* streme *Q*   17 goodliest. You] *Rowe;* goodliest you *Q;* goodliest, you *Q2*   20 seemed] *Pope;* seeme *Q*   21 eyes,] *Q2;* eyes *Q*   22 dropped. In] *Q2* (dropt; in*);* dropt in *Q*

KENT   Made she no verbal question?   25

GENTLEMAN

    Faith, once or twice she heaved the name of father

    Pantingly forth as if it pressed her heart;

    Cried 'Sisters, sisters, shame of ladies, sisters!

    Kent, father, sisters! What, i'the storm, i'the night?

    Let pity not be believed!' There she shook   30

    The holy water from her heavenly eyes,

    And clamour mastered her; then away she started,

    To deal with grief alone.

KENT   It is the stars,

    The stars above us govern our conditions,

    Else one self mate and make could not beget   35

    Such different issues. You spoke not with her since?

GENTLEMAN   No.

KENT

    Was this before the King returned?

GENTLEMAN   No, since.

KENT

    Well, sir, the poor distressed Lear's i'the town,

    Who sometime in his better tune remembers   40

26–7 heaved . . . heart Compare 1.1.91–2, where Cordelia was unable to heave her heart into her mouth at her father's request.

30 Let . . . believed perhaps 'let no one put any trust in pity', i.e. since her sisters have behaved so cruelly to their father. Of several proposed emendations (see textual notes), 'Let pity not believe it' seems the most plausible.

31 holy water the genuine thing, as opposed to *court holy-water*, or flattery; see 3.2.10. Milward sees an association with Catholic custom here; see 18–22 and n.

32 *clamour mastered her her vehement feelings overcame her. This emendation, suggested by Stone, of 'moystened her' (Q) makes sense of nonsense; her tears, not her *clamour*, moisten Cordelia. Many editors drop *her*, and explain awkwardly that her tears silence her outcries by moistening them.

34 conditions personal qualities, natures

35 one . . . make the selfsame husband and wife

38 King returned King of France went home

39 distressed distressèd

40 sometime sometimes

tune frame of mind; compare 4.7.16

30 pity] *Q;* piety *Oxf*   pity . . . believed] *Q;* it not be believed *Capell;* pity not believe it *Jennens (Pope)*   believed] *Q2, Q (*beleeft*)*   32 mastered her] *Stone;* moystened her *Q;* moistened *Capell*   mastered *Oxf*   35 and make] *Q;* and mate *Q2*

What we are come about, and by no means
Will yield to see his daughter.

GENTLEMAN   Why, good sir?

KENT

A sovereign shame so elbows him. His own unkindness
That stripped her from his benediction, turned her
To foreign casualties, gave her dear rights   45
To his dog-hearted daughters, these things sting
His mind so venomously that burning shame
Detains him from Cordelia.

GENTLEMAN   Alack, poor gentleman.

KENT

Of Albany's and Cornwall's powers you heard not?

GENTLEMAN   'Tis so; they are afoot.   50

KENT

Well, sir, I'll bring you to our master, Lear,
And leave you to attend him. Some dear cause
Will in concealment wrap me up awhile.
When I am known aright, you shall not grieve,
Lending me this acquaintance.   55
I pray you, go along with me.   *Exeunt.*^Q

43 one of several long, unwieldy lines in
   the scene in Q; most fall into blank
   verse, but this one breaks the pattern
   sovereign overpowering
   elbows him keeps thrusting him back
44–5 **turned . . . casualties** dismissed
   her to the uncertainties of life abroad
46 **dog-hearted** ruthless; compare *Oth*
   5.1.62, 'O damned Iago! O inhuman
   dog!'
48 **Detains him** holds him back

49 **powers** armies, as at 4.2.16
52 **dear cause** never named, but it means
   that Kent can remain in disguise,
   known only to Cordelia (4.7.10–11),
   until he comes to bid Lear farewell at
   5.3.233–5. Kent thus parallels Edgar,
   who also remains disguised until the
   final scene, only revealing himself at
   5.3.165–7.
54 **aright** correctly (as Earl of Kent)

50 so;] *Capell;* so *Q*   52 him.] *Rowe;* him *Q;* him, *Q2*   56 SD] *Pope; Exit. Q*

[4.4] *Enter* ᶠ*with drum and colours*ᶠ CORDELIA, Gentleman,
[*Officer*] ᶠ*and soldiers.*ᶠ

CORDELIA

Alack, 'tis he. Why, he was met even now
As mad as the vexed sea, singing aloud,
Crowned with rank fumiter and furrow-weeds,
With burdocks, hemlock, nettles, cuckoo-flowers,

4.4.0.1 **with . . . soldiers* In Q Cordelia is
described in 4.3 on her return to
England as an emblem of pity in the
Gentleman's account, and 4.4 calls for
a doctor and attendants to accompany
her when she appears in the next
scene. Her forces in Q were to be led
by the King or Marshal of France (see
note to 4.3) as general, though in both
texts she refers to *our arms* (4.4.27) as
if she is in charge of the army. 4.3 is
missing from F, so that her reappear-
ance in this text for the first time since
1.1 is abrupt and unheralded; she
enters in soldierly fashion as at the
head of the French forces somewhere
near Dover, and the drum and colours,
or flags, are important signals of this;
see Introduction, pp. 139–40, also
Warren, 'Kent', 66–8, and Appendix 1,
pp. 400–1. The '*Doctor*' who accompa-
nies Cordelia in Q may be more appropriate to an intimate or domestic scene
(see Taylor, 'War', 30), if he is different from the Gentleman of 4.3, who
goes off to attend on Lear at the end of
that scene. In F a '*Gentleman*' replaces
the '*Doctor*' of Q here and in 4.7;
Mahood, 166–8, thinks the change is
deliberate, and links him with the
'Gentleman' who speaks with Kent in
3.1, as someone who would be familiar
to Lear. See 4.7.24–5n.

1   **he** Lear

2   **mad . . . sea** Titus compares himself
to a mad sea in *Tit* 3.1.223–6.

3–7 **Crowned . . . field** Lear wears this
'crown' when he enters in 4.6; see
4.6.80 SD and n., and it is important in
relation to the golden crown he has on
in 1.1; see Introduction, pp. 20–1. All
the weeds and flowers mentioned here
belong to the summer season in
Britain, and provide the only indication of a time of year in the play. Lear
seems to emerge from the storm scenes
into a more summery world burgeon-
ing with plant-life in the *high-grown
field*; but the *rank* weeds may suggest
disorder and a rejection of civilization
which depends on *sustaining corn*. For
further comment on this passage, see
Frank McCombie in *N&Q*, n.s. 2
(1981), 133–4, and F. G. Butler, 'Lear's
crown of weeds', *English Studies*, 70
(1989), 395–406.

3   **fumiter** fumitory, a weed known as
smoke of the earth (Latin *fumus
terrae*), because it sprawls vigorously;
see *H5* 5.2.45, where it is also associated with hemlock and darnel. Q and F
suggest that 'femiter' or 'femitar' was
Shakespeare's spelling, the 'n' in
'Fenitar' (F) being no doubt a minim
error.

     furrow-weeds weeds that grow in
ploughed fields

4   **burdocks** a common weedy plant
that produces burrs. Q and F (see
textual notes) 'probably represent the
same word', which could have been
misread as 'hor-docks'; see *TxC*, 521.

4.4] *F (Scena tertia); not in Q*   0.1–2 Gentleman . . . soldiers] *F; Doctor and others Q   Officer*] *this edn*
2 vexed] *F;* vent *Q*   3 fumiter] *Theobald;* femiter *Q;* Fenitar *F*   4 burdocks] *Hanmer;* hor-docks
Q; Hardokes *F;* hardocks *F3;* harlocks *Steevens² (Farmer)*

Darnel and all the idle weeds that grow   5
In our sustaining corn. [*to Officer*] A century send
        forth;
Search every acre in the high-grown field
And bring him to our eye. What can man's wisdom
In the restoring his bereaved sense,
He that helps him take all my outward worth.   10

                                     [*Exit Officer, with soldiers.*]

GENTLEMAN
    There is means, madam.
    Our foster nurse of nature is repose,
    The which he lacks: that to provoke in him
    Are many simples operative, whose power
    Will close the eye of anguish.
CORDELIA   All blest secrets,   15
    All you unpublished virtues of the earth,

Charlock or harlock, another common weed, has also been proposed, but does not fit the group of plants as well; see 3–7 and n., and Kathryn Sprinkle-Jackson, *ELN*, 26 (1989), 15–23.

hemlock a weed that produces a powerful sedative

cuckoo-flowers the various plants that flower when the cuckoo is calling, in late May or June

5 **Darnel** a kind of grass that invaded fields of corn

6 **sustaining** supporting life, as opposed to *idle weeds*

century literally a hundred soldiers, a division in the Roman army (marking Cordelia's anxiety, that she sends so many?). The word may have been prompted by its echo of 'centaury', a herb noted for its medicinal powers, linked by Turner in his *New Herball* (1551), Ii^r, with marjoram (see 4.6.93), and said by him to heal 'the ake of the

mother'. In his *Herbal* (1597), 437, Gerard also remarks on the healing virtue of common 'centorie', and notes that it grows especially well on 'the chalkie cliffes of Greenehith in Kent', and suchlike places.

8 **can man's wisdom** human knowledge can do

9 **bereaved** bereavèd

10 **outward worth** worldly possessions (Weis)

14 **simples operative** The syntax is ambiguous, and the phrase could mean both 'many medicines are effective', and 'there are many effective medicines'. A *simple* was so-called because it was prepared from a single herb.

16 **unpublished virtues** undisclosed or secret restorative herbs. Their *virtues* are the powers they have to do good, but the image is of plants springing up, fertilized by Cordelia's tears; compare *R2* 3.4.104–7.

6 SD] *this edn*   century send] *F (*Centery send*);* centurie is sent *Q;* sent'ry send *Johnson*
10 helps] *F;* can helpe *Q*   SD] *Capell (after* eye, 8)   11 SP GENTLEMAN] *F; Doct. Q*

Spring with my tears. Be aidant and remediate
In the good man's distress. Seek, seek for him,
Lest his ungoverned rage dissolve the life
That wants the means to lead it.

Enter Messenger.

MESSENGER   News, madam: 20
The British powers are marching hitherward.
CORDELIA
'Tis known before. Our preparation stands
In expectation of them. O dear father,
It is thy business that I go about;
Therefore great France   25
My mourning and important tears hath pitied.
No blown ambition doth our arms incite,
But love, dear love, and our aged father's right:
Soon may I hear and see him.   *Exeunt.*

17 **aidant and remediate** helpful and remedial. These unusual words, Hunter suggests, fit the 'incantatory atmosphere' of Cordelia's prayer.
18 ***distress** F's 'desires' may be a misreading of a manuscript; it too makes sense, but is less appropriate to Lear's condition.
19 **rage** madness; the original meaning of the word, as at 4.7.78
    dissolve release from; a proper use in relation to dying (*OED* 6)
20 **wants the means** i.e. lacks sanity
21 **British powers** In 4.2, according to Oswald, Albany merely smiles at the news of a French invasion, and yet in F his army is on the march here in the very next scene (in Q the news is heard at 4.3.49–50); Shakespeare telescopes time, and the action moves rapidly as a result. See 4.5.1–5.
22 **preparation** deployed forces. See *Oth* 1.3.221, 'The Turk with a most mighty

preparation makes for Cyprus'.
23–4 **O . . . about** echoing Christ's words, 'I must go about my father's business', Luke, 2.49 (Bible). This most direct Christian reference in the play is deeply ironic, for Cordelia's *business* is to fight to restore Lear's *right* (28), whereas Christ's was to leave his parents to attend to God's affairs in the Temple. See Introduction, pp. 22, 34–5.
25 **France** the King of France, her husband; see Appendix 1
26 **important** importunate, urgent, as at *MA* 2.1.74, where Beatrice advises Hero, 'If the Prince be too important, tell him there is measure in everything'. Most editors prefer 'importuned' (F), which implies that the King of France has been importuning Cordelia.
27 **blown** swollen
    our arms incite provoke us to make war
28 **aged** pronounced as one syllable

17 be aidant] *Q2, F;* beaydant *Q*   18 good man's distress] *Q;* Goodmans desires *F*   26 important] *Q;* importun'd *F*   27 incite] *F;* in sight *Q;* insite *Q2*   28 right] *Q;* Rite *F*   29 SD] *F; Exit. Q*

[4.5]   *Enter* REGAN *and* OSWALD.

REGAN   But are my brother's powers set forth?
OSWALD   Ay, madam.
REGAN   Himself in person ᶠthereᶠ?
OSWALD   Madam, with much ado; your sister is the better
    soldier.   5
REGAN   Lord Edmund spake not with your lord at home?
OSWALD   No, madam.
REGAN   What might import my sister's letter to him?
OSWALD   I know not, lady.
REGAN

    Faith, he is posted hence on serious matter.   10
    It was great ignorance, Gloucester's eyes being out,
    To let him live. Where he arrives he moves
    All hearts against us. Edmund, I think, is gone
    In pity of his misery to dispatch
    His nighted life; moreover to descry   15
    The strength o'th' enemy.
OSWALD

    I must needs after him, ᶠmadam,ᶠ with my letter.

4.5.0.1 OSWALD A messenger brings a letter from Regan to Goneril at Albany's house at 4.2.83, and Goneril exits there to answer it. That answer has now, it seems, been brought by Oswald, who also carries a letter from Goneril to Edmund. Meanwhile Edmund has gone off to locate Gloucester or the enemy (13–16). The scene could be imagined as taking place at Gloucester's house or Regan's.

1–10 Although Regan's questions at 6 and 8 fall into blank verse lines, Oswald seems to be speaking prose, and the lineation is doubtful.

4 **with much ado** making a lot of fuss about it

6 *****lord** Q has 'lady', probably a mistaken expansion of 'L.' in manuscript (Duthie, 411).

8 **import** both 'What might my sister's letter convey?' and 'What might her writing to him signify?'

10 **is posted** has ridden off hastily

11 **ignorance** of the political consequences

12 **Where** wherever

15 **nighted** blacked-out (by blindness); compare *Ham* 1.2.68 (Q2)
    descry discover

4.5] *F (Scena Quarta); not in Q*   **0.1** OSWALD] *Dyce; Steward Q, F*   **2+** SP OSWALD] *Dyce; Stew. Q, F*   **6** lord] *F;* Lady *Q*   **8** letter] *F;* letters *Q*   **13** Edmund] *F;* and now *Q*   **16** o'th' enemy] *F;* at'h army *Q;* of the Army *Q2*   **17** him, madam, with] *F;* him with *Q;* with *Oxf* letter] *F;* letters *Q*

REGAN

Our troops set forth tomorrow; stay with us.

The ways are dangerous.

OSWALD   I may not, madam;

My lady charged my duty in this business.   20

REGAN

Why should she write to Edmund? Might not you

Transport her purposes by word? Belike –

Some things, I know not what – I'll love thee much;

Let me unseal the letter.

OSWALD   Madam, I had rather –

REGAN

I know your lady does not love her husband,   25

I am sure of that; and at her late being here

She gave strange oeillades and most speaking looks

To noble Edmund. I know you are of her bosom.

OSWALD   I, madam?

REGAN

I speak in understanding; y'are, I know't.   30

Therefore I do advise you take this note.

My lord is dead; Edmund and I have talked,

And more convenient is he for my hand

---

20 **charged my duty** commanded
exact obedience
22 **Belike** – Perhaps – ; Regan is
flustered, as Oswald's refusal to co-
operate leaves her uncertain what to
do.
23 **I'll . . . much** On stage Regan may be
played as lascivious towards Oswald
here, and often 'comes close, may
caress, even kiss him, as she reaches for
the paper' (Rosenberg, 261; Bratton,
173). This is a modern interpretation
that hardly squares with her passion
for Edmund; as a ruler talking to a
servant, she is probably saying, 'I'll

reward and favour you if you show me
the letter'; compare Lear at 1.4.86–7
saying to Kent, 'Thou serv'st me and
I'll love thee.'
27 **oeillades** amorous glances
28 **of her bosom** in her confidence
31 **take this note** take note of this
32 **have talked** There has been no chance
for them to speak about love or marriage in the play so far; Shakespeare
again short-cuts the action. Goneril
made advances to Edmund in 4.2.
33 **convenient** suitable, fitting the
circumstances

18 troops set] *F;* troope sets *Q*   22 Belike –] *Oxf;* belike *Q;* Belike, *F*   23 Some things, I . . . what
–] *Oxf;* Some thing, I . . . what, *Q;* Some things, I . . . what. *F;* Some thing – I . . . what. *Pope*
24 I had] *F;* I'd e *Q*   27 oeillades] *Rowe, after Q (*aliads*), F (*Eliads*)*   30 y'are,] *F (*Y'are:*);* for *Q*

Than for your lady's. You may gather more.
If you do find him, pray you give him this;   35
And when your mistress hears thus much from you,
I pray desire her call her wisdom to her.
So fare ᶠyouᶠ well.
If you do chance to hear of that blind traitor,
Preferment falls on him that cuts him off.   40

OSWALD

Would I could meet ᵠhimᵠ, madam, I should show
What party I do follow.

REGAN   Fare thee well.   *Exeunt.*

[**4.6**]   *Enter* GLOUCESTER *and* EDGAR [*in peasant's clothing
and with a staff*].

GLOUCESTER

When shall I come to the top of that same hill?

34 ***gather more** conjecture further. I
follow the pointing in F ('gather
more:'); Q has no punctuation here,
and Weis inserts some to make 'gather;
more.', which he thinks conveys
urgency.

35 **this** a token, or perhaps a letter. When
Oswald is killed he has *letters* about
him (4.6.244), though only the letter
from Goneril that he now withholds
from Regan is read by Edgar
(4.6.257–65).

36 **thus much** your report of what I have
said

42 **party** so F. Q has 'Lady', which is
incongruous in relation to Oswald's
steadfast loyalty to Goneril shown in
20–9.

4.6.0.1 *in . . . staff* Edgar is now wearing
the clothes the Old Man has brought
him (see 4.1.52), looks like a *peasant* to
Oswald at 227, and no longer speaks

like Poor Tom, as Gloucester notices at
7–8. They too are imagined here as
somewhere near Dover. One of them
has a staff or 'bat', used by Edgar to
fight Oswald at 239. The blind
Gloucester might more naturally have
a staff and, if so, Edgar borrows it
from him to defend himself against
Oswald's attack.

1 **hill** Dover cliff. He had it on his mind
at 4.1.76–81.

1–10 In these lines Shakespeare seems
anxious to dispel illusion and make us
conscious of the trick being played on
Gloucester, as he draws the attention
of the audience to Edgar's deception
of his father, in pretending to be
climbing, in claiming to hear the sea
and in lying about his change of
speech; see 41 SD and n. In leading his
father to suicide, Edgar is playing the
traditional role of the devil; see

34 gather more.] *F (*gather more:*);* gather more *Q;* gather; more. *Weis*   41 should] *F;* would *Q*
42 party] *F;* Lady *Q*   SD] *F; Exit. Q*

4.6] *F (Scena Quinta); not in Q*   0.1 EDGAR] *F; Edmund Q*   *in . . . clothing*] *Hunter (Theobald)*
0.2 *and . . . staff*] *Oxf*   1 I] *F;* we *Q*

EDGAR

You do climb up it now. Look how we labour.

GLOUCESTER

Methinks the ground is even.

EDGAR   Horrible steep.

Hark, do you hear the sea?

GLOUCESTER   No, truly.

EDGAR

Why then, your other senses grow imperfect   5

By your eyes' anguish.

GLOUCESTER   So may it be indeed.

Methinks thy voice is altered and thou speak'st

In better phrase and matter than thou didst.

EDGAR

You're much deceived; in nothing am I changed

But in my garments.

GLOUCESTER   Methinks you're better spoken.   10

EDGAR

Come on, sir, here's the place. Stand still: how
    fearful

And dizzy 'tis to cast one's eyes so low.

The crows and choughs that wing the midway air

Show scarce so gross as beetles. Half-way down

Hangs one that gathers samphire, dreadful trade;   15

Methinks he seems no bigger than his head.

The fishermen that walk upon the beach

Appear like mice, and yon tall anchoring barque

3.4.53–4 and n., and 72 below.

7–8 **speak'st . . . didst** a change marked for the audience by the verse; as Poor Tom, Edgar usually spoke in prose; for *matter* = sense, compare 170, and see 1.1.55 and n.

13 **choughs** jackdaws, a member of the crow family; pronounced 'chuffs'

14 **gross** large

15 **samphire** a plant with aromatic leaves used in pickles. The name derives from the French, 'herbe de Saint Pierre', St Peter's herb.
   dreadful fearsome

18 **barque** small sailing vessel. 'Barke' (Q, F) was a common spelling.

2 up it] *F;* it vp *Q*   8 In] *F;* With *Q*   15 samphire] *Rowe, Q3 (*Simphier*);* sampire *Q , F*
17 walk] *Q;* walk'd *F*   18 yon] *Q;* yond *F*

Diminished to her cock, her cock a buoy
Almost too small for sight. The murmuring surge   20
That on th'unnumbered idle pebble chafes,
Cannot be heard so high. I'll look no more,
Lest my brain turn and the deficient sight
Topple down headlong.
GLOUCESTER   Set me where you stand.
EDGAR
Give me your hand: you are now within a foot   25
Of th'extreme verge. For all beneath the moon
Would I not leap upright.
GLOUCESTER   Let go my hand.
Here, friend, 's another purse, in it a jewel
Well worth a poor man's taking. Fairies and gods
Prosper it with thee. Go thou further off;   30
Bid me farewell and let me hear thee going.
EDGAR
Now fare ye well, good sir.
GLOUCESTER   With all my heart.
EDGAR [*aside*]
Why I do trifle thus with his despair
Is done to cure it.
GLOUCESTER (ᵠ*He kneels.*ᵠ)   O you mighty gods,

---

19 **cock** cock-boat, or rowing-boat towed
behind
21 **unnumbered** uncounted
idle pebble barren pebbles. The singular *pebble* was used collectively to
mean a deposit or beach of pebbles.
23–4 **Lest . . . headlong** lest I become
dizzy, cannot see properly, and so topple headlong over the cliff
26 **beneath the moon** i.e. on earth
27 **not leap upright** not jump up verti-
cally so as to land on the same spot (in
case I went over the cliff); see *OED*

Upright *adv.* 2
28 **another purse** Gloucester gave him
one at 4.1.67.
29–30 **Fairies . . . thee** Fairies might
make wealth multiply, but Gloucester
may also be asking for secrecy, since
'Fairies treasure . . . but reveal'd,
brings on the blabbers ruine' (Philip
Massinger and Nathan Field, *Fatal
Dowry*, ?1617–19, 4.1.191–2); see also
WT 3.3.123–6.
32 **With all my heart** most earnestly
33–4 **Why . . . it** Edgar may be seen as

19 a buoy] *F;* a boui *Q;* aboue *Q2*   21 pebble chafes] *F;* peeble chaffes *Q;* peebles chafe *Q2*
22 heard so high.] *F;* heard, its so hie *Q;* heard: it is so hie *Q2*   32 ye] *F;* you *Q*
33 SD] *Capell*   34 Is] *Q, F;* tis *Q2*   SD] *Q (opp.* gods*)*

328

This world I do renounce and in your sights   35
Shake patiently my great affliction off.
If I could bear it longer and not fall
To quarrel with your great opposeless wills,
My snuff and loathed part of nature should
Burn itself out. If Edgar live, O, bless ᶠhimᶠ!   40
Now, fellow, fare thee well.   ᵩ*He falls.*ᵩ

EDGAR   Gone, sir; farewell.
[*aside*] And yet I know not how conceit may rob

playing a game with his father, one that has an element of cruelty, since it leads Gloucester to expect, and then denies him, the one thing he wants, death (see 48). It is often said that 'Gloucester in his despair is brought to accept his lot' (Hunter), but although he does so for the moment, 75–7, his encounter with Oswald later in the scene leads him again to desire death, 226–7, and he is 'in ill thoughts again' at 5.2.9. No wonder that there has been much debate about the nature of this episode, which may be seen as grotesque, comic, absurd, tragic, or a combination of these; see Introduction, pp. 62–3, and Bratton, 175.

34–40 **O . . . out** The Christian prohibition against 'self-slaughter' (*Ham* 1.2.132) was based on the biblical commandment 'Thou shalt not kill' (Exodus, 20.13), but in this ostensibly pagan play Shakespeare exploits an ambivalence by invoking the Stoic defence of suicide; see 62–4 and n.

37–8 **fall . . . with** give way to challenging

38 **opposeless** irresistible; Shakespeare's coinage

39 **snuff . . . nature** smouldering candle-end and hated remnant of my vital force. For *nature* in this sense, see 3.4.69.
    loathed loathèd

41 SD   *He falls* so in Q; not in F, where it may have been omitted by an oversight. The fall can be staged in various

ways. Editors since Capell have often expanded the SD to 'Gloucester throws himself forward and falls', and this is a common way of playing it, though sometimes he is made to jump, and in Peter Brook's 1962 production he fainted as he fell, giving point to the enormous risk Edgar is aware he is taking, that his father may really die. An older stage tradition established by Edmund Kean had Edgar move forward and 'catch Gloucester as he prepared to fall' (see Bratton, 175–7). The effect of this incident on the audience and its relation to stage illusion have been much debated by those who believe the audience is always conscious of the trick being played on them, and those who assume the audience shares the illusion. I think that from the opening lines onwards the scene makes the audience aware that Edgar is hoaxing his father with conscious deception, and contriving to have him 'die' in order to bring him to life again. But see Alan Dessen, 'Two falls and a trap', *ELR*, 5 (1975), 291–307; Derek Peat, ' "King Lear" and the tension of uncertainty', *SS*, 33 (1980), 47–9; and Jonathan Goldberg, 'Perspectives', 145–57; also Foakes, 202–3.

42–4 **I . . . theft** I'm not sure whether imagination (*conceit*) may bring about his death, when he is so willing to die. Edgar's image of 'the treasury of life'

39 snuff] *Q2, F;* snurff *Q*   41 Gone, sir;] *Q, F;* Good sir, *F2*   42 SD] *Capell*   may] *Q2, F;* my *Q*

329

The treasury of life when life itself
Yields to the theft. Had he been where he thought,
By this had thought been past. [*to Gloucester*] Alive or
    dead?   45
Ho, you, sir! ᶠFriend,ᶠ hear you, sir? Speak! –
[*aside*] Thus might he pass indeed. Yet he revives. –
What are you, sir?

GLOUCESTER   Away and let me die.

EDGAR

Hadst thou been aught but gossamer, feathers, air,
So many fathom down precipitating,   50
Thou'dst shivered like an egg; but thou dost breathe,
Hast heavy substance, bleed'st not, speak'st, art sound.
Ten masts at each make not the altitude
Which thou hast perpendicularly fell.
Thy life's a miracle. Speak yet again.   55

GLOUCESTER   But have I fallen, or no?

EDGAR

From the dread summit of this chalky bourn.
Look up a-height: the shrill-gorged lark so far

---

ironically contrasts with Gloucester's image of his life as a burnt-out candle-end.

46–8 **Ho . . . sir?** Edgar puts on yet another voice, at least for the moment, addressing his father as *friend* (F only, but required for the metre; prose in Q), even as Gloucester had earlier called him friend (28). He proceeds at 67–74 to rid himself finally of the image of Poor Tom.

47 **pass** die, pass away

51 **shivered** smashed

53 **at each** 'End to end' is the usual explanation, though no parallel has been noticed for this phrase, and some ingenious emendations have been pro-

posed; see textual note.

55 **miracle** Edgar has staged as a device, which is to say created as a fiction, what he now, and at 72–4, tries to persuade Gloucester is a miracle; the play no more supports the idea that miracles happen, unless contrived by human agency, than it does the existence of the gods; see Goldberg, 151–2.

57 ***summit** correcting 'Somnet' (F). Q has 'sommons', which I think is an error, since Edgar is inviting his father to see how high it is.

bourn boundary (of England, the cliff at Dover)

58 **a-height** on high (Abbott, 24, 140;

---

45 SD] *this edn*   47 SD] *aside Capell*   49 gossamer] *Q* (gosmore), *F* (Gozemore)   50 fathom] *F;* fadome *Q*   53 at each] *Q, F;* at least *Rowe;* attacht *Pope;* at length *(Jervis);* a-length *Oxf (Stone)*   56 no?] *Q2, F;* no I *Q*   57 summit *F (Somnet);* sommons *Q*   58 a-height] *Warburton;* a hight *Q;* a height *F*

Cannot be seen or heard. Do but look up.

GLOUCESTER

Alack, I have no eyes.   60

Is wretchedness deprived that benefit

To end itself by death? 'Twas yet some comfort

When misery could beguile the tyrant's rage

And frustrate his proud will.

EDGAR   Give me your arm.

Up, so. How ᶠis't ᶠ? Feel you your legs? You stand.   65

GLOUCESTER

Too well, too well.

EDGAR   This is above all strangeness.

Upon the crown o'the cliff what thing was that

Which parted from you?

GLOUCESTER   A poor unfortunate beggar.

EDGAR

As I stood here below methought his eyes

Were two full moons. He had a thousand noses,   70

Horns whelked and waved like the enraged sea.

---

compare 'afoot' = on foot)
shrill-gorged shrill-sounding (from
'gorge' = throat)
62–4 **'Twas . . . will** Shakespeare may, as
Hunter suggests, have had in mind the
defence of suicide offered by Stoic
thinkers, notably Seneca, who knew
the tyranny of Roman emperors such
as Nero, and who, in his epistles and
moral essays, argued that to have
power over oneself is the greatest
empire, as it makes the self superior to
arbitrary external power. Montaigne,
1.237, also praises suicide as a means
'to frustrate the Tyrants cruelty'.
63 **beguile** cheat
64–5 **arm . . . stand** Has Gloucester
been prostrate for twenty lines? Edgar
now helps him to stand, and

Honigmann², 86, suggests that he may
struggle first into a kneeling position,
providing a visual parallel with Lear,
who kneels to Cordelia at 4.7.58.
65 **Feel you** do you have any feeling in
71 **whelked** twisted and ridged like the
shell of a whelk
***enraged** enragèd; from F. Q has
'enridged', preferred by many editors
as a rarer word. F may offer an indifferent variant, an inadvertent change
made by the author, who, as noted in
TxC, 537, describes the sea as
'enraged' eleven times elsewhere. A
frenzied sea fits better with the idea of
a *fiend*, while 'enridged' may have been
suggested by the ridges on a whelk's
horn.

---

65 How is't? Feel] *F;* how feele *Q*   66–7 strangeness. / . . . cliff] *Q2;* strangenes / . . . cliffe *Q;*
strangenesse, / . . . Cliffe. *F*   68 beggar] *Q2, F;* bagger *Q*   69 methought] *Q2, F;* me thoughts *Q*
70 He] *F;* a *Q*   71 whelked] *Q (*welk't*),* *F (*wealk'd*);* whelk'd *Hanmer*   enraged] *F;* enridged *Q*

It was some fiend. Therefore, thou happy father,
Think that the clearest gods, who make them honours
Of men's impossibilities, have preserved thee.
GLOUCESTER
I do remember now. Henceforth I'll bear   75
Affliction till it do cry out itself
'Enough, enough' and die. That thing you speak of,
I took it for a man. Often 'twould say
'The fiend, the fiend'; he led me to that place.
EDGAR
Bear free and patient thoughts.

Enter LEAR ^Q*mad* ^Q [*crowned with wild flowers*].

But who comes here?   80
The safer sense will ne'er accommodate

72 **fiend** as the devil was popularly
supposed to tempt people to suicide;
see 3.4.53–4 and n.
happy father lucky old man. Here, as
Hunter notes, Edgar's true relationship is expressed 'in a context which
muffles its specific meaning', and
Gloucester does not notice; see also
280, 282.
73 **clearest** free from all faults
73–4 **make . . . impossibilities** gain
renown by doing what is impossible for
men to do; alluding to Matthew, 19.26,
'With men this is vnpossible, but with
God all things are possible', and see
Luke, 18.27 (cited by Cam²)
80 **free** untroubled, innocent, as at *Ham*
3.2.241–2, 'we that have free souls, it
touches us not'
patient See 2.2.458–60 and n.
Patience, or the capacity to endure suffering, is demanded of Lear and
Gloucester.
SD ******mad . . . flowers* F has a simple

entry here, and Q, placing it after 82,
has '*Enter Lear mad*'. Many editors,
including Ard² and Hunter, have
retained Capell's expansion, '*Enter
Lear, fantastically dressed with wild
flowers*', which would seem to miss the
point. Cordelia reports at 4.4.1–6 that
Lear has been seen crowned with
flowering weeds, and this is suggestive
as an internal stage direction. The
mock-crown is ironically related to the
royal crown Lear wore in 1.1, and
curiously helps to restore regality to
him even in his madness; see 106, and
Introduction, pp. 20–1. On the stage,
most actors have worn a crown of
weeds or flowers, and have often carried a 'sceptre' made of straw or a
bunch of flowers, pointing up the contrast between the unselfconscious king
of nature in this scene and the angry
tyrant of the court in the opening
scene; see Bratton, 177–9.
81–2 **The . . . thus** No one in his right

73 make them] *F;* made their *Q;* make their *Halio*   78 'twould] *F;* would it *Q;* would he *Q2*
80 Bear] *F;* Bare *Q*   SD *Enter . . . mad] Q (after 82);* Enter Lear. *F   crowned . . . flowers] this edn;
fantastically dressed with wild flowers / Capell*   81 ne'er] *Q2, F;* neare *Q*

His master thus.

LEAR   No, they cannot touch me for coining. I am the
King himself.

EDGAR   O thou side-piercing sight!   85

LEAR   Nature's above art in that respect. There's your
press-money. That fellow handles his bow like a crow-
keeper: draw me a clothier's yard. Look, look, a mouse:
peace, peace, this ᶠpiece ofᶠ toasted cheese will do't.
There's my gauntlet, I'll prove it on a giant. Bring up   90
the brown bills. O well flown, bird, i'the clout, i'the

---

mind would be got up like this (so
Ard², Cam²). For 'safe' = sane, see *Oth*
4.1.269, 'Are his wits safe? is he not
light of brain?' (cited *OED a.* 4); and
with *accommodate* = furnish or equip,
compare 3.4.105.

83–4 *****touch . . . himself** censure me for
making coins, which was a royal pre-
rogative; *coining* is ambiguous, and
could mean fabricating something
specious, but it seems to me unlikely
that the word would give offence; also
it links with another sense of *touch*, to
test gold by rubbing it on a touchstone.
If F's variant 'crying' was prompted
by censorship, as Taylor, 'Date' thinks
(483), then Q is to be preferred. As
Duthie, 183, pointed out, Lear comes
on with money, which he hands out as
if impressing soldiers (see 86–7 and
n.). Michael Warren (*SQ*, 35 (1984),
319–21) defends 'crying', largely
because of the prominence of weeping
in the play and the references to it in
Lear's speech at 172–6.

85 **side-piercing** heart-rending; and
recalling Christ on the cross, whose
side was pierced by a soldier's spear;
see John, 19.34.

86 **Nature's above art** Lear's disjointed
speeches, representing his madness,
resist explanation, even if threads of
connection can be found. Here he may
respond to Edgar by saying that nature

offers more heart-rending sights than
art; or he may allude 'to a stock theme
of the period, the relation between
Nature and Art – a king who coins by
divine right standing for Nature & a
forger for Art' (Cam¹).

86–7 **There's . . . press-money** Lear
may give real or imaginary press-
money, paid to recruits when they
were 'impressed' or enlisted, to Edgar
or Gloucester, or to imaginary soldiers;
he is evidently wandering in mind.

87–8 **like a crow-keeper** clumsily? A
crow-keeper was one who guards crops
against crows, or possibly a scarecrow,
as at *RJ* 1.4.6.

88 **draw . . . yard** draw the bow to the
full extent of the arrow. Arrows for the
longbow were called in ballads 'cloth-
yard shafts', the 'cloth-yard' being
fixed by a sixteenth-century statute as
36 inches plus one (*OED*).

89 **will do't** Lear is trying to catch the
imagined mouse.

90 **There's . . . giant** Lear appears to
challenge the *mouse*, and is ready to
make *it* good (his claim about toasted
cheese?) even on a giant.
   gauntlet Lear issues an imaginary
challenge; later Albany and Edmund
exchange gauntlets at 5.3.94–8.

91 **brown bills** soldiers with halberds,
weapons consisting of a long shaft
with a blade and spear-head at the top,

---

83 coining] *Q;* crying *F*   91–2¹ i'the clout . . . Hewgh] *F;* in the ayre, hagh *Q*

clout! Hewgh! Give the word.

EDGAR   Sweet marjoram.

LEAR   Pass.

GLOUCESTER   I know that voice.   95

LEAR   Ha! Goneril ᶠwith a white beard?ᶠ They flattered
me like a dog and told me I had ᶠtheᶠ white hairs in my
beard ere the black ones were there. To say 'ay' and 'no'
to everything ᶠthatᶠ I said 'ay' and 'no' to was no good
divinity. When the rain came to wet me once and the   100
wind to make me chatter; when the thunder would not

painted brown against rust. An
anachronism, as these weapons were
developed in the late fifteenth century.

91–2 **O . . . clout!** Lear may imagine he
sees a falcon, which becomes an arrow
hitting the *clout*, or target in archery.

92 ***Hewgh** representing the whizzing
sound of the arrow, or simply Lear's
startled awareness of Edgar, as 'hagh'
(Q) might suggest

93 **marjoram** 'Sweet Marierome is a
remedie against cold diseases of the
braine and head', according to John
Gerard's *Herbal* (1597), 540, so
Edgar's password relates to Lear's
madness, and is not merely fanciful;
see also 4.4.6 and n.

96–104 Lear at last understands what
Cordelia and Kent tried to make him
see in the opening scene, that there
may be a wide gap between words and
meaning, or words and deeds; see
1.1.55 and n.

96 ***Goneril . . . beard** The change in
F from Q's 'Ha *Gonerill*, ha *Regan*'
makes Lear specifically identify
Gloucester with Goneril and flattery.
Rosenberg, 270, and Cam² see hints of
the demonic, 'transsexuality . . . , a
demon witch, the inversion of child
and parent' here, but this is to press

the text very hard; Lear at once shifts
to a concern with himself and flattery
in general. Hunter suggests Gloucester 'falls to his knees' at this point,
his obsequiousness prompting Lear,
but see 106n.

97–8 **told . . . there** told me I was wise
when I was still a child. If this could be
taken literally, it might suggest that
Lear has been King for more than sixty
years. Shakespeare frequently associates dogs with fawning, as at *JC* 3.1.43.

98–100 **To . . . divinity** probably
influenced by Christ's injunction
against swearing, Matthew, 5.36–7:
'Neither shalt thou swear by thine
head, because thou canst not make one
hair white or black. But let your com-
munication be, Yea, yea: Nay, nay' (so
Hunter)

100 **divinity** theology; suggesting they
treated him as a god, and perhaps
alluding to the divine right of kings,
claimed by James, who said in a speech
to Parliament in 1609, 'Kings are justly called Gods, for that they exercise a
manner or resemblance of Divine
power upon earth' (*Works*, 307). See
Introduction, pp. 14, 69.

101 **chatter** shiver with cold, or talk nonsense

93 marjoram] *Q (*Margerum*);* Mariorum *F*   96 Goneril] *F; Gonorill,* ha *Regan Q*
99 everything . . . was] *Oxf (Blayney);* euery thing I saide, I and no toe, was *Q;* all I saide: I and no
too was *Q2;* euery thing that I said: I, and no too, was *F*

peace at my bidding, there I found 'em, there I smelt
'em out. Go to, they are not men o'their words: they
told me I was everything; 'tis a lie, I am not ague-proof.

GLOUCESTER

The trick of that voice I do well remember: 105
Is't not the King?

LEAR   Ay, every inch a king.
When I do stare, see how the subject quakes.
I pardon that man's life. What was thy cause?
Adultery?
Thou shalt not die – die for adultery? No!   110
The wren goes to't and the small gilded fly
Does lecher in my sight. Let copulation thrive,
For Gloucester's bastard son was kinder to his father
Than were my daughters got 'tween the lawful sheets.
To't, luxury, pell-mell, for I lack soldiers.   115
Behold yon simp'ring dame,
Whose face between her forks presages snow,
That minces virtue and does shake the head

102 **peace** keep quiet
104 **ague-proof** immune to shivering, or
fever
105 **trick** distinguishing feature
106 **Ay . . . king** Some actors have played
this line with great dignity, others have
turned it into caricature; see Bratton,
179–80; Rosenberg, 271–2. It would
seem that Gloucester kneels here
rather than at 96, his homage being
taken by Lear as the sign of a guilty
criminal begging for mercy.
108 **cause** case, or matter that brought
you to a court of law
109–10 **Adultery . . . adultery?** Lear
zooms in on Gloucester's sin, punish-
able by death according to the biblical
law, Leviticus, 20.10, but modified by

Jesus, who pardoned the woman taken
in adultery; see John, 8.3–11 (Noble;
Milward, 190).
111 **gilded** gold-coloured
112 **lecher** copulate
115 **luxury** lust, lechery
pell-mell in headlong promiscuity
117 **face . . . snow** (a) face between her
legs predicts snow (or chastity); the
grotesque image then has sexual
implications that contradict the overt
meaning; or (b) face predicts snow or
coldness between her legs (if the line
inverts the normal order of words)
118 **minces virtue** by her mincing walk
affects virtue. The word *minces* was no
doubt suggested by *forks* = legs.

102–3 'em . . . 'em] *F;* them . . . them *Q*   103 o'their] *F;* of their *Q*   104 ague-proof] *F;* argue-
proofe *Q*   106 every] *Q2, F;* euer *Q*   110 die – die] *F (*dye: dye*);* die *Q*   112 Does] *F;* doe *Q*
114 were] *Capell*   116 yon] *Q;* yond *F*   117 presages] *F;* presageth *Q*   118 does] *F;* do *Q*

ᶠToᶠ hear of pleasure's name –
The fitchew, nor the soiled horse, goes to't with a more   120
riotous appetite. Down from the waist they are
centaurs, though women all above. But to the girdle do
the gods inherit, beneath is all the fiend's: there's hell,
there's darkness, there is the sulphurous pit, burning,
scalding, stench, consumption! Fie, fie, fie! Pah, pah!   125
Give me an ounce of civet, good apothecary, ᵠtoᵠ
sweeten my imagination. There's money for thee.

GLOUCESTER   O, let me kiss that hand!

LEAR   Let me wipe it first, it smells of mortality.

119 **of pleasure's name** sex mentioned
120–7 Most editions print as irregular verse as far as *there's hell*, 123; Q prints the whole speech as prose, F as prose from 116. Lear's verse becomes more and more uneven, and finally breaks down into prose as his disgust with his daughters leads to his misogynistic outburst against all women here; the exact point at which verse gives way to prose is indeterminate.
120 **fitchew** polecat, proverbial for its *stench*, 125 (Dent, P461), and slang for a prostitute
soiled; lively or skittish, being fed with fresh green fodder
goes to't slang for sexual indulgence. *The Birth of Merlin* (1662, acted ?1604) has a character named Joan Go-to't who enters 'great with child' in Act 2, not knowing who the father is (Udall, 131).
122 **centaurs** legendary creatures, with the trunk of a human, and a horse's body and legs, the lower half typifying the beast, or animal lusts, in human beings
girdle waist
123 **inherit** have possession, inhabit
the fiend's With reference to this passage, Dent, 31, cites from a list of heresies and falsehoods said to be pro-

mulgated by the Popes and the Catholic Church in Christopher Carlile's *A Discourse of Peters Lyfe* (1582), 104: 'Seuerus said that a woman was the worke of the deuill, and the vpper part of a man of God, but from the nauell downe of Satan: and therefore they that mary do fulfill the workes of the deuill.' Lear's is a badly distorted view of women, as is shown also by Albany's comment on Goneril at 4.2.60–2. The priests in Harsnett's account of exorcisms assign 'the inferiour parts for a peculiar lodge for the devil' in the women they treat (Brownlow, 252).
125 **consumption** destruction (by fire). Q has 'consumation', which could mean both fulfilment of the sex act and the end or death of things, as at *Ham* 3.1.63, ''Tis a consummation / Devoutly to be wished'. Here, as at 130–1, is glimpsed also an apocalyptic vision of the end of the world; see 5.3.261–2.
126 **civet** perfume. Lear addresses Gloucester as if he were a druggist (*apothecary*).
129 **smells of mortality** smells of death; also of the condition of being human, which links with the *stench* of 125: 'his own flesh – traditionally

120 The fitchew] *F*; to fichew *Q*   124 sulphurous] *F*; sulphury *Q*   125 consumption] *F*; consumation *Q*   129 Let me] *F*; Here *Q*

336

GLOUCESTER

O ruined piece of nature, this great world   130
Shall so wear out to naught. Dost thou know me?

LEAR   I remember thine eyes well enough. Dost thou
squiny at me?
No, do thy worst, blind Cupid, I'll not love.
Read thou this challenge, mark ᶠbutᶠ the penning of it.   135

GLOUCESTER

Were all thy letters suns, I could not see ᵠoneᵠ.

EDGAR [*aside*]

I would not take this from report: it is,
And my heart breaks at it.

LEAR   Read.

GLOUCESTER   What? With the case of eyes?   140

LEAR   Oh ho, are you there with me? No eyes in your
head, nor no money in your purse? Your eyes are in a
heavy case, your purse in a light, yet you see how this

---

derivative from the woman's part in conception – carries that stench within it, as the mark of female corruption' (Adelman, 113)

130–1 an apocalyptic speech, one of several in the play that culminate in 'the great doom's image' at 5.3.261–2

130 **piece** part or fragment, but perhaps also suggesting the idea of a masterpiece, the great king, as Schmidt proposed, citing Cleopatra's words at *AC* 5.2.99–100, 'to imagine / An Antony were nature's piece 'gainst fancy'
   great world universe (everything, not only the *piece* or part of nature that is Lear; compare *little world*, 3.1.10)

133 **squiny** squint. See 3.4.114 and n.

134 **blind Cupid** Love, proverbially blind (Dent, L506), was imaged in the figure of a blindfolded Cupid shooting his arrows at random, an image used,

if Benedick can be trusted, as the sign at the door of a brothel; see *MA* 1.1.253–4.

135–6 **Read . . . one** Lear may imagine or produce a piece of paper; either way, this document offered to a blind man is another of the many letters that circulate in the play, and recalls Gloucester's 'Let's see, let's see' (1.2.43), when he reads but fails to *see* the letter Edmund says Edgar wrote.

135 **penning** handwriting

137 **take . . . report** believe this if I heard it reported. Edgar thus is witness to the 'reality' of the encounter between Lear and Gloucester.

140 **case** socket, protective covering; plight, condition. See also 143.

141 **are . . . me?** variously explained, usually as some variant of 'is that your meaning?' (Hunter, Cam² and others); perhaps better, 'so that's your excuse?'

---

131 Shall] *F;* should *Q*   Dost thou] *F;* do you *Q*   132 thine] *F;* thy *Q*   133 at] *F;* on *Q*
135 this] *F;* that *Q*   of it] *F;* oft *Q;* on't *Q2*   136 thy] *F;* the *Q*   137 SD] *Hanmer*   140 What?]
*Q (*What!*);* What, *Q2;* What *F*   eyes?] *F;* eyes *Q*

world goes.

GLOUCESTER   I see it feelingly.   145

LEAR   What, art mad? A man may see how this world goes
with no eyes. Look with thine ears. See how yon justice
rails upon yon simple thief. Hark in thine ear: ^Fchange
places and^F handy-dandy, which is the justice, which is
the thief? Thou hast seen a farmer's dog bark at a   150
beggar?

GLOUCESTER   Ay, sir.

LEAR   And the creature run from the cur – there thou
mightst behold the great image of authority: a dog's
obeyed in office.   155
Thou, rascal beadle, hold thy bloody hand;
Why dost thou lash that whore? Strip thine own back,
Thou hotly lusts to use her in that kind
For which thou whipp'st her. The usurer hangs the
    cozener.

---

145 **feelingly** by feeling or touch; with
strong emotion, passionately
146 **art mad?** Lear takes *feelingly* in the
first sense noted above.
148 **rails upon** castigates, rails at
simple common, humble
149 **handy-dandy** take your choice;
from a game in which a child has to
guess in which hand a small object is
hidden
153–5 This passage marks the great shift
that has taken place in Lear from the
first act in which he was the image of
authority; it recalls Lear's hiring of
Kent, who sees 'authority' in Lear, and
Lear's abuse of Oswald, 'you whoreson dog, you slave, you cur!' (1.4.30,
78–9).
153 **creature** creature was often used to
mean 'human being' (*OED* 2, 3); paradoxically the phrase makes the beggar

seem a mere animal
156 **beadle, hold** parish constable,
restrain. On the whipping of vagabonds, see 3.4.130 and n.
157–9 **Why . . . her** Matthew, 7.1–6,
beginning 'Judge yee not, that ye be
not judged', seems to underlie this
whole passage, as well as the pardon by
Jesus of the woman taken in adultery;
see 109–10 and n.
158 ***Thou** so F; Q has 'thy bloud',
changed perhaps to avoid the repetition of 'bloody' / 'blood'
kind same way
159 **usurer . . . cozener** the moneylender
hangs the swindler. Compare Dent,
T119, 'The great thieves hang the little ones'. Although usury had been
made legal in 1571, the practices of
capitalism were still new enough for
usurers to be regarded with suspicion

---

146 this] *F;* the *Q*   147 thine] *F;* thy *Q*   147–8 yon . . . yon] *Q;* yond . . . yond *F*   148 thine] *F;*
thy *Q*   149–50 justice . . . thief] *F;* thief . . . justice *Q*   153 And] *Q, F;* An *Oxf*   154–5 dog's
obeyed] *F;* dogge, so bade *Q*   157 thine] *Q;* thy *F*   158 Thou] *F;* thy bloud *Q*   159 cozener] *Q2,
F;* cosioner *Q*

Through tattered clothes great vices do appear;   160
Robes and furred gowns hide all. ^FPlate sin with gold,
And the strong lance of justice hurtless breaks;
Arm it in rags, a pigmy's straw does pierce it.
None does offend, none, I say none. I'll able 'em;
Take that of me, my friend, who have the power   165
To seal th'accuser's lips.^F Get thee glass eyes,

or hatred, and associated with the sin of covetousness; compare Antonio's attitude to Shylock in *MV* 1.3. Notable comedies contemporary with *King Lear* make greed their theme, like Jonson's *Volpone*, and Thomas Middleton's *A Trick to Catch the Old One* (1605–6?), which has characters named Lucre, Hoard, Moneylove and Dampit 'the Usurer', all satirized and associated with lechery too. In *Seven Deadly Sins of London* (1606), Thomas Dekker writes, 'The Usurer lives by the lechery of money, and is Bawd to his own bags, taking a fee that they may ingender' (*Non-Dramatic Works* (1885), 2.28). The spelling 'cosioner' in Q may be phonetic.

160 ***great vices . . . appear** The vices of the poor are perceived as great (while the rich can get away with anything); 'small vices' (Q) makes more obvious but less complex sense.

161–6 ***Plate . . . lips.** These lines in F (not in Q) were probably dovetailed in to expand the commentary on justice in this sequence, that begins by putting Gloucester on trial at 107. F omits the mock-trial of Lear's daughters at 3.6.20–55, perhaps to give greater weight to the present scene; see R. Warren, 52–3.

161 ***Plate . . . gold** Theobald's emendation of 'Place sinnes' (F) to 'plate sin' has been generally accepted, as the idea of giving sin armour-plate parallels 'Arm it in rags' (163). Gold is a soft metal, so the idea of a lance breaking

on it is ironic; a lance would penetrate it easily. In secretary hand 'c' and 't' can look alike, and are readily confused. At the same time, 'place' could be correct, as giving the sense, 'place sinners in office by bribery'; compare *Tim* 4.3.34–8, 'This yellow slave [i.e. gold] / Will . . . place thieves, / And give them title, knee and approbation / With senators on the bench.' The singular *sin* is required by *it*, 163, and the plural in F probably comes from a misreading of a tail on the final 'e' of 'sinne' as 's'.

164 **able 'em** empower (all of) them (compare 'enable' in modern usage); Lear's ultimate cynicism is to say none offends, because all do, and he authorizes sinners and criminals to go on sinning. He goes beyond the teaching of Christ about forgiveness (see 157–9 and n.) to give a free rein to subversion and wickedness. Cam² interprets the line as meaning, 'If everyone sins, then no-one does', but I think this misses the point; Lear is ridding himself of his own compulsion to punish (Rosenberg, 277).

165 **Take . . . me** learn that from me (*OED v.* 34c), as at *TS* 2.1.190–4, 'Take this of me, Kate . . . / Myself am moved to woo thee for my wife'. Many editors, and Rosenberg, 277, unnecessarily suppose Lear hands Gloucester an imaginary document of some kind.

power as King; see 107

166 **glass eyes** spectacles; false eyes made

160 Through . . . great] *Q2, F (*Thorough*); through tottered raggs, smal *Q*   161 hide] *F;* hides *Q*
Plate sin] *Theobald;* Place sinnes *F;* Plate sins *Pope*

And like a scurvy politician seem
To see the things thou dost not. Now, [F]now, now, now,[F]
pull off my boots; harder, harder, so.

EDGAR [*aside*]

O matter and impertinency mixed,
Reason in madness.

LEAR

If thou wilt weep my fortunes, take my eyes.
I know thee well enough, thy name is Gloucester.
Thou must be patient. We came crying hither:
Thou knowst the first time that we smell the air
We wawl and cry. I will preach to thee: mark [Q]me[Q].

GLOUCESTER Alack, alack the day!

LEAR

When we are born we cry that we are come
To this great stage of fools. This a good block:

of glass were first mentioned in the late seventeenth century

167 **scurvy politician** scabby, and hence contemptible, intriguer. The earliest meaning of *politician* was 'crafty schemer'.

168 **Now . . . now** Is Lear consoling the weeping Gloucester, or ignoring him and concentrating on his boots, real or imagined?

170 **matter and impertinency** sense and nonsense (Ard[2])

172–3 **If . . . Gloucester** It seems that Gloucester's weeping prompts Lear's recognition of him, but his 'trial' for adultery, 107–25, suggests that Lear has had some idea of the identity of Gloucester all along.

174 **patient** Lear can now preach patience; see 2.2.458–60 and n.

174–6 **We . . . cry** Compare Wisdom (Apocrypha), 7.3, 6: 'I was borne . . . crying and weeping at the first as all other doe . . . All men then have one entrance vnto life, and one going out in like maner' (Noble; Shaheen); also the common proverb, 'We weeping come into the world and weeping hence we go' (Dent, W889).

176 **wawl** yell

179 **this . . . fools** As Cam[2] notes, Lear combines two old commonplaces, that 'All the world's a stage' (*AYL* 2.7.139, and see Dent, W882) and that the world is full of fools (Dent, W896). Lear implicitly reveals his awareness of playing the role of King, and of his own folly.

This . . . block Usually taken to mean a mould for a hat, by association with *felt*, 181. Actors playing Lear have taken a hat off Gloucester's head, or Edgar's, at this point, or, in a tradition begun by Garrick, have removed the crown of flowers from their own head on 'I will preach to thee' (176), since 'Lear would not preach with his hat on' (see Rosenberg, 279). The block

168 not. Now] *F;* no now *Q* 170 SD] *Capell* 172 fortunes] *F;* fortune *Q* 176 wawl] *F;* wayl *Q*
179 This a] *Q, F;* 'Tis a *(Ritson);* This's a *Cam;* This' a *Singer*[2] *(W. S. Walker)*

It were a delicate stratagem to shoe   180
A troop of horse with felt. ᶠI'll put it in proofᶠ
And when I have stolen upon these son-in-laws,
Then kill, kill, kill, kill, kill, kill!

Enter a Gentleman [*and two attendants*].

GENTLEMAN
O, here he is: lay hand upon him. Sir,
Your most dear ᶠdaughter – ᶠ   185
LEAR
No rescue? What, a prisoner? I am even
The natural fool of fortune. Use me well,
You shall have ransom. Let me have surgeons,
I am cut to the brains.
GENTLEMAN   You shall have anything.
LEAR
No seconds? All myself?   190
Why, this would make a man ᶠa manᶠ of salt,
To use his eyes for garden water-pots.

---

could also be a mounting-block, by
association with horses, or simply an
imaginary tree-stump.
180 delicate ingenious
181 in proof to the test
183 kill . . . kill! parodying a battle-cry;
see *VA* 652 (so Malone). Various stage
business is possible, as noted by
Rosenberg, 279. If Lear imagines himself leading his troops in a revenge
attack, he may strike out with an imaginary weapon, a straw dagger (as
Edwin Booth did), or simply with his
arms; Hunter thinks he 'throws down
his flowers and stamps on them'.
183.1 and two attendants See textual
note. Q has '*three Gentlemen*', which is

the basic number needed, two to *lay
hand* on Lear, and one who is in
charge, speaks and remains behind at
200 to talk with Edgar.
186 prisoner It would be appropriate
irony if Lear were seized on each side
by his arms, even as Gloucester was at
3.7.23–9.
187 natural . . . fortune born to be the
dupe of fortune. Compare *RJ* 3.1.136;
but a *natural fool* is also a fool by birth,
a simpleton.
190 seconds supporters (especially in
fighting a duel, so possibly recalling
Lear throwing down his gauntlet at 90)
191 salt salt tears

180 shoe] *F (shoo); shoot Q*   181 felt] *F; fell Q*   182 stolen] *F; stole Q*   son-in-laws] *Q, F;*
sonnes in law *Q2*   183.1] *Hunter (Rowe); Enter three Gentlemen. Q; Enter a Gentleman. F*
184 hand] *F; hands Q*   him. Sir,] *Johnson (Rowe);* him sirs *Q;* him, Sir. *F*   186 even] *F; eene Q*
188 ransom] *Q, F;* a ransom *Q2*   surgeons] *F;* a churgion *Q;* a Chirurgeon *Q2*

ᵠAy, and laying autumn's dust.ᵠ
ᵠ²GENTLEMAN   Good sir.ᵠ²
ᵠLEARᵠ

I will die bravely, like a ᶠsmugᶠ bridegroom.
What? I will be jovial. Come, come,   195
I am a king, ᵠmyᵠ masters, know you that?

GENTLEMAN

You are a royal one and we obey you.

LEAR

Then there's life in't. Come, an you get it,
You shall get it by running. ᶠSa, sa, sa, sa.ᶠ
                    Exit ᵠ*running*ᵠ [*followed by attendants*].

GENTLEMAN

A sight most pitiful in the meanest wretch,   200
Past speaking of in a king. Thou hast one daughter
Who redeems nature from the general curse

193 ***Ay . . . sir!** The first part of 193 is found only in Q, where Lear's speech ends, but is immediately followed by another speech prefix for him. The Gentleman's 'Good sir' comes from Q2, where this phrase, the only addition made there to the Q text, fills a gap. The interruption by the Gentleman turns Lear's attention from weeping to fighting, as he thinks he is threatened with death. It is possible that Q2 here was printed from a lost corrected state of Q, which included the line.

194 **bravely** both courageously, and handsomely or in fine clothes, as the word relates to *smug*
like . . . bridegroom like a spruced-up bridegroom; playing also on dying as sexual climax, as at *TC* 3.1.121–3: 'These lovers cry, O ho, they die! / Yet that which seems the wound to kill, / Doth turn O ho! to ha, ha, he!'

195 **jovial** majestic (like Jove), and merry

(Cam²)

195–6 **Come . . . king** Lear asserts his royalty, and this may be the point at which the attendants back off, or even kneel, as in several recent productions, so allowing him to make his exit running at 199.

198 **there's . . . in't** there's no need to die bravely, for I can still get away! The phrase is proverbial; see Dent, L265.
it perhaps the *ransom*, 188

199 **Sa . . . sa** 'the King challenges his pursuers: "Come on! come on! Catch me if you can!" ' (Kittredge, who cites a number of other examples from the drama of the period). *Sa, sa* is not in *OED*, but Kittredge has evidence to show that it was an old hunting cry derived from the French 'ça, ça' = 'there, there'.

200 **meanest** of lowest rank, poorest
202–3 **general . . . to** The universal curse of original sin was brought on human nature by Adam and Eve, the first

198 Come] *F;* nay *Q*   199 by] *F;* with *Q*   SD *running*] *Q (Exit King running)*   SD *followed by attendants*] *Hunter (Capell)*   201 speaking of] *Q, F;* speaking *Oxf*   one] *Q;* a *F*

Which twain have brought her to.

EDGAR   Hail, gentle sir.

GENTLEMAN

Sir, speed you. What's your will?

EDGAR   Do you hear aught,

ᶠSir,ᶠ of a battle toward?

GENTLEMAN   Most sure and vulgar.   205

Everyone hears that, which can distinguish sound.

EDGAR

But, by your favour, how near's the other army?

GENTLEMAN

Near, and on speedy foot. The main descry

Stands on the hourly thought.

EDGAR   I thank you, sir.

That's all.   210

GENTLEMAN

Though that the queen on special cause is here

Her army is moved on.

EDGAR   I thank you, sir.   *Exit [Gentleman]*.

GLOUCESTER

You ever gentle gods, take my breath from me;

---

twain, who lie behind the more immediate pair, Goneril and Regan.
204 **speed you** short for 'God speed you',
or may God prosper you
aught anything
205–9 **battle . . . thought** a reminder of
the battle anticipated with the arrival
of Cordelia and French forces in 4.4;
her army has *moved on*, 212, so the
clash is postponed while she searches
for Lear
205 **toward** impending
vulgar generally known
206 ***sound** so F, possibly referring to

drums, heard in 4.4, and again in this
scene at 279; 'sence' (Q) would relate
rather to reports or rumours
207 **other army** the *British powers*, led by
Goneril and Regan; see 4.4.21
208 **on speedy foot** marching rapidly
208–9 **The . . . thought** the discovery or
sight of the main body of troops is
expected any hour
211–12 **Though . . . on** The *special cause*,
to take care of Lear, becomes clear in
the next scene, when Cordelia is no
longer accompanied by the soldiers of
4.4. The Gentleman's information

---

203 have] *F;* hath *Q*   206 hears] *Q2, F;* here's *Q*   which] *F;* that *Q*   sound] *F;* sence *Q*
208 speedy foot] *F;* speed fort *Q*   descry] *F;* descryes, *Q*   209 Stands . . . thought] *F;* Standst . .
. thoughts *Q;* Stands . . . thoughts *Q2*   212 SD] *Johnson; Exit. Q, F (after* moved on*)*

Let not my worser spirit tempt me again
To die before you please.

EDGAR   Well pray you, father.   215
GLOUCESTER   Now, good sir, what are you?
EDGAR

A most poor man, made tame to fortune's blows,
Who, by the art of known and feeling sorrows,
Am pregnant to good pity. Give me your hand;
I'll lead you to some biding.

GLOUCESTER   Hearty thanks.   220
The bounty and the benison of heaven
To boot, to boot.

Enter OSWALD.

OSWALD   A proclaimed prize; most happy!
That eyeless head of thine was first framed flesh

---

helps the audience, but is awkwardly
inserted here, without relevance to
Edgar's questions.

214 **worser spirit** evil angel or devil as
tempter; compare *Son* 144, which
plays on the idea of two spirits 'of
comfort and despair' (so Horsman).
Gloucester's encounter with Lear does
as much as Edgar's device of the imaginary fall from Dover cliff to strengthen him against suicide, but he is soon
again eager to die at the hands of
Oswald, 226–7.

215 **father** See 72 and n.

217 ***tame to** (F) habituated to. Q has
'lame by', which may be an error, as
Edgar is anything but lame in fighting
Oswald.

218–19 **art . . . pity** By the knowledge
(art) he has acquired in being exposed
to feel what wretches feel, and to

encounter his father blind and Lear
mad, Edgar may rightly claim to be
open to (or, like a pregnant woman, big
with) compassion for others.

220 **biding** dwelling

221 **benison** blessing

222 ***To . . . boot** in addition, to compen-
sate you. This is from Qc (see
textual notes); F was here set up from
an uncorrected copy of Q, which has
'to saue thee', and the Oxford editors
argue that the F variant must derive
from consultation with a manuscript
(*TxC*, 537). However, no one has
offered a convincing explanation of F's
'and boot'; possibly it is equivalent to
the reading of Qc, but I know of no
analogy for it.

   prize See 4.5.39–41.
   happy lucky, opportune, as at 2.2.173

223 **framed flesh** conceived and born

---

217 tame to] *F;* lame by *Q*   221 bounty . . . benison] *Qc, Q2, F;* bornet and beniz *Qu*   222 To . .
. boot] *Qc, Q2;* to saue thee *Qu;* To boot, and boot *F;* send thee boot, to boot *Halio (Blayney)*   SD
OSWALD] *Dyce; Q , F (Steward)*   222+ SP OSWALD] *Rowe; Stew. Q , F*   222 happy!] *Rowe;*
happy, *Q;* happy; *Q2;* happie *F*   223 first] *Qc, Q2, F; not in Qu*

To raise my fortunes! Thou old, unhappy traitor,
Briefly thyself remember. The sword is out   225
That must destroy thee.

GLOUCESTER   Now let thy friendly hand
Put strength enough to't.

OSWALD   Wherefore, bold peasant,
Dar'st thou support a published traitor? Hence,
Lest ᶠthatᶠ th' infection of his fortune take
Like hold on thee. Let go his arm.   230

EDGAR   Ch'ill not let go, zir, without ᶠvurtherᶠ 'cagion.

OSWALD   Let go, slave, or thou diest.

EDGAR   Good gentleman, go your gait ᶠandᶠ let poor volk
pass. And 'ch'ud ha' been zwaggered out of my life,
'twould not ha' been zo long ᶠas 'tisᶠ by a vortnight.   235
Nay, come not near th'old man; keep out, che vor ye, or

---

224 **unhappy** unfortunate
225 **thyself remember** recall your sins (and prepare yourself for dying)
226 **friendly** Gloucester wants to die; see 48.
227–30 **Wherefore . . . arm** Edgar already holds Gloucester by the hand (219), so that he may here threaten with his staff (see 237), thrust himself in front of his father, or make some other gesture of *support*.
228 **published** proclaimed. As Weis notes, the irony is that Edgar was earlier proclaimed a traitor by Gloucester at 2.1.60–3.
231–40 **Ch'ill . . . foins** Edgar puts on another verbal disguise, as a West Country yokel, using what for dramatists of the period was the more or less standard dialect; Kittredge lists numerous examples, the most apposite being in *The London Prodigal*, published in 1605 with Shakespeare's name on the title-page; see *The*

Shakespeare Apocrypha, ed. C. F. Tucker Brooke (1908, reprinted 1968), 206–8. F amplifies some indications of dialect, notably by substituting 'z' for 's'; this was typical of Jaggard's printshop, according to *TxC*, 537.
231, 238, 240 **Ch'ill** I (Ich) will
231 **'cagion** occasion, reason
233 **go your gait** be on your way (from 'gate' = road or path; *OED* Gate *sb.²* 2b)
234–5 **And . . . vortnight** If I (Ich) could have been bullied out of my life, it would have been shorter by a fortnight. This is what Edgar *says*, but what he seems to mean is rather Cam²'s interpretation, 'I would not have lasted a fortnight'.
236 **che vor ye** I warrant you, *vor* standing for 'warn', a dialectal contraction of the verb 'to warrant' (Helge Kökeritz, *MLN*, 57 (1942), 98–9). Kökeritz adduces examples from a number of works, including several in

---

224 old,] *F;* most *Q*   228 Dar'st] *Q2, F;* durst *Q*   231 zir] *F;* sir *Q*   'cagion] *Q* (cagion); 'casion *F*   234, 235 ha' been] *F* (ha'bin); haue beene *Q*   234 zwaggered] *F;* swagger'd *Q*
235 'twould] *F;* it would *Q*   zo] *Q2, F;* so *Qu, Qc*   vortnight] *Qc, Q2, F;* fortnight *Qu*

I'se try whether your costard or my baton be the harder.
Ch'ill be plain with you.

OSWALD　　Out, dunghill.　　[*Draws his sword.*] �𐞥*They fight.*ᐟ

EDGAR　Ch'ill pick your teeth, zir. Come, no matter vor　　240
your foins.　[*Oswald falls.*]

OSWALD

Slave, thou hast slain me. Villain, take my purse.
If ever thou wilt thrive, bury my body,
And give the letters which thou find'st about me
To Edmund, Earl of Gloucester. Seek him out　　245
Upon the English party. O untimely death, death!　ᐟ*He dies.*ᐟ

The London Prodigal (see 231–40n.), to support his argument; it seems to me, however, that Edgar is warning Oswald here, as Dr Johnson thought.

237 **I'se** I shall
costard derisively = head; literally, a kind of large apple. The rustic clown in *LLL* is named Costard.
***baton** cudgel. 'Ballow' (F) has no convincing parallels, and 'battero' (Qu) could be a misreading of 'batton', assuming that the tilde in manuscript 'battõ' was misread as an 'er' suspension after 'tt'. This is the same word as the modern *baton* but with a stronger meaning, as shown in Spenser's *Faerie Queene*, 6.7.46, 'And with his yron batton, which he bore, / Let driue at him' (cited *OED*). John Gwillim, *A Display of Heraldry* (1611), 53, explains that 'This word *Batune* . . . signifieth a *Wand* or *Cudgell*'.

238 **Out** out upon you!; compare 3.7.86

239 **pick . . . teeth** be more than a match for you. Dent cites this phrase as proverbial, T424.1. Hunter thinks that Edgar, fighting with Oswald, has taken a dagger from him with which to 'pick his teeth', and this may be how it was

played. In some modern productions Edgar has brutally driven a staff or dagger into the body of Oswald as if in hatred or to punish him, an action that may seem very much at odds with the idea of a noble Edgar (as in Jonathan Miller's BBC film, in which Poor Tom wore a crown of thorns, linking him visually with images of Christ).

241 **foins** thrusts; implying that Oswald uses his sword against Edgar's staff

244, 251 **letters** See 4.5.35 and n. Oswald may carry a letter from Regan as well as the one from Goneril but, if so, we hear no more about it.

246 A five-beat line would end at *untimely*, and Hunter makes 'Death! – Death –' a separate line. Perhaps these words were meant to be muttered as Edgar speaks.
***English** F's change from Q's 'British' may be an indifferent variant, a casual equivalent put in by actor, author or compositor; but see 3.4.180 and n. Duthie, 158–9, argues that *English* was what Shakespeare first wrote.

---

237 I'se] *F (ice)*; ile *Q*　whether] *Q, F (whither)*　costard] *Qc (costerd)*, *Q2*, *F*; coster *Qu*　baton] *Oxf (OED)*; battero *Qu*; bat *Qc*, *Q2*; Ballow *F*　238 Ch'ill] *Q2*, *F*; ile *Q*　239 SD *Draws . . . sword*] *this edn*　240 zir] *Q2*, *F*; sir *Q*　vor] *F*; for *Q*　241 SD] *Cam*; *Edgar knocks him down. / Rowe*　246 English] *F*; British *Qu*, *Qc (Brittish)*, *Q2*

EDGAR

  I know thee well; a serviceable villain,
  As duteous to the vices of thy mistress
  As badness would desire.

GLOUCESTER   What, is he dead?

EDGAR

  Sit you down, father; rest you. –   250
  Let's see these pockets: the letters that he speaks of
  May be my friends. He's dead; I am only sorry
  He had no other deathsman. Let us see:
  Leave, gentle wax; and manners, blame us not.
  To know our enemies' minds we rip their hearts,   255
  Their papers is more lawful.

  (^F*Reads the letter.*^F) 'Let our reciprocal vows be
  remembered. You have many opportunities to cut him
  off. If your will want not, time and place will be
  fruitfully offered. There is nothing done if he return   260
  the conqueror; then am I the prisoner, and his bed my
  gaol, from the loathed warmth whereof, deliver me and
  supply the place for your labour. Your (wife, so I would

---

247 **serviceable** diligent, ready to do anything; compare 2.2.17–18
253 **deathsman** executioner
254 **Leave** by your leave; compare *TN* 2.5.91–2 (Cam¹). Edgar tears open the letter, sealed, as was usual, with wax, which Weis thinks was 'sealed with a noble crest' (*gentle* meaning well-born, of gentle birth)
255 **rip their hearts** i.e. by killing them (the obvious meaning), or torturing them?
257 **reciprocal vows** exchanged at 4.2.19–25

258 **him** Albany
259 **will want not** purpose, and lust (for me), do not fail; for *will*, compare 266
260 **fruitfully** plentifully, but also suggesting sexual fulfilment
260–1 **done . . . conqueror*; F makes a separate sentence of 'There . . . done', perhaps taking the capital 'I' in 'If' in Q as indicating a new start. But Q has commas only, and Pope seems to have interpreted them better in placing a stop after 'conqueror'; this makes better sense than F.
263 **supply . . . labour** fill his place, both

250–1 you. – /Let's] *F* (you/Let's); you lets *Qu*; you, lets *Qc* 251 these] *F*; his *Q* the] *F*; These *Q* 252 sorry] *Q2, F*; sorrow *Q* 254 wax; and manners, blame] *Q* (waxe, and manners blame); waxe, and manners: blame *F* 254–5 not. / To] *Pope*; not / To *Q*, *F*; not, / To *Q2* 255 we] *F*; wee'd *Q* 257 SD] *F*; *not in Qu*; *A letter. Qc* our] *F*; your *Q* 260 done if] *Q* (done, If) *Q2*; done. *If F* 261 conqueror;] *Pope*; conqueror, *Q*, *F* 262 gaol] *Qc, Q2* (iayle), *F* (Gaole); gayle *Qu* 263–4 (wife, so . . . say)] *F*; wife (so . . . say) your *Q*

say) affectionate servant ^Qand for you her own for
venture.^Q Goneril.'   265
O indistinguished space of woman's will!
A plot upon her virtuous husband's life
And the exchange my brother. Here in the sands
Thee I'll rake up, the post unsanctified
Of murderous lechers; and in the mature time,   270
With this ungracious paper strike the sight
Of the death-practised duke. For him 'tis well
That of thy death and business I can tell.

[Exit dragging the body.]

GLOUCESTER
The King is mad: how stiff is my vile sense,
That I stand up and have ingenious feeling   275

---

as a reward for your labour, and as a
lover or *servant* (264) 'labouring' in his
bed

264–5 *and . . . venture Q's apparently
clumsy phrase (not in F) has not been
explained, may well be corrupt and is
usually omitted from editions of the
play. Goneril may be saying 'and for
you (to be) her own whatever the risk
(or venture)', but the repeated *for* is
confusing. Richard Proudfoot suggests
emending to 'for you her own to
venture', meaning, 'ready to take
responsibility for herself in the venture of love for you'. Q's 'Venter'
could mean 'wife in a second marriage'
(*OED* Venter 1. 1b), first citation 1707,
but Goneril has already said she would
be his wife.

266 *O limitless expanse of woman's lust!
It is *indistinguished* because the boundaries of it cannot be made out. Edgar
for the moment shares Lear's misogyny, but it was a common proverb
that 'Women will have their wills'
(Dent, W723). Q has 'wit', due probably to a misreading of 'l' as 't'.

268–9 Here . . . rake up Edgar says he
will bury (*rake up*) Oswald, but neither
Q nor F has any directions here.
Capell's arrangement makes the best
sense, to have Edgar drag off the body,
leaving Gloucester briefly alone, and
return for his final lines; see SDs at
273 and 279. The couplet at 272–3
supports this interpretation. The
reference to sands, as Weis notes, suggests that Edgar wants Gloucester still
to imagine he is on a beach, unless
Shakespeare still had the seashore in
mind.

269 post unsanctified unholy letter-
carrier, or go-between; perhaps also, as
Hunter notes, suggesting unhallowed
ground, as at *Ham* 5.1.22

270 in . . . time when the time is ripe

271 ungracious wicked, as devoid of
spiritual grace

272 death-practised whose death has
been plotted

274 stiff stubborn, unyielding
sense power of sensation (the senses
as a single faculty, *OED, sb.* 3)

275 ingenious perceptive, fully responsive

264–5 and . . . venture] *Q (Venter); not in Q2, F*   266 indistinguished] *Q;* vndistinguisht *Q2;*
indinguish'd *F*   will] *F;* wit *Q*   273 SD] *Capell subst.*

Of my huge sorrows? Better I were distract;
So should my thoughts be severed from my griefs,
And woes by wrong imaginations lose
The knowledge of themselves.   *Drum afar off.*

[*Enter* EDGAR.]

EDGAR   Give me your hand.
Far off methinks I hear the beaten drum.   280
Come, father, I'll bestow you with a friend.   *Exeunt.*

4.7   *Enter* CORDELIA, KENT [*disguised*] *and* Gentleman.

CORDELIA
O thou good Kent, how shall I live and work

276 **distract** mad
277 **severed** 'fenced' (Q) also means sep-
    arated, but perhaps with an overtone
    of being protected; the words could be
    confused in secretary hand.
278–9 **woes . . . themselves** my sorrows
    would be forgotten in wild delusions
281 **bestow . . . friend** lodge you with a
    friend. No more is heard of this friend.
4.7 *This scene, incorrectly numbered
    'Septima', should be 4.6 in F, which
    omits 4.3. There are no scene numbers
    in Q. It has often been argued, as by
    Greg, *First Folio*, 388, and Duthie,
    418, that 4.3 was omitted after the
    copy for F was prepared, and therefore
    Shakespeare was not responsible. Gary
    Taylor, however, shows that numerical
    errors in scene headings are not
    uncommon in plays by other authors
    as well as in F itself, and the mistake
    could just as well have originated in the
    printing-house; see *TxC*, 417–18. In
    stage productions, Lear has often been

discovered lying on a couch or sickbed
(Bratton, 189), in accordance with a
stage direction added by Steevens, but
the scene seems intended to echo 1.1;
see 20.1 and n.
0.1 **Enter . . . Gentleman** As she does in
    4.4 (F), Cordelia may display arms and
    the *colours*, flags or emblems of France,
    leading Lear to think he is in that
    country at 76 (so Rosenberg, 283),
    although she is no longer accompanied
    by soldiers; see 4.6.211–12 and n. F
    has '*Gentleman*', as a substitute for the
    '*Doctor*' called for in Q, so reducing
    the number of parts by one. This is
    presumably the same Gentleman who
    attends on Lear in 3.1 and on Cordelia
    in 4.4; see headnote to that scene. The
    Gentleman takes over some of the
    Doctor's lines from Q, and also his
    knowledge (19), though the advice he
    gives about Lear requires no specialist
    medical knowledge.

277 severed] *F*; fenced *Q*   279 SD *Drum . . . off*] *F (after 278); A drum a farre off. Q*
279.1 *Enter* EDGAR] *Capell subst.*   281 SD] *F; Exit. Q*

4.7] *F (Scena Septima); not in Q*   0.1 *disguised*] *Oxf (Riv)*   *and Gentleman*] *Fc; Gentleman Fu;
and Doctor Q*

To match thy goodness? My life will be too short,
And every measure fail me.

KENT

    To be acknowledged, madam, is o'erpaid.
    All my reports go with the modest truth,   5
    Nor more, nor clipped, but so.

CORDELIA   Be better suited;
    These weeds are memories of those worser hours.
    I prithee put them off.

KENT   Pardon, dear madam;
    Yet to be known shortens my made intent.
    My boon I make it that you know me not   10
    Till time and I think meet.

CORDELIA

    Then be't so, my good lord. [*to the Gentleman*] How
        does the King?

GENTLEMAN   Madam, sleeps still.

CORDELIA

    O you kind gods!
    Cure this great breach in his abused nature;   15
    Th'untuned and jarring senses, O, wind up

---

3 **every . . . me** nothing I can do will measure up to your goodness
4 **To be acknowledged** to have recognition (for my service)
5 **All . . . truth** all my accounts (of Lear and myself) correspond to the truth without exaggeration; *modest* = moderate, or free from exaggeration (*OED a*. 4)
6 **Nor . . . clipped** neither overstated nor understated
7 **weeds** clothes. Kent was hired as Lear's follower in 1.4, and wears clothes for that role; see 1.4.0.1 and n.
8 **I prithee** I pray thee
9 **to . . . intent** to be known at this time would undercut the plan I have made.

Shakespeare's plan, it seems, is to have Kent revealed as himself later (see 5.3.231–3 and 5.3.228.1n.), not in a scene devoted to the recognition of Cordelia by Lear. Thus he gives Kent an *intent*, mentioned earlier in Q at 4.3.52–3, to further this dramatic purpose. Kent's design is not mentioned again.
10 **My . . . it** the favour I ask is
11 **meet** fit
15 **abused** abusèd; maltreated, done violence to; but see 53
16 **wind up** put in tune (as if by tightening pegs to adjust the strings on a musical instrument)

---

8 Pardon] *F;* Pardon me *Q*   12 SD] *Theobald*   13+ SP GENTLEMAN] *F (Gent.); Doct. Q*
14 gods!] *F;* Gods *Q*   16 jarring] *F;* hurrying *Q*

Of this child-changed father.

GENTLEMAN   So please your majesty,
That we may wake the King? He hath slept long.

CORDELIA
Be governed by your knowledge and proceed
I'the sway of your own will. Is he arrayed?   20

ᶠ*Enter* LEAR *in a chair carried by servants.*ᶠ

GENTLEMAN
Ay, madam. In the heaviness of sleep
We put fresh garments on him.
Be by, good madam, when we do awake him.
I doubt ᑫnotᑫ of his temperance.

ᑫCORDELIA   Very well.

GENTLEMAN
Please you draw near; louder the music there.ᑫ   25

---

17 **child-changed** changed by his children (so that he now needs to be cared for like a child)
    majesty a proper address to the Queen of France, but Cordelia continues to address her father as *your majesty* at 44
20 **I'the ... will** as your inclination (*will*) guides you, or as you see fit
20.1 This SD, not in Q, is probably, as Granville-Barker noted, 182, intended to echo visually 1.1, by bringing on Lear in a chair, and clothed in royal robes again ('arrayed'), as suggested by 44 (see 1.1.32.1 and n.). Taylor, *Division*, 412–13, also points to a connection with Gloucester bound to a chair in 3.7. In many productions Lear is dressed in white to signify humility, and the scene is played simply for pathos; see Bratton, 189, and Rosenberg, 284. See also Introduction, p. 20.

21–2 Lear tried to tear off his clothes (royal robes?) at 3.4.106–7. Apart from his crown of weeds and flowers (4.4.3–6), his costume in the mad scenes is not described; now he is properly clothed once more, and possibly in early performances was visibly a king again. The imagery of taking off and putting on clothes is important in the play; see also 1.1.49 and n. These lines are given to the Doctor in Q.
23 **Be by** Does Cordelia stand apart, though within call, not wanting to wake him? Hunter suggests Cordelia may fall to her knees on Lear's entry, but this would undercut her kneeling later in the scene at 57.
24 **temperance** self-control
24–5 *CORDELIA ... there* F has no reference to music, or to the Doctor. Music was 'the best comforter / To an unsettled fancy' (*Tem* 5.1.58–9), and so is appropriate here, and may always

---

21 sleep] *F;* his sleep *Q*   23 Be ... madam] *F; Gent.* Good madam be by *Q; Kent.* Good madam be by *Q2; Doct.* Good madam be by *Capell*

CORDELIA

O my dear father, restoration hang
Thy medicine on my lips, and let this kiss
Repair those violent harms that my two sisters
Have in thy reverence made.

KENT   Kind and dear princess!

CORDELIA

Had you not been their father, these white flakes   30
Did challenge pity of them. Was this a face
To be opposed against the warring winds?
^QTo stand against the deep dread-bolted thunder,
In the most terrible and nimble stroke
Of quick cross-lightning? To watch, poor perdu,   35
With this thin helm?^Q Mine enemy's dog
Though he had bit me should have stood that night
Against my fire; and wast thou fain, poor father,
To hovel thee with swine and rogues forlorn
In short and musty straw? Alack, alack!   40
'Tis wonder that thy life and wits at once

have been played. The main purpose
of the omission from F is probably to
get rid of an unnecessary part, the
Doctor.
29 **reverence** venerable condition, as
deserving respect
30 **flakes** locks of hair
31 **challenge** claim, as at 1.1.53
32 ***warring** F's 'iarring' here is no doubt
an error, by attraction from *jarring
senses*, 16.
33–6 ***To . . . helm** F's omission of this
passage in Q leaves a dangling half-line
at 36, but the verse is irregular anyway
33 **dread-bolted** sending dreaded thun-
der-bolts
35 **cross lightning** forked lightning
watch stay awake, be on the alert
perdu a sentinel placed in such an
exposed position that he can hardly

escape death (hence *perdu*, French for
'lost')
36 **helm** covering or helmet (of hair)
38 **Against** before
fain glad (for want of anything better)
39–40 **hovel . . . straw** recalling the *hovel*
of 3.2.61, 71, and 3.4.170, where Poor
Tom mutters in the *straw* (3.4.43).
Short straw makes poor bedding
(Weis). For a possible allusion to the
parable of the prodigal son in Luke,
15.11–32, see Susan Snyder, *SQ*, 17
(1966), 361–4.
39 **rogues forlorn** wretched vagrants.
The line, as Cam[2] notes, provided
some basis for Grigori Kozintsev's
representation in his film version of
the *hovel* of 3.6 as crowded with such
figures.
41 **at once** at the same time

31 Did challenge] *F;* Had challengd *Q*   32 opposed] *F;* exposd *Q*   warring] *Q;* iarring *F*
36 enemy's] *F (Enemies); iniurious Q*

Had not concluded all. He wakes; speak to him.

GENTLEMAN   Madam, do you; 'tis fittest.

CORDELIA

How does my royal lord? How fares your majesty?

LEAR

You do me wrong to take me out o'the grave.   45
Thou art a soul in bliss, but I am bound
Upon a wheel of fire that mine own tears
Do scald like molten lead.

CORDELIA   Sir, ᶠdo youᶠ know me?

LEAR

You are a spirit, I know; where did you die?

CORDELIA   Still, still far wide.   50

GENTLEMAN

He's scarce awake; let him alone awhile.

LEAR

Where have I been? Where am I? Fair daylight?
I am mightily abused. I should ev'n die with pity

---

42 **concluded all** come to an end altogether
44 In this most moving of recognition scenes, it is notable that Cordelia addresses her father as King, as restored to the *right* she has invaded England to reclaim for him (4.4.28). See Introduction, p. 35.
45 Lear, like Gloucester, wants death; both are restored to life after an imagined death, and forced to endure almost more than they can bear.
46–7 **soul . . . fire** Lear imagines Cordelia as in a Christian heaven, and himself as suffering one of the torments of the damned. The image recalls the suffering of Ixion, punished by Jupiter for seeking to seduce Juno, and bound on an ever-whirling wheel in hell, but it has wider resonances which are explored by Elton, 236–8. Perhaps the

most important connections are, first, with the sun, depicted as a wheel of fire worshipped in pre-Christian England by Richard Verstegen in *A Restitution of Decayed Intelligence* (1605), 69, and linked with Lear at 1.1.110; and second, with the wheel of fortune that comes *full circle* for Lear even as it does for Edmund at 5.3.172; see also 2.2.171. In 'Myth and history in *King Lear*', *SQ*, 26 (1975), 227–42, O. B. Hardison documents traditional interpretations of the Ixion myth 'as a political allegory showing the disastrous result of irresponsible rule, and as an allegory of ingratitude' (232), but it is uncertain whether Shakespeare was aware of these.

47 **that** so that
50 **wide** wide of the mark, bewildered
53 **abused** The primary meanings are

---

48 scald] *Q, Q2; F* (scal'd)   do . . . me?] *F;* know me. *Q;* know ye me *Q2*   49 where] *Q, F;* when *Q2*   53 ev'n] *F;* ene *Q*

To see another thus. I know not what to say.
I will not swear these are my hands: let's see –   55
I feel this pinprick. Would I were assured
Of my condition.
CORDELIA [*Kneels.*]   O look upon me, sir,
And hold your hands in benediction o'er me!
[*She restrains him as he tries to kneel.*]
�QNo, sir,�Q you must not kneel.
LEAR   Pray do not mock ᶠmeᶠ.
I am a very foolish, fond old man,   60
Fourscore and upward, ᶠnot an hour more nor less;ᶠ
And to deal plainly,

misused or maltreated; and deceived or imposed upon. Both meanings function here as Lear is still 'in a strange mist of uncertainty' (Johnson); see also 15 and 77.

ev'n indeed, to be sure (*OED adv.* 8b)

55–6 let's . . . pinprick an indication of stage business. Lear may use 'a brooch or some other ornament from his costume to test himself' (Cam²).

56–7 Would . . . condition I wish I could feel confident about my state of being.

57–8 SDs *Kneels . . . kneel* There are no directions in Q or F, but the text suggests that Lear tries to rise from his chair, causing Cordelia to kneel and ask for his blessing, and that he then attempts to kneel to her. The scene thus echoes visually Lear kneeling in mockery to Regan at 2.2.343, and could relate also to 1.1, where Goneril and Regan have in some productions knelt before Lear to deliver their flattering speeches, while Cordelia remains standing to say *Nothing*. Here at last the kneeling is meaningful and moving, not only as an emblem of mutual reconciliation, but because it may suggest 'effigies on a tomb that face each other with hands uplifted in perpetual prayer' (Muriel St Clare

Byrne's review of the 1959 production at Stratford, with Charles Laughton as Lear, *SQ*, 11 (1960), 201); this is the supreme moment for Cordelia and Lear, and they might say with Othello, 'If it were now to die, / 'Twere now to be most happy'. Shakespeare got the idea from *Leir*, 2298–348, where Leir kneels and rises twice, and Cordelia three times, in their reconciliation scene, reducing the process by repetition almost to farce. See also 4.6.64–5 and n. for a possible parallel with Gloucester and Edgar; and Introduction, pp. 20–2.

60–3 Lear's admission that he is senile is the more moving because, even as humility replaces his earlier obsession with power, he is once again treated as King and given back his royalty by Cordelia.

60 fond in my dotage (Ard²), silly

61 not . . . less F's added phrase here does not make good literal sense in relation to *upward*, but is curiously apt as stressing (a) that Lear is not yet fully in command of himself, and (b) the overwhelming sense of his great age.

62 deal plainly speak bluntly; with Lear's concern here for matter over words, compare 1.1.55 and n.

57 SD] *Oxf*   58 your hands] *Q;* yours hand *Fu;* your hand *Fc*   SD] *this edn*   59 me] *Q2,* F; *not in Q*

I fear I am not in my perfect mind.
Methinks I should know you and know this man,
Yet I am doubtful; for I am mainly ignorant   65
What place this is and all the skill I have
Remembers not these garments; nor I know not
Where I did lodge last night. Do not laugh at me,
For, as I am a man, I think this lady
To be my child Cordelia.
CORDELIA   And so I am, ᶠI amᶠ.   70
LEAR
Be your tears wet? Yes, faith; I pray weep not.
If you have poison for me, I will drink it.
I know you do not love me, for your sisters
Have, as I do remember, done me wrong.
You have some cause, they have not.
CORDELIA   No cause, no cause.   75
LEAR
Am I in France?
KENT   In your own kingdom, sir.
LEAR   Do not abuse me.
GENTLEMAN
Be comforted, good madam, the great rage
You see is killed in him, �and yet it is danger
To make him even o'er the time he has lost.ᵟ   80

---

64 **this man** probably Kent, who speaks
to him at 76
65 **mainly** entirely (*OED adv.* 2)
66 **skill** knowledge
70 ***I am, I am** The second *I am*, added
in F, is extra-metrical, but seems a
deliberate expansion, expressing
Cordelia's love, and anticipating her
repetition in 75. The F compositor had
space to spare here, however, and could
have been stretching his copy to fill it.
The line invites stress on *am*: 'And so I
am, I *am*.'

71 **Be . . . wet** Here Garrick touched her
cheek in a moving gesture, and Henry
Irving went further, putting his finger
to his mouth as if to taste the saltiness
of her tears.
76 **France** See 0.1 and n.
77 **abuse** deceive; or, perhaps, do me
wrong. See 53 and n.
78 **rage** madness, as at 4.4.19
79–80 ***and . . . lost** By the omission of
these words in Q, F converts what is
prose in Q into irregular verse.
80 **even o'er** make sense of; literally,

63 in . . . mind] *Q, F;* perfect in my mind *Q2*   79 killed] *F;* cured *Q*

Desire him to go in. Trouble him no more
Till further settling.

CORDELIA   Will't please your highness walk?

LEAR   You must bear with me. Pray ᶠyouᶠ now, forget and
forgive; I am old and foolish.

Exeunt. ᵠ*Kent and the Gentleman remain.*ᵠ

ᵠGENTLEMAN   Holds it true, sir, that the Duke of Corn-   85
wall was so slain?

KENT   Most certain, sir.

GENTLEMAN   Who is conductor of his people?

KENT   As 'tis said, the bastard son of Gloucester.

GENTLEMAN   They say Edgar his banished son is with   90
the Earl of Kent in Germany.

KENT   Report is changeable; 'tis time to look about. The
powers of the kingdom approach apace.

GENTLEMAN   The arbitrement is like to be bloody. Fare   94
you well, sir.   [*Exit.*]

KENT

My point and period will be throughly wrought,

---

smooth out

82 **Till further settling** till his mind is
more composed

83–4 **Pray . . . forgive** In F the scene
ends on this note, with Lear making a
general appeal, perhaps asking not just
Cordelia but everyone to forget and
forgive all the horrors of the past. It is
especially poignant that Cordelia
cannot forget, but insists on trying to
put him back on the throne by means
of war; see Foakes, 205, and Introduction, pp. 22, 32.

85–97 *Q's passage, foregrounding Kent,
and reminding us yet again of the
coming battle (see 4.6.205–9), was perhaps cut from F as unnecessary, and as
removing an apparent contradiction:
in both Q and F Kent is identified by
name by Cordelia in line 1, but in Q at

91 the Gentleman thinks Kent may be
in Germany. Q has no entry for this
Gentleman (unless he is the same as
the 'Doctor'), but the SD at 84, '*Manet
Kent and Gent.*', shows he is already on
stage at 85, and so presumably comes
on at the beginning of the scene (as in
F), in which case he would hear
Cordelia's opening words. The role of
Kent is much reduced in F; see
Michael Warren in *TxC*, 70–1, and
Introduction, p. 143.

85 **Holds it true** is it still believed

88 **conductor** leader or commander
(*OED* 4)

92 **look about** take stock of the situation

93 **powers . . . kingdom** the British forces

94 **arbitrement** deciding of the quarrel

96 The culmination and end (of my life)
will be finally shaped; *point* and *period*

84 SD] *Q (Exeunt. Manet Kent and Gent.); Exeunt. F*   95 SD] *Theobald*

Or well or ill as this day's battle's fought.   *Exit.*^Q

5.1   *Enter* ^F*with drum and colours*^F EDMUND, REGAN, *gentlemen and soldiers*

EDMUND [*to a gentleman*]
Know of the Duke if his last purpose hold,
Or whether since he is advised by aught
To change the course. He's full of alteration
And self-reproving. Bring his constant pleasure.
                                                            [*Exit gentleman.*]

REGAN
Our sister's man is certainly miscarried.   5
EDMUND
'Tis to be doubted, madam.
REGAN   Now, sweet lord,
You know the goodness I intend upon you:
Tell me but truly, but then speak the truth,

---

both suggest a critical moment in time, but the latter word also carries the idea of completion. Compare *Oth* 5.1.131–2.
throughly a common equivalent of 'thoroughly'
97 **Or . . . or** either . . . or; a common usage
5.1.0.1 *with . . . colours* Here and at 16.1, F calls for martial drums and *colours*, the standards or flags displaying the emblems of two armies; however the badges of Goneril and Albany might be distinguished from those of Edmund and Regan, both presumably would include some indication that they are British, as distinct from the French forces who enter in 5.2. The location is somewhere near Dover.
1 **Duke . . . hold** Albany seemed to be in two minds at the end of 4.2, but in 4.3

(Q) his army was marching, and at 4.4.21 and 4.6.205–9 come further reports of British forces on the move, so his *last purpose* was to fight.
2 **since** more recently
advised warned or counselled
3 **the course** his course of action
3–4 **full . . . self-reproving** keeps changing his mind and reproaching himself
4 **constant pleasure** settled purpose; compare 1.1.42
5 **man** Oswald, killed by Edgar at 4.6.246
miscarried come to harm, been killed, as at 45
6 **doubted** feared
7 **goodness . . . you** benefit I mean to confer on you (i.e. her hand in marriage)

5.1] *F (Actus Quintus. Scena Prima); not in Q*   0.1–2] *F; Enter Edmund, Regan, and their powers. Q*
1+ SP EDMUND] *Theobald; Bast. Q, F*   1 SD] *Duthie*   3 alteration] *Qc, Q2, F; abdication Qu*
4 SD] *Hunter (Capell)*

Do you not love my sister?

EDMUND In honoured love.

REGAN

But have you never found my brother's way   10
To the forfended place?

^QEDMUND That thought abuses you.

REGAN

I am doubtful that you have been conjunct
And bosomed with her, as far as we call hers.^Q

EDMUND No, by mine honour, madam.

REGAN

I never shall endure her. Dear my lord,   15
Be not familiar with her.

EDMUND Fear ^Qme^Q not –

Enter ^F*with drum and colours*^F ALBANY, GONERIL,
[*and*] *soldiers.*

She and the Duke her husband.

^QGONERIL [*aside*]

I had rather lose the battle than that sister
Should loosen him and me.^Q

---

9 **honoured** honourable or virtuous
10 **brother's** Albany's, her brother-in-law's
11 **forfended place** forbidden bed or body (of Goneril). Regan jealously, and with reason, suspects Edmund of adultery; see 4.2.19–28 and 4.5.25–8 (so Cam²).
11–13 *EDMUND . . . hers.* perhaps omitted from F as mere expansion of what is already clear enough
11 **abuses** does you wrong, or dishonours
12 **doubtful** apprehensive, worried
12–13 **conjunct . . . hers** coupled and intimate with her, to the fullest extent (Hunter). Imagining Edmund in possession of all Goneril calls her own

does not reduce Regan's desire for him, but intensifies her hostility to her sister.
16 **familiar** intimate
16.1 *colours* flags presumably showing British insignia, such as heraldic lions
17 **She . . . husband** It is not clear whether Edmund sees Goneril and Albany coming, or is interrupted as he is on the point of saying something about them.
18–19 *GONERIL . . . me* This aside is not in F, and may have been cut in order to enhance the immediate dramatic irony of Albany addressing Regan as *loving* after what she has just been saying. For the quibble on *lose* and *loosen* (= make a breach between), see 1.4.295 and n.

9 In] *F; I, Q*   16.1 *soldiers*] *F; with troupes Q*   18 SD] *Theobald*   19 and me] *Qc, Q2;* nd mee *Qu*

ALBANY

   Our very loving sister, well be-met.   20

   Sir, this I heard: the King is come to his daughter,

   With others whom the rigour of our state

   Forced to cry out. ^QWhere I could not be honest

   I never yet was valiant. For this business,

   It touches us as France invades our land,   25

   Not bolds the King, with others whom I fear

   Most just and heavy causes make oppose.

EDMUND

   Sir, you speak nobly.^Q

REGAN   Why is this reasoned?

GONERIL

   Combine together 'gainst the enemy,

   For these domestic and particular broils   30

   Are not the question here.

ALBANY   Let's then determine with the ancient of war on

   our proceeding.

---

21 ***heard** so F. This reading or 'heare' (Q) could be due to the common confusion between final 'e' and 'd', which look alike in secretary hand.

22 **rigour . . . state** harshness of our government

23–8 ***Where . . . nobly** These lines are omitted from F, together with 34. Horsman suggests that the repetition of *with others whom*, and the parallelism of 22–3 and 26–7, may point to Shakespeare as having two shots at the same thought. I think the lines were cut from F in order to remove another reference to the King of France; see Appendix 1. In Q Albany announces his support for Lear, stressing that his sole concern is to deal with the French invasion, and the response of Regan at 28 is to ask, 'Why are you telling us again about your worries?'; in F she

interrupts Albany, in effect saying, 'Why tell us again about Lear and Cordelia?' (see Urkowitz, 96–100). In Q Edmund twice defers to Albany, at 28 and 34, somewhat oddly in view of what happens in 5.3, but enhancing Albany's role here.

26 **Not . . . King** not as it makes Lear bold, or encourages him to *oppose* British forces

27 **heavy** weighty, serious

30 ***domestic . . . broils** internal and private quarrels. Q has 'domestique dore particulars', which could mean roughly the same, but is a strange phrase, possibly the result of error of some kind.

32 **ancient of war** those experienced in war, senior officers

33 **proceeding** course of action

---

21 Sir,] *F;* For *Q*   heard] *F;* heare *Q*   26 Not bolds] *Q;* Yet bold's *Oxf (Blayney)*   30 domestic . . . broils] *F;* domestique dore particulars *Q*   31 the] *F;* to *Q*   33 proceeding] *F;* proceedings *Q*

^QEDMUND

    I shall attend you presently at your tent.^Q   [*Exit.*]

REGAN   Sister, you'll go with us?   35

GONERIL   No.

REGAN

    'Tis most convenient; pray ^Qyou^Q go with us.

GONERIL

    O ho, I know the riddle. I will go.

          Exeunt [Edmund, Regan, Goneril and] ^F*both the armies.*^F

    [*As Albany is leaving,*] *enter* EDGAR [*in peasant's clothing*].

EDGAR

    If e'er your grace had speech with man so poor,

    Hear me one word.

ALBANY [*to his soldiers*] I'll overtake you.   40

    [*to Edgar*]   Speak.

EDGAR

    Before you fight the battle, ope this letter.

    If you have victory, let the trumpet sound

    For him that brought it. Wretched though I seem,

    I can produce a champion that will prove

    What is avouched there. If you miscarry,   45

---

34 **presently** right away

35–8 **Sister . . . go** The sparring of the sisters here prepares for their full-blown hostility in 5.3. Regan presumably wants to be with Edmund and keep Goneril in view, while Goneril at first hopes to talk with Edmund, but changes her mind when she understands the *riddle*, and realizes Regan knows her design. Her *go with us* in 35 and 37 seems to refer to herself, adopting a royal plural, as equivalent to 'let's keep together'. No exit is marked for

the silent Edmund in Q or F, and in Q line 34 could signal his departure.

37 **convenient** appropriate, or proper

38 **I . . . riddle** I see what you are up to (understanding that Regan wants to keep an eye on her)

38.2 **in peasant's clothing** Edgar is still disguised, as in 4.6

41 **letter** found on Oswald; see 4.6.257–65

44 **champion** fighter in my cause

45 **avouched** avouchèd; affirmed
    miscarry lose and perish

---

34 SD] *Oxf (Exit with his powers)*   38.1 *Exeunt*] *opp. word, 40 Q Edmund . . . and*] *Theobald*
38.2 *As . . . leaving*] *this edn (Theobald), in . . . clothing*] *this edn; Enter Edgar. Q , F* 40 SD *to his soldiers*] *this edn (Hunter)* SD *to Edgar*] *Hunter*

Your business of the world hath so an end
^FAnd machination ceases.^F Fortune love you.

ALBANY

Stay till I have read the letter.

EDGAR   I was forbid it.

When time shall serve, let but the herald cry   49

And I'll appear again.   *Exit.*

ALBANY

Why, fare thee well. I will o'erlook thy paper.

Enter EDMUND.

EDMUND

The enemy's in view; draw up your powers.

[*Hands him a note.*] Here is the guess of their true
    strength and forces,

By diligent discovery; but your haste   54

Is now urged on you.

ALBANY   We will greet the time.   *Exit.*

EDMUND

To both these sisters have I sworn my love,

Each jealous of the other as the stung

---

47 ***And . . . ceases** perhaps omitted by
accident from Q. For *machination*,
plotting or intrigue, compare 1.2.113.
***love** so Q; the subjunctive, 'may
Fortune love you', must be correct. F
has 'loues', another case perhaps of a
long tail in a manuscript being misread
as 's'.

48 **forbid it** by Shakespeare, to avoid
anticipating Albany's knowledge of
Edmund's treachery and arrest of him
at 5.3.83 (Hunter)

51 **o'erlook** read through

52 **powers** troops

53 ***Here** so F, suggesting a bit of stage

business with a note; the word could be
misread in secretary hand as 'Hard'
(Q)

54 **discovery** reconnaissance

55 **We . . . time** We will be ready to do
what the time requires. Albany falls
into using the royal plural, perhaps as
a deliberate snub to Edmund, if he has
read the letter Edgar gave him; see
5.3.61.

56–70 Edmund's last soliloquy in the play
marks his near-desperation; see 1.2
and n.

57 **jealous** suspicious

---

47 love] *Q;* loues *F*   51 o'erlook] *Q, F* (ore-looke*);* looke ore *Q2*   thy] *F;* the *Q*   52 enemy's] *F;*
enemies *Qu, Qc, Q2*   53 SD] *this edn (Jennens)*   Here . . . the guess] *F;* Hard . . . thequesse *Q;*
Hard . . . the guesse *Q2*   true] *F;* great *Q*   56 sisters] *Q2, F;* sister *Q*   57 stung] *F;* sting *Q*

Are of the adder. Which of them shall I take?
Both? One? Or neither? Neither can be enjoyed
If both remain alive. To take the widow   60
Exasperates, makes mad her sister Goneril,
And hardly shall I carry out my side,
Her husband being alive. Now then, we'll use
His countenance for the battle, which being done,
Let her who would be rid of him devise   65
His speedy taking off. As for the mercy
Which he intends to Lear and to Cordelia,
The battle done, and they within our power,
Shall never see his pardon; for my state   69
Stands on me to defend, not to debate.   *Exit.*

5.2   *Alarum* ᶠ*within*ᶠ. *Enter* ᶠ*with drum and colours*ᶠ
          LEAR, CORDELIA *and soldiers,* [*they pass*] *over the stage*
                              ᶠ*and exeunt.*ᶠ

          Enter EDGAR [*in peasant's clothing*] *and* GLOUCESTER.

62 **carry . . . side** fulfil my side of the
    agreement, the *reciprocal vows*
    (4.6.257) exchanged with Goneril
64 **countenance** authority, prestige
66 **taking off** murder
69 **Shall** they shall
69–70 **my state . . . debate** my state of
    affairs is such that I need to act, not
    argue. For *Stands on me*, see *Ham*
    5.2.63.
5.2.0.1–3 *Alarum . . . exeunt* So F, call-
    ing for a display of French *colours*,
    banners or coats of arms, to match the
    British ones shown in 5.1. Both Q and
    F require actors to '*Enter . . . over the
    stage*', apparently in a processional
    fashion; how they crossed the stage is
    not known – whether, for instance,

they came in by one door and out the
other, or marched round the perimeter,
or did it some other way (see Gurr,
189). The entry may list Lear first as a
matter of precedence, and not mark
any significant difference from Q, but
Cam² thinks his 'strength and defiance
are suggested, not his weakness and
infirmity; regally attired, he may also
carry a sword'. In Q Cordelia holds her
father by the hand, and appears to be
following the French forces; it is not
clear who leads the 'powers of France',
and the SD in Q may be left over from
an earlier draft in which the King of
France led the invasion, as indicated at
4.2.57 (Q); see Appendix 1, p. 393. Edgar
is still in the costume he wore in 4.6.

59 Both? One?] *F;* both one *Q*   65 who] *F;* that *Q*   66 the] *F;* his *Q*   67 intends] *Q (*entends),
F; extends *Q2*

5.2] *F (Scena Secunda); not in Q*   0.1–3 *with . . . exeunt*] *F;* the powers of France ouer the Stage,
Cordelia with her father in her hand. *Q*   0.2 *they pass*] *this edn*   0.4 *in peasant's clothing*] *this edn*

EDGAR

Here, father, take the shadow of this tree
For your good host. Pray that the right may thrive.
If ever I return to you again
I'll bring you comfort.

GLOUCESTER   Grace go with you, sir.   *Exit [Edgar].*

Alarum and retreat ᶠ*within. Enter* EDGAR.ᶠ

EDGAR

Away, old man, give me thy hand, away!   5
King Lear hath lost, he and his daughter ta'en.
Give me thy hand; come on!

GLOUCESTER

No further, sir; a man may rot even here.

EDGAR

What, in ill thoughts again? Men must endure
Their going hence even as their coming hither.   10
Ripeness is all. Come on.

ᶠGLOUCESTER   And that's true too.   *Exeunt.*ᶠ

---

1   **father** See 4.6.72 and n.
    this tree For the tree or 'bush' (Q) one
    of the pillars supporting the canopy
    over the stage at the Globe may have
    served. Property trees were in use, and
    one could have been brought on stage
    for this scene, or painted on a hanging;
    see Gurr, 187–9. Alternatively, the audi-
    ence may have been left to imagine it.

2   **host** as providing shelter

4.1 *Alarum . . . within* The call to arms is
    followed by the signal for a retreat; the
    battle is heard, not seen, and is over
    quickly, with the visual emphasis on
    the blind figure of Gloucester left
    alone on stage. Shakespeare avoids
    showing the battle; the emphasis is to
    be on the fight between Edgar and
    Edmund in the next scene. Some
    directors, however, and Kozintsev in

his film, have chosen to stage more or
less elaborate fighting here; see
Bratton, 197; and Rosenberg, 296.

8   **a man . . . here** See 4.6.33–4 and n.;
    Edgar's attempt there to cure his father
    of despair is not altogether successful.

9–10 **Men . . . hither** The linking of birth
    and death recalls biblical passages
    such as 1 Timothy, 6.7, 'For we
    brought nothing into the world, and it
    is certaine, that wee may cary nought
    out' (Milward, 197–8); Edgar goes fur-
    ther in preaching to his father, for
    endure seems to imply the necessity of
    suffering, and his assumption of the
    moral high ground leaves many read-
    ers uncomfortable. Compare Lear
    preaching to Gloucester at 4.6.174–9.

11 **Ripeness is all** Does this mean we
    must be ready for death (Ardᵉ); or that

---

1   tree] *F;* bush *Q*   4   SD *Exit Edgar] Pope; Exit. Q (after* comfort*), F*   8   further] *Fᶜ;* farther *Q*
11   all. Come] *Roweᵉ;* all come *Q, F*   SD] *F; Exit. Q2; not in Q*

5.3   *Enter* ᶠ*in conquest with drum and colours*ᶠ EDMUND, [*with*]
          LEAR *and* CORDELIA *as prisoners;* ᶠ*soldiers* [*and a*]
          Captain.ᶠ

EDMUND

Some officers take them away – good guard,
Until their greater pleasures first be known
That are to censure them.

CORDELIA   We are not the first

Who with best meaning have incurred the worst.
For thee, oppressed King, I am cast down;   5

providence or the gods control our
existence and determine when the
time is ripe (Cam²); or that we must
await the time of ripeness, 'which is
the time appointed for death'
(Hunter)? If ripeness refers to a time
appointed by the gods, it is outside
human control and there is no way to
anticipate when it will happen. Again,
Edgar's moralizing seems hardly adequate to the nature of the action, and is
undercut by the next scene; and yet the
phrase has great evocative power, and
'the ring of a conclusive cadence'
(Brooke, 49). This power derives in
part from the echo of Ecclesiastes,
3.1–8, beginning 'To all things *there is*
an appointed time' (Geneva Bible), in
part from a long tradition of Stoic and
Christian thinking about endurance
and time, reviewed by Elton, 99–107,
and partly from the shadow behind
this passage of the proverb 'Soon ripe,
soon rotten' (Dent, R133). There may
be a conscious echo of Hamlet's 'The
readiness is all' (*Ham* 5.2.222), but
Hamlet speaks for himself when faced
with the possibility of being killed,
whereas Edgar speaks as if his words
apply to everyone.

11 **And . . . too** In F only, these words
complete the blank verse line with an
ambiguity. They perhaps qualify
Edgar's last utterance by implying it is
no more true than what Gloucester
said at 8. It would then appear that to
Gloucester, who has endured so much,
all moral sayings now sound equally
true; but the phrase could also be taken
in a positive sense to suggest that
Gloucester is finally cured of *ill
thoughts*.

5.3.0.1–3 *Enter . . .* **Captain** The entry
in F is more elaborate than in Q, and
again calls for the *colours* of the British
forces to be displayed.

1   **good guard** guard them carefully
2–3 **greater . . . them** In public, and in
front of Albany's soldiers (see 104),
Edmund defers to the decision of
Albany, Goneril and Regan (*greater*
serving as a transferred epithet apply-
ing to them), who will pronounce sentence on (*censure*) the prisoners. His
private intentions emerge at 27.

3   **censure** pass judgement on
4   **meaning** intentions
5   **oppressed** oppressèd

5.3] *F (Scena Tertia); not in Q*   0.1–3] *F subst.; Enter Edmund, with Lear and Cordelia prisoners. Q*
1+ SP EDMUND] *Bast. Q, F*   2 first] *F;* best *Q*   5 I am] *F;* am I *Q*

Myself could else outfrown false fortune's frown.
Shall we not see these daughters and these sisters?

LEAR

No, no, ⌜no, no⌝. Come, let's away to prison;
We two alone will sing like birds i'the cage.
When thou dost ask me blessing I'll kneel down   10
And ask of thee forgiveness. So we'll live
And pray, and sing, and tell old tales, and laugh
At gilded butterflies, and hear poor rogues
Talk of court news; and we'll talk with them too –
Who loses and who wins, who's in, who's out –   15
And take upon's the mystery of things
As if we were God's spies. And we'll wear out
In a walled prison packs and sects of great ones
That ebb and flow by the moon.

EDMUND [*to soldiers*]   Take them away.

8–26 **No . . . come** In this moving speech, which is deeply ironic in relation to Lear's banishment of her from his sight at 1.1.124–7, Cordelia alone seems to exist for Lear. He insulates himself against reality in a vision that is at once self-centred, absurd, pathetic, and a renunciation of power. As the end approaches, he seems to retreat into himself, no longer conscious of other sufferers, or concerned with justice, or able to feel what wretches feel. At the same time, a number of biblical allusions in his lines, and in a play that is overtly pagan, add a special dimension to what are the last words he speaks to Cordelia while she is alive; see the notes below.

9 **cage** not only a birdcage, but a 'prison for petty malefactors' (*OED sb.* 2, citing Dr Johnson)

10–11 **When . . . forgiveness** recalling 4.7.57–9

13 **gilded butterflies** fashionably vain and ephemeral courtiers (see *OED* Butterfly *sb.* 2), though the literal resonance of *gilded butterflies* enhances the dreamy quality of Lear's speech

16 **take . . . things** claim to understand the 'hidden workings of the world' (Cam², after Ard²); but the word *mystery* in a political context, as here, may have recalled its use in 2 Thessalonians, 2.7, in the well-known phrase 'the mysterie of iniquitie', which is appropriate to the play. See *OED* Mystery *sb.* 1, 5e.

17 **God's spies** spies of the gods or of God? An audience hears *God's*, though neither Q nor F has an apostrophe before 's', and the play nowhere else directly refers to the Christian God. **wear out** outlive

18 **packs and sects** cabals and factions. With *packs*, compare *packings*, 3.1.26.

---

13 hear poor rogues] *Q; heere (poore Rogues) F*   19 by the] *F (by th'), Q2;* bith' *Q*   SD] *Oxf*

LEAR

Upon such sacrifices, my Cordelia,　　　　　　　　　20
The gods themselves throw incense. Have I caught
　thee?　[*Embraces her.*]
He that parts us shall bring a brand from heaven,
And fire us hence like foxes. Wipe thine eyes;
The good ᶠyearsᶠ shall devour them, flesh and fell,
Ere they shall make us weep!　　　　　　　　　　25
We'll see 'em starved first: come.
　　　　　　　　　　ᶠExeuntᶠ [*Lear and Cordelia, guarded*].

EDMUND

Come hither, captain, hark:

---

20 **sacrifices** The word seems to anticipate the human 'sacrifice' of Cordelia
in her death, while referring more
obviously to the sacrifice she has made
in attempting to save her father, and to
the loss of freedom both have suffered.
The idea of doing good as a sacrifice
may echo Hebrews, 13.16, 'To doe good,
and to distribute, forget not, for with
such sacrifice God is well pleased'
(Brockbank, 13; cited by Cam²).

22–3 **He . . . foxes** The idea is that 'no
human power shall ever part us again'
(Kittredge), and the image refers to
smoking foxes out of their holes, as in
Harsnett (Brownlow, 278), 'to fire him
out of his hold, as men smoke a Foxe
out of his burrow'. The word *brand*
also recalls the story of Samson punishing the Philistines in Judges, 15.4–5
by tying firebrands to the tails of foxes,
'And when he had set the brands on
fire, he sent them out into the standing
corne' (Shaheen, 155).

23–5 **Wipe . . . weep** Compare 4.7.71;
Cordelia's tears of pity are for him, not
on account of *them*. Lear's refusal to
weep recalls his stance at 2.2.471–2.

24 **good . . . them** as long as Lear can be
with Cordelia, the years, as he imagines them, will be good. This phrase
may recall biblical comments on the
wicked, who may live many years, but
'cometh into vanity and goeth into
darkness' (Ecclesiastes, 6.3–6), and
echo Genesis, 41.1–36, where Pharaoh
dreams of seven *good years* (35),
followed by seven years of famine; the
word 'devoured' occurs in verse 24.
The term *good years* (F) is often, but I
think mistakenly, interpreted as the
expletive 'goodyear', 'denoting some
undefined malefic power or agency'
(*OED*; so Cam²), and Oxf emends
accordingly; see Taylor in *Division*,
489.
　flesh and fell entirely (*OED* Flesh, *sb.*
1c); *fell* literally = skin

26 **starved** i.e. to death
　SD Oxf supposes the stage cleared
here except for Edmund and the
Captain, but, as Cam² notes, they could
simply talk apart from others, the
soldiers and the drummer, who are
needed for the dead march at the end
of the scene. See Taylor, 'War', 33.

---

21 SD] *Hunter*　24 good years] *F;* good *Q;* goodyear *Oxf*　flesh] *F;* fleach *Q*　26 'em starved] *F*
*(*e'm staru'd*);* vm starue *Q*　SD Exeunt] *Theobald; Exit Q2, F (Exit.); not in Q*
SD *Lear . . . guarded*] *Theobald; all but Edmond and the Captain. Oxf (Blayney)*

Take thou this note. Go, follow them to prison.
One step I have advanced thee. If thou dost
As this instructs thee, thou dost make thy way   30
To noble fortunes. Know thou this, that men
Are as the time is; to be tender-minded
Does not become a sword. Thy great employment
Will not bear question: either say thou'lt do't,
Or thrive by other means.

CAPTAIN   I'll do't, my lord.   35

EDMUND

About it and write 'happy' when thou'st done't.
Mark, I say, instantly; and carry it so
As I have set it down.

ᵠCAPTAIN

I cannot draw a cart, nor eat dried oats.   39
If it be man's work, I'll do't.ᵠ   ᶠ*Exit*.ᶠ

ᶠ*Flourish*.ᶠ *Enter* ALBANY, GONERIL, REGAN [*and*]
soldiers [*with a Trumpeter*].

28 **note** warrant for the death of Lear and
   Cordelia; see 243–4
31 **noble fortunes** great wealth or promotion
31–3 **men . . . sword** often seen as a doctrine of expediency, as by Cam², and
   compare the proverb, 'Times change
   and we with them' (Dent, T343); but,
   as Kittredge noted, Edmund also
   seems to be echoing the exhortation
   of Henry V in his speech before
   Harfleur, *H5* 3.1.1–17, in saying men
   'may be merciful in time of peace, but
   must be savage in war'.
34 **bear question** allow debate
36 **happy** fortunate, prosperous (in the
   reward he will get)

37 **carry it** manage the matter (as if
   Cordelia were to commit suicide, see
   251–3)
39–40 *CAPTAIN . . . do't** Mahood,
   175–6, thinks these lines in Q (not in
   F) depict a 'cynical and reckless
   desperado prepared to go anywhere
   and do anything', and she argues that
   their omission from F, in which the
   Captain merely says, 'I'll do it, my
   lord' (35), shows him pausing to make
   a moral choice, and improves the
   scene; but see 31–3 and n. above.
40.2 The trumpeter is not mentioned
   here in Q or F, but is required later in
   the scene; see 91 and 113–15.

29 One] *Qc, Q2, F*; And *Qu*   36 done't] *F (*dont*)*; don *Q*   40 SD *Exit*] *F (Exit Captaine, opp.*
38)   40.1–2 ALBANY . . . *soldiers*] *F*; *Duke, the two Ladies, and others. Q*   40.2 *with a Trumpeter*]
this edn (Oxf)

ALBANY

Sir, you have showed today your valiant strain
And fortune led you well. You have the captives
Who were the opposites of this day's strife:
I do require them of you, so to use them
As we shall find their merits and our safety   45
May equally determine.

EDMUND   Sir, I thought it fit
To send the old and miserable King
To some retention ^Qand appointed guard,^Q
Whose age had charms in it, whose title more,
To pluck the common bosom on his side,   50
And turn our impressed lances in our eyes
Which do command them. With him I sent the queen,
My reason all the same; and they are ready
Tomorrow, or at further space, t'appear
Where you shall hold your session. ^QAt this time   55
We sweat and bleed; the friend hath lost his friend

---

41 **strain** quality (and, perhaps, lineage, though Edmund is, of course, a bastard)

43 **opposites** opponents

44 **require . . . you** insist on having them from you
use treat

45 **merits** deserts

46 **equally determine** justly decide (what is to be done)

48 **retention** place of detention
*and . . . guard] Qc (see textual notes). The phrase is necessary for the metre, and it is not clear why it was omitted from F, unless F here was set from Qu, or because of some oversight; the problem has been much debated, as by

Taylor, 'Date', 361–2, and Howard-Hill[1], 427–33.

50 **pluck . . . side** draw the sympathy of the common people

51 **turn . . . eyes** turn the weapons of our enlisted soldiers against ourselves (to blind us, as Gloucester was blinded?)
impressed 'imprest' in Q and F; compelled to serve

55 **session** judicial investigation

55–60 ***At . . . place** Edmund has been lying to Albany, and the touch of arrogance in his speeches in the scene, marking the height of his success in the play, surfaces strongly in these lines in Q, though nothing material is lost if they are cut, as in F.

---

41 showed] *Q* , *F;* shewne *Q2*   42 well.] *Q2, F (*well*:); well *Qu;* well, *Qc*   43 Who] *F;* That *Q*
44 I] *F;* We *Q*   them of] *F;* then of *Q*   47 send] *Qc, Q2, F;* saue *Qu*   48 and . . . guard] *Qc, Q2;*
not in Qu, F   49 had] *F;* has *Qu, Qc*   more,] *Qc, Q2, F;* more *Qu*   50 common bosom] *Qc, Q2, F;*
coren bossom *Qu*   on] *F;* of *Q*   55–6 session. At . . . time / We] *Theobald;* session at . . . time,
mee *Qu;* session at . . . time, wee *Qc;* Session at . . . time: we *Q2*

And the best quarrels in the heat are cursed
By those that feel their sharpness.
The question of Cordelia and her father
Requires a fitter place.^Q

ALBANY   Sir, by your patience,   60
I hold you but a subject of this war,
Not as a brother.

REGAN   That's as we list to grace him.
Methinks our pleasure might have been demanded
Ere you had spoke so far. He led our powers,
Bore the commission of my place and person,   65
The which immediacy may well stand up
And call itself your brother.

GONERIL   Not so hot!
In his own grace he doth exalt himself
More than in your addition.

REGAN   In my rights,
By me invested, he compeers the best.   70

ALBANY
That were the most, if he should husband you.

57–8 best . . . sharpness *Quarrels* appears to refer both to the trial of Cordelia and Lear, and to the battle just fought, and I take the sense to be 'best causes (in war and in law) are cursed in the heat of passion by those who feel the hardship and pain (of battle)'. As Hunter notes, Edmund is stalling for time, to ensure that Lear and Cordelia will be executed, while pretending that they will get a fair hearing.

60 by your patience if you will allow me to say so

61 subject of subordinate in

62, 67 brother equal, but with the hint of 'brother-in-law', as at 4.2.15, 4.5.1

62 we list I choose. Regan uses the royal plural to assert her authority over Albany.

65 commission . . . place authority of my high rank or dignity

66 immediacy being next in place to myself

69 *your addition honours you bestow; compare 1.1.137. Q has 'aduancement', which likewise suggests promotion.

70 invested endowed
compeers equals, is the peer of

71 *That . . . most that would be fully realized. This line is given to Goneril in Q, but the change in F, interrupting the exchange between Goneril and Regan, enlivens the situation, and helps to establish Albany as in control.

---

58 sharpness] *Qc, Q2;* sharpes *Qu*   63 might] *F;* should *Q*   66 immediacy] *F;* imediate *Q*
69 addition] *F;* aduancement *Q*   rights] *F;* right *Q*   71 SP] *F; Gon. Q*

REGAN

    Jesters do oft prove prophets.

GONERIL   Holla, holla!

    That eye that told you so looked but asquint.

REGAN

    Lady, I am not well, else I should answer

    From a full-flowing stomach. [*to Edmund*] General,   75

    Take thou my soldiers, prisoners, patrimony;

    ᶠDispose of them, of me, the walls is thine.ᶠ

    Witness the world, that I create thee here

    My lord and master.

GONERIL   Mean you to enjoy him ᵠthenᵠ?

ALBANY

    The let-alone lies not in your good will.   80

EDMUND

    Nor in thine, lord.

ALBANY   Half-blooded fellow, yes.

REGAN [*to Edmund*]

    Let the drum strike and prove my title thine.

---

72 **Jesters . . . prophets** proverbial; Dent, W772

73 **asquint** with a prejudiced eye, or distorted vision. Goneril responds with another proverb, Dent, L498, 'Love, being jealous, makes a good eye look asquint.'

75 **From . . . stomach** in modern idiom, 'from a heart bursting with anger'. The stomach, as often as the heart, was referred to as the seat of the passions (*OED sb.* 6).

77 ***Dispose . . . thine** Regan surrenders all her wealth and herself as if she were a castle taken by storm; the image here in F of a woman's heart as a castle defending itself against attackers had, as Kittredge noted, a long

ancestry, and was popularized by *The Romance of the Rose*; compare *Cym* 2.1.62–3, 'The heavens hold firm / The walls of thy dear honour'. A plural subject with a singular verb is 'extremely common' in F; see Abbott, 333.

80 **let-alone** power to interfere

81 **Half-blooded** as a bastard, and as having only one parent of noble blood (so Cam²); Albany reacts to *thine*

82 *In Q this line is given to Edmund, who boldly issues a challenge to Albany to prove his title 'good'; in F Regan calls on Edmund to establish his right to be her *lord and master*, by accepting any trial. Note also the addition in F at 91; F leads more

---

75 SD] *Hunter*   77 the walls is] *F;* the walls are *F2;* they all are *Hanmer (Theobald);* the whole is *(anon.)*   80 let-alone] *Capell;* let alone *Q , F*   82 SP] *F; Bast. Q*   SD] *Malone*   thine] *F;* good *Q*

ALBANY

Stay yet, hear reason: Edmund, I arrest thee
On capital treason, and in thine attaint
This gilded serpent.   [*Points to Goneril.*]
[*to Regan*]   For your claim, fair sister,   85
I bar it in the interest of my wife:
'Tis she is sub-contracted to this lord
And I her husband contradict your banns:
If you will marry, make your love to me;
My lady is bespoke.

^FGONERIL   An interlude!   90

ALBANY^F

Thou art armed, Gloucester. ^FLet the trumpet sound.^F
If none appear to prove upon thy person
Thy heinous, manifest and many treasons,
There is my pledge.   [*Throws down his gauntlet.*]
                       I'll make it on thy heart,
Ere I taste bread, thou art in nothing less   95

directly to the crucial clash between
Edmund and Edgar. See Appendix 1,
p. 402.

83 **hear reason** hear the reasons for these
quarrels and accusations. As Weis
notes, Albany is making a public statement before proceeding to the challenge and trial by combat.

84 **attaint** condemnation. Attaint or
attainder signified the legal consequences of being condemned for treason, i.e. death and forfeiture of wealth
and honour, as if the blood were, by
false etymology, irretrievably stained.

85 **sister** sister-in-law

86 **bar . . . interest** ironically using the
legal terms for staying a claim in order
to protect someone's rights

87 **sub-contracted** already betrothed;

Shakespeare's coinage (*OED*)

90 **bespoke** already engaged. Albany's
humour in this scene adds a new
dimension to his character, as he sees
the absurdity of his own situation.
  *****GONERIL . . . interlude** An interlude
or farce was originally a comic entertainment staged to fill an interval in a
longer feast or play. F adds Goneril's
interjection here, a conscious dramatic
pointer to a little play within the play.

91 *****Let . . . sound** See 82, 102–15 and n.

92 *****person** so F, replacing 'head' (Q),
probably so as to avoid the clash with
heart, 94

94 *****make it** make the proof. Q has *prove*,
and the change in F avoids the repetition of *prove* in 92.

95 **in nothing** in no particular

84 thine attaint] *Q;* thy arrest *F*   85 SD *Points to Goneril*] *Johnson*   SD *to Regan*] *this edn*   sister]
Q; Sisters *F*   86 bar] *Rowe²;* bare *Q, F*   88 your] *F;* the *Q*   banns] *Q* (banes*)*, *F* (Banes*)*
89 love] *Q;* loues *F*   92 person] *F;* head *Q*   94, 98 SD] *Malone*   94 make] *F;* prove *Q*

Than I have here proclaimed thee.

REGAN   Sick, O, sick!

GONERIL [*aside*]

If not, I'll ne'er trust medicine.

EDMUND

There's my exchange.   [*Throws down his gauntlet.*]
                                        What in the world he is
That names me traitor, villain-like he lies.
Call by the trumpet: he that dares approach,   100
On him, on you – who not? – I will maintain
My truth and honour firmly.

ALBANY   A herald, ho!

                         ᶠ*Enter a* Herald.ᶠ

[*to Edmund*] Trust to thy single virtue, for thy soldiers,
All levied in my name, have in my name
Took their discharge.

REGAN   My sickness grows upon me.   105

ALBANY

She is not well; convey her to my tent.

                                        [*Exit Regan, supported.*]

---

97 ***medicine** drugs, as a poison, or
'cure' for Regan's love-sickness.
Goneril's 'sick' joke is stronger in F; Q
has 'poison'.
98 **What** whoever; see 3.1.15 and n.
100 **Call** summon
102–15.1 ***ALBANY . . . *within* In F
Albany is firmly in charge, calls for the
Herald, and, on the third sound of the
trumpet, Edgar's trumpet is heard
'*within*' before he appears on stage. In
Q Edmund is more dominant, speaks
82, given to Regan in F, takes up the
call for a Herald after Albany (102)
and interrupts the Herald to cry

'Sound!' at 116; for a discussion of the
textual variants here, see Appendix 1,
p. 402.
103–5 **Trust . . . discharge** How and
when the soldiers who entered with
Edmund at 0.2 melt away from him is
not indicated. Possibly they drift away
during the quarrel between Goneril
and Regan, 62–90. Compare *2H4* 4.2,
where Prince John tricks rebels into
discharging their army while keeping
his own intact.
103 **single virtue** unaided strength or
courage

---

97 SD] *Rowe* medicine] *F*; poyson *Q* 98 he is] *Q*; hes *F* 100 the] *F*; thy *Q* 102.1] *F (after
firmly, 102)* 102–15 SDs] *as F; for text in Q, see Appendix 1* 103 SD *to Edmund] Oxf* 105 My]
F; This *Q* 106 SD] *Hunter (Theobald)*

Come hither, herald; let the trumpet sound
And read out this.   ^F*A trumpet sounds.*^F

HERALD (^F*Reads.*^F)   'If any man of quality or degree within
the lists of the army will maintain upon Edmund,   110
supposed Earl of Gloucester, that he is a manifold
traitor, let him appear by the third sound of the
trumpet. He is bold in his defence.'   ^F*First trumpet.*^F

Again!   ^F*Second trumpet.*^F

Again!   ^F*Third trumpet.*^F   115

^F*Trumpet answers within.*^F

Enter EDGAR ^F*armed.*^F

ALBANY

Ask him his purposes, why he appears
Upon this call o'the trumpet.

HERALD   What are you?

Your name, your quality, and why you answer
This present summons?

EDGAR   ^QO^Q know my name is lost,

By treason's tooth bare-gnawn and canker-bit;   120
Yet am I noble as the adversary

---

109 **quality or degree** noble birth or
  high rank
110 **lists** roster
115.1–2 *Trumpet . . . armed* The SD in Q
  requires Edgar to enter at the third
  sound of the trumpet; F maintains sus-
  pense by a delay as an answering trumpet is heard offstage before he comes
  on. Edgar is in yet another
  disguise, but it is not described. Is he
  immediately recognized by the audience? His name is *lost* (119), so he has
  no coat of arms, or identifying marks,
  but Edmund sees a *fair and warlike*
  appearance (140), so Edgar may be in

bright armour (stripped from a dead
knight in Peter Brook's film), and wearing a helmet, but he has been effectively costumed in black, a masked, anonymous figure of nemesis for Edmund, as
in the Granada tele-vision version of
1983; see Rosenberg, 304–5. This formal trial by combat symbolizes a show-
down between the forces of good and
evil in the play, represented as brothers,
recalling Cain and Abel; but see
Introduction, pp. 45–8.
120 **canker-bit** eaten by canker-worms
  or caterpillars (*OED* Canker 4); compare *Ham* 1.3.39–40

109–10 within . . . lists] *F;* in the hoast *Q*   112 by] *F;* at *Q*   118 your] *F;* and *Q*   119–20 lost, /
By . . . tooth] *Theobald;* lost by . . . tooth. *Q;* lost / By Treasons tooth: *F*   121 am . . . as] *F;* are I
mou't / Where is *Q*

I come to cope ^Qwithal^Q.

ALBANY   Which is that adversary?

EDGAR

What's he that speaks for Edmund, Earl of Gloucester?

EDMUND

Himself. What sayst thou to him?

EDGAR   Draw thy sword,

That if my speech offend a noble heart,   125

Thy arm may do thee justice. Here is mine.   [*Draws his sword.*]

Behold: it is the privilege of mine honours,

My oath and my profession. I protest,

Maugre thy strength, youth, place and eminence,

Despite thy victor sword and fire-new fortune,   130

Thy valour and thy heart, thou art a traitor:

False to thy gods, thy brother and thy father,

Conspirant 'gainst this high illustrious prince,

---

122 **cope** encounter in combat

124 **thou . . . thy** The use of the second person pronoun is appropriate for this quarrel between equals, and slides readily into the intimacy of brothers. See Introduction, pp. 7–8.

125–6 **That . . . justice** that if my charges give offence (as being unsound) you may vindicate your true nobility in combat

127–8 ***it . . . profession** It is Edgar's privilege, on account of his noble rank (see *OED* Honour *sb.* 5), and the oath he swore when he made his profession or accepted the principles of knighthood, to draw his sword and challenge his adversary. F, I suspect by some inadvertence, repeats *privilege*, making two inept lines: 'it is my priuiledge, / The priuiledge of mine Honours'. In

place of *honours* Q has 'tongue', which seems unrelated to Edgar's act of drawing his sword.

129 **Maugre** in spite of

place and eminence elevated rank (as at 65) and status

130 **victor sword** so F. *Victor* was often used attributively, more or less as an adjective, as here (so *OED sb.*¹ 2, citing Spenser, *Faerie Queene*, 2.10.23)

fire-new fortune brand-new (as fresh from the forge) success in battle, and promotion as leader of an army. Edgar cannot know of Edmund's questionable *fortune* in love, but the audience does. Edgar's speech depicts Edmund at the very height of his fortunes.

131 **heart** spirit or courage

---

122 Which] *Q, F*; What *Q2*   126 SD] *Hunter*   127 the . . . honours] *Pope;* the priuiledge of my tongue *Q;* my priuiledge, / The priuiledge of mine Honours *F*   honours] *F;* honour *Oxf*
129 Maugre] *F;* Maugure *Q*   youth, place] *Q;* place, youth *F*   130 Despite] *Q (*Despight*);* Despise *F*   victor sword] *F;* victor, sword *Q*   fortune] *F;* fortun'd *Q*   132 thy gods] *Q, F;* the gods *Q2*   133 Conspirant] *F;* Conspicuate *Q*

And from th'extremest upward of thy head
To the descent and dust below thy foot   135
A most toad-spotted traitor. Say thou no,
This sword, this arm and my best spirits are bent
To prove upon thy heart, whereto I speak,
Thou liest.

EDMUND   In wisdom I should ask thy name,
But since thy outside looks so fair and warlike,   140
And that thy tongue some say of breeding breathes,
ᶠWhat safe and nicely I might well delayᶠ
By rule of knighthood, I disdain and spurn.
Back do I toss these treasons to thy head,
With the hell-hated lie o'erwhelm thy heart,   145
Which for they yet glance by and scarcely bruise,
This sword of mine shall give them instant way,

---

134 **extremest upward** very top or crown
136 **toad-spotted** The toad typified everything loathsome, and its spots were thought to be venomous (see *AYL* 2.1.13); in Milton's *Paradise Lost*, 4.800, Satan is found 'squat like a toad' at the ear of Eve.
139–43 **In . . . spurn** Edmund was not obliged to fight with an unknown antagonist, as Goneril says at 150–1. Some have seen here a 'sentimental side' in Edmund, the 'softness that the hard rationalist frequently falls into' (Heilman, 244, and Cam²); but it could just as well be the unbounded confidence of someone flushed with success, who has no doubt of victory.
141–54 *In these lines F changes several words in Q, including *tongue* for 'being' (141), *rule* for 'right' (143), *Back* for 'Heere' (144), *war* for 'armes' (150) and *name* for 'thing' (154); F also inserts a new line, 142. F is generally more precise, and avoids the clumsy

echo of 'being' in *breeding* (141).
141 **some say** some evidence or proof; an aphetic form of 'assay', very common until the seventeenth century
142 ***What . . . delay** This line is not in Q, and may have been accidentally omitted. Stone, 68–9, however, suggests that *By rule*, 143, in Q may be a misprint for 'My rule', and that a reviser added a line to make sense of the passage. Oxf and Cam² incorporate this emendation in their editions of the Q text.
safe and nicely without risk, and scrupulously according to the rules
145 **hell-hated lie** the lie (that I am a traitor) I hate as I do hell
146 **for . . . by** because they as yet pass by scarcely touching me. The earliest meaning of *glance* had to do with a weapon failing to deliver the full effect of a blow, or missing altogether (*OED* v.¹ 1a and b).
147 **give . . . way** give them immediate passage (by opening a way into Edgar's

---

135 below . . . foot] *F;* beneath . . . feet *Q*   137 are] *F;* As *Q*   141 tongue] *F;* being *Q*   some say] *Q;* (some say) *F*   142 delay] *F;* demand *Oxf (Hudson)*   143 rule] *F;* right *Q*   144 Back] *F;* Heere *Q*   these] *F;* those *Q*   145 hell-hated lie] *F;* hell hatedly *Q*   o'erwhelm] *F;* oreturnd *Q*

Where they shall rest for ever. Trumpets, speak.
ᶠ*Alarums. Fight.*ᶠ [*Edmund falls.*]
ALBANY [*to Edgar*]
    Save him, save him!
GONERIL   This is ᵠmereᵠ practice, Gloucester.
By the law of war thou wast not bound to answer   150
An unknown opposite. Thou art not vanquished,
But cozened and beguiled.
ALBANY   Shut your mouth, dame,
Or with this paper shall I stop it.
[*to Edmund*]   ᶠHold, sir,ᶠ
Thou worse than any name, read thine own evil.

---

heart, where the *treasons* will lodge for
ever)
148.1 *Fight F has '*Fights*', the 's'
perhaps being a compositor's error
(compare 4.6.161 and n.); not in Q.
This bare direction does not mean that
the fight is perfunctory; there is a stage
tradition of making it a strenuous and
extended encounter between two
strong adversaries, Edgar winning
with difficulty.
149 **Save . . . him*! most probably a cry
to Edgar to keep Edmund alive so that
he may be questioned. Possibly Albany
could be calling on soldiers to save a
threatened Edgar, which would give
point to Goneril's 'This is practice'.
This interpretation could be reinforced if the emendation by Oxf of the
speech prefix '*Alb.*' (F) to '*All*' were
accepted, but I think it unnecessary.
practice trickery
151 **opposite** antagonist
152 **cozened and beguiled** cheated and
deceived
152–8 **Shut . . . know* The changes
made in F in these lines (see textual
notes) are dramatically significant: in
Q Albany addresses Goneril only, and

she replies to his question, 'Knowst
thou this paper?' The words, *Hold, sir,*
in 153, added in F, are linked by the
comma to the next line, and are
addressed to Edmund, who perhaps
tries to grab the letter Edgar took from
Oswald and gave to Albany (see
4.6.257–65 and 5.1.41). Thus in F
Albany, observed by Goneril, shows
the letter to Edmund, who answers
Albany's question at 158. In Q Goneril
exits at 158, 'Ask me not what I know',
in F she leaves at 157, after 'Who can
arraign me for't?' In F she leaves on a
note of defiance; Q is more ambiguous,
and she could be thought to leave the
stage 'defeated and shamefaced'
(McLeod, 188). Urkowitz, 113, sees
here a 'pattern of delay' developing in
Albany's responses in F, a hesitancy, or
weakness of character, and stresses his
'negative qualities' (126) in opposition
to those, e.g. Leo Kirschbaum in *SS*,
13 (1960), 20–9, who treat Albany as
simply great and good.
153 **Hold, sir,** Stop, sir! The words have
been variously interpreted, as
addressed either to Edgar or to
Edmund, and as meaning 'take,

148 SD *Fight.*] *Hanmer; Fights.* F   *Edmund falls*] *Capell (Hanmer)*   149 SP ALBANY] *Q, F*
(Alb.); ALL. Oxf (Blayney)   SD] *this edn (Hunter)*   150 war] *F;* armes *Q*   wast] *F;* art *Q*
152 Shut] *F;* Stop *Q*   153 stop] *F;* stople *Q*   SD] *Capell*   154 name] *F;* thing *Q*

[*to Goneril*] ^QNay^Q, no tearing, lady; I perceive you
  know it.   155

GONERIL
  Say if I do, the laws are mine, not thine.
  Who can arraign me for't?   *Exit.*

ALBANY   Most monstrous! ^FO!^F

  [*to Edmund*] Knowst thou this paper?

EDMUND   Ask me not what I know.

ALBANY [*to an officer, who follows Goneril*]
  Go after her; she's desperate, govern her.

EDMUND
  What you have charged me with, that have I done,   160
  And more, much more; the time will bring it out.
  'Tis past and so am I. [*to Edgar*] But what art thou
  That hast this fortune on me? If thou'rt noble,
  I do forgive thee.

EDGAR   Let's exchange charity:

---

receive' (Cam²), 'Just a moment!'
(Kittredge) or 'Wait' (Cam¹). Hunter
follows Capell in supposing Albany is
addressing Edgar here, and in effect
says 'Don't kill Edmund', but in F the
comma after 'sir' suggests that these
words and the next line are spoken to
Edmund; see 152–8 and n.

155 **no tearing** Goneril tries to destroy
  the letter, as Albany shows it to
  Edmund.

156–7 **the . . . for't?** Goneril claims that
  as Queen she cannot be indicted,
  because she is above the laws.

158 ***Knowst . . . paper? / EDMUND** In
  Q Goneril replies to Albany's question, though she has already shown she
  knows the letter at 155; F makes much
  better sense.
  Ask . . . know Compare Iago's
  'Demand me nothing', *Oth* 5.2.303;

unlike Iago, Edmund has a change of
heart as he faces death.

159 **govern** restrain or take care of. In Q
  Albany's command follows directly on
  Goneril's exit; in F he speaks to
  Edmund first. The slight delay hardly
  justifies the perception by Urkowitz,
  113, of an emerging 'pattern of delay'
  in Albany.

163 **fortune on** victory over (implying
  also an element of luck)

163–4 **If . . . thee** At the point of death,
  Edmund relapses from the revolutionary ideas of his soliloquy in 1.2 'into
  traditional conceptions of nobility and
  breeding' (Hunter).

164 **Let's exchange charity** There is little charity in Edgar's next lines; but
  the alternation in him of moral stern-
  ness in relation to his father's sin and
  compassion for him as a suffering man

---

155 SD] *Oxf* 157 can] *F*; shal *Q*   SD *Exit*] *as F*; *opp. 158 Q* (*Exit Gonorill.*)   158 SD] *Hunter*
SP EDMUND] *F (Bast.)*; *Gon. Q*   159 SD] *Capell subst.*   162 SD] *Hudson*   163 thou'rt] *F*; thou
bee'st *Q*

I am no less in blood than thou art, Edmund;   165
If more, the more thou'st wronged me.
My name is Edgar and thy father's son.
The gods are just and of our pleasant vices
Make instruments to plague us:
The dark and vicious place where thee he got   170
Cost him his eyes.

EDMUND   Thou'st spoken ^Fright, 'tis^F true;
The wheel is come full circle, I am here.

ALBANY [*to Edgar*]
Methought thy very gait did prophesy
A royal nobleness. I must embrace thee.
Let sorrow split my heart if ever I   175
Did hate thee or thy father.

EDGAR   Worthy prince, I know't.

ALBANY
Where have you hid yourself?
How have you known the miseries of your father?

---

may be seen as his attempt to find moral coherence in what has happened to Gloucester; see 168–9, 181 and notes.

166 **If more** as legitimate, while Edmund is *half-blooded* (81)

167 **My . . . Edgar** Edgar reveals himself to Edmund and Albany by removing some part of his disguise, a mask or a helmet (so Oxf)

168–9 ***The . . . us** a biblical commonplace, as at Wisdom (Apocrypha, always included in early Bibles), 11.16, 'wherewithall a man sinneth, by the same also shall hee be punished' (Noble, 232; Milward, 200). Edgar's moralizing applies to Edmund and to Goneril and Regan, as for all of these the wheel comes full circle in this scene. Q oddly has 'vertues', which makes no sense, for *vices*, and 'scourge' for *plague*.

170 **got** begot

172 **The . . . circle** both in the larger sense of appropriate punishment for sins, and invoking the traditional idea of the wheel of fortune, which, ironically, Edmund had initially scorned. His own words at 1.2.118–26 about attributing to fortune 'the surfeits of our own behaviour' now come home to him.

173 **gait** bearing

174 **royal** used loosely to mean dignified, but perhaps anticipating Albany's invitation to Edgar, Lear's godson (2.1.91), to share the rule of the realm at 318–19

---

165 art,] *F4;* art *Q, F*   168 vices] *F;* vertues *Q*   169 plague] *F;* scourge *Q*   171 true] *F;* truth *Q*
172 circle] *F;* circled *Q*   173 SD] *Hanmer*   gait] *Johnson;* gate *Q, F*   175–6 ever I / Did] *F;* I
did euer *Q*

EDGAR

By nursing them, my lord. List a brief tale,　　　　　180
And when 'tis told, O, that my heart would burst!
The bloody proclamation to escape
That followed me so near – O, our lives' sweetness,
That we the pain of death would hourly die
Rather than die at once! – taught me to shift　　　185
Into a madman's rags, t'assume a semblance
That very dogs disdained; and in this habit
Met I my father with his bleeding rings,
Their precious stones new lost; became his guide,
Led him, begged for him, saved him from despair,　190
Never – O fault! – revealed myself unto him

180 **List** hear, listen to
181 **O . . . burst!** Edgar here takes on the function of a messenger, as Hunter notes, and his initial rhetorical flourish energizes his narrative. If he means that he would wish to die, he might seem to repudiate all that he did to persuade his father to stay alive; see, for example, 4.6.72–80. His compassion here also seems unrelated to his oddly objective moral condemnation of his father's sin at 168–71, in what are almost his first words to Edmund. It is odd that he begins a speech wishing his own heart would burst, and ends it describing how his father's heart did burst (195–8). See Rosenberg, 306–8, for a discussion of Edgar's inconsistencies, and Introduction, pp. 46–8.
182 **bloody proclamation** sentence of death proclaimed by Gloucester at 2.2.172 (so Weis)
184–5 *****That . . . once!** that we choose to stay alive, even if we have to endure every hour anguish like that of dying. Gloucester wanted to *die at once* rather than endure suffering, and it was Edgar who kept him alive in 4.6. Weis

defends 'with' (Q) in preference to *we* (F) as making the whole sentence an apostrophe to *lives' sweetness*, but the meaning is much the same, and F seems to me both clearer and more dramatic.
185 **shift** change clothes (*OED v.* 9)
187 **habit** clothing
188–9 **rings . . . stones** sockets . . . eyeballs
190 **despair** the denial or loss of faith in God, and so the ultimate sin in Christian (Catholic) terms. In this pagan play Edgar seeks to save his father from a Christian sin; see 4.6.34–40, 62–4 and nn. Shakespeare was also well aware of the Stoic defence of suicide in the Senecan tradition of accepting it as a proof of having the ultimate power over oneself, (killing oneself, as Cleopatra puts it, *Ant* 4.15.87, in the 'high Roman fashion'), and the two attitudes overlap disturbingly in *King Lear*, a play in which it is hard to believe finally that, if the gods exist, they have any interest in human affairs; see Introduction, pp. 32–3.
191 *****Never . . . him** It was necessary for

184 we] *F;* with *Q*　189 Their] *F;* The *Q*　191 fault] *F;* Father *Q*

Until some half-hour past, when I was armed,
Not sure, though hoping of this good success.
I asked his blessing and from first to last
Told him our pilgrimage. But his flawed heart,   195
Alack, too weak the conflict to support,
'Twixt two extremes of passion, joy and grief,
Burst smilingly.

EDMUND   This speech of yours hath moved me,
And shall perchance do good; but speak you on,
You look as you had something more to say.   200

ALBANY

If there be more, more woeful, hold it in,
For I am almost ready to dissolve
Hearing of this.

ᵠEDGAR   This would have seemed a period
To such as love not sorrow, but another

---

the structure of the play that Edgar should maintain his anonymity, but the *fault* he acknowledges here is part of his character too, for it is appropriate that he should be morally perceptive about himself, as well as about others, as at 164–71. If Gloucester dies with a glimpse of happiness (see 197 and n.), Edgar nevertheless reveals himself at a time and in a way that brings about his father's death. Q has the neutral 'O Father' instead of 'O fault!'

193 **good success** fortunate outcome

195 **pilgrimage** course of life, all that had happened. The word is used in this neutral sense by Othello in reference to the story he tells Desdemona, *Oth* 1.3.155; see also 190 and n.
flawed cracked

197 **joy and grief** joy at knowing Edgar to be alive, and grief for what he has suffered; also, a kind of happiness in dying at such a moment, and grief for the pain he has caused. Compare the death of Lear, 309–10 and n.

198–9 **moved . . . good** See 163–4 and n.

202 **dissolve** faint, or melt in tears

203–20 *****EDGAR . . . slave** F omits these eighteen descriptive lines, which are unnecessary dramatically, and something of an anticlimax following on Edgar's account of the death of his father. Weis thinks the lines necessary to explain Edgar's recognition of Kent at 228, but it seems more likely that Kent has there shed his disguise and appears in court dress as in 1.1. The omission speeds the action, and shortens the interval between Edmund's talk of doing good and his doing it at 241–3; it also further diminishes the role of Kent, who in Q can be seen either 'as spokesman for deep human feeling' (Warren, 'Kent', 67, and see 4.7.85–97 and n.), or as channelling our sympathies in a coercive way (Foakes, 108). See Introduction, p. 143.

203 **period** limit or extreme point (of sorrow)

204–6 **another . . . extremity** Edgar

195 our] *F;* my *Q*

To amplify too much would make much more   205
And top extremity.
Whilst I was big in clamour, came there in a man
Who, having seen me in my worst estate,
Shunned my abhorred society, but then finding
Who 'twas that so endured, with his strong arms,   210
He fastened on my neck and bellowed out
As he'd burst heaven, threw him on my father,
Told the most piteous tale of Lear and him
That ever ear received, which in recounting
His grief grew puissant and the strings of life   215
Began to crack. Twice then the trumpets sounded
And there I left him tranced.

ALBANY   But who was this?

EDGAR

Kent, sir, the banished Kent, who in disguise
Followed his enemy king and did him service
Improper for a slave.^Q   220

Enter a Gentleman ^Q*with a bloody knife.*^Q

GENTLEMAN
Help, help, ^FO, help!^F

EDGAR   What kind of help?

^FALBANY   Speak, man.

elaborated his account of his father,
and he now says that to enlarge or spin
out another tale of sorrow (Kent's)
would generate much more distress,
and go beyond what can be endured.
He amplifies the story nevertheless.
207 big in clamour loud in lamentation
208 estate condition
209–10 finding . . . endured Edgar
revealed who he was, and that he had
endured as Poor Tom.
212 As as if (Abbott, 107)

threw . . . father threw himself on the
dead body of Gloucester
214 which in recounting in recounting
which
215 puissant overpowering
strings heart-strings.   Kittredge
compares *KJ* 5.7.55, 'My heart hath
one poor string to stay it by'.
217 tranced stupefied, lost in grief
219 enemy See 1.1.176–9.
220 Improper unfitting
221–2 *GENTLEMAN . . . knife? See tex-

212 him] *Theobald;* me *Q*   213 Told . . . most] *Q;* And told the *Q2*   216 crack. Twice] *Theobald;*
cracke twice, *Q*   220.1 *a* Gentleman] *F;* one *Q*   221 SP EDGAR] *F; Alb. Q*

EDGAR^F

What means this bloody knife?

GENTLEMAN 'Tis hot, it smokes,

It came even from the heart of – ^FO, she's dead!^F

ALBANY Who ^Fdead^F? Speak, man.

GENTLEMAN

Your lady, sir, your lady; and her sister 225
By her is poisoned; she confesses it.

EDMUND

I was contracted to them both; all three
Now marry in an instant.

EDGAR Here comes Kent.

Enter KENT.

ALBANY

Produce the bodies, be they alive or dead.
Goneril's and Regan's bodies brought out.

---

tual note: in Q Albany alone interrogates the Gentleman, whereas in F one
phrase of his, 'What kind of help?', is
given to Edgar, who also speaks the
question in 222. Cam², following
Warren ('Albany', 101, 105), sees
Edgar as beginning to take over
'responsibility for events'. The text
does not seem to me to justify such an
interpretation, but this slight strengthening of Edgar's role in F is no doubt
connected with the assignment of the
final speech in the play to him. See 322
and n.

222 **smokes** steams; a common usage

223 **O, she's dead!** In Q the Gentleman
breaks off at *heart of*, unable to speak.
F's addition has point: does everyone
at first suppose he means Cordelia?

228 **marry** See 4.6.194 and n.; the hint
of sexual consummation provides a
bitter irony.

228.1 *In F tension is maintained as Kent
enters unregarded by Albany; in Q
Edgar announces him in the middle of
Albany's speech at 231, and Albany at
once responds, 'O, tis he'; see textual
notes. Kent, I take it, is no longer in
disguise, but is costumed as in the
opening scene, according to his
promise at 4.7.10–11; but see 203–20
and n.

229 *Produce the bodies It is unusual
for bodies to be brought on stage (produced); the concern more commonly
is to get them off, as Edmund is carried
out at 254. Here Shakespeare wanted
to have all three of Lear's daughters

---

222 this] *F; that Q* 'Tis] *F; Its Q* 224 dead? Speak, man.] *F; man, speake? Q* 226 confesses]
F; hath confest Q 228 EDGAR . . . Kent] *F; Edg. . . . Kent sir. Q (opp. pity, 231)* 228.1] *F; after
allow, 232 Q* 229 the] *F; their Q* 229.1] *F; The bodies of Gonerill and Regan are brought in. Q
(opp. Kent?, 237)*

This judgement of the heavens that makes us tremble 230
Touches us not with pity – O, is this he?
The time will not allow the compliment
Which very manners urges.

KENT   I am come
To bid my King and master aye good night.
Is he not here?

ALBANY   Great thing of us forgot! 235
Speak, Edmund, where's the King? And where's
    Cordelia?
Seest thou this object, Kent?

KENT   Alack, why thus?

EDMUND

Yet Edmund was beloved:
The one the other poisoned for my sake,
And after slew herself.

ALBANY   Even so; cover their faces. 240

---

dead on stage in this final scene, in order to recall and to contrast with the opening scene; see 254.1 and n. In Q the SD calling for bodies to be brought on stage follows 'Kent?' at 237, but Albany's 'This judgement . . .' (230) becomes stronger if he can point to them. In F the bodies are '*brought out*', in Q '*brought in*', both phrases meaning 'brought on stage'.

232 **compliment** ceremonious greeting
233 **very manners** common courtesy (let alone personal motives)
234 **aye** for ever
235 **Great . . . forgot!** I have heard members of an audience titter with nervous laughter on this line, perhaps because so much action involving fights and murders has taken place in the two hundred lines since Lear left the stage that indeed his unfinished business has

been forgotten. It is understandable that for Albany the death of his wife and Regan, and their bodies on stage, the horrible *object* or spectacle that confronts him, absorbs his immediate attention. His reaction, it seems to me, hardly justifies the claim that he 'reveals an inability from here on to take effective and timely action' (Cam²). See 221–2 and n.

237 **object** spectacle (of the dying Edmund and the bodies of Goneril and Regan)
238 **Yet . . . beloved** Ard² suggests these words provide a motive, namely that he felt unloved by others, for Edmund's whole course of action.
240 **Even so** Albany's words may mark a pause as he looks at the bodies; the phrase extends the line into a hexameter.

---

230 judgement] *F*; Iustice *Q*   tremble] *Q* *(tremble,)*; tremble. *F*   231 is this] *F*; tis *Q*   233
Which] *F*; that *Q*   235+ SP ALBANY] *F*; *Duke Q*

EDMUND

I pant for life. Some good I mean to do,
Despite of mine own nature. Quickly send –
Be brief in it – to the castle, for my writ
Is on the life of Lear and on Cordelia;
Nay, send in time.

ALBANY   Run, run, O run.   245

EDGAR

To who, my lord? Who has the office? [*to Edmund*]
    Send
Thy token of reprieve.

EDMUND

Well thought on, take my sword; ᵠthe captain,ᵠ
Give it the captain.

EDGAR [*to Gentleman*]   Haste thee for thy life.

[*Exit Gentleman.*]

EDMUND

He hath commission from thy wife and me   250
To hang Cordelia in the prison and
To lay the blame upon her own despair,
That she fordid herself.

---

242 **Despite . . . nature** See 163–4 and n.
243 **writ . . . life** formal warrant for the execution; *writ* is the proper legal term
248 ***the captain** F follows Q2 in omitting these words; as Cam² notes, Edmund's 'gasping repetition' is dramatically effective.
249 SP ***EDGAR** Albany in Q (see textual note): there are no stage directions here in Q or in F, but in Q it seems that Edmund gives Edgar his sword, and that Albany addresses *Haste thee* to Edgar, who rushes off to try to save Lear and Cordelia, and returns with them; Duthie, 191, and Sisson, 424,

think this is how it should be played. In F Edmund's sword is received by an attendant, or an officer; Edgar remains on stage, and urges him to hasten to save Lear. F here again strengthens Edgar's role, making him a little more authoritative; see 221–2 and n.
253 **fordid** killed; compare Kent's report of the deaths of Goneril and Regan at 289–90 (so Hunter). Shakespeare may have got the idea of suicide from Spenser's *Faerie Queene*, 2.10.32, in which Cordelia is said to have hanged herself after being long imprisoned; see 272.

---

242 mine] *F*; my *Q*   246 has] *F*; hath *Q*   SD] *this edn*   248 the captain] *Q*; *not in Q2, F*
249 SP EDGAR] *F*; *Duke Q*   SD *to Gentleman*] *this edn*   SD *Exit Gentleman*] *Oxf*; *Exit Messenger. / Theobald; Exit Edgar. / Malone*

ALBANY

The gods defend her. Bear him hence awhile.
[*Edmund is carried off.*]

Enter LEAR *with* CORDELIA *in his arms* [*followed by the* Gentleman].

LEAR

Howl, howl, howl, ᵓhowlᵓ! O, you are men of stones!   255
Had I your tongues and eyes, I'd use them so
That heaven's vault should crack: she's gone for ever.
I know when one is dead and when one lives;
She's dead as earth.   [*He lays her down.*]
            Lend me a looking-glass;

---

254 **Bear . . . awhile** Edmund is carried off so that the final tableau will group Lear with his three daughters, all dead; see 229 and n. If Edmund was taken out at one door with the audience watching him, Lear's entry at another door with his great cry *Howl* may have been especially shocking.

254.1 **with . . . arms** Many editors have repeated Rowe in adding the word '*dead*', but all that follows depends upon a measure of uncertainty, both in Lear and in the audience, who may hope against hope until the very end that Cordelia will revive; Lear thinks she is alive for the moment at 263. Honigmann², 91, suggests that Cordelia 'returns to consciousness and then dies . . . the final twist of the knife is that she is unable to speak'; but would an audience spot this? Others have seen here a kind of 'secular *pietà*', or echo of the Virgin Mary holding the dead body of Christ, which suggests one way in which the image exerts its force (see Introduction, pp. 31–2, 35), but the pathos of the scene depends upon its ambiguity. Actors have managed this difficult entry in various ways; a frail old Lear on the point of death himself has to carry a sometimes heavy actress on stage, usually laying her down on the stage, or on a litter, to utter his first words as a cry of anguish; see Bratton, 209; Rosenberg, 311–12.

255 **Howl . . . howl!** These words may represent an extended cry of anguish, or, if the verb is imperative, could be a last command that others howl out their grief. Lear's entry here marks a cessation of the busy activity of the preceding lines, and abruptly establishes a most affecting tableau, with all eyes fixed on him and Cordelia.

255 **men of stones** like statues, silent and unresponsive; compare *R3* 3.7.25

256–7 **tongues . . . crack** tongues for clamour, and eyes for weeping, recalling the raging thunder and drenching rain of the storm in 3.2

259 **Lend . . . looking-glass** Evidently Lear has by now laid Cordelia down, and has his hands free. The stage business in these lines has been variously

---

254 SD *Edmund . . . off*] *Theobald*   254.1 CORDELIA] *Q, F; Cordelia dead / Rowe   arms.*] *Q, F; arms, Edgar, Officer and others / Malone*   254.1–2 *followed . . . Gentleman*] *Oxf*   255 you] *Q; your F* 256 I'd] *F (I'I'd); I would Q*   259 SD] *Oxf*

If that her breath will mist or stain the stone,   260
Why then she lives.

KENT   Is this the promised end?

EDGAR

Or image of that horror?

ALBANY   Fall, and cease.

LEAR

This feather stirs, she lives: if it be so,
It is a chance which does redeem all sorrows
That ever I have felt.

KENT   O, my good master!   265

LEAR

Prithee, away!

EDGAR   'Tis noble Kent, your friend.

LEAR

A plague upon you murderers, traitors all;

interpreted, according to the fragility of Lear, and whether the actor suggests a wholly sane figure, or someone who is again losing his wits; there are no stage directions in Q or F. He may be given a mirror by someone, or imagine it, or forget at once what he has said, and many actors prefer to emphasize the feather at 263. For discussion of the problems of staging here, see Meagher, 248–57 (he suggests that a mirror may have been to hand, attached to Goneril's costume), and Rosenberg, 314. Allan R. Shickman, in *ELR*, 21 (1991), 85–6, less convincingly associates this mirror with the Fool; see 1.4.137–48n. Steevens noted the echo of this passage in Webster's *White Devil* (1612), 5.2.38–40, where Cornelia hopes to revive the dead Marcellus: 'fetch a looking-glass, see if his breath will not stain it; or pull some feathers from my pillow, and lay them to his lips'.

260 **stone** specular or semi-transparent

stone, such as mica, used as a mirror (*OED* Specular *a.* 1)

261 **promised end** Kent may refer to Lear's hope that he might 'Unburdened crawl toward death' (1.1.40, F), or his own anticipated death (see 234), but Edgar interprets the words for us as signifying the 'great doom's image' (*Mac* 2.3.78), the end of the world, or the last judgement, as foretold by Christ in Matthew, 24, Mark, 13, and Luke, 21. See Introduction, pp. 73–5.

262 **Fall, and cease** in general terms, 'Let everything come to ruin, and cease to be', but the immediate thought may be a wish to release Lear from the anguish of his grief

263 **feather** Actors have found feathers in their own costume, or in the attire of others on stage, or they have plucked a hair from their own or another's head, or they have imagined the feather; see 259 and n.

267 **you murderers** so F (Q has 'your murderous'). Lear seems to denounce

263 stirs, she lives:] *F;* stirs she lives, *Q;* stirs; she lives! *Capell*   265 O] *F;* A *Q*   267 you murderers] *F;* your murderous *Q;* you murdrous *Q2*

I might have saved her; now she's gone for ever.
Cordelia, Cordelia, stay a little. Ha?
What is't thou sayst? Her voice was ever soft,   270
Gentle and low, an excellent thing in woman.
I killed the slave that was a-hanging thee.

GENTLEMAN
'Tis true, my lords, he did.

LEAR   Did I not, fellow?
I have seen the day, with my good biting falchion
I would have made him skip. I am old now   275
And these same crosses spoil me. [*to Kent*] Who are
    you?
Mine eyes are not o'the best, I'll tell you straight.

KENT
If Fortune brag of two she loved and hated,
One of them we behold.

LEAR
ᶠThis is a dull sight:ᶠ are you not Kent?

everyone as if all are to blame for Cordelia's death.

269 **stay a little** Now she is *gone for ever*, he wants her to stay for him, in moving contrast to his dismissal of her at 1.1.265–6 with the words 'nor shall ever see / That face of hers again'.

272 so much for the *noble fortunes* the Captain was promised by Edmund at 31 (Hunter). Cordelia hangs herself in Spenser's version of the story; see 253 and n.

274 **falchion** curved broadsword

275 ***him** F, suggesting that Lear, as so often in this sequence, doesn't quite grasp what has been said. Many editors prefer Q's 'them', which Cam² thinks makes 'better sense'.

276 **crosses spoil me** troubles ruin me. Lear's sequence of thought is inconse-

quential: he refers generally to all his afflictions, and it is not merely as a swordsman (so Ard², Cam²) that he is 'spoiled', though *crosses* could refer to the art of parrying in swordplay; see James L. Jackson's note in *SQ*, 31 (1980), 387–90.

277 **Mine . . . best** Hoeniger, 96, shows that failing eyesight was regarded medically as a symptom of approaching death (so Cam²).
straight at once; compare 285

278–9 **If . . . behold** If Fortune boasts of two people she (most) loved or (most) hated, then we see that Lear is the latter (most unfortunate of all). With this allusion to fortune, compare 163, 172 above, and Lear's image of himself as the 'natural fool of fortune', 4.6.187.

280 ***This . . . sight** These words, only in

271 woman] *F;* women *Q*   273 SP GENTLEMAN] *F (Gent.); Cap. Q*   274 have] *Q, F;* ha *Q2*
with my good] *Q, F;* that with my *Q2*   275 him] *F;* them *Q*   276 SD] *Oxf*   277 not o'the] *Q,
F;* none o'th *Q2*   278 brag] *F;* bragd *Q*   and] *F;* or *Q*   280 you not] *F;* not you *Q*

KENT   The same;   280
   Your servant Kent; where is your servant Caius?

LEAR
   He's a good fellow, I can tell ᶠyouᶠ that;
   He'll strike and quickly too. He's dead and rotten.

KENT
   No, my good lord, I am the very man –

LEAR   I'll see that straight.   285

KENT
   That from your first of difference and decay
   Have followed your sad steps –

LEAR   You're welcome hither.

KENT
   Nor no man else. All's cheerless, dark and deadly;
   Your eldest daughters have fordone themselves
   And desperately are dead.

LEAR   Ay, so I think.   290

ALBANY
   He knows not what he says and vain is it

F, emphasize Lear's failing sight, and accentuate the pathos in his inability fully to acknowledge the presence of his most faithful follower. But the *dull sight* could possibly be the body of Cordelia; the implications are considered in Booth, 30–1.

281 **Caius** This is the only mention of Kent's name when disguised. It was a common name in ancient Rome, occurs in all of Shakespeare's Roman plays except *AC*, and is given to Dr Caius, a French physician in *MW*.

285 **see that straight** look into that right away. Lear resists being distracted from Cordelia. His *welcome* of Kent at 287 is equally casual, as Cam² notes.

286 ***your . . . decay** the start of the

change and decline (in you and your fortunes). Instead of F's 'first' Q has 'life', which makes good sense too.

288 **Nor . . . else** completing 'I am the very man – and no one else', but also responding to Lear's *welcome*, the negatives implying 'I'm not welcome, nor is anyone else' (so Hunter)

289 **fordone** killed; see 253 and n. Q has 'foredoome', probably a misreading. Goneril in fact poisoned Regan (out of jealousy, to deny her the freedom to marry Edmund?) before killing herself.

290 **desperately** in despair

291 ***says** Hunter prints 'sees', from Q, arguing that 'Lear's *sight*, rather than his utterance, has become imperfect'; but 'saies' points up the incoherence of

---

284 man –] *Pope;* man. *Q, F*   286 first] *F;* life *Q*   287 You're] *Q (*You'r*);* Your are *F*   289 fordone] *F (*fore-done*);* foredoome *Q;* fore-doom'd *Q2*   290 Ay . . . think] *F;* So thinke I to *Q;* So I thinke too *Q2*   291+ SP ALBANY] *F;* Duke *Q*   291 says . . . is it] *F;* sees . . . it is *Q*

That we present us to him.

Enter a Messenger.

EDGAR   Very bootless.
MESSENGER [*to Albany*]   Edmund is dead, my lord.
ALBANY
   That's but a trifle here.
   You lords and noble friends, know our intent: 295
   What comfort to this ᶠgreatᶠ decay may come
   Shall be applied. For us, we will resign
   During the life of this old majesty
   To him our absolute power;
   [*to Edgar and Kent*]   you to your rights,
   With boot and such addition as your honours   300
   Have more than merited. All friends shall taste
   The wages of their virtue and all foes
   The cup of their deservings. O, see, see!

Lear's words, and inattention to what
others are saying, for he appears to
sink into a kind of trance here. See 303
and n. *OED* lists 'seis' or 'ses' as possible variant spellings of 'says' (*v.*¹ 2d),
and 'sees' (*TNK* 2.3.51) has generally
been emended to 'says', as demanded
by the context.

292 **us** ourselves; but passing in Albany's
next speech into the royal plural, as he
is now head of state

292 **bootless** useless

295 **intent** Compare 1.1.36–40; as Lear
began with a *fast intent* to retire, so
now Albany expresses his intent to do
the same; the wheel has come full circle in this way too (Cam¹).

296 **great . . . come** it is possible to bring
to Lear. Although Albany, like Kent at
286, is conscious of the dissolution of
Lear, he still seeks to return power to

him; see Introduction, p. 22.

299 **you to** i.e. as for you, I intend you to
have. In expressing his *intent*, 295,
Albany speaks first for himself (*For
us*), then for Edgar and Kent.

300 **With . . . addition** with advantage
(*boot*) and such distinctions as your
honourable deeds (in battle) have more
than deserved. For *addition*, see
1.1.137.

301–3 **All . . . deservings** These lines,
promising a restoration of order,
would appropriately round off a more
conventional ending, and have often
been compared, as by Cam², to the final
speech by Malcolm in *Mac*. Here the
presence of the dead Cordelia renders
almost absurd the idea of virtue
rewarded.

303 **O, see, see!** Lear draws attention by
some movement, roused out of the

292 SD] *F; Enter Captaine. Q*   293 SP MESSENGER] *F (Mess.); Capt. Q*   SD] *Oxf*   299 SD]
Malone; To Edg. / Rowe   300 honours] *F; honor Q*

389

LEAR

And my poor fool is hanged. No, no, ᶠno**ᶠ** life!
Why should a dog, a horse, a rat have life					305
And thou no breath at all? ᵠOᵠ thou'lt come no more,
Never, never, never, ᶠnever, never.**ᶠ**
[*to Edgar?*] Pray you undo this button. Thank you, sir.
ᵠO, o, o, o.ᵠ
ᶠDo you see this? Look on her: look, her lips,
Look there, look there!		*He dies.***ᶠ**

absorption with Cordelia, or trance-like condition he seems to have fallen into at 290; actors have rocked Cordelia, mumbled over her, or even moved aimlessly about the stage (see Rosenberg, 317), but always out of touch, until this moment, when Lear speaks in mid-sentence, as if bringing to consciousness a continuing train of thought.

304 **fool** a term of endearment, referring to Cordelia, who has been hanged; but also recalling Lear's other favourite, the Fool, not heard of since he left the stage at the end of 3.6. The double reference, making us suppose the Fool dead too, gives a special poignancy to these six short words, which penetrate to the very heart of loss. Many have speculated that the parts of Cordelia and the Fool were doubled, since they never appear on stage together (see, for example, Booth, 32–3 and 129), but there is strong evidence that Robert Armin, a mature adult actor, played the Fool, while Cordelia would have been played by a boy; see Wiles, 144–5, 155, and Introduction, pp. 50–1.

307 **Never . . . never** perhaps the most extraordinary blank verse line in English poetry; the relentlessness of *no*, repeated five times in the preceding lines, is now matched by the repetition of *never*, making what follows the more startling. The line also recalls the

repetition of *nothing* in the opening scene; see Introduction, p. 78.

308 **Pray . . . button** Lear is usually taken as referring to a button on his own robes or doublet, echoing *come, unbutton here* at 3.4.107, and as having a last attack of the *mother* (see 2.2.246). It could also conceivably be a button on Cordelia's costume (some women wore bodices that buttoned at the front, a style of dress favoured by Queen Anne), or an imaginary button. We do not know how Cordelia was dressed in this scene; it is possible that she was in male attire, if she had been fighting with her army. To whom is Lear speaking? Oxf, following the suggestion of Warren, 'Kent', 71, adds the SD '*To Kent*', but it is Edgar who is close to Lear, notices that he faints and tries to revive him, and Edgar whose role is enlarged in the final scene, so it is likely that he responds here; see 249 and n. It is also possible to have an attendant help Lear, if a director wishes to maximize the sense of Lear's new-found humility and make the most of a king addressing a menial as 'sir'.

309–10 *****Do . . . there!** These lines, added in F, made it possible for Bradley, 291, to argue that Lear dies in joy, believing Cordelia to be breathing and alive. If Lear does think so, he is deluded, or perhaps delirious, and

305 have] *Q2, F;* of *Q*   306 thou'lt] *F;* thou wilt *Q*   308 SD] *this edn; to Kent / Oxf   sir.*] *F;* sir, O,o,o,o. *Q;* O,o,o,o,o. *Q2*   309 look, her lips] *Johnson;* Looke her lips *F;* looke on her lips *F2*

EDGAR   He faints: my lord, my lord!   310

KENT

Break, heart, I prithee break.

EDGAR   Look up, my lord.

KENT

Vex not his ghost; O, let him pass. He hates him
That would upon the rack of this tough world
Stretch him out longer.

EDGAR   ^QO^Q he is gone indeed.

KENT

The wonder is he hath endured so long;   315
He but usurped his life.

ALBANY

Bear them from hence. Our present business
Is ^Qto^Q general woe. [*to Edgar and Kent*] Friends of my
    soul, you twain,
Rule in this realm and the gored state sustain.

---

others have insisted that the ending is
painful, and there is nothing here to
indicate 'a transition from grief to joy'
(J. K. Walton, 'Lear's last speech', *SS*,
13 (1960), 17; see also Peat, 44–6, and
Clayton, 135). It is impossible to say
what Lear sees, or thinks he sees, but
these lines complicate the ending by
their very ambiguity. Lear's death is at
once painful and a welcome release, for
who, as Kent says, would wish this
decayed old figure to live longer with
such grief, when, even if he is deluded,
he dies with all his attention focused
on Cordelia, not any longer on
himself. See Introduction, p. 78. Q has
'O,o,o,o', a conventional representation of a dying groan, which has often,
unnecessarily, been taken as an actor's
interpolation.

310 SD   F only; Q has no direction for
    the death of Lear
311 **Break . . . break** given to Lear in

Q, where he returns to dwelling on his
own misery. Kent may refer to both
Lear and himself.
312 **ghost** soul or departing spirit
313 ***rack** instrument of torture. The
    word is spelled 'wracke' in Q and F,
    meaning 'ruin', which also applies to
    the destruction brought about in
    Lear's *tough world*.
316 **usurped** stole or clung on to (beyond
    the natural term); compare 4.2.28
317 **Bear . . . hence** perhaps best regard-
    ed as a signal within the text for the
    soldiers and attendants in the scene to
    begin to take up the bodies of Goneril
    and Regan (which could have been
    brought in on stretchers at 229), Lear
    and Cordelia, in preparation for a pro-
    cessional ending with a '*dead march*'
    (F)
319 **Rule** Is Albany restoring Edgar and
    Kent to their titles and power as nobles
    so that they can *sustain* order in the

---

311 SP KENT] *F; Lear. Q*   313 rack] *Q , F (*wracke*)*   318 SD] *Johnson*   319 realm] *F;* kingdome *Q*

KENT

I have a journey, sir, shortly to go;   320
My master calls me, I must not say no.

EDGAR

The weight of this sad time we must obey,
Speak what we feel, not what we ought to say.
The oldest hath borne most; we that are young
Shall never see so much, nor live so long.   325

ᶠ*Exeunt with a dead march.*ᶠ

FINIS

realm, or inviting them to govern jointly with him?

gored deeply wounded; bleeding (gore = blood)

320 **journey** following Lear beyond the grave

322 SP *EDGAR F; Albany in Q (see textual notes). The royal plural in the last four lines is appropriate to Albany; but the change in F completes the enhancement of Edgar's role (see above, 249 and n.), and may make for a stronger finish. There are various ways of staging the end. Edgar may, in effect, be accepting Albany's invitation to be restored to his rights; but if *rule*, 319, means 'to exercise sovereignty' (*OED* 5, citing from Ben Jonson, 1616, 'a prince who rules by example'), then an intriguing possibility for staging might be that Albany has the crown (taken from Edmund, who took it from Lear, as Rosenberg suggests, 322) and offers to share it with Kent and Edgar at 319, an offer Kent declines. Edgar may mark his acceptance by taking hold of it; thus at the end Albany and Edgar would each have a hand on the crown, and Edgar could appropriately speak himself in the royal plural. The presence of the crown here would recall the crown and coronet in 1.1; see

Introduction, pp. 14–15.

weight burden of sorrow

323–5 **feel . . . see so much** feeling and seeing have powerful resonances in the play, recalling Lear's call to the powerful to 'feel what wretches feel' (3.4.34), and Gloucester's complaint about the rich and lustful man who 'will not see / Because he does not feel' (4.1.71–2). In 1.1, Goneril and Regan spoke dutifully what they *ought to say*, while Cordelia thought she had to conceal her feelings. It would seem that for Edgar and Albany the overwhelming events of the play have freed them to speak feelingly, as Edgar found compassion through 'the art of known and feeling sorrows' (4.6.218), and have also given them insight while young, so they will not need to suffer in order to *see* properly; they can perhaps already say what Gloucester learned only through physical blindness, 'I see it feelingly' (4.6.145). But the idea of 'feeling' in the play is complex and ambivalent; see Introduction, p. 79.

324 **hath** keeping the emphasis on Lear; 'haue' (Q) includes Gloucester too.

325 SD *dead march* music suitable for a funeral, reinforcing the mood of sadness. Oxf adds, '*carrying the bodies*', but see 317 and n.

321 calls me] *F;* cals, and *Q*   no.] *Q, F; F2 adds SD: Dies.*   322 SP EDGAR] *F; Duke Q*
324 hath] *F;* haue *Q*

APPENDIX 1
TWO TEXTUAL PROBLEMS

There are three places in the texts of *King Lear* where the differences between Q and F are especially hard to interpret without seeing the texts together, and where they have considerable importance for the interpretation of the play. Two of these, in 3.1 and 5.3, are examined here; the third, the ending of the play, is discussed in the Introduction, pp. 75–80, where the Q and F versions are reproduced.

(a) 3.1.17–39: The texts in Q and F differ markedly here at the only point in the play where there are two different versions of a substantial speech.

There has been much debate as to whether these passages are alternatives or supplementary to one another. From 1733, when Lewis Theobald's edition appeared, to the 1970s, nearly all editions of the play conflated the two passages to give Kent a long, unwieldy speech. Some there were, however, who found the F version inadequate, and complained that Kent gives the Gentleman no commission, but sends him off 'he knows not why, he knows not whither' (*Johnson on Shakespeare*, 79; Doran, 75). In the 1980s, when the idea that Shakespeare might have revised the play gained ground, both Urkowitz, 67–79, and Taylor, 'War', 31–2, argued that F offers an intentional revision of Q, a revision calculated, in Taylor's view, as one of several that remove or obscure references to a French invasion of England. It has also been suggested that 'here we may have a Q/F difference in which the same speech by a prominent character has been differently cut' (Weis, 30). Those who regard the passages as alternatives may prefer that in Q, claiming that it is

The Hiſtorie of King Lear.

The too and fro conflicting wind and raine,
This night wherin the cub-drawne Beare would couch,
The Lyon,and the belly pinched Wolfe
Keepe their furre dry, vnbonneted he runnes,
And bids what will take all.

    Kent. But who is with him?

    Gent. None but the foole,who labours to out-ieſt
His heart ſtrooke iniuries.

    Kent. Sir I doe know you,
And dare vpon the warrant of my Arte,
Commend a deare thing to you, there is diuiſion,
Although as yet the face of it be couer'd,
With mutuall cunning, twixt *Albany* and *Cornwall*
But true it is, from *France* there comes a power
Into this ſcattered kingdome, who alreadie wiſe in our
Haue ſecret feet in ſome of our beſt Ports, (negligēce,
And are at point to ſhew their open banner,
Now to you, if on my credit you dare build ſo farre,
To make your ſpeed to Douer,you ſhall find
Some that will thanke you, making iuſt report
Of how vnnaturall and bemadding ſorrow
The King hath cauſe to plaine,
I am a Gentleman of blood and breeding,
And from ſome knowledge and aſſurance,
Offer this office to you.

    Gent. I will talke farther with you.

    Kent. No doe not,
For confirmation that I much more
Then my outwall, open this purſe and take
VVhat it containes, if you ſhall ſee *Cordelia*,
As feare not but you ſhall, ſhew her this ring,
And ſhe will tell you who your fellow is,
That yet you doe not know, fie on this ſtorme,
I will goe ſeeke the King.

    Gent. Giue me your hand,haue you no more to ſay?

    Kent. Few words but to effect more then all yet:
That when we haue found the King,
Ile this way,you that, he that firſt lights

                                  Enter

22 Quarto text of *King Lear* 3.1.17–34

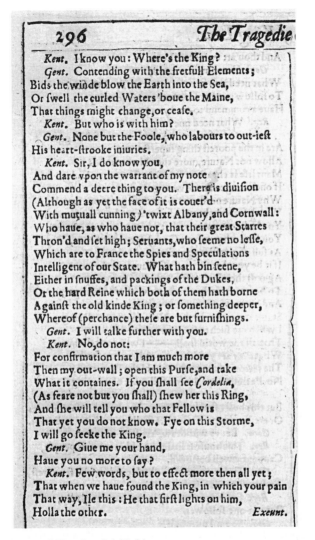

296   *The Tragedie*

 Kent. I know you: Where's the King?
 Gent. Contending with the fretfull Elements;
Bids the winde blow the Earth into the Sea,
Or swell the curled Waters 'boue the Maine,
That things might change, or ceafe.
 Kent. But who is with him?
 Gent. None but the Foole, who labours to out-ieft
His heart-ftrooke iniuries.
 Kent. Sir, I do know you,
And dare vpon the warrant of my note
Commend a deere thing to you. There is diuifion
(Although as yet the face of it is couer'd
With mutuall cunning) 'twixt Albany, and Cornwall:
Who haue, as who haue not, that their great Starres
Thron'd and fet high; Seruants, who feeme no leffe,
Which are to France the Spies and Speculations
Intelligent of our State. What hath bin feene,
Either in fnuffes, and packings of the Dukes,
Or the hard Reine which both of them hath borne
Againft the old kinde King; or fomething deeper,
Whereof (perchance) thefe are but furnifhings.
 Gent. I will talke further with you.
 Kent. No, do not:
For confirmation that I am much more
Then my out-wall; open this Purfe, and take
What it containes. If you fhall fee *Cordelia*,
(As feare not but you fhall) fhew her this Ring,
And fhe will tell you who that Fellow is
That yet you do not know. Fye on this Storme,
I will go feeke the King.
 Gent. Giue me your hand,
Haue you no more to fay?
 Kent. Few words, but to effect more then all yet;
That when we haue found the King, in which your pain
That way, Ile this: He that firft lights on him,
Holla the other.   *Exeunt.*

23 Folio text of *King Lear* 3.1.17–34

coherent and stylistically superior, in contrast to the Folio version, which is then branded as 'stylistically awkward if not unintelligible' (Knowles[2], 37). Value judgements in such matters are uncertain, and both versions have generally been accepted as by Shakespeare, F being in a 'style more typical of Shakespeare's later work' (Cam[2], 269).[1] The debate is summed up and analysed, from the perspective of a scholar who believes in the superiority of Q, in Knowles[2], 32–46.

Following a suggestion made by Peter Blayney, Knowles has proposed that the eight lines added in F are not a substitution but 'two passages intended for two different locations in the Q text' (Knowles[2], 42). He would insert F's lines 'Who have, as who have not ... Intelligent of our state' to follow '*Albany* and *Cornwall*' (as they do in F); the remaining lines from F he would place after 'The King hath cause to plaine' in Q, where 'What hath bin seene' then would complete the line beginning 'The King hath cause to plaine'. He would thus combine Q and F, but in a new way, to make a very long speech for Kent. He observes of this proposal, 'Except that such an addition would make a long speech four lines longer, I can think of no reason why both the added F lines about spies and the original Q lines about invasion should not coexist in the speech' (Knowles[2], 43).

According to Knowles, Blayney, in unpublished notes, in fact argued that the first three and a half lines added in F were intended to replace the statement in Q that a French force has landed in England; his view was thus more in line with those of critics who have supposed that changes were made in F because of censorship in relation to some sensitivity about the French (see, for example, Doran, 74–6, and Greg, *First Folio*, 387). Gary Taylor later sought to establish that the lines in F were a replacement intended to suggest an idea of civil war rather than a French invasion, an idea rejected by Honigmann ('Do-it-your-

---

1 See also E. A. J. Honigmann, 'Shakespeare's revised plays: *King Lear* and *Othello*', *The Library*, 6th series, 4 (1982), 153. Clare, 46–7, shows that Q has most often been preferred in recent British productions.

self *Lear*', *New York Review of Books*, 25 October 1990, 58–60)
and by Foakes (106–7) on the grounds that other references to a
French invasion were not cut from F, notably 3.7.2–3, 'the army
of France is landed' (Q and F).

It seems to me that Blayney and Taylor were right to feel that
the Q lines about invasion and the F lines about spies were not
meant to coexist in one speech, but that they may have mistaken
the reasons for the change in F. Furthermore, the idea that the
lines in F might represent two separate passages to be inserted at
different points in the Q text seems to me an unnecessary
hypothesis. The sequence of action here from the ending of 2.2
into 3.1 appears to have been subject to some deliberate reworking. After Lear goes off into the storm F inserts two half-lines at
2.2.485–7:

> GLOUCESTER   The King is in high rage.
> ^FCORNWALL   Whither is he going?
> GLOUCESTER
>   He calls to horse,^F but will I know not whither.

This insertion is consistent with and recalls the way Lear had
called for horses when leaving Goneril's house at 1.4.244, 250 and
1.5.46. A king would be expected to travel by horseback or in a
coach, but, of course, no horses are brought on stage. If Lear goes
off on horseback, as this insertion suggests, it would help to
explain why Kent cannot easily find him. When Lear returns, in
3.2, he is on foot, as always. At 3.1.7–15 in F eight lines are neatly
excised from the report of a Gentleman or Knight about Lear in
such a way as to preserve the metrical pattern. These lines
describe Lear as hatless and tearing his hair, and may have been
cut as merely expanding what the Knight has said in his first four
lines, or as describing what we are shortly to see Lear do on stage.

The assignment of speeches is also changed; two of Regan's
are assigned to Cornwall (484, 488), and a speech of Cornwall's
is given to Goneril (482–3). This redistribution makes Cornwall
a little more prominent after Regan has for some time had the

lion's share of the dialogue with Lear. The Folio editor appears to have got all these changes right, but it looks as though the markings for rearrangement and deletion were found confusing by the compositor when he came to Kent's speech. The simplest solution, as I now see it, is to suppose that the eight lines added in F were intended to replace the four irregular lines in Q (nearly five if set out as blank verse) that relate to France, and the passage is printed in this way in the text of this edition. I also suppose that the punctuation is erratic, as so often in F, and that the full point after 'State' is no more reliable than the semicolon after 'set high', and that both should be commas. I take it that Kent's message is meant to be mystifying, its hesitations and alternatives expressing his own uncertainties. I also assume that the passage beginning 'What hath bin seene ...' is in indirect apposition with 'Intelligent of our State', and speculates on the nature of the intelligence conveyed to France; and that Kent changes the subject on the word 'furnishings' to give directions to the Gentleman or Knight. The text then reads as follows when modernized:

> KENT   Sir, I do know you,
>   And dare upon the warrant of my note
>   Commend a dear thing to you. There is division,
>   Although the face of it is covered
>   With mutual cunning, 'twixt Albany and Cornwall,
>   Who have, as who have not that their great stars
>   Throned and set high, servants, who seem no less,
>   Which are to France the spies and speculations
>   Intelligent of our state – what hath been seen
>   Either in snuffs and packings of the dukes,
>   Or the hard rein which both of them hath borne
>   Against the old kind King; or something deeper,
>   Whereof, perchance, these are, but furnishings. –
>   Now to you:
>   If on my credit you dare build so far

To make your speed to Dover, you shall find
Some that will thank you, making just report
Of how unnatural and bemadding sorrow
The King hath cause to plain.
I am a gentleman of blood and breeding,
And from some knowledge and assurance
Offer this office to you.

This arrangement has the advantage of making Kent's speech consistent. He speaks of 'division' between Albany and Cornwall, echoing Gloucester's reference to the 'division of the kingdom' at 1.1.4. He refers to spies reporting English affairs to France, using the word 'intelligent', which is picked up at 3.5.11 by Edmund, who discovers Gloucester to be 'an intelligent party to the advantages of France', or one of the spies Kent has heard of. Kent's long parenthesis, 'what hath been seen … furnishings', offers possible explanations of the condition of 'our state' and the specific matters on which the spies may be reporting. These matters include the resentments and intrigues ('snuffs and packings') of Cornwall and Albany and their harsh treatment of Lear. It is sometimes said that we do not see Albany treat Lear badly, which is true, but a Knight comments at 1.4.58–9 on the 'great abatement ^{F}of kindness^F' that 'appears as well in the general dependants as in the Duke himself also' (the words 'of kindness' are not in Q) and, since he has done nothing to mitigate Goneril's harshness to her father, as her husband he is a party to the way Lear has been treated. The emphasis of the whole speech is thus on three matters, quarrels between Cornwall and Albany, spies passing intelligence to France, and, above all, the sufferings of Lear.

I suggest two reasons for the changes made in F. The first has to do with the time scale of the action. A reference to a French invasion in 3.1 is premature not only because Kent is only now conveying news of the way Lear has been treated, but also in relation to the announcement made by Cornwall at the beginning of 3.7, an announcement made on the basis of a letter stolen by Edmund from Gloucester's closet (3.5.10). When Gloucester advises Edmund to 'incline to the King' in 3.3 he says 'There is part of a power already landed' (Q), or 'footed' (F), a change in F that is consistent with that in 3.1 in obscuring another reference to an invasion before 3.7; here 'footed' could refer to the forces of Albany or Cornwall. (The word 'footed' is used again at 3.7.45, but with explicit reference to 'traitors' landing in the kingdom). In 3.1 Lear has just gone off into the storm, and the news of this could hardly have reached France. If the reference to a French invasion is omitted, Kent sends the Gentleman to Dover, where he may see Cordelia, who presumably informed Kent, in the letter referred to at 2.2.163, that she was planning to return to England.

The second reason has to do with an ambiguity in the word 'France', which may refer to the King of France, as at 1.1.127, 1.2.23 and 2.2.401, or to the country; at 3.1.24 in Kent's speech the reference could be to either. The changes in F in 3.1 and 3.5 remove references to the landing of a French army in England, references that suggest Shakespeare may have had an initial conception of an action in which French forces led by the King of France invaded England to rescue Lear; so in the old play *Leir*, after Cordella is reconciled to her father, the King of Gallia invades England to defeat in battle Cambria and Cornwall and their British forces, and restore Leir to his throne. F also omits Goneril's hostile question to Albany at 4.2.56–7:

> Where's thy drum?
> France spreads his banners in our noiseless land …

Here 'France' refers to the King of France, as does 4.3 (Q), in which we are told that the King of France has returned to his own country, leaving his Marshal in charge of his forces; these references, now mysterious, since the King of France left the stage in 1.1 and has not been seen since, also appear to be residual from a conception of the play that was modified. In 4.4 in both texts the

King of France ('great France') has succumbed to Cordelia's pleading, and sent an army, apparently under her command, to England. But there is another significant omission in F at 5.1.24–6, where in Q Albany, entering with an army, says

> For this business,
> It touches us as France invades our land,
> Not bolds the King …

here 'France' must mean the King of France, as 'the King' refers to Lear.

The changes in F in 3.1, 3.5, 4.2 and 5.1, and the omission of 4.3, all may thus be seen as modifying an earlier conception of the action of the play that has left its traces in Q. That earlier conception apparently included an invasion by French forces with the King of France at their head. In F, the streamlining of 4.2 by the omission of about thirty-five lines, followed by the complete omission of 4.3, means that Cordelia appears abruptly, with no preparation, after scenes of the meeting of the blind Gloucester with Edgar as Poor Tom (4.1), and of Albany and Goneril quarrelling (4.2). In F she enters in the next scene '*with Drum and Colours*' and '*Souldiours*', at the head of an invading army. In Q, on the other hand, she appears after two references to the King of France landing in England, and after a Gentleman's saintly description of her as an emblem of pity in 4.3, and she is accompanied on her entrance in 4.4 by a '*Doctor, and others*'. It would seem that in F Cordelia takes over the role of leader of the French invading army, which was originally to be commanded by the King of France. The difference between the entry at the beginning of 5.2 in Q and F would also seem relevant. Q has '*Enter the powers of France ouer the Stage, Cordelia with her father in her hand*', an entry that may be another trace of an early version of the play, since it seems to imply that the army is led by someone other than Cordelia, who follows on, guiding her father. The entry does not clearly indicate who is leading the French forces; 'France' here is ambiguous, and again might relate to a version of the play that brought on the King of France at the head of his troops. F by contrast has '*Enter with Drumme and Colours, Lear, Cordelia, and Souldiers, ouer the Stage, and Exeunt*', so putting Lear and Cordelia at the head of their (French) army. The evidence might suggest that Q presents us with an intermediate stage in the evolution of the texts of *King Lear*, and not a first draft. The only evidence we have is the texts as they appear in Q and F, so all interpretation must be speculative. For further comment, see Introduction, pp. 130–3.[1]

(b) 5.3.102–15: The challenge to the fight between Edgar and Edmund in 5.3 is differently orchestrated in Q and F. In F Albany initiates matters by calling 'Let the trumpet sound' (5.3.91), a phrase not in Q.

In Q Edmund (*Bastard*) caps Albany's call for a herald by shouting 'A Herald ho, a Herald', and then, after a Captain has ordered the trumpet to sound, Edmund again intervenes twice to command the second and third sounding of the trumpet. So in Q Edmund appears to take charge of the occasion with a boldness, even an anxiety to get on with the duel. In F, by contrast, Albany seems to be in charge, staging a more formal ceremony in which the Herald calls for the trumpet to sound, while Edmund simply waits for his challenger to appear. In F the role of Albany is diminished by the omission of substantial passages in 4.2.32–70, and some lines at 5.1.23–7, and the changes here in 5.3 may be designed to confirm the restoration of Albany's authority in the last scene of the play.

1 A fuller consideration of the changes in 3.1 and the problem of the King of France may be found in *SS*, 49 (1996), 217–23.

APPENDIX 2
LINEATION

It is not always easy to distinguish between prose and verse in the play, especially in some of the later scenes; in 4.6, for example, Lear's longer speeches are a mixture of verse and prose, but scholars disagree about where the boundaries lie. The Quarto prints long stretches of verse as prose, possibly because the verse lines in the manuscript had no initial capitals, as in the manuscript of *STM*, and were run on by the printer. In the Folio, by contrast, a number of verse lines are printed as two half-lines, probably because, in casting off copy, or estimating how much text he would need to fill a page, the compositor miscalculated, had more space on the page than he expected, and filled it by turning a single verse line into two. The differences between the Quarto and Folio are so many that they are presented in this appendix rather than in textual notes. The lineation of the Second Quarto in a few instances where it tried to correct the lineation in Q1 is also recorded.

1.1

26–7	My ... friend.] *Q; F lines* Kent: / ... Friend. /
71–3	I ... joys] *F; Q lines* short, / ... ioyes, /
75–6	And ... love.] *F; one line Q*
76–8	Then ... tongue.] *F; Q lines* sure / ... tongue. /
85–6	what ... sisters?] *F; Q lines* opulent / ... sisters. /
91–3	Unhappy ... less.] *F; prose Q*
99–104	Why ... all.] *F; Q lines* all, / ... hand / ... him, / ... neuer / ... all. /
118–19	Or ... shall] *F; Q lines* generation / ... appetite /
122–3	Peace ... wrath!] *F; one line Q*
137–8	The ... rest,] *F; Q lines* King, / ... rest, /

145–52 Let … judgement,] *F; Q lines* rather, / … heart, / … man, / … dutie / … bowes, / … folly, / … consideration / … life /

161–2 Now … vain.] *F; one line Q*

164–7 Kill … evil.] *F; Q lines* Physicion, / … disease, / … clamour / … euill. /

190–4 My … love?] *F; Q lines* you, / … daughter, / … present / … loue? /

194–6 Most … less?] *F; Q lines* than what / … lesse?/

196–200 Right … pieced,] *F; Q lines* vs / … fallen, / … little / … peec'st, /

206–7 Pardon … conditions.] *F; Q lines* vp / … conditions. /

214–20 This … degree] *F; Q lines* now / … praise, / … deerest, / … thing, / … fauour, / … degree, /

235–6 Better … better.] *Pope; Q lines* borne, / … better. /; *F lines* had'st, / … better. /

238–41 Which … stands] *F; Q lines* do, / … Lady? / … stāds /

243–6 Royal … Burgundy.] *F; Q lines* portion / … *Cordelia* / … *Burgundie,* /; *Q2 lines* … portion / … take / … *Burgundy.* /

249–51 Peace … wife.] *F; Q lines* respects / … wife. /

264–5 Thou … see] *F; Q lines* thine, / … see /

267–8 Without … Burgundy.] *F; one line Q*

270–3 The … father.] *F; Q lines* father, / … are, / … faults / … Father, /

278–80 Let … scanted,] *F; Q lines* Lord, / … almes, / … scanted, /

285–7 Sister … to night.] *Capell; Q, F lines* say, / … both, / … tonight. /

1.2

1–26 Thou … news?] *F; prose Q*

41–2 I … blame] *Q; F lines* it: / … them, / … blame. /

1.3

4–5 By … other] *F; Q lines* me, / … other /

13–16 Put … one,] *F; prose Q*

17–21 Not … abused.] *Theobald; prose Q*

a

| 23–4 | And ... so.] *Capell; prose Q , F* |
| 25–7 | I ... dinner.] *Hanmer; prose Q , F* |

1.4

1–7	If ... labours.] *F; prose Q*
80–1	I ... pardon.] *Q; F lines* Lord, / ... pardon. /
86–7	I ... thee.] *Q ; F lines* fellow. / ... thee. /
116–25	Have ... score.] *F; prose Q*
130	Why ... nothing.] *Q; F lines* Boy, / ... nothing. /
166	Then they] *part of song Theobald; prose Q , F*
166–9	for sudden ... among.] *F; prose Q*
180–1	How ... frown.] *Q; prose F*
187–8	Mum ... crumb,] *Cam; one line Q , F*
189–90	Weary ... peascod.] *Capell; one line Q , F*
191–204	Not ... proceeding.] *F; prose Q*
206–7	The ... young.] *Pope; prose Q , F*
211–14	I would ... are.] *F; prose Q*
215–16	May ... thee.] *F; prose Q /*
217	Does ... Lear.] *Rowe; F lines* me? / ... *Lear.* /; *prose Q*
218–21	Does ... am?] *F; prose Q*
228–46	This ... daughter.] *F; prose Q*
247–8	You ... betters] *Rowe²; prose Q , F*
249–344	Woe ... th'event.] *F; prose Q*
282	Now ... this?] *Q; F lines* adore, / ... this? /
288	I'll ... ashamed] *Rowe; prose Q ; F lines* thee: / ... asham'd /
291	Should ... thee] *Rowe; prose Q ; F lines* them, / ... thee: /
296–7	To ... daughter,] *Pope; prose Q ; F lines* so. / ... daughter, /
308–9	Nuncle ... thee] *Q; F lines Lear,* / ... thee: /
315	This ... knights!] *Rowe; F lines* Counsell, / ... Knights? /

2.1

2–5	And ... night.] *Q ; F lines* bin / ... notice / ... Duchesse / ... night. /
14	You ... sir.] *Q ; F lines* time, / ... Sir. /
15–97	The Duke ... consort.] *F; prose Q*
31	Draw ... well.] *Capell; prose Q; F lines* selfe, / ... well. /
103–4	That ... there.] *F; one line Q*

104–6	Nor … office.] *F*; *prose Q*
111–17	If … on.] *F*; *prose Q*
128–30	Lay … use.] *F*; *Q lines* councell / … vse. /

2.2

66–7	Peace … reverence?] *Q*; *F lines* sirrah, / … reuerence? /
78–80	Knowing … fool?] *Q2, F*; *Q lines* epeliptick / … foole? /
87	Why … fault?] *Q (*Why … offence.*); F lines* Knaue? / … fault? /
93–102	This … nicely.] *F*; *Q lines* praysd / … ruffines, / … nature, / … plaine, / … so, / … know / … craft, / … ducking / … nisely. /
113–15	I … misconstruction,] *F*; *Q lines* maister / … misconstruction, /
122–3	None … fool.] *F*; *one line Q*
125–7	Sir … you.] *F*; *Q lines* me, / … you, /
130–1	Fetch … noon.] *F*; *Q lines* honour, / … noone. /
133–4	Why … so.] *F*; *prose Q*
157	The … taken.] *Q*; *F lines* this, / … taken. /
170–1	This … wheel.] *Pope*; *Q F lines* goodnight, / … wheele. /
194–6	As … remove.] *F*; *Q lines* was / … remoue. /
198–201	Ha … nether-stocks.] *F*; *Q lines* garters, / … beares / … men / … at legs, / … neatherstockes. /
202–3	What's … here?] *Rowe*; *prose Q*; *F lines* he, / … mistooke / … heere? /
203–4	It … daughter.] *F*; *one line Q*
226–7	Commanded … looks;] *F*; *Q lines* leasure / … lookes, /
238–43	Fathers … poor.] *Pope*; *F lines* blind, / … kind. / … poore. /
251	Made … of?] *Q*; *F lines* offence, / … of? /
252–3	None … number?] *F*; *one line Q*
277	Deny … weary,] *Q*; *F lines* me? / … weary, /
280–6	My … wife.] *F*; *prose Q*
290	The … father] *Q*; *F lines* Cornwall, / … Father /
295–8	Infirmity … forbear,] *F*; *Q lines* health / … oprest / … forbeare, /
300–3	To … her] *F*; *Q lines* man, / … here? / … her /
336–40	Nature … return;] *F*; *Q lines* confine, / … discretion, / … selfe, / … returne, /

351–3	All ... lameness!] *F; Q lines* top, / ... lamenes. /
357–8	O ... on.] *F; Q lines* me, / ... mood – /
360–3	Thy ... train,] *F; Q lines* or'e / ... burne / ... traine, /
378	Thou ... heavens!] *Pope; Q, F lines* on't / ... Heauens! /
379–81	If you ... part!] *F; Q lines* alow / ... cause, / ... part, /
387	Will ... stocks?] *Q; F lines* hold? / ... Stockes? /
401–2	Why ... brought] *F; Q lines* dowerles / ... brought /
413–14	A ... thee:] *F; Q lines* my / ... thee, /
420–3	Not ... passion] *F; Q lines* yet, / ... welcome, / ... those / ... passion, /
434	Why ... ye] *Q; F lines* Lord? / ... ye, /
472–4	No ... flaws] *Steevens; Q, F lines* weeping, / ... flawes /
482–3	So ... Gloucester?] *F; one line Q*
491–2	Do ... bush.] *F; one line Q*

3.1

46–7	Give ... say?] *F; one line Q*
47–50	Few ... other.] *this edn; Q lines* yet: / ... King, / ... lights / ... other /; *F lines* ... yet; / ... pain / ... him, / ... other. /

3.2

2–9	You ... man!] *F; Q lines* drencht, / ... and / ... to / ... head, / ... flat / ... natures / ... make / ... man. /
10–13	O ... fools.] *F; Q lines* house / ... doore, / ... blessing, / ... foole. /
18–24	You ... foul.] *F; Q lines* plesure / ... & / ... seruile / ... ioin'd / ... white / ... foule. /
27–34	The ... wake.] *Johnson; prose Q; F lines* any; / ... many. / ... make, / ... wake. /
42–60	Alas ... sinning.] *F; Q lines* here? / ... these, / ... the / ... caues, / ... fire, / ... of / ... remember / ... cary / ... force. / ... dreadful / ... now, / ... thee / ... Iustice, / ... and / ... incestious, / ... couert / ... life, / ... centers, / ... grace, / ... sinning.
60–7	Alack ... courtesy.] *F; prose Q*
70–2	The ... heart] *F; Q lines* can, / ... poore, / ... heart /
74–7	He ... day.] *F; prose Q*

| 79–80 | This … go:] *Malone; F lines* Curtizan: / … go: / |
| 91–2 | Then … confusion:] *Pope; one line F* |

3.3

| 1–19 | Alack … careful.] *F; Q lines* this, / … leaue / … me / … paine / … him, / … him. / … vnnaturall. / … Dukes, / … receiued / … spoken, / … iniuries / … home / … landed, / … and / … talke / … him / … gon / … me, / … is / … careful. / |
| 20–4 | This … fall.] *F; Q lines* know / … deseruing / … lesse / … fall. / |

3.4

1–3	Here … endure.] *F; prose Q*
5	I … enter] *Q; F lines* owne, / … enter. /
19–22	In … that.] *F; Q lines* this! / … father / … lies, / … that. /
73–4	Judicious … daughters.] *F; Q lines* flesh / … daughters. /
75–6	Pillicock … loo!] *Johnson; one line Q , F*
117–20	Swithold … thee.] *F; prose Q*
133	Horse … wear.] *F; prose Q*
141–2	Our … gets it.] *Pope; prose Q , F*
144–9	Go … ready.] *F; prose Q*
151–2	Good … house.] *this edn; one line Q; F lines* offer, / … th' house. /
153–4	I'll … study?] *F; prose Q*
157–8	Importune … t'unsettle.] *F; one line Q*
166–8	The … company.] *F; Q lines* wits, / … Grace. / … company. /
171–2	With … philosopher.] *F; one line Q*
173	Good … fellow.] *Q; F lines* him: / … Fellow. /

3.6

15–16	To … 'em!] *F; prose Q*
25	Come … me.] *Capell; prose Q*
26–7	Her … speak] *Capell; one line Q*

29–32	The … thee.] *Theobald; Q lines* nightingale, / … herring, / … thee. /
33–4	How … cushions?] *Theobald; prose Q*
35–9	I'll … too.] *Theobald; prose Q*
41–4	Sleepest … harm.] *Theobald; prose Q*
62	Tom … curs!] *Q; F lines* you / … white: /
63–8	Be … wail;] *F; Q lines* bite, / … him, / … waile, /
69	For … head,] *F; prose Q*
71–2	Do … dry.] *Q; F lines* Fayres, / … dry. /
73–8	Then … changed.] *F; Q lines* her / … hardnes, / hundred, / … say, / … chang'd. /
83	Come … master?] *Q; F lines* Friend: / … Master? /
87–93	There … provision] *F; Q lines* frend, / … master, / … thine / … losse, / … prouision/
96–8	Which … behind.] *Theobald; Q lines* cure, / … behind. /
99–100	When … foes.] *Q2; prose Q*

3.7

1–3	Post … Gloucester.] *F; Q lines* letter / … *Gloster.* /
6–12	Leave … Gloucester.] *F; Q lines* company. / … father, / … going / … like, / … vs, / … *Gloster,* /
15–19	Some … friends.] *F; prose Q*
26–7	Shall … traitor?] *F; Q lines* blame / … traytor? /
29–31	What … friends.] *F; Q lines* consider, / … friends. /
34	To … find –] *Q; F lines* him, / … finde. /
35–6	By … beard.] *F; prose Q*
37–8	Naughty … chin] *F; one line Q*
42	Come … France?] *Q; F lines* Sir. / … France? /
44–5	And … kingdom?] *Rowe; prose Q, F*
45–6	To … Speak.] *F; one line Q*
51	Wherefore … peril –] *Q; F lines* Douer? / … perill. /
53	I … course.] *Q; F lines* Stake, / … Course. /
60–1	And … rain.] *F; Q lines* heart, / … rage, /
73–4	But … hold.] *F; one line Q*
75–6	If … mean?] *F; prose Q*
80–1	O … O!] *F; prose Q*
84	All … Edmund?] *Q; F lines* comfortlesse? / … *Edmund?* /

86–9	Out … thee.] *F; prose Q*
92–3	Go … you?] *F; prose Q*
95–7	Turn … arm.] *F; Q lines* vpon / … vntimely / … arme. /
99–101	If … monsters.] *Theobald; prose Q*
105–6	Go … him!] *Theobald; prose Q*

4.1

10–11	But … world!] *F; one line Q*
14–15	O … years –] *Q; F lines* Tenant, / … yeares. /
37	Was … since:] *Q; F lines* him. / … since: /
39–41	How … master.] *F; prose Q*
49	'Tis … blind.] *Q; F lines* plague, / … blinde: /
57	And … bleed.] *Capell; F lines* must: / … bleede. /
59–61	Both … fiend.] *F; Q lines* foot-path, / … wits, / … fiend, /
61–6	Five … waiting-women] *Pope, who omits* So, bless thee, master; *Q lines* once, / … dumbnes, / … *Stiberdigebit* of / … chambermaids / … maister. /
68–9	Have … still!] *F; Q lines* thee / … still, /
80–2	With … thee.] *F; Q lines* me, / … need. / … thee. /

4.2

3–11	Madam … offensive.] *F; prose Q*
30–1	O … wind] *F; one line Q*
48–9	Send … come:] *Malone; one line Q*
50–1	Humanity … deep.] *Pope; one line Q*
53–4	Who … honour] *F; one line Q*
54–8	that … threat,] *Theobald; Q lines* pitty / … mischiefe, / … land, / … threats /
60–2	See … woman.] *F; prose Q*
71–3	O … Gloucester.] *F; prose Q*
79–82	This … eye?] *F; Q lines* Iustices, / … venge. / … eye. /
82–3	Both … answer;] *F; one line Q*
87–8	Upon … answer.] *F; Q lines* tooke, *[for* tart *F] /* … answer. /
89	Where … eyes?] *Q; F lines* Sonne, / … eyes? /
95–8	Gloucester … knowst.] *F; Q lines* King, / … friend, / … knowest. /

4.3

13–15 Her … moved her?] *Pope; Q lines* passion, / … her. /
33–4   It … conditions,] *Theobald; one line Q*
41–2   What … daughter.] *Pope; one line Q*
46–8   To … gentleman.] *Johnson; Q lines* mind, / … *Cordelia.* /
       … Gentleman. /
55–6   Lending … me.] *Delius; one line Q*

4.4

8–10   And … worth.] *Pope; Q, F line* wisdome / … him / …
       worth. /
15–16 All … earth,] *F; one line Q*
20–1   News … hitherward.] *F; one line Q*
24–5   It … France] *Johnson; one line Q, F*

4.5

4–5   Madam … soldier.] *Q; F lines* ado: / … Souldier. /
14–16 In … enemy.] *F; Q lines* life, / … army. /
19–20 I … business.] *F; prose Q*
21–2   Might … Belike –] *Q; one line F*
37–8   I … well.] *F; one line Q*

4.6

3–4   Horrible … sea?] *F; one line Q*
11   Come … fearful] *Q; F lines* Sir, / … fearefull /
25–7   Give … upright.] *Q; F lines* hand / … Verge: / …
       vpright. /
33–4   Why … it.] *F; one line in Q*
41–8   Gone … sir?] *F; prose Q*
49   Hadst … air,] *Q; F lines* ought / … Ayre, /
80   Bear … here?] *Q; F lines* thoughts. / … heere? /
81–2   The … thus.] *F; one line Q*
105–15 The … soldiers.] *F; prose Q*
116–19 Behold … name –] *Johnson; prose Q, F*
120–4 The … darkness,] *Q, F; Johnson lines* to't / … appetite; /
       … centaurs, / … above; / … inherit, / … darkness,

126–7	Give … thee.] *Q*, *F; Johnson lines* apothecary / … thee. /
129	Let … mortality.] *Q; F lines* first, / … Mortality. /
130–1	O … me?] *Rowe; prose Q; F lines* world / … naught. / … me? /
134–5	No … it.] *Cam; prose Q*, *F*
137–8	I … it.] *Theobald; prose Q; F lines* report, / … it. /
156–9	Thou … cozener.] *Pope; prose Q*, *F*
160–7	Through … seem] *Rowe; prose Q*, *F*
170–1	O … madness.] *F; one line Q*
172–203	If … her to.] *F; prose Q*
204–5	Do … toward?] *this edn; one line Q*, *F*
205–6	Most … sound.] *F; Q lines* that / … sence. /; *Q2 lines* … heares / … sense. /
207	But … army?] *Q; F lines* fauour: / … Army? /
220–2	Hearty … boot.] *F; prose Q*
222–30	A … arm.] *F; prose Q*
231	Ch'ill … 'cagion.] *Q; F lines* Zir, / … 'casion. /
245–6	To … death!] *F; Q lines* vpon / … death. /
248–9	As duteous … desire.] *F; one line Q*
250–4	Sit … not] *F; Q lines* pockets / … friends, / … deathsmã / … not /
274	The … sense] *Q; F lines* mad: / … sense /
279–80	Give … drum.] *F; one line Q*

4.7

1–3	O … me.] *Rowe; Q lines* goodnes, / … me. /; *Q2 lines* … Kent, / … goodnesse, / … me. /; *F lines* Kent, / … worke / … goodnesse? / … short, / … me. /
6–8	Be … off.] *Q2*, *F; Q lines* those / … off. /
12	Then … King?] *Q; F lines* Lord: / … King? /
14–15	O … nature] *F; one line Q*
17–18	So … long.] *F; Q lines* king, / … long. /
26–9	O … made.] *F; Q lines* lips, / … sisters / … made. /; *Q2 lines* … father, / … lippes, / … harmes / … made. /
36–8	Mine … father,] *Q; F lines* me, / … fire, / … Father) /
44	How … majesty?] *Q; F lines* Lord? / … Maiesty? /
51–2	He's … daylight?] *Q; F lines* awake, / … while. / … bin? / … light? /

56–7	I feel … condition.] *F; one line Q*
57–9	O … kneel.] *Q2, F; prose in Q*
61	Fourscore … less;] *Capell; F lines* vpward, / … lesse: /
71	Be … not.] *Q; F lines* wet? / … not, /
78–82	Be … settling.] *Theobald; prose in Q; F lines* rage / … in, / … setling. /
83–4	You … foolish.] *Q; Q2, F line* me: / … forgiue, / … foolish. /
92–5	Report … sir.] *Johnson; Q lines* about, / … apace. / … sir. /

5.1

12–13	I … hers.] *Q2; prose Q*
15–16	I … her.] *F; prose Q; Q2 lines* her, / … her. /
16–17	Fear … husband.] *Capell; one line Q, F*
18–19	I had … me.] *Theobald; prose Q; Q2 lines* battell / … me. /
32–3	Let's … proceeding.] *Q; Q2 lines* determine / … proceedings. /; *F lines* warre / … proceeding. /
48–50	I … again.] *Q2, F; prose Q*
54–5	By … you.] *F; one line Q*
57–9	Each … enjoyed] *F; Q lines* Adder, / … inioy'd /; *Q2 lines* … Adder, / … one / … enioy'd /

5.2

| 3–4 | If … comfort.] *F; one line Q* |
| 9 | What … endure] *Q; F lines* againe? / … endure / |

5.3

3–5	We … down;] *F; Q lines* incurd / … downe, /
21	The … thee?] *Q; F lines* Incense. / … thee? /
25–6	Ere … come.] *F; one line Q; Pope lines* first, / … Come. /
47–8	To … guard,] *Q2; one line Qc; one line Qu, (omitting and appointed guard) F*
53–5	My … session.] *F; Q lines* morrow, / … hold / … bleed, /
55–60	At … place.] *Theobald; Qc lines* bleed, / … quarrels / … sharpnes, / … father / … place. /
61–2	I … brother.] *F; one line Q*
67–9	Not … addition.] *F; prose Q*

413

69–70	In … best.] *F; one line Q*
72–3	Holla … asquint.] *F; one line Q*
91	Thou … sound.] *Rowe; F lines* Gloster, / … sound; /
104–5	All … discharge.] *F; one line Q*
117–19	What … summons?] *F; Q lines* qualitie? / … summons. /
119–22	know … withal.] *F; Q lines* tooth. / … mou't / … with all. /; *Q2 lines* tooth: / … canker–bit, / … with all. /
125–6	That … arm] *F; one line Q*
127	Behold … honours,] *Q (reading* tongue *for* honours*); F lines* priuiledge, / … Honours, /
137–9	This … liest.] *F; Q lines* spirits, / … liest, /
149–52	This … beguiled.] *F; Q lines* armes / … opposite, / … beguild, /
152–5	Shut … know it.] *F; prose Q*
156–7	Say … for't?] *F; one line Q*
157–8	Most … paper?] *Capell; one line Q, F*
160	What … done,] *Q; F lines* with, / … done, /
169–71	Make … eyes.] *F; Q lines* vitious / … eies. /; *Q2 lines* … place / … eyes. /
171–2	Thou'st … here.] *Q2, F; prose Q*
175–6	Let … father.] *F; one line Q*
180–8	By … rings,] *F; Q lines* Lord, / … told / … proclamation / … neere, / … death, / … once. / … rags / … disdain'd / … rings, /
202–3	For … this.] *F; one line Q*
203–6	This … extremity.] *Theobald; Q lines* such / … much, / … extreamitie /
222–3	'Tis … of –] *Capell; one line Q; prose F*
231–3	O … urges.] *F; Q lines* allow / … vrges. /
233–4	I … night.] *F; one line Q*
246–7	To … reprieve.] *Q; F lines* Office? / … repreeue. /
250–3	He … herself.] *F; Q lines* me, / … lay / … despaire, / … selfe. /
273–7	Did … straight.] *F; Q lines* day, / … would / … now, / … you? / … straight. /
280–1	The same … Caius?] *Capell; one line Q; F lines* Kent, / … Caius? /
288	Nor … deadly;] *Q; F lines* else: / … deadly, /

414

294–301 That's … merited.] *F; prose Q*

301–3 All … see!] *Pope; prose Q; F lines* shall / … Foes / … see. /

304–8 And my … sir.] *F; prose Q*

312–14 Vex … longer.] *F; Q lines* passe, / … wracke, / … longer. /

ABBREVIATIONS AND REFERENCES

Some general usages are described at the end of the Introduction, p. 148. In references to books, the place of publication is London unless otherwise indicated. Biblical quotations are from the 'Bishops' Bible' (1568), and reprints of Old Testament till 1602 (New Testament till 1618), except where otherwise specified.

ABBREVIATIONS

ABBREVIATIONS USED IN NOTES

anon.	anonymous
ed., eds	editor, editors
edn	edition
n.s.	new series
opp.	opposite
SD	stage direction
SP	speech prefix
subst.	substantially
this edn	a reading introduced in this edition
vol., vols	volume, volumes

( ) surrounding a Q or F reading in the textual notes indicates original spelling; surrounding an editor's or scholar's name indicates a conjectural reading.

SHAKESPEARE'S WORKS AND WORKS PARTLY BY SHAKESPEARE

AC	*Antony and Cleopatra*
AW	*All's Well that Ends Well*
AYL	*As You Like It*
CE	*The Comedy of Errors*
Cor	*Coriolanus*
Cym	*Cymbeline*

Ham	*Hamlet*
1H4	*King Henry IV, Part 1*
2H4	*King Henry IV, Part 2*
H5	*Henry V*
1H6	*King Henry VI, Part 1*
2H6	*King Henry VI, Part 2*
3H6	*King Henry VI, Part 3*
H8	*King Henry VIII*
JC	*Julius Caesar*
KJ	*King John*
KL	*King Lear*
LLL	*Love's Labour's Lost*
Luc	*The Rape of Lucrece*
MA	*Much Ado About Nothing*
Mac	*Macbeth*
MM	*Measure for Measure*
MND	*A Midsummer Night's Dream*
MV	*The Merchant of Venice*
MW	*The Merry Wives of Windsor*
Oth	*Othello*
Per	*Pericles*
PP	*The Passionate Pilgrim*
R2	*King Richard II*
R3	*King Richard III*
RJ	*Romeo and Juliet*
Son	*Sonnets*
STM	*Sir Thomas More*
TC	*Troilus and Cressida*
Tem	*The Tempest*
TGV	*The Two Gentlemen of Verona*
Tim	*Timon of Athens*
Tit	*Titus Andronicus*
TN	*Twelfth Night*
TNK	*The Two Noble Kinsmen*
TS	*The Taming of the Shrew*
VA	*Venus and Adonis*
WT	*The Winter's Tale*

Line references to works by Shakespeare other than *King Lear* are keyed to *Riv* (to which the *Harvard Concordance to Shakespeare* is keyed), but quotations may be emended or modernized.

REFERENCES

EDITIONS OF SHAKESPEARE COLLATED

Alexander	*William Shakespeare: The Complete Works*, ed. Peter Alexander (1951)
Ard¹	*King Lear*, ed. W. J. Craig (1901)
Ard²	*King Lear*, ed. Kenneth Muir, The Arden Shakespeare (1952; reissued with corrections, 1972)
Cam	*Works*, ed. W. G. Clark, J. Glover and W. A. Wright, 9 vols (Cambridge, 1863–6)
Cam¹	*King Lear*, ed. John Dover Wilson and George Ian Duthie (Cambridge, 1960)
Cam²	*The Tragedy of King Lear*, ed. Jay L. Halio (Cambridge, 1992)
Capell	*Comedies, Histories, and Tragedies*, ed. Edward Capell, 10 vols (1767–8)
Collier	*Works*, ed. John Payne Collier, 8 vols (1842–4)
Collier²	*Works*, ed. John Payne Collier, 6 vols (1858)
Delius	*Works (Werke)*, ed. Nicholas Delius, 7 vols (Elberfeld, 1854–61)
Duthie	*Shakespeare's King Lear: A Critical Edition*, ed. G.I. Duthie (Oxford, 1949)
Dyce	*Works*, ed. Alexander Dyce, 6 vols (1857)
F or F1	*Comedies, Histories and Tragedies*, The First Folio (1623)
Fc, Fu	The First Folio text in corrected or uncorrected state
F2	*Comedies, Histories and Tragedies*, The Second Folio (1632)
F3	*Comedies, Histories and Tragedies*, The Third Folio (1663)
F4	*Comedies, Histories and Tragedies*, The Fourth Folio (1685)
Grant White	*Works*, ed. Richard Grant White, 12 vols (Boston, 1857–66)
Halio	*The First Quarto of King Lear*, ed. Jay L. Halio (Cambridge, 1994)
Hanmer	*Works*, ed. Sir Thomas Hanmer, 6 vols (Oxford, 1743–4)
Horsman	*The Tragedy of King Lear*, ed. E. A. Horsman (Indianapolis and New York, 1973)
Hudson	*Works*, ed. Henry N. Hudson, 20 vols (Boston and Cambridge, Mass., 1886)
Hunter	*King Lear*, ed. G. K. Hunter (1972)
Jennens	*King Lear: A Tragedy* ed. Charles Jennens (1770)
Johnson	*Plays*, ed. Samuel Johnson, 8 vols (1765)
Keightley	*Plays*, ed. Thomas Keightley, 6 vols (1864)
Kittredge	*The Tragedy of King Lear*, ed. G. L. Kittredge (Boston, 1940)
Knight	*Works*, ed. Charles Knight, 8 vols (1838–43)
Malone	*Works*, ed. Edmond Malone, 10 vols (1790)

Oxf	*Works*, ed. Stanley Wells, Gary Taylor, John Jowett and William Montgomery (Oxford, 1986)
Pope	*Works*, ed. Alexander Pope, 6 vols (1723–5)
Q or Q1	M. William Shaks-peare: *HIS* True Chronicle Historie of the life and death of King LEAR and his three Daughters, 1608 (The First Quarto)
Qc, Qu	The First Quarto (1608) in its corrected or uncorrected state
Q2	*King Lear*, The Second Quarto (1619)
Q3	*King Lear*, The Third Quarto (1655)
Rann	*The Dramatic Works of Shakespeare*, ed. Joseph Rann, 6 vols (1786–91)
Ridley	*King Lear*, ed. M. R. Ridley, The New Temple Shakespeare, 1935
Riv	*The Riverside Shakespeare*, textual ed. G. Blakemore Evans (Boston, 1974)
Rowe	*Works*, ed. Nicholas Rowe, 6 vols (1709)
Rowe[2]	*Works*, ed. Nicholas Rowe, 8 vols (1714)
Singer	*Dramatic Works and Poems*, ed. S. W. Singer, 2 vols (New York, 1834)
Singer[2]	*Dramatic Works*, ed. S. W. Singer, 10 vols (1856)
Staunton	*Plays*, ed. Howard Staunton, 3 vols (1858–60)
Steevens	*Plays*, ed. Samuel Johnson and George Steevens, 10 vols (1773)
Steevens[2]	*Plays*, ed. Samuel Johnson and George Steevens, 10 vols (1778)
Theobald	*Works*, ed. Lewis Theobald, 7 vols (1733)
Var	*King Lear*, A New Variorum Edition, ed. Horace Howard Furness (New York, 1880)
Warburton	*Works*, ed. William Warburton, 8 vols (1747)
Warren	*The Parallel King Lear 1608–1623*, ed. Michael Warren (Berkeley and Los Angeles, 1989)
Weis	*King Lear: A Parallel Text Edition*, ed. René Weis (1993)
Werstine[1]	*The Tragedy of King Lear*, ed. Barbara Mowat and Paul Werstine, New Folger Library (New York, 1993)

OTHER WORKS

Abbott	E. A. Abbott, *A Shakespearian Grammar* (1886)
Adelman	Janet Adelman, *Suffocating Mothers: Fantasies of Maternal Origin in Shakespeare's Plays, 'Hamlet' to 'The Tempest'* (New York, 1992)
Anderson	Judith R. Anderson, 'The conspiracy of realism: impasse and vision in *King Lear*', SP, 84 (1987), 1–23
Anderson[2]	Peter S. Anderson, 'The fragile world of *Lear*', in Clifford

Davidson, C. J. Gianakaris and John H. Stroupe (eds), *Drama in the Renaissance: Comparative and Critical Essays*, (New York, 1986), 178–91

Andresen   Martha Andresen, ' "Ripeness is all": sententiae and commonplaces in *King Lear*', in *Some Facets*, 145–68

Armstrong   Edward A. Armstrong, *Shakespeare's Imagination* (1946; reissued Lincoln, Nebraska, 1963)

Barker   Howard Barker, *Seven Lears* (1990)

Barker, *Violence*   Francis Barker, *The Culture of Violence: Tragedy and History* (Chicago, 1993)

Bate   Jonathan Bate, *Shakespeare and Ovid* (Oxford, 1993)

Bayley   John Bayley, *Shakespeare and Tragedy* (1981)

Bickersteth   Geoffrey Bickersteth 'The Golden World of *King Lear*', *Proceedings of the British Academy*, 32 (1946)

Blau   Herbert Blau, *The Impossible Theater: A Manifesto* (New York, 1964)

Blayney   Peter W. M. Blayney, *The Texts of 'King Lear' and their Origins*, vol. 1: *Nicholas Okes and the First Quarto* (Cambridge, 1982)

Bond   Edward Bond, *Lear* (1972), ed. Patricia Hern, Methuen Student Editions (1983)

Bono   Barbara Bono, ' "The chief knot of all discourse": the maternal subtext tying Sidney's *Arcadia* to Shakespeare's *King Lear*', in S. P. Cerasano and Marion Wynne-Davies (eds), *Gloriana's Face* (Detroit, 1992) 105–27

Booth   Stephen Booth, *King Lear, Macbeth, Indefinition and Tragedy* (New Haven, 1983)

Bradley   A.C. Bradley, *Shakespearean Tragedy* (1904; 2nd edn, 1905)

Bratton   *King Lear*, ed. J. S. Bratton, Plays in Performance (Bristol, 1987)

Bratton[2]   J. S. Bratton, 'The Lear of private life: interpretations of *King Lear* in the nineteenth century', in Richard Foulkes (ed.), *Shakespeare and the Victorian Stage* (Cambridge, 1986), 124–37

Brockbank   Philip Brockbank, 'Upon such sacrifices', *Proceedings of the British Academy*, 62 (1976)

Brooke   N. S. Brooke, *King Lear* (1963)

Brownlow   F. W. Brownlow, *Shakespeare, Harsnett, and the Devils of Denham* (Newark, Delaware, 1993)

Bullough   Geoffrey Bullough (ed.), *Narrative and Dramatic Sources of Shakespeare*, vol. 7 (London, 1978)

Carroll   William C. Carroll, ' "The base shall top the legitimate": the Bedlam beggar and the role of Edgar in *King Lear*', *SQ*, 38 (1987), 426–41

Cavell   Stanley Cavell, 'Disowning Knowledge' in *Six Plays by Shakespeare* (Cambridge, 1987)

Chaloner	Erasmus, *The Praise of Folie*, translated Sir Thomas Chaloner, ed. Clarence H. Miller, EETS 62 (Oxford, 1965)
Chambers	R. W. Chambers, *King Lear*, W. P. Ker Memorial Lecture, 1939 (Glasgow, 1940)
Chambers, *ES*	E. K. Chambers, *The Elizabethan Stage*, 4 vols (1923)
Clare	Robert Clare, ' "Who is it that can tell me who I am?" ': the theory of authorial revision between the Quarto and Folio texts of *King Lear*', *The Library*, 6th series, 17 (1995), 34–59
Clare²	Janet Clare, '*Art Made Tongue-tied by Authority': Elizabethan and Jacobean Dramatic Censorship* (Manchester, 1990)
Clayton	Thomas Clayton, ' "Is this the promis'd end?": revision in the role of the King', in *Division*, 121–41
Coleridge	Samuel Taylor Coleridge, *Lectures on Literature 1808–1819*, ed. R. A. Foakes, in *The Collected Works of Samuel Taylor Coleridge*, 5, 2 vols, (Princeton, 1987)
Colie	Rosalie L. Colie, 'Reason and need: *King Lear* and the crisis of the aristocracy', in *Some Facets*, 185–219
Colie²	Rosalie L. Colie, 'The energies of endurance: biblical echo in *King Lear*', in *Some Facets*, 117–44
Cox	Brian Cox, *The Lear Diaries, The Story of the Royal National Theatre's Productions of Shakespeare's Richard III and King Lear* (1992).
Danby	John F. Danby, *Shakespeare's Doctrine of Nature* (1949)
Davison	Peter Davison, *Contemporary Drama and the Popular Dramatic Tradition in England* (1982)
Dent	R. W. Dent, *Shakespeare's Proverbial Language: An Index* (Berkeley and Los Angeles, 1981)
Division	Gary Taylor and Michael Warren (eds), *The Division of the Kingdoms: Shakespeare's Two Versions of 'King Lear'*, (Oxford, 1983)
Dobson	E. J. Dobson, *English Pronunciation, 1500–1700*, 2 vols (Oxford, 1957; 2nd edn, 1968)
Dollimore	Jonathan Dollimore, *Radical Tragedy* (Brighton, 1984; 2nd edn, 1989)
Doran	Madeleine Doran, *The Text of King Lear* (Stanford, 1931)
Dowden	Edward Dowden, *Shakspere: A Critical Study of his Mind and Art* (1875; citing 3rd edn, 1886)
Drakakis	John Drakakis, 'Theatre, ideology and institution: Shakespeare and the roadsweepers', in Graham Holderness (ed.), *The Shakespeare Myth* (Manchester, 1988)

Dutton
Richard Dutton, '*King Lear, The Triumphs of Reunited Britannia*, and "The Matter of Britain"', *Literature and History*, 12 (1986), 139–51

Edwards
Thomas Edwards, *The Canons of Criticism* (1750)

EETS
Early English Text Society

Ekeblad
Inga-Stina Ekeblad, '*King Lear* and *Selimus*', *N&Q*, n.s. 4 (1957), 193–4

ELH
English Literary History

ELN
English Language Notes

Elton
William R. Elton, *King Lear and the Gods* (San Marino, 1966)

Erasmus
Erasmus, *The Praise of Folie*, translated Sir Thomas Chaloner, ed. Clarence H. Miller, EETS 62 (Oxford, 1965)

Farmer
Richard Farmer, *An Essay on the Learning of Shakespeare* (Cambridge, 1767)

Felperin
Howard Felperin, *Shakespearean Representation* (Princeton, 1977)

Fly
Richard Fly, *Shakespeare's Mediated World* (Amherst, Mass., 1976)

Foakes
R. A. Foakes, *Hamlet versus Lear: Cultural Politics and Shakespeare's Art* (Cambridge, 1993)

Foakes²
'Textual revision and the Fool in *King Lear*', *Trivium*, 20, Essays in Honour of Peter Davison (1985), 33–47

Freud
Sigmund Freud, 'The theme of the three caskets', *Complete Psychological Works*, translated James Strachey in collaboration with Anna Freud, assisted by Alix Strachey and Alan Tyson, vol. 12 (London, 1958), 291–301

Gardner
Helen Gardner, *King Lear*, The John Coffin Memorial Lecture, 1966 (1967)

Gaskell
Philip Gaskell, *From Writer to Reader: Studies in Editorial Method* (Oxford, 1978)

Gibbons
Brian Gibbons, *Shakespeare and Multiplicity* (Cambridge, 1993)

Goldberg
S. L. Goldberg, *An Essay on King Lear* (Cambridge, 1974)

Goldring
Beth Goldring, '*Cor*'s rescue of Kent', in *Division*, 143–51

Granville-Barker
Harley Granville-Barker, *Prefaces to Shakespeare*, vol. 2 (Princeton, 1946; reissued 1963)

Greenblatt
Stephen Greenblatt, *Shakespearean Negotiations* (Oxford, 1988)

Greg, 'Date'
W. W. Greg, 'The date of *King Lear* and Shakespeare's use of earlier versions of the story', *The Library*, 20 (1940), 377–400

Greg, *First Folio*
W. W. Greg, *The Shakespeare First Folio* (Oxford, 1955)

Greg, *Variants*
W. W. Greg, *The Variants in the First Quarto of King Lear* (1940)

Guazzo	*The Civil Conversation of M. Steeven Guazzo*, translated George Pettie (1581), in Tudor Translations, 2nd series, 8, ed. Charles Whibley (London and New York, 1925)
Gurr	Andrew Gurr, *The Elizabethan Stage 1574–1642*, 3rd edn (Cambridge, 1992)
Hardison	O. B. Hardison, 'Myth and history in *King Lear*', *SQ*, 26 (1975), 227–42
Harrison	William Harrison, 'An Historical Description of the Iland of Britaine', in Holinshed, vol. 1
Harsnett	Samuel Harsnett, *A Declaration of Egregious Popish Impostures* (1603), reprinted in Brownlow
Hawkes	Terence Hawkes, 'Lear's maps: a general survey', *Deutsche Shakespeare-Gesellschaft West Jahrbuch* (1989), 134–47
Hazlitt	*The Complete Works of William Hazlitt*, ed. P. P. Howe, 12 vols (1930–4)
Heilman	Robert Bechtold Heilman, *This Great Stage: Image and Structure in King Lear* (Baton Rouge, Louisiana, 1948)
Henslowe	*Henslowe's Diary*, ed. R. A. Foakes and R. T. Rickert (Cambridge, 1961)
Hibbard	G. R. Hibbard, '*King Lear*: a retrospect 1939–1979', *SS*, 33 (1980), 1–12
Hinman	Charlton Hinman, *The Printing and Proof-Reading of the First Folio of Shakespeare*, 2 vols (Oxford, 1963)
Hoeniger	F. D. Hoeniger, *Medicine and Shakespeare in the English Renaissance* (Newark, Delaware, 1992)
Holinshed	Raphael Holinshed, *Chronicles of England, Scotland and Ireland* (1587), reprinted 6 vols (1807)
Holland	Peter Holland, 'Shakespeare performances in England, 1992–3', *SS*, 47 (1994), 199–202
Holloway	John Holloway, *The Story of the Night: Studies in Shakespeare's Major Tragedies* (1961)
Honigmann	E. A. J. Honigmann, *The Stability of Shakespeare's Text* (1965)
Honigmann[2]	E. A. J. Honigmann, *Myriad-Minded Shakespeare* (New York, 1989)
Howard	Skiles Howard, 'Attendants and others in Shakespeare's margins: doubling in the two texts of *King Lear*', *Theatre Survey*, 32 (1991), 187–213
Howard-Hill	Trevor Howard-Hill, 'The problem of the manuscript copy for Folio *King Lear*', *The Library*, 6th series (1982), 1–24
Howard-Hill[2]	Trevor Howard-Hill, 'The challenge of *King Lear*', *The Library*, 6th series, 7 (1985), 161–79
Howard-Hill[3]	Trevor Howard-Hill, 'Q1 and the copy for Folio *Lear*', *Papers of the Bibliographical Society of America*, 80 (1986), 419–35

Hulme	Hilda Hulme, *Explorations in Shakespeare's Language* (1962)
Ioppolo	Grace Ioppolo, *Revising Shakespeare* (Cambridge, Mass., 1991)
Jackson	MacD. P. Jackson, 'Fluctuating variation: author, annotator, or actor?', in *Division*, 313–45
James I, *Works*	*The Political Works of James I*, reprinted from the edn of 1616, with an introduction by Charles Howard McIlwain (Cambridge, Mass., 1918)
D. G. James	D. G. James, *The Dream of Learning* (Oxford, 1965)
Jervis	Swynfen Jervis, *A Dictionary of the Language of Shakespeare* (1868)
Johnson	Samuel Johnson, *Samuel Johnson on Shakespeare*, ed. H. R. Woudhuysen (1989)
Jorden	Edward Jorden, *A Briefe Discourse of a Disease Called the Mother* (1603)
Judges	A. V. Judges (ed.), *The Elizabethan Underworld* (1930)
Kahn	Coppélia Kahn, 'The absent mother in *King Lear*', in Margaret W. Ferguson, Maureen Quilligan and Nancy J. Vickers (eds), *Rewriting the Renaissance: The Discourses of Sexual Difference in Early Modern Europe* (Chicago, 1986)
Kaiser	Walter Kaiser, *Praisers of Folly: Erasmus, Rabelais, Shakespeare* (Cambridge, Mass, 1963)
Keats	*The Letters of John Keats*, ed. Hyder Rollins, 2 vols (Cambridge, Mass., 1958)
Kennedy	Dennis Kennedy, *Looking at Shakespeare: A Visual History of Twentieth-Century Performance* (Cambridge, 1993)
Kerrigan	John Kerrigan, 'Revision, adaptation, and the Fool in *King Lear*', in *Division*, 195–245
T. J. King	T. J. King, *Casting Shakespeare's Plays* (Cambridge, 1992)
Knowles	Richard Knowles, 'The printing of the Second Quarto (1619) of *King Lear*', *Studies in Bibliography*, 35 (1982), 191–206
Knowles[2]	Richard Knowles, 'Revision awry in Folio *Lear* 3.1', *SQ*, 46 (1995), 32–46
Kott	Jan Kott, *Shakespeare our Contemporary*, translated Boleslaw Taborski (1964)
Kozintsev	Grigori Kozintsev, '*Hamlet* and *King Lear:* stage and film', in Clifford Leech and J. M. R. Margeson (eds), *Shakespeare 1971*, Proceedings of the World Shakespeare Congress, Vancouver, August 1971 (Toronto, 1972), 190–8
Kozintsev[2]	Grigori Kozintsev, *King Lear: The Space of Tragedy*, translated Mary Mackintosh (Berkeley and Los Angeles, 1973)

Lamb	*The Works of Charles and Mary Lamb*, ed. E. V. Lucas, 7 vols (1903)
Law Reports	*The All-England Law Reports Reprint 1558–1774*, ed. G. F. L. Bridgman, revised Miss M. R. Plummer, 38 vols (1968)
Leggatt	Alexander Leggatt, *King Lear: Shakespeare in Performance* (Manchester, 1991)
Leir	*The History of King Leir*, Malone Society Reprints (Oxford, 1907; reprinted 1965)
Lockyer	Roger Lockyer, *The Early Stuarts: A Political History of England 1603–1642* (1989)
McGuire	Philip C. McGuire, *Speechless Dialect: Shakespeare's Open Silences* (Berkeley and Los Angeles, 1985)
Mack	Maynard Mack, *'King Lear' in our Time* (Berkeley and Los Angeles, 1965)
McKenzie	D. F. McKenzie, *Bibliography and the Sociology of Texts*, The Panizzi Lectures, 1985 (1986)
McLeod	Randall McLeod, *'Gon. No more, the text is foolish.'*, in *Division*, 153–93
McLuskie	Kathleen McLuskie, 'The patriarchal bard: feminist criticism and Shakespeare: *King Lear* and *Measure for Measure*', in Jonathan Dollimore and Alan Sinfield (eds), *Political Shakespeare* (Manchester and Ithaca, 1985)
Mahood	M. M. Mahood, *Bit Parts in Shakespeare's Plays* (Cambridge, 1992)
Marowitz	Charles Marowitz, 'Lear Log', *Encore*, 10 (1963), 20–33, and *Tulane Drama Review*, 8 (1963), 103–21
Marcus	Leah Marcus, *Puzzling Shakespeare* (Berkeley and Los Angeles, 1988)
Mason	John Monck Mason, *Comments on the Last Edition of Shakespeare's Plays* (1785)
Matchett	William H. Matchett, 'Some dramatic techniques in *King Lear*', in Philip C. McGuire and David A. Samuelson (eds), *Shakespeare: The Theatrical Dimension* (New York, 1979), 185–208
Maxwell	J. C. Maxwell, 'The technique of invocation in *King Lear*', *MLR*, 45 (1950), 142–7
Meagher	John C. Meagher, 'Vanity, Lear's feather, and the pathology of editorial annotation', in Clifford Leech and J. M. R. Margeson (eds), *Shakespeare 1971*, Proceedings of the World Shakespeare Congress, Vancouver, August 1971 (Toronto, 1972)
Meyer	Ann R. Meyer, 'Shakespeare's art and the texts of *King Lear*', *Studies in Bibliography*, 47 (1994)

Milward   Peter Milward, *Biblical Influence in the Great Tragedies* (Tokyo, 1985)

Miola   Robert S. Miola, *Shakesespeare and Classical Tragedy: The Influence of Seneca* (Oxford, 1992)

MLR   *Modern Language Review*

Montaigne   *The Essays of Michael Lord of Montaigne*, translated by John Florio (1603), 3 vols, Everyman's Library (1910)

MSR   Malone Society Reprint

Muir   Edwin Muir, 'The politics of *King Lear*', The W. P. Ker Memorial Lecture, 1946 (Glasgow, 1947)

Muir, *Sources*   Kenneth Muir, *The Sources of Shakespeare's Plays* (1977)

Nichols   John Nichols, *The Progresses, Processions, and Magnificent Festivities of King James the First*, 7 vols (1828)

Noble   Richmond Noble, *Shakespeare's Biblical Knowledge* (1935)

N&Q   *Notes and Queries*

Odell   George C. D. Odell, *Shakespeare from Betterton to Irving*, 2 vols (New York, 1920; reissued 1966)

OED   *The Oxford English Dictionary*, ed. J. A. H. Bradley, W. A. Craigie and C. T. Onions, 13 vols (Oxford, 1933)

Parker   Brian Parker, '*Ran* and the tragedy of history', *University of Toronto Quarterly*, 55 (1986), 412–23

Partridge   Eric Partridge, *Shakespeare's Bawdy* (1947; 2nd edn, 1968)

Patterson   Annabel Patterson, *Shakespeare and the Popular Voice* (Cambridge, Mass., and Oxford, 1989)

Patterson[2]   Annabel Patterson, *Censorship and Interpretation* (Madison, 1984)

Peat   Derek Peat, ' "And that's true too": *King Lear* and the tension of uncertainty', *SS*, 33 (1980), 43–53

Perrett   Wilfrid Perrett, *The Story of King Lear from Geoffrey of Monmouth to Shakespeare*, Palaestra 35 (Berlin, 1904)

Pettie   *The Civile Conversation of Mr. Steeven Guazzo*, the first three books, translated George Pettie (1581); Tudor Translations, ed. Charles Whibley, 2nd series, 8 (1925), vol. 2, Book 3, 65–74

PMLA   *Publications of the Modern Language Association of America*

Reibetanz   John Reibetanz, *The Lear World* (Toronto, 1977)

RES   *Review of English Studies*

Richman   David Richman, 'The *King Lear* Quarto in rehearsal and performance', *SQ*, 37 (1986), 374–82

Ringler   William A. Ringler, Jr, 'Shakespeare and his actors: some remarks on *King Lear*', in Wendell M. Aycock (ed.), *Shakespeare's Art from a Comparative Perspective* (Lubbock, Texas, 1981), 183–94

Ringler[2]   William A. Ringler, Jr, 'Exit Kent', *SQ*, 11 (1960), 311–17

Ritson   Joseph Ritson, *Remarks, Critical and Illustrative, on the Text and Notes of the Last Edition of Shakespeare* (1783)

Ronan	Clifford J. Ronan, '*Selimus* and the blinding of Gloucester', *N&Q*, n.s. 33 (1986), 360–2
Rosenberg	Marvin Rosenberg, *The Masks of King Lear* (Berkeley and Los Angeles, 1972)
Rubinstein	Frankie Rubinstein, *A Dictionary of Shakespeare's Puns and their Significance* (1984)
Ryan	Kiernan Ryan (ed.), *King Lear* (New Casebooks, 1993)
Salingar	Leo Salingar, *Dramatic Form in Shakespeare and the Jacobeans* (Cambridge, 1986)
SB	*Studies in Bibliography*
Schmidt	Alexander Schmidt, revised and enlarged by Gregor Sarrazin, *Shakespeare-Lexicon and Quotation Dictionary*, 2 vols (Berlin, 1902; New York, 1971)
SEL	*Studies in English Literature*
Sewall	Richard B. Sewall, *The Vision of Tragedy* (New Haven, 1959)
Shaheen	Naseeb Shaheen, *Biblical References in Shakespeare's Tragedies* (Newark, Delaware, 1987)
Shrimpton	Nicholas Shrimpton, 'Shakespeare performances in Stratford-upon-Avon and London, 1981–2', *SS*, 36 (1983), 149–55
Sidney	Sir Philip Sidney, *The Countess of Pembroke's Arcadia*, ed. Victor Stretkowicz (Oxford, 1987)
Sisson	C. J. Sisson, *New Readings in Shakespeare*, 2 vols (1956)
Skeat	*Chaucerian and Other Pieces: Being a Supplement to the Complete Works of Geoffrey Chaucer*, ed. W. W. Skeat (Oxford, 1897)
Snyder	Susan Snyder, '*King Lear* and the Prodigal Son', *SQ*, 17 (1966), 361–9
Some Facets	Rosalie Colie and F. T. Flahiff (eds), *Some Facets of King Lear* (Toronto, 1974)
SP	*Studies in Philology*
Spurgeon	Caroline Spurgeon, *Shakespeare's Imagery and What it Tells Us* (Cambridge, 1935)
SQ	*Shakespeare Quarterly*
SS	*Shakespeare Survey*
Sternfeld	F. W. Sternfeld, *Music in Shakespearean Tragedy* (1963)
Stone	P. W. K. Stone, *The Textual History of King Lear* (1980)
Strier	Richard Strier, ' "Faithful servants": Shakespeare's praise of disobedience', in Heather Dubrow and Richard Strier (eds), *The Historical Renaissance: New Essays in Tudor and Stuart Literature and Culture* (Chicago, 1988)
Swinburne	A. C. Swinburne, *A Study of Shakespeare* (1880; 3rd edn, revised, 1895)

Taylor, 'Date'   Gary Taylor, '*King Lear:* the date and authorship of the
                       Folio version', in *Division*, 351–451
Taylor, 'Folio   Gary Taylor, 'Folio compositors and Folio copy: *King
   copy'   Lear* and its context', *Papers of the Bibliographical Society
                       of America*, 79 (1985), 17–74
Taylor,   Gary Taylor, 'Monopolies, show trials, disaster and
   'Monopolies'   invasion: *King Lear* and censorship', in *Division*, 75–119
Taylor, 'New   Gary Taylor, 'A new source and an old date for *King Lear*',
   source'   *RES*, n.s. 33 (1982), 396–413
Taylor, 'War'   Gary Taylor, 'The war in *King Lear*', *SS*, 33 (1980), 27–34
Tennenhouse   Leonard Tennenhouse, *Power on Display: The Politics of
                       Shakespeare's Genres* (1986)
Thompson   Ann Thompson and John O. Thompson, *Shakespeare
                       Meaning and Metaphor* (Brighton, 1987)
Tilley   M. P. Tilley, *A Dictionary of Proverbs in England in the
                       Sixteenth and Seventeenth Centuries* (1950)
TLS   *The Times Literary Supplement*
Turner   John Turner, 'King Lear', in Graham Holderness, Nick
                       Potter and John Turner (eds), *Shakespeare: The Play of
                       History* (Iowa City, 1988)
TxC   Stanley Wells and Gary Taylor, *William Shakespeare: A
                       Textual Companion* (Oxford, 1987)
Tynan   Kenneth Tynan, *A View of the English Stage 1944–63*
                       (1975)
Udall   Joanna Udall, *A Critical, Old-Spelling Edition of 'The Birth
                       of Merlin'*, Modern Humanities Research Association
                       Texts and Disssertations, 31 (1991)
Urkowitz   Stephen Urkowitz, *Shakespeare's Revision of King Lear*
                       (Princeton, 1980)
Urkowitz,   Stephen Urkowitz, 'The base shall to th' legitimate: the
   Division   growth of an editorial tradition', in *Division*, 23–43
Walker   D. P. Walker, *Unclean Spirits: Possession and Exorcism in
                       France and England in the Late Sixteenth and Early
                       Seventeenth Centuries* (Philadelphia, 1981)
Walker[2]   W. S. Walker, *A Critical Examination of the Text of
                       Shakespeare*, ed. W. N. Lettsom, 3 vols (1860)
Warren, 'Albany'   Michael J. Warren, 'Quarto and Folio *King Lear*: the inter-
                       pretation of Albany and Edgar', in David Bevington and
                       Jay L. Halio (eds), *Shakespeare Pattern of Excelling Nature*
                       (Newark, Delaware, 1978), 95–105
Warren, 'Kent'   Michael J. Warren, 'The diminution of Kent', in *Division*,
                       59–73
R. Warren   Roger Warren, 'The Folio omission of the mock-trial:
                       motives and consequences', in *Division*, 45–57
Wells   Stanley Wells, 'The once and future *King Lear*', in
                       Division, 1–22

Welsford	Enid Welsford, *The Fool: His Social and Literary History* (1935)
Werstine[2]	Paul Werstine, 'Folio editors, Folio compositors, and the Folio text of *King Lear*', in *Division*, 247–312
Whiter	Walter Whiter, *A Specimen of a Commentary on Shakespeare* (1794), ed. Alan Over, completed Mary Bell (1967)
Wickham	Glynne Wickham, 'From tragedy to tragi-comedy: *King Lear* as prologue', *SS*, 26 (1973), 33–48
Wiles	David Wiles, *Shakespeare's Clown* (Cambridge, 1987)
Wittreich	Joseph Wittreich, *Image of that Horror': History, Prophecy, and Apocalypse in 'King Lear'* (San Marino, 1984)
Young	Alan R. Young, 'The written and oral sources of *King Lear* and the problem of justice in the play', *SEL*, 15 (1975), 309–19

INDEX

This index covers the Introduction, Commentary and Appendix 1.

430